The Phoenix and the Flame

Also by Henry Kamen

European Society 1500–1700 (1984)
Golden Age Spain (1988)
Inquisition and Society in Spain (1985)
Spain 1469–1714: A Society of Conflict (1991)

The Phoenix and the Flame

Catalonia and the Counter Reformation

Henry Kamen

Yale University Press · New Haven & London 1993

Set in Sabon by Best-set Typesetter Ltd., Hong Kong
Printed and bound in Great Britain by The Bath Press, Avon

Library of Congress Cataloging-in-Publication Data

Kamen, Henry Arthur Francis.
 The phoenix and the flame: Catalonia and the Counter Reformation/
Henry Kamen.
     p. cm.
 Includes bibliographical references and index.
 ISBN 0–300–05416–5
   1. Counter-Reformation—Spain—Catalonia.   2. Catalonia (Spain)—
Church history.   3. Catalonia (Spain)—Religious life and customs.
4. Catholic Church—Spain—Catalonia—History—16th century.
5. Catholic Church—Spain—Catalonia—History—17th century.
I. Title.
BR1027.C3K36 1993
282'.46709031—dc20   92–41268
                                                                         CIP

A catalogue record for this book is available from the British Library.

The publication of this book has been generously assisted by a subvention from
The Program for Cultural Cooperation Between Spain's Ministry of Culture and
United States Universities.

Contents

Glossary

Catalan words are here presented in capital letters and Castilian words in italic. See introduction to Notes for usage in text. For a more detailed attention to political definitions, see the entries in J.H. Elliott, *The Revolt of the Catalans*, Cambridge 1963.

ALBAT. A child who died before reaching the age of reason; generally applied to children who died before reaching the age at which they could go to confession and communion.

Alumbrados. Illuminists, groups of mystics who minimised the role of the Church and ceremonies.

APLEC. A celebration, normally of people going on an outing to a country shrine, when the religious ceremony would be followed by a meal and dancing.

Arbitrista. Writers who drew up *arbitrios* or proposals for economic and political reform in seventeenth-century Spain.

AUDIÈNCIA. The REIAL AUDIÈNCIA, sometimes called the CONSELL REIAL, was the supreme royal court in Catalonia, with seventeen judges divided into three chambers.

Auto de fe. The ceremony at which accused were sentenced by the Inquisition, either in public or within a Church building.

BATLLE. Bailiff, the chief judicial official at town and village level, appointed by whoever (king, lord, bishop) controlled the jurisdiction, and usually answerable to the VEGUER.*

Beata. Holy woman, usually not connected with any religious order, dedicated to a solitary hermit life.

BENEFICIAT. A priest holding a benefice.

BUTIFARRA. Catalan sausage, a traditional element of meals in Catalonia.

CAPÍTOLS MATRIMONIALS. The clauses forming a marriage contract.

CENSAL. The interest payable annually on a sum of money borrowed or advanced.

CIUTADANS HONRATS. 'Honoured citizens', the highest civic rank granted by major towns in the Crown of Aragon; applied specially to the civic elite of Barcelona.

COBLA. Small orchestra which plays at folk dances, specifically for the SARDANA.*

Comisario. Official of the Inquisition, always a priest, entrusted with various administrative duties.

CONSELL. A town 'council' made up of JURATS.* In Barcelona the city council was known as the CONSELL DE CENT or Council of One Hundred.

CONSELLERS. In Barcelona, the executive councillors of the city, elected annually. Their president was the CONSELLER-EN-CAP.

CÓNSOL. Town councillor in some towns, mainly in Rosselló.

Conversos. Christians of Jewish descent.

CORTS. The Catalan parliament, consisting of three estates and summoned by the king. Frequently it met at the same time as the Corts of Valencia and Aragon, in the town of Montsó, when the sessions were referred to as CORTS GENERALS.

DIPUTACIÓ. The standing committee of the Corts, consisting of two members (DIPUTATS) from each of the three estates. Also known as the Generalitat, the Diputació was the supreme representative of Catalonia.

ESCREIX. Sum paid by the bridegroom as complement to the dowry of the bride.

FADRISTERN. Brother to the HEREU*; applied in general to a young unmarried man of the community.

Familiar. Official of the Inquisition, layman appointed to help the Inquisitors with their duties.

FESTA MAJOR. The main annual festival of the community, usually coinciding with the feast-day of a saint.

FURS/*fueros*. The laws and constitutions of a town or, in later usage, of an entire state such as Catalonia.

GAVATX. Term of abuse, of obscure origin, used by Catalans of the French.

GOIG. 'Joy', printed leaflet celebrating in verse the praises of the Virgin or of a saint.

HEREU. The male heir to the family property.

JURAT. Town councillor.

Licenciado. Title generally used by those having a university degree in law.

Limpieza de sangre. 'Purity of blood', freedom from Jewish or Moorish racial origins; a condition required for membership by various Castilian institutions.

MAS, MASIA. The traditional Catalan farm-house and by extension the estate associated with it. The farm-hands working the estate are MASOVERS.

MOSSÈN. Title given to Catalan clergy.

NINOT. Figure of man, made of wood or plaster, applied specially to figures used in processions.

Observance. Reformed branch of religious order, as against unreformed or Conventual branch.

PABORDE. Ecclesiastical functionary in some communities.

PAGÈS, PAGESOS. Peasant(s), used without distinction of economic status.

PEDRENYAL. Small firearm using a flintlock mechanism, sometimes translated here as 'pistol'.

PUBILLA. The heiress to the family property.

Regidor. Member of town council. The word passed into Catalan use.

ROMERIA/*romería*. Pilgrimage, usually to local shrine.

Sanbenito. Penitential garment imposed by the Inquisition.

SARDANA. Traditional popular dance in the Catalan lands.

SÍNDIC. Agent or representative.

SOMETENT. Voluntary armed force called out in emergency to pursue delinquents.

TERME. Territory.

TRENTENARI. 'Thirty', the memorial masses said for a soul in Purgatory.

UNIVERSITAT. Community, description used by towns.

VEGUER. Royal official in charge of each of the seventeen VEGUERIES into which Catalonia was divided.

Visita. Formal visit to examine and enquire, used in this book for the visitations made by diocesan visitors to the parishes, and the visits made by inquisitors to the areas of their competence.

Preface

Well do I know that writing a history requires a life of
application, but happy is he who spends it on so worthy a task.
Preface to Esteban Corbera, *Catalonia illustrated*, 1678

'The Phoenix of Catalonia is in search of new life',
wrote a Catalan merchant of the late seventeenth
century,[1] reflecting the use of the same image by a writer of the
previous generation.[2] Catalans like the lawyer Narcis Feliu de la
Penya, who wished to see his homeland rise 'like a phoenix from
the ashes', were concerned not only with economic regeneration but
also with preserving the flame of faith in a province 'where there
have never been heretics or heresiarchs'.[3] As the first province in
Spain to receive what we now call the 'Counter Reformation',
Catalonia had reason to be proud of its faith. The principality is the
historic setting for this study, but the enquiry is more specifically
directed to the impact of religious change on a small pre-industrial
community, and by extension on the life of the society of which it
formed a part. The focus therefore centres at first on the people of
Mediona, then moves out immediately to the broader perspective of
Spain and Catalonia before coming back finally to a view of the
communities of the Penedès.

The traditional presentation of religion in Catholic Europe at the
time of the Reformation had little to do with the lives of the people
it affected and dwelt primarily on the struggle against Protestantism,
the reform of religious orders, and the achievements of saints. Seen
from this perspective there appeared to be no need for reform in
Spain and there are consequently no studies of it, the assumption
being that a few administrative changes and a revision of spiritual
attitudes were enough to bring the peninsula into line with the post-
Tridentine world. Spain is prominently absent from every published
work, ancient and modern, on the religious changes of the time;

and a historian specialising in the field has claimed that 'Spaniards turned down, in most of the senses which can be given to that term, the Counter Reformation.'[4] While good work has emerged on the reform movement in Italy, France (a fine study by Hoffman) and the Netherlands (a thorough survey by Lottin), Spain has remained in the shadows, condemned perhaps by the learned belief that there was no change and therefore nothing that could be studied.

Though light is at last beginning to penetrate the darkness, notably with a recent thesis by Sara Nalle on the diocese of Cuenca, our ignorance of the process of change in the peninsula is immense and in the case of Catalonia total. To write this book there were few guides available and nearly every scrap of information collected had to be mined from the archives. To avoid being overwhelmed by the material I have tried not to make it a tedious learned exposition and have deliberately avoided the systematic presentation of data – lists of dates, councils, bishops, reforms – which needs to be done some day but which did not form part of my programme. What this book offers is quite simply a perspective of the impact the religious changes had on society and culture, in an attempt to understand the rhythms underlying the life of early modern Mediterranean Spain.

Much ink has been spent on trying to define what the Counter Reformation was or whether it existed; I have assumed that it did exist, for the evidence suggests that something happened in Spain to which we must put a name. In his enquiry into local religion in New Castile, William Christian asserted that local practice in Spain 'was little affected by the Council of Trent' and that the Counter Reformation 'merely tried to correct excesses' without changing anything,[5] a conclusion similar to that of Soulet in his study on the central Pyrenees. My impression is somewhat different, and as readers will see my narrative points to a substantial reshaping of the dimensions of faith.

Little of value exists in English on Catalan society in early modern times other than the recent fine studies by Amelang and Sahlins, and in Spanish there is no social history of Catalonia nor surprisingly any history of the Catalan Church. For what orientation I could obtain I am indebted particularly to the writings of the great historians of early modern Catalonia, Pierre Vilar and father Miquel Batllori, and to the latter as well as to Dr Jan Lechner of Leiden University I am particularly grateful for help in sorting out some problems in my Chapter Eight. My lasting debt is to the late Fernand Braudel, who many years ago was the first to direct my steps towards Spain.

Three main types of historical evidence have been used: archival papers and especially the episcopal archives; printed books of the epoch; and sources relating to traditional culture and folklore. Printed books, most of them in Castilian, presented the problem of whether they reflected ideas also current among the educated in Catalonia. I have attempted to resolve this issue by concentrating mainly on those Castilian works circulating in Catalonia, and occasionally (in Chapters Two and Eight) I have brought in aspects of the Castilian experience, which dictated much that went on in Catalonia. Folklore has been less trustworthy as a source: the great work of Amades (and others) has saved for us the traditions of the nineteenth-century countryside, but up to two centuries separate those customs from the period studied in my book. The large and interesting corpus of Catalan folklore unfortunately has paid little attention to evidence of historical continuity, which severely reduces its value for trying to study pre-industrial society. Inevitably then the approach adopted here is not always that of the traditional political historian with his comforting store of documentary sources or state memoranda.

The themes for exploration – and the sources – are virtually limitless. The material I have used has been severely pruned, and text, notes and bibliography reduced to a minimum so as to spare both publisher and reader. Economy rather than ignorance explains a reluctance to elaborate some subjects. It should be emphasised that the book is not an ecclesiastical history, so a consistent study of personnel and events will not be found here. And the rich visual aspects of the theme – the imagery of altarpieces, *goigs*, *festes majors*, mountain-top shrines – wait to be presented in another volume.

Research for the book (recommenced in 1984 after all my previous archival notes were destroyed) was made possible by the generosity of the Institute for Research in the Humanities, University of Wisconsin-Madison, which through its then director Bob Kingdon invited me as Herbert F. Johnson Professor during the academic year 1984–5; and by subsequent generous grants from the British Academy and the trustees of the Leverhulme Foundation. Research in early printed books was facilitated by the kindness of John Tedeschi, director of special collections at the Memorial Library, Madison, and by the staff of the Biblioteca de Catalunya and the Institut Municipal of Barcelona. I am also specially grateful to the staff of several archives, in particular the diocesan archives of Barcelona (where by a happy chance I came across the parish manuals of the rector of Mediona) and those of Urgell.

Along the way I made the acquaintance of now forgotten Catalan scholars who tried in the face of indifference to record the past of their country, men such as Narcis Camos, canon of Barcelona, who

spent three years wandering round the war-torn province in the
1650s, braving rains and heat, to collect information on the shrines
of the countryside; fray Joan Roig, historian of Gerona, struggling
to unearth 'manuscripts buried and totally forgotten in volumes
rotting with the dust and worms of the archives of this principality';
fray Sigismund of the Holy Spirit, chronicler of his order, describing the search for 'fragmented, scattered and forgotten scraps of
historical information, which have to be unearthed, unwrapped and
set out, at the cost of much time, good health, grit and especially
much patience; because much of the information is in papers
thrown aside, shelved as useless, torn up, damp, the writing half
blotted out, and sometimes in such quantities that even in a week or
a fortnight you would not find anything; and when you are fed up
and want to give up, suddenly you light upon a rich treasure'.[6]

A Navarrese scholar of the sixteenth century suggested that the
difference between reading novels and history was that 'to read the
imaginary books of Amadis and suchlike, is sinful; but to take
pleasure in a historian's prose is not sinful.'[7] For me the pleasure in
composing this history has been fostered in no small measure by
one who in her active research-companionship through the many
hours spent in libraries, archives, and along the valleys, roads and
mountains of rural Catalonia, trudging along inaccessible paths to
find ruined and forgotten *masies*, sharing the adversities of El
Superbo, En Barrufet, Paula Ponsa and all the others who people
these pages, conjured up for me an intimate acquaintance with the
past of her country without which this book could never have been
written.

St Quintí de Mediona

One may say of Catalonia that it is a little world within one province.
A Carmelite chronicler, 1689

CHAPTER ONE

Mediona: A Community in the Counter Reformation

I have written this so that those born hereafter may know, and as a record of how it was in Mediona.
mossèn Pere Santacana, rector of Mediona, 1600

Mediona today is a rural community cradled in a mountain valley of the Alt Penedès just under an hour away by car from Barcelona. In the early sixteenth century it was a grouping of scattered settlements known as 'the district (*terme*) and castle of Mediona', dotted through the valley in an almost continuous chain of houses which seemed to confirm the view of contemporaries that 'on any road you take you will find towns or villages or at least houses,'[1] and that 'you cannot go a quarter of a league without discovering a town or settlement, house or cottage, as if they were sprinkled everywhere.'[2] Farmhouses (*masos*) and settlements such as Orpinell, Mas Martí, Puigfret, Conques, Agulladolç, Prades, each forming a small nucleus of people dedicated to exploiting the red soil on the slopes around the river Mediona, made up the 'university of Mediona', which took official shape when its representatives in the *consell* met (as they did up to at least the early eighteenth century) 'in the castle square in the accustomed place where matters of interest to the república are normally discussed'. At each meeting of the consell, in the shadow of the ruined castle walls overlooking the precipitous pine-covered slopes of the river valley, the minutes were taken and all official business recorded by a qualified notary who in Mediona was, and had been since the beginning of continuous records in the fourteenth century, the parish priest.

Because the consell met seldom, only to perform the annual election of the civic representatives (*jurats*) of the terme or to settle financial business such as taxes, the scattered settlements of Mediona lived a communal life primarily through the medium of the parish church of Santa Maria, which for over six centuries performed the difficult task of acting as the focus of religious and social activity. A Romanesque structure of the early eleventh century, when the castle was entrusted with the defence of the valley, the church of Santa Maria with its typical bell-tower stood in striking isolation one thousand feet above the winding river, preserving a grandeur that moved the bishop's visitor much later, in 1777, to pen a Gothic description of the church, 'isolated together with the house where the vicar lives, in a ruined castle, situated in uninhabited mountains and bare rocks, the nearest house being a league and a half away from the church'.[3] The isolation of the church was unchanged by 1812, when the rector reported that 'since the neighbourhood of the parish of the castle of Santa Maria of Mediona consists entirely of scattered houses, the vicar needs to maintain a mule for the administration of the sacraments.'[4] All the parishioners of Santa Maria – the census of 1553 lists forty-five hearths (*focs*) – depended on the vicar and the church for the rites of passage which marked the transition from birth to death, but religion did not necessarily form the centre of their lives. The vicar was crucial far more as notary than as priest: as in most Catalan country parishes, the ability of the parish-priest alone to authenticate marriage contracts, property transactions, and testaments (the three most important legal documents of the time), gave him a unique importance in rural society and a role that extended beyond the liturgical since he was literally the arbiter of all social and economic transactions in the community.[5] Despite this central role, the vicar was seldom in a position to impose religious practice on the people of his parish.

The rural grandeur of Santa Maria was complemented by the more urban setting of the parish of St Quintí de Mediona, a little town of closely-packed houses grouped on the slopes around the river Mediona some four kilometres downstream from the castle, and served by an old Benedictine priory in the middle of the town. With thirty-nine households in 1553, St Quintí was the only large settlement in the terme. In the Middle Ages the priory, a dependant of the monastery of Ripoll, had been responsible for both parishes, but as the population grew it became necessary to create permanent vicars for Santa Maria. In November 1586 the old prior retired and the 'priorate of St Quintí and rectorate of Mediona' was transferred, with papal permission, to the ownership of the cathedral chapter of Barcelona.[6] Control of the priory building, whose mediaeval walls overlooking a little tree-lined square remain virtually unchanged today, and of part of the tithes of the two parishes, now went directly to the chapter.

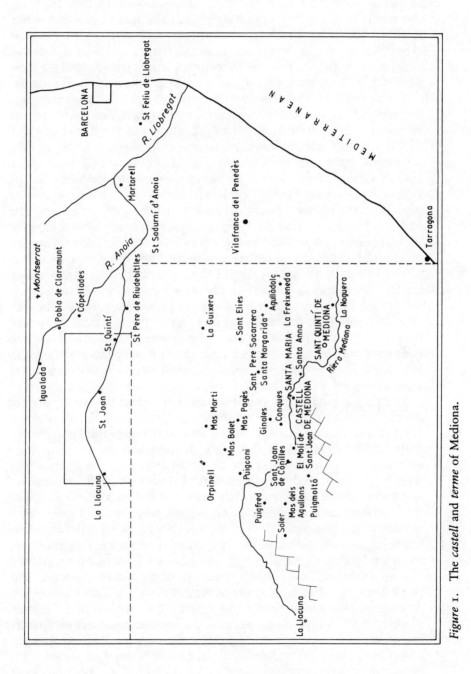

Figure 1. The *castell* and *terme* of Mediona.

In terms of political government, Mediona fell within the royal *vegueria* of Vilafranca del Penedès, but it was not ruled by the king: the seigneur of the town and terme was the most powerful feudal lord in Catalonia, the duke of Cardona, who nominated the chief law officials of Mediona, the bailiffs (*batlles*), and also received part of the tithe. Since the thirteenth century Mediona had been aggregated to a grouping of seigneurial towns within the Conca d'Odena, part of the neighbouring area of Anoia; the Conca was represented by a Consell General of three deputies (*síndics*) and administered by a governor in the name of the duke.[7] At one and the same time, then, Mediona was subject to the jurisdictions of the bishop of Barcelona, the cathedral of Barcelona, the king of Spain, and the duke of Cardona. Of the two benefices endowed on the main altar of Santa Maria, one was in the gift of the duke, the other in that of the bishop, a neat illustration of the joint rule of secular and spiritual powers over the terme. Apart from the loss of tithes to the Barcelona chapter and to the duke, little of this apparent burden of multiple authority created problems: the duke, for example, granted in 1544 to the Conca d'Odena a string of privileges which effectively gave its towns autonomy; and even the bailiff – a decision confirmed by the supreme royal court of Catalonia, the *Audiència*, in 1605 – could be selected only from a short-list of three presented by the terme to the duke every three years. Mediona and its area continued to be a community theoretically dependent on outside authorities but in practice enjoying an autonomy that typified a great part of the Catalan countryside.

The people of the Alt Penedès have been forgotten by historians and omitted from the itinerary by all recorded travellers,[8] yet their story is a microcosm of the history of Catalonia in the epoch of the Counter Reformation. Maintaining themselves largely out of their own resources, with a good stock of animals and a comparatively fertile soil dedicated to wheat, barley, vines and olives,[9] the inhabitants of Mediona tried to preserve their way of life without the interference of outsiders. Representing what Braudel once called a 'hillside civilisation',[10] economically fragile but hardy and long enduring, separated from the coastlands but looking to them for trade and succour, they formed a mid-point between the isolation of the Pyrenean valleys and the expanding urban nuclei of the Mediterranean. The most detailed census available is that of 1553.[11] The thirty-nine households huddled into St Quintí were an integral peasant community with an active communal life dedicated to exploitation of the surrounding soil; assuming they had a domestic structure similar to other small settlements in Catalonia,[12] the households were nuclear families of around four persons each, totalling 156 souls. The rest of the population of Mediona consisted of forty-five multiple households, each living in the large traditional farmhouse known as the *mas*, from which they organised the exploitation of the land. The population of each hearth was substantially bigger in the rural environment, with approximately seven persons per household, a total in 1553 of 315 souls.[13]

Though each of the parishes was fully autonomous, together they formed a single intimate community,[14] and for formal occasions convoked joint meetings in the castle ruins of Mediona. Election of jurats – each parish had one bailiff and two jurats – was done on 17 January each year, the feast of St Antoni Abat, 'the people of Mediona and of St Quintí being joined together in the castle of Mediona in the accustomed place to elect the jurats of the said terme of Mediona and town of St Quintí',[15] in the presence of the bailiffs and with the token presence of a couple of dozen citizens. St Quintí was small enough to maintain a wholly traditional community structure. Its bailiff, appointed in rotation from among local residents, was responsible both to the governor of the Conca d'Odena and to the royal *veguer* in Vilafranca del Penedès. He supervised the election of jurats and maintained law in the parishes. The jurats, in their turn, helped to run the town and took care of the finances. All important decisions in the terme, however, could only be made by a general council of all the residents, 'after ringing the bells to summon the Consell General, as is the custom'. In St Quintí, which then as now had no large public square, the residents had to meet 'assembled in the entrance of the priory'. By the late sixteenth century in much of Spain and western Europe the assembly of residents was no more than a memory, but in Mediona it was still taken very seriously. The names of all those attending were noted, as 'representing the whole university of the said town', and account was taken of the absence of 'young, widows, sick, absent and others', so that their wishes not be neglected. If there was a serious difference of opinion, the names were recorded of 'those who did not consent to the said matters in this Consell', and if a decision was commonly agreed then it was announced 'with the agreement of the whole town and terme of Mediona and of its chief men'.[16]

In the later middle ages St Quintí had been well under the control of the Cardonas, who in 1335 conceded the town a butchery, and in 1419 a bakery, but as seigneurial monopolies;[17] and the principal mill available, at the grotto known as Les Deus, was a monopoly of the Barberà family, hereditary castellans of the castle of Mediona.[18] By the sixteenth century the bakery and butchery, though still owned by the duke, were operated by licence from the jurats, and when a storm wrecked the mill at Les Deus the town in a general council in 1598 decided to build their own,[19] subject to the permission of the duke. The greater independence and initiative of the town, expressed fluently at recorded meetings of the general council, extended also into all areas of Church activity.

Mediona and its neighbours were wholly Catalan in speech and culture: apart from standard Latin phrasing used in business and similar contracts, all documentation (marriages, testaments) done by the local notaries was in Catalan. Not until the middle of the eighteenth century did Castilian creep in, but exclusively when links with the outside world, such as personal or official correspondence, were involved; internally, Catalan remained the only language spoken or written.

The surviving records leave no doubt that Mediona was a Catholic society, but with significant differences from the Catholicism of the twentieth century. Everyone got baptised almost immediately after birth, because of the imminent threat from infant mortality. Entry into the Christian community was however the only regular (and by its nature involuntary) sacramental link with the Church that people had throughout their lives. Religious practice in the pre-Tridentine period was not governed by regular observance of the sacraments: attendance at mass could be as frequent as once a week (on Sunday) if there was a priest available to officiate, but if the priest were only empowered to say one mass a day, which was normal, parishioners living far away from him might have to wait two weeks for their next mass. As late as 1609 in neighbouring La Llacuna the townspeople complained that Sunday mass was available only three weeks out of four, 'and for that reason many people go without mass in this town of about one hundred households'.[20] Mediona was more fortunate: St Quintí had a rector more or less in residence, and Santa Maria usually had two vicars. In theory there were more priests available: Santa Maria, for example, had four benefices attached to the church, but all the clergy involved were absentees (mainly in Barcelona), and restricted their interest to drawing their meagre salaries. As a result the vicars in Santa Maria had to minister not only to the parish church but to a suffragan church in Conilles, and chapels in Sant Elies, Sant Pere Sacarrera, Orpinell, Santa Anna, Pareres and Santa Margarida. It was to these local altars and not to the distant parish church that the faithful in Mediona went for mass; only in St Quintí did the people have an accessible parish building.

The distance to the parish church in rural Catalonia – it takes, for instance, well over two hours to walk from Orpinell to Santa Maria – was one reason why most sacraments were not associated with it and when performed took on more of a communal than a religious significance. In Mediona the records show that it was habitual well into the seventeenth century for baptisms to be performed at the place of birth, in the home. When the vicar made an exception to this he said so: the baptism entry in Santa Maria for 6 August 1589 says for example, 'I Pere Santacana ... baptised a son in the church of Mediona ...'; it is an exceptional entry and there were no further baptisms in the church until July 1591.[21] Lack of physical contact with the church had to be compensated for by the parish priest, who usually performed the minimum duty of bringing mass to the people, trekking around the parish on mule-back as the vicars of Mediona were wont to do. Though there were normally two vicars in Santa Maria, they were not empowered to say more than one mass a day, and consequently depended heavily on other available clergy in the area, and possibly also on itinerant clergy, for the general availability of mass.

Apart from mass there was little or no recourse to sacraments. Confirmation, normally administered by a bishop, was notable for its almost total absence from the religious life of Mediona. A few perished notes on children who were confirmed in Mediona and in neighbouring St Pere de Riudebitlles during the sixteenth and eighteenth centuries, are the only surviving record of the very infrequent episcopal visits.[22] By contrast confession in Mediona took place with great formality once a year. Early in Lent, 'tempore Quadragesima', the rector warned parishioners that it was time to fulfil the precept that mature Christians – canon law specified that girls were mature from the age of twelve and boys from fourteen – should confess at least once a year.[23] The names of those who confessed were carefully noted down, providing us with an invaluable record of the names and addresses of the residents in Santa Maria.[24] In 1551, the first year for which the record survives, out of some 225 parishioners noted, at least 34 – some 15 per cent – did not perform the obligation. The highest proportion was in the mas at Conques, where out of twelve people six did not go to confession that year, at least two of them being noted as 'shepherds', itinerant and therefore probably absent during the due time. Sporadic non-observance is noted through the next two decades (in 1570 about thirteen people did not confess), but by the 1580s the record appears to show a total observance by the parishioners.

The precept of annual communion at Easter followed logically from the annual confession, but in Catalonia the change to recording communions seems not to have been enforced before the eighteenth century, and in Mediona there is no evidence of whether people went to the sacrament, which it was more common to administer to the dying rather than to the living. Occasionally the curtain is lifted to give us some information: in 1621 when Tony Totasans of the settlement at St Joan de Conilles died, the vicar noted that 'he did not receive the sacrament because he did not send for us; in any case, he never used to come to communion.'[25] We may assume that the annual communion was generally observed, but these minimum norms were not always sustained. Over a century and a half later, in 1754, the bishop observed of the Alt Penedès that 'in nearly all the parishes the fact is that not everyone complies with the precept of annual communion within the period stipulated.'[26]

Formal attendance at the sacraments may reflect only an external observance of religion, but it is difficult to make the documents tell us much about internal observance. Positive evidence of piety is consequently elusive. The negative aspects stand out more sharply as a result: nothing is more incontrovertible than the refusal of parishioners to pay their tithes or to contribute to the expenses of the church, a problem that the episcopal visitors to Mediona denounced repeatedly in all their reports between the 1580s and the 1680s. Throughout the sixteenth century excommunication was used as a regular instrument to bring hardened offenders to heel, but it was an instrument of limited use in a society not educated to take it seriously, and by the seventeenth bishops dissuaded their clergy from using it. At Mediona in the 1570s and 1580s there was about one excommunication a year (the ban was usually lifted within a few weeks), a number too small to warrant a special record-book, so the vicar used to slip in records of excommunication among the marriages, where they lie uneasily, testimonies to distress, among the happier histories of young couples beginning a new life.

Marriage in Mediona was not a Church matter nor sealed in church.[27] The families of the terme between them supplied enough young people for there to be continuous intermarriage through the generations, but in practical terms the catchment area for partners extended beyond the valleys to other neighbouring communities within, roughly, a ten-kilometre radius.[28] Young people from the western extreme of the terme found partners in La Llacuna and Miralles, those in St Quintí could find them in Vilafranca and Pontons, those in the area of Agulladolç might find them in Capellades, Piera and Pobla de Claramunt. In eighty-three (38 per cent) of the 215 marriages celebrated in the parish of Santa Maria between June 1575 and December 1630, both partners came from within the terme; so that in rounded terms the surrounding communities supplied new life to Mediona in some two-thirds of the marriages within that period. French immigrants, who helped powerfully to raise population levels in coastal Catalonia in these years, had litle impact: only fifteen Frenchmen were spouses during the period, and there was none between 1621 and 1630. Twenty-one (10 per cent) of the marriages in the period were second marriages, with the curious feature that widows normally remarried not with men from the terme but with outsiders.[29]

Assuming that age at first marriage was similar to that elsewhere in Catalonia, girls in Mediona got married at about twenty-two years, men at about twenty-seven.[30] Except among the very poor, marriage was a major transaction which linked families and property and was regulated by formal marriage 'clauses' (*capítols* in Catalan) agreed by both parties before a notary. In Mediona, where there was an effective equality of social condition among the population, everybody seems to have drawn up marriage clauses, which invariably laid down a date for the marriage. When the marriage ceremony took place, before family and friends, it was always performed in the presence of a priest but seldom took place in church. In Santa Maria, with its additional problems of distance from the parish church, the situation was very clear: within the period 1575–1630, long after the Church authorities had attempted to alter the long-standing practice of not marrying in church, only some sixty (or 28 per cent of 215) marriages were performed within a church. The great majority of unions took place in the secular environment of a private house or a mas, with the priest functioning as notary rather than as minister of a sacrament, and the ceremony taking place before assembled friends; if it were a nice sunny day, as with the marriages performed in May and June of 1597 in Mas Prades and Mas Ginoles, the function took place in the open air 'in the patio of the house'. Couples who were married at home were supposed to go eventually to their local church to receive a clerical blessing, but not all couples in Mediona bothered to go, and the problem was general throughout Catalonia. Two generations later, when official rules had continued to insist on marriage in church, there was still no uniformity. Between 1692 and 1700 inclusive, out of forty-nine marriages performed in the parish of Santa Maria thirty-eight took place in church, five at home, three in the rector's house, two in the public square of the village of Pareres, and one in the castle ruins of Mediona. The trend was clearly towards marriage in church alone, but the goal was not yet achieved.

Although religious festivities and holidays took up much of the leisure time of the people of the terme, who took great civic pride in improving and embellishing the parish church, sacramental religion based on the ritual performance of duties and the receipt of corresponding benefits through the clergy played litle part in their lives.

The image of the priest as the dispenser of graces and ritual healer cannot be found in this Catholic community. If people went to the parish priest with great frequency it was primarily so that he could notarise their contracts, leases, sales, marriage clauses and testaments; for the rest he had no unusual status in the community. When significant disputes took place, outside arbiters were called in, and the priest attended simply to notarise. In a dispute in 1599 when one of the confraternities of St Quintí threatened to bring a lawsuit against the jurats of the town, a canon of Barcelona cathedral came as arbiter.[31] Similarly, in another threatened court case of 1605 the governor of the Conca d'Odena came in as arbiter.[32] Only at the point of death, when in reality they were passing out of his jurisdiction, did the people feel a pressing need for the religious services of the priest, and only then was there unqualified resort to the sacraments of the Church. Death in Mediona represented a permanent state of confrontation that began at the moment of birth. Infant mortality in pre-industrial Europe was the first great threat to survival, and in Catalonia the death rate among the young was high.[33] In Santa Maria in the period 1573–1630 infants made up 28.5 per cent of all deaths,[34] with the highest mortality in the days immediately after birth. All adults who died were given all the sacraments, namely confession, communion and extreme unction, and apart from those who showed a clear wish to receive none,[35] or who could not be reached in time, the people of the terme seem to have been fully protected against the eventualities of the next life. Those who were forewarned by a grave illness drew up testaments which were devised not so much to distribute their property, a task normally catered for by the marriage clauses, as to protect their souls.

Testaments drawn up in the sixteenth century seldom expressed personal sentiments but merely followed a standard phrasing recommended by the diocese for framing the text of wills, which decade after decade in Mediona started with the formula: 'In the name of God, since none that is of flesh can escape death, and since there is nothing more certain than death nor more uncertain than its hour . . .', a pious but routine phrase which the clergy imposed on a population unable to express its own piety eloquently. In Mediona almost without exception testaments were drawn up only when the subject was very ill or dying,[36] with the notary-priest carefully recording last wishes and legacies. After providing for all debts to be paid, the testator in early modern Mediona invariably left a sum of £5 or more for the costs of burial, the celebration of a *trentenari* of masses – thirty masses 'commonly called masses of St Amador'[37] – and asked for a novena mass to be celebrated after death. Those with money available asked for much more: a further quantity of masses, and possibly the foundation of an anniversary mass for which a due capital sum was allotted. The more important members of the community could ask for two or three trentenaris, and for a number (usually twelve) of priests to accompany the coffin to its resting-place, which in the masies and country areas was often 'in the tomb in which my forebears are buried'. Those with no family tomb were interred in the cemetery of St Quintí or, if they lived elsewhere in the terme, down by the river in the cemetery of St Joan de Conilles.

Virtually all charitable bequests remained within the terme, the major external beneficiary in the early seventeenth century being the hospital of Holy Cross in Barcelona. Occasional bequests went to the shrine at the monastery of Montserrat, whose gaunt profile dominated the skyline of the Penedès. A typical disbursement was that by Bertomeu Tort, *pagès* of St Pere Sacarrera, whose testament in 1632 left £4 to the altar of the Rosary in Santa Maria, 40s to the Sant Crist of Mediona, 40s to the chapel of Sts Nicholas and Isidore, 20s to the hospital in Barcelona, and 20s to Montserrat.[38] Though the people of Mediona spent their lives in the ambit of the mas, in death they abandoned it. The majority of those subject to the parish of Santa Maria asked for their masses to be said at its altar, but in view of the difficult access to the church they preferred to be buried in the valley in the cemetery of St Joan. Among the leading men in the parish was Miquel Gostems, pagès of Puigmoltó and head of his family: his testament in 1629 asked that twelve priests accompany his coffin (each to be paid 20s for the duty), that he be buried in St Joan 'in the tomb in which my forebears are buried', and that two trentenaris be said for him 'in the said church of St Joan de Conilles'.[39] The extraordinary use of the services of the Church at death contrasts strangely with their relative neglect during life. No doubt precisely because of this, there appears to have been no brooding fear of the other life among the people of Mediona. Purgatory, in official theology the major obstacle facing the soul on its journey, was amply taken care of by the ritual of the masses of St Amador, which guaranteed an effortless passage; and the novena mass, celebrated within about a month after burial, brought together as many priests as the deceased could afford in order to speed the passage, with novenas in the 1570s in Santa Maria employing as many as twenty-three priests (for a soul from Mas Ginoles) and twenty-four (for one from Orpinell), ferried in from the environs since the terme had no such resources. Increasingly, from the late sixteenth century, it became the practice for richer testators to set aside a small capital sum for the saying of an anniversary mass, intended always (in Mediona) as a *memorial* (record) rather than as a propitiatory rite with an eye to Purgatory.[40] The impressive absence of Purgatory in rural Catalonia before the seventeenth century confirms what we know of popular practice elsewhere in the Catholic world.[41]

Though death came early to the very young in Mediona, there were always hardy survivors: Miquel Gili of St Quintí stated proudly as he dictated his will in 1601 that 'I am over eighty years old'.[42] Time, however, weighed more heavily on those who lived in an era with much lower life expectancy than ours. When mossèn Pere Santacana drew up his will in 1603 he claimed to have arrived 'at my old age, for I am over fifty years old'. Even more cogent was the case of the farming couple who in 1602 decided to pass the masia to their son and heir on his marriage since they were 'old and aged over forty'.[43] Sudden death was no stranger to the terme, and the apparent tranquillity of life in the valleys was frequently punctuated by acts of unusual violence. In July 1584 a young man of Mas St Martí was murdered 'beside his house in his own land and for no fault whatever'; in June 1585 a man of Agulladolç lingered two weeks in dying 'from a wound by a *pedrenyal*'; in August 1600 'they murdered Joan Camps', pagès of Mas Pasqual in Agulladolç; in October 1610 a young man of Mas Corteges died 'of a stab-wound given him in his house by his brother'; in January 1612 'they murdered Sebastià and Jaume Castellvi, brothers' of Mas Pagès; in November 1613 in Mas Freixeneda a woman 'died violently from an axe-blow before daylight, delivered from all the signs by her husband Salvador Puigdengoles when she was sleeping'; in December 1617 'persons induced by the devil murdered with three gunshots at round about eight o'clock in the evening' young Joan Santacana of St Pere Sacarrera, and burnt all his hayricks; in December 1620 Joan Mallofre of Orpinell cut the throat of his wife Jerónima and repeatedly shot to death the young man with her, Nicolau Via of Font Rubí.[44] It was a society where every household (the inventories for Mediona leave no doubt) had a weapon, but violence was not the order of the day and the cases, which visibly shocked the priest who recorded them, may be seen as exceptional. In contrast, the ravages caused by epidemic were a continuous threat to the community.

The first recorded arrival of plague in the locality was dated precisely by the vicar of Mediona: on 28 May 1589, he wrote, the fiesta in La Pobla de Claramunt had to be cancelled because of rain, and a married couple selling clothes had to take their wares to Igualada instead. There the man died in the hospital from the plague, but the matter was hushed up so as not to create alarm; but others died, and rumours grew. 'People in Igualada were terrified how quickly some died,' but the secret was kept 'until the day of St Joan [24 June] and the day before was a Sunday, entertainers were hired, it was a big fiesta. But on the day of St Joan the secret got out, there was an enormous hue and cry, most of the people fled out of the town into the masies and set up huts.' From Igualada death spread through the countryside: children died in their numbers, clergy fled from the villages, settlements were depopulated. The vicar of Mediona, Pere Santacana, heard that the epidemic had hit Barcelona, where 'many people have died, they say five thousand' (the real figure was twice that). Worst of all, in his view, was the moral impact on people and communities. In September 1589 Melchior Torrens, whose father lived in Mas dels Agullons, fled to the terme from Barcelona with his wife and two infant children, but his wife died a month later and the neighbours refused to help him bury her. He was forced to carry her corpse downhill to the river at St Joan, where she was to be buried, and when the two infants ran after him crying 'Mummy, mummy' he put down her body to go and comfort them and promptly fainted with grief. The bailiff and jurats were there to see that the body was dealt with, and when Torrens fainted the officials yelled at him and warned him they would shoot him and his two children if he did not bury the body and remove the threat to the terme. After the burial they were moved by grief and bought new clothes for the family (it was common practice to burn infected clothing) and the next day Torrens left for Barcelona, with the further grief that on the way his elder child died. Under the impact of plague the unity of the community shattered. The vicar grimly notarised the death in October 1589 of Joan Andreu, who died when a son of the Totasans family, which the bailiff and jurats were trying to quarantine because of a plague death, stabbed him during an argument: 'a tragic case', Santacana noted, 'for they had been neighbours and friends'.

The exposure by plague of so many sores in the soul of Christian society drew the following carefully signed and dated memoir from the vicar:

The hue and cry has been such that although the whole terme of Mediona was touched by the plague, today and all this year there has been good health, thanks be to God. I cannot write down the cruelties used in guarding the towns, the outcry, the penalties they impose, people not trusting each other, they do not let people move from their termes, trading has stopped, there is evil in the souls of men, little charity, nobody is allowed to approach the towns and the masies, or

each other when they go along the roads . . . People killing each other
mercilessly . . .

It is believed that the plague was brought into Catalonia by heretics
in order to kill the people . . . Pray to Our Lord to preserve us from
such evil . . . Written by me, Pere Santacana, one of the two vicars of
Mediona, today the twentieth of September 1589.[45]

Despite the alarm the terme remained completely free of plague,
and in gratitude they solemnly vowed at the end of 1589 to make
the day of St Sebastian, traditional protector against the plague,
into an obligatory annual feast-day.[46]

Death did not come to everyone on the same terms. When the
noble lady Dionisa Barberà died in 1578 'her body was buried in
the church before the altar of St Miquel of Mediona, there were
twelve priests at her burial'. All others had to be content with the
cemetery outside the church, where the principal masies had their
family tombs. The terme had its share of poor vagrants, who were
all given Christian burial. In May 1578 'a poor man from the
kingdom of Aragon died in St Joan de Conilles'; another 'poor man,
a stranger' was interred in September 1583; in May 1585 it was the
turn of a French woman, 'who died begging, she was found dead in
the barn, her body was buried in the cemetery of Our Lady of
Mediona'; in 1592 'on the fifth of May a poor man who went
begging, a stranger, died in the castle of Mediona, he was given a
Christian burial.'[47]

Poverty was not unknown in a community wholly dependent on
the caprice of the elements, and freak weather was common: 'in the
present year 1598 the *pagesos* sowed the wheat with good fortune.
The whole year was abundant in rain. The wheat and fruits of the
soil were all ready to give a big and fertile harvest. But in the month
of May God sent fog and mist and humid weather which did great
damage to the fruits and vines.'[48] But the local market extended up
to La Llacuna and the Segarra, and down to the coast of Penedès,
so that imbalances in production were soon remedied; and the
following year 'it was a good crop for wheat' and 'a good and
plentiful harvest' in wine,[49] a story of constant ups and downs that
never, in the period we are considering, collapsed into misery.
When in February 1603 snow covered the Penedès, an event which
might happen once in a century and in Mediona meant that 'people
were shut up in their houses, and to go along the roads and paths
they had to clear the way with sticks, and the snow brought bitter
cold and ice – something never seen or heard of by old or young in
this part of the country,'[50] the consequence was severe but not
fatal: 'the snows and ice killed many crops and animals in Segarra
and Urgell, and in St Joan and La Llacuna the harvest was bad . . . ,

in the Penedès they harvested two parts of every three, a sufficient crop.'[51] In Mediona the main produce centred on wheat, barley and rye, together with wine and oil and a very limited quantity of local meat, usually goat meat; even in bad years production seems to have been 'sufficient'. A general failure of the harvest, however, could not fail to affect the terme. At the end of 1604 Pere Santacana noted that

> there are many lawsuits and threats of actions, people cannot pay because the harvest was very poor and they have no money, so that people are suffering because they cannot pay and cannot get loans on *censal* or in any other way ... In Barcelona many of the common people rioted against a Conseller and wanted to burn his house in the Born, because there was no wheat in the market.[52]

The following year was worse, 'people are in a bad state ... Catalonia is in great need ... People are worn out and in trouble and there are many begging.'[53] In 1606, when wheat in the local markets doubled in price, 'people are frightened and do not know where it will end.'[54]

Economic problems were accompanied by conflict and distress, in the experience of the local parish clergy. In 1598, when Pere Santacana recorded that 'king Philip the Second has died in Madrid', and that 'in the country there is good health and no talk of wars', he also observed that 'everything is expensive ... Between villages and between individuals, great complaints and quarrels and all out of self-interest'.[55] Inevitably the phenomenon of banditry extended into the Alt Penedès: from the 1560s at least there were bands active in the area,[56] and both the royal veguer in Vilafranca and the bailiffs in Mediona had to cooperate in summoning the voluntary police force known as the *sometent*, in order to flush bandits from their local hideouts. In 1603 Santacana noted that 'there are great disorders in Catalonia, comrades killing each other treacherously, murders on the roads; in this area there are cavalry soldiers'; in 1604 'in this countryside there are bandits ... the main gang in the Camp of Tarragona is called "The Catalan Land"'; in 1605 the bandits 'do not dare to go in gangs, they kidnap some of the rich for ransom but get little out of it ... Many lawsuits between people ... In the country there is good health among both men and beasts; but among the men little charity. Abundabit iniquitas et refrigescet charitas.'[57]

In its political and economic life Mediona seems to have undergone no significant change before the eighteenth century, when the expansion of viticulture brought new life to the Penedès. The relative isolation of the terme did not however insulate it from the great events that created modern Catalonia, for Mediona was on the main route from Igualada to Tarragona and all troop movements (the observation of the rector in 1603 is significant) seem to have made use of the road. In the early sixteenth century French troops 'when they came to Catalonia to help the king of Aragon, on coming to St Quintí met firm resistance from the church and priorate and burnt the one and demolished the other'.[58] The pattern was repeated faithfully once in every century.

After its many travails St Quintí was restored, and little seemed to have changed. Over those centuries none the less a major presence made itself felt, reshaped religion in the Penedès and transformed the settlements and parish churches of Mediona: that presence was the Counter Reformation.

Part of the duty of prelates, whether bishops or abbots, was to make regular pastoral visits, in person or through a representative, to institutions under their jurisdiction to see that everything was in order. In the autumn of 1522 when the diocesan visitor came to the Penedès, he made a brief report on Santa Maria, with its little stock of two silver chalices and four velvet chasubles, and found nearly everything to be 'bene'; a visit the same day to St Quintí, where he found items to criticise, was rather briefer, since the priory was directly under the jurisdiction of the abbot of Ripoll.[59] Already at this date the vicar of Santa Maria had to deal single-handed not only with two altars in his church (the second was that dedicated to St Michael) but with the seven country chapels at Conilles and the other settlements.[60] The churches were not visited thereafter for thirty-seven years, confirming Mediona in its effective isolation from the see of Barcelona. Improvements were made in some of the churches during these years: in 1518 a new bell was installed at Santa Maria; in 1523 silver crosses were made for the churches of Santa Maria and St Joan by Pere Camps, silversmith of Barcelona.[61] The activity of foreign artisans in the principality at this time is demonstrated by the contract made by St Quintí in 1538 with a Flemish and an Aragonese artist to paint the reredos of the high altar and the altarpiece of the Virgin.[62] Similarly, in 1545 and 1547 French builders were contracted to repair the church.[63] The highpoint for the church of Santa Maria in these years was the installation on the high altar of a statue of the Virgin (with a silver crown) and Child, taken up the mountain in a long procession in which 'a great part of the people of the terme' took part, on the day of the *Festa Major*, 15 August 1549.[64]

In 1556 prior Sebastià Ric baptised a new bell for St Quintí that had been imported from Vizcaya, and 'nearly everybody from

St Quintí and many other people from the terme' attended the ceremony.[65] When the next diocesan visitor came to Santa Maria in the summer of 1559 he was pleased that the high altar was 'decenter' and noted that there were new altars to St Sebastian and to St Nicholas. Three years later, in the autumn of 1562, another visitor came.[66] In all these visits, which were short and summary, one gets the feeling that both visitors and clergy were acting within an unchanging scenario which included themselves alone and from which the parishioners were permanently absent; the country parish was approached as though it were a quiet outpost in which all that was required was an occasional brushing of the dust off the altars.

Suddenly in 1566 all this changed. It was two years after the closure of the Council of Trent, and the provincial Council of Tarragona was ending its sessions in Barcelona, but it is unlikely that these events touched the people of the Penedès, who were more directly affected by the crippling drought of that year.[67] On 31 October, the feast of St Quintí, a committee of the town discussed the state of the church – 'the present one is tiny, old, hardly looks like a church, and was burnt by the French' – and decided to reconstruct it. A contract was made with Pere Terrassa, of Barcelona but a native of Vilafranca, for an extensive re-modelling of roof and choir, the construction of fourteen chapels, and a main door to be built like that of 'the chapel of the Virgin of Montserrat in the city of Barcelona'. Additional work was contracted with Pere Oriol of Vilafranca in 1566, and Esteve Forner in 1567. The contracted time of work was eighteen months, and on 6 March 1567 prior Ric laid the first stone of the new church.[68] Very shortly, the available money ran out. In June 1570 a general council of the town heard that 'since the jurats are burdened with many other matters they cannot take part in carrying on the work'; but since 'it has seemed to the whole people of the town of St Quintí' that the work should proceed, the bailiff and jurats and thirty-seven heads of households elected a committee of two 'to negotiate and contract with any necessary artisans'.[69] There is no record of when the fabric was completed.

In 1574 there was another historic event. For apparently the first time since the beginning of the century, the bishop made a personal visit round his diocese, and at the end of September he came to Mediona. Bishop Martín Martínez del Villar[70] had already been trekking round his diocese through April, May and early June, with a break in July and August to escape the summer heat. He came armed with the decrees of Trent, the resolutions of the provincial Council of Tarragona, and his own diocesan edict of reformation passed on 8 October 1572.[71] Essentially, he came to tidy up, not to change. In Santa Maria he pointed to improvements that were required: a curtain before the sacrament on the altar, repairs to a gilt wooden cross, 'a little crown' of silver 'for the baby Jesus' to go with the silver crown his mother had in the image on the high altar, new shirts for the celebrant, two of the new Roman missals; but he also enquired into the vacant benefices and asked (the first visitor to do so in the century) for details of their income and duties. At St Quintí, which at this period still had only one altar and few furnishings, he ordered that a Roman missal be purchased and that the cemetery be locked to exclude animals. There was a hint of new things in the air, but in Mediona no one stirred and the provisions made by the bishop were politely noted and quickly forgotten.

When the bishop's visitor came four years later, in October 1578, he found that nothing had been done.[72] At Santa Maria the curtain had not been made, the infant Jesus was still without his crown, the Roman missals had not been bought, no information was available on the benefices; at St Quintí the animals were still roaming around the unlocked cemetery. From this period the episcopal visitors recognised that there was a problem of discipline involved in trying to make the country parishes fall into line. The visitor to Santa Maria in 1578 repeated all the provisions that the bishop had made, ordered further repairs, noted approvingly that the altar of St Sebastian was maintained by the faithful, ordered that altar lamps be installed and lit on the appropriate saint's day, and that a Roman missal be bought for each of the country chapels. He also for the first time made a provision intended to deal with local practices on marriage: in future no betrothed man was to visit his fiancée at her home or visit her elsewhere, unless they were first married before witnesses.[73]

The episcopal visitor in November 1581 continued the pressure. The town of St Quintí was now growing, the structure of the church had been rebuilt, and a new altar, to St Martí, was made available; but the visitor still found much to criticise. He found the old high altar, made of wood, to be rotting and dangerous, and ordered a new one of stone; he also found the tabernacle to be 'indecenter' and ordered a new one constructed. A historic innovation was introduced into Mediona with the order that 'two confessionals be made, to hear confessions'.[74] With these provisions St Quintí gradually began to move up to the size and level of Santa Maria, which in this 1581 visit showed that it was lagging, since despite the previous visit lamps had not been installed on the altars and the infant Jesus was still crownless. The last decades of the century, however, were the take-off period for investment in the Counter Reformation, and Mediona played its part. In 1586 they began to rebuild the chapel of Sta Anna, which had fallen down three years before, and contracted a builder from St Pere de Riudebitlles; in 1587 censers of silver were bought from a silversmith in Vilafranca.[75] The town of St Quintí in 1589 further took the expensive step, since it had recently changed the wooden high altar to one of stone, of commissioning a Barcelona sculptor, Joan Llunell, to make a new altarpiece of the Rosary at a contract cost of £800, with delivery in four years (he made it in one, and it was installed in 1590).[76] In 1592 a wall of Santa Maria was opened in order to construct a chapel of the Rosary, and the contract agreed with the builder Sebastià Santacana of Riudebitlles.[77] In 1595 one of the most noted sculptors of Catalonia, Agustí Pujol, who worked in Tortosa but was at the time living in St Quintí, was contracted to sculpt images of St Salvador, St Peter and St Paul for the sacristy, and to carve the angels at the foot of the Rosary altarpiece.[78] If his work at this period was as accomplished as the reredos of the Rosary he did for the church of St Vicenç of Sarrià in 1618, St Quintí had obtained a small masterpiece.

Within the last two decades of the century, then, the external and visible aspects of religion in Mediona began to take on a new character, and may have been accelerated by the transfer in 1586 to the jurisdiction of the cathedral of Barcelona. Though some pressure came from above, all developments touching the churches of the terme were brought about exclusively by the decisions of the people or by their gifts, for the church building belonged to the community alone. 'The jurats of the town', the rector noted in June 1598, 'as ordered by the visitation have had made a silver case to keep the Blessed Sacrament on the altar; they used eight ounces of silver costing £6 16s, it was made by Pau Messalla silversmith of Barcelona.' But community cash was complemented by other items, corporals and towels, bought by individuals: 'all the aforementioned items were received today, 12 June 1598, and taken to Barcelona to be blessed.'[79]

Two fundamental signs of the changes in Mediona merit comment. The first, touching worship, was the reservation of the sacrament on the altar. In the pastoral visits of 1559 and 1562 the presence of the sacrament was noted briefly as being that of 'the body of Christ'. In the visit of 1578 for the first time the term 'consecrated forms' was used, as though to call attention to the special nature of the wafers, and attention began to be paid to the place where the forms were housed. On the visit of 1581 the visitor advised the rector of St Quintí that the 'consecrated forms' be kept in a case which could be 'suitably locked with a key'. With this development the church became confirmed as a building where God was physically resident, as could be seen by the permanent flame burning visibly (a provision of the 1580s in Mediona) before the high altar. Since reservation – a practice with ample mediaeval precedents – was not practised in any of the country chapels around Mediona, the parish church became the only acceptable centre for divine worship, and its role and importance correspondingly increased.

The second development touched the people of the terme. In the scattered parish of Santa Maria there was limited scope for con-certed action among the scattered farming community; for its part the old church of St Quintí had only one altar other than the high altar for indulging popular devotions. Now all this changed. The popular devotion to the Rosary, actively fostered by Dominicans, reached the area; St Quintí led the way by creating a confraternity in August 1578, but Santa Maria followed with one in June 1595, and both churches now had altars dedicated specially to Our Lady of the Rosary. Adults of the parishes, both men and women, for the first time became active helpers in the administration of devotional aspects of the parish. Elsewhere in Spain and in Europe con-fraternities could trace their origins back to mediaeval times; in Mediona it was a new departure, which tied a growing population more closely to the parish. Other saints also quickly obtained confraternities. In 1589, as thanks for its immunity from the great epidemic, the terme held a public meeting at which the day of St Sebastian, protector against the plague, was declared a formal feast-day.[80] In June 1595 the confraternity of Sts Roc and Sebastian had its constitution approved by the bishop.[81] The success of the confraternities was shown when the chapel of the Rosary at Santa Maria was formally opened by the rector of neighbouring La Llacuna in June 1598, with solemn mass celebrated by the vicar; the membership of the confraternity of the Rosary was put at 475 persons,[82] virtually the whole adult population of Mediona.

In June 1599 four leading pagesos of the terme contracted with *mestre* Antoni Calmeix of Piera to have an altarpiece of the Rosary made for Santa Maria 'at a price of £75', with delivery in one year.[83] The new altar became the beneficiary of several testaments in the period; in 1601, for example, Samson Montluc, described as a 'labourer from Comminges' in France, willed that 'all the other goods [apart from small gifts to the parish church and to the hospital in Barcelona] that I have in this land I wish to be spent for annual masses to be said in the chapel of Our Lady of the Rosary of the parish church of Mediona'.[84] In February 1600 the church in St Quintí commissioned the painting of the altarpiece of the Rosary, but because it cost so much (£110) the jurats felt they should have a public 'adjudication' of the work in the presence of the whole town; and so on 3 July 1601 'after first ringing the bells to hold a Consell General as is the custom' they asked the artist, Antoni Rovira of Vilafranca, to present the work, and arranged to bring mestre Felix Ros, silversmith, all the way from Barcelona to give his opinion. The reluctant silversmith, who protested in vain that he was not qualified to adjudicate works of art, nevertheless rendered his judgment in a scene that is itself a cameo of the life of that era.

> Senyor bailiff, jurats and gentlemen [he said] by the commission you have given me and to satisfy both your conscience and mine, I have seen the said reredos and in my judgment I can tell you that the finish and gilt though not as subtle and delicate as it might be is none the less tolerably well done and quite well polished . . . The gilt is delicate, and if the gold appears white it is because of the reflection from the white walls of the church; the gold is not thin, and I find no fault in it. The painting in the lower half of the reredos is good and adequate, as required. The other sections are good representations of the Nativity, the Flagellation, the Agony in the Garden, and the Coronation of Our Lady. But in the painting of the Salutation the angel has to be re-done. All the rest is honestly and adequately done, and can well pass . . . [85]

The artist immediately accepted the verdict. 'I have listened to the report', he said, 'to paint the angel again and to retouch other things, as Ros directs.'

By the end of the sixteenth century, Mediona had established contact with the religious changes of the new epoch, and in 1600 was gratified to find that the outside world was also interested in it. Thanks to the diligent pen of mossèn Pere Santacana, who had moved from Santa Maria to become rector of St Quintí, 18 November 1600 remains on record as a great day in the history of the parishes. For the first time in twenty-five years, a bishop of Barcelona, Alonso Coloma, came on visitation:

> Saturday the eighteenth of this month at sunset he entered and was received in this town . . . The day after, Sunday, he said mass, then visited the sacristy and the baptismal font, preached a sermon and confirmed a great many people, bestowed first orders on six students, blessed the extension to the cemetery, blessed the vestments for the images of St Roc and St John the Evangelist. After lunch he went up to Mediona, did the visitation and confirmed a great many people and then came back to sleep in St Quintí. On Monday morning he confirmed sixty-seven more people who remained to confirm . . .

The rector was moved to record the town's impression of the bishop: 'He is a man of fifty years, of good height, polite, friendly, gentle, a charitable preacher, a stealer of the wills and hearts of people, everyone speaks well of him, everyone wishes him well, everyone prays God that Our Lord preserve him.'

And Santacana adds, in a moving final note that records the impact of the bishop's presence on the community served by this humble and unknown country priest:[86] 'I have written this so that those born hereafter may know that they should be confirmed, since all those going before have been confirmed; and as a record of how it was in Mediona, so that there be a record that a bishop came to Mediona, endowed with divine grace and goodness and worthy of honour.'

By 1600, indeed, the churches of both Santa Maria and St Quintí had taken on the form they were to conserve till the nineteenth century.[87] The latter was now a flourishing place with six altars apart from the high altar; it had twelve benches to accommodate worshippers, and a good tower with four bells. Santa Maria in its turn now had four altars apart from the high altar; it had fourteen benches and four bells in the tower, and like St Quintí had two confessionals and reservation of the sacrament on the high altar. The bishop had three provisions to make in Santa Maria: that after the collection at mass every feast day the vicar add up the cash so as to prevent fraud; that 'since the church is isolated and in an uninhabited place and for fear of thieves and evil people, the money cannot be kept there', the parishioners each year should appoint a treasurer; and that every Sunday after vespers the vicar should ring the bell and summon 'the people to the church to be taught catechism'.

Just before bishop Coloma's visit, the cathedral chapter of Barcelona had had to intervene in a dispute in St Quintí over administration of confraternities. Members of the successful confraternity of the altar of Sts Roc and Sebastian claimed that it could have its own form of electing officers, and keep its cash-box separate from that of the church. Canon Jaume Nebot came from Barcelona to try to talk sense into them: 'I've come to listen to your demands and help you reach agreement and concord for the service of Our Lord.' A Consell General was called and continued in session until one in the morning. After listening to the arguments of the confraternity spokesman the canon responded:

My good man, from what I have seen and understood from the bailiff, the jurats and the other chief men here present, they have not agreed and do not agree with your request and demand, nor do they want this privilege, and their wish is that the confraternity of St Roc and St Sebastian be administered like other confraternities and charities of this church ... As for what they say of the cash-box, I have observed that the said bailiff and jurats at the wish of the whole village have had made in the church a strong-box with five strong locks in which the wish of all is that the money from the charities of the church be put, from what I can see written in this book.

The meeting ended with the confraternity agreeing to abide by community rules, and accepting election by lot, which was then immediately carried out with the ten-year-old son of the bailiff picking out the names of officials from a drum.[88]

After 1600 there was a further visit by a bishop in 1609 and no further episcopal visits until 1636.[89] Thereafter there appears to have been only one further episcopal visitation before the end of the century (in 1685), so that the sacrament of confirmation remained virtually unknown to the rural population.

Despite its Romanesque portal and low-vaulted ceilings, the church at Santa Maria was well on the way to becoming a full-fledged Counter Reformation building. The first decade of the seventeenth century brought several decisive developments to Mediona. Following the painting in 1601 of the Rosary altarpiece of St Quintí by Rovira, in 1602 the Rosary altarpiece of Santa Maria was painted by Francesc Gomar of Igualada for the much higher figure of £150.[90] For the first time the word *daurar* (to gild) appears regularly in the contracts: over and above its expenditure on churches, Mediona was committing itself to the gold of the Baroque. The biggest expenditure of the period was the contract agonised over by the town council of St Quintí in the two years 1605–6, to 'paint and gild' the main altarpiece and other parts of the church; eventually the contract was signed in March 1607 by the cathedral chapter of Barcelona in the name of the town, with the Milanese painter Juan Baptista Toscano, then living in La Llacuna. The cost was a stunning £1400,[91] made more impressive by the fact that the terme was going through a crisis in that decade. The work was put in hand immediately, and completed three years later, in 1610 (the contract had allowed five years). In 1618 Santa Maria in its turn undertook a major contract to install a reredos of the Assumption, to be done by Bernat Perelló, carpenter of Arbós, at a cost of £550.[92] The investment of these enormous sums – worth contrasting with the prices of a generation before – is impressive testimony to the cultural change represented by the Counter Reformation, capable of encouraging farming communities to spend their surplus on religious piety. In 1625 Santa Maria contracted Rovira to do further painting in the church for £62, and in 1628 the French artist Claude Marc Antoni was contracted to paint the altarpiece of St Isidore in St Quintí.[93]

By the time of the diocesan visitation of 1683 both the parish

churches were worthy witnesses to the Counter Reformation. Santa
Maria had a gilt and painted reredos on the high altar, four altar
lamps of which one burned perpetually, and a total now of six side
altars, of which one was dedicated to St Isidore. The purging of
unseemly imagery was completed by the provision of the visitor that
the vicars 'remove an image of Our Lady from the entrance to the
choir, since it is very unbecoming, and put it in the deposit where
similar images are put'.[94] St Quintí had seven altars other than the
high altar, and a similar range of decoration. Both churches had a
good display of silver.[95] Rural piety and investment had created a
good environment for worship.

Moving our focus from the little world marked out by Mediona
within the mountains of the Penedès to the broader horizons of
Catalonia, the perspective changes but the features are recognisably
similar. In the sixteenth century the Catalan countryside was made
up of small settlements which in the interior regions of Urgell and
Pallars and in the Pyrenees fell to a population density of no more
than one household per square kilometre. Demographic movement
was continuously towards the coast, which offered better land,
commerce and employment: Barcelona absorbed the immigration
and grew throughout the period, but the typical environment of the
time was less urban than rural. When Arthur Young made a quick
tour through the province in 1788 he noted that 'we travelled
about three hundred and forty miles through the province and may
conclude that not one acre in a hundred is under any sort of
cultivation,' but his route took him through the forested foothills of
the Pyrenees and the rocky terrain around Montserrat, so that to
him most of inland Catalonia was miserable: 'the poverty of the
people in the interior country is striking, their houses old, ill built,
dirty and wretched.'[96] As he correctly concluded, the weight of
economic activity was in 'the towns upon the coast, and they are
very numerous and very populous'; but like other travellers down
to modern times he underestimated the part played by the interior
in the make-up of the country, and expressed only grudging admiration for what the Catalans had been able to achieve 'in a country
submitted to numerous festival days by its religion'.

As in Mediona, it was the peasant family in the mas, the traditional farm-house, that cultivated the land and provided political
and cultural continuity in the countryside.[97] In the seventeenth
century there were some thirty-three masies in the terme of
Mediona;[98] some had been there for four centuries already, most
have continued their existence until today on hillside and valley,
surviving in some cases merely as spectacular ruins. The mas safe-

guarded its own existence, and therefore the economic stability of rural society, by a careful ordering of succession and property rights, which can be followed in the meticulous marriage contracts of the period. By ruling out any division of the lands exploited by the masia, and restricting succession rights to only one heir, the masia gained economic stability at the expense of social stability, since younger sons were left propertyless and had to reconcile themselves either to working with the family or emigrating, creating an unstable element which both contemporaries and historians have blamed for the phenomenon of banditry in the principality.

The masia was a complete unit of exploitation, usually owning twenty to forty hectares of land, sufficient for the family. In its simplest form, it might have a proportion of soil directly worked by the master, who lived in the mas, while the remainder of the estate was worked by *masovers* living in their own dwelling on the land. In a scheme which has changed little through the centuries, the family house would lie in the middle of the estate, with the surrounding soil given over to cultivation of grain and vegetables, while the outlying areas would be reserved for wood and pasture. In early modern Mediona the masies changed their personnel frequently as masovers came and went, but the mas itself remained rock-steady in the hands of the same family from century to century. The land was worked through short-term contracts which in the mid-seventeenth century varied from three to five years: in a typical lease in 1665[99] Joan Gostems of Puigmoltó let out to Isidre Santacana for three years a portion of the estate, on which Santacana had to pay all taxes including those to the monastery of Santes Creus, and had to give to Gostems each year one-sixth of grain, and one-third of oil, wine and almonds, as well as rear a fat pig which Gostems would buy from him each Christmas. The masia combined within itself most rural activities, and its independence made it the backbone of the individuality which characterised the mentality and religion of rural Catalonia.[100]

The masies of Mediona, accounting for some three-fifths of the terme's population, were enclaves of multiple families of the traditional type: three generations, including brothers and sisters, and not omitting the servants, lived under the same roof. In Mas Pagès the Castellvi family, which in 1552 had one of its members as vicar of Santa Maria, united twelve people under one roof, and the same number made up the Puigdengoles family in neighbouring Conques; in Mas Ginoles at the same date there were at least fourteen people, forming the Farrera family. Though apparently separated by the ample fields and woods that divided one mas from the other, in practice the families formed a continuous community, marrying among themselves and settling at will throughout the terme without affecting the integrity of the masies: in the early seventeenth century there were Puigdengoles also in La Freixeneda, Farrera also in Mas Ubach and St Joan, Tort in both St Quintí and St Pere Sacarrera.

The masters of the masies and their peasants, besides being the focus of traditional society and the economy, were also the mainstay of traditional religion. As in Mediona, they were the support of the local church and invested part of their surplus in the only insurance then available, pious endowments which would pave their way to heaven; they built altars, founded benefices, and made loans (censals) to the Church. It was common for a larger mas to have its own chapel, so that there was no need to leave the household even for religion. But though loyalties centred on the household they also took active account of society outside it, and of the demands of trade, marriage, the parish and the local community. The complex seigneurial regime of Catalonia reinforced this localism, by splitting up jurisdictional loyalties.

In the *vegueria* of Vilafranca during the early seventeenth century, of 123 communities only thirty-two were wholly in the king's jurisdiction, thirty-three were governed by several Church entities, and all the rest, covering the greater part of the landscape and representing roughly half the communities of the region, were in the hands of secular lords. In the neighbouring vegueria of Tarragona, only three towns (Tarragona and two others) were in royal jurisdiction: all the other communities were seigneurial, with the lion's share going to the see of Tarragona.[101] This picture was repeated over the rest of Catalonia, with some 72 per cent of the towns and cities and roughly two-thirds of the population not subject to royal jurisdiction in the crucial areas of taxation, justice and law and order; a situation with immense implications for government policy.

The fragmentation of civil and religious units, aggravated in the north by the geography of the Pyrenees, had profound consequences for the history and society of the Catalan lands. At the same time that an apparatus of royal government and constitutional organisation was developing in Barcelona, in the countryside the traditional community substructure continued to persist almost undisturbed, aided powerfully by the subdivisions of jurisdiction. As in other western nations, the shared elements of a common ruling dynasty, a common spoken tongue and a common territory were slow to impose a firm identity on a Catalonia within which many and different societies preserved their autonomy intact. Of these, the most striking were in the Pyrenees.

The Catalan lands of the central and eastern Pyrenees, a spectacular area that stretched from the Vall d'Arán through Andorra and Cerdanya to Rosselló and represented about one-third of the surface of the principality, were fragmented by their geography into small communities whose isolation gave them effective independence from each other and from all outside authority. Each valley or group of valleys constituted an autonomous community,[102] as in the valleys of Carol and Osseja, governing itself through assemblies of the heads of families which imposed community norms that in some cases extended to full community ownership of certain amenities, in particular the rights of pasture. This communal collectivism was a type of social organisation quite different from the individualism of the masies, but no less an aspect of rural independence in Catalonia. Ultimate feudal lordship rested with kings, nobles and bishops, but in practice the valleys were given full freedom to run themselves. Typical was the Vall d'Arán, which since the fourteenth century had enjoyed rights to almost complete freedom from taxation and military service and had communal use of land and water. In the neighbouring Vall d'Aneu the Bon Consell de la Vall consisting of all heads of families elected a popular council of six, which governed the valley in the name of its seigneur the duke of Cardona. The valleys traded and treated with each other as sovereign states, regardless of their lords, and from 1293 to 1725 the major valleys of the central Pyrenees maintained a series of 'peace' treaties or *patzeries* by which they regulated trade and transhumance; even more notable was the 1513 treaty, subsequently renewed, by which several valleys (including Arán) on both the French and the Spanish sides of the Pyrenees guaranteed to preserve peace among themselves in the event of war between their countries,[103] thereby giving the communities priority over the nation.

Local autonomy, jealously preserved and where possible extended, generated local forms of economic and social organisation and religious practice, and strengthened regional solidarity. Not only in the mountain valleys but throughout Catalonia, the loyalty of people to their community and its way of life preceded all other loyalties. As elsewhere in Mediterranean Europe, the bonds that united people, dictated principally by their religious aspirations and their concern for economic survival, were always local. In mediaeval Catalonia, the Christian parish offered the necessary nucleus for action;[104] but as settlements extended and the feudal regime asserted itself, parishes were submerged in larger groupings of village communities protected by a lord.

The nature of a 'community' depended on the legal agreements which brought it into existence.[105] It might be a town grouping in which certain key decisions were made by the inhabitants and in which the lord normally had a voice;[106] it might also be a multiple grouping of towns, united by common geography or a common seigneur, meeting under the same conditions. Two functions in particular defined the historic community: its role in religion, and in the use of natural resources.[107] In religion its jurisdictional limits tended to coincide with those of the rural parish, and the church was often used as the centre for communal meetings. The fact that the parish priest was, in Catalonia, frequently appointed by an external secular authority might appear to have been a threat to the solidarity of communal religion, but at least in Mediona this was not so: throughout the early modern period the rectors and vicars were regularly recruited from among the local families. When the population census of 1553 was made, the rector of St Quintí was Mateu Busquets, from a leading family in the town, and the vicar of Santa Maria was mossèn Castellví, whose family lived in Mas Pagès. Possibly every parish priest in Mediona in the early modern period was either a local son or came from the immediate vicinity: rectors such as Tort (1565), Puigdengoles (1595), Esteve (1620), Gili (1610), Gostems (1747), were from the terme, while others such as Santacana (1583, of La Llacuna), Ferrer (1606, of St Pere de Riudebitlles), and Valtá (one in 1579, one in 1595, of Capellades) completed the panorama of local recruitment. Families such as the Busquets and Santacana played an active part in the ordering of the community (a Busquets made the statue of the Virgin for the Rosary altar of Santa Maria in 1595) and have survived down to the present century. The recruitment of clergy from the masies made the mas into the focal centre of traditional religion in Catalonia. The picture that we find in Mediona was duplicated in the Pyrenees. In the little community of Egat in Cerdanya, subject to the jurisdiction of the bishop of Urgell, the rector throughout the seventeenth and early eighteenth centuries was drawn exclusively from one family, that of Aymar, which together with the families Fabra and Margall constituted the core of the population of some forty people.[108]

A traveller through the towns would have been impressed by the dominance of bells, conventual and cathedral, over the urban landscape, seemingly confirming the sovereign authority of God. The impression reflected the growing concentration of property in the hands of the Church, which by the seventeenth century came to own up to half of all real estate in the major cities of Spain. But out in the countryside the bells had a different story. There they tolled for mass and sacraments, vespers and Sunday school, but they did so because these were services to the community; and it was the community, which had paid for them out of its meagre resources, that relied on them to be called to assemblies, to be warned of disaster, or to be rallied in case of attack. In traditional society the bells were not religious but communitarian.

The community dimension was fundamental to Christianity, for the concept of a 'personal' faith was unknown or at best limited to mystics; the practice of religion coincided almost wholly with the functioning of the community. In a society with an almost exclusively agrarian economy, the cycle of seasons and agrarian production dictated all aspects of communal and religious life; work could not be divorced from religion. The absence of intensive work schedules outside the rhythm of sowing and harvesting meant moreover that leisure time was considerable and was also ordered by the community and its religion. 'Work' and 'leisure' were not sharply distinguished from each other: both formed part of a continuous cycle of events and customs that repeated themselves year after year in a well-ordered calendar which regulated the life of the local community, and in which all parts of the community, rich and poor, played a recognised role.[109] The outward form of the calendar was ecclesiastical, with dates and seasons determined by official saints and established observances such as Lent; within that framework the parishes had since time out of memory evolved their own customs, nurtured their own saints, established their own timetable for work and for leisure, creating a series of practices and customs which helped to give the local community an identity of its own. Religion in former times was so intimately interwoven with the life of the community that it may appear difficult to define it, but at least in Catalonia it seems clear that traditional religion was more social than sacramental, and the rites on which Trent (like the Lateran Council before it) placed so much emphasis played a subordinate part in the life of the community and the Church.

In the mild climate of the Mediterranean, religious and social life was intimately tied to the seasons. The Jesuit Pere Gil in 1600 commented that

> all of us who live in this principality have to give many thanks to the Lord for placing us in this land, where we neither suffer the cold that they suffer who live in northern parts and have always to be shut up with stoves or to leave off their labour, nor do we suffer the heat that they suffer who live in the torrid zone. Rather we have in this principality a wholly temperate clime, with the change and variety of three months of winter, three of spring, three of summer and three of autumn, with no great excess of heat or cold. And this variety is the reason why the year is no trouble to us, and life no burden, and man always has time to devote himself to spiritual things.[110]

The most fundamental component of the annual cycle was the calendar of work, in which the various days and seasons for sowing, shearing, harvesting, threshing and other duties were fixed in accordance with local climate and the nature of the local economy. The allotted days were described by names of saints,[111] but their primary importance was agrarian, not liturgical; the saints functioned as symbols and signposts, indicating the traditional rotation of duties, and had restricted sacred significance. When a pagès of Vic wished to record the excess of rain in the winter of 1641 he put it this way: 'When we were in the middle of sowing it began to rain and the earth took a long time to dry out, but for all that we sowed by St Andreu, and by Ninou the tips of the blades of wheat were just coming out. This year it rained all summer, we couldn't harvest a blade until after St Miquel.'[112]

Interleaved with the work calendar came the calendar of leisure, fundamentally a ritual of rest and reproduction, in which fell the seasons of courtship, marriage and birth which gave life to the community. Within this cycle of rest there were also days which by custom allowed the communal expression of feelings of conflict and protest,[113] and in which the young of the parish were given licence. Once again, the major points of the leisure year were indicated by saints' days. The great festivities of the Church were the signposts to all activity in the parish, but their content was not necessarily religious; sacred and secular were interwoven in a perpetual cycle which remained unchanged for centuries even after the attempts of the Counter Reformation to regulate it. By integrating work and leisure the calendar helped to integrate the sacred and the profane in the social life of communities, producing for example community rituals and celebrations that were at one and the same time both sacred and profane, both work and play;[114] but there were also areas and rites which were recognisably only sacred, and which each member of the community might experience in his transition from one part of his life to the next.[115] The role of the sacred, highly ritualised when applied to the whole community, became more real when applied to the individual.

The environment within which men worshipped was not fixed but constantly changing. Though religion was rooted in local experience,[116] it also recognised universal symbols that retained their validity over great distances, and defects in the local practice of religion were compensated by the search for symbols elsewhere. At its most extensive, popular faith of this type resorted to pilgrimages, which in the middle ages were assiduously cultivated to promote the financial viability of sites such as the shrine of St James in Galicia. But it was not necessary to go so far. The everyday world had its own moving frontier of faith, typified by the crucial role in rural life of transhumance. The herds of sheep and goats on which every community depended, above all in the Pyrenees, had to be moved towards pasture in a cycle of transhumance that took place on explicitly allotted feast days, resulting over the centuries in long routes of migration which extended all the way from the Pyrenees to the hills of southern Catalonia. As they moved, the shepherds took with them their own local faith but along the way they also developed a whole range of practices and beliefs that entered into the fabric of Catalan religion.[117] The isolated chapels and hermitages of the mountains were the centres of devotion of the shepherds, to whom primarily is due the discovery and proliferation of the numerous mediaeval shrines to the Virgin, based on the miraculous discovery by a sheep or an ox of a statue which would be immediately venerated by the local population. On remote or inaccessible heights to which no one but a shepherd would have dared to venture, cults of the Virgin sprang into existence and endured for centuries, outstanding among them the cult of the Virgin of Núria, six thousand feet above the valley of the Freser, or the shrine of Montgarri, five thousand feet above the Noguera in Pallars. The shepherd who as I write can be seen slowly moving his sheep and goats, their bells tinkling, over the rocky hillsides of Mediona, is the survivor of a long agrarian tradition that helped to shape a profound dimension of Catalan religion. The annual cycle of feasts in Catalonia shows clearly the interaction of secular and sacred in daily life.[118]

The four major liturgical cycles of the year were those which led up to Christmas, Easter, Midsummer, and harvest. The calendar year in traditional Catalonia commenced at Christmas, as decreed in 1350 and observed throughout this period. It consisted of a series of rituals carefully signposted by long custom and marked out, for ease of comprehension, to coincide with the feasts of the Church. The Christmas season, a time of rest for agriculture and working adults, was dominated from the Feast of the Innocents (22 December) to the Feast of Kings (6 January) by the needs of the young, who received gifts on the latter feast. New Year's day was celebrated in Barcelona by the Consellers with a procession, and at the church of Santa Maria del Mar cakes were distributed after mass. One of the saints most invoked against epidemic was St Sebastià (20 January): in Monistrol de Montserrat the confraternity of the saint, headed by its 'abbot', elected its committee of *pabordes*, who had to perform a dance. By Candlemas (2 February) winter in the Mediterranean was preparing to take its leave: the ball de l'Os (dance of the bear), danced in Arles at Candlemas, ended with the symbolic killing of the bear, symbolising winter. On the same day, the people in Valls danced and celebrated with the construction of *castells* (also called *moixigangues* elsewhere), in which the pyramid of humans surmounted by a young child enacted magical ceremonies of growth and fertility for the fields. By early February the cycle of rejoicing that had commenced at Christmas completed itself with the outburst of Carnival (in Catalan, *Carnestoltes*), covering the days that preceded Ash Wednesday. At the end of the rejoicings and rituals a figure representing the licence of Carnival was ritually buried (the 'burial of the sardine') or burned (a mock-figure) to the accompaniment of dancing and feasting. In parts of the Penedès, and specifically in St Quintí, there was also a community purging in which a *moixo-foguer*, or man dressed as a bird, ran through the village pouring scorn on husbands who were dominated by their wives or whose wives were being unfaithful to them.[119] St Quintí was typical of communities in which the figure burned as Carnestoltes was a *ninot*.[120] The long weeks of Lent were a time of waiting: human reproduction itself ceased, as marriages could not be sanctified in that period. Dancing was generally forbidden, though in April on Thursday of Holy Week the village of Verges put on a unique Dance of Death; while at Perpinyà a confraternity put on a solemn Procession 'de la Sanch' (of the Blood). With Easter Sunday joy and resurrection returned: bells rang, the vestments of mourning were changed for robes of white, eggs (a classic symbol of fertility) were decorated and consumed. Just after this there was general celebration of St George (Jordi), the 'patró del Principat' (23 April). From this time the whole community dedicated itself to the task of survival and production: marriages were blessed, and the erection of trees as May-poles on the first of May, with dances around them, symbolised the return of life. When Henry Cock accompanied Philip II to Catalonia in 1585 he observed the custom in many parts. On Holy Cross day (3 May) the parish boundaries were beaten and the fields blessed. On the feast of St Isidore (15 May) 'the feast of all the farmers, in all the villages musicians play the evening before, and on the day itself there is music at mass and processions and dances in the evening in the square'.[121] In the village of Sant Privat d'En Bas in the Pyrenees of Rosselló, a dance was performed in which St Isidore symbolically ploughed the ground with a stick, while little girls dressed as angels strewed rose-petals behind him. As the sun mounted in the sky the agrarian cycle reaffirmed its priority in the rural calendar of duties.

By June, Sant Joan (St John's) (24th) or Midsummer's Eve brought to a climax the human and the agrarian ritual: purifying and life-giving fires were lit, and under the symbol of fire – made famous in the wooden *fallas* that were burnt in Valencia – the sun was asked to render the fields fruitful. In towns throughout the principality *corre-focs* or fire-runs were made through the main streets, with fireworks. 'There is a lot of bustle in the streets,' a resident of eighteenth-century Barcelona noted, 'and not a few disturbances, people going to bathe in the sea and looking for excitement; music, and fires on the mountains – what used to be in the old days the fire of St Joan in the houses, streets and squares of this city.'[122] At the same time, the night became a witching-time for lovers, who were supposed then to succeed in finding partners. Rites of fire were accompanied by rites of water. Rose-water was used in ceremonies, reflecting an old belief that whatever it touched on that night would not age. Maidens who washed their faces at midnight would preserve their beauty. The ritual of fire was followed almost immediately by that of blood, with the celebration a week later of Corpus Christi (29 June), the central religious devotion of the Church in the Catalan lands, typified at the secular level by a procession of giant statues.

The end of summer, with the (hopefully) successful gathering-in of the wheat sheaves, began the season through July and August of *Festes Majors* in the villages and towns of Catalonia. In July festivals of bread were common in many towns, accompanied by communal meals of thanks. In Arles the Festa Major was chosen to coincide with the ancient feast of Sts Abdón and Senén (30 July), patron saints of farmers, when the town exhibited its relics of its patrons. In St Quintí the Festa Major was celebrated on the Sunday after the feast of the Assumption (15 August); the town paraded its giant statues (which had been used during Corpus), and among other dances performed one which was to be found throughout the Penedès but for which it became particularly well known, the *ball dels Diables*.[123] As celebrated today, the Festa Major of St Quintí displays all the typical characteristics of the traditional feasts. On the eve of the Festa the procession, introduced and accompanied by the steady rhythm of drums, is led first of all by the diables, who go through the streets spouting fire (the corre-focs); they are followed by a group of ninots and by the giant statues, which dance as they wind through the town; some way behind come the *bastoners* with their traditional dance of the sticks; then the procession is closed by a group of little girls. Outside the town hall, a group of castellers display their skills to the public; then the diables perform their dance while a series of satirical verses is read out to the laughter and acclaim of those present. For many places throughout Catalonia, the feast of the Virgin of August (the fifteenth) was that of their own Virgin: in Bellver de Cerdanya the Virgin of Talló, in

Cotlliure the Virgin of Consolation, in Prats de Molló the Virgin of Coral. It was followed the next day by another popular feast, that of St Roc (16 August), always bearded and with a dog, and revered as protector against illnesses and the plague. In Capellades, neighbour to Mediona, it was the custom to have a big communal feast in honour of St Roc's dog.

Where communities were more dependent on the wine harvest at the end of September, the Festa Major was correspondingly later, and coincided with days of the Virgin, whose feasts began in September (Nativity, 8 September, celebrated in the Pyrenees as the feast of the Virgin of Núria) but whose particular month was October, when the confraternities of the Rosary were most active. It was also the month of St Galderic (16 October), the principal saint of Rosselló, whose remains rested on the spectacular mountain of Canigó. The closing of the productive year in autumn brought a lull also in religious activity, with the opening of the advent season that led to the Christmas feasts.

The calendar dominated the life of all communities both large and small, but a special place must be assigned to the city, where on top of the normal seasonal rituals was superimposed the ceremonial of the urban elite. As performed in, for example, pre-Reformation Coventry,[124] the year for the citizen was divided up into its own seasonal ceremonials, determined in part by the guilds, in part by the traditional celebrations – May Day, Midsummer, Christmas, 'Misrule' – that provided a safety-valve for urban tensions. Catalonia had only one city whose urban ceremonial was complex enough to be compared to that of other European centres, and during the epoch of the Counter Reformation Barcelona continued to develop its ritual calendar. If in Coventry, as no doubt in other cities, ceremony 'was a societal mechanism ensuring continuity, promoting cohesion and controlling conflicts',[125] in Barcelona it became something more: a means to establish both spiritual and political hegemony over the principality.

The participation of religion in leisure produced what we may call 'rites of joy', a concept accepted by the Church synod at Augsburg which in 1548 divided its public processions into two categories, 'those of sadness and those of joy',[126] and reflected in the vision of the feasts and feastings in spring given by a Catalan nobleman of the eighteenth century:

Happy days in this time of May, the most joyful and florid of the year, men and women in celebrations in the countryside in their country houses and villas, and villages feasting the delicious season of spring...
Time now to take lunch at tables in the open air, eating broad beans

with black pudding and pickled pork, and a green soup with peas and other vegetables; and for dessert, for those who can, delicate strawberries all covered in sugar. It is Maytime, the days are longer, and for some now is the time to set out on their travels, such as the friars, who know well how to seek their creature comforts by going now to their provincial chapters. Days outside in the green fields crowned with ears of corn and other crops, and on the trees the first beautiful leaves and tiny fruits, roses on bushes and other flowers... The sweet song of birds, and everything that is beautiful in this loveliest season of the year.[127]

But the universe was also menaced with insecurity and fear.[128] The diary of the peasant farmer Joan Guàrdia of Vic[129] shows the presence at every turn of insecurity: death, which took away four of his six children during his lifetime, and his first wife at the early age of twenty-five; war, which spread misery throughout the area in which he lived; drought, which blighted the fields, and rains, which ruined them; plague, which in 1650 devastated the province. One year of disaster could follow another: 'this year 1650 is the year of misery', but then, hard on its heels, 'the year 1651 is the year of the tribulations of hunger, plague and war', three of the horsemen of the apocalypse.

Because all life was uncertain and only death certain, through the centuries use was made of 'rites of deliverance' that were an accepted and sometimes efficacious remedy. Three enemies, traditionally exorcised in ceremonies of the Church, invited formal measures of protection: hunger (through drought, locusts, rains), epidemic, and war. At a popular level all these natural disasters were deemed to be controllable through the agents that brought them about, and the intervention of the priest was frequently called upon: 'I must admit', the seventeenth-century Franciscan Noydens admitted, 'that in many parts the common people are not satisfied until they see the parish priest at the church or cemetery entrance, with his cope and stole, sprinkling holy water and with his cross pointed to the clouds.'[130] The most notorious form of exorcism used against pests was the so-called 'excommunication', condemned by prelates and theologians in the early sixteenth century.[131] It went on nevertheless: the cursing of pests was practised in Provence in the mid-sixteenth century, and in Italy a writer of the late century condemned its use.[132] Inquisitor General Valdés was widely reputed to have excommunicated rats out of his diocese of Oviedo in the mid-sixteenth century, and as late as 1650 in a case of excommunication of locusts in Segovia the priest who performed the ritual cited in his justification previous excommunications directed against locusts in Avila, rats in Osma and swallows in Córdoba.[133] Majority opinion, resumed by Noydens, agreed however 'that creatures without feeling and reason, such as clouds, thunder, lightning, locusts, insect pests and other brute animals, cannot be conjured'.[134]

In Spain the lack of rain was a permanent hazard. The ideal climate of the principality, pinpointed by Pere Gil as one of God's favours to Catalans, did not exclude the perpetual concern for adequate water: it dominated the private annotations of all diarists of the time, and in Mediona prompted mossèn Santacana to record every significant presence or absence of rain. In October 1600 he noted how 'for two hours it rained in torrents with thunder and wind... the gutters could not take the water since they were too full and the water entered through the tiles and through the doors of houses with the force of the wind; so much water came into the houses that people were terrified, fearing that the houses would collapse and that the world would come to an end with water.'[135] More usually, Santacana noted the scarcity of water, and his record for 1602 lists every day of rain in the year: 'it rained in October and November [1601] a good bit, but then it did not rain till the April of 1602, that is on the first of April when it rained for three days. In addition it rained from the sixteenth to the twenty-first to the great satisfaction of everybody, because in this way wheat was at 40s [a load] and in good demand.' In times of drought the normal procedure was to resort to rain rituals, pleading with specific saints (whose efficacy in times past had been proven) to intervene with heaven for relief. Despite much scepticism among educated clergy the rituals continued unchanged through the Counter Reformation and into modern times. In Segovia in 1586 a synod forbade the popular practice of dipping into streams and wells 'the bodies and relics of saints' to obtain rain; in Saragossa another in 1615 called for an enquiry into the same custom.[136] The bishop of Barcelona in 1611 referred with disapproval to the common practice in many places of 'in times of storm, fire, war or similar cases, taking out the Blessed Sacrament from the church, and in times of drought bathing the true cross or relics of saints'.[137]

In Barcelona the most used saint was Santa Madrona, whose body was kept in the monastery on Montjuic. In times of drought the Consellers would make a formal request to the monks for 'the holy body of the glorious Virgin, through whom this city obtains many graces in times of drought, and many miracles',[138] and the body would be escorted in procession around the parishes. Rain processions usually took place in April or May, and in Barcelona were frequent enough to be almost annual. The ritual was usually successful, as in 1561 when the secretary of the city council noted that 'this morning the clergy went to the chapel and took out the holy bodies of Sta Madrona and other glorious martyrs ... And the night of the same day it began to rain.'[139] Sometimes the normal relics would not produce the desired effect, so further and more desperate approaches to other relics would be made. Typical was the drought of 1627, which continued through the winter: in April 1628 'in Barcelona there was a big procession which went from the cathedral to the convent of Santa Clara, carrying the body of St Sever to plead for water ... This is usually the very last procession undertaken in times of need,' but this final measure was not enough and a special procession (not done since 1571) was made to Sta Eulàlia at Sarrià, and three days after that the church of Santa Maria del Mar brought out its most sacred relics, of Sts Isidore and Philip Neri, both recently canonised and thus the very final word in appeals to heaven. However, 'our sins kept the heavens shut'.[140] At this stage the bishop had to step in and perform a public ceremony, and 'the next day it rained a bit', proof of 'the power of the Church, which shuts and opens the heavens'; but his power seems not to have extended to Empúries where this diarist, Jeroni Pujades, was then living, and the local clergy there had to exorcise the heavens for themselves.

In Rosselló the saint most invoked was St Galderic, whose remains had been preserved since the tenth century by the monks of the Benedictine abbey of Sant Martí on the mystical peak of Canigó. In times of great distress the communities of Rosselló claimed to be able to borrow the body of the saint to rid them of their problems, a right they were capable of insisting on to the point of war.[141] At Perpinyà it was the practice, of remote origins and followed throughout the period of the Counter Reformation, to borrow the relics in times of drought. In the manuscript memoirs of the community of priests of the church of Sant Jaume in Perpinyà, it was recorded that 'in the year 1566 on the 22nd of March the town sent an embassy to the convent of Sant Martí de Canigó' for the relic of the saint. 'On the twenty-fifth of the month it arrived in the town and a procession began from the New Bridge with all the clergy, the governor and the *Cónsols* ... and on the twenty-ninth of the month between five and six in the morning a general procession set out for the sea with the saint ... and when they arrived at the sea they wet the saint with the salt water.' Other saints were used for the same purpose in later years (in 1605 the community chronicler noted that 'in May they carried in procession to the sea the arm of the glorious Saint Agatha virgin and martyr, to obtain rain from heaven through her intercession').[142]

A special committee of the city council decided in 1668 'that because of the great drought of water that there is at present in the whole land of Rosselló and Vallespir, and the great harm suffered by the fruits of the earth which are necessary to sustain the human body, the relic of the body of the glorious saint Galderic be sent for'.[143] A delegation of three was appointed to go and ask the monastery for the body, a sum of money had to be allotted for the expenses of the transport, and a notarised agreement had eventually to be drawn up in which the city promised to return the body (not an idle consideration, since the monks in the tenth century had themselves robbed the body from another monastery). From the documented evidence it appears that the city asked for and obtained the body roughly every two years in the seventeenth century, and that because of this frequency long-term financial agreements were made (a typical agreement signed in 1646 remained valid until 1692). There remained the practical problem of transport. Security was involved, since the saint's head was encased in gilded silver, his body had to be accompanied by a large number of ornaments including a gilded crown, garments worked in silver, and a crucifix of crystal; and the distance travelled, over difficult mountain routes, was such that the pious procession winding its way back to Perpinyà took four days and three nights to cover one hundred miles, with overnight stops in the towns of Prada, Vinça and Millars.[144] Once in Perpinyà, the saint formed the head of yet another procession, this time bound for Santa Maria la Mar, where the civic authorities, the confraternities of the city and the local population, a total of several thousands, assisted at the ritual dipping of the relic into the sea accompanied by prayers for rain:

> Puig t'agrada Deu de vos   Since God favours you
> com de altre just Abel,   as another just Abel,
> feu baixar pluja del cel   bring the rain from heaven
> Galderich, sant glorios.   glorious St Galderic.

If it did not rain the saint could be scolded; he also faced another dipping into the sea on a subsequent day if he failed to perform. Tradition says that he invariably obliged with rain.

Because the land depended wholly on the heavens, rain rituals formed a fundamental part of agrarian life, and the majority of goigs[145] to local saints include petitions for rain. The diary of a farmer in Vic reflects the measures taken in the face of a long drought in the winter of 1649–50: 'the earth could not germinate, we could well say it was the year of the drought, the number of processions that people made was frightening, and we carried Our Lady of the Rosary in two processions, and others in mourning carried Christs and went to St Genis, and two weeks later we went to St Sebastian in the same manner, and each time it rained a little and the weather got cooler...Then on 12 June it began to rain very hard.'[146] A generation later, his son was performing the same rituals: 'it didn't rain from All Saints to the end of May, everyone was terrified, all the villages went in procession and afterwards it rained a lot.' In Barcelona the majority of public processions and prayers conducted by the city council were for rain. It has been calculated that 'from 1515 to 1631, sixty-four dry spells occasioned over six hundred processions in the streets of Barcelona, five times more than for all other reasons combined':[147] within that period, the body of Santa Madrona was brought out fifty-one times, processions to churches of the Virgin occurred forty-six times, there were processions to the Wounds of Christ twenty-three times, the body of St Sever was taken to the convent of Santa Clara thirteen times, and the relics of the True Cross were dipped in the sea twelve times, the last such occasion being in 1584, after which it was presumably forbidden by the bishop as superstitious. One-third of all public prayers in the city during the eighteenth century, each time accompanied by a procession, were likewise for rain. It was identical in the villages: in one eighteenth-century parish a third of the processions, concentrated between May and August, were related to agrarian production and pleas for rain.[148]

Although processions for rain formed the major part of all the communal rituals of deliverance, there were other less frequent disasters that invited action, notably the onset of epidemic. Catalonia in early modern times was a nation with good population growth and a healthy economy, which makes it the more remarkable that it suffered frequent and – in the Pyrenees – continuous epidemics. Rosselló suffered major epidemics of plague in 1560–4, 1586–92, 1628–32 and 1648–54; the city of Perpinyà, with a possible population of 10,000, suffered around 4000 deaths in the years 1589–92, and 6700 deaths in 1631–2.[149] In February 1593 the city council minutes, the Llibre de Totis, comment that 'in the past days there has been such mortality of persons in the present town, with such ferocity and havoc, that many and almost an infinite number have died without being able to receive the holy sacraments of confession, eucharist and extreme unction'; and that the costs occasioned were such that 'it would be fearful and terrible to state them'.[150] The ravages of the plague destroyed communities and spread misery everywhere. It was before the threat of such an epidemic that in 1639 the Consell General of Prada, twenty strong, met on a cold December day in the valley, to discuss 'the great illnesses that there are today in this town and other villages and

places and counties around it', and 'if it seemed one should send for
the relic of the glorious St Galderic of the monastery of St Martí de
Canigó and bring it down to the town and perform the accustomed
services and processions', for the saint to 'intercede with Our Lord
and God Jesus Christ to remedy the many great needs caused by the
illnesses, and also the wars that there are in the counties and
principality of Catalonia'.[151]

With a bigger population and even higher levels of epidemic
mortality, Barcelona had greater need of protection. In 1466 it had
'vowed' (a procedure we have seen in the case of St Quintí) to adopt
St Sebastian as patron against the plague, but waited until 1563
before it 'vowed' St Roc in the same cause.[152]

The coming of the Counter Reformation to Catalonia may be
pinned down for convenience to one date – the provincial council of
Tarragona in 1565 – but should more properly be seen within the
broader context that favoured its reception and growth. Four distinct dimensions, imperial, economic, spiritual and civic, provided
the parameters within which it was able to take root and flourish.

The active European foreign policy of the Habsburgs intensified
the links that Spain had already had with Italy and northern Europe
under the Catholic Kings, and by his regular use of Barcelona as a
point of departure Charles V drew Catalans inevitably into more
intimate contact with their neighbours. Though Philip II was less
itinerant than his father, he perforce had to use Barcelona for
diplomatic links and the transport of men and bullion, while the
growth of heresy in France aroused concern for the security of
Catalonia. Barcelona consequently remained at the centre of
international currents, and open to the influences that came to the
peninsula from Italy.

In the mid-sixteenth century both Castile and Catalonia were in a
phase of economic expansion fed by demographic growth, good
climatic conditions, favourable trade patterns with European
markets and the new possibilities available in America.[153] In Castile
there were growing problems in the later century, but in the principality by contrast the growth momentum of the early century
was maintained, so that the high tide of the Counter Reformation
coincided with a period of social expansion. A population rise in
Catalonia of about 75 per cent between 1553 and 1626 has been
suggested, an expansion unparalleled in western Europe and common to both the interior and the coastal areas of the principality.
Though Barcelona with about 30,000 people was the only large
urban centre, the smaller towns also raised their population levels,
with the possible exception of Perpinyà, soon to become a prey to

military struggles and epidemic. The special factor which made demographic expansion possible was a stream of immigrants from France, precisely from the mid-sixteenth century to the early decades of the seventeenth.[154] Most (some 80 per cent) came when young, and though they tended to live on the coast about half were employed in agriculture. A high proportion married and settled down permanently: one of every six men marrying in this period in Barcelona was French. In much of the principality the period from the second half of the sixteenth century up to 1630 was one of stability in agrarian production:[155] this was precisely the setting in which investment and reconstruction became possible.

As in Mediona, everywhere in Catalonia population growth and agrarian stability were direct stimuli to reconstruction, and a veritable fever of rebuilding seized the principality. In his dialogue on Tortosa the contemporary Despuig commented that 'the city is being improved and extended in a thousand ways and specially in buildings both public and private.'[156] In Esparraguera the process of expansion could be clearly measured. The old mediaeval parish church of Santa Maria del Puig had sufficed when the village was still small, but with growth in the late fifteenth century a need became apparent for a new parish, and the church of Sta Eulàlia was accordingly built in 1523 and became the main parish church just before 1580. Since then, 'the number of parishioners has kept on increasing continually and the town is so much bigger that in 1587 and indeed long before it was clear that the said two churches were not enough nor sufficient for the parishioners, from which it was agreed that another and new parish church needed to be built,' which was done that year.[157] The generation that grew up at the end of the reign of Philip II witnessed a growth in religious foundations without equal in the history of Catalonia.[158] Pere Gil, rector of the Jesuits in Barcelona, testified in 1600 that 'in the past fifty years there have been constructed or renovated very many churches in Catalonia, both for religious orders and for parishes, and many monasteries have been founded for different orders, and few or no churches have been pulled down.'[159] His testimony for Catalonia is supported by the evidence for Valencia, where during the years that Juan de Ribera held the see (1569–1611) at least eighty-three religious houses were founded.[160]

Within a favourable economic climate the sporadic disasters could also be a stimulus to religious activity: droughts, floods, frost, epidemic, intensified rather than diminished rituals of deliverance and the adoption of patron saints, and consequently the founding of altars and confraternities. The great freeze of 1573–4, the great floods of 1581–2, were for Pere Gil the notable points of the ten lean years 1574–84 which desolated the interior and especially Urgell;[161] but the reverses came within a half-century when the population of the area effectively doubled. After about 1630 the situation changed. In much of western Europe 1630 was a year of great mortality: in Catalonia the phenomena of harvest failure and epidemic combined to produce a major crisis. Demographic levels managed to remain steady rather than fall; but it was different with the war of secession in mid-century and the great plague epidemic of 1651, events which affected population seriously (possibly one-fifth of the people of Catalonia died) and also hit hard at production levels in the countryside. The Counter Reformation effectively ended its formative phase with this negative period.

The spiritual origins of the Counter Reformation had many sources.[162] Two events mark the pre-reform period in Catalonia: the occupation of the abbey of Montserrat by the Observance of Castile, and the conversion of Ignatius Loyola in 1522 during his visits to Montserrat and Manresa. Reforming trends were already visible in the 1540s, with two central influences: the Jesuits and Trent.[163] There was a vital formative phase in the Catholic reform movement that coincides largely with the years during which Trent was in session, but the beginning of the active phase of the Counter Reformation in the Mediterranean can be fixed precisely at 1565, when Carlo Borromeo arrived in his diocese of Milan, and when the provincial councils convened in Spain.

Focus of radical spirituality – the *Devotio Moderna*, Lullism – and also of the new Ignatian spirit,[164] with undefined traces of the Erasmian outlook, Catalonia leapt from pre-Reformation to Counter-Reformation Catholicism without undergoing the painful transition of flirting with the forces unleashed by the Lutheran tide. Not without reason could Catalan writers boast of their nation's unswerving loyalty to the faith, a 'Catalan faith that has never suffered heretics or heresiarchs'.[165] The painless transition from one mode to another can be seen acutely in the 1557 publication of the constitutions of the councils of Tarragona, a volume which is accompanied by an anonymous homily in Latin entitled 'Institution of a pious Christian man', and addressed to 'the Christian reader'.[166] Redolent of the intense spirituality of the Netherlandish school, the homily is primarily an exposition of the Creed and the Lord's Prayer, and takes all its phrasing directly from scripture, the only non-scriptural reference being a phrase from Denis the Carthusian. When discussing the 'Holy Catholic Church' the author makes no mention of the pope, stresses that the only head of the Church is Christ, and that unity of faith and charity is only in Christ. No mention is made of the mass, but only of the need to observe 'mystical ceremonies' and feast days. Though heresy is denounced, no specific heresies are mentioned, and Luther is prominently absent. The whole homily is fluent testimony to the existence in the Catalan Church of the visionary pre-Reformation spirituality of the *Devotio Moderna*,[167] at the very time that its ecclesiastical apparatus was beginning to integrate itself into the programme of Tridentine reform. At the same time, the complete contrast in language between this document, issued with the blessing of a provincial council of the Church, and the subsequent vocabulary of Catholic writers, emphasises the reality of the change that now began to influence the faith and conduct of pious Christian men.

The civic context of the changes, finally, has a crucial importance. No scholar today can ignore the community environment within which the Reformation took place in Germany, and by the same token the Catholic societies of the Mediterranean played an active role in the acceptance of a new cultural outlook.[168] Within Catalonia, civic piety[169] was the vehicle for the introduction and imposition of the reform. Each city took care, when the elites could agree, to adopt the new religious orders and favour them with sites; foster the cults of new saints; and establish appropriate institutions and ceremonial for the relevant days of the year. The era of civic splendour in Barcelona began with the Habsburgs and the institution of the Golden Fleece (1519), but the evolution of a full-blooded civic piety more properly centred on the canonisation a century later, at the peak of the Counter Reformation, of St Ramon de Penyafort.

Devotions, like loyalties, were rooted in the local communities, and were as volatile as they were. When contemplating the landscape of Mediona it is easy to visualise it as the seat of an unchanging traditional faith, tied down by devotion to places and shrines that remained unaltered through time. Yet religion was not a perennial landscape:[170] though the calendar of seasons and the inherited ritual of generations would continue to retain their validity, they also, like the landscape itself, were remorselessly worked upon and changed by men and ideas which intruded into the localities and compelled them to come to terms with the world outside. In the process much that was old managed to endure and was reaffirmed, but there were also significant new departures that for many Catalans in the epoch of the Counter Reformation changed the conditions and aspirations by which they lived.

CHAPTER TWO

Philip II and the Catalans

Attempt by all available means to see that the orders for the reformation are carried out, applying yourselves with all the zeal and energy possible.

Philip II to viceroy of Catalonia, 1567.[1]

Philip II knew Barcelona well: he first passed through briefly with his father in November 1542, and subsequently made brief visits in October 1548[2] and July 1551. His only prolonged visit was for the *Corts* at Monzón in 1563–4, and he did not return for over twenty years, until the Corts of 1585. Such studied neglect might lead to the conclusion that there was little contact with the king, but the reverse is true: he took a close interest in the politics of the principality, and all correspondence relating to it that crossed his desk invariably earned a comment in his hurried, undecipherable scrawl. His memories of the Barcelona of 1564 were those of a Renaissance prince, all music and festivity. He approached the city from Monzón in the first week of February, and after a visit to Montserrat was met by the *Consellers* outside Barcelona at Molins. 'He came on horseback, dressed in a velvet doublet, cloth cloak and hat of black taffeta with a white feather, and leather boots', and the nervous *Conseller en Cap* kept uncovering his head every time the king spoke to him, and then covering it when the king told him to, much to Philip's amusement. A Renaissance arch greeted him at the entrance to the city, with three boy choristers singing a 'Te Philippum laudamus' in his honour.[3] The king came in time for Carnival, days full of 'dance, sounds, masks and costumes as never seen before', when the count of Aitona put on a great two-day feast in his house 'and the king went one day masked to visit the celebration and the ladies'.[4] A few days later, on 2 March, he received the homage of the communities of Catalonia in the Sala del Tinell of the *Audiència* and swore the constitutions of the province; 'the clergy and officials came to over four hundred men, the hand-kissing lasted some two hours'.[5] Three days later, Sunday the fifth, he assisted at an *auto de fe* held in his honour in the Born, just outside the city; for the inquisitors it was a special occasion, since they had never before been permitted to use the public square.

Though the visit was dedicated to the Corts it also coincided with the closure of the Council of Trent, whose progress Philip had followed closely, and he was eager to talk to the first prelates returning from its final session in December 1563. The bishop of Barcelona, Guillem Cassador, returned in mid-February,[6] and by the end of that month many other prelates had also assembled in the city, including those of Tarragona, Urgell and Gerona; some were old and ailing, and two – the prelates of Valencia and León – came back only to die before they could even leave Catalonia. There is no record of Philip's talks with the bishops, but he certainly communicated his plans for the immediate implementation of the decrees of the Council.

The Church in Catalonia and the northern realms of the peninsula had through the centuries helped to civilise and settle Spanish territory, earning in the process a highly privileged status not only as pastor but also as secular lord. In 1500 the great mediaeval sees of Spain were still semi-feudal enclaves, exercising temporal lordship over cities, villages and fortresses, and with extensive landholdings that included jurisdiction over taxes, administration and justice. The see of Toledo, which in 1517 controlled 1754 benefices and had jurisdiction over 19,000 vassals and twenty fortresses, was the most impressive example of feudal power, but there were parallels in Catalonia, notably the sees of Tarragona and Urgell. In the *vegueria* of Tarragona the archbishop had complete jurisdiction over thirty-three of the seventy-six towns and partial over twenty-four more, as well as jurisdiction over a further eight in other areas; the bishop of Urgell, in addition to his lordship of the city of Urgell, had jurisdiction over twenty-seven towns and was joint ruler of the principality of Andorra.[7] The bishops were only one part of the landed power of the Church.

In the mountains of Galicia, Asturias and Catalonia the monasteries had been the cradle of culture and authority, and their lands were still immense: in Catalonia the abbot of Ripoll was feudal lord of the town itself and of twenty-three other towns in the territory with a total population in the early seventeenth century of some six thousand vassals.[8] The abbot of St Miquel de Cuixà had jurisdiction over thirty-three towns in Conflent, one in Rosselló and ten in Cerdanya.[9] In the principality as a whole ecclesiastical lords had jurisdiction over one-fourth of all the towns; in the dioceses of

Solsona, Vic and Urgell they controlled at least one-fifth of the towns and population.[10] Effective income of the sees varied considerably: the richest was Tarragona, with an annual income of over £22,000 in 1600, ranging through the see of Barcelona, with an income of some £9000, to the smaller and poorer bishoprics such as Solsona – 'this my church, a new growth in the vineyard of the Lord', as the bishop saw it in 1603 – with an income of around £4000.[11]

On the eve of the Council of Trent, which started its sessions in the last few days of 1545, the ecclesiastical map of Spain was divided into seven metropolitan sees of which Toledo and Seville among others fell within the Crown of Castile, and Tarragona with Valencia and Saragossa within that of Aragon. Like the autonomous ecclesiastical provinces of Canterbury and York in pre-Reformation England, there was complete autonomy between the Castilian and Aragonese provinces. In Castile the clergy had their own Assembly, which in effect substituted for the non-attendance of the clerical estate in the Cortes, but the body had infrequent meetings and apart from an historic session at Seville in 1478 it appears to have had no significant convocations. In the realms of the Crown of Aragon, where Cortes met more regularly, the clergy took their places with the other estate representatives but seldom emerged as a coherent group with their own voice, though individuals might occasionally play an outstanding role, such as Pau Claris in 1640. Tarragona, whose jurisdiction coincided roughly with the principality of Catalonia, contained within its province the eight sees of Lérida, Tortosa, Gerona, Barcelona, Solsona, Urgell, Vic and Elna.

The churches of Catalonia had their own chamber in meetings of the Corts and were entitled to appoint two of the members of the *Diputació*, the standing committee of the Corts which was made up of two representatives from each estate. Since the Corts met seldom, the Diputació (or *Generalitat*, as it was also known) was the effective government of the principality and spokesman for Catalan aspirations, in which evidently the clergy had a continuing voice. All the prelates recognised the crown as sovereign lord, but firmly within the framework of the constitutions of Catalonia and without compromising their own feudal lordship or their independence in a broad range of spheres; and crown control was exercised only at the most crucial point, that of appointment, a privilege which had been fully acquired by the reign of Philip II.

Crown initiative came to play a crucial role in the history of both Reformation and Counter Reformation. The groundwork for royal supremacy was laid down by the Catholic Kings Ferdinand and Isabella, who aimed principally to pacify the Church and assert their control over it. In 1478 they defied the rebellious archbishop of Toledo, Carrillo, by calling an Assembly of loyal Castilian clergy to meet in Seville; the proceedings of this council were of seminal importance, and foreshadowed the reform aspirations of a whole generation of clergy. In the same year and the same city, the monarchs sanctioned the commencement of the notorious Inquisition. Many reformers saw in the growth of royal assertiveness an opportunity to bring some order into the Church, and the Seville council made it plain that papal interference would not be welcomed. Enthusiasm in these years was invigorated not only by the coming of peace to Castile and Aragon under the new united monarchy, but also by the initiation of a ten-year crusade against the Muslims of the kingdom of Granada. Zeal for the faith no less than zeal for reform lay behind the ambitious programme to alter monastic discipline in the peninsula by enforcing the *Observance* on religious houses. Guided by advisers such as her confessor Talavera (who in 1492 became the first archbishop of Granada), Isabella sought to appoint righteous prelates to the sees under her control.[12]

By the end of the fifteenth century the rulers of Spain had become impatient with a papacy that not only enjoyed considerable jurisdiction in Spain through the 'exempt sees', but also used Spanish bishoprics as gifts to be handed round to favoured (and absentee) Italians. For their part many cathedral chapters jealously guarded their right to elect and approve their bishops, and strenuously opposed or blocked nominations made by the papacy. Bit by bit, and thanks in some measure to their undoubted utility to papal political interests, the rulers of Spain managed to secure for themselves the right to provide to sees within their jurisdiction. They obtained in 1504 and 1508 the Patronato Real over appointments in the New World, and the patronage rights granted to Charles V in 1523 by his former tutor Adrian of Utrecht, now pope Adrian VI, which gave to the king absolute control of the property of the Military Orders and rights of presentation to all the sees and monasteries in Castile and Aragon. These astonishing concessions, taken together, gave the rulers of Spain an autonomous control over their Church unequalled not only in Christendom – since the privileges were fuller than those granted to France in the Concordat of Bologna – but in the entire history of the Catholic Church. From this time the king had full authority to interfere in the internal life of the Church in Spain, a factor of supreme importance for the development of the Counter Reformation. In Catalonia, as in the rest of the peninsula, the power to make appointments and to guide Church policy also extended to finance: the steady intrusion of the central government into the income of the sees was confirmed in

1653 when the Council of Aragon reported that 'His Majesty has reserved to himself the power to make payments out of the income of the bishoprics of Catalonia up to a value of one-third of the value of the sees,' testimony corroborated by the bishop of Tortosa who reported in 1661 that such payments 'represent one-third' of his see's income.[13]

For generations, prelates, cathedral chapters and diplomats had battled against the ambitions of Italians and the pretensions of the Holy See, so that outright hostility to Rome could be found as a normal attitude among many Spaniards. Reform was the common programme of many clergy who saw Rome as the centre of decadence within the Church; there remained in Spain a hope that some future ecumenical council might take up the task in earnest. The crown actively promoted anti-papalism when it served its purposes, notably after the sack of Rome (1527), used by Charles' secretary Alfonso de Valdés to launch a bitter attack against Roman corruption; and in the epoch of the Council of Trent, when Charles V's German policy fell out of line with that of the papacy. In 1536 we find the extraordinary case of Alfonso Alvarez Guerrero, a distinguished legist who served Charles V and ended his career as a royal official of Philip II in Italy, whose *Treatise on the manner in which the General Council is to be held* (Valencia 1536) is an extreme example of anti-papal sentiment in Spain.

In the last phase of the Council of Trent profound criticisms were directed by Spanish prelates against Rome, and one of the reasons for subsequent hostility to the Jesuits in the peninsula was the feeling that these had prejudiced the cause of reform by their support of the papacy.[14] As late as 1555 the noted theologian Melchor Cano had emitted the memorable opinion that 'he who thinks Rome can be purified doesn't know Rome', and in 1607 Cardinal Zapata drew up a famous 'Memorial to the king on the abuses of the Roman see', in which he regretted that Trent had failed to control the papacy.[15] Ironically, the anti-Roman trend reached its peak at the height of the Counter Reformation, with the setting-up in Madrid in 1632 of a committee on Roman abuses, and the presentation to the pope in 1633 of an historic memorial of protest by two officials of the Spanish government.

It is sometimes assumed that the thirst for reform in Spain was amply met by the policy of the Catholic Kings and Cisneros,[16] and that this helped to avert a Reformation; but the view has no evidence to support it. Under Ferdinand and Isabella the quality of some men appointed to bishoprics improved (one, Talavera, was widely considered to represent the ideal prelate); many religious houses in Castile, mainly those under the Franciscans and Dominicans, were disciplined and reformed; some bishops called synods and tried to upgrade their clergy; and much important reformist literature, particularly in the area of devotional piety, was written. Seen from the perspective of a subsequent generation, little of this was convincing gain. One half of the peninsular Church, that in the Crown of Aragon, remained almost untouched by change (Montserrat was the prominent exception); the majority of the religious orders were unaffected by any disciplinary reform; sees continued to be held by men who were partial or total absentees; decrees of synods were not enforced and therefore remained so much paper; no steps whatsoever were taken to improve the parish clergy; and the religion of the people survived, through all this, in the form it had retained for generations. Many Spaniards in the 1540s therefore looked on reform as a project that had to be undertaken *ab initio*, and commented negatively on previous attempts: in 1546 Francisco Borja, discussing the reform of monasteries in both Catalonia and Castile, could write of 'the little fruit secured, either in the time of Queen Isabella of blessed memory, or in our own time'; and the Observant reforms of Cisneros were implicitly condemned by an official in 1566 for their self-defeating use of force: 'nothing done by force can last or endure; the last time these monasteries were reformed, by Queen Isabella, it lasted as little as the others, from which Your Majesty can well understand the great problems involved, and that one should take care that it not be a three-day reformation, but one that is permanent.'[17]

If the Reformation in these years passed Spain by, it was certainly not because Spain had a reformed Church.[18] From about 1520, when the court in Castile became conscious of the existence of a Lutheran threat, defensive methods were adopted, but it was a threat that remained unrealised for over thirty years.[19] From about 1540 Charles V began a policy, later to be followed by Philip II, of arresting outside Spain those Spaniards who seemed to be likely to take their contagion back home. In 1541 he ordered the arrest in Regensburg of a native of Burgos called Francisco de San Tomás, and provided an order for him to be taken by ship to Spain and handed over to the Inquisition of Valladolid. The Suprema was informed that 'just over seven years ago he apparently went to Antwerp and there was misled and then he was sent to Augsburg where he remained a few days and did much harm of the sort that is done in those parts'.[20] These were isolated cases abroad, and the peninsula felt itself secure from the European storm until rudely shaken out of this complacency by the events of 1558. In the pre-1558 period, Spanish reformers continued to pursue their hopes for change, not as a response to the events abroad but as a conscientious follow-through from the programmes for improvement that had been launched in the peninsula long before Luther appeared on the horizon. The very many proposals for reform[21] launched in Spain within those generations have never been studied, but some managed to take shape in the epoch of the Council of Trent. One of the most influential was that drawn up in 1551 by Juan de Avila and submitted to Pedro Guerrero, the archbishop of Granada who left that year for Trent where he headed the Spanish delegation. For a general perspective of the Spanish bishops' views we have the excellent memoranda they drew up for presentation to the Council of Trent, touching partly on religious practice but dealing mainly with discipline.[22]

The crown wished to restore discipline in the Church in order to bring under its control institutions that seemed to escape its authority; bishops wished to convert into reality the jurisdiction over their own clergy which they exercised more in theory than in practice; clergy themselves, including cathedral canons and leaders of religious orders, looked for a clearly defined autonomy within their own spheres. A particular concern of all three – crown, bishops, and clergy – was to liberate themselves from the obstacle of lay jurisdictions.

The feudal authority exercised by the Church over towns and vassals was only one face of a mediaeval panorama in which secular barons also exercised feudal authority over the Church. Throughout Catalonia the magnates, great and small, had taken over rights of presentation to benefices and the enjoyment of taxes nominally payable to the clergy. Both Church and crown consequently shared a common interest in trying to bring under their authority institutions which were in theory ecclesiastical but in practice out of their control. Bishops reported that the number of benefices in lay presentation formed the biggest single obstacle to reform of any sort. In Mallorca in 1590, according to the bishop, of the six hundred benefices in the diocese only about forty corresponded to the ordinary (that is, the bishop), the rest being 'virtually all in the hands of lay persons and of the founders'.[23] In the diocese of Pamplona (Navarre) the immense majority of the parishes were of independent appointment, with parish priests being nominated by the village community, a situation that continued unchanged into modern times. In 1714 the bishop of Pamplona explained that 'they appoint and nominate by majority vote and since to obtain these benefices no great learning is required and little grammar and enough wit to understand the nature of the orders they receive, the bishops have come to terms with ordinating them so that the churches are manned.'[24] In the late eighteenth century the bishop

complained that virtually all the parishes were in lay appointment, with clergy succeeding each other 'as though by hereditary
succession'.[25] In Asturias in 1630 the bishop stated that 'the majority
of the parishes are in lay patronage, and with this excuse the lords
of the province present to their benefices persons unworthy of the
ministry.'[26] It followed that bishops were unable to reform the
structure of their own churches. As late as the 1650s in the diocese
of Barcelona, three-fourths of benefices taken up by new clergy
were in lay patronage, and the remaining quarter were shared
between the Church and lay institutions outside the bishop's
control.[27]

The tensions and abuses created by secular lords having jurisdiction over benefices can be illustrated through the court case brought
before the Royal Audiència at Barcelona by the rector of Sentmenat
(Vallès) in 1593, with the support of his bishop.[28] The rector
claimed, with ample support from local farmers as witnesses, that
the baron of Sentmenat had deprived the parish of its income
and its tithes. The baron, it appears, had freely in previous years
appointed whom he wished to the benefice and had freely usurped
all its lands and income. As one witness, a weaver of seventy years,
affirmed:

> before the Council of Trent the rectors at Sentmenat resided very little in
> the rectory because it was rented out and not looked after ... And since
> the lord baron appointed whichever rector he liked it is to be supposed
> that the rector did only what the baron wanted ... And this witness has
> seen with his own eyes that whenever the rectorate fell vacant the lord
> of the castle came with a lot of armed men and remained behind closed
> doors and did not emerge until he had given the rectorate to whom he
> wished, and that was before the Council ... And he has seen that
> administrators and instructors of the household of Sentmenat, after
> serving some years in the household, were afterwards made rectors of
> the rectorate ... and the rector only used to do what the lord baron
> wanted and the baron rather than the rector controlled the rectorate.

The statement, from one whose memory clearly encompassed the
transition from old to new, shows a consciousness that the Counter
Reformation in Catalonia was attempting to change matters. No
immediate solution appears to have been reached in the case, but
in the long run it was the seigneur who triumphed, and by the
eighteenth century the entire tithe was going to the lord and none to
the parish priest. The problem was common throughout Catalonia.
In the diocese of Urgell in 1610 the clergy complained that 'laymen
make themselves absolute lords of the church collections and of the
money of the confraternities and claim absolute power', and the

synod of 1616 denounced 'the abuse in this diocese whereby many barons and owners of tithes dare to take their tithe without summoning the rectors and other clergy', thereby appropriating the better part of the tithe.[29]

Bishops also suffered from the long-standing rights of patronage exercised by monasteries and religious orders. In some parts of the country, notably in Galicia and in Navarre, the great mediaeval abbeys eclipsed the wealth and authority of the bishops: in Navarre in 1575 the abbey at Roncesvalles controlled appointments to forty-five churches, whose revenue it shared not with the bishop but with Rome.[30] It is not surprising that when the first missionaries went to the New World in the early sixteenth century, they set about expressly to create for themselves a spiritual structure that was wholly free of the possibility of interference by secular lords.[31] In the whole of Spain, the only see to experience no serious obstacles to reform was ironically the one which had the highest proportion of non-Christians, Granada; as the archbishop explained to Philip II in 1565, in the provincial council held that year 'the business to deal with is less in volume and substance than in other sees, since Your Majesty has the right of presentation to all the benefices and enjoys all the Church revenue.'[32]

Though the Council of Trent had expressed itself firmly against lay patronage, the government in Spain dared not include the subject in its plans for reform, and one of the king's advisers warned him in 1565 that the matter should be excluded from the agenda of the provincial councils, because 'it would provoke grave complications and cause much unease and disquiet in these realms, being a matter which touches everything and affects many.'[33] In Catalonia the great monasteries had extensive rights of presentation which inevitably prejudiced episcopal authority but which the authorities were powerless to touch. When the crown finally at the end of the sixteenth century dared to reform the Benedictines and Augustinians of Catalonia, it was obliged to leave all the rights of patronage of the orders intact, but insisted that ecclesiastical jurisdiction be vested in the bishops. The king's visitors explained in 1588 that in the case at least of these two orders, 'the parishes and benefices are filled unsatisfactorily and they do not observe the Council of Trent and are badly served; and since they do not recognise the jurisdiction of the bishops these do not go to give the sacrament of confirmation, to the great disservice of the people.'[34]

The reaction of the Spanish bishops to the holding of a Council at Trent was wholly favourable, though Spaniards began to play a significant role only in the last phases. Meeting together on foreign soil, the bishops found their aspirations to be surprisingly similar, and their pride in the power of Spain shows through in their discourses. Italians were visibly offended, and one Jesuit said that a distinguished Italian 'complained to me about these Spaniards and said they were troublesome and spoke too freely'.[35] Certainly the Spaniards were excited and felt they were in the vanguard of the reformers: 'we Spaniards', the bishop of Gerona wrote to Philip from Trent in 1562, 'are with those who are full of zeal.'[36]

Trent did not by itself constitute the Counter Reformation, but was of extraordinary importance because it provided a programme to the revitalised machinery of the Church. It has been traditional to suppose that this programme was a progressive movement of reform and regeneration, dedicated to the eradication of abuses and the renovation of ideas, and that opposition to it was necessarily reactionary. In practice the Tridentine reform, like the Gregorian reform of the eleventh century, also implied an extension of Italian cultural hegemony, a tendency to ecclesiastical elitism and centralism, and a clear challenge to secular power: all these features attracted opposition, not only in Spain but throughout the Catholic world. The programme of the Counter Reformation, like that of Gregory the Great, attempted to create a power system that would stand the test of time: the effort was magnificent, but the results were inevitably conditioned by their environment, and in Spain the obstacles to success were considerable.

The reception of Trent in Spain was never a problem, despite the somewhat misleading image conveyed by Pastor, the historian of the papacy.[37] In the 1540s and 1550s individual bishops and clergy were already applying the directives of the Council, and in 1554, for example, the regent Juana was exhorting the archbishop of Granada 'to observe the decrees of the Sacred Council of Trent and have them carried out and executed in your church and diocese'.[38] When the Tridentine decrees were finally issued in 1564, Spain was the first European country to give its complete and unequivocal acceptance. Philip's correspondence shows his anxiety to bring the decrees into operation at once. In January 1565 a special meeting of the Council of Castile studied plans for the calling of provincial councils throughout Spain to give effect to the Tridentine decrees. Subsequent events, however, revealed the inescapable gap between aspiration and implementation, the sharp difference of opinion among many about how to achieve the one desired end, the single-minded and stubborn purpose of the king to keep all aspects of reform within his own hands, and the accelerating distrust by the papacy of a monarch who seemed to be taking his Church into schism from Rome.

Although the word 'reform' has been used here repeatedly for convenience, in practical terms the whole Counter Reformation in both its genesis and its evolution implied an exercise in the transfer of power. To the king 'reform', in the sense of putting order into the belief[39] and practice of the Church, was inseparable from the means – the power – necessary for implementing it, indeed the means logically took precedence over the objective. In the same way, all attempts to modify the role of a lay-appointed clergy, to suppress popular folk practices, to restrict the scope of municipal religious processions, to abolish rural saints, must be seen not simply as religious 'reforms' (which they no doubt were) but as part of an extensive attempt to change the frontiers of power within society. The Counter Reformation constituted a deeply conflictive chapter in the evolution of western civilisation and generated problems which might call in doubt its success in achieving so-called reform.

The political tension is easily explained. From the very inception of his reign Philip had inherited from his father a state of war with the papacy. Conflict between the two over their respective interests both in Italy and in the rest of Europe had become a constant of diplomatic life, colouring attitudes on both sides and infusing into public relations a hostility which soured all policy-making. On almost every single issue of importance, Spain and the papacy agreed on objectives but disagreed on the means.[40] This applied equally to the implementation of reform in the peninsula. From the very beginning Philip made it plain that reform in Spain, though conforming to the principles of Trent, would be carried through as a clear act of state and on terms dictated by the state.

Moreover, there was another important principle[41] that sheds light on all Philip's subsequent policy towards Rome. The king's instructions to ambassador Vargas, dated 22 September 1563, show that his haste to accept Trent was motivated by a desire to accept the Council on its own terms, terms to which moreover his own bishops, theologians and officials (all those in short who 'have been in the Council and were paid by me') contributed in great measure, *before* the Council decrees could receive the official stamp of the papacy. Philip was determined that his conformity with Trent should in no way appear as a mute and unquestioning reception of papal decrees, and he had already, probably in this year 1563, requested of his bishops their response to six questions, which we summarise as follows:

1. Do they think that the papal confirmation is necessary to the decrees of the Council?
2. If His Majesty were to subscribe to papal confirmation, as it seems he may have to, should this be done without reservations, or with?

3. If the pope in his confirmation adds some document to the decrees of the Council, how will this affect publication of the decrees here?
4. Since there will be differences of opinion about how the Council decrees be put into practice, what suggestions do they have for going about it?
5. If the use of royal authority is necessary for putting the decrees into effect, how should the royal authority be used?
6. Could they give their opinion about what seems important in the Council decrees, and what other measures may be necessary?

The questions are excellent evidence of Philip II's methods of government: his readiness always to receive advice, and his reluctance to make any important decisions without being sure that no negative consequences would follow. The only surviving reply to this letter appears to be from the bishop of Barcelona, dated 1564.[42] The substance of his reply was as follows:

1. 'Although we would not give as much importance to the confirmation as some do who hold that it alone gives authority to what has been decreed in the Council', it is still true that all recorded ecumenical councils have asked for papal confirmation; that the papal power and privilege is unique and necessary; and that this confirmation does not detract from the authority of the Council but in fact completes it.
2. Without reservation.
3. All the documents, including the papal, should be published.
4. He is willing to accept any order of priority given to the decrees by the king.
5. Royal authority may be used, with penalties for those disobeying.
6. A useful guide to what seems important would be 'the memoranda of abuses which the Spanish bishops gave to the legates at Trent, of which a volume was made which no doubt some bishops have'; but no public hint must be given that the Council in some way failed to deal with certain complaints.

Philip was also anxious to talk to all the Tridentine delegates, and as we have seen he made a point of meeting those who had returned to Barcelona; a week later, he left the city. By this time, the papal confirmation had been issued: the date of 26 January 1564 was affixed to the bull Benedictus Deus, which was formally issued in Rome on 30 June. Two weeks later, on 12 July, Philip in Madrid issued a royal *cédula* approving the decrees of Trent as issued by the papacy. He was the first head of state to accept Trent, and the manner of acceptance, openly and without reservation, was remarkable evidence of his commitment to the cause of reform. Even more remarkable is the fact that the acceptance of the papal bull coincided with a political decision to break off diplomatic relations with Rome and recall the Spanish ambassador, Requesens.[43] The two apparently contradictory acts are clear proof of the unusual nature of relations at this epoch. The Catholic King was determined that, once issued officially within the country, the implementation of the decrees be treated as a matter wholly Spanish and therefore wholly to be decided by himself alone, without the intervention of the papacy. It was with this fundamental principle in mind that instructions were sent out on 8 April 1565 to all the metropolitans of Spain ordering that provincial councils be summoned.[44]

The policy of holding local synods to implement the decrees had been recommended in the Tridentine session of November 1563. Philip from the first made sure that every aspect of the situation in Spain be controlled by the Royal Council, and on 4 September 1564 a royal cédula prohibited any publication of the decrees without official approval.[45] He was not prepared for what took place in Catalonia.[46]

The archbishop of Tarragona, Fernando de Loazes, a distinguished Valencian jurist who had been inquisitor of Catalonia in the early century, attended Trent in 1551 and had occupied his present see since 1560, was eager to implement the long-desired reforms that had now been decreed both by the pope and by his own king. On 30 August 1564, unaware of the forthcoming royal cédula, he accordingly sent out letters to his prelates summoning them to a provincial council to meet in his cathedral on 2 October. It was no novelty to hold such a council in Tarragona for there had been regular assemblies in the 1550s; moreover, the province of Tarragona had always had close links with the Holy See. The assembly thus opened with optimism. On 10 October they sent a letter to the king, consulting on a question of appointments, and in solemn session on 24 October the clergy officially received the decrees of the Council of Trent for their province. At the session on 7 November 1564, however, the delegates were startled to receive a letter from Philip II, dated 27 October, which thanked the bishops for their zeal in holding a council but said that it would have been better to have consulted first with the crown: 'although we thank you greatly for the attention and respect and zeal for our service which you have shown in advising us of it, it would have pleased us more and been more suitable if you had met and begun to deal with these matters at the same time as in my other realms, and not before, so that going forward together in one mind and understanding and agreement we could better put into effect what the Sacred Council of Trent disposes and orders.' Unknown to the delegates, the king had also on the same date sent a letter to the viceroy of Catalonia, Diego Hurtado de Mendoza, ordering him to suspend the council in the king's name and giving him directions about what should be done in the case of resistance by the archbishop.

Fortunately, no extreme measures were necessary. The stunned delegates heard their archbishop, 'for certain just reasons which motivate me', as a secretary who was present noted, suspend the session and prorogue the council to Easter Day 1565, in either Barcelona or Tarragona. The date was only a temporary expedient: on 14 April Loazes, who was then in Barcelona, issued an order proroguing the meeting yet again, to 29 July 1565. Meanwhile, the Royal Council had been working to make sure that no councils would meet unless with official permission and with the presence of a royal representative. It was not until 18 September that the Tarragona provincial council, meeting in fact in Barcelona, received letters from the king allowing it to proceed.

The traditional method of introducing change in the Church had been through the medium of 'provincial' councils, that is councils which covered a specific ecclesiastical province. As elsewhere in Europe, 'national' councils were almost unknown, since they implied the collaboration (and control) of the state;[47] initiatives therefore usually came from the 'ecumenical' or papal-inspired councils. No national councils met in Spain: the assembly at Seville in 1478, called at the initiative of the crown, was classified simply as a 'Congregation' and had no canonical status. Few provincial councils took place from the fifteenth to the early sixteenth century, with the prominent exception of those held with regularity by the archdiocese of Tarragona. There is record of a provincial council of Toledo held at Aranda by archbishop Carrillo in 1473, and in 1512 fray Diego Deza held one for his province of Seville: both these pre-Reformation councils are notable for their exhaustive coverage of the major reforms demanded by prelates and later emphasised by the Counter Reformation, but there is no evidence that the decrees were ever enforced or observed. The role of provincial councils was to pass decrees, which relied for their implementation on diocesan synods, or meetings of a bishop with the clergy of his diocese. It has been calculated that some 143 synods were celebrated between 1475 and 1558 in the territory of the crowns of Castile, Aragon and Navarre.[48] Whatever the real total, one cannot be far out in calculating that during the eighty years preceding the closure of the Council of Trent, the average number of synods held in Spain was just over three for each diocese, or about one every thirty years, a frequency which is not only derisory but reveals the real state of neglect in the Church and needs to be set against the canonical stipulation, reaffirmed in repeated general councils, that synods be held annually in each diocese. The decisions of many of these synods have survived,[49] and the texts leave no doubt that there existed a keen awareness of the need for reform, but there is not the slightest evidence that any of the resolutions was ever put into practice.

In diocese after diocese the picture of lethargy was the same. Sees like Ciudad Rodrigo and Zamora, which appear to have had only one diocesan synod in the one and a half centuries from 1400 to 1565, must have suffered a total lack of liaison between local clergy and the bishop. When St Tomás de Villanueva celebrated a synod in his diocese of Valencia in June 1548[50] he stated in his opening address that it was the first to be held 'for over a century', the last recorded one being in 1422. Villanueva was one of the luminaries of the early Counter Reformation, and his decrees illustrate the areas in which prelates felt reform to be due: all excommunications issued by his predecessors were revoked as being perilous to souls, the number of feast-days was reduced 'so that they be better observed and the people not be burdened by too many feasts', night-time vigils in churches were banned, as also popular rituals on Innocents Day, the sacrament of baptism was to be given only in church, religious instruction for adults on Sundays was introduced, and clergy were to wear clerical dress. With the pressing problem of the Moriscos on their doorstep, the Valencian prelates were more aware than most of the need for change.

The infrequency of provincial councils tended to aggravate disunity and disorder, leaving bishops, religious houses and clergy free to follow their own whims in every aspect of discipline and worship. Particularly disturbing for the crown was the fact that a breakdown in ecclesiastical order threatened its own interests. With an inevitability rendered even more dangerous by the political fragmentation of the country, the Church in Spain was rapidly becoming ungovernable. When the councils of 1565 eventually took place, there had been no provincial assemblies anywhere in Spain (apart from Catalonia) for forty-three years, and there had been no diocesan synods in Oviedo for 115 years, in Salamanca for sixty-nine years.

It is impossible not to be impressed by the king's stubborn determination to do things his way, against the opposition of prelates many of whom had been hardened by their experience in international affairs and in the Council of Trent itself. Following in the tradition of Ferdinand the Catholic, Philip insisted that reform must be initiated and controlled by the crown, and as with Tarragona would allow no council to commence without his personal delegate

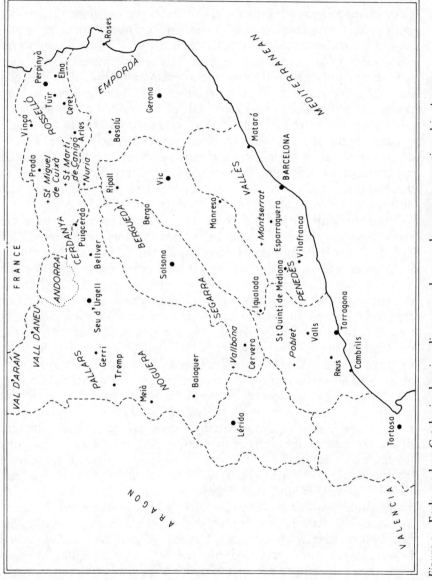

Figure 2 Early modern Catalonia showing dioceses and some place-names mentioned in the text.

present: in Granada, archbishop Guerrero in autumn 1565 was ordered to postpone the council for two weeks to await the arrival of 'the person who is to take part and attend in our name'.[51] In Barcelona the delegate was Joan de Montcada, count of Aitona. The instructions given to Aitona for the 1565 session of the Tarragona council were explicit and uncompromising:[52] deem the session at Tarragona invalid, do not touch royal patronage, press forward with reforms on residence and other matters, count on royal support for complaints against Rome. It is not surprising that the papal nuncio should subsequently comment that in the Royal Council there was a devil in human form intent on leading the king down the way trodden by Henry VIII of England.[53] Complete state control over the proceedings of 1565 was made patent in the king's circular letter of 29 December that year, ordering that all the decisions of each council must be submitted to the Royal Council for approval, a determined act of regalism.[54] In these circumstances the meeting of the councils deepened rather than eliminated the differences between Spain and the papacy.

The split with Rome had come at a most inconvenient time for everyone involved, and most of all for archbishop Carranza of Toledo, who had appealed to the papacy to investigate his case.[55] In October 1565 a mission led by cardinal Boncompagni (later pope as Gregory XIII) arrived in Madrid with the purpose of healing the rift and with instructions to look into the matter of Carranza and the question of reform in the religious orders. Boncompagni returned to Rome in December, on the death of Pius IV, having resolved nothing. The new pope, elected with passive Spanish support,[56] was Pius V, who renewed diplomatic relations with Spain and so opened a more positive phase. What did not change was the strong suspicion by Rome of the nature and purpose of the provincial councils in Spain. In November 1565 the secretary of state of the Curia, cardinal Altemps, complained to Boncompagni of the content of the decrees that Philip had issued as instructions for the new councils.[57] At the same time he complained strongly of 'the scandalous phrase which has been used by a person in the Royal Council, saying that "there is no pope in Spain" (che in Spagna non hai Papa)'. The reference, which immediately acquired notoriety in Rome, was taken by Altemps from a report he had before him from cardinal Castagna, who had accompanied Boncompagni and succeeded him as nuncio. Castagna dwelt in some detail on 'the attacks made in Spain by the civil power against Church jurisdiction', and in particular accused Figueroa, president of the Council of Castile, of having said openly before many people 'che non habbia Papa in Spagna'.[58] Taken in conjunction with other comments which Castagna and Boncompagni made at the time about the Inquisition, it is obvious that the papal diplomats were intensely annoyed by the obstructions they encountered in Madrid; and it is equally obvious that one single problem was at the root of their grievances: the case of Carranza. The provincial councils seemed to confirm Rome's suspicions that Spain wished to carry out a reform of its own, independent of the universal Church (it was also no doubt relevant that Pius V, who hoped to call his own provincial synod in the autumn of 1566,[59] had no wish to be outdone in zeal). Writing from Rome in March 1566, Requesens reported that all the cardinals now possessed a copy of the 'secret' instructions that Philip had sent to his bishops in October, and urged the king that in view of Curial suspicions, it would be better to end the councils soon.[60] Philip II's perhaps naive belief that he could hold national councils without causing any offence to Rome was speedily called in question by the ensuing complications. The business of the councils was controversial, and from the very beginning invited papal intervention; in July 1566 Requesens informed Philip that 'some days ago there came here delegations from some cathedral chapters of Castile to appeal against things decreed in the provincial councils'.[61] The Spanish councils, in effect, provoked misunderstanding and suspicion at a time when the king was extremely anxious to obtain papal cooperation over a broad range of issues, from the tensions in England and the Netherlands to the escalating war with the Turks.

The councils of 1565 were the central episode of the Spanish Counter Reformation, fulfilment of the aspirations of a generation of reformers, and an historic step in the evolution of the peninsular Church: as such they require some mention in order to put the situation in Catalonia into focus. They were the key feature of a triple reform – to include also the bishoprics and the religious orders – that Philip was anxious to push through at all costs and as soon as possible. Having brought Tarragona into line, Philip personally directed every stage of the councils, which in a circular letter of 8 April 1565 he summoned to meet under their metropolitans not only in Spain but throughout the monarchy, in Mexico, the Netherlands (the council of Cambrai met here from June 1565 to July the next year), and the Italian realms of Milan, Naples and Sicily. For convenience, the clergy subject to Santiago met in Salamanca and those of Tarragona met in Barcelona; otherwise, meetings were in the relevant metropolitan cities. Each council, as we have seen, was to have the presence of a royal representative to sanction its proceedings,[62] and all proceedings had to be submitted to the Royal Council, presided over at this period by Diego de Espinosa, for ratification. These fundamental controls were complemented by other firm indications of government diktat.

A glance at the council of Toledo gives us a good perspective of the sessions, their significance and their problems.[63] Since Toledo had no archbishop (it was Carranza's sixth year in captivity) Philip appointed the pliant bishop of Córdoba, Cristóbal de Rojas y Sandoval, as president, the seat next to him being occupied by the royal representative Don Francisco de Toledo (subsequently viceroy of Peru), who had precedence over all the bishops. Despite its theoretical importance as the largest archbishopric in Spain, the Toledo council was a relatively small affair: apart from Rojas, only five bishops attended, with a handful of other delegates, and only three short sessions took place, in September 1565 and in January and March 1566. The cathedral chapter of Toledo objected vigorously to the council on the grounds that it could not meet without their archbishop and in May sent a long petition to the king asking for indefinite postponement; the 'exempt' (that is, directly subject to the papacy) sees of Oviedo and León sent no prelate; and the prelate of the exempt see of Burgos, cardinal Francisco de Mendoza, 'the cardinal of Spain', refused to come and sent deputies instead. Of the five other bishops attending, four were close to the government: the bishop of Cuenca, Bernardo de Fresneda, was a member of the Royal Council, the bishop of Segovia, Diego de Covarrubias, was a distinguished legist who ended his career as president of the Royal Council, the bishop of Osma, Honorato Juan, was tutor to the prince, and Pedro de la Gasca of Sigüenza was the famous subduer of the Pizarro revolt in Peru. This pliant assembly was, however, neither meek nor unproductive. Conscious that with the full support of the state they were now in a position to reform the entire Church and thereby implement Trent to its fullest, the prelates took on board long and radical proposals from every quarter: from the tireless Juan de Avila (a major influence on the final constitutions of the council), from the Jesuits (who sent a stream of letters from Rome), from the absent but reforming cardinal Mendoza (a list of forty-four items), and even from the king himself, who in December 1565 despatched to the council a list of measures which he felt needed urgent attention. Though there was complete freedom in the sessions to raise and discuss any and every matter, the government was careful not to allow the prelates to be carried away by their enthusiasm, especially when it came to the reform not simply of the clergy but of the laity as well. Philip observed to Francisco de Toledo in February 1566 of the suggestion that 'after the reformation of the prelates and clergy one should deal with the reform of the laity and of public sins', that 'this is an important matter, in which however the prelates have had pretensions to the detriment of our royal jurisdiction,'[64] specifically referring to the claim by Church courts that they could arrest laymen for moral crimes and seize their goods, all of which the king ruled to be beyond ecclesiastical jurisdiction. When the deliberations and decisions had all been completed, they amounted to a formidable compilation of fifty-seven leaves.[65] Similar painstaking efforts were made in the other provincial councils.[66]

The council of Compostela, summoned by archbishop Gaspar de Zúñiga, was attended by twelve bishops and other clergy, with the count of Monteagudo as royal legate. Three sessions, all held in Salamanca cathedral, took place in September 1565 and April 1566, and thirty-six constitutions were issued. In Valencia the council met under archbishop Martín de Ayala in five sessions lasting from November 1565 to February 1566, and in each session passed a series of innovatory constitutions. In Saragossa the council was called by archbishop Fernando de Aragón, with the assistance of four bishops; only one session was held, in which ten constitutions were passed. In Granada archbishop Guerrero, who had led the Spanish delegation at Trent, was assisted by two bishops: the council here opened in September 1565, with the marqués del Carpio as royal legate, and closed in April 1566, to allow the archbishop to carry out a visitation of the diocese.[67] Since the closing of Trent Guerrero had continued to receive memorials from Juan de Avila outlining a programme of missionary activity, and these undoubtedly helped to orientate his policy. Avila suggested[68] that preachers be sent through the diocese, that clergy teach doctrine not only at mass but also in the village schools, that Sunday mass be made obligatory for children, that in the villages 'rosaries and images should be made available, and the rich should buy them from the cities', that since few confess properly confessors must be trained. Only in the archdiocese of Seville was no council held.[69]

The constitutions passed by the provincial councils reflected to their fullest the reform aspirations of the Counter Reformation, and with the experience of Trent in mind concentrated on reform of both clergy and people. Toledo limited the food menu of prelates, ordered synods to be held annually, laid down rules on preaching and instruction, and ordered 'extreme care that the music used in divine praise should not imitate the profane sounds of the theatre, nor the strains of shameless love or of war'. Valencia had perhaps the fullest programme, with controls over schoolbooks and a ban on the works of Ovid and Martial, the closing of churches at night ('since at night many bad things tend to be done'), a ban on dancing, and 'that the images of saints be painted and carved with decency'. Although many of the constitutions merely repeated mediaeval rules, the hundreds of stipulations added up in their totality to a comprehensive programme for religious reform.

The excitement and conflict of those months had all the air of a revolution, albeit a revolution carried out (as in England) at the elite level; but inevitably the practical consequences were another matter. It was not too difficult to pass decrees, rather more difficult to implement them. The fate of provincial councils was in part dictated by the negative reaction that prelates faced when they took the council decisions back to their dioceses. From the first the cathedral chapters throughout Spain rejected the decisions as impinging on their rights: in Córdoba in July 1566 the bishop had to throw some of the canons into prison, and 'the churches receive the council with hostility'.[70] The cold breath of hostility and inertia blew over the flame of reform. Synods of the clergy were generally distrustful and uncooperative: when bishop Fuenleal of Pamplona summoned a diocesan synod in May 1566 on his return from the provincial council at Saragossa, he could not foresee that disputes would delay the closure of the synod for twenty-four years, until 1590, three prelates later;[71] and no further synod was called before 1634.

In Toledo one more provincial council was called, by Gaspar de Quiroga. It opened in September 1582 and closed in May the next year. In its early weeks it had the inconvenience of coinciding with the papal reform of the calendar, so that the day after 5 October had to be re-dated 16 October; but thereafter it proceeded successfully to deal with a number of issues that the more strife-ridden council of 1565 had been unable to touch on. At this council, for example, it was decreed for the first time that confessionals be constructed, and that women be divided from men during worship.[72] No further provincial councils were held in the Crown of Castile. Numerous synods continued to be held by reformist prelates, but by the seventeenth century they too were disappearing. When canon Villanueva visited the see of Segorbe in the nineteenth century he learnt from the records that there had been no synod there since 1668.[73] Of all the realms of Spain, only Catalonia continued with an uninterrupted programme of councils and synods.

Though the religious orders will take up little of our attention, they occupy a crucial place in the scenario since they represented the bulk of the clergy in Spain, and were the most affected by the reforms of the period. During the fifteenth century important changes had occurred in their structure, provoked by the spread of the Observant discipline, and among the Dominicans and

Franciscans the majority of religious houses in Castile had been converted, often by force, to the new 'reform'. Perhaps the most interesting aspect of the new trend was the emergence and rapid growth of the Jeronimite order. Under Ferdinand and Isabella, whose policy in these matters has been exhaustively studied, important steps were taken towards carrying out with papal permission the ordering and reform of individual religious houses in various parts of the peninsula; but though the resort to royal initiative would continue to bear fruit in subsequent years, it is clear that the 'reforms' (which involved the imposition of the Observance) were limited in scope to a few religious houses, were only partially successful, and did not extend to any other sector of religious life, either among clergy or people.[74]

The attempt by the Catholic Kings to reform the religious houses for women in Catalonia provides an example of the difficulties involved.[75] Ferdinand plunged into the reform of the Catalan female houses when he was in Barcelona with the queen in the eventful year 1492–3. Permission was received from the pope to visit and if necessary reform the thirty-nine convents, in their majority belonging to the order of Santa Clara, but including important Cistercian and Dominican foundations. From the beginning, there was strong opposition. The convents refused to accept the imposition of the strict enclosure, which was contrary to the vows they had taken; and they rejected visitors who emanated not from their own superiors but from an outside authority, namely the crown. The nuns were powerfully backed up by their families, and in the case of the Barcelona convents by their links with the *Consell de Cent*. Faced by this opposition the king, writing from Salamanca in February 1506, observed angrily that 'we know from experience that people in Barcelona, both clergy and others, have at all times tried to destroy the reformation.' Several houses were forced to accept new constitutions, but the hasty methods of the king's visitors were high-handed and ultimately self-defeating, so that the whole exercise ended in failure.

The Observance reforms of Cisneros were always looked upon in Spain as a task left uncompleted, and there was unanimous agreement on the need to bring about a sweeping change in the religious houses of the peninsula: no clearer proof of it existed than the energetic attempts under Charles V to proceed with reform. Evidence of the continuing neglect in Catalonia emerges from the report in 1532 of the official (French) visitor to the Cistercian monasteries: at Santes Creus he found that 'there was little observance of the ceremonies of the order, and what there was was corrupted', and at Poblet found the younger monks 'extremely dissolute, irreverent and undisciplined'.[76] Disputes over jurisdiction were always to the fore, with the result that the Observance by the early sixteenth century was satisfactorily rooted in Castile but hardly known in the Crown of Aragon, where subsequent attempts to introduce change were carried through with violence and inevitably also met with violence. In 1534 the Dominican friar charged with enforcing the Observance on the convents of Aragon, Domingo de Montemayor, was assassinated by two aggrieved friars who immediately fled to north Africa and turned Muslim. In Catalonia a subsequent viceroy, Francisco de Borja (1539–43), collaborated with the bishops in trying to impose reform on the religious houses, especially those of women, but little was achieved. The emperor's instructions to the viceroy call his attention to 'the dissolution and evil customs and excessive liberty in some monasteries in Barcelona and in Catalonia'; but though Borja was aware of the measures being attempted by the bishops, he wrote to Los Cobos in December that year that the reform 'could and should be better'.[77] By mid-century, then, when Philip II officially took over the government of Spain, much still remained to be done. Moreover, though in many areas of Spain the Observance had now established itself, and one may therefore assume a certain improvement in discipline and religious practice, little or no evidence exists of any change in the social and economic context of the monasteries, or whether their internal life had any effect on the population as a whole. It is no surprise to find the bishop of Oviedo complaining, a full century after Trent, that 'the convents of nuns of this diocese are as needy as those in Castile of a thorough reform.'[78]

The papacy down to the death of Pius IV in December 1565 collaborated with the proposals of Philip, but not without considerable doubts, which it was the task of special nuncios, especially cardinal Boncompagni, to try to dissipate. There always remained serious differences of opinion and conflicts of approach, with Philip repeatedly insisting that Spain had its own proposals for reform of the orders, that 'what was laid down by the Council is not remedy enough',[79] and that if Rome (this was in 1563) did not approve the Spanish proposals he would 'depopulate the monasteries rather than let them live as they do'. Pius IV felt that Spanish truculence threatened his authority: 'if the king wishes to be king in Spain,' he stormed, 'we wish to be pope in Rome.' The unease on both sides was provoked not simply by political obduracy but also by the two problems we have touched on above: the case of Carranza, and Philip's summoning of the provincial councils of 1565.

The succession of the austere Dominican Michele Ghislieri to the see of Peter as Pius V in 1566 augured well for the Spanish reform programme, but the pope had doubts about how to proceed and it was not until the very end of the year, in December, that he began to issue the necessary briefs to give the Spanish authorities power to proceed.[80] The central feature of the programme was the reorganisation of each religious order, and the definitive imposition on all of the Observance. It is probably inappropriate to use the word 'reform' for the events which now followed, since no obvious abuses were tackled and no changes made in the interior practice of the major orders. What did take place was an attempt to restructure the religious orders by abolishing all smaller orders and smaller monasteries, and handing them over to the major bodies: thus the Premonstratensians and Isidrites were to be dissolved and absorbed into the Jeronimite order. There was to be no consultation on the changes; instead all the measures were decided upon and executed by the organs of state, notably by a Committee of Reform made up of the royal secretary Zayas, various royal councillors, the confessors of the king, and the inquisitor general Fernando de Valdés, a man who notoriously was never tolerant of opposition.[81] Wherever necessary, armed troops were used to occupy monasteries and drive out the incumbents, and at every stage force was employed in order to effect an immediate 'reform'. Some monasteries gave in helplessly and accepted the reorganisation. The extent of the changes that took place has never been properly assessed, but it would not be unjust to compare the abolition, closing and fusion of Spanish religious houses with the English Dissolution of the Monasteries, the difference being that in Spain all confiscated property was retained for Church use. As may be imagined, there was widespread opposition to the measures: monks and nuns barred their buildings against the soldiers, took up guns and engaged in hand-to-hand struggles. Defying orders for their arrest, leaders of the threatened orders went underground, then fled the country and turned up in Rome, where they canvassed support for their cause and pleaded with the pope for help; others gave up the cloth and took service as soldiers in Italy and in the French religious wars.[82] Fray Rodrigo de Oporto, superior of the threatened Third Order of Franciscans, and fray Gonzalo de Salas, abbot of the Premonstratensian house at Medina del Campo, were among those who managed to make it to Rome and gain the pope's ear. The struggle went on, nevertheless, within a context of considerable freedom. It is interesting that Martín de Azpilcueta, the greatest canonist of his day, who had already stuck his neck out by firmly supporting the cause of the disgraced archbishop of Toledo, Carranza, now again braved official displeasure by issuing a considered 'opinion' or *parescer* in which he affirmed that the Franciscans had a canonical right to be excepted from the changes.

Seeing the extent of the opposition to the 'reform', Pius V backtracked. In January 1568 he guaranteed to the Franciscan Tertiaries a limited autonomy within the main order, and thus ensured their survival. Then in March he issued a brief claiming that his purpose had never been to dissolve the Premonstratensians but only to reform them; this opportunely saved the order. In the event, the only group to be dissolved and absorbed was the Isidrites, a tiny grouping that was fused with the Jeronimites in 1568. Philip II was particularly angry at being frustrated in the attempt to fuse the Premonstratensians with his favourite order of Jeronimites, but was obliged to accept the situation. True reform, in terms of the religious life and of discipline, was something that evolved more slowly, but again the state insisted on playing a role, clear evidence of Philip II's almost obsessive concern with the re-ordering of the Church in his realms. In subsequent years each order was subject to visitations from royal commissioners, but any changes were usually made in consultation with the papal nuncio in Spain; thus both king and pope entered into a period of reasonable co-operation. These limited achievements, however, applied only to the Crown of Castile.

During Borja's tenure of the viceroyalty of Catalonia he had cooperated enthusiastically with the efforts of bishop Cassador of Barcelona to look into the religious orders, but his conclusion on it all was that 'when I left office in Catalonia the work had only begun.'[83] Philip II was starting virtually from scratch. In March 1567, armed with the brief granted him by the pope, he wrote to the bishops of Catalonia 'on the reformation of the monasteries of Conventual friars and nuns of the Order of St Francis and their conversion to the Observant rule', asking them to send him a full inventory of all the property of the Franciscans in the diocese. Three weeks later he informed all the Franciscan religious houses in Catalonia of his plans,[84] and on the same day wrote to the veguers of the principality on the same subject. A letter was also sent to the Conventual provincial, with the hope 'that you will collaborate willingly in this task'. The unsuspecting Franciscans were given no details of the 'task', which was outlined in a confidential letter of the same date to the royal high court in Catalonia, the Audiència.[85] From this we learn that the 'reform' was to be entrusted entirely to the bishops, as specified by the brief of Pius V; that the first step each bishop would take would be to order the seizure and embargo of all the assets of the Conventual Franciscans; that each bishop would appoint an ecclesiastical commissioner to visit the religious houses, but that each such commissioner must be accompanied by a secular magistrate; and that at each visit the brief for the reform must be read and a demand made that all keys be handed over.

Shortly after, the king wrote identical letters to the bishop of Barcelona and to the provincial of the Observant Franciscans, asking them to use their good offices to 'attempt as far as possible to win over and persuade by favourable means the said friars' of the Conventual wing of the order, and assuring them that force by the secular authorities would be used only as a last resort. Since the seizure of Conventual assets was only the first stage of the royal programme, Philip was concerned that no one must suspect that further religious orders would be affected, and asked them to make sure 'that nobody learns that a reformation of the other orders is planned, since it would cause as you can imagine serious complications'.[86]

It was not long before the next blow fell. In September the king wrote to the viceroy and to the bishops, informing them that it was his intention now to reform the Carmelites, the Trinitarians and the Mercedarians, and asking the viceroy to devote to the task 'all the zeal and energy possible'.[87] This time, according to the king's figures, fifty-six religious houses in total were involved. Subsequently, in November, he extended the programme to the only Premonstratensian religious house in Catalonia, that of Bellpuig de les Avellanes in the bishopric of Urgell.[88] By the end of the year information was being collected preparatory to an order for the reformation of all the Benedictine abbeys and nunneries of Catalonia, and in a letter to the viceroy the king specified that all the great abbeys (Ripoll, St Cugat, St Miquel de Cuixà, Poblet) fell within the programme.[89]

Time and again in his correspondence, as though it were an obsession, the king insisted on the need for a 'reformation'. In April 1567 he termed it 'the task of the reformation', and that December he expressed 'the desire we have that the friars and nuns of all the orders in my realms keep the purity of the rule they professed'.[90] The king's concept of 'reform' followed the thinking of his predecessors but also coincided with the outlook of the Counter Reformation: houses with an inadequate number of religious must be suppressed and the personnel sent to larger foundations, larger houses must be purged and the numbers made up with Observants or if necessary with personnel from Castile, all religious houses must conform to the original rule of foundation, all female convents must practise the strict cloister. These principles were not so easy to sustain in practice. With some orders the original rule was itself defective by the standards of Trent, and in the case of the Benedictines the king had to concede that a secret ('as secretly as possible') meeting be held with the already reformed Observants of the order to see 'to what extent the said Benedictine rules coincide with the original rule and to what extent they deviate, and how far they differ from the decrees of the Sacred Council of Trent'.[91] The convents of Catalonia, moreover, did not always have the cloister in their original rules of foundation, a fact that the nuns were able to use in their favour when rejecting the pretensions of the royal commissioner.

The king, however, was in a hurry. In June 1568 he sent a long letter to the bishops of Catalonia, reminding them of the instructions he had already sent them the preceding August and November:

> And though much time has passed since then for the business to have been completed, there is still much to be done . . . If everything is not carried out as has been stated there can be little confidence that the reformation will be permanent and even less in what has been done so far. To that effect we are sending you more copies of the said instructions, just in case you do not have the others to hand . . . It is clear and obvious that if the smaller houses, where the reformation cannot be carried out for lack of religious, are not suppressed and their revenues applied to other larger ones, that would be to leave an opportunity for the friars and nuns to return to the same past abuses and excesses.[92]

The reform was not proceeding as smoothly or as rapidly as the king had hoped. Philip reported to the viceroy a case in Rosselló that bore out the need for reform:

> The bishop of Elna has written to us saying that he carried out the reformation in a monastery of Conventual friars of the Order of St Francis that he has in his diocese. The prior who lived there sold wheat and supplies that had come for the provision of the house, together with the jewels he could seize, and fled taking with him over two hundred ducats. Another of the same monastery stole some clothing and went into the mountains where they say he has dropped his habit and turned bandit, threatening the Observant friars who are said to be terrorised.[93]

The changes in Catalonia took much longer to effect than the king could have imagined. The transfer of Franciscan religious houses from the Conventuals to the Observants was carried out by force, and some houses were suppressed altogether, the one in Cervera being used as the basis for a university in 1592.[94] But the Benedictine houses were untouched by the Observance, and changes were only gradually introduced through the agency of the diocesan authorities; finally in 1592 a papal bull laid down the norms to be accepted by the order and after some resistance was accepted in 1597 by the monks of the province. Similar rules for the Cistercians of the Crown of Aragon, now autonomous from the French, were not achieved until 1616. Change was likewise slow in penetrating the other orders. Prominent among them were the Mercedarians, based in Catalonia; though Philip managed to draw up proposed rules for them at Guadalajara in 1574, it was not until 1593 that the order agreed to accept a new system of regulations. The Carmelites were also slow to change: it must be remembered that the famous reforms of Teresa of Avila did not emerge until the 1580s and only in 1593 were the Discalced Carmelites given recognition. In one other major sphere – female religious houses – success was also limited. Traditionally, nunneries in Spain had never practised the full cloister, and most female religious also practised mendicancy in order to maintain themselves, thereby coming into contact with the secular world. The enforcement of the strict cloister, laid down by Pius V in constitutions of 1566, could not therefore be carried out in Spain without coming into grave conflict with all the female orders. Reformers pointed out the scandals, particularly those involving male religious, that resulted from the existing situation, but though some steps were taken to impose the Tridentine rules no lasting change occurred in the matter within Spain.[95]

The reform programme was in effect postponed until the last years of Philip's reign,[96] by which time the king's methods had changed. The four visitors appointed to visit the Benedictine order and the Augustinian Canons in 1586 were instructed to proceed 'with great gentleness and kindness'. In Catalonia the king tried to enforce his general rule that all houses have a minimum of thirteen religious, failing which they should be merged or abolished. Some were easy to abolish because they were neglected and undermanned, and changes of personnel were salutary: the bishop of Elna in a report to the visitors recommended the transfer of a monk of St Pere de Rodas who had murdered another but 'the case against him could not be proven', of one in St Miquel de Fluvià 'a haughty person, hated by everyone in that area for being a troublemaker and a friend to vagrant and bad people', and so on. Despite objections from the orders, eight out of twenty-four Benedictine houses and two out of seven Augustinian houses were finally suppressed by a bull of 1592, which elicited long objections until a compromise was reached in 1616. It was typical of Philip II's careful policy that even when insisting firmly on forcing through change, he took care that all aspects of policy in Catalonia 'should be entrusted only to the nuncio'.[97]

The visitors' report, issued in 1588,[98] no doubt exaggerated to some extent but serves to dispel any illusion that all was well in the religious houses of rural Catalonia. The Augustinians have no provincial chapters. They have no visiting inspectors and are not visited. They are not cloistered and everyone lives in his own house. They have almost no rule of obedience and go where they like. They have women in their houses. They give no account of their income. In some monasteries they stopped performing the masses and anniversaries to which they were obliged by the terms of their foundation. They carried offensive weapons. They have no teachers to teach them grammar and so most of them are totally ignorant and cannot even read. They used to dance publicly with women. Some have been found guilty of very serious crimes, adultery, fornication, theft, homicide, simony, enmity, and of letting bad people enter and of being friendly with bandits.

The judgment on the monks of St Benedict was no less severe:

They have no cloister and go out when they please. Their obedience to their superiors is almost nil. Some cohabited publicly with women. They had nobody to teach them grammar and so remained ignorant, as nearly all of them are, and most of them do not even know how to read. They slept not clothed as the rule demands but naked. They carried weapons. They took part in all types of gaming. They went to dances and danced with women. Those monks who were not mass-priests did not go to confession or communion outside Lent...

The pastoral efficiency of the houses was questioned: 'the parishes and benefices are badly staffed and they do not observe the Council of Trent and are badly served.' The report may be compared with the frank views of the first provincial of the new Discalced Carmelites of Catalonia; writing to the king in 1590, he said of the abbeys of the see of Urgell that 'they are truly nothing more than sinks of sin and a meeting-place for bandits and evil people, those who go to live there do not do so out of a wish to serve God but as a way of life, certain that they will never lack for food.'[99] The monks had been in Catalonia for five centuries and were being called to account by the reforming standards of a new generation.

Even after the measures of Philip II, much remained to reform. The king's rule that there be a minimum of thirteen religious in a monastery was seldom seriously followed, and late into the next century the notable monastery of Bellpuig de les Avellanes, belonging to the Premonstratensians, did not have more than eight religious, 'and today [1665] there are five'.[100] When in 1690 the bishop of Lérida made an official visit he found disorder and neglect, and 'we have found no evidence of any previous visit nor the slightest sign of its decrees.'[101]

From all this it is clear that prolonged and intensive efforts were being made, both by the crown and by Church authorities, to bring order and discipline into the religious houses of the peninsula, and that some rationalisation was achieved; but it would be naive to think that a purification of the religious community occurred. Old mentalities persisted, and it was difficult to achieve effective change where all the old structures continued unaltered. Moreover, the delay of a reform programme until as late as the 1580s meant that two quite different countervailing currents came into operation, because the wish of the crown and the reformers to restructure, and where necessary abolish, conflicted with a Counter-Reformation piety that desired to multiply religious communities. A case from the diocese of Urgell in 1584 illustrates the point. The crown had planned to suppress the two convents of the order of Santa Clara at Puigcerdà and Conques, each of which 'had only two or three nuns, and because of their poverty could not maintain more, nor did the nuns have the cloister'; the nuns were to be transferred to a convent at Balaguer. However, the civic piety of Puigcerdà was aroused at the possible loss of a religious house, and the government was therefore informed that 'those of the town of Puigcerdà, which is populous and rich, together with the whole territory, wish to restore the said monastery,' and the requisite financing was eventually made available.[102]

In Catalonia, moreover, there were sensitive problems which a reformer could ignore only at his peril. Any change from above was bitterly opposed by those defending local privileges and traditional practice. When in addition the changes were introduced by outsiders to the province then the spectre of Catalan sentiment was aroused. Typical of the problem was the case of the monastery of Ripoll, where in January 1628 serious conflicts arose because of the attempt to purge the existing (Catalan) monks by sending in new personnel from Castile. The Diputació opposed the changes 'on the basis that the reformers and the new abbot were Castilians and could not hold office in Catalonia'; and a contemporary in the privacy of his diary criticised the fact 'that the king wishes to exile our poor Catalans, and to let the dogs of Castile come and eat the bread of our sons and drink the blood of our fathers'.[103] It was a problem to be seen at its most acute in the long history of conflict between the Castilian and the Catalan monks within the great abbey of Montserrat.[104]

In line with his wish to bring order into the peninsular Church, Philip in 1566 proposed to the papacy that new sees be created, partly to take account of population changes and partly to readjust the political map. Changing the areas covered by bishoprics was nothing new: the conquest of Granada in 1492 had led to readjust-ment of the sees in Andalusia, and later in 1517 Charles V had attempted, against the bitter and successful opposition of the chapter there, to dismember the enormous archbishopric of Toledo.[105] Philip's suggestions were met everywhere without enthusiasm: in Rome some cardinals accused the king of wishing to create more bishops so as to have a bigger representation in universal councils, and in Spain there was stubborn resistance from the clergy in the sees affected. It is also worth recalling that Philip's introduction of new bishoprics into the Netherlands in 1561 had by now provoked a major crisis, so that the king was well aware of the likely obstacles. Nevertheless, he went ahead. Giving in to his persistence, Pius V sanctioned the changes, most of them in the Crown of Aragon, which took place over the next few years. In July 1564 a papal decree created the see of Orihuela, in the south of Valencia, and transferred the neighbouring see of Cartagena, which was 'exempt', to the province of Toledo. In June 1571 the large Aragonese see of Huesca was dismembered, and two additional sees, those of Barbastro and Jaca, were erected to share the area with it. Indubitably the most important change of the period was the erection of Burgos, which had been 'exempt' since the eleventh century, into an archbishopric in October 1572. The city had been for about a century the most prosperous urban centre in Castile, and there seemed to be every good reason for elevating its status by granting it authority over the bishoprics of Pamplona and Calahorra, both formerly subject to Saragossa. The latter was com-pensated in 1577 by being allotted the new sees of Albarracín and Teruel. The next important change was the carving out of the Catalan diocese of Solsona, in July 1593, from the sees of Urgell and Vic. Although the then bishop of Urgell approved of and probably suggested[106] the move, he strongly opposed the removal of 258 of his parishes and eventually in 1623 a compromise was reached whereby only 114 of the parishes of Urgell were integrated into the new diocese. Finally, at the end of his reign, Philip in September 1595 resolved a long-running dispute by giving Valladolid its own diocese and separating it from the see of Palencia, which was transferred to the province of Burgos while Valladolid entered the archdiocese of Toledo. Apart from the last change, which was frankly made in order to settle a quarrel, most of these reorgan-isations can be called 'reforms' in the sense that they were made in response to perceived needs, such as the desire (in Albarracín) to provide greater episcopal control over the lands settled by Moriscos; but they were not obviously 'reforms' of improvement, and by no means rationalised the structure of episcopal authority, since the unwieldy mediaeval provinces of Santiago and Toledo were allowed to maintain their structure and the latter was even made bigger. In Catalonia the request by the archbishop of Tarragona in 1603 that the island of Ibiza be erected into a see (since he could never find time to visit it) fell by the wayside.[107]

In Catalonia one further change took time to come about. Possibly since 1538, when the emperor Charles V had visited Rosselló, there were proposals to move the seat of the bishopric of Elna from that town to Perpinyà. One year after the transfer of the see from the jurisdiction of the archbishop of Narbonne to that of Tarragona in 1564, a petition by the cathedral repeated the request,[108] and by 1579 application had been made to Rome. Philip II in a letter to the pope in August 1579 supported the move, but on condition that the Catalan parishes of Rosselló and Cerdanya which were still subject to the French sees of Narbonne and Alet, be transferred to Elna. It is unclear whether these conditions were known to the town of Perpinyà and the bishop of Elna when they wrote to Philip II in January 1582 supporting the transfer.[109] The next year the Council of Aragon decided that 'we agree that the cathedral of Elna be translated to the town of Perpinyà', the main motive being that 'we must proceed with the proposal of His Majesty the Emperor'; but the decision was strongly opposed by the viceroy on the grounds that Elna was a tiny town which depended entirely on the cathedral for its economic survival.[110] The campaign was vigorously renewed in 1591, and in 1599 the bishop and the clergy of Perpinyà came to a broad agreement[111] on the terms of the move. Finally in 1602 a papal bull sanctioned the change, but fierce objections were raised by the canons of the collegiate church of St Joan in Perpinyà, whose building was the proposed cathedral, and they tied the whole matter up in violence and lawsuits until 1607; not until 1620 was agreement reached. After the loss of Rosselló to France in 1659, the see remained in the anomalous position of being subject to a Spanish province, and in 1678 was reunited with Narbonne.

A cornerstone of Philip II's policy was his determination to make the authority of his Church coincide with national frontiers. In the 1560s he managed to secure from Pius V a firm division of the frontier area between Spain and France: the archdeaconate of Baztán in Pamplona and the archpriesthood of Fuenterrabía in Guipúzcoa, both formerly subject to the French diocese of Bayonne but within Spanish territory, were removed from this jurisdiction and put under the see of Pamplona; the Vall d'Arán, on the Spanish side of the Pyrenees but within the French diocese of Comminges, was transferred to the jurisdiction of the bishop of Urgell; and the entire diocese of Elna, which covered Rosselló and fell within the French province of Narbonne, was put under the archbishopric of Tarragona (1564).[112]

Whenever the king reverted to the theme of 'reformación', he tended to cite as a crucial factor the dangers of foreign intrusion into Spanish affairs. Superiors of the orders resident in Rome, he said, neglected the state of their religious in Spain; many superiors were French, and therefore unreliable; foreign contacts allowed the infiltration of Protestant ideas; religious in sensitive frontier areas could present a threat to security.[113] Whatever the real spiritual concern of the king over the need for reform of the orders under his jurisdiction, there can be no doubt of the explicitly political motivation. Writing to his ambassador in Rome in 1569 on the issue of reforming the Franciscans of Sardinia, he stressed that in order to achieve 'the good administration and reformation of that province, it is not acceptable in any way that it come under foreign religious, for many legitimate and sufficient reasons that motivate us'.[114] Fortunately for Philip, the papacy was inclined to agree with the nationalising of the orders. As a consequence, the king managed to achieve the unique distinction of presiding over a wholly autonomous Church, in which not only the nomination of all bishops and prelates but of all heads of religious orders passed under the survey and control of the crown. The friars of the order of Calatrava, who came under the jurisdiction of the French abbot of Morimond, were in 1560 removed from that control; in 1561 the Spanish Cistercians were removed from the jurisdiction of the mother house at Cîteaux, and put directly under papal control; the Trinitarians were likewise released from obedience to their superior in France, and given a Spanish head; the Carmelites were given a Spanish vicar-general; and the Mercedarians, normally based in Catalonia, were in future to have Castilians as alternate superiors.[115] In 1578 the French general of the Premonstratensians declared the new Spanish constitutions of the order void, which provoked a direct conflict with the Spanish authorities; in 1584 no Spanish monks attended the chapter general held in France, and from 1600 the Spanish wing became wholly autonomous.[116] In each case, the change involved release from obedience to a foreign superior, specifically France. The policy reflected Philip's own distrust of events in France and the rapid advance in the 1560s of important sectors of the French elite towards the Reformation; but there was also a distrust of things foreign which continued in later years to prejudice his relations with the Society of Jesus.

For Catalonia, the nationalisation carried different implications. Control from within the peninsula meant, in effect, control from

Castile. There is no secure evidence that Philip II was a conscious Castilianiser, but since the majority of his servants were Castilians they were more likely to be preferred for posts in the Crown of Aragon. Up to 1500 most bishops appointed in Catalonia had been Catalan. With control of presentation in crown hands after 1523, more and more there was a tendency for non-Catalans to receive preferment: between 1563 and 1640, of seventy-three new bishops appointed in Catalonia, thirty-five were non-Catalan; between 1640 and 1715 of forty-six new appointments twenty-four were non-Catalan.[117] In the chief prize, the archiepiscopal seat of Tarragona, the figures were even more unequivocal: twelve out of fifteen appointments in the years cited were non-Catalan. The problem was commented on frequently by public authorities in Catalonia, but to no result. In 1588 the Council of Aragon noted that only two of the bishops of Catalonia at that date – those of Barcelona and Urgell – were Catalans.[118] The diarist Pujades remarked on the people of Barcelona being 'very pleased' when a native of the city, Joan de Montcada (brother of the marqués of Aitona), became its bishop in 1610, but he commented unfavourably when he heard of the death in September 1622 of 'Don Luis Tena, bishop of Tortosa, a Castilian and bitter enemy of Catalans'.[119]

The bishopric of Elna-Perpinyà experienced stormy scenes in 1613, when the appointment of the Andalusian Francisco de Vera to the see outraged the canons who were already protesting over the recent transfer of the see from Elna. Vera provoked further opposition by wishing to make an official visit to the cathedral in Perpinyà. In 1616 the *cónsols* of Perpinyà complained to Madrid of 'the great troubles and upsets caused in this town by the bishop',[120] and violence broke out. In one incident inside the cathedral the angry canons shot at the bishop and wounded him in the hand, while rioters in front of the bishop's palace chanted, 'Come out, morisco Castilians, now you'll see what those of Perpinyà are made of'; and the bishop eventually had to flee for his life to the old seat of Elna.[121]

The vital impulse of the provincial councils of 1565 was not sustained. Though the royal directive called for regular councils, virtually none was called in Castile after that year (the exception of Toledo has been mentioned), and the practice died out completely. In the Crown of Aragon, only the archdiocese of Tarragona (that is, Catalonia) continued throughout the early modern period to maintain a regular series of councils. Between the beginning of the reign of Charles V and the council of 1565 some thirteen provincial councils are known to have been held in Tarragona. Between 1565 and 1757 a further thirty-six were held.[122] Catalonia thus played a uniquely vigorous role in the evolution of Spanish Catholicism.

The pioneering role of Tarragona in the peninsula can be seen clearly in the comprehensive publication by the provincial council of 1555 of all its preceding constitutions. This major work, published at Barcelona in 1557, presents a clear guide to the evolution of reform efforts and establishes the continuity of Trent with preceding Church legislation. Few reforms of the sixteenth century lacked antecedents: clandestine marriages in Tarragona had been prohibited by constitutions since the year 1129, the obligation to confess and communicate once a year had been laid down in 1329, details of clerical dress had been decreed since 1338, since 1429 rectors had been obliged to explain doctrine to the people, and in the same year the sacraments of baptism and matrimony were ordered to be performed only in church and not in private houses.[123] The council of 1555 added to all these a list of further constitutions, including the obligation to maintain registers of baptisms and deaths in all parishes.[124] It was in this active spirit of discipline that the provincial council of 1565 decreed constitutions that were to remain a fundamental reference point for Catalan churchmen over the next two centuries. Though in principle the constitutions of provincial councils required the approval of Rome, royal policy prevented such approval being sought; and only on rare occasions (as with the bitter dispute in 1637 over the use of the Catalan language) did the Tarragona councils apply for a decision from Rome.

The council of 1565 was a stormy one in which several objections were made to the decrees of Trent, particularly over tenure of benefices. The objections gathered force in the lengthy council summoned by cardinal Cervantes which lasted from November 1572 to 1574. In the session of February 1573 a decree was passed accepting the new Roman missal and breviary, but a formal protest was lodged by the then bishop of Lérida, Antonio Agustín, on the grounds that his see had a rite older than that of Rome. Agustín himself, when he in turn became archbishop of Tarragona (1577–86), summoned a council in 1577 and synods in 1569 and 1573. His successor Joan Teres (d. 1603) held councils in 1598 and 1602, the latter being particularly active. Councils seem to have been held thereafter at intervals of roughly five years, usually with little business to discuss apart from taxation to be paid to the crown. This politicisation of their function provoked serious problems. In the 1630s the cathedral chapters of Vic, Urgell and Gerona led the way in resisting royal taxation imposed through the councils, combining their stand with popular rioting. In June 1634 the bishop of Gerona reported that 'the resistance and obstinacy of these three chapters is the most outrageous ever seen', and when commissioners were sent to Urgell (where the resistance was led by canon Pau Claris) 'the clergy came out armed to kill them and would have done so if they had not escaped.'[125] After 1637 the see of Tarragona remained vacant for seventeen years as a result of the problems provoked by Olivares' intervention in the principality, but was filled again from 1653 and the series of provincial councils continued.

Prelates and clergy attending the provincial assemblies were meant to implement and reissue the constitutions in their own areas of authority, primarily, at episcopal level, through the medium of diocesan synods. The close links between Tarragona and Barcelona were reflected in the regularity of synods held by the latter diocese over the next two centuries. The first post-Tridentine synod of Barcelona was held in the chapter house in April 1566 and brought together 104 parish rectors.[126] Subsequent synods were held every year, with good participation and few evident problems. In the synod of May 1572 there were 142 clergy in attendance and thereafter with few exceptions the number remained at this high level, 202 being present at the synod of 1586, 210 at that of 1605 and 196 in 1669. The order of business was usually straightforward: relevant officials of the diocese were elected, and then the assembly would discuss before the bishop petitions brought by individual clergy; if after discussion the bishop agreed to the petitions, they would be adopted ('placet synodo') and then later issued as constitutions. The final item of business would be decrees issued by the bishop for the government of his diocese. The synod which met on 20 April 1574 consisted of 197 clergy and 25 constitutions were adopted by the assembly.

In some other sees synods were less frequent and often not published. In Urgell[127] there appear to have been no synodal constitutions between those of 1557, issued by bishop Juan Pérez García in Castilian, and those of 1585 issued by Hugo de Moncada, when for the first time attention was given to the stipulations of Trent; thereafter synods drew up constitutions in 1610, 1616, 1622 and 1635, with a long break until the late seventeenth century in 1665.

When Philip II came again to Barcelona in the spring of 1585 it was to a city and province that had experienced twenty years of religious development, much of it due to his initiative. The city had nineteen male religious houses and ten female, in addition to ten hospital foundations; it had some sixty professional confraternities without counting the confraternities of the seven parishes.[128] Unlike the previous visit, sparkling with optimism, this one took place in quite a different atmosphere. On arriving in Catalonia the king took the royal party to stay in Poblet and then in Montserrat. In Montserrat, however, the situation was abnormal, and though a Catalan source claims that the king was 'well looked after by the fathers who were all Catalans, there being at the time no Castilian monks or friars since they had been expelled',[129] we may doubt whether Philip felt at ease in the strained environment. The purpose of the visit to Catalonia was to see off his youngest daughter, the beautiful infanta Catalina, who had just married the duke of Savoy; but in Montserrat the infanta Isabel caught a fever, the young infante Felipe was taken violently ill with vomiting, and the king was suffering seriously from his gout. To avoid the fuss of a solemn entry into the city, and with the excuse that he was making a private visit on his daughter's account, Philip and his party slipped in unannounced in the first week of May, and and were met by a storm of protest for doing so. 'The Consellers were angry', reports Henry Cock, 'for they felt they had been tricked, the citizens were angry because His Majesty had not entered in triumph, everybody was angry that the confraternities had not greeted him.'[130] The city insisted on laying on six days of fiestas during which, as Cock says succinctly, 'everything else was dropped and the citizens simply did nothing'. The royal party took little part in the celebrations, for in addition to the others the duke of Savoy was also laid low with fever. The king stayed in Barcelona for five weeks, during which he celebrated his fifty-eighth birthday, on 21 May. On 13 June, after a leave-taking at the quayside which lasted two hours because Catalina was weeping and unhappy to leave her sister and father, the infanta and duke set sail in the fleet, forty galleys strong, of admiral Andrea Doria.[131] It was the ailing Philip's last visit to the principality.

Five years previously, in 1580, the Jesuit Pedro de Ribadeneira had already commented on the disillusion of many with the king's policies: 'the people, the grandees, the nobility, the clergy, even the friars, all embittered, disappointed and discontented with His Majesty'. Shortly before the king's visit, Diego Pérez in 1583 had preached publicly from the pulpit of Santa Maria del Mar in Barcelona in similarly pessimistic terms on 'the king don Felipe, an old and sick man; the kingdom poor and worn out, for many a year nothing has gone right; the land full of thieves, murderers, idlers, the sick and the wretched; everything in ruins'.[132] Even allowing for the moralising rhetoric, it appeared that the tide, once full of promise, was changing. In Catalonia the reform in the religious orders was running into trouble. The problems in Montserrat[133] were symptomatic of those facing the Counter Reformation in the principality. Changes could not be brought about simply by royal fiat, nor was it possible to implement them rapidly. Very much more than a generation would be required for carrying out the 'reformation' that the king so ardently wished to bring about.

CHAPTER THREE

The Revolution in Public Worship

Experience has shown that within Spain there are Indies, and mountains in this case of ignorance.
Felipe de Meneses, *Light of the Christian soul*, 1554

R eligion in pre-industrial Europe was conditioned at the level of belief by symbols related to the non-material universe and at the social level by modes of action arising out of the material environment.[1] Christianity among the people was more than the corpus of creed and conduct laid down by the Church; it also consisted of inherited attitudes and practices relating both to the invisible and the visible world that were as deeply ingrained as the official culture. The relationship between official belief and informal, traditional practices was an uneasy one, and long before the outbreak of the Reformation there were Catholic writers, among them many Spaniards, who insisted that much remained to be done in bringing the people to a proper sense of Catholic religious living.[2]

Though the symbols and ritual of the Church were, as we have seen, universally used as a means of coming to grips with the environment, they supplied only the outward form of popular beliefs, which found their justification in a variety of other traditional sources. It would be unconvincing to argue, at least for Spain, that 'it was above all with the sacraments of the Church that such [unofficial] beliefs arose',[3] for it was precisely because the sacraments played little part in religion that the people resorted to alternative rites rooted in folk practice. Mass and the sacraments, even when used, were regarded 'less as acts of personal salvation than as expressions of group solidarity'.[4] Far from the institutional Church being regarded as 'a vast reservoir of magical power',[5] it was because the Church was often unable to respond to psychological needs that the people took refuge in other sources of power, natural and supernatural. Implicit, indeed, in much of the Catholic writing of the early Reformation period is the criticism that the people were not resorting enough to the rites of the Church and were instead using practices for which there was little sanction in official theology or official practice. This specifically was the 'superstition' that they attacked, with perversions of Church ritual as only one component of the broader span of popular practice.

Although much 'superstition' was explicitly to be found among the uneducated, the beliefs were never limited to those sectors and could be found among all sections of the community, in both village and town. Our best guide to apparently superstitious aspects of religion in the first decades of the sixteenth century can be found in the treatises by Martín de Castañega and Pedro Ciruelo, fortuitously published in the same year, 1529. Though the books deal at some length with witchcraft (which the bishop of Calahorra in his preface to Castañega said 'some parts of our bishopric have suffered in these past years') they were principally concerned with the deterioration in all aspects of religion and culture, the 'vain superstitions and witchcraft which in these times', to cite Ciruelo, 'are widespread in our Spain'.[6] The works can be viewed as an attempt to recover for official religion control over the rites and symbols of everyday existence; but there is in both authors an insistence on the unreason and ignorance which governed popular beliefs, so that their studies may also be seen as an attempt to reject outmoded attitudes in favour of the educated discipline of the Church. Apart from expressing some standard prejudices of his time and of his sex,[7] Castañega showed considerable understanding of some of the social reasons for superstition, and directed his comments to the three great areas of uncertainty that were of particular import to pre-industrial cultures: defence against the unknown, the combating of sickness, and conjuring the weather. 'We see in our experience every day' that the role of witches, curers and finders is often taken up by poverty-stricken women and clergy 'to maintain themselves and earn a living . . . and through this they have their houses crowded with people'. Of healing, he recognised that it could not be written off as witchcraft and that there were methods of curing which were difficult to explain, but his criticism was directed primarily at deceits and at alleged miracles. Finally, he was unsparing of the stupidity of attempts to control the weather: 'the conjuring and exorcism of clouds and storms are so widespread in the realm that there is hardly a farming village which does not have a sum set aside for it'; and explained to his (clerical) readers that excommunication should not be used in such absurd ways as putting curses on locusts when they attack the harvest.[8]

Although clergy at all levels differed in their perception of superstition, an uncompromising guide to the standard official view at the end of the sixteenth century may be found in the pages of the moral theologian Manuel Rodríguez, who stated firmly that 'using arts of divination is a mortal sin', 'the art of chiromancy for divining is prohibited', zodiac readings at birth are 'vanity, superstition and mortal sin', 'it is forbidden and a mortal sin to use astrological enquiries to find stolen objects', 'the art of magic is prohibited', and 'they sin mortally who think that witches are taken from one place to another, as the witches themselves sustain'.[9] All these offences, Rodríguez said, fall under the jurisdiction of bishops and of religious orders: by implication, the Inquisition has no automatic jurisdiction over the matter, a view (we should note) shared by the Inquisition itself, since heresy was not involved. When considering superstition, in fact, heresy was not an issue. In his authoritative *The Practice of Curates*, the seventeenth-century Franciscan theologian Noydens defined superstition as 'vain or false religion with an illicit cult', but then went on immediately to discuss popular superstition not as a 'falsa religio' but as 'vanities', indulged in by people who were 'simple and ignorant', the only danger being when diabolism intruded.[10]

Ignorance, rather than heresy, was considered the principal enemy by the new generation of reformers, and humanists looked to education as the effective solution. The first Church council of the sixteenth century in Spain to take note of the problem was that of Seville in 1512, which observed that 'it has come to our notice that many of our subjects arrive at the age of discretion without knowing the prayers laid down by the Church, through the neglect and carelessness of the parish priests, wherefore we order that both priests and confessors admonish them to learn the general confession, the Our Father, the Ave Maria, Credo and Salve,' all of which the priest was also to teach at mass.[11] Knowledge of these prayers constituted over the next century the basic requirement for Christian Spaniards, but it was a long time before the programme of instruction would be put into effect. The experience of the mendicant orders, who had in that decade started their drive to evangelise the New World, provided valuable information on the problems involved and the solutions to be adopted.[12] As more and more experience was accumulated, clergy adopted the view that the problem of ignorance was primarily a geographical one, at its gravest among isolated rural and mountain communities which clergy had seldom visited. From the mid-century it became common practice to label these sectors 'Indies', and to recognise that there were also extensive Indies within the peninsula, over and beyond the extensive areas where Islam was still the effective religion despite government decrees to the contrary.[13] When using the label clergy tended to refer explicitly to regions where the population was traditionally Christian. 'The fathers and brothers here say that they have another Indies here,' wrote the rector of the Jesuits from Monterrey in Galicia to Laínez in 1561; and another Jesuit reported that 'in these Indies of Galicia we are pressing ahead with the work'.[14] The rector of Alcalá advised Laínez in 1564 that when Jesuits 'ask to go to the Indies it is important to be careful to concede it very rarely, for here we have real Indies and the labourers are few'.[15] Four years later, in 1568, a canon of Oviedo writing to Francisco Borja asked him to send Jesuits to the north: 'These are veritable Indies that we have within Spain,' 'no Indies need to hear the word of God more than these Asturias.'[16]

What were 'Indies'? Even those with direct experience of what they were describing do not explain exactly what they mean. In the 1520s – when Ciruelo and others were writing – there was considerable concern over cases of witchcraft, leading many experts to suggest that the problem was a combination of rural ignorance and diabolic influence. In a government committee which met in 1526 at Granada, where the court was accompanying Charles V on his honeymoon with Isabel of Portugal, the bishop of Mondoñedo suggested the following remedies to a current outbreak of superstition in the mountains of the north of Spain : 'send preachers to those parts, to tell the people of the errors of the witches and how they have been deceived by the devil; the inquisitors and secular judges should proceed with caution; the monasteries of that region should be reformed.'[17] The cures suggested are revealing: preaching, caution, reform; with an equal distribution of blame between the people (for being deceived) and the clergy (for being unreformed and failing in their duty). The clergy were blamed by the bishop of Sigüenza when in 1533 he complained that for lack of instruction 'we see that many men do not know the Creed, nor how to cross themselves, nor anything about Christianity.'[18] 'Indies' seems to have implied areas of ignorance rather than areas practising pre-Christian rites, and despite occasional exaggerations the writers of this period do not assert that their people were non-Christian.

One of the clearest definitions of the problem was made in 1581 relative to the Pyrenees of Catalonia and Aragon by an Aragonese, Dr Pedro Hervás, whose information so disturbed Philip II that he sent Hervás to Catalonia with special letters for the bishops of Barcelona and Urgell, and for the provincial of the Jesuits. The king's concern was over 'the Pyrenees from the county of Cerdanya to Sobrarbe, twenty leagues long and as many wide', and the danger to the faith of the people living there 'in having nobody to instruct them in the things of our Holy Catholic Faith, for the monasteries through whom those parts were in times past conquered and instructed are almost ruined and those who live in them totally ignorant'.[19] Hervás' report was summed up by the author himself in the following terms:

> The causes of the ruin of those people are these: *1*: Ignorance both in matters of faith and in matters of civil customs.   *2*: Not having anyone to teach them, since the parish priests are like the rest, as are the canons regular who live among them.   *3*: Not having the Inquisition visit them in those parts, since the terrain is difficult.   *4*: Not having the bishops make personal visits.[20]

The tenor of this report was confirmed in 1590 by Joan de Jesús Roca, provincial in Catalonia of the newly-founded Discalced Carmelites: 'In the mountains of Catalonia there is such ignorance that through it alone the people living there fall into great sins of murders, robberies, killings, betrayals and other evils, besides which they are ripe for heretics who come from France to sow among them errors against the faith.' Writing to the king, specifically about the mountains of Urgell, he stressed also 'their great ignorance and lack of doctrine'.[21] When the viceroy of Aragon in 1594 asked for Jesuits to come and teach the mountain people of the region of Jaca (the 'montañeses') he referred mainly to their 'great ignorance and little doctrine', and to the absence of schooling, 'from the lack of which they live like wild beasts'.[22] When Pedro de León undertook his missions in the early seventeenth century in Andalusia, he categorised some of the remoter populations as 'very barbarous and bestial' (around Fregenal, towards the Portuguese border) and 'the refuse of all Spain' (the new immigrants who replaced the Moriscos on the Granada coast), but he limited his analysis to saying that the latter, for example, 'had heard no sermon or catechism in over twenty years'.[23]

In none of these reports does heresy appear as the primary issue, and we may safely judge the views which the Inquisition found among the people as reflections of common belief rather than as echoes of infiltrated heterodoxy. The existence of the Reformation almost never appears in the sources as a stimulant to the drive against ignorance. So important a book as bishop Díaz de Luco's *Advice for Curates* (1543) concentrates exclusively on problems of behaviour and culture, and devotes not a single word to the existence of heresy; when he denounces 'these wretched times so full of wicked books which bring no benefit to the state and so much harm to the souls of those who read them',[24] the reference is patently to books of chivalry and not to heresy. The central issue on which Luco concentrated was how the parish priest could teach and instruct. Drawing on his personal experience, fray Felipe de Meneses in 1554 commented on the real ignorance of religion among Spaniards:

> This ignorance is to be found not only among the barbarous and uncivilised mountain people but also in those presumed to be civilised ...; not only in people with no preachers, but also in those bubbling with doctrine...; and in this land not only in small hamlets and villages but even in cities and populous towns ... If you ask what it is to be a Christian ... they can no more give an answer than savages can ... In every two words they will utter three errors or heresies, though in reality those are not heresies but idiocies and foolishness.
>
> There are so many such people that in any village, and not just in one but in many, out of three hundred residents you will find barely thirty who know what any ordinary Christian is obliged to know ... and the same proportion in large and important towns.

Meneses cited specific examples he had encountered among both upper and lower classes:

> A merchant, an important man of experience and informed in worldly matters and of mature years, was questioned on the main points of the Christian faith and could not more give an answer than a one-year-old child ... If we descend to the common people, it is pitiful to see the absurd things they say, the blasphemies they utter on matters which touch the first principles of Christianity. If I were to give an account of what I have seen and heard on this matter, there would be no end to it.[25]

Ignorance leads to unchristian living, and unchristian living to heresy, so the Inquisition should begin to pay attention to the reform of morals (it was in fact just beginning to do this). Spaniards unfortunately have too much inclination to liberty (in the sense of licence): 'I find a greater inclination to liberty in Spain than in Germany or any other nation, a taste for not being subjected, for living free... If with this situation in Spain the drum of Lutheran liberty were to sound, I fear that it would win as many people as it has done in Germany.'

Fortunately the Inquisition with its 'smoke from the sacred fire' had protected the country from heresy (a naive hope this, soon to be shattered by the events of 1558!). In any case, a new Church was arising in America that would compensate for the loss of the Church in Germany. Meneses concluded: 'It was about seven or eight years ago that I began to comprehend this sickness which is the ignorance in Christian souls ... In all those years I have tried to succour ignorant souls and teach them, both up in the mountains and here in Castile. For, as I have said already, experience has shown that there are Indies in Castile and that in the very heart of Castile there are mountains, in this case of ignorance.'[26]

Heresy then was merely a symptom, the real illness was ignorance. This emerges clearly from the pages of one of the most significant writers of the mid-century, Alfonso de Castro, whose major works *Against Heresies* (1534) and *On the Just Punishment of Heretics* (1547) have been judged by their titles alone rather than by their content. An active participant at Trent, Castro was profoundly conscious that the clergy had little right to punish heresy if they had made no prior attempt to dissipate ignorance; and earned himself a place in English history in 1556 by preaching before Philip and Mary Tudor against the persecution of heretics in England.[27]

In Catalonia, which shared an open frontier with Huguenot territory, the perception of heresy was perhaps stronger, as Pere Màrtir Coma's best-selling *Directory of Curates* (Barcelona 1566), written at the outbreak of the troubles in France, points out:

> The heretics labour tirelessly to extend everywhere the poisonous cancer of their ideas, sending everywhere their little books written not only in Latin but also in the vulgar tongue. And they are not content simply to preach as often as they do, but also send their false apostles through every land. And Catholics, who have the true faith, remain dumb like dogs who cannot bark, stay silent, and do not preach or write more than seems fit ... They are many who groan and weep for the misfortune of these times, and few who present themselves as a wall and rampart for the defence of the house of the Lord.

Despite the threat from heretics, however, Coma saw an even greater threat:

> Though there are many causes of this deplorable misfortune, I think that not the least important among them is the ignorance that today reigns generally among Christians ... In conclusion, the fact that the sacraments and other things and rites of the Church are not held in due reverence, is the cause of the great ignorance to be found today among Christians.

Looking back to what seemed to be the mediaeval age of faith, he concluded that 'those truly were the golden times, and these our times are times of blood.'[28]

The preference of clergy for the comfortable towns rather than the harsh mountains was also seen by many as a root cause of ignorance, affecting both clergy and people. The testimony in 1593 of the bishop of Urgell, speaking of his own diocese, is revealing:

> There is a need for the clergy to know more and to attend more to their duties. Most occupy themselves in merchandise and trade, and since the region is austere, the rectorates poor and the benefices as well, no one wants to be stuck out there, and in general one sees much damage from the clergy attending very little to the things of God or to study, and once they are entitled to say mass they do not open a book. The clergy of some worth prefer to be in the populated cities, and no matter how many monasteries you set up in these mountains it is certain that the only ones to enter them would be those who are of least worth, the scum of the province, as one knows from experience.[29]

The clergy wrote their annals with hindsight and inevitably tended to exaggerate the degree of ignorance they had found on their arrival; even so, their comments must not be swept aside, and most were explicit that ignorance was just as extensive in the cities as in the countryside. An historian of the Carmelites, writing in 1709 about the situation they found in Mataró in the 1580s, observed that 'there was so much ignorance of the Christian doctrine that many old people knew nothing of and did not understand the mysteries of our holy faith, for no one had taught them'; thanks to their ministrations, went the claim, 'not only was this ignorance expelled from Mataró but also from all surrounding towns, and now all frequent the sacraments.'[30]

If we view religion not as a system of dogmas but as a cultural framework within which various functions and beliefs, not always compatible, managed to coexist, the concept of 'irreligion' loses its force, since nearly everyone participated to some extent in the rituals and attitudes of their society. Dissidence with received beliefs was always widespread. Systematic dissidence, based on alternative premises of belief, was what we might call heresy, and cannot be found in Catalonia. Partial dissidence may be considered as 'doubt' or 'unbelief', and is easier to identify but difficult to quantify or explain. The problem was approached by Febvre through the printed word,[31] but when we enquire into the minds of those for whom the printed word did not on the whole exist, the question changes its focus. The vocabulary of irreligion was to be found among educated people in Europe from at least the 1580s, when in France for example the writer Pierre Crespet said of the burning of a man for atheism at Metz that 'il faisait mal aux juges de condamner un athéiste, attendu que si on les voulait tous brûler, je ne sais si l'on ne dépeuplerait point les forêts'.[32] Scepticism and dissidence were the hallmarks of sections of the elite throughout western Europe in the Renaissance and during the Counter Reformation,[33] but it could also be found at various levels among the common people.[34]

The impression given by the available evidence is that many Catalans held views which were part of their own local cultural environment and which were in no sense intended as disagreements with the Church. The most significant of these views, discussed below,[35] looked on sex as a normal, healthy activity. Another widespread attitude, common enough for it to appear in a volume of refrains published in Castile in 1541, asserted that enjoyment of this life would not prejudice the life hereafter: 'you won't see me do badly in this life nor suffer for it in the next', or to take the words of a Catalan parish priest of 1626, 'there is as much glory in this world as in the next'.[36] Other views seem to be based on simple reason rather than on ignorance or on heresy. A Valencian writer of the 1590s commented on the scepticism about miracles among 'those who in these times reject miracles, nor accept anything no matter how marvellous as a miracle, basing themselves on St Paul saying that miracles are allowed by God for the conversion of unbelievers, and since we are all believers now there are no miracles'.[37]

Scepticism about the after-life seems to have been common. A merchant of Cambrils, who was also a familiar of the Inquisition, maintained in 1583 that 'the travails of this world are hell and there is no hell or purgatory',[38] and a citizen of Camprodón in 1602 asserted that 'I don't believe there is a hell, it's something they say to frighten us.'[39] There is no resurrection of the dead, claimed a young *pagès* of Blancafort in 1584, and a sixty-year-old farmer of Vilanova de Cubells in 1585.[40] A farmer of Viladrau said in 1593 that 'he did not believe there was any heaven or hell, and God feeds Moors and heretics just as he feeds Christians.'[41] There was a common feeling that, as a farmer of Vilavert said in 1602, 'Moors can be saved just as much as Christians, what blame do Moors have if they were born in a Moorish land?';[42] a view shared by the bailiff in Rosselló who said to a priest in 1603 that 'Moors can also be saved in their own faith if they wish to be saved in it.'[43] It was the opinion also of the parish priest of Torroella de Fluvià (Gerona), who believed that Moors would not go to hell but to limbo.[44] Such views were part of the common heritage of popular reason, in a Mediterranean land where there was frequent contact with Muslims and not a little understanding of their culture. It is much rarer to find views subversive of society, such as the textile worker of Artes who held in 1598 that 'theft is not a sin, some of us have to live off others, those who have must help those who have not.' He did not go to confession – 'I do not confess because they would not absolve me' – and when asked how long it was since he had last confessed replied, 'over fifteen years', and when rebuked for going to confession in mortal sin, 'replied shrugging his shoulders, So what?'[45]

In a somewhat different category are sentiments which went beyond anticlericalism and seemed to reflect hostility to Church discipline or dogma. A farmer of Lio (Tarragona) was heard to exclaim 'damn the person who invented saying mass', and it was said of him that 'he keeps being excommunicated over and over again', presumably for not paying tithes.[46] The mysteries of the mass were questioned by the farmworker of Urgell who stated in 1594 that 'Our Lord is not in that consecrated host.'[47] In 1596 a woman of thirty-two in the parish of La Roca, Barcelona, believed that 'Our Lord in the consecrated host is not as high and powerful as he is in heaven,' and told neighbours 'what you say is nonsense, my God and Lord is only in heaven.'[48] The inquisitors dismissed this as ignorance, and told the woman to recite the rosary, but the statements in fact reflect a common view that God's mightiness could not be imprisoned inside a piece of bread. Did unbelief lie behind the anger of the farm-labourer of Corcó (Vic) who in 1613 smashed a wayside cross to the ground and vilified it as 'the great bogey'?[49] Something more than unbelief lay behind the assertion in 1632 of the forty-year-old weaver of Reus who 'questioned if he believed in God said he did, and asked what it was to believe in God replied that it was to eat well, drink well and get up in the morning at ten o'clock', for he hanged himself in the cells of the Inquisition.[50] Such episodes present the historian with insoluble problems of interpretation. Assuming all the statements and events to be factually correct, we have litle information about the context and emotions involved, we do not know if anger or malice was at work, or if drink was to blame; above all, there is no way of deciding how typical the incidents were.

If 'irreligion' can be seen in these varying human reactions, how do we identify 'religion'? There are probably no better criteria than those adopted by the character witnesses who spoke up on behalf of those accused by the Inquisition. In 1539, when events in distant Germany were still so unreal that they made no mark on the Catalan countryside, Joan Antich, a farmer of Teyà, was accused of saying frequently 'that in this world you'll not see me do badly and you'll not see me suffer in the next', and 'that there is no heaven or hell, and at the end we all have to go to one place, and where the good go the bad will also go and where the bad go the good will go as well'. Apparently he also stated 'that there is no heaven, purgatory or hell', joked about confession, and said 'that it was better to die rich and go to hell than die poor and go to heaven'. The case terminated with a reprimand, for the malice of his accusers was clear, but he was also condemned to a very heavy (300 ducats) fine.[51] Several witnesses were firm about his good character, and their testimony sets out what in their view were the criteria of a good Catholic: 'he speaks like a good Catholic and does many good works and hears masses and performs other charities, and often when talking of the Turk and of Barbarossa said he marvelled that these infidels didn't convert to our holy faith,' and 'he has always been seen to do many good works and give good advice as a very good and Catholic Christian,' and 'he has always been seen to do good works and hear masses and perform charities,' and 'I have seen him hear masses and sermons, confess and go to communion every year, and do good works as a good Christian.' The emphasis on good works in these definitions of a good Christian is striking, with a parallel emphasis on mass-going and the annual confession. In another case, that of a doctor of law of Barcelona, a witness in 1537 stated that he 'confesses and goes to communion every year, and goes to mass on Sundays and feast-days',[52] which was meant to show that he went to more masses than ordinary people. However, frequenting the sacraments was not in itself a sure guide to religion, for in 1536 in Mataró a *comisario* of the Inquisition was happy to declare of an accused person that he was 'a good man and a good Christian', but added that 'I do not know and have not seen whether he goes to confession and communion,'[53] a significant admission in a small community where everybody knew who did and did not go to communion. Testimonies of this type inevitably took into account the fact that the criteria had to be acceptable to the inquisitors, but within their context are also fairly credible reflections of ordinary opinion.

The last cited testimony, of a 'good man and good Christian' who apparently did not go to the sacraments, reveals that religious observance did not necessarily form part of the definition of Catholicity. Nor, for that matter, did knowledge of the basic prayers and practices. Joan Ganer of Barcelona was in 1535 accused of never going to mass or to confession (by his own testimony 'for over sixteen years'), and of saying, when rebuked for eating meat in Lent, that 'in the fine cities and fine towns they do not practise Lent, everyone eats'. A witness for him admitted that 'he does not know the Our Father', but declared stubbornly all the same that 'he is a man of good character (*seny*) and a person who gives a good account of himself.'[54]

There is no easy way to strike a balance between the differing

testimonies to the nature of belief in Catalonia on the eve of the
Counter Reformation, since the criteria clearly varied. One may
also be permitted a certain scepticism about what some uncritical
diocesan visitors claimed to observe on their visits. If the evidence
of *mossèn* Pere Pros, visitor to the region of Oliana (diocese of
Urgell) in July 1575, can be trusted, all the people lived in a state of
Christian perfection: in Castelvedre 'no one is critical of our Holy
Catholic Faith or has spoken any word against it,' in Cortinda 'all
the parishioners went to confession and communion in Lent, there
is no usury nor public concubinage, nor anyone who criticises
our Holy Catholic Faith nor blasphemers nor perjurers,' in Pla de
Trego, 'all the parishioners confessed and went to communion in
Lent, there is no concubinage nor public usury nor marriages either
clandestine or within prohibited degrees, nor anyone who is critical
of our Holy Catholic Faith, and the rector teaches the catechism to
his parishioners every Sunday and holyday of obligation.'[55] The
reports may well be true, but if they were then there was no need
for a Counter Reformation in the region of Oliana.

The early mediaeval Church in the west had faithfully copied
Roman usage in the public liturgy, but at the same time had added
to and adapted it in the light of local customs, with the result that
every significant area and sector of the Church ended up with its
own special variant of ritual. The reformers at Trent were determined to put an end to this 'disorder'. In the time of Charlemagne
the clergy at Narbonne adopted the Roman liturgy and diffused
it throughout the *marca hispanica*, but at the same time added to it
some Visigothic forms, creating in this way a unique liturgy that
predominated in the churches of Languedoc and Catalonia. The
Catalan–Languedoc liturgy which resulted was, moreover, not
merely a clerical imposition but absorbed popular influences and
rites.[56] Catalonia came to possess a liturgy which differed from
the practice of both France and Spain and of Rome as well. The
Tarragona rite, as it was called from the period when that see
assumed primacy among the Catalan churches, could rightly claim
both antiquity (over five centuries) and popular attachment. None
of this impressed Rome, which pushed ahead with plans for change
and abolition.

The two principal instruments of change in the public worship of
the Counter Reformation were the new Roman breviary, issued by
Rome in July 1568, and the new Roman missal, issued in February
1569; both were authorised by Trent as part of the corpus of
reforms that included the Tridentine Index of Prohibited Books
(1564) and the new catechism (September 1566). The breviary (that

is, the prayers meant to be recited daily by clergy) and missal (containing the text and order of the masses to be said throughout the year) were ordered to supersede all rites currently in use, except for churches which could prove that their rite was more than two centuries old (this saved, for example, the Ambrosian rite of Milan and the Mozarabic rite of Toledo), and for certain religious orders which could also claim ancient use (such as the Benedictines). The changes, though asked for by the bishops themselves and reflecting their aspirations for order in worship, caused consternation in the Catholic world and many parts of the peninsula, and provoked mute opposition for generations. Ironically, the see of Tarragona, which shared with most of the Catalan lands an old and fascinating rite and which might have been expected to be the most truculent, was as always the most eager to conform with Roman directives: from 1565 on, provincial councils and prelates continued to insist on the use of the new manuals.

For some, the uniformity was welcome. The Spanish Jesuits in 1564 deplored the lack of a common mass: 'there is no uniformity in this [Jesuit] province nor has it been attempted, indeed if there was any uniformity it has slowly disappeared in this college, and in saying the mass one observes neither the Roman ritual nor the one approved by the previous provincial, and so there is not only confusion in the colleges but even among personnel of the same college.'[57] In Castile, by contrast, the higher clergy felt that the move towards order was being imposed at the expense of legitimate variations, and in 1571 they sent to Rome a long and reasoned protest against some implications of the new rite.[58] Since the crown normally had to be kept informed of all correspondence with the papacy, a copy of the memorial reached the hands of Philip II, and nothing is more indicative of the king's zeal to impose Trent in Spain than his careful instructions to his ambassador in Rome that the memorial be presented to the pope but that the pope be discouraged from making any concessions to the Castilian clergy.

Opposition to change should not be viewed as reactionary or mediaeval. The modifications changed the public face of Catholicism, imposing unwelcome novelties on clergy and people alike, and caused confusion at all levels to a degree comparable only with the innovations of the Second Vatican Council of the twentieth century. Like the changes of the Vatican Council, those of Trent were not a quick, neat revolution imposed in a day, but consisted of alterations dribbled out from year to year, as we learn from the remarkable and definitive studies by the Toledan priest Pedro Ruiz Alcoholado, who in 1584 and 1589, some twenty years after the Tridentine decrees, published two manuals, one for the breviary and one for the missal, summarising and explaining the changes. Commenting on the breviary, Alcoholado explained that 'since in this reformed Roman breviary which was first published in 1568 it has been desirable to revise some details according to the province, in particular for our Spain', further changes had become necessary:

> And since in the said Roman breviary from the said year 1568 in which it was issued up to the present year 1583, both in Rome and in other parts, there have been touchings up, clarifications, additions, corrections, and deletions; all of which has made it very difficult not only for those over here but even for those in Rome, with the result that it became necessary to keep on adding and correcting every day in the printed editions, so that in the end all the calendars (which are regulated by the breviary) differed from each other and became wholly confused and even today many have not sorted themselves out....[59]

The confusion was undoubtedly compounded by the fact that in 1582 the old Julian calendar had just been substituted by the Gregorian, with the fifth of October that year being re-dated the fifteenth, a loss of ten days.

Reluctance to use the new books was understandable in those sees which had only recently put order into their rites and taken the care and expense of publishing new missals (Pamplona, for example, had issued its own missals in 1489, 1545 and as recently as 1561; and its own breviaries in 1500, 1518 and 1551, this last published in Lyon). For many years the acceptance of the new rite (*nuevo rezado*) reduced itself to a simple quarrel over the finances of the matter. In Catalonia there was no hurry to respond to the changes. Both the dioceses of Gerona and Urgell, for instance, had just had new manuals printed in Lyon: in 1561 the Barcelona bookseller Joan Guardiola held among his stock 232 large Gerona missals, costing just over £1 each, 725 quarto missals costing about 15s each, and 404 ordinaries or ritual books at about 10s each: at a total value of nearly a thousand pounds, neither diocese nor bookseller could afford to write off the books. Guardiola similarly held a stock of Urgell manuals worth about £700.[60]

In Castile, Philip II on 15 July 1573 issued an order to the Council of Castile that only the breviaries and missals distributed by the Escorial could be used in Castile; others could be neither printed nor imported nor sold.[61] The order was extended to the Crown of Aragon on 18 August, and on 1 December the Escorial's monopoly was also extended to the Indies. All the religious orders, with the exception of the Carmelites, Carthusians, Benedictines, Cistercians and Dominicans, were to use the official publications. In 1574 a large book-store was set up for the new manuals in the

Jeronimite monastery in Madrid, and remained in use for the next two centuries. The Escorial privilege is commonly said to be associated with a monopoly in missals granted to Plantin of Antwerp in February 1571, but there is no evidence of such a monopoly and it appears that Philip II was simply attempting to give priority to his contract with the Plantins.[62]

Subsequent events offer a classic example of the inefficacy of state legislation. The Castilian clergy in their official assembly protested strongly to the king in 1575 against the lucrative Jeronimite privilege, and in 1613 took the protest to the pope. The new Plantin books, moreover, were both expensive (the Jeronimites received one-third of the sales price) and long in arriving. Many Spanish bishops therefore placed contracts for printing the Roman text within the country, and manuals were printed in the late sixteenth century in Burgos, Salamanca, Saragossa, Alcalá, Toledo and Madrid. In the Crown of Aragon, the bishops felt themselves free to order missals directly from Italy and France: in 1586, for instance, we find the parish church of Sabadell in possession of a 'missale romanum impressum Venetiis anno MDLXXVII'.[63] In 1590 the Barcelona bookseller Antoni Oliver stocked not only a selection of missals produced by Rouillé in Lyon, but also missals issued 'by Cassador', bishop of the city.[64] The Escorial was thus faced with a clear undermining of its monopoly. In about 1603 the prior complained that 'from Rome, Venice and France there have entered and still enter Spain an enormous quantity' of alternative breviaries. In an effort to save the situation, the Escorial in 1607 ordered breviaries from Venice (11,000 were received between 1607 and 1615) and sold them through its distribution channels. For over thirty years, then, there was considerable confusion over the texts of the nuevo rezado. The Escorial continued to operate its privilege (in 1615–25 further large contracts were agreed with the Moretos, who now ran the Plantin presses), but in practice many areas, such as the archdiocese of Tarragona, received their missals directly from Italy. Between the delays in introducing the new manuals, the heavy costs involved and the passive resistance of many churches and communities, the official texts of the new liturgy took well over a generation to become established, and well into the seventeenth century many churches were still unfamiliar with the rites and did not possess the relevant books.

Important financial problems arose with the new chant-books, which had to have special type-face not only for the words but particularly for the music and the requisite illustrations, and were traditionally done on parchment not on paper, all representing an enormous cost; if, moreover, a local expert could not be found to prepare the books, these had to be imported. For a generation after the closure of Trent, churches throughout Spain followed the pre-Tridentine music because they had no financial alternative: in a parish in Pamplona in 1589 the clergy, when asked why they did not follow the new rite, replied that 'because the church is poor it had no way to pay for those books and had to continue using the old books.'[65]

The numerous rites and liturgical practices in Spain were of very long standing and inevitably deeply rooted in the habits and affections of both clergy and people, so that official decrees by themselves were powerless to bring about change. In Gerona, which had several centuries of traditional rites, bishop fray Benito de Tocco assembled the cathedral chapter on 2 October 1574 and gave them a homely allocution on the desirability of accepting the new rites and reforms,[66] which had been officially admitted in the cathedral on 4 February that year, a year after their promulgation by the provincial council of Tarragona. The innovations injured sensibilities both in big matters and in small. As recently as 1557 Gerona had printed in Venice its own missal, which included among its saints St Feliu; the new Roman breviary omitted the saint entirely. In 1567, the year after the provincial council in Tarragona, when it was known that changes in rite were forthcoming, the chapter of Gerona made a contract with the Barcelona printer Miguel Ortiz for the production of 700 missals and 1500 breviaries.[67] In 1567 Lérida also brought out its own new missal and was horrified when the new Roman rite was issued. The cathedral chapter asked their spokesman in Rome whether any choice was possible, and bishop Antonio Agustín, assuming that it was, went further and ordered a complete new printing of 1500 copies of the Lérida breviary.[68] Thus several sees had good financial reasons for holding out against acceptance of the new books: Lérida, which formally accepted the new Roman ritual in November 1573, made a substantial financial loss. For well over half a century, far from unity reigning in the public liturgy of the post-Tridentine Church, there was nothing but chaos and confusion. In Barcelona's second largest parish, that of Santa Maria del Mar, it took a direct order from bishop Dimas Loris in 1596 to make the clergy stop using a copy of the church's printed missal of 1498.[69]

Many old practices which were deemed to be inappropriate for the interior of a church were under attack already, and it was difficult to resist change for long. In 1473 the provincial council of Aranda, legislating for the archdiocese of Toledo, ruled that 'since it is an old custom in metropolitan cathedrals and other churches of our province at the feasts of Christmas, St Stephen, St John, the Innocents and on

other days, for comedies, mummeries, spectacles and many other
and very varied indecent entertainments to be performed during
divine service, and for a loud racket to be made while reciting crude
verses and burlesque speeches, in such a way as to disturb the celebration of divine worship and to remove all sense of devotion from
the people',[70] such rites were in future prohibited; a ruling which
seems to have been entirely ignored. With the coming of the Counter
Reformation the determination to make changes was firmer.

Among the most traditional of Catalan popular rites was that of the
boy bishop. Known over much of western Europe, it constituted
one of the many forms of rite inversion practised during the great
feasts of the Christian year. The ritual usually occurred on the
feast of the Innocents, when the clergy left their places during
the proceedings in the cathedral and a young boy (the 'innocent')
dressed as a bishop took their place and officiated over the ceremonies, among his duties being the reading of a sermon. The word
'innocents' was in many areas extended to mean 'fools', and the
Feast of Fools, a series of rite inversions which affected not only the
Church but all sectors of society, was observed on the feast-day of
Innocents and became to some extent mingled with the rites of the
boy bishop.[71] Gerona had a particularly active tradition of the boy
bishop, known there as the *bisbetó*.[72] In the church of St Joan in
Perpinyà the practice laid down in the 1420s gave the sermon and
the ceremony to two separate children: 'there should be one infant
who preaches the sermon and another who guides the six cantor
infants who participate in the mass; and there should be priests
available who that day ride through the town with the bisbetó.'[73] In
Lérida, costumes for the participants were kept in the cathedral as
early as 1344; a text of the rite of the same period specifies that
'the lord bishop shall be removed from his seat and the boy bishop
put in his place ... After the office the boy bishop shall give the
episcopal blessing and during the mass the sermon shall be given by
the boy bishop.'[74] But the ritual of the boy bishop brought with it
many elements that disturbed the authorities, for in some places
major changes of ritual took place. Inversion of rites at Christmas
could be found in many parts of mediaeval Europe, and in a fully
developed form in France in the twelfth century, with astonishing
scenes where the very ritual of the mass was burlesqued, censing
was done with a sausage, and the celebrant of the mass was called
upon to bray like an ass; the cathedral chapter at Sens in 1444
deemed it to be a reform when they specified that 'not more than
three buckets of water' could be poured over the priest celebrating
vespers.[75] The direct participation of the people in religious rites

was basic to the practice, but the confusion of sacred and secular, and the festive celebrations that occurred at the same time, led to incidents that throughout the fifteenth century invited the criticism of Church leaders and eventually paved the way for suppression of the practice in most areas by the seventeenth century.

In 1512 the practice was stopped in Seville cathedral by arch-bishop Diego de Deza, and replaced by a wholly religious ceremony at which choir-boys and canons changed places during the words of the Magnificat 'He has put down the mighty from their seats and exalted the humble', thereby preserving the element of rite inversion while avoiding the popular element. In Gerona, where the practice lingered on and assumed some quite incredible aspects, the chapter and vicar-general in 1541 issued an order 'that the beneficed clergy carry the candles in their holders in the due and customary manner, and that no one in the said church throw cream or mud, ashes or other rubbish, nor fall on top of each other, nor bring the bisbetó dancing through the church, nor on Innocents Day or other days go in costume or mock the reading of the gospels, epistles and psalms'.[76]

Rite inversion was not a revolutionary or anticlerical gesture, for the disorders of participants occurred within a clearly conservative context, as we see by the sermon of a fifteenth-century boy bishop, possibly of Gerona, where clergy and people were invited to be good Christians, peasants were exhorted not to reserve the worst tenth of their harvest for tithes, and husbands were warned not to take wives fully into their confidence.[77] The chapter of Gerona were worried about the disorders during the ceremony, and in 1475 agreed 'that it would be desirable either to totally abolish the rite of the boy bishop or to reform it';[78] but not until the end of the tenure of Arias Gallego in the episcopate in 1565 was it agreed to abolish the ceremony of the bisbetó in Gerona, and this and similar prac-tices were banned by the Tarragona council of 1565. In the same year the provincial council at Toledo also ordered that 'there be no boy bishop in the churches nor any profane rejoicing on the day of Innocents'.[79] The rite lingered on in various forms and in various parts of Catalonia. In Tarragona cathedral, where a rite or *consueta* of 1369 laid down precise rules for the ceremony, and the boy bishop preached a satirical sermon, the practice disappeared at the end of the sixteenth century.[80] In 1771 the diocesan visitor to the parish of Piera, near Mediona, criticised the rite inversion whereby at Christmas time 'a child carrying a sword and crown' took the place of the town *regidors* and preceded them in the procession to the altar.[81] In Montserrat on the feast of Innocents a boy was chosen from among the members of the monastery school to preside over the ceremonies of the day; in the eighteenth century the feast-day was changed to that of St Nicholas, and the practice continued into the twentieth century. The history of the boy bishop illustrates the process of liturgical change brought about by the Counter Reformation, and the firm decision of the post-Tridentine clergy to impose a respect for their status that the mediaeval practices seemed to deny; but there were limits to the efficacy of change, and the practice lingered on long afterwards.

A multitude of other less prominent practices which had added a popular dimension to the Church liturgy were also on their way out. On the feast of the Guardian Angel in Gerona, celebrated there since 1450, a boy had usually dressed as the angel and sung secular couplets in the common tongue: the practice was stopped in 1585.[82] At the bishop's mass at Christmas in Gerona it was the practice for the assisting priests to kiss the officiating bishop directly on the mouth; this was discontinued, and the priests instead learned to kiss the shoulders of the bishop.[83] A number of popular liturgical practices were linked directly to the everyday world of the street and the field, and will be considered later within their context; our concern here is with customs that affected the ceremonial within the church building. One of the most curious of these was the Song of the Sibyl. The ancient Roman Sibyl had been cited by St Augustine in his City of God as a pagan witness to the coming of Christ, and consequently many churches incorporated her alleged prophecies into their Christmas rites, the text of her 'song' being common in the liturgical uses of the French, Catalan and Provençal lands. It was in use in the cathedral of Vic as early as the twelfth century, achieved official status by appearing for example in the 1464 breviary of the see of Valencia, and made an appearance in the Holy Week ritual used in Valencia in 1533. In the non-Catalan parts of Spain, the Sibyl seems to have existed only in the cathedrals of Toledo and León.[84] The Urgell rite has a variation which was used there in 1545; and versions of the song appear in the liturgical manual of Gerona in 1550 and of Barcelona in 1569. The reform of the liturgy by Trent raised doubts as to the status of the Sibyl, who was not only pagan but had no Biblical foundation whatsoever; the council of Tarragona consequently prohibited the ritual. However, the cathedral chapters had their own view of the matter. In 1572 the chapter of Tarragona voted to continue the practice.[85] In Barcelona the chapter at their meeting on 23 December 1575 debated the Christmas arrangements. 'The question was raised whether this coming Christmas one should have the Sibyl sing the verses of the Judgment, as she used to before, and also whether she should recite the Book of Generations, and when.' There was a heated discussion: 'there were many differing views on it, many saying that one should have neither the Sibyl nor the "Liber Generationis", since they were not in the Roman breviary, and could not be introduced into the Christmas matins.' Finally, though there was 'a lot of disagreement over this point, the resolution taken was that immediately after matins the Sibyl should say her verses'.[86] The Song was gradually phased out in Catalonia by the end of the sixteenth century, no doubt thanks to the action of the bishops, though there is no record of a formal decision by the province to discontinue its use. By contrast, it survived in some other parts of Spain, notably in Mallorca where there is a text of the Song dated to 1575, despite a clear decision of the chapter of the cathedral in December 1572 to stop using the ceremony.[87]

The imposition of the new Tridentine rite in Spain took very long to achieve, at least a generation as a minimum and in some cases more than half a century. In Pamplona the bishop, Antonio Manrique, decreed that the rite come into force by December 1576,[88] but in 1580 efforts were still being made by the vicar-general to ensure that the new books were available throughout the diocese; in the church of San Llorente within the city the old rite was still being sung in 1589, and the town of Garde did not begin to use the plainsong until 1594. Delays cannot be attributed exclusively to non-availability of books: there is irrefutable evidence that many clergy rebelled against having to adopt strange new ways, not only in the mass but even more in the unfamiliar chant. Some poor parishes which had been unable to buy the old books could hardly have been expected to buy the new: in the decayed Mallorcan parish of Llucmajor the bishop in 1562 ordered 'that four missals be bought since there are none in the church apart from old ones which are almost illegible'.[89] In the parish church of Santa Maria del Pi in Barcelona, the community of priests in September 1576 appointed a music teacher who 'must teach all the priests, both beneficed and chaplains... and also the students, plainsong and organ song, and how to say the masses on Sundays and feast-days',[90] good evidence of the willingness to learn; by contrast, in the cathedral the canons complained that the new chant was alien and impossible to learn. In a country as large as Spain, where individualism, local custom and historical tradition all militated against the acceptance of unity, it is no surprise to find that the Tridentine use took generations to impose itself. In Mallorca in 1588, over fifteen years after the introduction of the new rites, less than a third of the clergy were using the Roman missal – 'there is not one in three of the priests who uses it' – and the bishop had to rule that in future no priest could say mass without first being examined in his knowledge of the Roman rite.[91] Mallorca was a typical case where formal acceptance of the new liturgy (accepted by the bishop in 1569, by the cathedral chapter in 1572) did not necessarily mean implementation, since the traditional Mallorcan rite included many small practices and customs which managed to survive despite attempts to eradicate them. The use of the Sibyl continued down to today, and the dance of the *cossiers*,[92] frowned on by most reformers, was permitted to continue. In 1601 bishop Juan Vich y Manrique de Lara published a *Manuale Sacramentorum* which standardised the changes from the traditional island rite, but many priests ignored it.

In Catalonia the use of the new breviary and missal was decreed in February 1573 by the provincial council at Tarragona, despite a formal protest made on behalf of the see of Lérida by its bishop, Antonio Agustín, on the grounds of its own ancient rite. To get the parishes to adopt the new books was no easy task, and in visitation after visitation the bishops bullied their clergy into line. In 1574 bishop Martín Martínez de Villar had to specify purchase of the new missals in parishes as central as Sarrià, Besós, and Vilafranca, and the task of uniformity was no easy one. In Esparraguera in 1578, for example, the bishop's visitor had to order that new missals and choir books be bought, and that 'no priest may celebrate mass without the newly printed Roman missal'; yet the clergy made no move to obey, and again in 1581 precisely the same provisions had to be made. One might imagine that this was sufficient pressure, but when the next visitation was made in 1585 the visitor was obliged to repeat the very same demands that the new books be purchased, and by the end of his visitation to the town he was undoubtedly in a state of desperation, for the secretary noted that 'not one of the provisions made in the previous visit has been carried out.'[93] Esparraguera, as we shall see, was no exceptional case, and every stage of the new reforms cost unimaginable effort to impose, and even then did not take root. We can be sure that the opposition did not come exclusively or even primarily from the clergy, since the purchase of books was in fact the obligation of the local community, not of its clergy.

Thirty years after the official adoption of the new liturgy in Catalonia, in January 1602, the provincial council at Tarragona in its seventh session observed that the Roman rite was still not being followed in Catalonia, and set up a committee headed by the bishop of Barcelona and including the abbot of San Cucufat and deputies of the sees of Barcelona, Lérida and Tortosa, to examine the rite and report whether there was any problem about its acceptance in the province.[94] As late as 1634, seventy years after the official acceptance of Trent in the archdiocese of Tarragona, the diocesan synod of Barcelona could decree that 'in the matter of the rite and ceremonies of the Church, different styles and rituals are observed. We therefore decree that from now on the new ritual be followed, as well as the customs of the churches which observe it'; it also ordered the appointment of officials to check 'that all pray in one manner and observe one rite'. One may well express astonishment that after seventy years the current form of the mass could be referred to as a 'new rite'.[95]

The attempt to renovate the liturgy had two fundamental characteristics: a desire to impose uniformity of discipline on the Church, by encouraging all Catholics to worship in the same way and use the same rites in a commonly acceptable way, with the standardisation of clerical dress, altars, vestments and other external aspects of worship; and a determination to supersede local variations of piety by a universally shared Catholic piety.

The most important instrument of disciplinary reform in the post-Tridentine Church was the bishop. Despite their enormous secular power in terms of jurisdiction, income and status, the prelates of Spain had over the ages been losing their religious authority over the clergy and the people, notably through their lack of control over appointments to benefices. In the century prior to Trent there had already been a widespread resolution to restore the authority of bishops and confirm them in their powers to carry out change. Spain was second to none in its emphasis on episcopal power, mainly because the crown considered bishops to be the best mechanism for bringing order into the Church. Several contemporary writings defined what seemed to be desirable in the ideal bishop; and by a happy accident all the ideals came together in reality in the person of archbishop Hernando de Talavera of Granada. As late as 1583 Jerónimo de Lemos in his *Tower of David* was still looking back to Talavera as the most ideal of all bishops, and did not hesitate to criticise the bishops of his own day: Talavera, he said, 'did not put on the show and dignity that is now used, nor any great train and following, nor did he have a large house as bishops now have; rather he went through Granada with two or three clergy, and his cross before him'.[96] Though nothing is known of the higher clergy in Catalonia at this period, it would appear that some measures of reform and improvement took place in Castile, and that some Castilian clergy were as conscientious and qualified as any in Europe.[97]

Perennial failings remained difficult to eliminate. Though all paid lip service to the campaign against absenteeism of bishops, non-residence continued. The problem had already been raised by the Congregation of 1478 in Seville, and was still common in the early sixteenth century. Barcelona was no exception. In 1512 bishop Martín García was appointed but six years later the *Consellers* were still demanding his residence. His successor spent most of his time in Italy. In 1531 Joan de Cardona was appointed to the see but not actually consecrated for fifteen years, until 1545, the year in which he also died. The series of reforming bishops in the see did not start properly until the appointment of Jaume Cassador in 1546. When the reformer Diego de Arnedo arrived at his see of Mallorca in 1561, his flock had not seen a bishop for forty years; it is significant that one of the absentees (1532–61) had been the son of cardinal Lorenzo Campeggio.[98] Spaniards had never ceased to protest at such papal appointments, and the emperor gave them his active support: a decree of Charles V issued at Toledo on 26 January 1526 protested that 'foreign persons take the revenues from our realms without residing in their churches, which are left without care, order or administration, wherefore divine worship decays every day and our realms and estates are left without money.'[99] In Pamplona from 1481 to 1540 no bishop was in residence.[100]

Absenteeism at episcopal level was less tolerated and less frequent during the Counter Reformation, but by no means disappeared. Bishop Pere de Copons of Urgell was absent from his see for the seven years 1664–71, with the not unnatural consequence that his subjects (he was also feudal lord of most of his diocese) learned to live happily without him, and he himself, once back in his diocese, yearned for the good life elsewhere. 'There is nothing', he wrote to a colleague in Barcelona, 'like going from fiesta to fiesta, from flower to flower, yet here is the poor bishop of Urgell buried between cliffs and crags without any solace other than to look at the bare mountains.' In 1673 he left his diocese once again and came back a year later, informing a friend that 'having left Barcelona I am back in these mountains . . . I arrived so shattered that I shall not again go down there only to have to come back'; but two weeks later, tired already of the problems in Urgell, he wrote to the same, 'I am not at all at ease in these mountains and when the good weather comes I hope to go again to the lowlands.'[101]

The whole pace of change when instituted by the episcopacy depended on the character of the bishops, some of whom showed little inclination to be pioneers of reform. Some guide to their activity is provided by the records of the *ad limina* visits to Rome, which were made compulsory by a constitution of Sixtus V in 1585, the frequency depending on distance from the Holy See, in the case of Spain the rule being that visits be made every four years.[102] In

Catalonia, Tarragona dutifully made its first report in 1590, but many sees delayed for years: the first *ad limina* report of Barcelona was in 1594, that of Urgell in 1598, that of Gerona in 1606, Solsona in 1602 and Vic in 1610.[103] When the reports were made, they were often brief and uninformative, but even more galling for the papal officials must have been the fact that frequently they were merely word-for-word copies of the previous report. Astonishingly, bishops did not make their report in person, the normal practice being to send a representative; possibly the only exception to this rule during the period was the visit made by Jaume Copons, bishop of Vic, in 1668.[104] This situation, clearly in accordance with royal policy, was described by a Catalan bishop in 1803 as being 'the ancient practice of the bishops of Spain, confirmed in the past by the fact or by prescriptive right or else dissimulated through the pious connivance of the Holy See',[105] so that Rome appears to have accepted it.

Absenteeism by prelates caused particularly notorious problems in the so-called 'exempt territories', subject directly to the Holy See and including the sees of Oviedo, León and Burgos. In these dioceses the papacy tended to appoint Curial officials who necessarily lived and worked in Rome instead of in their sees, with the result that the lack of direct episcopal control encouraged laxity of discipline. In Catalonia the exempt territories included those of Ager, Gerri, Mur and Meià in the diocese of Urgell; the bishop here complained to the pope in 1675 of the situation, and in 1717 gave a long and interesting account of the scenes that took place when he went to administer confirmation – the first prelate to do so in seventy years – in the area.[106] In exempt areas, the bishop was usually given direct licence by the pope to operate, but papal jurisdiction was only one of the many problems that confronted bishops when they tried to carry out visitations, since the renewed pretensions of episcopal authority were resented equally by local nobility, religious orders, and parish clergy, leading in some cases to the employment of force against the bishop's officials. As late as 1679, when the bishop of Lérida visited his diocese he was personally prevented from entering some twenty towns where the order of St John did not recognise his jurisdiction.[107]

Visitations were, in the long run, the only effective way that a bishop could try to assert his authority, but though canon law required that visitations be made, both tradition and common sense militated against it, the former since the practice had died out in preceding generations, the latter since the realities of geography and of time available made it impractical for a prelate to spend time visiting his flock. Numerous reports of the period leave us in no doubt that in many parts of the peninsula generations would come and go without ever once laying their eyes on a bishop, and there were consequently problems for those who required the sacrament of confirmation, normally dispensed only by a prelate. When the bishop of Avila, for example, made a pastoral visit in 1617 (after holding the first recorded synod in his diocese) he reported that 'it is eight years since confirmation was last given, and in many villages because of their difficult terrain there is no record of any bishop ever having been or visited.'[108] During the period, newly-appointed bishops would usually initiate their pontificate by making a visitation of the cathedral and its clergy, a courtesy visit in which care was taken not to give offence to the latter; as soon as possible thereafter, the bishop would attempt a visitation of his diocese, in order to make contact both with clergy and with people. This was the minimum norm but some did not attain it and few prelates ever exceeded it. In 1672, eight years after taking over his diocese, bishop Pere de Copons of Urgell informed his flock in Cerdanya that 'it has not been possible for me, for various reasons and duties, to personally visit until now the flock of my see...'[109] If visitations had to be made, the bishop preferred to send out a personal representative, such as a canon of the cathedral, or the vicar-general of the diocese, to act in his place. In part, the sub-stitution was because the visitor had to be absent in the field for several months. In Mallorca the first visit made by bishop Arnedo occupied six months of 1562 and ten months of 1563, a heroic effort that very few paralleled; but subsequent ones by his rep-resentative were also lengthy, seven months in 1570 for instance.[110] All these Mallorcan visits continued straight through the summer months, a feat made possible by the benign island climate. In a relatively accessible area, such as Burgo de Osma (Aragon), the visitation in 1657 took fifty-seven-year-old bishop Palafox six months of the year;[111] it followed that in more difficult territory such visits were out of the question for many prelates. Claims in the *ad limina* reports that regular visits had been made are misleading: the bishop of Urgell reported in 1598 that 'every year visits of the whole diocese were made', and that of Vic in 1618 claimed that 'the whole diocese is visited every year', but the claims were not wholly accurate; in practice the bishop would limit himself to one great sweep of the principal areas, with the primary aim of administering the episcopal sacrament of confirmation, leaving annual visits of smaller areas to be made by his officials. There is evidence that some bishops, given the rarity of personal visitations, tried to do the job thoroughly. In Solsona in 1626 bishop Miguel de Santos, com-menting that his diocese had not been visited 'for many years', possibly since its foundation in 1593, went round his 140 parishes in person, 'seeing everything with my own eyes, touching with my own hands', despite the prevalence of banditry and bad weather, going through inhospitable mountains and visiting parishes 'which had never been visited by the bishops of Urgell, and whose pastors and faithful had never seen the face of their bishops, with the result that many of them have died without the sacrament of confirmation'.[112] In the same see bishop Puigmari claimed to have given communion to over 26,000 persons during his visitation from 1632 to 1633; and bishop Serrano in his visitation of 1637 gave confirmation to some 4600 men and women.[113] In León in 1669, bishop fray Juan de Toledo went on a lengthy visitation to dispense confirmations – 'never performed by my predecessors' – and claimed to have administered it to 50,000 people.[114] When there was clear evidence of an extensive personal visitation, such as made by the bishop of Urgell in 1692 ('I personally visited the greater part of the diocese'), a Curia official could not refrain from commenting in the margin of the report, 'laudandum', a comment conceded also to the archbishop of Tarragona when he claimed in 1697 that 'I visited the whole of my diocese personally.'[115] Despite the rarity of episcopal visitations, they were usually carried out at least once during the term of tenure by every Catalan bishop (when bishop Copons of Lérida made two visits, he took care to inform Rome of it in 1679).[116] The same diocese of Lérida seems to have suffered from infrequent visitations: in the first three-quarters of the seventeenth century the subject is mentioned only twice in the Vatican documentation: by bishop Serra in 1626 to say that three years after his appointment he has not yet found time to make one; and by Joseph Ninot in 1670 to say that nine years after his appointment he has not yet been able to do it. It is no surprise then to find Francisco de Solis, who was driven from his see by the turmoil of the War of Succession, making this report on his visitation in 1702:

I began my visit in the spring of 1702 through the harshest and most inaccessible part of the mountains and the Pyrenees, where in some villages according to the books no bishop has been for a century and in many for over sixty years. I continued the visit in the subsequent weeks up to the summer of last year, and in all I visited about four hundred towns and villages, administering in them the holy sacrament of confirmation to over 22,000 souls; and if the troubles of Catalonia had not intervened I would this autumn have concluded the visit of the whole bishopric, since there only remained the town of Monzón with a few villages near it, and after that the visit of the cathedral and parishes of Lérida. In this general visit I found among the lay-people little to reform in terms of abuses and superstition, but I did find a great ignorance of Christian doctrine, so I ordered all the parish priests to read and explain to the people a chapter of the Roman catechism at the offertory on feast days, and in the afternoon to collect the young people and instruct them in Church doctrine.[117]

In many neglected or isolated communities the bishop's visit, thanks to its rarity, took on historical proportions. We have seen that when bishop Alonso Coloma of Barcelona visited Mediona in November 1600, the rector noted that the last visit had been by Martínez del Villar, a quarter of a century before. The most serious spiritual consequence of these rare episcopal visitations was that the sacrament of confirmation, which only the bishop could dispense and which in theory was a rite of passage from childhood to adulthood (boys became eligible for it at fourteen years, girls at twelve), had virtually ceased to exist within the experience of parishioners[118] and reduced even further the effective contact of the faithful with the Church. Philip II commented to the canons of the cathedral of Mallorca in 1568 that 'we understand that it is a long time since the sacrament of confirmation was ministered to the island of Menorca,'[119] and since bishops were disinclined to travel to the island the problem no doubt continued. In the area of Meià in the bishopric of Urgell, according to a report of 1717, confirmation had not been given for seventy years; but then Meià and its neighbours were 'exempt' territories which refused to recognise the jurisdiction of the bishop and claimed to be subject only to the pope. The refusal of some of these autonomous territories to admit episcopal authority endured throughout the Counter Reformation, with the bishop of Urgell complaining in 1692 that the clergy of the Vall d'Aneu would not let him visit.[120]

Visitations varied greatly in nature: those made to churches, monasteries and church communities tended to emphasise liturgical order and religious discipline; while those made to parish churches sometimes looked in addition to questions of communal morality and doctrinal instruction. Enough evidence survives, in the form of diocesan records as well as the parish 'visitor's books' in which the comments of the visitor were recorded, to give us a reasonable idea of the nature and impact of the reform movement. The clearest evidence of Trent forming a watershed in Church discipline is the abrupt change in the nature of visitations. In the records of visitations made in the diocese of Barcelona there is a notable difference between the early years of the sixteenth century, when altars, ornaments and discipline were all deemed to be in good order and not calling for reformation, and the visits after the 1560s, when a detailed and relentless campaign was undertaken to introduce improvements. This clear contrast between the pre-reform and the reform years can be followed in every diocese, and is a good guide to the coming of the Counter Reformation to different areas of Spain. Inevitably, the disciplinary pressure varied greatly according to the nature of the person making the visit: in 1574 in Barcelona visitations made by bishop Martín Martínez del Villar were models of rigour, whereas those made in the same months by his diocesan visitor were rapid and undemanding. Rigour might also sometimes be self-defeating: the reforming bishop of Mallorca, Arnedo, was notoriously harsh, intractable and violent; and practised nepotism while at the same time trying to weed out absentee foreigners.[121] Arnedo, indeed, fell foul of everybody in Mallorca and asked to be transferred from that see; translated to his home-town of Huesca, he also aroused bitter opposition there, and died a year later.[122] Pressure was however necessary when dealing with stubborn parish clergy: in June 1609 in the Barcelona parish of Sant Just a dispute flared up when the vicar insisted on using more than the canonical quantity of candles at mass, leading a diarist to observe that 'the bishop has taken great care all this season that there are no excesses or vanities in the churches, which he visits personally.'[123] Change took a long time to penetrate, and the only firm impulse provided throughout this period was the clear provisions of Trent and of the provincial councils of 1565, which continued to be cited repeatedly in admonitions of the next one and a half centuries.

Many bishops since the early century had carried out occasional visitations and attempted to implement reforms. They were, however, voices in the wilderness, given moral support by the opening of Trent in the 1540s but otherwise unable to enforce their own constitutions. Few or none of the reforms decreed in the early century can therefore be taken seriously. Even into the 1560s the spirit of change had not penetrated the diocese of Vic. The bishop at this time was fray Benet de Tocco, but his visitations and those of his vicars show no consciousness of the spirit of Trent, which they seem not to mention, and in their rapid visits they judged virtually everything in the churches of Vic to be 'bene et decenter'. When the bishop's visitor visited the parish church of St Pere and St Feliu in Rodos in May 1566 he found the church locked, the bell cracked, the rectory in ruins, the mass vestments torn, and no baptismal font in existence; while requiring that these things be seen to, he nevertheless concluded that everything else was 'bene', and made no stipulation about keeping parish registers.[124] By contrast, there is a marked change with the visitations of the 1570s, which call for extensive improvements, and particularly notable in Vic were the visitations made in the year 1580 by the vicar-general, Onofre Montserrat Granollachs, who made thorough and detailed recommendations in each parish. By about 1587, when parish churches such as those in St Joan de Olo and St Joan de Avinyó were in possession of the 'new Roman missal', the Counter Reformation may be said to have been established in Vic.[125]

Other prelates, such as abbots, also had the duty of carrying out visitations in their jurisdictions, and seem to have carried them out with the same degree of success and failure. The Benedictine abbey at Bages seems to have attempted faithfully to enforce order in the various parishes under its control, but encountered a refusal to obey mandates, and falling rather than rising standards in the case of one parish where as late as 1606 the visitor was obliged to complain of the 'dirt on the altars of the church and a lack of ornaments... the altars of the Conception in ruins... the high altar a mess'.[126]

A fundamental concern of visitors was to restore decency and order to the church premises, making sure that the building and its limits were respected, properly cared for and financed, and that religious services were conducted correctly: these matters occupy over ninety per cent of the written text of all visitors' reports. The programme represented a major effort to alter the character of sacred premises. It has been observed that 'the mediaeval church was a storehouse,... a civic centre,... a theatre';[127] it was also a place where blood was often shed. All these uses were now to be done away with and the entire space occupied by the church was to be restored and sacralised. Space for worship was frequently insufficient: late mediaeval structures could not cope with the demographic increase of the late fifteenth century, and all over Spain parish churches were ordered to be enlarged or rebuilt. In the Mallorcan episcopal visitations of 1562–70 nearly every church on the island was ordered to be made bigger: in Santa Eulàlia in 1570 the visitor judged the church 'small and unable to accommodate the great number of parishioners'.[128] It may be imagined that the extent of repairs ordered to churches was normally beyond the financial means of the parishes: on their visits through Mallorca the visitors said the bell-tower of Santa Cruz was 'stinking and full of dung' (1562) and ordered repairs to it and also to the roof which the rain was coming through (1570); in Bunyola in 1562 the roof was ordered to be repaired at once ('statim'), but six years later the order had to be repeated, and in 1570 the roof was still letting in the rain.[129] The episcopal visitations undoubtedly played a crucial role in the great rebuilding that marked the Counter Reformation. Throughout Catalonia churches were ordered to be repaired, altered and made bigger. In Sta Maria de Miralles, near Mediona, the visitor in 1578 ordered a complete renewal of the fabric of the church.[130]

Many developments during the period are impossible to understand without bearing in mind that in Catalonia, as in most of Spain, the church and its space (cemetery, gardens) belonged effectively to the community, not to the Church. Though the building and its land might legally be the property of some other authority, the community was responsible for it and financed it, and the rector was no more than a tenant. It is significant that during the sixteenth and seventeenth centuries all directives of diocesan visitors relating to the maintenance of the church, even to aspects such as the need to buy missals, are addressed to the 'parishioners', or to the 'churchwardens and councillors'. If there was opposition to directives it was the people and churchwardens, rather than the parish priests, who were the real obstacle to the imposition of control by the Church.[131]

The church building had always been the social centre of the parish, and explicit moves were made to eliminate its social role and to reserve it for religious purposes. Bishop Dimas Loris of Barcelona insisted 'that in the church one preserve quiet, rest and silence. And not permit dancing on Sundays and holydays of obligation, or in the morning during mass and sermon, or in sacred places, nor permit the performance of farces and divine comedies either in churches or in sacred places.'[132] The sacred theatre of mediaeval times was immediately affected by the new rules. Up to the end of the fifteenth century it had been the custom at Cervera to perform a mystery play within the church on Good Friday, and there survives a script of 1534; but thereafter there is no mention of the play taking place indoors, and the Tridentine regulations seem to have compelled it to move out into the town square.[133] In 1600 bishop Coloma of Barcelona inveighed against the practice of having meals within the church on feast-days: 'it is outrageous that people have meals in churches for baptisms, and in the octave of Corpus, and at Conception and other days, and therefore we prohibit it and order that no such abuses of eating in churches be committed.'[134] Half a century later the authorities in Barcelona were still trying vainly to eliminate the practice of having 'dinners, meals and other refreshments' within church premises during Holy Week.[135]

The restoration of decency and holiness did not, however, resolve all problems. Mass and other rites were always a social function, to which people went regardless of piety; going to mass during the week 'is not out of devotion', it was observed, 'but to seek sociability, of which there is no shortage there'.[136] From the beginning the reformers found that they had to condemn the many things

that went on in the church building under cover of religious observance. Since the church was one of the few communal buildings
available to all and a refuge from the elements, it was frequently
used as a storehouse. In the diocese of Vic it was common as late as
1628 for both clergy and people to store their wheat, barley, wine
and oil in the church.[137] In St Nicolás de Porto Pi (Mallorca) in
1564 the church seemed more a cellar: the high altar was thick with
dust ('pulvere plenum') and all the sacred vessels were filthy; in the
corners lay sacks of grain which the visitor tactfully ('prudenter')
ordered to be removed at once; the room next door was stacked
high with timber; and the roof was in a parlous state. There were
similar scenes in other Mallorcan churches: probably the worst
parish was Llucmajor, where everything required change or repair,
the bell-tower was a rubbish-dump, and the almost permanent
('largam et antiquissimam') absence of the rector had reduced his
rectory to a ruin used as a sheep-run.[138]

The building was often a shelter for people. Moralists gave
serious consideration to whether the entire building should be
reconsecrated because young people had fornicated inside it. A
question posed by one, in 1573, was whether 'to fornicate in the
convent dwellings built on top of cloisters, chapels and churches, is
sacrilege of the same type as when it is done inside the churches and
chapels';[139] Vicente Mexía in 1566 ruled that even married people
could not have sex in these places,[140] a judgment undoubtedly
based on real happenings; and Ortiz Lucio summarised in 1598 that
'it is not licit to sleep with one's wife in a sacred place in a bed and
make love, for this is to violate the church.'[141] It was no solution to
close the church outside of mass hours, since the whole philosophy
of the reservation of the sacrament was that Christ be accessible at
all times. Despite undoubted successes, such as the imposition of
some silence on the congregation, there is little evidence that abuses
of the building as a community centre were everywhere eliminated.
By the late seventeenth century Juan de Zabaleta was able to
provide an unedifying picture of a typical mass in Madrid;[142] and
Galindo in 1682 was condemning night vigils in churches, 'which in
the name of devotion are left open at night . . . and if some go out of
devotion others feign it and exploit it, both men and women, for
their vile and illicit meetings, which would otherwise not be so easy
for them to carry out; and at the very least what takes place are
many encounters of men with women, and other irreverences such
as eating, drinking, talking, laughing, sleeping and snoring.'[143]

The reform of popular liturgy, touched on below, called for
changes in attitude to the church building; it is all the more surprising to find the survival as late as 1734, at Palautordera, of what

the diocesan visitor called 'the puzzling ceremony carried out by the church in Holy Week and known as *fasols*' (fasols was popularly known as 'going to kill Jews'),[144] in which the people rushed round the church beating the benches and altars.

The area immediately adjacent to the building, which in many cases meant the cemetery, was now to be cordoned off and fenced. Cemetery land belonged to both church and community, and the community had always used it for its own purposes.[145] In Santa Cruz (Mallorca) in 1570 the village women used the space to hang out their washing;[146] more commonly, it was used for pasturing animals. In La Llacuna, the visitor in 1578 thought the cemetery a pigsty, 'indecentissime et irreligiose'[147] because of the animals in it. His comments made no impact on the churchwardens.

The slow pace of change in some churches can be attributed to two main causes: opposition or indifference of clergy and people, and lack of money. Both can be seen in the case of the principal Dominican religious house in Catalonia, the convent of Santa Catarina in Barcelona. As a great international order, the Dominicans had an Italian general and therefore had to suffer Italian-inspired reform ideas. The chronicler of the convent, fray Francesc Camprubi, gives us this account of events in 1585:

> Fra Sexto Fabri de Lucca, general of the whole order, came to this priorate during his visit to Spain from Italy. The said general on his visit wished to attempt a most difficult thing, namely to place the choir for singing divine office behind the high altar, in the manner of Italy. To this there was strong opposition and objections, even from the Consellers of Barcelona, who as patrons of the convent rejected the attempts and said that had they known in advance they would also have opposed introducing confessionals. The result was that he failed, and I was witness to all of this.

Though this resistance succeeded, and confessionals had only been accepted after great reluctance, the rejection of change was not uncompromising. Three years later, when the same general 'was scandalised to see the condition of the place where the Blessed Sacrament was kept, which looked like a rat-hole and was a disgrace', the friars accepted the order to construct a new sanctuary behind the high altar. And other changes, albeit Italian in origin, were slowly introduced. In 1588 the prior 'introduced in the convent that solemn and devout procession which is celebrated on Easter morning, which was not done before'. The great attraction of the new procession was that it had dramatic appeal; it used, among other things, 'a child who would sing the Regina Caeli, dressed as an angel'. These elements of theatrical show, together with the music, inevitably attracted more worshippers, and the friars were overjoyed:

> All this aroused great devotion in the people, who were pleased with the time and the gathering and the performance of the procession: it was something worth seeing. And there was no small attendance of people, indeed despite the early hour the church and chapels and cloister were all full, provoking fear and wonder, and it was thought to be a great honour to the convent, and the procession has been continued to this day with the same simple devotion of the people but with even higher attendance.[148]

By adopting the show-business of the Counter Reformation Santa Catarina had reached its peak in religious popularity. Indeed, so great was the public that in 1588 the clergy decided to take their Rosary procession out of the cloister, where it had always been performed, and let the participants 'go round the streets', thereby taking the church to the street. Ten years later, they invited the street into the church: 'in this year [1598] there began to go through our church the procession of Our Lady of Solitude which was introduced into Barcelona six years ago.' Meanwhile, whenever the money would permit they set about renovating parts of the fabric: in 1588 they replaced the old organ, so old and battered that 'it looked like a boiler', and in this manner regularly continued rebuilding, restoring, and innovating.

Though visitations were made to parishes, and precepts were recorded in the parish register, it would be naive to imagine that much attention was paid to them. In the San Sebastián parish of San Vicente, a detailed visitation of 1564 introduced for the first time the norms of Trent, but a subsequent incumbent had revealing comments to make on the precepts of the visit as recorded in the register. On the order that children be taught regularly he commented, 'till now this has been of little importance'; on the rule that marriage banns be published so as to combat clandestine marriages, the remark is, 'this is done but is of little use'; and against the precept that catechism be preached on all Sundays and feasts he recorded in the margin of the register, 'this has never been done.'[149] The local community felt free to pick and choose from, or even to ignore completely, the directives handed down from the bishop. The parish of La Llacuna, Mediona's neighbour, is a prime example. In 1574 the visitor had ordered the baptismal font to be rebuilt, but on the next visit in 1578 nothing had been done, nor indeed had it been done by the visits of 1581 or 1585. In 1578 the visitor ordered the cemetery to be fenced; in 1581 he repeated the order; by 1585 a stone wall had been put round it, but with a large gap for a non-existent gate, so that the animals still used it.[150] Esparraguera, as we have seen, was impervious to the visitations of 1578, 1581 and 1585.[151] 'It is of little use', concluded the episcopal visitor to the churches of Monzón, Dr Juan Mora, in 1598, 'to make all the above stipulations if there is no one to report whether they are observed or not carried out,' and he therefore ordered the vicar of Santa Maria, on pain of excommunication and a fine of twenty-five ducats, to denounce any infringements of his precepts.[152] But what could be done if the clergy themselves refused to observe the precepts? After a visit to the parish church of Sóller (Mallorca) in 1599 the visitor reported: 'The priests and beneficiats of this church are stubborn (durae cervicis) and refuse to pay attention to what is ordered in the visits.'[153] Resistance could not be unending, and within half a century most of the changes demanded by visitors had been implemented. When bishop Manrique visited the Barcelona diocese in 1635 he was able to observe that in all the parishes the cemetery had a wall round it and was well-kept.[154]

To look only at the bishops would give a false sense of the structure of authority in the Church. One of the major and in great measure unsolved problems provoked by an emphasis on episcopal power was the balance to be achieved between the prelate and the cathedral chapter. We have seen that authority in the Church was in some disorder, that bishops and clergy had little contact because of the lack of synods, and that the crown had no direct method of interfering apart from the power to appoint prelates. As if this were not enough, there was energetic opposition to the pretensions of pope, crown, and bishop, from the chapter. The chapter, a legally constituted community consisting of the canons and clergy who administered the cathedral, operated independently of the bishop, who was merely the temporary administrator of the diocese. By tradition they controlled the revenues (*mensa*) of the diocese, appointment of officials, schools and charities; they also frequently had the right to elect the bishop. Their communal duties included financial organisation, policy-making with the right to vote at meetings, and obligatory participation in the prayers of the community. Not surprisingly, given that bishops came and went, they were the only element of continuity in the see and considered themselves as the keepers of the diocese, a position which repeatedly brought them into conflict with pope and king when these attempted to touch their revenues or appoint prelates of whom they disapproved. Self-appointed oligarchies (only the existing canons could appoint new canons), they inevitably represented one of the major obstacles to change, and consequently played an unusually large role in the history of the Counter Reformation.

In the Castilian Cortes of 1527 the deputies of the chapters deliberated apart from the bishops. In April 1545 the chapter of Toledo proposed a meeting of representatives of all Castilian chapters in Avila or Segovia (cities which still preserved a memory of the revolt of the Comunidades) to discuss the threat from the Council of Trent, but in May that year prince Philip wrote to all the chapters of Spain forbidding them to attend the proposed meeting.[155] However, in 1551 a committee representing eight Castilian chapters did meet in Valladolid, and sent to Rome a representative who in 1553 obtained from the pope a decree suspending the right of Spanish bishops to visit their cathedral chapters. It initiated a long period of bitter conflict which endured throughout the Counter Reformation. In November 1554 regent Juana informed the archbishop of Granada, Guerrero, that 'I have been informed that some chapters in some churches in these realms are trying by every possible means to block' the reception of the decrees of Trent, and ordered him to put the decrees into effect in his jurisdiction,[156] Granada being the only see in Spain where this could be done since it was directly under crown control.

In Catalonia the problem of the chapters seems not to have been resolved throughout the entire period, and the case of Lérida was typical. We have seen that the chapter there petitioned Rome against its bishop during the sessions of Trent. In 1588 the bishop complained that 'he cannot reside in his cathedral nor do anything that needs to be done nor can he visit it', and pleaded for a papal visitor to be sent.[157] In the same year an official report, probably by the Audiència, referred to 'some disorders in many chapters of the province and particularly in Barcelona, showing themselves to be very active in revolt and in taking up the popular cause'.[158] In their *ad limina* visits of the seventeenth century the bishops did not fail to remind the pope of the problem, and Francisco de Solis in 1702 blamed the loss of the city to the allies primarily on the chapter.[159]

Pre-Tridentine Catholicism in Catalonia was largely non-sacramental, a religion which comprised a broad range of observances but in which the only regular sacramental theme was that of penitence. The seven sacraments, when used, did not have to be administered within the church, and their significance was frequently more communitarian than religious. Trent and the Counter Reformation placed a new emphasis on the place of the sacraments in the Church.[160] Baptism[161] had seemed more often a rite of entrance into the community of citizens than into the community of believers, and other sacraments were more noteworthy for their absence than for their use. In Toledo there appears by the 1570s to have been a sudden new rigour in the administration of baptism, with the priest being accorded a more prominent role.[162] In the Barcelona diocese there were constant directives, made through synods and during pastoral visits, that baptism be restored to its place in the church: the synodal constitutions of 1669 continued to insist 'that baptisms not be celebrated in any private dwelling but only in the churches'.[163] One consequence was the erection throughout the diocese during the second half of the sixteenth century of baptismal fonts conforming to the new standards.[164] Already in 1512 the provincial council of Seville had insisted that mass and the sacraments (such as marriage) be celebrated within the church and not outside it; but only in the late sixteenth century was this attitude both repeated and enforced.

For sacraments to recover their significance they needed to be identified with a fixed location, the church. In pre-Tridentine Spain mass was not necessarily celebrated in church, and one could receive the sacraments in a variety of circumstances and places, so that attendance at church was not seen as essential. This fragmentation of function was clearly displeasing to the reformers, who from the beginning insisted on focusing Christian attention on the church building, an emphasis that brought some important changes.

The mass became, first of all, standardised,[165] as we have seen above. From the late sixteenth century the decrees of the provincial synods ordered the substitution of all old forms by the new Tridentine mass; a few minor variations were subsequently permitted, but the only major survival allowed was the Toledan Mozarabic rite.

The mass was also made more available. There had been no great stress on the obligation to hear or say mass in church, with the result that the ritual was not as available as we might suppose. A worshipper looking for mass might have to travel a long way indeed to find one;[166] and in their treks between mass centres the clergy were the first to complain of the travails. One long-standing problem, the absence of clergy in remote parishes, was countered by the bishop allowing parish priests to say two masses a day in order to attend to the needs of neighbouring churches. In 1611, for example, licences were granted to priests of Torrellas, Olivella, St Feliu de Llobregat, and Orta to say two masses:[167] in each case the problem was twofold, the dispersal of the rural population and the inability of the local church to afford to pay for an assistant priest. In Orta 'the houses in the said parish are so far apart and separated from the parish church that it is impossible for all the parishioners to meet together on Sundays and feast-days,' a case similar to Mediona and many other rural communities throughout Catalonia. Where mass was said regularly, it might still be unavailable if said at an unusual hour, and successive regulations laid down specific times at which masses should be said so that parishioners could attend.

Attendance at mass had been notoriously irregular, and well before the Reformation various authorities had tried to impose discipline. The comment on attendance in fifteenth-century Flanders could well be extended to Spain: 'few go to church, even fewer attend mass . . . For many it is enough just to enter the temple, sprinkle themselves with holy water, genuflect, and glance at the Lord's body in the priest's hands.'[168] In 1495 the provincial council of Tarragona stipulated that 'he or she who is absent from mass for three consecutive Sundays should be expelled from the church by the curate or vicar and publicly banned.'[169] After Trent, mass attendance remained one of the Christian duties that the parish priest was enjoined to record in a book, but even attendance at the weekly Sunday mass was not general practice: in 1593 the bishop of Gerona remarked that 'we are informed that there is notable laxity in keeping feast-days and hearing the whole of mass';[170] and in 1598 the bishop of Barcelona stated that 'some men and women out of human scruples' were failing to comply with the precept of going to mass.[171] The real problem always remained one of defining how one fulfilled the obligation. Theologians accepted that there were many circumstances in which attendance was not binding: Rodríguez cited, among other curious reasons, 'if hearing mass is a risk to life, honour or income, for example if the man of rank has no adequate cloak or shoes;[172] likewise are excused from mass those who are travelling and share good company and would lose it if they went to mass; nor does a woman sin if she does not hear mass because her husband does not want her to leave the house and would quarrel with her if she left and give her no peace.' Nor was the shepherd on the mountain bound by the obligation, nor the carter taking his load nor the messenger carrying an urgent message.[173]

Before the firm application of the rules – dating back to mediaeval times and repeated in the 1512 provincial council of Seville – which restricted mass to the parish church, it was common for clergy to celebrate masses in private dwellings, partly for convenience and also because of distance from the church building. Díaz de Luco in 1543, however, ruled that 'the parish priest should exhort his parishioners to come to the church to hear divine office and not hear mass in their houses,' and that permission to have mass in the home had been given too freely in the past, 'and because of this many people do not go to church even on feast days... The parish priests must work to drive out this evil custom from their parishes.'[174]

For very many, both before and after Trent, mass was primarily a communal gathering (reflected in Rodríguez' comments on the need for proper dress) of which the part over which the priest officiated was not necessarily the most important. Much more relevant to many – the situation has not changed today – was the bustling activity and social intercourse afforded by the occasion. Many ('multi ex parrochianis', complained the bishop of Mallorca of one of his parishes in 1570)[175] came when mass was halfway through and then left before it was finished. In Mallorca at the end of the same century it was common 'to leave the church on Sundays and feast-days after the consecration, before the priest had taken communion', and by the moment of the Ite Missa Est the people had 'the evil and abominable custom of talking and beginning to discuss their affairs',[176] terminating all participation in the mass. In the same decade bishop Dimas Loris of Barcelona denounced 'the abuse of those who arrive late at mass, when it is long since started; and the abuse of others, especially women, who at or just after the consecration leave the church and go to their homes to devote themselves to their housework'.[177] A common custom in the warm Mediterranean Sundays, widespread down to modern times, was to leave the main church doors open and linger outside, chatting or playing at dice, within sound of the priest's voice: this was supposed to satisfy the obligation, but was duly condemned in the late sixteenth century by the bishop of Barcelona. Another variation was for only the women to go in and assist at the mass, while the men waited outside. In Andalusia in the 1560s, Juan de Avila commented on the fact that children were not taken in to Sunday mass but were left to play in the streets.[178] As late as the eighteenth century in Provence, it was quite normal for only the women and children to attend mass,[179] while the men busied themselves elsewhere, particularly in the inn. No doubt some improvement in mass-attendance was achieved, but it is unlikely that this was widespread. A Portuguese traveller in 1605 commented favourably on mass-goers in Madrid that 'all hear mass every day... and hear the whole mass with much devotion... and not outside the church or at the door, as in Portugal, where nothing can be heard,'[180] but it is more likely that he was exaggerating Spanish practice in order to point a moral to his own people. In the record of the diocesan visit to St Vicente (San Sebastián) in 1564, when the visitor stipulated that people must not leave before the end of mass and that the clergy must admonish the people not to so do, a later hand has written: 'this order can be ignored because it is not the duty of the priest to control the parishioner, but to teach him what is correct.'[181]

The people certainly went to mass, but hardly in a way that fulfilled the obligation. Near Mediona, at Pobla de Claramunt, the continuing practice of aural attendance at mass as late as 1772 was condemned by the bishop of Barcelona, who exhorted the local clergy to 'drive out the deep-rooted abuse of the people remaining in front of or near the church on feast-days, talking and playing, with the result that they do not even go into the church' to hear mass, while 'many arrive at the church too late to fulfil the precept'.[182] Nor did attendance at mass imply any sacralising of Sunday: having fulfilled the obligation, many went about their daily work as normal. Juan de Avila in the late sixteenth century in Andalusia was scandalised at this, and pleaded that at least 'while at church, they should shut the shops in which they sell those items they need for sustenance, and with more reason should they shut the houses of public women until after mass has been said, since it is only for a short while.'[183]

Incomplete and infrequent assistance at mass, and in the case of men frequent non-assistance, was therefore common practice and we cannot treat as exceptional the cases prosecuted by the Inquisition of men who refused to go to church. Church-going was looked upon as being for women only, an attitude which has persisted through time but which also had a quite logical reason, since men possessed in the inn a centre where they could congregate but women had no other meeting place than the church. The tavern was, as it has remained, an alternative church, and one over which the curate had no control; successive Church authorities therefore attempted to impose the rule that the tavern should not be open during hours of divine service. In practice, outside of the major cities there were few drinking-houses, and rural taverns seem to have functioned to serve wayfarers as much as the settled population.[184]

Assistance at mass was a constant confusion of activities. The Mallorcan prior Pere Caldes was moved to write his *Instructio* in 1588 because he could find no more than 'five or six pages' written by learned men about 'the method and order of hearing mass'. Basing himself on short works by Carranza and Domingo Soto, he composed in Catalan the first Spanish manual for everyday worshippers. From him we get a delightful picture of the disorder among them:

frequently they are sitting when they should be standing, and standing when they should be kneeling, and when they kneel they use only one knee... They busy themselves crossing their foreheads, their chests, their sides and all over their bodies, saying that that is efficacious for headaches and pains in the chest and sides or for other ills.[185]

Pere Font, canon of Barcelona, described what he had undoubtedly seen many times at mass in the city, people

turning their faces from one side to the other and looking at what they should not, and talking and chatting with others and combing their heads or beards, and when they should be kneeling with two knees kneeling with one, and wishing that mass be as short as possible and getting angry if it goes on for long.[186]

Though the new mass after Trent emphasised the liturgical participation of the people, it also very clearly separated priest from congregation and defined sacred areas into which the people could not intrude. The appearance of rails in churches gave functional validity only to the clergy and, despite intentions to the contrary, reduced the congregation to the status of spectators. In the cathedral of Valencia in the fourteenth century the celebrant kissed the sacred host and passed the kiss to acolytes and from them to the congregation; after Trent the kiss of peace was restricted to those in the altar space.[187] Pere Caldes commented that the custom of the kiss 'is still continued in some religions and countries, because they do not have such depraved intentions as we have in our Spanish nation, with the result that it was not possible to continue it in our Spain nor is it right that it should be, given the clear and evident dangers'.[188]

There was much difference of opinion on the social function of both priests and sacraments, most notably in the question of the frequency of sacraments and the frequency of saying mass. As late as 1566 a reformer such as archbishop Juan de Ribera of Valencia could state that 'I think it would be useful to seek some remedy for the problem of priests saying mass with such frequency, which has brought into disrepute a high ministry, and many even celebrate daily';[189] sentiments which a century later might have earned the subsequently canonised prelate a denunciation for heresy.[190]

Opposition to frequent communion was likewise still widespread, and throughout the period strongly differing views were openly held by respected theologians. In the 1550s the Castilian bishops, in a list of standard demands for reform, spoke out clearly against frequent communion: 'In some parts the devotion to communion has grown so much that many lay-people, men and women, married and unmarried, go to communion so often that they receive the Blessed Sacrament every day. This seems to be excessive frequency, and it should be considered whether at this time the people should be encouraged to receive the Blessed Sacrament more than once a year.'[191]

Since regular communion on this scale was rare, it is clear that the bishops had in mind some local movement of piety, possibly the *alumbrados*. Their objection, it would appear, was to lay-people taking communion, and not to clergy; pious opinion had long recommended that religious should take communion regularly. In the mid-sixteenth century it was still daring to advocate frequent communion for the laity: Vicente Mexía had to find reasons for stating that thrice a year was desirable.[192] So well known a confessor's manual as Azpilcueta's, which dominated the field for half a century, made few concessions to frequency: for laymen, 'men of honour should go to communion at least four times' in the year, and as for religious 'the Council of Trent has now ordered that all nuns confess and go to communion at least once a month.'[193]

From the very beginning of its activity in Spain, the Society of Jesus made no compromises about its insistence that both confession and communion be used as frequently as possible by the faithful, but a strong and persistent tradition openly contradicted this, and as in many other matters there was no unity of theory or practice in Spain for the entire period of the Counter Reformation. In 1551 a Jeronimite friar, Francisco de Villalba, publicly attacked the Jesuits for their position over communion[194] but was rebuked by the regent Juana. In 1592 canon Francisco Farfán of Salamanca, commenting on 'the question, hotly disputed among some preachers and confessors, as to whether it is good to resort often to this sacrament', concluded: 'I wish that the ministers of the Lord in their pulpits would stop entering into disputes and rivalries.'[195] Similarly the Carthusian friar Antonio de Molina, in a work published in Barcelona in 1610, confessed that 'I do not cease to wonder at the reserve and restraint with which many serious, learned and spiritual persons talk, as though to go to communion were a grave danger for the soul.'[196] In Barcelona the prevailing opinion among clergy was certainly in favour of frequent communion, and the publication by Diego Pérez of a work on the theme seems to have been influential.[197]

Farfán recognised that too many people were 'not used to this sacred table and are alienated from the use of the sacraments', a statement he went on to apply to 'the greater part of the Christian people'. It is quite possible to view this as exaggeration, but the evidence appears to suggest that attendance at communion beyond the annual duty was very infrequent.[198] Communion on Sundays and feasts was virtually unknown in Mallorca in the 1580s: 'it is no longer the practice for Christians to go to communion after the priest,' commented a writer, drawing a contrast with the idyllic 'early Church'.[199] Manuel Rodríguez in the 1590s, reflecting no doubt the view preponderant among Franciscans, ruled that 'as to persons who wish to go to communion every day or frequently, and as to making a rule that everyone should go every week, it does not seem right to me, because not all persons have the same devotion... They should not be bidden to go to communion so often, but only on some major feast-days.'[200] A practical lack of piety among common people, then, seems to have been a major influence in the opposition to daily communion, which persisted throughout the period. Nearly a century later, Joseph Gavarri in 1673 felt constrained to criticise those among his fellow clergy who 'oppose daily communion', and the most favourable figures that he could suggest for the whole of Christian Spain were that 'it is a fact that today over a hundred thousand persons take communion every day,'[201] an obviously optimistic estimate which, taken at face value, in a total Castilian population of possibly four million people of communion age came to 2.5 per cent. There is no evidence to corroborate Gavarri's claim, which looks very much like the habitual exaggeration of a partisan writer. In the almost solidly Catholic countryside around Paris in the 1660s, a generation after the French Counter Reformation had been at work, annual communion was still the common practice, and monthly or even weekly communion rarely existed outside the pages of books promoting it.[202]

Possibly more than any other sacrament of the Church, confession during the Counter Reformation was revolutionised in its nature, style and context.

Though the notion of penance and penitence still permeated all the ritual and literature of the Church, by the early sixteenth century the practice of confessing had lost its rigour: many clergy did not know how to minister the sacrament properly, and the task was often left to roving clergy, usually friars but sometimes clerics who made their living exclusively out of going from town to town and using their own unique methods of shriving. In Guissona in 1581 an itinerant Franciscan told an elderly *beata* that 'she must accept the penance he imposed, and the friar said he had to give her a slap on the buttocks, and he made her raise her skirts and gave her a pat on the buttocks and said to her, "Margarida, next time show some shame."'[203] Laymen did not think it obligatory to entrust their problems to one person, the rector, who in any case was not deemed to be sufficiently detached from the community to be able to listen to intimate problems, and there was consequently regular recourse to outside clergy. When in 1612 Paula Ramada of Montroig (Tarragona) refused to confess her intimate sins to the local parish priest he got angry with her and denounced her to the Inquisition.[204]

The infrequency of confession affected every aspect of Christian life, and there were no easy or rapid solutions. Toussaert's suspicion that in fifteenth-century Flanders the sacrament of confession was little used[205] may be extended to Spain. The Fourth Lateran Council (1215) had stipulated confession at least once a year; insistence by later Spanish synods on this duty indicates non-compliance with the legislation. It is likely that the habit of confession had become, as in pre-Reformation Germany, reserved for emergencies;[206] and even by the end of the sixteenth century the bishop of Barcelona was lamenting that 'in the cities, towns and villages many remain and continue stubbornly in their sins for many years.'[207] The pre-Tridentine ideal was expressed in the 1495 constitutions of Tarragona which laid down that[208] 'all faithful Christians aged over seven years should confess two or three times a year or at least once in Lent, and go to communion at Easter, and he who does not should be expelled from the church'; but this was a counsel of perfection and every episcopal directive of the subsequent century shows that it was a struggle to impose on the faithful the minimum obligation of an annual confession. Those fulfilling the obligation had to receive and keep a certificate showing they had done it; in Barcelona the bishop ordered rectors to give 'the receipts of confession, written in their own hand, to the penitents'; and in 1610, informed of the refusal of domestic personnel to perform their annual confession, decreed that in future the master of the household could receive the certificates, which gave them the responsibility of getting their servants to church.[209]

The first great pastoral publication of the sixteenth century, Bernal Díaz's *Advice for Curates* (1543), inevitably put the proper administration of confession as a priority, and within the same period several manuals for confessors were published, culminating in the authoritative volume by Azpilcueta, written in 1552 and first published in 1555. The manuals for confessors were complemented by guides to making confession: in Catalonia the most used included Juan de Dueñas' *Confesionario* (1545) and Juan de López de Segura's work of the same title (1555).

The appearance of good manuals improved moral theology but did not begin to touch the social problem of confession. In order to control the ministering of the sacrament and order it within the context of the parish structure, bishops attempted to outlaw the phenomenon of wandering confessors. All confessors within the diocese had to be licensed, and their names were regularly reviewed. The cooperation of the laity was sought by decreeing that the annual schedule of confession be obtainable only within one's native parish. The firm localisation of the sacrament of confession clearly had a disciplinary objective, but as in other matters it was never easy to enforce. There were sporadic prosecutions in the diocese of Barcelona, but the problem did not come simply from licensed clergy. In July 1599 an unlicensed priest in the parish of St Llorenç Savall was prohibited from hearing confessions: 'he has confessed many persons both men and women in the parish and in particular in the house of Jaume Busqueta in the bedroom, a place more suitable for sleeping than for administering this sacrament.'[210]

Fortunately, the Inquisition rendered the valuable service of acting as a prosecuting tribunal and supplementing the jurisdiction of the bishop. Even by the end of the seventeenth century it was faithfully attempting to enforce norms that had been decreed a century and a half before. We find the following order issued in Barcelona:

> We hereby make known to all curates, prelates and confessors of this city and other cities, towns and villages of our district that by repeated orders of ours, the last dated 15 April 1692, we have ordered that confessions not be heard in secret cells and chapels of convents and parish and other churches, or in other hidden places; but only in the body of the church and the sacristy, cloisters and chapels therein, with the doors wide open. And since experience since that date has obliged us to tighten up this measure, we order that from now on all women must confess only through the grille of the confessionals, in the body of the church, and not in chapels, cloisters or sacristies; and that in parishes and convents where there are not enough confessionals one should construct wooden screens with a grille and confess through that, with the confessor on the other side seated on a chair or bench; and since this provision costs so little it should be used to make up for the lack of confessionals on feast-days when there are a lot of people.[211]

Enforced slowly but firmly, the new standards of confession constituted perhaps the most fundamental tool of Counter-Reformation morality and religion. Parish clergy were enjoined to keep a register of confession along with their other registers, and though few appear to have done so it is likely that the rule helped to promote resort to the sacrament. In the Barcelona diocese clergy in the late sixteenth century were told to keep records of the annual confession and to bring them to the annual diocesan synod.[212]

Introduction of the wooden structure of a confessional, popu-
larised by Carlo Borromeo in Milan, may have helped to restore
confidence in the sacrament by affording a degree of anonymity and
helping to discourage amorous confessors. The Jesuits were the first
in Catalonia to adopt the practice: a report on their college in
Barcelona in 1561 mentions 'some confessionals set up in the
church'.[213] But it took a long time for the novelty to be adopted. In
the church of St Vincent in San Sebastián, only in 1600 did the
bishop stipulate that they be introduced.[214] The Barcelona bishops
were diligent, Dimas Loris pressing that 'there be confessionals
in the churches, well-made and suitable for confessing women
respectably'.[215] Mediona had confessionals from 1581, and in
the Penedès the parishes adopted the innovation with a surprising
alacrity. Capellades bought two confessionals in 1581 as soon as
the diocesan visitor stipulated it, and so did Collbató in 1585.[216]
Elsewhere in Catalonia there were certainly delays, and it seems
that the parish of Sant Martí in Sant Celoni did not have any even
in 1756, when the diocesan visitor ordered their introduction.[217]

By itself the new structure was still no secure protection, for
earlier confessionals merely had a curtain to separate confessor
from penitent; and in the 1560s the Jesuits were trying to introduce
conformity since 'in some churches the confessionals are partly
open, in others they are closed... An effort is being made to close
them, leaving a third of the door with a grille.'[218] By the end of the
sixteenth century many curtains had been replaced, and in the
church of the Pi in Barcelona, for example, the bishop ordered in
1607 that 'confessions may not be heard in the confessionals of the
church until the windows have railings of wood or iron.'[219] There
seems however to have been resistance to installing grilles, and the
Inquisition, which was particularly concerned since it exercised
jurisdiction over clergy who solicited in the confessional, reported
in 1719 that many churches in Catalonia still lacked grilles in their
confessionals.

The reformation of confession through dogmatic manuals,
enforcement of practice, and use of confessionals, opened the way
to the evangelisation of the common people. Confession became the
means most frequently used by missionaries[220] to penetrate the
normally impenetrable souls of the common people, and bishops
tried to ensure that the sacrament coincided with Tridentine norms.
The instruction issued by the bishop of Barcelona in 1580[221] to
rectors in his diocese specified that only licensed clergy could hear
confessions; that all rectors 'are obliged to draw up and complete in
time the list of those who have the duty to confess, and should take
special care to check afterwards if all have confessed, and who has

not done so, and if they have gone to communion in their own parishes'; 'and when starting the confession the rector has to find out if the penitent is from that parish, because if he is not the confession cannot be heard without licence'.

In rural Mediona death was the only point at which the people made intensive use of the Church, with a full use of sacraments and an unusual concentration of clergy to help ferry the soul into the next world. Early modern piety in Catalonia seems to have offered ample security to Christians departing this life, particularly if they made use of the votive masses of St Amador. Denounced by Ciruelo and other Spanish writers of the early century as superstitious,[222] the masses were also denounced at Trent, which decided not to condemn them outright 'since they are used by many' and instead recommended churches not to use the rite, 'which appears to be more a superstitious rite than one based on true religion'.[223] In practice, they continued to be a cornerstone of popular piety not only in Catalonia but throughout Spain in the sixteenth and seventeenth centuries. Originating in the Middle Ages, the mass 'commonly known as of St Amador' was reputed to have the power to liberate souls from Purgatory. Known in Catalan as a *trentenari*,[224] the mass had to be celebrated on thirty specified feast-days during a twelve-month period, with a fixed number of candles on the altar at each feast-day, for example seven candles on Christmas day but twelve on the feast of Sts Peter and Paul. The cycle was normally completed by three masses on the three days leading up to All Souls, making thirty-three masses in all.[225] In testaments, requests for the trentenari were normally supplemented by requests for a few more masses and then for a single 'novena' mass of commemoration. In this way, all the requirements of the Christian soul were met, and Purgatory posed no problems.

For the Catholic reformers, this was superstition comparable to the belief that buying indulgences freed one from Purgatory. The Counter Reformation insisted instead that access to salvation was not automatic and that only the continuous operation of the official machinery of the Church offered security. The slow change from one security system to another can be followed in the testaments of Mediona where the demand, common since mediaeval times, for a trentenari and a few votive masses, was gradually supplemented but not replaced by the custom of founding an *aniversari*, whereby a priest would say a mass on a fixed day every year at a fixed location. Since the premise was that the soul was lingering in Purgatory, the anniversary masses would act as a perpetual chain of pleas addressed to the creator asking for release. The doctrine was not only an apparently comforting one that allowed the faithful, and even the dead faithful, to continue storming heaven with demands for salvation; it also provided the basic income of a considerable section of the clergy, the *beneficiats*, whose office was based not on the cure of people in the parish but on the cure of the souls represented by the anniversaries. The Counter Reformation brought with it an increased emphasis on the mechanics of salvation, and boosted the endowment both of memorial masses and of anniversaries.[226] The process can be measured easily by the rapidly accumulating number of masses which the beneficed clergy had to say. In testaments the masses experienced an inflation commensurate with that which existed in more worldly sectors: by the 1700s testators could be found charging that 3000 masses be said for their souls on 3000 successive days;[227] and the burden of pressure on favoured altars of required masses meant that often anniversaries could not be fixed for a desired day because it was fully booked up. A study of masses requested in Barcelona wills suggests that from the sixteenth to the seventeenth century there was in rounded terms an eightfold increase in the volume demanded.[228] Even worse for religious foundations which had allowed the anniversaries of several generations to accumulate to such an extent that it was physically impossible to find either the priests or the time to say all the masses, the result was a wholly unacceptable situation in which clergy drew their incomes from masses which they would never be in a condition to say, and so the salvation of souls, both on earth and in Purgatory, was imperilled.

The higher demand for anniversaries and masses suggests that Counter-Reformation piety, in contrast to that of previous generations, increased the sense of insecurity in the face of death, and by implication increased the perception in popular piety of the idea of Purgatory, which had been only marginal to popular piety and on which the first study to appear in Catalonia was published as late as 1600.[229] The insecurity was fostered by the Church in order to encourage greater use of the recommended propitiatory rites, but the people continued to hope for the security offered by other routes, and the masses of St Amador continued in use until modern times. There is evidence of continuing popular scepticism over the official Church's formulae for a safe journey to the other life. In 1594 the Inquisition disciplined a young farmworker of Tarragona for saying that praying for souls in Purgatory 'doesn't help them' and that 'we do not know if there is a purgatory or a heaven or a hell'; and a fifty-year-old smith of Cervera who affirmed that 'there is no hell or heaven' and that 'after death there is nothing'.[230]

Every church was faced with the problem of accumulated and unsayable masses brought into being by the search for more security.

The problem was so serious that it formed the principal item on the agenda[231] of the first post-Tridentine diocesan synod of Barcelona, meeting in May 1566. In the parish of the Pi in Barcelona the existing burden was reduced by episcopal authority in 1593: the total of daily masses was reduced to twenty-seven daily, the weekly masses were reduced to five, and the annual masses to 341. Despite the reductions the total was an impressive nine thousand masses a year, still too much for the community of clergy to handle, and in 1606 the bishop sanctioned a drastic rearrangement by which all the annual and weekly masses were merged into a reduced daily total of ten masses, or just over three thousand.[232] Even to say these masses, the clergy had to commence at 4.30 a.m. to be able to fit them into the daily routine.

The ordering of mass was, the reformers intended, to be accompanied by a return to the tranquillity of worship of an idealised early Church. The Counter Reformation in consequence set in train one of the most profound revolutions of the period: the imposition and invention of silence.[233] Pre-Tridentine religion was unmistakably noisy: the bustle of a disorganised mass, with people entering and leaving throughout the ritual and, in the larger churches, several public masses being said simultaneously at separate altars, as if to further the confusion; women and men chatting together loudly throughout the proceedings, 'doing dealings in all their worldly business, both illicit and profane, effectively using the church as though it were the market-place or the merchants' exchange'; with the active worshippers 'busy saying or reading their prayers' aloud, irrespective of what the priest was doing;[234] inactive worshippers 'turning their faces this way and that, and talking and chatting';[235] instead of listening to the music in church 'they ignore the music, talking and laughing among themselves and with the women';[236] marginal activities taking place around the building, such as beggars jostling among the worshippers for alms, young men paying court to local girls or even to nuns whom they would have no opportunity to encounter in another place, 'flirting and laughing loud and disrespectfully';[237] men sitting at the church door during high mass and nominally assisting but in reality playing at cards or dice; all this was the commonplace scenario of mass on a feast-day. The conduct of the clergy was no better. The notorious persistence of cathedral canons in chatting during divine office, quarrelling in the aisles, and shouting across the building; the neglect of the priest himself, yelling at his congregation, shouting insults at and (a case of 1574)[238] hitting a member of the parish during mass, or cursing and abusing the congregation (a Morisco congregation in this case, as reported by a Castilian grandee):[239] all constituted a recipe for noise and chaos. In a Mallorca parish in 1562 'in the choir of Santa Eulàlia during divine service there is no order but only constant confusion'; in another (Alaró) the people chattered so loudly during mass that the priest could not continue, and in Llucmajor 'there is no order nor is silence observed'.[240] In rural parishes, it seems, it was common to chatter during mass. All the examples we have cited were the object of disciplinary measures, so the issue was clearly being dealt with. At the same time writers were at pains to educate both clergy and people about the need for silence within religious buildings. Perhaps the most explicit instructions come from Diego Pérez's important work *Salutary Documents*, published in Barcelona, in which the author ruled out verbal prayer at mass:

> I beg those who go to mass to remain in complete silence... Do not talk, nor look this way and that, for both these things are discourtesies to God; nor dedicate yourself to praying aloud, but let your chief care (without omitting to say, should it help your devotion, some verbal prayers) be to recall the passion and death of Jesus Christ... Those who pray should pray softly, so that neither the priest nor anybody can hear, so that mass can be said in total silence, which gives authority and majesty to that mystery.[241]

Antonio de Torres in his *Manual* (1598) forbade, among things to avoid during mass: 'praying aloud: because it disturbs the priest and others who are present. And even more must one avoid talking and yawning, and making a noise, something which is most impolite and rude.'[242]

The effort was bound to take decades to achieve, given that both clergy and people needed to be educated out of a previous concept of church use. The search for silence sometimes transcended church and cloister: Cristóbal Acosta in 1592 considered it the key to a happy marriage, not only because, as a general principle, 'speaking too much leads to mistakes, silence to security'; but also because restrictions on use of the tongue were helpful to a good relationship between husband and wife, and 'silence comes from a good understanding.'[243]

Since in practice religious ceremonies were never restricted only to the church building, the noise of external rituals constantly intruded and helped to perpetuate noise: of fiestas, carnivals and *romerías*, of group celebrations and of Corpus Christi, of community music and weddings. Interminable detail is available of the displeasure caused to several bishops by the intrusion of street ceremonies into their cathedrals, and the uncontrollable rowdiness of fiestas when the public, aided by clergy, burst in, danced, sang, and let off fireworks on the altars; less obvious was the unexpected noise at weddings, when a quiet family ceremony might be interrupted by the hysterical ritual of the charivari. It took possibly two centuries for the reformers to exclude street religion completely from the church premises. Thereafter noise was restricted to the street, and in the church a blessed silence descended. The campaign was driven home by repeated directives issued by prelates to their parish clergy: the priest must observe silence when vesting himself, must say mass in subdued and respectful tones, must always address his congregation with respect.[244] Pastoral letters from the bishop encouraged congregations to assist at mass in total silence; private devotions were discouraged. Gradually a discreet silence fell upon the Counter-Reformation Church, which thereby achieved something which the Protestant Reformation, with its emphasis on praying, preaching and singing, did not during its first century consider desirable.

Local piety remained at all times the most impenetrable barrier to the infiltration of new ideas, and both before and after Trent Catholic thinkers were agreed that for change to be lasting it must register among the local communities, where the piety and practice of generations must be modified in order to establish true religion. Over the mediaeval centuries, towns and villages had enjoyed extensive religious autonomy which allowed them to evolve their own local variations in worship, their own special devotions to local apparitions and saints, their own feast-days and their own peculiar practices and observances. Some practices were so popular and generalised that they eventually became prevalent in entire regions, to such an extent that it is now difficult for the historian to follow the course of their evolution.

Of primary importance from the liturgical point of view was the need to bring under control the number of saints, mythical or otherwise, celebrated in the Church calendar. The Tridentine papacy imposed control on the issue by decreeing that a rigorous procedure of examination be adopted before individuals could be considered 'saints'. At the same time, the bishops in each diocese issued an abbreviated list of saints' days, eliminating those whose cult was doubtful or excessively local, and introducing into the calendar new saints whose cult could be considered beneficial in that they were representative of broad interests in the universal Church. The task of suppressing local devotions was not easy and inevitably aroused opposition; in any case, no sooner was one saint suppressed than the population created another. The local saint, in the society of the time, was the personification of regional traditions and aspirations, both past and future, so that any attempt at change was a threat to the community as a whole, not simply to its religious beliefs. Modifications to the calendar were therefore to be broached with care. In Galicia in the village of Coirós the Church ordered the removal of the image of St Pedro Manzado, but the people continued to venerate the saint none the less.[245] In Valencia the abolition of the *fueros* after 1707 and the introduction of Castilian law and language was accompanied by attempts to Castilianise the Church, but the Valencian clergy fought successfully to keep their saints, as we learn from a friar of the Dominican convent in Valencia:

> around the year 1715 the Castilians tried to introduce in this city the Castilian church calendar, so that we should observe here the feasts they observe over there, but on this point some reasoned objections were made, since it seemed unsuitable to introduce here unknown saints and exclude Valencian saints and some feast-days celebrated since antiquity. It was consequently necessary to draw up a statement in favour of what is rightly observed here, and it was so successful that thanks to it we avoided having them take away even a single day of our ancient holidays and venerated festivities . . .[246]

In Barcelona after Trent the bishops dutifully reissued to their flock the latest instructions from Rome about saints, but did not always achieve a positive response. In 1617 bishop Sans had to enforce in his diocese the new office of the Stigmata of St Francis, because 'we understand that in the churches of the present city and bishopric of Barcelona they have stopped celebrating the said office.'[247]

With its roots in the antiquity of Christian Rome, Catalonia shared with the rest of western Europe the invasion of the cult of saints. As the tides of the new faith lapped at the pagan shores of rural Europe, they bestowed on the villages new concepts of belief which came to be focused on the power and presence of objects (relics) and persons (saints).[248] Isolated from the fully developed Christianity of the great towns, the villages through their careful nurturing of the local cult felt that they were still part of a great chain of Catholic faith, and saw no conflict between official ideology and the often unique and magical forms of local piety. The local saint, indeed, gave to the local community not only an unparalleled and direct link with heaven, thereby freeing it to some extent from the apparatus of the institutional Church, but provided a centre on which the social activities, agrarian rites and political identity of the community could focus. All this was enhanced to a further degree when the saint produced miracles, and the shrine then became a centre of pilgrimage, the ultimate assertion of identity by a local community, and one that might easily lead to conflict with other saints venerated in neighbouring localities. Even by the sixteenth century the vast bulk of local 'saints' in Catalonia were drawn from the remote and mythical past, largely from Roman times on which there survived narratives of early Christians giving their lives in the struggle against paganism, possibly the best known being Santa Eulàlia, patroness of Barcelona.

The Catalan Franciscan Joseph Dulac stated in 1680 that 'Marineo Siculo lists over one hundred [local] saints in different parts of Spain, taking into account only the principal ones; but in our Catalonia alone there are ninety-six native saints, and of saints' bodies brought in from outside, 426.'[249] Aside from the lugubrious image of 426 dead bodies being brought into Catalonia by pious believers, the figure given for the principality is substantially confirmed by other sources, of which the most authoritative is by the Dominican Antonio Vicente Domenec, published in 1602 in Barcelona.[250] Domenec carefully compiled a list of all the saints, both Catalan and foreign, whose remains rested in the province, and in the process included some of whom all trace had disappeared:

> and I say disappeared, because my experience has shown me that some of their histories have already been lost, and in places where no one would know or expect I have found almost without looking traces of some saints whom everyone had given for lost, and so I think I have done no small service to my country in looking for these histories and printing them here.

To the saints from Roman times Domenec added a large number of ancient prelates, and finally a substantial number (forty-four in all) from the religious orders; his final total of 145 saints was distributed by dioceses: Barcelona thirty-nine, Gerona thirty-four, Urgell seventeen, Vic sixteen, Tarragona fourteen, Elna fourteen, Tortosa two and Solsona two. All of these, he informs us, were canonised merely by popular tradition; the only exception, canonised according to the new rite introduced by Rome, was Ramon de Penyafort, in 1601. The analysis leaves us with some 144 pre-Counter-Reformation 'saints' whose origins lay mostly in the remote past, whose credentials were doubtful, and whose very existence, in some cases, might be doubted.

The cult of saints was a highly controversial issue during the Reformation era, with many humanists (notably Erasmus) questioning its value and all the Protestant reformers united in abolishing it. Ironically, then, the religiously charged sixteenth century was the very epoch when Rome dropped its old privilege of canonising saints: none was made after 1523 for a space of sixty-five years,[251] and only with the progress of the Counter Reformation did Rome regain its confidence and, on the prodding of Philip II, resume the process with the canonisation of San Diego de Alcalá. Thereafter the rules for making saints were tightened up considerably. Caution in the face of local and mythical saints, and hostility to the abuses which accompanied venerations, was a legacy that Catholic leaders continued to share. They aimed to modernise by getting rid of the great number of saints of dubious origin, and attempted to prune the calendar in Catalonia and throughout Spain. Among the saints for Gerona included by Domenec, for example, was the emperor Charlemagne, whose feast had been established in the cathedral in 1346, but whose veneration had been discontinued since 1473, at which time an annual sermon in his honour replaced the old liturgy.[252] St Charlemagne disappeared along with many other saints: at the provincial council of 1565 a new and shortened list of the obligatory feast-days of the year was introduced, and subsequently the bishops in each diocese modified their own lists to suit local custom and their own policies. It was impossible to abolish altogether local devotion to fictional saints, but these were henceforward deprived of any official status, were removed from the text of masses, and could not have confraternities. Their bits and pieces remained carefully preserved none the less: when canon Villanueva visited Vic in 1803 he was able to draw up a long list of feet, ankles, toes and other parts of holy bodies, most of them accumulated in the fifteenth century, 'on whose authenticity I preserve my customary silence'.[253]

Changes in the canon of saints among the parishes occurred exclusively through popular demand, and devotions changed because of services rendered by the saint to the people. Where the cult of a saint was so old that its origins were out of memory, it was because his services were proven and there was no need to change: in one Castilian village in 1540, the falling-away of devotion to a saint who had saved the village from locusts was castigated with another visit from the locusts, and the village promptly renewed its devotions.[254] In the countryside, the 'miracles' sought from a saint were not the modern ones associated with personal bodily healing, but communal ones related to material survival, deliverance from floods, tempests, hail, locusts and drought. Miracles as such seem to have played a very tiny part in the daily experience of religion, and wonder-working was usually limited to the great pilgrimage shrines such as Montserrat, which depended on cures for credibility.[255] Protection rather than cure was the guiding principle: if a saint could prove himself more efficacious than another in granting this protection, he was immediately adopted in the other's place, a circumstance which explains the variation in cults between one generation and another. Often the reasons for a cult had happened within the memory of villagers, as we see from the case of Felanitx (Mallorca). When the bishop's visitor in 1569 enquired about the parish's devotions to saints Margaret and Michael he was informed by those who could date the cults to living memory:

> As for the feast of Sta Margarita ... in Felanitx there was no water and on one feast-day of Sta Margarita they found water in front of the church and so the jurats (the witness has heard say) held consell and with permission from the cathedral declared a feast ... Certainly before the water was discovered there was no feast ... As for the feast of the Apparition of St Michael ... Gabriel Montserrat says that the day of St Michael there was a big hailstorm, when he was ten years old ... and from that day on there has been a cult. About Sta Margarita, his father told him of it.[256]

In the epoch of the Counter Reformation the official Church itself put forward saints for consideration through the new medium of canonisation, and the new religious orders imposed cults simply by naming their churches for specific saints. However, the newly canonised, though eagerly accepted into the pantheon, were there only on a trial basis and could easily be ejected if they were no more effective than the older saints. One success story in Catalonia was that of St Isidore, who gradually edged out the veneration of Abdón and Senén, Medin and Galderic in agricultural rites.[257] When St Isidore was canonised in March 1622 there was an immediate rash of dedications in Catalonia, explicable more in terms of the novelty than of any extension of Castilian influence. 'Wednesday the eighteenth,' recorded Pujades in October 1623, 'the relic of St Isidore of Madrid came to Barcelona. Devotion to the saint has grown in Barcelona.'[258] In the Barcelona diocese in 1624 alone there were confraternities of St Isidore founded in Granollers, Arbós and the parish of Santa Maria del Mar.[259] Throughout Catalonia the peasant communities eagerly embraced the worship of a modern saint with roots in the rural world:[260] in the Vallès, part of the Barcelona diocese, there were altars to St Isidore in Lliçà d'Amunt in 1626, in Samalús in 1628, in Canovelles in 1626, in La Roca del Vallès in 1627, in Malanyanes in 1627, in Llerona in 1630.[261] We have seen from the example of Mediona that these years of agrarian crisis were fertile ground for the adoption of a new farmer saint who might compensate for the deficiencies of previous protectors of the countryside. In practice the hold of the old saints on popular consciousness was too powerful to be broken, and many parishes simply took on board the new with the old: in the church of the Pi in Barcelona, the confraternity of Abdón and Senén added Isidore to its devotion,[262] and the same combination could be found in 1635 in the churches of Argentona, Vilamajor and Vilassar.[263] In Sitges, the confraternity of Abdón and Senén was in 1602 allowed to add to its title the name of St Ramon de Penyafort;[264] in St Llorenç de Cerdans (Rosselló) the foundation of a confraternity of St Isidore did not displace the continued celebration, common throughout the Pyrenees, of St Galderic as the patron of farmers.[265]

The revision of the calendar of saints represented not only a move to a standard universal calendar for the Catholic Church but also quite obviously the intrusion of universal (and therefore foreign) saints into the local liturgy. Most such intrusions occurred because of religious orders promoting their favourite members as saints, but even then few foreign names were introduced, the only outstanding exception being St Antony of Padua, whose cult seems to have flourished in Catalonia from about 1620, a phenomenon which requires explanation since the saint was a thirteenth-century Portuguese domiciled in Italy. On the whole, Spaniards firmly resisted any intrusion by Italian saints. It comes as a surprise to find in 1635 in Mataró an altar dedicated to St Carlo Borromeo, the only such dedication in the whole Barcelona diocese.[266] By contrast, the canonisation in 1601 of Ramon Penyafort, a native son of the Alt Penedès, was a happy choice that satisfied the wish of the Catalan governing elite to present one of themselves as a candidate for worship, met the aspirations of national sentiment in the province, and reflected the desire of the papacy to control the process of saint-making.

Writers such as the Catalan Jesuit Pere Gil adopted a more critical approach in narrating the lives of the saints.[267] But the pruning of saints, and the corresponding attempt to uproot superstitious practices connected with them, was by no means a step towards the simpler, purer religion that reformers wished for. On the contrary, the many campaigns to foster more devotion among the people led inexorably in the opposite direction. Despite the attempt to substitute universal for local heroes, local devotions continued to proliferate and extend themselves. In the cathedral of Valencia, for example, a new feast of the Holy Grail was established in 1607, even though the chalice in question had been in possession of the canons since 1437. It is possible that the new universal feast of the Guardian Angel, decreed in 1608, was little more than the projection on a broader plane of a local devotion originating in the 1390s in Valencia and the Catalan lands.[268] In Barcelona the remains of St Pacià, an ancient bishop of the see, were authorised as genuine by bishop Dimas Loris, a local feast was established in

1600, and by 1654 the relics were being publicly venerated.[269] The devotion of the local population to sacred symbols which identified with their customs and privileges, and the concern of the official Church to promote piety through the cultivation of similar symbols, combined to foster rather than modify the resort to religious relics, with the result that the Counter Reformation, far from purifying the addiction to magical symbols, merely intensified and vulgarised their use, however much individual clergy might dissent.

It was an essential aspect of the cult that a saint had to be local, though imported saints might be adopted provided always that they were physically present. As a dimension of the cultural plunder in which they participated during the age of empire, Spaniards also developed the custom of collecting relics, in which they were given a lead by Philip II, whose collection of over seven thousand relics at the Escorial was one of the great cultural achievements of his reign.[270] It was in a real sense a dimension of imperialism, since relics were symbols of power and their acquisition an assertion of hegemony. From all over Europe, from Hungary, Flanders, Germany, Rome, the stream of fragments of bodies and sometimes of entire cadavers, made its way to the peninsula. The Council of Trent, which had been critical of the late mediaeval superstitions attached to relics and had therefore insisted on tighter controls over authenticity and caution over worship, was no match for the body-hunters, who sent their trophies back home in the wake of their diplomatic and military manoeuvres. In 1610 a bemused Consell de Cent received a report from a Catalan officer in Flanders that he had discovered there the head of Santa Eulàlia, and that he wondered whether the patroness of Barcelona (preserved in the cathedral crypt) still retained hers;[271] the bishop had to enquire and certify that the saint was still in full possession of her parts, and the Consell wrote to Flanders advising that the alternative head not be acquired. Barcelona continued however to be the gateway through which the sacred relics of Italy and central Europe flowed. In 1623 when Gaston de Montcada, marquis of Aitona, returned from his post as ambassador to the Empire, he brought with him 'a large number of saints' relics, such as heads, shins, arms, ribs and so on, which were for some years kept in the sacristy of Sta Maria del Pi, from which on some annual feasts they are brought out and revered; and I,' adds the diarist Pujades, 'among others, paid reverence to them many times'.[272]

Conscious of the attacks made during the Reformation period both by Protestants and by reformist Catholics (Alfonso de Valdés' *Dialogue on the events in Rome*[273] was one of the most vivid attacks penned in that period), no Counter-Reformation writer or preacher in Spain ever made a direct attack on the abuse of relics. The case against them therefore went by default, and the cult was one of the few aspects of traditional Catholicism in Spain that continued into the early modern period with an even greater intensity.[274] Spanish imperialism was undoubtedly the principal impetus to the collection of sacred memorabilia, just as British imperialism in a later epoch brought together curious memorabilia from around the globe. But there were also factors such as status rivalry which impelled churches and communities to accumulate as many relics as possible. By the early eighteenth century, a splendid example of the fruits of such accumulation may be seen in the monastery of Scala Dei (Tarragona),[275] where the high altar on its epistle side boasted fifty relics and on its gospel side seventy-two: the fifty included fragments of a tunic of St Bernard, an arm of St Cyprian, a rib of St Agnes, and the skin of St Bartholomew, while the seventy-two included bits of the tunic of St Francis, a knee of St Matthew, the head of Sta Lucia, a tooth of St Calixtus, a rib of St Cyprian, a stone of Calvary on which Christ's blood fell, pieces of the emperor Constantine and St Mary Magdalen, and the stone on which Christ stood before his ascension. In addition to these treasures the church possessed thousands of other relics – to count them would have been 'to try to count the stars', reported a visiting clergyman in wonderment – including bits of wood from the Cross, fragments of a nail of the same, a thorn from the crown of thorns, bits of the sandals of Christ, some myrrh offered by the wise men, hair and milk of the Virgin, relics of saints Peter and Paul, Andrew and John, and many many more.

The hold of such symbols over the local community was impressive. In 1612–13 one of the most outstanding uses of the *mà armada* (literally, the 'armed hand'), the right of the citizens of Perpinyà to take up arms, took place when the city sent officials to the monastery of St Martí de Canigó to borrow the relics of St Galderic for use in a procession for rain. The officials were detained in Vilafranca de Conflent, which objected to the removal of the relics from their territory, whereupon Perpinyà proclaimed the mà armada, sent an army out to besiege Vilafranca and release their officials, and brought the relics triumphantly back.[276] Relics could not merely provoke war, they were themselves the symbols of war, and indeed of all other expressions of the will of the community. When Perpinyà again raised the mà armada in February 1629, but this time against Barcelona, the citizens of Barcelona were thrown into a feverish state of excitement and threatened to 'advance the banner of Sta Eulàlia against Perpinyà'.[277] Saints became weapons of power, wielded by community against community, city against city, and the moving of relics – as in the case of St Galderic – implied a moving, a subtraction, of power.

In 1623 the people of Besalú rioted against the local Benedictine monastery of Sant Pere because the abbot had dared to transfer the relics of Sts Prim and Felicià from Besalú to his own home town of Olot.[278] Any arrival of relics was, by definition, an augmentation of power. In 1609 the bishop of Barcelona held a solemn conference of thirty-two theologians to declare genuine a relic of St George, patron of Catalonia, which originated in Cologne and was presented to the cathedral by the viceroy; in 1625 Santa Maria del Mar held solemnities and a procession to receive a relic of Philip Neri; and in 1628 Figueres put on great festivities for the reception of new relics of Sts Clement and Anchim, which had been brought from Germany five years before by the marquis of Aitona.[279] No doubt Catalonia also received some of the venerable parts of the great Italian Counter-Reformation saint Carlo Borromeo, who died in 1584 and of whose person some ninety-two relics (clothes rather than his body) were distributed between 1608 and 1630.[280]

It would be misleading to present Catalans as a society of un-questioning saint-worshippers. Popular irreligion also mocked the saints. A clothworker of Santa Coloma de Farners maintained in 1632 in conversation that the saints were really in hell, that 'all this about indulgences and medals is a joke', and that even if he were denounced to the Inquisition (as he was) 'he would defend himself, and prove how some saints had been canonised in exchange for money'.[281] A peasant of Castellgali (Vic) claimed in 1628 that 'painted saints are worth nothing'; worse, 'speaking of St Philip Neri he asked if he were a Castilian, because if he were a Castilian he couldn't be a saint or anything good'.[282] Scepticism about the efficacy of saints and their images was, however, not looked on with favour. A rational-minded parish priest would have to be brave to stand up to the beliefs and prejudices of his people. When the rector of Passamonte (Tarragona) did so in 1584, he was denounced to the Inquisition; his parishioners claimed that 'on a stormy day he refused to take the cross out of the church and said that he didn't want to carry a hunk of wood on his shoulders.'[283] The Holy Office decreed that he say five masses 'in the presence of the people at the altar where the cross is', and that 'in his sermons to the parishioners he should encourage the veneration of images'. The case would only have confirmed the people in their belief that sacred images could really stop storms. The other face of this continuing magical use of images was the criticism and sometimes punishment of saints who did not duly respond to petitions. When a widow of Cassá de la Selva (Gerona) obtained no relief of the pain in her leg, she upbraided the Virgin: 'Come down, you useless rubbish, since you don't wish to help me, you're as much rubbish as I am!'[284]

The persistence of local religion was powerfully helped by the advance of printing, which preserved permanently for the faithful many oral traditions that might otherwise have disappeared or been distorted. Late mediaeval lives of saints in Catalonia were collected in the *Flos Sanctorum*, which from the end of the fifteenth century came out in numerous printed editions in Catalan.[285] The material from the *Flos* was frequently used by parishes in dramatised form, and the verses took on a standard style when invoking the saints. Rural parishes began to follow urban parishes in producing *goigs* ('joys'), fly-sheets consisting of the versified praises of a saint. Goigs originated in the later Middle Ages in the Provençal-Catalan lands as a form of religious ballad addressed to the Virgin, whose 'joys' in Christ were set out in vernacular verse;[286] some of the earliest come from Rosselló and Valencia, the best surviving examples being from the fourteenth century, when the earliest accompanying music is also found. They were given real life by the spread of printing in the late fifteenth century, but their original and refined troubadour form was thereafter absorbed into a more popular, less literate tradition which gave them wider diffusion at the cost of quality and originality.

By the sixteenth century, when the Counter Reformation changed the religious context of the goigs, the praises of the Virgin were being supplemented by the praises of the whole company of saints. Some early fly-sheets lacked illustrations and had little popular appeal, but in the course of the century there was a rise in interest and throughout the seventeenth century an impressive stream of goigs was issued in the Catalan lands. Down to the nineteenth century they fulfilled an important role in rural piety, were preserved and revered as though they were icons and were sometimes supposed to have magical effects. The role of the lithograph is often cited as a crucial factor in the German Reformation;[287] an exact parallel occurs with the role of the goig in the Catalan Counter Reformation.

It is possible that by the late seventeenth century every parish in Catalonia had produced at least one, and most produced several; printing was done at the nearest urban press, with the largest number of surviving examples originating in Barcelona and Gerona. In principle the goig was simply testimony to a local devotion, with the five-foot strophes – composed in simple and often execrable verse by local clergy, some even written by the sixteenth-century poet and rector of Vallfogona – explaining the life and miracles of the saint or, more commonly, of the Virgin. In reality it was very much more than this, with four clear dimensions which identify the characteristics of faith in Catalonia: dedication to a concrete object of everyday religion, the holy relic or image; definition of the geographical area within which the cult flourished; invocation of the saint for specific functions relating believers to their natural environment; and exaltation of the social group most closely identified with the revered symbol. It was also the curious quality of the goig that neither its text nor its imagery changed: the verses, once issued, remained frozen testimony to the apparently unchanging and faithful nature of local religion, and were issued generation after generation without alteration.[288]

The chief pride of the goig writers was to show that their church possessed a tangible portion of the sacred, with relics ranging from entire bodies to minute fragments of the same, not to mention famous items such as drops of the Virgin's breast-milk. The town of Mataró in 1688 prided itself on having 'the sacred body' of St Desideri; Montjuic in 1677 prided itself on 'that rich treasure' of the body of Santa Madrona; the Carmelites of Tarragona in 1689 claimed to have the body of St Theodore; and at a later date even St Quintí de Mediona ended up with the body of St Justin Martyr. Fragments of bodies were inevitably more common, with organs of saints liberally distributed throughout Catalonia. 'Happy land of Tossa', proclaims a goig of 1696,

De bras, y galta Reliquia,	You venerate the relics
y una dent adorau.	of arm and cheek and tooth,
Si comptassen los que	counting those who come
venen	to worship
nos podrian acabar.	would be never-ending.

More intensely local than these stray portions of saints were the sacred images miraculously revealed by heaven and thereafter worshipped with burning devotion. The majority were images of the Virgin, discovered by shepherds or by oxen, and thereafter solemnly installed in the local church and worshipped for centuries: very many dated from mediaeval (*immemorial*) times, and it is impossible to date them with certainty. When was the origin of Our Lady of Gresolet, worshipped since at least the late sixteenth century; or of Our Lady of la Gleva, in the mountains near Sant Hipólit, and celebrated in a goig of 1635; or of the spectacular shrine of Our Lady del Far, whom one of 1647 locates as

rodejada de las valls	surrounded by the valleys
de Estoles, Mer, y Rupit...	of Estoles, Mer and Rupit...
a vista de tres ciutats	within sight of three cities
Manresa, Vich y Gerona?	Manresa, Vic and Gerona?

The numberless miraculous images never seem to have provoked doubts, and served to reinforce the conviction that heaven had in reality destined every church to have its own sacred object. Around 1630 Mediona was peculiarly blessed with its own sacred discovery, a crucifix uncovered accidentally by a peasant digging, as a goig composed much later explains:

Esta Imatge . . .	This image
fou també enterrada;	was also underground;
després doná mostra	thereafter it gave signs
de resuscitada:	of coming to life:
cavant ab porfía,	persistent digging
bella se ha mostrat.	uncovered its beauty.
Lo cávech feri	The spade wounded
la cama, y senyal	its leg, and left a mark
en ella imprimí	imprinted on it
lo colp casual:	the accidental blow:
mostra vuy en dia	it still shows today
un hermós morat.	the lovely bruise.
Lo poble y Rector	The people and rector
que de goig se banyan,	overwhelmed with joy,
aquest rich tresor	took the rich treasure
al temple acompanyan:	to the church:
allí ab armonia	there in splendour
lo deixan posat.	they placed it.

In this way the *terme* was able to create its own alternative to the already famous Sant Crist of Igualada, discovered a generation earlier, in 1590. Down to today, on the first Sunday in September the people of the terme hold a day-long *aplec* at the castle ruins, beginning with a high mass and adoration of the Sant Crist, followed by a picnic lunch on the hillside in the autumn sunshine and rounded off in the late afternoon with songs and *sardanas*.

The area encompassed by a cult depended in part on geography, in part on the favours of heaven. When a sacred image was located in remote territory, usually by transhumant shepherds, it was given its own shrine and then became an object of devotion for all neighbouring parishes equally, as in the case of Our Lady of el Far or Our Lady of Gresolet. With luck, such cults, not formally restricted to any town, might become hugely popular and attain universal status, as in the outstanding case of the Black Virgin of Montserrat. The Counter Reformation ironically became the direst enemy of most extra-parochial devotions, and continuous directives from bishops prohibited the joyous, extended pilgrimages that entire communities made up into the mountainsides on the pious excuse of devotion to remote Virgins. The prohibitions seem, at least in rural Catalonia, to have failed; and a goig of 1669 celebrated Our Lady of Gresolet,

rodejada de las valls	surrounded by the valleys
Caldas, Gofol y Gisclareny,	Saldes, Gósol and Gisclareny,

who was 'visited by many in this remote place'. Movement of parishioners continued to be common because many parishes were not favoured by heaven with a magical object of their own, and it was common for goigs proudly to present their shrine as the preferred centre of believers in the region. The shrine of St Geroni at St Pere de Riudebitlles was supposed to guard all neighbouring towns as well: 'the people of Riudebitlles, and others from round about' (among whom Mediona was included). St Guillém was addressed in a 1664 goig by the parish of St Joan at Campins:

No te sols de vos reparo	You receive the attention
aquest poble de Campins,	not only of the people of Campins,
Patrò sou, y gran amparo	but are patron and succour
destos llochs circunvehins.	of all surrounding villages.

It was a feature of the more successful images and shrines that their appeal, without ceasing to be purely local, was based on the devotion not simply of one parish but of the many parishes that fell within a *comarca*, so that local saints had quite an ample area to supervise, and popular shrines became the preserve of entire counties.[289]

The major function of local saints was to protect the community from all ills that capricious nature might bring. A 1618 goig to Our Lady of Bellver, 'discovered in the terme of Santa Coloma de Farners', besought her to

En lo terme en que esteu	Protect the *terme* where you are
guardaulo de tot perill.[290]	from all danger.

Approaches to the deity or to Christ were irrelevant: the goigs are quite specific that the day-to-day care of the countryside and its people was directly in the hands of the Virgin and the saints, who alone had the spare time to care over details while God remained more concerned with the governance of the universe. Although some saints might be allotted specific functions, and for that reason possessed numerous dedications throughout the principality – such as St Elmo for sailors, Sts Abdón and Senén for farmers – the particular glory of a local saint was that he or she intervened in a broad range of activities. St Desideri in Mataró, for example, had heavy responsibilities:

Tota aquesta vila está	This whole town
ab esperança segura,	has the secure hope
que molts bens alcançará . . .	of receiving many benefits . . .
Espera que ha de tenir	It hopes to be
molt libre de tempestats	free of storms
a sas vinyas y sembrats,	on its vines and crops,
y molts fruits que recullir	and have a good harvest
y tots los seus navegants	and all its sailors
ab bonança en la Mar . . .	safe at sea . . .

Santa Madrona, we have seen, had a permanent obligation to bring rain, as a 1677 goig informs us:

Y quant per nostres pecats	And when for our sins
estan los camps molt axuts;	the fields are parched;
per ella tots los sembrats	through her all the crops
daygua son socorreguts.	are succoured with rain.

The image of Our Lady of Mercy in Canet de la Costa, according to a goig of 1663, had a universal care over her community:

Los de Canet son ditxosos	The people of Canet are fortunate
en tenir tal advocada,	to have such a patron,
curau malalts y febrosos,	you cure the sick and fevered,
guardaulos de pedragada:	you protect them from hail:
guerra, pesta, y mal passar.	from war, plague and misfortune.

In Barcelona the image of Our Lady of the Port was addressed in these terms:

Sou llanterna resplandent	You are the shining lamp
per los pobres navegants,	for poor sailors,
desensaulos del turment,	you protect them from the storm,
de borrascas, trons y	from wind, thunder and
* llamps.*	lightning.

Some saints proved their powers on one or more clear occasions and so reinforced their position in the devotion of the people. In the parish of St Pere in Gavá, a relic of St Nicasi turned the saint into a protector against plague:

Miracle fereu molt grau	You worked a big miracle
en est lloch de Gava, y es	in this village of Gavá
que invocantvos en lo any	when you were invoked
mil siscents sinquanta y tres	in the year 1653
apretats de pestilencia	we were pressed by plague
la fereu en punt parar.	and you stopped it at once.

Similarly, the priory of the Mercè in Barcelona claimed, in a goig of 1688, that their image of the Virgin had saved the city from the French in 1652, had brought rain in 1680, and in 1687 had preserved the city from locusts. In St Quintí de Mediona, although many other devotions also flourished the name-saint was still invoked for many purposes:

Vos invocan los devots	The faithful invoke you
en las malaltias grans . . .	in great sicknesses . . .
Cuan alguna tempestat	When a storm
amenasa pedregada,	threatens hail
esta comarca es guardada	this comarca is protected
de San Quintí lo veinat.	and the people of St Quintí.

The great majority of goigs, as a reflection of the environment from which they come, were concerned with crops and the need for rain, giving saints a strictly utilitarian role within rural religion. In Mediona the image of the Sant Crist was a constant benefit:

ella l's remedia	it brings aid
en la sequedat.	in times of drought.

In the same terme of Mediona, St Elies, who had his own chapel, was also regularly invoked against drought. It followed that saints who failed to succour their communities were soon discarded, and there was an impressive turnover of devotions from one generation to the next in many communities. By the late nineteenth century in St Quintí, for example, care of the fields was passing into the hands of St Justin and of Our Lady of the Snows. The former was besought:

De pèdras, de ayguats, y	From hail, flood and
llamps,	lightning
esta Parroquia devota,	this devout parish
devant vòs rendida tòta	prostrate before you
prèga defenseu sòs camps.	begs you to protect the fields.

And the latter was told:

A causa de pedregadas	Because of hail
a vegadas	St Quintí frequently
Sant Quintí molt trastornat	harrowed
ploraba desconsolat	wept bitterly
ven trinxadas	to see destroyed
las vinyas y los sembrats;	its vines and crops;
a qui acudir no sabia	with no one to go to
O Maria!	O Maria !

It was a rash person who publicly doubted the power of saints' statues to bring rain. When a farmer of Biosca did so in 1620, he was denounced to the Inquisition, which did not take the matter seriously (he was reprimanded) but which, simply by accepting the denunciation, helped to legitimise popular beliefs.[291] Legitimation went further than this: during a visit to Moja in 1598 the inquisitor inexplicably accepted an accusation made against a local Frenchman who, in response to a conversation where others had said that the Huguenots smashed images, had said 'that images have no feeling'.[292] He was reprimanded, but for what? Did the inquisitor maintain that images of saints had physical feeling? Or was the statement seen merely as an extenuation of the Huguenots?

The saints, finally, were images of power among men. Their names and reputations were used to promote the power aspirations of groups within and between communities, and goigs imply clearly that the relevant saint was supporting their cause. The group might be a fairly large one, such as a convent or a religious order: in Barcelona in the 1690s, for example, goigs emanating from religious orders (which usually wrote in Castilian, because of their cosmopolitan membership) included one to Our Lady of Mercy, for the order of the Mercé, one to Our Lady of Consolation, for the Carmelites, and one to Our Lady of Copacabana, for the convent of Santa Monica. Throughout the principality so many local Virgins, each with a distinguishing local name, were honoured that one readily comprehends the comment of a parish priest in 1597 that 'there are more Virgins than *butifarras*'.[293] More commonly, however, goigs in Catalonia were the work of parish confraternities, which took upon themselves the defence of the honour of the community and its saints. That to St Ferriol in the parish of St Vicenç in Falgons, Gerona, was issued in 1618 by the confraternity in defence of the saint's relics. In Núria in 1675 the goig informed St Gil

Seus ha fundat Confraria,	You have a confraternity,
y cada any lo voste die	and every year on your day
festeja gente Pastoril:	the shepherds feast you:
advocat sou dels Pastors.	you are patron of shepherds.

The miraculous properties of the relics and images celebrated by goigs became by extension transmitted to the goigs themselves, and the little fly-sheets with their attractive woodcuts were treasured, revered, used as prayers and employed in cures: thousands have consequently survived, and the same texts would be used from century to century, since the form of words itself took on something of the sacred. Their survival is due mainly to the efforts of nineteenth-century folklorists to preserve evidence of popular culture, and for some the fly-sheets had a fundamentally important role in Catalan history, since during 'the seventeenth and eighteenth centuries, when there was a marked decline in every branch of language and spirituality and nothing was printed in Catalan apart from the goigs, these kept alive the sacred flame of our printed tongue'.[294] We shall have occasion later to comment on this verdict.

One effect of Tridentine piety was to provoke a remarkable growth of devotion to the Virgin Mary, who emerged everywhere as the universal patron and interceder, her name invoked as the protector of all that required protection: travellers, sailors, crops, plants (in a work of botany published at Basel in 1584 the name of Mary was given to forty plants).[295] The growth of her cult was perhaps the most impressive development of the Counter Reformation in Catalonia, and can be followed in detail thanks to the rigorous scholarship of the contemporary Dominican Narciso Camos, whose 1657 work, *The Garden of Mary*, was based on his extensive travels throughout the province in search of shrines to the Virgin. 'I visited her shrines and chapels in the years 1651, 52 and 53, when this province suffered great miseries of famine, plague and war', he tells us; and despite the travails of extreme heat and bad weather 'I never faltered . . . And it cost me seven years from the time I began my searches to when I saw the book in print'.[296] In the course of visiting personally virtually every shrine to Mary in Catalonia, he calculated also that the province had seven cathedrals, 468 parish churches, 112 religious houses, and 441 chapels dedicated to her. Though it was difficult to establish when many shrines first began to function, Camos nevertheless put together enough information for us to make a reasonable analysis of his data, from which the following estimate of the dating of shrines is made. In the diocese of Tarragona, of nineteen shrines possibly twelve were post-1540; in Barcelona, of thirty possibly ten; in Gerona of seventeen possibly four; in Tortosa, of seven possibly three; in Lérida, of eleven possibly three; in Urgell, of twenty-eight possibly nine; in Vic, of fifteen possibly five; in Elna, of fourteen possibly four; in Solsona, of nineteen possibly five; with six more mediaeval shrines in the area of Ager. Out of a total of 166 shrines, therefore, possibly fifty-four, or one-third, can be dated to the Counter Reformation.[297]

The growth of devotion to Mary was given particular emphasis in Narcis Feliu de la Penya's contemporary *Annals of Catalonia* (1709), which, apart from specifically dating over twenty 'apparitions' of the Virgin between 1540 and 1640, mentioned in his own day the foundation in 1690 of a convent at Oliana which had in its keeping a miraculous image of the Virgin painted by angels and discovered in that village, 'according to the authentic account which is kept in the archive of the convent and which I have before me'.[298]

In Catalonia the Virgin made herself known not through apparitions but through the medium of images. Although she often revealed
herself it was only momentarily, in order to draw attention to the
image or future shrine, and in no case was there encouragement to
use her appearance as the basis of the type of devotion that was to
become current in the twentieth century at Lourdes and Fatima.
Traditional religion, assailed on all sides by the uncontrollable and
the inexplicable in daily life, had little room for sudden irruptions
by divine visitors, and apparitions were extremely rare. Even fewer
were those which found acceptance and led to the establishing of
shrines: a recent scholar has commented on two Catalan visions of
1592 and 1618 but agrees that the holy places of Catalonia were
fundamentally those established by the early monks on mountain
peaks.[299] Claims to apparitions were suspected by neighbouring
parishes not so privileged, as well as by the Church, which always
disliked alternative revelations, so that there were structural factors
which immediately dampened their hope of credibility.[300] An
image, by contrast, was a single completed event, not (as an apparition was) one which promised to be repeated, and so could flourish
safely within the bosom of the community blessed with it. As if
to make her cult even more of a trial to outsiders, the Virgin
located some of her most successful images in locations which were
physically very difficult to reach, on the heights of Montserrat and
Núria.

The mechanism through which images of the Virgin were discovered seems not to have altered between ancient and modern
times.[301] All the images were discovered in virtually inaccessible
places in the countryside, underground or in caves or undergrowth,
with only a handful located in ruins; and over half were pinpointed
by the insistence of cattle (of fifty such cases, thirty-four were oxen
and sixteen were specifically bulls) which were drawn to the spot
while grazing. In a few cases the images were pinpointed by lights
shining from heaven. The rural and pastoral location of the discoveries was associated with the inevitably magical function of
the image as a propitiator of the forces of nature, but special
importance must be attached to the persistence of humble cattle as
discoverers of sacred images: in the Catalan lands cattle entered
into Christian symbolism because they had been the first animals in
creation to pay their respects to the newborn Jesus in his manger.[302]

A different kind of testimony to the Marian cult comes from the
spread of devotion to the Rosary in Catalonia, and the extension of
the practice of the Angelus. Often erroneously attributed to St
Dominic as its originator, the Rosary devotion was of much later
origin. It had a confraternity in mediaeval Barcelona, but only from

the late fifteenth century did its popularity begin to grow, fed by influences from Germany and the Netherlands which filtered in through the medium of the Dominican order.[303] At the same time, confraternities began to be dedicated to the Rosary: there are examples in Manresa in 1503, in Sant Boi de Llobregat in 1510, in Mataró in 1535,[304] in Malanyanes in 1559.

Two factors in particular helped the devotion to spread. The religious orders wherever they went made the Rosary a cornerstone of their piety, with particularly strong support from the Dominicans and later from the Jesuits. 'In the city of Barcelona', claimed Geroni Taix, Dominican author of a best-selling study of the Rosary which first came out in 1556, 'devotion to the Holy Rosary had grown cold, but began to renew in 1547 through the preaching of some friars of the Order of Preachers.'[305] It also became the rule for proposed confraternities of the Rosary to obtain the patronage of the local Dominican order (in St Quintí, for example, the foundation of the confraternity in 1578 was sanctioned by the priory of Santa Catarina of Barcelona, whose prior came to the village for the occasion).[306] The second and no less decisive factor was the naval victory over the Turks at Lepanto in 1571, attributed from the very beginning to Our Lady of the Rosary since it took place on her feast day, 7 October. Barcelona heard the news only on the thirty-first, but they received it 'with such great happiness and joy that men had tears in their eyes and others appeared almost out of their minds, it seemed to be something out of a dream and hardly to be believed'.[307] Don Juan brought home with him the crucifix from his galley and gave it to the cathedral, where it still has its own chapel. In April 1573 Gregory XIII put the cult on an official basis.

Catalonia, from which the Spanish contingent had set out, felt itself particularly indebted to the Virgin, and after 1571 there was a rash of dedications to the Rosary: new altars in 1572, for example, in Vilafranca and in Cabrera de Penedès, and a confraternity in Igualada in 1574.[308] In the Vallès the rapid spread of the Rosary was without precedent; altars or confraternities to it can be found in Palautordera in 1583, in Cardedeu in 1574, in Bigues in 1604, in Garriga in 1586, in Llerona in 1586, in Lliçà d'Amunt in 1578, in Samalús in 1588, in Vilanova de la Roca in 1614.[309] In the Pyrenees, though the cult was not unknown, it took longer to root itself; Estavar, with a confraternity of the Rosary in 1607, was among the first places in Cerdanya to adopt the devotion.[310] By the end of the century it had become an obligatory devotion in Catalonia, and in 1635, when bishop Manrique made a personal visitation of the Barcelona diocese, he found that every single parish church had an altar and a confraternity of the Rosary.[311] As in

Mediona, which spent considerably on installation and decoration, many churches invested money in beautiful altarpieces, the delightful reredos in Sarrià (1618) being one of the more outstanding testimonies to the piety of the people.[312] In the Vallès, other splendid examples of altarpieces to the Rosary survive in St Pere de Bigues (1626), La Doma (1586), St Sadurni de la Roca (1620), and Vilanova de la Roca (1628).[313]

Inevitably the public rituals of the Rosary mingled with older customs, and added to the enormous range of rites that went to make up the cult of the Virgin. The most enduring of all customs was the cult of the rose, increasingly associated with the Virgin in the scattering of roses in processions, and the sprinkling of rose-water in church ceremonies.[314]

In many communities the confraternity of the Rosary became the principal social organisation, but the Church frowned on the freedom that young women associated with membership. In the diocese of Solsona the women would go in groups playing rosary-drums (*panderos*) and begging for the confraternity. The bishop's synod in 1629 ruled that the procedure was indecent 'because they encounter dissolute people who give them pushes and address them with amatory, loving and flirtatious words . . . The charity that men give them is not charity but sensuality, they do not give money for the love of God and the Blessed Virgin but out of the love and pleasure they get from seeing and hearing the young girls.' The begging was prohibited for the future, but the prohibition went the way of all such; in 1751 a diocesan synod once again had to prohibit the custom.[315] Inevitably the Rosary also had its own rich range of dances, called Danses del Roser but taking different forms according to the locality, and danced not only on feasts of the Virgin but also in Carnival. In Ridaura (Olot) the words of the dance –

El ball del Roser	The dance of the Rosary
Marieta, Marieta,	Marieta, Marieta,
el ball del Roser	the dance of the Rosary
Marieta jo el sé	Marieta, I can do it

– implied male and female dancers and must also have invited clerical criticism.

Prominent among the new devotions associated with Mary and stimulated by the Counter Reformation was that of the nativity crib. Although the existence of forms of the crib was very old (in Rosselló the monastery of Sant Miquel de Cuixà is said to have had one in the eleventh century), the cult of the crib, in the sense of lifelike images placed in the church, was probably Italian in origin (examples are known from Naples in the late fifteenth century) and was promoted vigorously by the Italian St Gaetano de Thienne in the first decade of the sixteenth century. The Reformation, by its rejection of imagery, encouraged Catholic missioners, notably St Ignatius and the Jesuits, to use such imagery for popular devotions, and significantly the first documented crib to be displayed within a church was mounted by the Jesuits in Prague in 1562. The Germanic lands, indeed, may have contributed as much as Italy to its introduction into Spain, since the oldest crib in Castile, in León cathedral, was brought from Germany by Charles V.[316]

In Catalonia there seem to be no references before the 1580s. A canon of Vic in 1585 is recorded as possessing 'some plaster images of the nativity', suggesting that the domestic crib was in use by this date.[317] Since the presence of shepherds was integral to the crib, the devotion identified itself with transhumance piety and shepherds featured in Christmas devotions both inside and outside church. In the Catalan lands possibly the oldest surviving Christmas drama to include a crib of living persons dates from Mallorca in 1599.[318] In accordance with old usage, the crib festivities involved dances (*carols* in English refers to dances, not to songs), so that the new devotion took over those very aspects which the Counter Reformation was trying to eliminate. Old Christmas carols in Catalonia include the earliest references to the sardana being danced before the crib to the accompaniment of flutes and other instruments:[319]

Anem, pastors, a Betlem,	Let's go, shepherds, to Bethlehem
caminem, anem, anem,	let's go, let's go,
allà farem sardaneta.	there we'll dance a sardana.

Or, in another song:

Ballem una sardana	Let's dance a sardana
davant de l'infantet	before the baby child
i aixi la seva mare	and so his mother
es distraurà un xiquet.	will relax for a while.

The act of dancing before the crib underscores an interesting feature of Catalan carols: their concern to participate in the Nativity and not simply to adore, an attitude which may explain the surviving presentation of living cribs in many villages, among them St Quintí de Mediona. Carols of the early sixteenth century had Joseph and Mary dancing, and the participating shepherds celebrating in a manner we might not immediately identify with transhumance piety:

En esta nit de Nadal	On this night of Christmas
ab gros capó	with a fat chicken
begueren del vi del barral	they drank wine from the barrel

e del flascó.	and from the jug.
De les neules me torrau;	Toast me some *neules*:
tot me sap bo.[320]	everything tastes fine.

In the Catalan Pyrenees animals were brought into the midnight mass of Christmas. The Counter Reformation set its face firmly against the practice, both for religious and for hygienic reasons, and in time seems to have succeeded also in expelling animals from paintings of the nativity.[321] The beautiful Nativity carved by Joan Grau in 1642 for the altarpiece of the Rosary in St Pere Màrtir of Manresa represents to perfection the scene as the official Counter Reformation preferred it.

A number of devotions were brought in or renewed and in time seemed always to have been part of the landscape of popular piety. Among them was the Angelus, made familiar to modern generations by Jean-François Millet's evocative painting of peasants in France. The prayer was only partially known in Spain. Its use was enjoined by diocesan synods in Oviedo as early as 1381, and in León from 1526, in Tuy from 1528, in Mondoñedo from 1534, in Orense from 1543, and in Astorga from 1553; it apparently gained in popularity during the early sixteenth century.[322] In this period, its practice was imposed generally throughout the churches, but by no means uniformly: the Salve and Angelus were first used in the parish of San Vicente (San Sebastián) only in 1591.[323] In 1588 Diego Pérez commented of the Angelus that 'it seems that it is being forgotten and little used' in Catalonia, and urged that 'it would be good for all Christian people to use this prayer'.[324]

A devotion due exclusively to the Counter Reformation was that of the 'Forty Hours'. In 1580 the Capuchins were the first to introduce it from Italy into Catalonia, where it was taken up immediately in Perpinyà[325] but apparently slow to catch on elsewhere, particularly in Barcelona, where in 1604 we find Pere Gil, then serving his second term as rector of the Jesuit college, claiming to have introduced it. A devotion consisting of day and night vigil before the Sacrament, the Forty Hours was utilised by the Jesuits specifically on the last two nights of Carnival as a counter-attraction. 'Since it was something new in the city it attracted a very large attendance of people ... and was continued in subsequent years ... The devotion of the Forty Hours drew an amazing number of people.' This may well be an exaggeration, for Pere Gil's conclusion on the impact of the devotion reads suspiciously like wishful thinking: 'the dances and masked entertainments were not a success.'[326]

The liturgical changes were slow to make a visual impact, and Spain remained a prominent example of a country where Baroque failed to become a pace-setter and filtered in only fitfully. The visitor who turns from the riches of Prague and Vienna to the Mediterranean in the hope of finding there the sources of visual opulence, may be disappointed with Catalonia. Resistance to Baroque was in part due to a general resistance to importations and a stubborn preference for the native tradition. Little leadership was given in cultural matters, and there is no evidence of the bishops actively fomenting new art or censoring older forms. Diego Pérez in 1588 gives the impression of a battle still to be fought:

> Painters who paint the saints and particularly female saints gaily dressed, commit a serious sin, for they dressed not that way but with decency. It is a particularly serious sin to paint Our Lady in a dress that is not worthy and decent. The truth is that these unsaintly paintings of saints do harm to simple people, and because of this the sacred Council of Trent recommended that bishops examine the painting of images to see that unless they are painted as they should be, they be removed.[327]

In Catalonia the artistic forms normally associated with the Counter Reformation seem to have come in only from the later years of the seventeenth century, and resident foreign artists (principally Italians) worked within an existing tradition rather than branching into a new one. From the early 1600s churches throughout the principality – as in Mediona – had begun to invest in the new ornateness, but the trend was restricted by the continuing influence of traditional forms. The Counter Reformation was not therefore conspicuously an age of Baroque in the province.[328] Only at the end of the century did Catalans begin to establish an initiative, with Xurriguera and Rates playing an important role in the extension of Baroque (brought directly from Italy) to Castile.

The pace of religious construction and decoration remains to be studied, but we can follow one part of it in perhaps the most typical place, the Jesuit college of Betlem in Barcelona. Though the church there began to be constructed in 1553[329] it was many years before the priests had enough money to embellish it, and in any case the early theories of the Jesuits forbade ornate churches. As donors gave funds, bits were added. A milestone was reached in 1592: 'in this year an effort was made to complete the reredos of the high altar, which had been started sixteen years before, and the carving of the reredos of the chapel was also completed and painted; and a wooden pulpit was also erected. The reredos and the sanctuary were put in place on Christmas Day.'[330] The next major stage was in 1627, when 'the church was further extended and the monument and reredos for saints Francis Xavier and Francisco Borja were painted in gold, and the painting of the chapel of St Gertrude was continued and remained in the unfinished state in which it now is in 1633.'[331] By 1671 the Baroque church was complete, richly furnished and decorated. That year, unfortunately, it was totally destroyed by fire, and all trace of the first Jesuit church of Catalonia was effaced. It was ten more years before, in 1681, the foundation stone of the new building was laid,[332] but the church took another sixty years to complete.[333]

Outside influences never wholly dictated the forms of religious worship and art in Catalonia, the best example of Catalan compromise between native tradition and external influence being the shrine of Montserrat. It is perhaps too often forgotten that the building of the new Montserrat (1560–92) coincided precisely with the building of the Escorial, and that the former was, like the latter, a product of the Counter Reformation. To all Catalans, the monastery had since the fifteenth century assumed the mantle of national leadership that perhaps only Ripoll had been able to offer in mediaeval times; but to Castile it was also a political symbol, since the deliberate imposition of Castilian control over its government, at the time of the reforms of abbot Cisneros, allowed a convenient intrusion into the heart's core of Catalan sensibility. It is no surprise to find that Philip II had a keen interest in the monastery, becoming in effect its most prominent patron. Montserrat, like the Escorial, became a mirror to several key aspects of the Counter Reformation. It was in the monastery that Philip first met his bishops who were making their way home from Trent: when some of them arrived in Barcelona they learned of the king's presence at the sanctuary and joined him at high mass there on the feast of the Purification, February 1564. As in the Escorial, so here the king came to examine the progress of the work he had set on foot in 1560 for the construction of a new basilica. The church took thirty-two years to complete, and was officially consecrated in 1592 on the same feast-day, of the Purification, by the bishop of Vic in the presence of the hierarchy of Catalonia. To make sure that the altar was a worthy one, in October that year Philip II sent an artist to make sketches for altarpieces. Their construction, carried out in Valladolid, took two years and the items were eventually transported laboriously from Castile in sixty-five carts.[334] It cannot be said that the House of Austria neglected Montserrat: the famous Black Virgin was ceremoniously enthroned in the new church in July 1599 in the presence of Philip III, and in 1626 Philip IV also made a visit.

A recurrent problem which reflected tensions elsewhere in public life was the conflict within the monastery between Catalans and

Castilians. The extension of the Castilian Observance to the Crown of Aragon in 1493 involved the imposition of fourteen Castilian monks from the mother-house in Valladolid, under the leadership of abbot García de Cisneros. The Castilian dominance provoked constant problems, felt both internally and in Catalonia as a whole. In 1563, a compromise was introduced with the imposition of the *alternativa*, by which Castilians and Catalans were to take turns in holding the posts of abbot and prior.[335] This may have quieted troubled spirits, but any external crisis was likely to provoke further tension. In the 1580s there was an active plot among some of the Catalans to separate from the control of Valladolid, and in March 1585 the twenty-two Castilian monks were expelled by force. A visit by the bishop of Vic in 1586 restored the Castilians, three ringleaders were expelled and the tension was allowed to settle down; but two years later, in 1588, the Castilian prelates in Catalonia were still nervous about how to handle the monks.[336] In 1612 there was an internal revolt when the Castilian monks were deprived of their offices; it turned out to be an extended problem, and in 1616 eighteen Catalan monks put their names to a petition asking that 'a neutral person' be appointed to look into their case.[337] There were repercussions among the surrounding towns, and the communities of the Camp of Tarragona issued a joint protest against 'the grave suffering in that sacred house and the injustices suffered by the Catalan nation through the misgovernment of the Castilians who are trying to ruin it by removing the Catalans and sending them to Castile so as to rule as they see fit.'[338]

The problem continued down to the revolution of 1640, when all the Castilian monks were expelled from the monastery.

Montserrat occupied a unique role in Counter-Reformation Spain because it continued to be, unlike the Escorial, closely identified with both international and national, both elite and popular, religious culture. For foreign tourists it never ceased to be an obligatory stop. With a cultural radius that extended beyond the Catalan lands to the whole Pyrenean area and the Gascon provinces, the monastery remained central to the devotions of both French and Spaniards. In 1615 the cardinal duke of Joyeuse made a memorable visit into Catalonia simply to visit the shrine: 'he came', reported the regent of the Audiència, 'accompanied by many French messieurs and thirty or forty vassals from Conflent, all with arquebuses, as well as cavalry knights from Perpinyà and a gang of bandits'.[339] In July 1622 when Louis XIII was in Narbonne, 'many titled nobles from his court entered Catalonia to visit the sanctuary of Our Lady of Montserrat';[340] and in 1624 fray Oliver, as we have seen, estimated the French to be the largest contingent among visitors.

Given the role of Castilians in the monastery, devotion spread to Castile as well: 'devotion to the image grew,' wrote fray Gregorio de Argaíz in 1677, 'such that in many villages of Castile, León and Galicia they dedicated altars and chapels to it'.[341] The miracles at the shrine were carefully noted by the monks: Argaíz calculated that 'from 1596 till the present year 1617, in the span of twenty-three years we find recorded seventy-seven miracles worked by the Virgin and authenticated.'[342]

Montserrat was the clearest example in Spain of an ideological symbol with both religious and political validity, which despite its internal tensions merged effortlessly into the new world of the Counter Reformation and continued to be for Catalans the focus of penitential pilgrimage. Its gaunt profile, visible from every vantage point of the Alt Penedès, offered to the people of the terme of Mediona a security which transcended their experience of day-to-day religion in the community and drew their aspirations towards a more eternal horizon.[343]

CHAPTER FOUR

Community and Counter Reformation

In this city of Barcelona the masked entertainments are so
uncontrolled that people think everything is allowed at this time.
Diego Pérez de Valdivia, *Sermon on the Masques*, 1618

Though the theology of the teaching Church emphasised personal salvation and personal sin, its practical directives emphasised the extra-personal responsibilities of a Christian living among his fellow men. Church and religion took on meaning when practised within society, forming an essential component of the immediate community and of the broader universe beyond it; but though all the fundamental stages of a person's life and rites of passage – birth, baptism, marriage and eventually death and burial – took place within the shadow of the Church, it was not the Church but the community that laid down the parameters of behaviour.[1] The relationship between religious rules and community norms seemed for the most part to be happily defined, but there were significant areas of tension, into which the Counter-Reformation Church felt it had an obligation to intervene. Perhaps the most obvious area was that in which the Church had exercised its right to cut a person off from the community of believers, through excommunication. Few village rectors were without their short-list of excommunicates, placed in this category not for religious reasons but almost exclusively for the economic one of not paying tithes; it was an abuse of clerical sanctions that had been repeatedly denounced and which reformist prelates were sworn to eradicate. Excommunication remained a convenient weapon to use in communities where there was in reality no other form of coercion available to the clergy,[2] but the clergy themselves might also support non-payment, for in Catalonia a substantial proportion of tithes went directly to secular lords rather than to the Church, and inability to win back the tithes[3] tended to identify the village clergy even more closely with community interests. The interaction of Church and community was a delicately poised drama in which the specified roles were played out with care and respect, but in which there were always conflicting interests that tended to surface in times of crisis.

The basic administrative unit of the religious community, the parish, centred on a church building and was staffed by a parish priest working either alone or in conjunction with a group of beneficed clergy; in larger towns more than one parish was necessary to cater for the needs of the population. Parishes were not isolated units: many were based on monastic churches and so fitted in with the life of a religious order, others were visited frequently by wandering friars who kept them in touch with other parts of the Church. Since early mediaeval times parishes had come into existence through the willingness of settlers to arrange themselves into a community, with or without the sanction of a local lord, and construct their own church: the lands set aside for church use, such as the church building, the cemetery, and adjacent land, were therefore always looked on as community property even if the jurisdiction over those lands was technically claimed by a lord or an abbey. In some communities – frequent in the Basque country but unusual in the Catalan lands – the community might elect the rector. During the mediaeval period lords with a right of presentation limited their activity to nominating the rector and collecting the tithe: most other aspects of church organisation might be left to the community itself. It is not surprising that in these circumstances the church became absorbed into the community. By the fifteenth century in Catalonia the parish priest seems to have become simply a functionary of the community, catering for the rites of passage of his flock, participating in their everyday activities, and identifying himself with their spiritual and secular interests to an extent that made him consider outside loyalties, even to his own bishop, as alien. In those parishes where the bishop did not even exercise the right of appointment, the breakdown of control was evident.

In practical terms a parish could exist only if paid for by the community. Where rectorates and benefices were in the control of outside bodies, as was the case in Mediona, those same bodies also enjoyed all the normal income, so that the tithe was never used to finance the church. Instead clergy had to fall back on the so-called first-fruits (*primicies*), or on the cash available from funds for saying masses for the dead. Fortunate indeed were those parishes where, as again in Mediona, local families invested in the church and in return obtained special benefits, most commonly seats in the church and the right to be buried before the high altar. Where little or no steady income was available the parish would have to do without a resident priest; and even if they had a priest he might have to live elsewhere because the funds did not extend to finding a house for him. Where a modicum of financial independence was to be had, it did not make the priest arbiter of the parish, and there is no evidence to support the quite inappropriate image of a community where the clergy ruled and dictated. The financial and social position of clergy in the parishes, especially in the more poorly endowed rural parishes, represented unsuitable material on which to construct a clerical despotism.

The coincidence of church and community in the rural areas, that is in the greater part of Catalonia, was preserved throughout this period.[4] The financing of the church and its effective control was in the hands of *obrers*, officials of the community chosen by election or by lot, who had the authority to raise loans (*censals*) and make decisions on the church building. It is significant that when the diocesan visitors came around their directives were always addressed to the obrers, and only questions of religion were referred to the rector. In many communities the obrers were also the elected town council (in St Quintí the *jurats* of the town were also in charge of the church, for whose business they had a special committee); but this total identification could lead to problems, and in Sarrià in 1645 the resulting chaos led to moves to divide the two administrations.[5] Day-to-day organisation of church activities was usually in the hands of the various confraternities, which had charge of processions and festivities; some groups, such as that of unmarried men (the *jovent* or *fadrins*), were headed by a 'king' or 'abbot' who had specified ritual duties. Raising of cash for the poor and other purposes might be in the hands of confraternities or of administrators (*pabordes*), who took charge of the *obres pies*. The whole community in this way administered the parish and were not simply members of it. Significantly, all the treasures of the church (images, crosses, silver) were considered community rather than church property; and in times of crisis the community exercised the right to sell them to raise capital.

It is evident from this that the parish had always been at the centre of traditional religion, but only in so far as it was identified with the community. In other respects pre-Tridentine religion had been indifferent to the parish: clergy had roamed from one area to another, the faithful had performed their religious obligations anywhere they wished, runaways had married in any parish that would have them, pilgrimages and processions had no boundaries. The Counter Reformation attempted to bring significant changes into this schema of things by tying down religious observance to the limits of the parish, and by elevating the role of the parish priest: both policies had in mind administrative control rather than religious change. Henceforth, all the rites of passage of a Christian were in theory tied down firmly to his parish of origin: the new laws regulating marriage, for example, made it difficult for him to marry anywhere but in his parish. In practice, as we have seen from Santa Maria in Mediona, long after Trent the difficult geography of the countryside made resort to the parish church rare, and sacraments, including mass, were administered in local chapels or within the *masia*. In many areas collapse of administration had led to the virtual extinction of parishes: in the village of Bunyola (Mallorca) in 1562 the bishop found that 'those who have lands in the parish almost never in the whole year go to the parish church for divine services',[6] and the parishioners were warned on pain of excommunication that even if they went to other churches for mass their primary obligation was to their parish church. The neglect continued, and though in that year's visit the church roof, through which water poured when it rained, was ordered to be repaired 'statim', eight years later the visitor found that nothing had been done. Possibly the worst case encountered in 1562 was the parish of Llucmajor, where the rectory was 'totally collapsed, ruined and derelict', uninhabited and used only as a sheep-corral, thanks to the permanent absence of the rector; where the bell-tower was collapsing, the noise of the parishioners at mass unendurable and their oaths even more so, and where there were no missals, with the result that mass had to be said from memory.[7]

The renewed emphasis on the sacred character of the priestly office implied a distinction between the priest as minister of the sacraments and the priest as servant of the community.[8] The Church was attempting to reclaim the local priest as its agent, a process consonant with the Tridentine move towards centralisation of structures. Bishops would have been delighted with a reliable clergy on whom they could depend for information and advice, but the obstacles to such a programme were formidable. We have seen that a high proportion and in some areas the majority of benefices were not within the gift of the bishop but within that of local seigneurs; moreover, few local revenues were available for the Church. Failing the right to appoint, however, the bishop could still control all other aspects of the post: the qualifications of the appointee (his age and training) and the conditions of tenure (the authority to exercise, preach and administer). In practice, then, a lack of jurisdiction – to be found elsewhere in the western Church[9] – did not necessarily have negative consequences. Possibly more serious was the inability of the community to control its pastor, if he was nominated neither by them nor by the bishop. Cases in the Church courts show that villages seem to have tolerated the most extraordinary conduct from their clergy, and very rarely did they petition to have them removed. There may, of course, have been ties of locality and blood which bound them to their pastors. In the diocese of Barcelona many young men were first appointed to a benefice and only then did they study to take up orders: ten of the forty-five priests consecrated by the bishop in March 1600 were already in possession of their posts.[10] This practice had the important effect of keeping local men in local jobs (as in Mediona), and by ensuring the survival of the parish as a community unit rather than as an outpost of episcopal authority guaranteed the continuation of traditional and local religion. It did not guarantee good relations between pastor and people: although the interests of the priest were always essentially those of his people, there is also ample evidence of strife.[11]

Despite this, the nature of rural society guaranteed the survival of the traditional parish/community in the Catalan countryside, to the detriment of the interests of episcopal authority. In the mediaeval Church in Catalonia there had been heavy reliance on the warrior barons for the founding of benefices. By the fifteenth century, when barons were no longer what once they were, it was the gentlemen farmers in their masies who diverted their spare cash to endowing benefices; but it was not out of pure altruism. The benefice-holder was invariably a younger son of the family, and the pious foundations (*causes pies*) in the church were invariably funds for endowing marriages (of the family) or for educating children (of the family). A typical case was that of the monastery of la Portella, near Serrateix: ruined since the fourteenth century, it was in 1548 restored by the joint investment of seven masies, which restricted tenure of the benefice to members of the said families.[12] In much of the Catalan countryside, and more particularly in the Pyrenees, where as late as 1764 it was reported that 'there is not a church altar in Andorra that is not in the patronage of one house or another,'[13] the pattern was repeated.

Clergy ordained in Barcelona were overwhelmingly Catalan in origin, and from the rural classes. Of a sample of 511 ordained to first orders between 1595 and 1600, only a handful (about fifty, or ten per cent) can be identified as coming from the urban elite of merchants and notaries.[14] This was balanced by a growing preference, especially among the religious orders, for recruitment from the upper classes.[15] The attempted aristocratisation of the clergy, reinforced among the orders by resort to proofs of *limpieza*, which in the past had been used to exclude those of Jewish origin but were now clearly directed to excluding recruits of humble birth, no doubt formed part of the Church's intention to raise its own standards by choosing the best, but had to struggle against the local and rural roots of the Church and there is no evidence that it succeeded.[16]

Where parish priests had long been considered on the same terms as other members of the community, and where their role had been one of equality, they were logically treated as mere equals. In Cuenca in the 1560s it was noted that when the priest rebuked parishioners for not coming to church or not observing holy days, the latter answered back during mass; and in Burgos in the 1570s when the preacher singled out sinners by name the said persons, including *alcaldes* (town mayors), would stand up and direct abuse at the priest.[17] Synods tried to change the situation by emphasising the distinctive functions and status of the priest, but the problem was also a broader one of the relation between the priest and society.

It is commonly assumed that society in Catholic countries became more clericalised as a result of the Counter Reformation. Certainly Spaniards of the early seventeenth century never doubted that theirs was a nation with too many clergy, and the comment of the priest-historian Gil González Dávila in 1619 that 'there are more of us than there should be'[18] can be supplemented by other testimony. Of Barcelona the Council of Aragon commented in 1603 that there were 'so many clergy that in this city alone there are more than in an entire bishopric';[19] and in 1633 the Consell de Cent decided to ban any further religious in the city, on the grounds that there were too many clergy begging for alms in the streets.[20] Outside the major towns, where the clergy and important orders ensconced themselves, accumulated real estate and ended up by 1700 as owners of the bulk of urban property,[21] the role and presence of the priest was however smaller than often supposed.[22] A common mis-understanding has been to confuse 'clergy' with 'priests', leading to some over-inflated estimates of the number of priests in Spain. In fact only a small proportion of those in holy orders were priests with a benefice or other function. The clerical presence may in some major centres have been oppressive, but priests as such were often in short supply. In the diocese of Barcelona between 1546 and 1570 no less than 4502 men received the tonsure, the first grade of orders; but only 284 received the priesthood,[23] an output of only some eleven priests a year for the principal diocese of Catalonia. The figures did not improve during the Counter Reformation: between 1635 and 1717[24] 2667 clergy were created but only 622 diocesan priests, or some seven priests a year. The Council of Aragon was probably justified to complain as it did of the many who entered into holy orders, no doubt for some advantage (such as the obvious one of tax exemption), but the Church was by no means flooded by priests. Indeed, the data show clearly that ordinations to the priesthood in Barcelona declined dramatically during the seventeenth century, from about thirty in 1640 and the same in 1650, to about two a year in the 1680s and 1690s.[25]

The well-known licence of clergy, condemned repeatedly by diocesan and provincial councils since the middle ages, amounted to little more than participating on terms of social equality with laymen. Throughout the period vigorous efforts were made by bishops to discipline their priests, but not always with success, and in 1675 the bishop of Barcelona was still denouncing clergy in Vilafranca del Penedès who went 'to taverns and gaming houses, playing at games we prohibit, going out at night without clerical habit, playing guitars and other instruments, and going in disguise at Carnival time'.[26] The licence of clergy was, despite the denunciations, by no means the principal reason for tension between clergy and people, and if anticlericalism existed it probably drew on a more complex range of causes. Hostility to clergy is amply documented. The farmer who in 1581 lost his temper and claimed that 'the priests in this village are devils and I don't believe they elevate God [at mass] but the devil, and they think they have Our Lord but they have the devil,' was apparently driven by a personal quarrel.[27] A merchant of Besalú who did not like the Inquisition had no more love for the Church and said of the offerings in church: 'Offerings? So they can get fat like pigs?'[28]

Some of the anticlerical conflict latent in rural society was provoked by the tithe, on which the finances of the Church relied in part. Constant evasion and fraud on the part of the tithed, with regular outbreaks of violence, might suggest that the Church was hated as the exploiter, and the Inquisition records lend support to this impression. In 1578 a resident of Olesa de Montserrat stated that 'he would rather spend a shilling on a whore than pay it for mass to be said, and give offerings to the dogs rather than to the priests, and he would stop ploughing his land to avoid paying tithes and first-fruits; and he said that the priests got too fat, it would be better not to give them offerings and then they would not get fat.'[29]

In 1586 a citizen of Perpinyà, during a conversation in which someone said that 'the sacred Council [of Trent] had ordered that the tithe be paid in full', replied 'that the sacred Council had exceeded its limits'.[30] In 1593 a resident of Enveig in the Pyrenees 'mistreated his mother because she gave offerings in the village church, and he said that all it went for was to fatten the priests'.[31]

The examples are in reality likely to mislead, for opposition to secular tithes was possibly even more resolute, yet never prosecuted by the Inquisition since no criticism of the role of clergy was involved.

The clerical role in society came in for constant criticism both from idealist reformers and from impatient laymen, but seems not to have changed substantially within the period.

Our principal source for the history of the people of pre-industrial Europe came into being through pressure from the Council of Trent, which laid down by a decree of November 1563 that all parish clergy should keep sacramental registers of baptisms, marriages and burials. In Catalonia the requirement to keep registers was an old one: as early as 1502 the bishop of Gerona ordered all his parish clergy to keep a record of baptisms,[32] with the result that this diocese contains some of the oldest baptism series in Spain. The provincial council of Tarragona ruled in 1555 that all rectors should keep two books, of baptisms and burials.[33] Baptism records in the church of Santa Cruz in Mallorca had begun in 1508, but were immediately discontinued, and not until 1562 were they again systematically kept.[34] Bishops after Trent tried to tighten up administration of the rules and in some cases went beyond them: the parish priest was sometimes enjoined to keep up to six types of record, not simply the three main ones but also registers of finances, of excommunications and of confession and communion. In the diocese of Barcelona the normal requirement was that rectors keep four registers: baptism, marriage, burial, and confessions.[35]

The parish, in mediaeval times a civil unit of settlement,[36] began to emerge as a firmly defined ecclesiastical unit in which the administrator – the parish priest – was directly responsible to the bishop, regardless of who actually exercised jurisdiction; in this way, the formerly independent and dispersed parishes of the late mediaeval world were absorbed into the centralised Counter-Reformation system. Inevitably, in practice things were not quite like that. The universal Church was not always able to overcome the resistance of communities which treasured their old ways and their traditional religion. Many parishes failed to keep registers, indubitably because they had no wish to record their lives for the outside world.[37] Rectors were willing to open their books to the bishop or his visitor, but when, for example, in 1681 the *familiars* of the Inquisition insisted on consulting the baptism records of the parish of Aiguaviva (Barcelona) the parish priest, in front of his parishioners, berated them 'not to write lies, and it was not the first time they had done so, changing signatures and other things like that'.[38] In the light of such reactions, one may surmise the response of village rectors to the suggestion of bishop Dimas Loris of Barcelona in 1598 that they should, in addition to the other registers, keep a 'special secret register' with the names of the adults in the parish and comments on their conduct.[39] Unfortunately for historians, no such registers seem to have survived, if indeed they were ever kept.

Social organisation in the parish had always been based on the community and its units rather than on the rector, who had never controlled any of its structures, of which by far the most significant was the confraternity (*confraria*). The greater emphasis given by the Counter Reformation to the parish did little to alter this picture, and probably increased the role of the parishioners to the detriment of the priest, a result by no means the one desired. This outcome can be seen in the growth during this period of the various lay bodies which the priest needed to be able to run the parish successfully: confraternities, sodalities, obreries and pabordies.

Of mediaeval origin and to be found throughout the cities of western Europe, the confraternity was an association of people with a common purpose and sharing a common ritual. The oldest associations were professional, grouping together the artisans of a particular calling – textile, metal, transport, fishing – and had their period of greatest expansion in the fifteenth century. As their point of contact they adopted a particular church, fashioned their own trade banner, and celebrated annually with a dinner. By the very nature of their profession such confraternities were urban. The Counter Reformation brought in a different type of association, the pious confraternity, which had existed everywhere since the middle ages but in this period of religious change experienced a rebirth and change of direction. Because they shared the more general purpose of a pious intention (devotion to a saint, alms for the poor), the members of such a confraternity were not limited only to the urban environment and could be drawn from any single parish, urban or rural. A further significant difference between the types of confraternity was that pious associations invariably allowed women to be members, whereas the professional bodies were restricted to males. Beyond that, both their organisation and public function tended to be identical: they adopted a favoured saint, endowed and supported an altar to him in the parish church, helped to administer affairs of the church and of the community at large, participated in rituals and processions, and set up a fund to protect members and their families. Richer confraternities might have a common fund which they used to buy property and make endowments.

The older confraternities were usually given a bad press by writers of the Counter Reformation. Many reformers, notably Juan de Avila, were hostile to the old confraternities and favoured their abolition or modification. Criticisms dating to the middle ages were made of their excessive liberty, of their feastings and irreligion. Diego Pérez in Barcelona reflected the views of the reformers:

> those like me who are old and aged seventy years, heard when we were young from those who were then aged seventy, eighty, ninety and even over a hundred years old, of how they lamented that some confraternities had lost the quality and virtue they used to have, and instead of dedicating themselves to works of mercy did nothing but eat, drink and do things unworthy of Christian men.[40]

Their virtual independence from Church control was notorious. It was an area where bishops, with the support of Trent, were eager to intervene, and during the period considerable changes were made in their character and constitution.

The stimulus given to confraternities by the Council of Trent is unquestionable, and can be seen more clearly in the country parishes than in the cities where the continuity with mediaeval tradition obscured the real changes that took place. Many rural communities, like Mediona, had no confraternity before the epoch of the Counter Reformation. When associations were founded in smaller parishes they coincided with all the institutions of the population and so *were* the community, holding their meetings in the parish church and organising most communal activity, thereby 'facilitating the consolidation of communal autonomy'.[41] In some small towns, consequently, a confraternity might have a surprisingly large membership. In Mataró in 1620, with a population of some five hundred households, the confraternity of the Carmen, based on the Carmelite church, boasted a membership of 1267,[42] or an average of 2.5 persons from each household. Because small parishes could not organise single-profession associations as in the cities, they did the next best thing by merging together all the available professions into one body, so that the countryside saw the rise of confraternities which embraced most of the community and the major trades in it. In 1596 the town of Piera founded a confraternity for its jurats, tailors, clothiers, shoemakers and 'many other individuals', under the names of St Jacinto and Santa Lucia; in the previous year Sabadell founded one for its shoemakers, carpenters, builders and smiths, and put it under the protection of four saints: Joseph, Eulàlia, Eloi, and Crespi.[43]

Confraternities might take on some tasks associated with the whole community, such as maintaining order in the village. Down

to the sixteenth century many had a free hand in affairs of the
parish, organising charity and festivities and running all aspects
of the church to such an extent that many parish clergy could
complain, like one in Toledo in the 1580s, that laymen ordered the
priests around like labourers.[44] In towns with a long ecclesiastical
history the number of mediaeval confraternities together with
modern additions came to an impressive total: by the late sixteenth
century Florence with a population of 59,000 had seventy-five, but
in parts of Spain the proportion was even higher, and Valladolid for
30,000 people had about one hundred, while Zamora with 8600
residents had 150.[45] In Barcelona the thirty professional confraternities in 1519 were still only thirty in 1564 but had by 1588
increased to fifty-one,[46] which together with the numerous parish
bodies may have brought the number close to eighty.

Various measures of the late sixteenth century were climaxed in
1604 by the papal constitution Quaecumque of Clement VIII,
which has been described as 'the last piece of legislation attempting
to put an end to the independence enjoyed by mediaeval confraternities'.[47] In future all confraternities had to receive the formal
permission of the diocesan authorities: in the Barcelona diocese the
regulations of every new foundation had to be submitted to the
vicar-general for his approval, a policy which had been carried out
systematically since about 1570. The success of these measures must
be judged within the context of jurisdictions in Catalonia, for in
practice a confraternity would apply for approval to the seigneur as
well (baron, abbot or king) and not necessarily to the bishop alone;
while Rosary foundations invariably consulted with the nearest
Dominican religious house.

It was at parish level that the most profound changes took place,
in two respects: new confraternities were set up with rules and
devotions consonant with the new age, and in each case the rector
was made president of the grouping. In this way both the ideology
and the personnel of the Counter Reformation were given control.
The diocesan synod of Barcelona in 1600 attempted to organise
popular piety by instructing rectors to form in their parishes a
confraternity of the Name of Jesus, directed against swearing, and a
sodality of the Blessed Sacrament.[48]

There were always mediaeval antecedents to the pious foundations of the period, especially with devotions to the Virgin, but
though confraternities of the Rosary can be found in the fifteenth
century their expansion dates only from the sixteenth, in association
with the growth of altar dedications. In Rosselló the Rosary confraternities took off mainly in the early seventeenth century, with
foundations in Vinça in 1607, Elna in 1610, Vilafranca in 1614,

Banyuls in 1623, Nyer in 1625,[49] Tuir in 1644 and Rivesaltes in 1669.[50] The transition from old to new was often almost imperceptible, as in the case of the famous confraternity of the Blood (*de la Sanch*) of Perpinyà, founded by St Vincent Ferrer in about 1416, which was imitated throughout Rosselló during the Counter Reformation, with new foundations in Vinça, Tuir (1623), Millars, Canet and Prada.[51] The devotion to the Blood of Christ was usually associated with ritual flagellation, and was also popular in many other parts of Catalonia: in 1601 confraternities to it were founded in Olesa and in St Vicenç dels Horts.[52] In Vilassar a small group of *disciplinats* (flagellants) was active from 1614, and became so successful that it founded a confraternity of the Blood in the parish church in 1623.[53]

The distinctive contribution of Counter-Reformation spirituality is reflected in the nature of the newer foundations, which in general terms shifted their emphasis from traditional local devotions to the dogmatic emphases of Tridentine theology, without displacing entirely the older devotions. The newer devotions were virtually imposed from above, for they were brought in from outside and cultivated through the assiduous efforts of both clergy and missionaries. The Rosary is a classic example of the change, together with other devotions which during the period fomented the growth of confraternities, such as the dogma of the Immaculate Conception. In Vallbona the founding in 1575 of a confraternity to the Holy Name of Jesus was directed specifically against blaspheming. Perhaps the most significant of all in social terms was the confraternity of the Blessed Sacrament (commonly known as the Minerva), whose development was in line with the boom in celebrations of the feast of Corpus. In Rosselló the forming of a Minerva confraternity in Perpinyà in 1560 was followed over the next century by foundations in towns such as Ceret, Cotlliure, Prats de Molló (1645) and Tuir (1663).[54] Apart from these bodies based on dogma, the major growth area was in devotions to particular saints who took the popular imagination: the canonisation of Ramon Penyafort in 1601 created a fashion in which the way was led by Martorell, Vilafranca del Penedès, and Sitges, the first three towns in Catalonia to have confraternities of the saint.[55]

In the diocese of Barcelona, and almost certainly in the rest of Catalonia as well, the enthusiasm for founding confraternities was restricted to the half-century 1580–1630.[56] Few were founded in the remainder of the seventeenth century: the need did not arise within the parameters of existing piety, and adequate associations were available to the population. An interesting aspect of Catalan piety at this time was the low level of interest in the doctrine of

Purgatory: associations with devotions to the souls in Purgatory did not make an appearance before the mid-eighteenth century.[57]

The noble classes had their own confraternity, dedicated to chivalry and named after the patron saint of Catalonia, St George. In Barcelona the association seems to have been of mediaeval origin, but in the sixteenth century the vogue for chivalry and the ceremony of the Golden Fleece in the city in 1519 gave it new life. In 1555 a ban was put on 'the tourneys which some nobles of Barcelona are accustomed to celebrate',[58] with the consequence that the body was reformed in 1565.[59] Chivalric tourneys and festivities continued to take place in Barcelona and other Spanish cities.[60] In Perpinyà the confraternity of St George was founded only in 1562 for the nobility of the county of Rosselló, and held jousts and celebrations; but collapsed at the period of French annexation, in 1652, undoubtedly because virtually all the nobility remained faithful to the Spanish crown.

Long-established confraternities became privileged groups within the community, with their own altar in the local church, their own property and privileges, their own practices and processions which sometimes antedated the changes which the bishops and clergy were trying to initiate. Quarrels and rivalries inevitably followed: with the parish priest, with other newer confraternities, with the bishop. In St Quintí we have already seen that a canon of Barcelona had to come to the village to mediate in a dispute between a confraternity and the jurats. Among the most troublesome of the village groupings was the confraternity of young men, which went by different names in all parts of western Europe and was normally entrusted with important community duties such as organising feasts. The old 'abbeys of misrule' found in France and the Netherlands were also identifiable in the Catalan lands. In 1518 there is a reference to the head of the confraternity of the Rosary in the cathedral of Urgell being 'commonly known by the title of "the abbot of misrule"';[61] an 'abbot of misrule' was still active in the town of Tuir in 1562;[62] and in Perpinyà one of the duties of the 'abbot of misrule' was to keep order among the children who attended Sunday mass.[63] Wherever the Feast of Innocents, known otherwise as the Feast of Fools, was celebrated, organisation of the rites and election of the boy bishop tended to be in the hands of the youth groups of the parish, organised as 'abbeys' or as 'kingdoms'. The persistence of such bodies confirms the ineradicable hold of popular customs, regardless of clerical discipline. In Urgell down to modern times it was the custom for the youth groups to take control of the village on Carnival Monday, bring all work to a stop, and make a procession round the streets dressed in masks and outrageous garb.[64]

In 1630 in Sabadell the episcopal visitor lamented the holding in church of ceremonies of the local 'kingdom', 'since the young people enter the church with the insignias of king or count on solemn feasts and provoke laughter and disturbance in the whole church and distract those listening to divine service', and for the future prohibited 'in any way allotting a special place in church to these people, even if they do not carry the insignias of king or count, nor must they be allowed a seat in the church'.[65] The youths cannot be suspected of simple piety in their behaviour, and some of their Carnival customs, such as the *pedrades* (stoning),[66] were far from religious, but reform proved very difficult. 'Kingdoms of misrule'[67] were not, despite the views of the official Church, merely escape valves for frustrated energies; and Carnival time was only one season of their activities. Throughout the liturgical year, the 'kingdoms' were active on other feast-days, helped to organise community celebrations and claimed the right to preserve community norms, in particular through the rite of the charivari.[68]

The day-to-day business of the parish was inevitably in the hands of parish members. So simple but essential a business as the cleaning and decoration of the church was usually taken over by women's guilds. The important role of women in Sabadell, for instance, can be seen through the foundation in 1596 of their all-women confraternity, dedicated to the Virgin.[69] With the help of a cash gift from a noble lady, Dionisa de Sarrià, towards restoring a lady chapel in the church of St Feliu, a wife and a widow of the town helped to found the association, which was devoted mainly to organising the charity of the parish. The confraternity had its annual procession on the feast of the Assumption, when it carried an image of the Virgin lying in bed. Many other communities in the region, notably in the Vallès, had all-women guilds based on the altar of the Virgin. In Lliçà d'Amunt from at least 1508, and in other villages such as St Llorenç Savall, the parish churches had a women's sodality known as 'of the Eggs', which administered for the church all eggs laid on Sundays and feast-days.[70]

In urban settings the 'community' was a highly politicised structure with well-defined power strata supported by elaborate rituals of role and authority. As we know already from studies made of towns such as Lyon and Romans,[71] a complex community nurtured tensions and pressures that were not simply of lower against upper class, but of factions among the upper class, and tensions among sections of the lower, often grouped according to parish. Fortunately, the Catalan towns did not suffer from the religious divisions to be found in France. In Catalonia the oligarchies were usually firmly in control of politics, and both Barcelona and Perpinyà made use of a tightly-woven, traditional, set of public rituals that enhanced community solidarity and maintained the peace; it is this set of rituals that we shall term 'civic piety'.[72]

In a Catalonia that was predominantly rural, one urban grouping stands out clearly: the city of Barcelona.[73] Symbol and soul of the province's aspirations, it never ceased to generate rivalry from other cities which claimed an equally venerable history. Since political, economic and cultural life tended to focus on it, Barcelona determined the major aspects of the Counter Reformation in Catalonia. It is now commonplace to argue that the religious changes of the German Reformation were in part promoted by the civic awareness of the urban community,[74] but in a Catholic city too the community was capable of responding to its religious responsibilities. 'Piety' meant a concern not only for the existing political and religious traditions of the city but also for a broadening of identity by taking on new *penates*, such as new relics and new saints, in order to reinvigorate both community sentiment and religious feeling. Piety expressed in this way was civic power. The origins were mediaeval but the combination of civic association – guilds, confraternities, parishes – and religious allegiance – cults, feasts – could be clearly seen in many of the self-confident city-states of Renaissance Italy. 'Civic patriotism was permeated by religious symbols and myths promoting public consciousness.'[75] The cult of saints legitimised the secular power of the urban oligarchy.

The bulk of civic ritual in Barcelona, of late mediaeval origin, was organised strictly according to time (the fixed order of the agrarian year, interspersed with the relaxation of Midsummer and the Midwinter Carnival), participants (the confraternities), and place (the approved theatre for all public ritual was the Born, then on the outskirts of the city but now fringing the park of the Ciudadela).[76] The religious innovations of the Counter Reformation modified this routine and tended to give more initiative to the Church in the principal festivities. Briefly, there were three areas where the influence of novelty was felt.

First, the recruitment of new saints to the civic cause was a major priority. The new rite of beatification or canonisation by Rome had the benefit of sanctioning an immediate cult and permitting extensive public celebrations, to the extent that one can follow the growth of pride in Barcelona through the tourneys held by the knights of St George in the Born. At every announced canonisation the rites of chivalry were re-enacted in the city,[77] and St Teresa of Avila, who once confessed her weakness for novels of chivalry, would have been gratified to know that a joust was held in her honour in Barcelona when she was canonised. The most notable canonisation of the entire Counter Reformation, that of Catalonia's favourite son Ramon Penyafort (d. 1275) in April 1601, tied the city up for several days in celebration and unleashed a flood of writings.

> Ya a nuestra Barcelona   Now our Barcelona
> otro patron le concede[78]   has another patron

exulted a pamphleteer. The country priest from Mediona, Pere Santacana, summoned to Barcelona to participate, could not conceal his wonder:

> On the twenty-fourth of May they had fiestas in Barcelona in honour of St Ramon, in particular a solemn procession in which there took part all the bishops of Catalonia, all the rectors of the diocese of Barcelona (summoned by order of the bishop), all the religious orders of the city, all the musicians and jugglers of Catalonia, with minstrels placed on stands in all the streets through which the procession had to pass, and all the chief persons of the city and many from Catalonia . . . Everybody from Catalonia was there . . . There were other processions from all the parishes near Barcelona and from Mataró, Terrassa, Caldes and others, in great order and wearing pilgrim badges . . . People went with casks of rose-water with taps, which they filled in the houses and went through the streets sprinkling great quantities of rose-water, and the city and *Diputació* spent a lot of money on illuminations . . . There were musicians, jousts, tourneys and other things which I cannot possibly find space to mention.[79]

Accumulation of canonisations, though impressive, was only one dimension of the promotion of civic piety. It was yet more power-enhancing to obtain possession of the relics of the saint: we have already noted the celebrations for the arrival of the relics of St Isidore and St Philip Neri. The final step in the assertion of power was possession of the entire body of a saint. In 1604 a pamphleteer could write:

> Esta es la gran Barcelona,   This is the great Barcelona,
> madre, amparo, honor y   mother, refuge, pride and
>   guarda   protector
> de su reyno y de su Rey   of the kingdom and its king
> y de gran parte de España.   and the greater part of Spain.
> A esta pues le a dado el cielo,   Heaven now has given to it,
> para su gloriosa fama,   for its glory,
> seys cuerpos santos . . .[80]   six holy bodies . . .

The six, all deemed to be patrons of the city, were Sta Eulàlia, St Ramon Penyafort, Sta Madrona, St Sever, St Pacià and St Oleguer.

It is no exaggeration to say that in the context of civic piety Barcelona's dominance in Catalonia could be defined in terms of these six bodies,[81] a notable contrast to Perpinyà, which had none; and the search for new bodies was never-ending.[82] The only other body in the principality with recognised power was that of St Galderic, treasured by the monks of Canigó and which the city of Perpinyà had to plead for every time it required rain. We have seen that in 1612 Perpinyà declared a *mà armada* because it could not have the body, and sent an armed force out to besiege Vilafranca de Conflent and bring the relics back. A peak point in Barcelona's saga was reached when it also came into possession of St Galderic. The monks of St Martí de Canigó, fleeing in 1654 from the French occupation, brought with them the body of their saint, which stayed in Barcelona until at least 1661, in the church of St Pau del Camp, then later returned to Canigó.[83]

A second area of civic piety affected by the Counter Reformation was the coming of the new religious orders. One of the major factors which helped them to grow in Catalonia was the rivalry among towns to obtain their privileged services. As in the thirteenth century when the mendicant orders went out, municipalities were anxious to see what was on offer and were willing to adopt and house the missionaries who pleased them. In their turn, the new religious were eager to give their services generously and to demonstrate that heaven supported their ministry. Gerona, for example, was hardly an ungodly city, yet as early as 1551 the authorities were writing to Loyola to ask for a preacher, citing 'the great need this city has of a little light'. By 1579 or earlier the Jesuits were preaching missions there, and in 1581 they were given as their base the former Augustinian monastery of St Martí Çacosta.[84] The city council was specially interested in the opening of a school, 'in which true Christian letters can be learnt as is learnt in other places in colleges of the Company'. In the same way Perpinyà was anxious to receive both the Jesuits and the Discalced Carmelites; on obtaining the latter, the *cónsols* wrote proudly to the king that they hoped the Carmel 'can teach and instruct the people'.[85]

A third modification attempted was in the transformation of public space from profane to sacred use. Civic manifestations in Barcelona had always used the streets and squares freely, particularly in Carnival, but from the time of the viceroyalty of Francisco Borja the bishops received more support from the elite in their campaigns to sacralise public areas. The most common weapon for doing this was the procession, which by moving through defined areas effectively claimed them for Church use.[86] Though the Church authorities seem to have successfully asserted some rights, particularly in the important procession of Corpus Christi it is doubtful if any effective or lasting control of popular space was achieved.

Public festivities were central to the life of all pre-industrial communities. Church feasts were public holidays, when the population was expected to abstain from work and attend to spiritual duties; but there were also secular days of feast and celebration determined by the annual cycle of the agrarian economy. Catholic reformers in the sixteenth century felt that religious holidays were both excessive in number and celebrated haphazardly, with parishes choosing their feasts at will. In New Castile there were complaints throughout the late century that villages preferred to celebrate their local days of devotion rather than those laid down by the Church calendar.[87] The provincial council of Tarragona in 1565 attempted to legislate both obligatory and standard holidays, while cutting out undesirable feasts: apart from the fifty-two obligatory Sundays of the year, provision was made for thirty-three other obligatory holidays, giving a minimum of eighty-five days of obligation,[88] to which the council added thirteen days recommended as worthy of respect, and other days for local saints which parishes could choose at will. This gave a minimum total of religious holidays for Catalonia of about one day in three. To this one must add the number of local holidays celebrated by the community during the agrarian year, possibly about two weeks in all. The figures were consonant with practice in the peninsula and in much of Catholic Europe. By way of comparison, the official 'bank holidays' observed by the municipal bank (Taula) at Perpinyà in 1584 totalled 119 days in all, one-fifth more than the total recommended by the council of Tarragona.[89] A century later, in 1684, the total of Church and secular holidays observed in Catalonia was 110 days, without counting the many saints' days recommended for observance;[90] almost a third more than the figure recommended in 1565. These minimal figures leave out of account the many 'bridging' days in the year, notably Saturdays or Mondays, and the fact that the great feasts were never restricted to one day but frequently took in two or three; so that the official total should probably be augmented by at least thirty more days, making the real total of holidays close to one day in every two, a total quite consonant with the quality of life in a society not governed by strict time-keeping or work routine. In pre-industrial Catalonia leisure occupied the same amount of time as work.

The proper use of this leisure time was inevitably a major preoccupation of the Church. As we have seen, the chronology of work and joy was dictated by the feasts which marked the transition between seasons.[91] Though the central axes of the year, the winter and summer solstices, were celebrated with the religious feasts of Christmas and St Joan, there was an uneven distribution of holidays in the rest of the year, with a long stretch of months from November to March when the earth lay fallow and there were no significant celebrations. Only with the opening of spring, the festival of Easter, and the beginning of the period of transhumance, did the cycle of feasts develop, reaching their climax in the summer months from June to August. A 'feast' was essentially a rite of communication within each social grouping, celebrating a special or traditional event and expressing itself through symbolic or real means such as dancing, drinking, ceremonial, satire, and sexuality. In a Christian society the ceremonial used might be Christian but did not necessarily supersede all other forms of expression, which in agrarian societies might have no less validity for the people than the formal Christian ceremony. In attempting to bring some order into popular feasts the mediaeval Church had been obliged to accept the continued practice of folk rituals, but the Counter-Reformation clergy felt that it was possible to purge the disproportionate part still played by old rites.

As festivities of leisure time, celebrating release from work, feasts also celebrated release from society's norms and encouraged an atmosphere of merriment, relaxation and satire which contrasted vividly with the orderly world of conventional relationships. The disorder associated with feasts was not restricted to the inevitable chaos of drink and unruly behaviour but was also, by a process paralleled in other traditional societies,[92] transmuted into a series of rituals of mockery, laughter and social inversion that varied in form from community to community. At one level, inversion of roles might be regarded as a simple form of the community at play, indulging the freedom to jest and criticise, in much the same way as a king's jester might mock the king, without in any way presenting a threat.[93] At another level, role reversal, inversion and mockery can be regarded as alternative rituals offering a differing symbolism for crucial stages[94] of man's role in the community. One of the most typical of these rituals, and also one of the oldest, was the Feast of Fools, which mocked the values of wisdom and order and enthroned those of simplicity and misrule, spawning in the process a whole range of rites and practices which became institutionalised by late mediaeval times, produced a provocative literature,[95] and entered the domain of the Church in ceremonies such as the boy bishop. Was the disorder a real challenge to established society? The instinct of the official Church, long before the Reformation, was to restrict the extent to which nameless and disorderly rites, often associated with the lower classes, could be allowed to take place. Looking back to a previous generation Dr Diego Pérez in 1618 claimed that 'very few used to mask themselves, they were lowly and common people, and masks were used almost only for plays. Now the whole thing has become dissolute ... Over the last few years the masques and the jugglers and excessive eating and drinking and dressing-up and other vices have come in to Barcelona, and from here have spread through the province.'[96] At an intellectual level, many of the elite had long been conscious that inversion and disorder were essentially harmless, reflecting a dualism in the universe; Baltasar Gracián had affirmed that 'the things of this world can be truly perceived only by looking at them backwards.' The reforming clergy were less patient of such intellectual conceits.

Rite inversion could be found in all the major festivals. The winter festivities, from Innocents to Carnival, were perhaps the biggest group of inversions. On Innocents Day in traditional Catalonia the rules of order were allowed to be suspended: stealing was permitted (Sarroca de Bellera, Sant Llorenç de Muga), in church a young boy heard confessions (Gósol). In Santa Coloma de Queralt in the seventeenth century the 'king' and 'bailiff' of the confraternity of St Esteve were given control over the town for that day; in Igualada the town remained under the rule of the 'Innocents' until midday.[97] The inversion was extended to the role of women on the feast of Sta Agueda (5 February),[98] in rites still practised in Catalonia. On that day in Serós (Lérida) women were allowed to serve at mass; in several towns a woman was elected mayor for the day. The role reversal was evidently not a move to give status to women, but rather, by allowing the departure from the norm, a confirmation of existing status roles. The mixture of both sacred and secular in these rites made it very difficult for the clergy to attempt to change only those aspects affecting the Church, and inversion continued to be practised, usually in a modified form, throughout the Counter Reformation and down to today. As late as 1756 the parish of Llinàs (Llobregat) maintained a ceremony whereby 'on Innocents Day the parish elects a bailiff and town council commonly known as The Rogues, who enter in the church like ruffians and assist at divine service.'[99]

The merging of sacred and traditional affected all the major festival seasons. Carnival, or *Carnestoltes* as it was known in the Catalan lands, formally a part of the pre-Lenten celebrations permitted by the Church, coincided with the winter agrarian cycle and might cover several days over and above the specific religious days. In Menorca 'carnival' meant in practice the entire period between Christmas and Ash Wednesday; in the Baix Llobregat it began the day after Christmas.[100] In Barcelona there was similar liberality about the duration. Carnival in Barcelona always provoked protests about public and moral disorder, and the festivities were repeatedly banned. When Francisco Borja was viceroy there in 1540 he had great satisfaction in prohibiting the unruly aspects, an act which upset the city: 'if those of Barcelona speak ill of me,' he wrote to the government, 'don't believe them; it is because I prohibited the dances this carnival.' 'In any case,' he added, 'the masques went very well.'[101] The city was in fact also concerned to limit the disorders of carnival, and the Consell banned carnivals – denounced in 1558 because of 'many fights, quarrels, woundings, deaths and other serious offences and criminal acts' – on nine occasions between the mid-sixteenth and mid-seventeenth centuries. Carnival was so large a public celebration that all the responsible authorities – viceroy, city and bishop – took part in decisions on the matter, and issued their own regulations, some prohibitions of the late sixteenth century being issued by the city because of epidemic and not merely as a measure of law and order. There were occasionally differences of opinion: in 1587, when a total ban was declared because of epidemic, viceroy Manrique de Lara was reluctant to let the city proceed with the ban since in his opinion 'dances and masques in time of carnival are so rooted and traditional in this city that they would be difficult to stop, and the people would be very offended,'[102] implying that public dissatisfaction might be more of a threat than the epidemic. In the winter season of January 1623 the Consellers 'decreed that on pain of prison no one should put on masks or disguises'.[103]

As with most of the feasts of this period, popular celebrations differed in some respects from those put on by the elite. Carnivals[104] tended to include agrarian and folk rituals which subsisted until modern times, such as the ceremony of the 'burial of Lent', or the 'death' of the Carnival king, with its variant the 'burial of the sardine', performed on Ash Wednesday. The symbolism of death (still practised in parts of the country as the 'execution of the cock') and of subsequent resurrection, was basic to the celebration,[105] but the communities also had a wide variety of traditional rites to celebrate the culmination of the winter festivities.[106] Carnival practices sometimes intruded into the liturgy, from which they were very difficult to dislodge, and in 1662 in the diocese of Urgell there were 'priests and laymen who when singing the divine office in the choir on some days, and in particular at the vespers of Christmas, the Circumcision and Epiphany, mix profane songs and words with the psalms and hymns of Holy Church, in great contempt and irreverence of divine worship'.[107]

The nobles, while sometimes participating in the popular celebrations, had their own rituals, which were more markedly chivalresque and usually performed in the Born. Pujades in February 1604 was enthusiastic about one such noble tourney:[108] 'on the twenty-seventh in Broad Street [the carrer Ample] there was an armed combat, with two lances on each side ... It was very attractive, and never before seen in Barcelona.' Among carnival celebrations of the period was the interesting masquerade put on in January 1633 for the cardinal Infante, which was accompanied by a tourney among the nobility. The masquerade consisted largely of a version of Don Quixote presented to the public, who were invited to enjoy themselves:

Pus que Carnestoltes	Since Carnival
desterra a los trists,	drives out sadness,
viscan los alegres,	long life to the gay,
muyran los podrits.	and death to the sour-faced.
Los podrits son gent cansada	The sour-faced are a bore
y ningu sab lo perque,	and no one knows why
tenen la cara rugada	they have long faces
y de res no senten be.[109]	and grumble about everything.

Out of Carnival time the nobles had similar feasts, such as those put on in April 1630 for the queen of Hungary by the duke of Cardona in Barcelona 'in the garden of the house', with jousting, races and target practice with pistols, which Pujades witnessed with delight. 'They also had a bull-run. The games were splendid to see, but the bulls were a brutal thing.'[110]

Preaching in Barcelona on the eve of the Carnival of 1583, Diego Pérez energetically denounced 'what we see today in Catalonia':

Who cannot see that for the most part the masques end up in vileness and lewdness? In bad thoughts and wicked desires and in things that are done in secret which are shameful to mention in public? What happens in these streets? What happens in these houses where men and women in masks enter to do what they please? You know better than I do, and some are ashamed and keep quiet for their honour's sake.

During the masques all the bandits, all the scum of the earth come to Barcelona and wander at will through the streets and houses, and do what they wish, though the devil restrains them from killing and robbing. At this time crazy and dissolute men and sick women use the hellish holiday to settle their affairs. At this time everyone spends exorbitantly from St Antony (or even before) up to Ash Wednesday on masks, clothes, parties, entertainments, eating and drinking.

Despite his moralising, Pérez offers a documented commentary on aspects of the Carnival season: 'On carnival Tuesday [Shrove

Tuesday, Mardi Gras] the people dance beyond midnight and at one o'clock return home, and eat their supper on what is already Ash Wednesday . . . The masques of the day extend into masques at night, people go dancing, they go eating and drinking to excess; and how are they to get up on the Wednesday to go to mass? . . .'

The problem of abandoned children, which led Pérez to found a hospital for them in the city, was in his view compounded by the sexual licence during Carnival:

> It has been observed from many years' experience that counting from those days of carnival the time that lapses coincides exactly with the number of babies who are taken to the General Hospital. From which one can infer the unhappy dissoluteness of the masques, since they end up in so many secret births. And the truth is that not all of them are born, and it is likely that many are aborted or hidden in some other way.
>
> The masques begin almost from Christmas and keep on growing like a disease, and in the end what we have is not Barcelona but Babylonia.[111]

It was symptomatic of the elite's concern for order that the popular Carnival was often banned but little control was exercised over the noble entertainments. After the revolutionary disorders of Corpus in the city in 1640, the Consell decreed on 18 January 1641 'a perpetual ban by night and day on carnivals, masques, dances and other causes of disturbance and riot'. A similar decision was taken in Gerona where the city in 1641 decided to allow no public entertainments between Christmas and Lent, a decision repealed only in 1660.[112] In Barcelona relief came earlier: when the city was recovered for Spain, Carnival and its joys returned; and the celebrations of February 1653 in the Diputació, authorised by Don Juan of Austria, inspired a witness to claim that 'in no city of the world are there better fiestas of this type; the two days of Monday and Tuesday witnessed the biggest masques ever seen in Barcelona.'[113] Little new appears to have transpired until 1678, when a public controversy broke out in Spain over veils, masks and nudity;[114] the viceroy issued a ban on carnival, and on 5 January 1680 the Consell confirmed the ban throughout the principality. The prohibition appears to have been observed until the end of the century.[115]

Common to most feasts was the procession, a group activity which shared with Carnival the spirit of enjoyment but might also have the more solemn role of public intercession.[116] In rural villages, particular importance was given to processions made to local shrines, which took the form of community outings armed with packed lunches, drink and music. Since mediaeval times, complaints had been made that such outings and processions were the occasion for sin rather than piety, particularly if the distance to be covered was so long that it called for an overnight rest, with its attendant opportunities for licence. Criticisms were also levelled against group pilgrimages to well-known shrines, such as that of Montserrat. The Counter-Reformation clergy came out firmly against mobile devotions as they had been practised since mediaeval times. In 1629 the diocesan synod of Barcelona demanded 'that a remedy be found for the problems that arise from processions which go to hermitages far away from the villages, or which go to Our Lady of Montserrat. That processions not be undertaken unless they return the same day'.[117] This sort of ruling attempted to stop the previous practice by which communities used to make outings to several shrines far away from their own village; it also as a consequence gave a greater impulse to local religion by encouraging the development of accessible holy places and confining piety to the administrative limits of the parish. Whether the rulings were effective is another matter. In 1683 it still remained a cause for complaint by the Barcelona synod that 'in the present diocese there is an abuse by which many villages make annual processions "extra propriam parrochiam" . . . and when they arrive at the chapel or shrine they dedicate themselves more to buying and selling, eating and drinking, than to divine worship.'[118]

The procession in its most evolved form was both an exercise in piety and an exercise in power, demonstrating control over a given space and providing evidence of the masses who would give group testimony to their affiliation. In purely religious processions the area covered was strictly delimited by the Church, which was thereby able to control both the movement and the message; for the same reason, the Church always opposed processions which ventured beyond the areas it felt it could control, since that implied the entry of alien elements, nor was it happy with the participation of the secular powers unless they accepted a secondary role. In Church eyes, the ideal procession consisted only of clergy wending their way round a church or round a parish, distributing their blessing as a measure of magical protection to the area and the people using it; within a city the routes chosen by a Church procession would similarly define the accepted area benefiting from the protection of the clergy.[119] The participation of believers in a procession was peripheral to its main purpose. However, in pre-industrial society the dominance of rogational processions inevitably brought in public participation, and by the time of the Counter Reformation the Church was struggling to assert its privileged role in these acts.

In large processions made up of faithful from different parishes, there was always a danger of violence because of conflict between differing affiliations and arguments over the respective merits of confraternities and even of saints.[120] By contrast rites of deliverance such as processions to pray for rain united all the faithful in a common purpose and appeared to pass peacefully. In a climate more subject to drought than northern Europe, processions to intercede with heaven were common enough, though in crisis years their frequency could surprise even hardened souls like the seventeenth-century farmer Joan Guàrdia, whose comment on the year 1650 has been noted above: 'this year 1650 was the year of misery... the grain was lost because of the great drought... it could be called the year of the processions.'[121]

Since multiple functions and activities were involved in a procession it was difficult for authority to control all aspects, and inevitably differing views could be taken of the same phenomenon. One confraternity at Caldes de Montbui, for example, motivated no doubt by respect for the evangelical virtues of poverty, put twelve beggars to represent the twelve apostles into its annual procession on the feast of the Assumption, and the practice seems to have continued for some time until the diocesan visitor in 1771 took the view that it was 'the most horrifying contempt, irreverence and profanation' to put 'twelve men of the dregs of the people to represent the sacred persons of the twelve most holy apostles'.[122] The clear social preferences of the official Church were consequently imposed on the somewhat different perspective taken by a rural community.

Throughout Spain the most picturesque processions took place, as they still do, in Holy Week. In Barcelona there is no evidence of attempts at ecclesiastical regulation of the proceedings until the middle of the seventeenth century, from which it would appear that such processions played a less prominent part in popular celebration than the Midsummer feasts and Corpus, for which episcopal rulings appear at the very beginning of the century. The first detailed rules for Holy Week processions were issued in 1650, during the last epoch of Catalonia's ill-fated secession from the Spanish monarchy; from them we can see that many of the undesirable customs denounced since the early days of the Counter Reformation still remained.[123]

Many persons with little fear of God Our Lord and little care for the sovereign mysteries not only ignore them but even, with no respect and in great contempt, bring benches, chairs, gifts, snacks, meals and other refreshments, thereby introducing profanity and scandal into the temple of God. And in the churches and streets through which the mysteries pass they scoff and sneer at the priests and the devotions, when they should with tears and profound sorrow of heart be weeping. Others, wearing indecent clothes quite unsuitable for an act of mortification and penance, accompany the procession with immodest vests and tunics that do not cover their bodies but reveal their sins, and go covered with corsages of flowers and different perfumes that display their profane vanities.

In order to remedy the situation the following rules were specified: eating, noise-making and other disorder was forbidden; 'those who go by day or night to visit the holy monuments should not speak indecently nor sing profane songs, and those flagellants and penitents who wish to visit must be persons of rank' and not riff-raff; when processions enter churches they must not break order; no objects are to be thrown, 'there must be no throwing of lead pellets, balls, stones, water, earth or other things that hurt and damage'; flagellants must be adequately clad; people must not dress indecently, or be accompanied by their servants; everyone must behave properly, especially within the church.

These regulations were repeated in similar form for the rest of the century, with occasional variations which suggested that problems still remained. In 1657, for example, the bishop had to forbid the appearance in the procession of unusual and excessive penitences: 'no one may dare or presume to carry iron bars on the shoulders with the arms stretched out, nor be tied up in esparto- or hemp-cord, nor do any other unusual and rigorous penitence.'[124]

The best studied of all the popular feasts of the Church is Corpus Christi.[125] Instituted in honour of the Blessed Sacrament by a papal bull of 1264, and with a liturgical office composed by Thomas Aquinas, the feast of Corpus Christi took a long time to gain popularity. It was the Council of Vienne (1311) which gave it real impetus, and Barcelona was possibly the first city in the peninsula to hold a public procession in its honour, in 1319. Over the next two centuries the Crown of Aragon pioneered its celebration, and by the mid-fifteenth century the festivities also played a prominent part in both Seville and Toledo, with all the main components of the procession – street decorations, theatrical performances, floats, giants and *tarascas* (dragons), dances and music – already present. The mood of the feast was always a joyful celebration, but the theme varied according to locale: normally each corporate entity, mainly the city council and the respective parishes through their confraternities, put on a show with a religious or Biblical format; but elements of folklore and symbolic imagery also made their appearance (eagles, for no clear reason, turned up at the end of the fourteenth century). By the early sixteenth century in the Catalan lands Corpus was easily the most popular of the great civic festivities. Curiously enough the Eucharist, in whose honour the feast had been instituted, seems to have made little showing in the celebrations; and Catholic reformers were also scandalised by the profanity apparent in every aspect of the traditional festivities. Around this key cultural event, which took place on the Thursday after Trinity Sunday, at the beginning of the summer season which thereafter moved to its climax on Midsummer's Day (St Joan), a long and historic battle was waged by the forces of the Counter Reformation.

Like other great feasts, Corpus was governed by regulations issued by both civil and Church authorities; but the post-Tridentine Church considered that Corpus was par excellence a Christian feast and made great efforts to assert clerical control over its organisation and content. The Corpus procession, which formed the heart of the celebrations, had often given rise to conflicts in the past but now became the setting of a struggle for power between city and Church. Typical of the conflicts was that in Gerona. On 22 May 1573 bishop Tocco of Gerona made a determined attempt to have a say in those aspects of the Corpus celebrations that affected himself and his churches. He issued a decree denouncing

> the abuse in the said cathedral of Gerona and other churches of our diocese, in use on the vigil of Corpus and on the day, and no doubt used in other festivities, of people bringing into the church the giant, the giantess, the eagle, and dragons and other types of animals, and dancing and letting off fireworks ... embracing each other before the altar and the Blessed Sacrament, the musicians playing immodest songs and the people dancing *sardanas* ... as a result of which it is impossible to celebrate divine service ...[126]

In consequence, he forbade any of these practices in his churches. There was a sharp reply from the city council, which on 17 June affirmed that the traditional aspects of the ceremonies were done in the service of God, noted 'the little consideration Your Worship has for the city', and decided not to pay any attention to the bishop's decree. In 1575 Tocco agreed on a compromise by which the giants were allowed into the cathedral, but no fireworks were allowed inside and all dancing was forbidden. The firm attitude of the Church began slowly to mould the traditional Corpus festivities into the required shape, and by 1596, when an order of ceremonies called the *Llibre de Nou Redres* was drawn up in Gerona, the whole Corpus celebration began to settle down into the form it retained for over a century, with the exclusion from the procession of much of its old character. From now on Corpus, once a noisy combination of agrarian and religious customs, became a public celebration dedicated to the Sacrament.

From the 1590s the bishops of Barcelona issued partial instructions for the more efficient celebration of Corpus, banning completely the use of horses in the processions, since they defecated and thus made the road unpleasant for those on foot.[127] In 1608, bishop Rovirola for the first time, by an order dated 4 February and therefore coinciding with the Carnival season, attempted to control some aspects of religious processions: 'We order that on the day and octaves of Corpus and other solemn days the streets be well decorated and adorned, there be no dancing before the Blessed Sacrament, nor may men and women or even children dance in the procession, there be no chanting and singing of profane and lewd songs, nor may guitars and other unsuitable musical instruments be used.'[128] The first detailed regulation of Corpus by episcopal authority in Barcelona was in 1610, when the vicar-general issued an instruction on 4 June and the following day bishop Montcada issued an 'Edict on the procession for the day of Corpus'.[129] The former set a limit on the amount of decoration, so that 'in the illuminations for the Blessed Sacrament there be no more than three hundred candles', and ordered that 'in the music to be performed before the Blessed Sacrament guitars may not be played nor may any type of profane song be sung, and the words of songs have first to be approved by us,' while the bishop ruled that nobody could

> along the streets where the procession is to pass, go on horse or on mule or in a coach nor any similar manner; nor dance, sing or chant dances and songs which are lewd, profane and indecent; nor fire arquebuses or fireworks or similar things which can hinder the passage of the procession; nor do immodest and indecent things; nor make snacks or other meals in the churches through which the procession will pass.

The move was important enough for Pujades in his diary to attribute its need to 'the great outcry and riot that takes place in the churches on the days of the octave of Corpus, all more out of rivalry between people than out of a desire to serve God'.[130] Subsequent bishops issued similar orders (there is one by bishop Sans, for example, dated 1617)[131] and there seems to have been no major change until the tragic events of the Corpus of 1640.

The cooperation of bishop and city in the regulation of the civic piety of Corpus did not always meet with clerical approval. Some clergy demanded for themselves a much larger role than the authorities were willing to allow, and the restrictions placed on Dominicans participating in the 1625 procession provoked the chronicler of the convent of Santa Catarina to exclaim, 'If the Council of Trent were to see it, how it would complain of the bishop!'[132] By the late seventeenth century Corpus had a fixed ritual which began with high mass in the cathedral at 10 a.m., followed in the afternoon by the procession, which began at 5 p.m., passing through the streets of the city and the Born, and finishing at 9 p.m.[133]

The struggles of the Church to distinguish between sacred and profane, religious and popular, may be seen in some elements of Corpus such as the giants. The use of large figures of wood and paper painted to represent saints, historic heroes or symbolic creatures, seems to have become generalised throughout western Europe from its origins in the Netherlands in the fifteenth century. Often known as *tarascas* (dragons) in the Mediterranean lands, the giants were most popularly used in the Corpus Christi processions but also became the focus in others. For the Church, the evidently secular nature of giants made them unwelcome in processions, more so when – as frequently – attempts were made to bring the giants into church for the mass which climaxed the festivities.

The continuing tension between popular practice and ecclesiastical discipline may be seen as late as 1644, when the synod of Segorbe once again prohibited dancing in processions, complaining that 'many men take part dressed as devils or as women, and dance around gesticulating like devils.'[134] The dance of the devils, documented from at least the 1420s in the Corpus celebrations in Barcelona and Cervera, continued to be a popular diversion in lower Catalonia and the Counter Reformation never succeeded in controlling it. At the celebrations for the canonisation of St Ramon Penyafort in 1601 there were 'many dressed like devils with ugly masks, bells on their legs and a sort of stick in their hands from which they fired many firecrackers';[135] and in 1689 the bishop of Solsona, complaining that in the Corpus processions there were 'some men dressed in devils' clothes and making gestures as though they were demons, with which they moved the faithful more to laughter than to piety', solemnly pronounced that 'we extinguish and prohibit it'.[136] Today the dance remains as a typical component of festivities during Corpus and the *Festa Major* in St Quintí, Vilafranca and the major towns of the Penedès and Tarragona.

A number of other Corpus rituals were also called in question. The diary of the Consell de Cent in 1604 informs us of a dance of the eagles of Corpus inside Barcelona cathedral: 'the eagle went up to the altar and danced with the musicians before it, and then it came down to wait for the viceroy, and when he arrived it returned to the altar and danced.'[137] A similar dance had been banned in

Gerona cathedral since 1575, but in Barcelona the practice seems to have continued until 1753 when the bishop prohibited it. In 1723 the vicar-general of Solsona protested to the vicar of Berga, whose Corpus celebrations would become famous as the 'Patum', that during the proceedings the giants and devils ran in and out of the church, letting off firecrackers inside and filling the place with smoke.[138]

The limited success of the Church in controlling the content of Corpus celebrations was balanced by an apparently successful attempt to give the people sacred entertainment. Dramatic performances had been a regular part of most fifteenth-century Corpus celebrations in Spain, but from the early sixteenth century there are clear signs of the creation of *autos* or dramatised allegories written specifically to honour the Eucharist, and in the second half of the century an enormous number were written, with a highpoint of production in the autos of Calderón in the seventeenth century.[139] The encouragement of an officially approved theatre, however, went hand in hand with the suppression of late mediaeval sacred plays, principally because the old plays had a relatively fixed text which could not be modified to the new orthodoxy and therefore had to be scrapped. In Gerona there had been bans on such traditional Easter-week performances as 'Les Tres Maries' and 'La Magdalena' since 1538, but the bans were ignored and in 1560 we still find the cathedral giving permission for the performance of 'La Magdalena'. The tendency to ban gathered force, and the plays slowly disappeared. In 1684 the bishop of Gerona added the traditional Christmas play of 'Els Pastorets' ('The Shepherds') to the ban;[140] fortunately, the play still remains as the most popular Nativity performance for Catalan children. It is likely that Christmas plays ceased to be performed in churches, for we find in 1669 a firmly worded ban from the bishop of Barcelona, citing the 'fights, commotion and uproar arising from the performances which are habitual in some parishes and churches of this our diocese, in particular on Christmas night, and Thursday and Friday of Holy Week, because of the multitude of people who come to see the performances'; penalties for infringements of the ban 'will be rigorously carried out'.[141]

A late development in the campaign against uncontrolled spectacles, and often taken, rightly or wrongly, as typical of the spirit of the Counter Reformation in Spain, was the campaign against comedies and the theatre, in which the Jesuits came to play a leading role. The campaign gathered force in Castile at the end of the sixteenth century, precisely when Lope de Vega was popularising the theatre, and initiated a long series of condemnations by some Church authorities.[142] In Catalonia the Jesuit Joan Ferrer in 1618 joined in the attack[143] and the bishops decreed various restrictions. Since the beginning of their ministry in Barcelona the Jesuits had offered a sacred theatre as an alternative to the profane attractions of the city, and continued to employ different types of dramatic entertainment,[144] but also took offence when other clergy offered their versions of the theatre. In 1634 a zealous Jesuit went so far as to denounce the Inquisition itself for permitting plays to be performed on its premises. According to the Jesuit, Jeroni Vidal,

> Inquisitor Otero has introduced into his residence which is inside the palace of the Holy Inquisition the practice of putting on secular comedies from nine to twelve o'clock, as well as soirées, and this has continued all this year and there have been many complaints in the city.
>
> One consequence of this was what happened on the day of St Peter Martyr in the church of St Dominic, to the scandal of the whole city. The inquisitors asked to be allowed to put on a comedy on the saint's night in the church of those fathers, and when they received permission they began the performance, which was all about love affairs, between eight and nine o'clock. The Holy Office was present in a public and official way. The plot was about a woman who was always in love, and the comedy lasted until half past eleven. A lot of people came, with an infinite number of men and women there at night mixing promiscuously.[145]

In defence of themselves the inquisitors pointed out that 'in this city the custom is for actors who come there to ask for permission to perform from the tribunal, and they usually put on a play if the tribunal asks them to. And in the last year three companies have come, and they have put on three comedies.'[146]

This role of the tribunal in comedies had been true since at least 1620, when the inquisitors stated that 'when companies of actors arrive, before performing they ask the tribunal for permission and do not put on plays until they have been censored by a censor.'[147]

The purification of rites by the post-Tridentine clergy was not limited to great festivities and their exceptional celebrations. Through the generations popular custom in Catalonia had embroidered the liturgy with pieties and frivolities which the reformers now rejected as alien. Many parish clergy saw little to criticise in the folk practices, but their superiors had other ideas. One of the small battles of the period involved the use of rose-water in ceremonies. Belief in the properties of rose-water had old folk origins, and the belief later merged with the development of devotion to the Rosary. At least from the mid-fourteenth century,[148] rose-water was kept by confraternities in a special glass bottle (known as an *aiguarrós*) for use in church, at public dances and celebrations; in the confraternity of the Rosary at Vilafranca del Penedès, special officials were appointed to guard the aiguarrós. Among the people rose-water was widely used as a universal cure for all types of illness and even as an aid in childbirth.[149] In 1484 it was distributed during mass to the leading officials of the city in the ceremonies preceding Corpus Christi in Gerona; they were given bunches of dried flowers and rose-water with which to add perfume. The bishops however looked with disfavour on any secular water competing with the official holy water of the Church, and from the late sixteenth century there were firm attempts to ban its use in Catalonia. In the 1590s in Gerona bishop Jaume Cassador banned any further use 'in churches of the distribution of flowers and rose-water', but the ban was difficult to enforce, and the custom of using rose-water was still alive in 1622[150] and no doubt much later. Barcelona had the same problem: during the diocesan synod of March 1575 clergy favouring its use petitioned that 'permission be given to the churches to bring in players with tambourines and horns to play at the time of the offertory, and to give rose-water to those who are attending, since it is scandalous that some parishes do it while others cannot'; but the bishop ordered 'that rose-water not be given nor players and tambourines be allowed in at the offertory'.[151] It was difficult to enforce these rulings. In April 1597 the bishop of Barcelona ordered the parish priests of La Llacuna and Miralles, the parishes neighbouring Mediona,

> that in future they not allow certain improper things in their churches
> ... That in future they not permit or allow in their parish churches at
> Christmas or on other feast days of the year, performances of 'kings'
> nor dances and other performances, nor must rose-water be given at the
> offertory; and they must make sure that neither in Lent nor at any other
> time are songs composed known as *cantarelles*, for all these things are
> prohibited by the sacred canons and constitutions of the province of
> Tarragona, under grave penalties and censures.

The order, covering the major feasts of the year, was clearly made only after long experience of the contraventions; but threats were fruitless, for two years later, in December 1599, the injunction had to be repeated.[152]

Some other traditional rites were frowned upon because they offended against decency and decorum. At Lérida in the early sixteenth century the cathedral at Pentecost had a ceremony of '*la Colometa*', a dove descending, during which fireworks were let off inside the building; the nuisance compelled bishop Antonio Agustín in the 1570s to discontinue the custom.[153] In 1580 the bishop of Vic had to resort to the authority of a papal bull to suspend in his diocese the practice by which on the feast of the Purification the celebrant blessed candles and then threw them into the congregation, provoking a wholly unbecoming scramble, fights and casualties.[154] The custom continued nevertheless in Catalan parishes, and in 1608 the bishop of Barcelona also had to forbid that 'on the day of the Purification of the Virgin the curates throw blessed candles, which should instead be distributed and handed out.'[155]

The participation of the whole community in festivities could be seen most typically in dancing: everyone – adults, children, even the clergy – danced to songs and music in celebration of the great days of the Church. In the scattered communities of late mediaeval Europe, music and dance was the normal accompaniment to both secular and religious celebration. The fourteenth-century Catalan writer Eiximenis in his *Book of Ladies* (1396) reflected the common acceptance of dance when he presented to his readers a Christian paradise where all was 'games, songs, dances and laughter', and where 'when they sing of love then everybody leaps and jumps, like flames of fire.' Eiximenis may have drawn on his experience of the celebrations of Corpus in Catalonia, but dancing was common to all feasts, secular and sacred. Since the early Christian fathers, dance had been accepted in the Mediterranean lands as a form of sacred joy, and in Spain community practices had combined with religious usage to encourage the emergence of various types of dance during processions and festivals. As early as the seventh century St Isidore of Seville had condemned Carnival dances which combined men and women, where men dressed as women; and a mediaeval Spanish hymn to the Virgin described her as dancing in heaven.[156]

Religious dance did not necessarily take the same form as popular dance. The latter, more energetic, rhythmic and free, has been classified as 'high' dance, in contrast to 'low' dance, which used more ordered rhythms and sedate movements and by the sixteenth century was becoming more typical of the dance used by the upper classes in their celebrations.[157] The difference between the two might be minimal, for they influenced each other: 'popular songs and their melodies were used by the clergy to compose liturgical hymns, and popular dances offered them a choreographic format on which to organise religious dances.'[158] Music, movement and popular melody could all be used for religious purposes. Not only the people, therefore, but the clergy as well made use of dance, citing the well-known image of David dancing before the Ark of the Covenant. In the cathedral of Mallorca in 1392 the priests danced before the altars,[159] and innumerable examples from all over Spain show the persistence of a dancing clergy well into the seventeenth century. A regular custom common in the Catalan lands was for clergy saying their first mass to invite their families to it and to dance during the celebration of the mass. A Valencian writer of 1571 reproved 'the bad custom that some clergy have, or had, of dancing on the day of their first mass',[160] and the bishop of Barcelona in 1598 repeated previous orders that clergy 'not dance at their first mass or at any other time'.[161] The saints themselves, and in particular the Virgin, were invited to join in liturgical dancing, as surviving practices show: in Atienza on Pentecost Sunday the members of the confraternity of the Virgin visit the altar of the Virgin of the Star, their patron, and 'dance with the Virgin', each member in his turn.[162] An earlier generation of clergy, aware of the value of popular dancing to neophytes to Christianity, was willing to tolerate it, and archbishop Talavera in Granada allowed Moorish dances to be performed in the Corpus Christi procession.[163]

The new reforming spirit was hostile to all dancing which mingled secular and sacred, notably any dancing within the church building, or which permitted men and women any bodily contact. All dancing is bad, Francisco Ortiz Lucio had concluded in his *Compendium of all the Summas* (1598), 'save for women with women and men with men', with the exception, noted by other writers, that husbands could dance with wives and sisters with brothers.[164] The dictum had important consequences for it threatened the existence of all traditional secular dances of courtship and those dances that required a couple. When Pedro de León was in the area of Aracena, near Seville, in 1614, he observed that 'there was in this and other villages a very bad custom: on days of fiesta the unmarried men and women of the villages would go to the square and all would dance together, men with women; and although the people are healthy there is always the possibility of a maggot which rots the fruit; so we stamped firmly on the practice in all the villages.'[165] Diego Pérez in Barcelona in 1588 attacked dancing and commented sardonically that 'even the prudent gentiles condemn dancing, a practice the devil taught to men.'[166] Another work published in Barcelona[167] advanced the curious argument that 'our present life is a continuous run to death. Who ever heard of running to death dancing?' There were, inevitably, more liberal opinions, and Marco Antonio de Camos, a contemporary of Pérez in Barcelona, was willing to allow secular dancing.[168]

Liturgical dances tended to take place in the church building, where dancing of various types seems to have been common during the major feasts of the year, such as Carnival, Corpus and Christmas. The dances in church appear to have been of two types: popular participation in rites (such as a case, cited from 1544,[169] of the New Year's day mass in Rouen when the congregation danced through the church, often throwing off their clothes), and ritual homage to saints; the former were very firmly expelled from the church, the latter were modified and in most cases also expelled from the building, though some were officially allowed to survive. As early as 1543 Bernal Díaz de Luco warned that the parish priest 'must not allow in his church (even if it be for the joy of some major feast) dances, immodest farces, or the singing of ballads and profane songs'.[170] The provincial council of Valencia in February 1566 denounced 'some who think mistakenly that they do honour to the saints by dancing before the altars'.[171] In 1575, when bishop Tocco of Gerona made a compromise with the city council over the celebration of Corpus he was nevertheless adamant on some points: there would be no 'letting off fireworks' inside the cathedral, and 'in no way and at no time will we allow dancing in the church.'[172] The attempt to eradicate dancing and rite inversion in processions was continuous and seldom successful: as late as 1644 the diocesan synod of Segorbe denounced dancing in processions.[173] Perhaps the most detailed denunciation of a dancing clergy was that published by the Franciscan Juan de Dueñas at Toledo in 1583.[174] His view, as virulent as it is informative, was that

> those who are dedicated to God should not be present at the vain spectacles of this world. What can we say of some priests and religious who when they sing their first mass perform great dances and games in the churches and monasteries; who also dress in strange clothes, wear masks, and go to jousts and other inappropriate games, for which some dress themselves as women, others as shepherds, others as nobles? And what is worst of all is that he who is most dissolute and profane in these activities thinks that he is the most successful. They also perform profane farces, sing lewd songs, alien to all decency and purity, all of which is banned and prohibited and most specially condemned in ecclesiastical persons.

A rather more balanced judgment may be found in the widely used seventeenth-century authority Noydens, who ruled that 'it is not prudent to forbid peasants to dance on days of fiesta,' since they might find worse entertainments; and that although it was sinful for clergy to dance in public there was no sin 'in dancing privately among themselves, as they do in some religious communities', an intriguing glimpse into convent life.[175] The celebrated Jesuit Juan de Mariana in 1609 stated that 'these shameful customs have penetrated temples consecrated to God and have been absorbed into divine worship.' Speaking of the Corpus celebrations in Madrid, 'we know that in this very city on this feast-day in various nunneries they have music and dancing and of such a vile nature that it is necessary to cover one's eyes.'[176]

Though individual clergy could be rigorously opposed to dance, the Church authorities were in principle more liberal and were concerned simply to exclude it from religious premises. The provincial councils of both Tarragona and Valencia in 1565 decreed an end to the Corpus custom of dancing before the Sacrament or before church altars. In Mallorca, consequently, the dance of St Joan Pelós was in 1573 banned by the bishop. With what success, we may judge by the manual of ceremonies of the cathedral two centuries later in 1750, which says that 'St Joan Pelós may dance a while before the Sacrament, but most chastely'; chaste it may have been, but a clear infringement of repeated decrees. By the same token, despite criticism from high quarters Mallorcan dances such as the dance of the *cavallets*, or that of the *cossiers*, both derived from fifteenth-century Catalonia but in use on the island since the early sixteenth, prospered in the seventeenth century and have survived into modern times.[177] Elsewhere in Spain some dances survived, such as the Dance of the Seises in Seville cathedral, known there since before the fifteenth century and reformed into a more acceptable version during the seventeenth.

Constant bans inevitably took their toll, and religious dancing, with or without clergy, slowly faded from popular usage; but it would be unwise to imagine that there was any effective 'repression'. Some writers have viewed the decree of Charles III in 1777, which uncompromisingly banned all religious dancing throughout Spain, as the death-knell of the practice; yet the decree was ignored openly just after its issue – in Barcelona the vicar-general protested at the continuation of dancing in Sarrià and other parishes of the diocese[178] – and can be regarded as virtually a dead letter.

One of the targets of the attack on mixing secular and sacred was the *sardana*, a dance formalised only in the nineteenth century and by no means, despite a widespread belief to the contrary, either preponderant or typical among the Catalan people. Mythologised in modern times as the 'national' dance of Catalonia, for most of Catalan history it was simply one among many dances, danced in different ways in different parts of the Catalan lands. In its several forms it earned distinction for being regularly denounced by clergy (the bishop of Gerona in 1573 prohibited the use in churches of 'immodest songs and dancing of sardanas', and a synod in Vic in

1596 banned the use of the music).[179] Where town councils joined the attack (Olot in 1552 prohibited 'the dancing of the sardana and other indecent dances', and half a century later Igualada in 1610 ruled that 'sardanas may not hereafter be danced in the square because they are indecent') we may also suspect the intervention of the clergy.[180] It is no surprise to discover that a century or more after such bans, the sardana, perhaps in a more discreet form, was still being used within churches. In a fly-sheet of verses produced by Rafael Pastor in 1602, the short and nimble rhymes on a religious theme had to be danced and sung to its rhythm; though the poem began with the ironic call

Dexem estar la sardana	Let us leave the sardana
perques cosa molt profana	because it is most profane
y cantem de bona gana,	and let us sing instead,

the whole piece was in fact a religious sardana.[181] The dance continued to be an integral part of community celebrations, as shown by verses written for the 1616 carnival in Barcelona:

Molts dels que dancen	Many who dance
sens que no cancen	and do not tire
ab gentil ayre	gracefully
saltant en lo ayre	leaping in the air
com bolatins,	like balls
los matutxins	dance the
fan, y altres balls	*matutxins*, and other dances
portant plomalls	wearing plumed caps,
gorres de grana	caps of red,
fent la sardana	doing the sardana
y lo ball pla	and the slow dance
tots ma per ma	hand in hand
altres ab bandes	others with fine
fines de Flandes	belts from Flanders
y molt bisarres	and many trinkets
sonant guitarres.[182]	and playing guitars.

In the end, liturgical dancing was driven into the street, where it continued to thrive in processions and similar festivities. By contrast virtually no impact seems to have been made on secular and community dancing, in which the Church could not usually interfere though it disapproved and tried to make sure it would not taint sacred premises: the Barcelona synod of 1629 decreed that 'rectors are not to permit dancing within twenty paces of the church and should call for the help of the king's officials to enforce this.'[183] The sardana, in the form given to it in the nineteenth century by middle-class folklorists, evolved into a delicate but wholly chaste dance immediately acceptable to Catholic moralists, and was seen by Joan Maragall as the quintessence of the Catalan spirit.[184]

Clergy continued to dance. Bishop Miguel Santos of Solsona in 1624 stated that 'we are informed that some ecclesiastical persons on feast-days and celebrations and weddings and in carnival dance with women and wear masks and go publicly to dances.' The Barcelona diocesan synod in 1669 found it necessary to repeat that 'no ecclesiastic may dance or sing indecent and profane things at weddings, first masses or at any other festivity or *aplec*, nor play musical instruments for others to dance, nor go in costume during carnival.' The diocesan synod of Solsona in 1641 was seriously concerned that at 'gatherings in memory of the dead (known commonly as *cantars*) many abuses are committed',[185] among them the fact that the clergy danced at the funeral celebrations. In the diocesan synod of Urgell in 1689 complaints were made of clergy who 'dance publicly on days of the Rosary and other days of festivity and aplec, not only in private houses but also in public places'.[186]

Mediaeval practice had encouraged pilgrimages because they universalised the piety of Christian people, but the Counter Reformation (in common with mediaeval critics) frowned on them because they gave rise to superstitions and represented administrative disorder. All pilgrimages may be seen as potentially subversive of institutional religion,[187] since they contained elements of freedom of movement and worship that put them beyond official control. By the fifteenth century, the great international centres of pilgrimage were in decay, but the problem remained a real one, and at a local level the post-Tridentine Church reiterated mediaeval restrictions on uncontrolled visits to shrines. However, in a society such as the Spanish which offered considerable world horizons, there was a constant movement of population which made it difficult to tie people down.[188]

Traditionally, pilgrimages had taken place because of a search for miracles or in order to fulfil a penance (both Church and secular courts in the Middle Ages regularly imposed the penitential pilgrimage as a punishment). The late mediaeval emphasis on atonement for sins and the development of the concept of Purgatory tended to place further emphasis on the penitential system[189] and on spiritual relief through contact with relics, shrines and pilgrimages. This pre-Reformation system was carried through unchanged into early modern Spain, but with a significant difference that seems to distinguish the warm Mediterranean from the cold north of Europe. Pilgrimages in Catalonia were based on supplication and expiation, but the haunting presence of the purgatorial dead which permeated northern religion, as in Bavaria where the dead souls (*Armeseelen*) wandered up at night in the form of toads,[190] was less visible in the south. Penance in Catalonia seems to have been done primarily for the living. The cult of indulgences, a by-product of the doctrine of Purgatory, was active but not effusive, and criticisms of it can be found sporadically in the prosecutions brought by the Inquisition. The shrine at Montserrat was the principal focus of penitential pilgrimage in the Catalan lands and in Occitania, though Catalans themselves on occasion went elsewhere during an emergency: in times of plague it seems to have been traditional in both Barcelona and Perpinyà to send a special intercessory mission to the shrine of St James at Compostela: Barcelona is on record as doing it in 1476 and Perpinyà in 1589.[191]

Emphasis was placed on two functions of the shrine at Montserrat: to promote the sacrament of penance, and to elevate the cult of Mary. The heights of the holy mountain became a laundry for the sins of the living. A resident French monk, Mateo Oliver, recorded that 'in the year 1624 from the first of January to the last day of December I confessed 5552 French and Flemings and others of French speech.' His information is not reliable proof of long-distance pilgrimage (France was nearby, and many Flemings may simply have been soldiers serving the Spanish crown), but it is undeniably impressive to learn from him that 'on some feast-days in one single day 9715 persons have come and all have been given bread and wine and the rest.'[192] In that same year, he records, a total of 3829 clergy (of whom 2349 were secular and the rest religious) visited the shrine. We know that in old Catholic Europe a visit to a shrine was a regular way of expiating sins, and in fifteenth-century Belgium the pilgrimage was the most common sentence handed down by lower courts.[193] Similarly, the most common regular punishment handed out by the Inquisition of Barcelona in this period was its injunction to the accused – normally those with lesser offences such as swearing – that 'they go to Montserrat'.

Second only to Montserrat in Catalan devotion came the shrine of Our Lady of Núria, on a mountain height commanding 'seven valleys' leading from Ripoll to Cerdanya. Originating in the transhumance piety of the eleventh century, Núria enjoyed a widespread devotion throughout subsequent centuries and flourished during early modern times, so that the shrine had to be rebuilt in 1639.[194] Its seventeenth-century historian recorded only two miracles in the later sixteenth century, but eleven in the period 1600–6 and fifty-six between 1646 and 1666, suggesting a popularity that increased in the course of the Counter Reformation.

Primarily a summer shrine because of its location, Núria catered for pilgrims from every corner of the Catalan lands.

Even shrines such as Montserrat, watched over by clergy, were not exempt from the abuses provoked by the coming together of thousands of visitors, male and female. We have seen that in 1629 the synod of Barcelona commented on 'the problems resulting from processions that go to shrines far from the village or those that go to Montserrat', and decided that 'no processions be made unless they return the same day'.[195] The requirement had been in force since Trent and could be found also in mediaeval decrees, so that its constant repetition (for example, in a Barcelona synod of 1634) was testimony to the failure of the authorities to check pilgrimages at a local level. Episcopal decrees were directed against all freewheeling religion in the shape of vigils and *romerias*, inter-parish pilgrimages, and overnight pilgrimages to shrines. Diego Pérez, whose writings were addressed specifically to the situation within the diocese of Barcelona, upbraided those who

> in the guise of pilgrims wish to spend money and enjoy themselves and see the world and take their bad company with them. Those who wish to lead lives of doubtful character have found a way of living which suits them very well, and that is to become pilgrims and go on pilgrimage ... I am particularly concerned that young women become pilgrims for a whim and without any godly intention.

Criticising many who go dressed 'like nightmares, dressed in loose garb and crazy clothes and ragged clothing so that they look like actors', Pérez suggested that all intending pilgrims in the diocese should be licensed by the bishop before being allowed to go. Emphasising that a pilgrimage was not 'going on an outing or excursion, nor to relax, but to honour God', he pointed out that right preparation of fasting and communion must be made, and that because of the dangers to chastity involved pilgrimaging was not for 'young women, maidens or widows, but for married women of a good age who go with their husbands, or for unmarried women of a good age who go safely accompanied'. For many people, 'it is better not to go on pilgrimage and they would be safer in their homes, there quietly praying to Our Lady or to the saint whose shrine they wish to visit.' In conclusion, he lamented 'how different the pilgrimages now are from what good Christians used to make and still make, and this is to be seen not only in long-distance pilgrimages but even in short ones of a league and half a league.'[196]

It seems that all the authority of the Church was unable to prevail against popular practice, for in 1683 the synod in Barcelona complained (as we have seen) of 'the abuse whereby villages make annual processions "extra propriam parrochiam", and when they arrive ... dedicate themselves more to buying and selling, eating and drinking, than to divine worship'.[197] In the same decade the synod of Urgell in 1689 had to prohibit 'all processions made far away from the village or parish and that cannot return the same day to their houses; nor may food and drink be taken and the people must return and eat and drink in their houses'.[198]

A prime example of the problems that could arise can be seen in the Perdó of Marcevol.[199] Marcevol was a tiny village on the river Tet, six kilometres from Vinça in Rosselló. In the fourteenth century it benefited from an indulgence (or pardon, *perdó*) applicable to those who visited its church, Santa Maria de las Gradas, on 3 May, feast of the Holy Cross, in every year that the feast fell on a Friday. On the eve of that day the clergy at Vinça, who administered the church at Marcevol, would organise a big procession made up from all the surrounding communities to the shrine of Our Lady of las Gradas. The pilgrimage, with an overnight rest, followed difficult, winding mountainous routes to the shrine, where mass was said and an aplec held, after which the whole body of people wended its way back to Vinça and thence home. All the abuses of an overnight outing of thousands of people inevitably appeared, and in 1617 the tensions between participating French and Catalans broke out in bloodshed, a recurring problem to judge by the reference in 1627 to the 'passions aroused in the last Perdó' between the two nationalities. Despite everything, the Perdó endured down to the Revolution.

Constant admonitions by the bishop failed to put a stop to practices which were central to the functioning of life among the rural communities, and the accumulated evidence of the completely new genre of ex-votos[200] – gifts, wood-carvings, sometimes little paintings left behind at shrines as thanksgiving for answered prayers – proves that local pilgrimages never decayed. Throughout late mediaeval Spain, it had been common practice to use the regular visits to local shrines as an organised outing for the entire village, with several parishes sometimes combining their efforts. Pérez may have been concerned that the trekkers enjoy 'the streams and fountains, the flowers and trees, the sky, the clouds, the birds',[201] as testimony to the beauty of God's nature, but to the parishioners these things were, as they still remain, part of the pleasure of wandering through an exotic environment freely in the company of those one did not meet during the daily routine. It was this freedom, enjoyed under cover of devotion, that the clergy wished to curtail. There is no doubt that the prohibitions were new, a product of the Counter Reformation. Pérez explained carefully that 'many things are good in themselves but must change as times change': into this category fell *velas* or vigils, roundly condemned in this period. Customs 'which are not so important and which moreover are misused should sometimes be changed by the Church', and as a result the Church in recent practice banned night vigils, holding them instead by day, and introduced fast days to replace vigils: 'today, and for same time now, vigils are not practised by laymen and their place has been taken by fasts.' In fact, vigils were far from finished and Pérez knew it, for he stressed the preference of the Church 'that laymen should not go as they once did to night vigils in the churches, least of all in the countryside, where there is no one to control them and they respect nobody, and where men and women meet with so many dangers and opportunities of sin'. He cited moreover two whole pages of early Church fathers against the practice, 'so that nobody should think I got this out of my own head'. He also condemned 'the *cirios* that often accompany vigils', *cirios* being large candles carried in a popular procession in which the religious element was all but forgotten, so that 'they never hear a sermon, and seldom a mass, and they go with entertainers and then return home to eat, drink deep and dance.'[202]

Considerable difficulty was experienced, in a pre-industrial Spain which had no strict division between labour and leisure, in enforcing holy days of obligation as days of rest. As we have seen, from one-third to one-half of the days in the year were holidays, and once the duty of attending mass had been fulfilled many saw no harm in continuing secular duties, even on holidays. This indeed had been normal practice, the provincial council of Seville in 1512 specifying for instance that the ban on work applied to the period of mass alone.[203] Later opinion tended to favour a complete ban on work during feast-days. In April 1600 the bishop of Barcelona complained that 'some fail to observe Sundays and days of obligation, labouring, digging, sowing and doing other similar servile duties',[204] and ordered that on days of obligation traders should not keep their shops completely open, nor put stands outside; but only seven months later in November he was obliged to return to the problem of the 'great abuse among workers, shopkeepers and artisans ... keeping their shops open and causing scandal in the city', and imposed a fine of £5 for any future infringements. The scant attention paid to Church discipline is proved by bishop Rovirola issuing exactly the same order in August 1604.[205] It was recognised that some functions needed to be carried on regularly, but in 1610 the bishop of Barcelona commented on 'the abuses committed in granting to workers a licence to work on days of rest'.[206] In the synod of Urgell that year the clergy observed that 'on Sundays and holydays of obligation the people work publicly and violate the feast-days.'[207] In 1641 the bishop of Solsona stated that 'we are informed that the feasts ordered by the Church are not observed.'[208]

In Rosselló the bishop of Elna faced exactly the same problem, and the visitors' book of the small parish of Escaro in Conflent shows the efforts made by authority.[209] The diocesan visitor here in 1620 criticised the 'bad custom of parishioners' in working on feast-days, and banned labour on all feast-days and Sundays. In 1629 the visitor, canon Rafel Llobet, came armed with a detailed exposition by the bishop, drawn up clearly in the light of experience of 'the intolerable abuses introduced into this our diocese against the due observance of the holy feasts'. The statement took care to spell out even to the most ignorant peasant what was deemed to be a violation of the feast-day: 'on Sundays and holydays of obligation (which must be observed for the full span of twenty-four hours continuously from the midnight preceding the feast-day to the midnight following) one must not sell nor buy except what is essential for life that day'; and specified that shops could not sell, bakers could not bake, millers could not grind, barbers could not shave clients, smiths could not shoe, carters could not transport, and tailors could not sew.

The struggle was to establish a division between secular and religious[210] time, and by no means implied that the population was eager to work at all times or that the Church was opposed to work. As in nineteenth-century England, the clergy played a crucial role in educating the working man to understand the clear difference between work and leisure. Certainly part of the problem in the sixteenth century was the inability or reluctance of labourers to create a firm division between the two, with the result, criticised by commentators everywhere,[211] that they introduced leisure into their work and work into their leisure, in a pattern common to all pre-industrial societies. As late as 1673 a missionary was condemning 'an error widespread in many parts of Andalusia', whereby at peak seasons farm workers contracted to work straight through feast-days, and went to mass only once a fortnight.[212] In Catalonia the problem seemed insoluble; workers in many parishes both failed to attend mass and also worked on feast-days, inflexibly separating their conduct from that dictated by the Church. Throughout the Llobregat area, in Llinàs, St Feliu and other parishes, the diocesan visitor in 1757 found that working on days of precept was an ineradicable practice; and in Sant Boi he denounced 'the intolerable abuse of working on feast-days without licence from the rector, and that in contempt of the sacred ritual of the Church, dances and public gaming are carried on during divine service'.[213] In Pobla de Claramunt, neighbour to Mediona, he found 'widespread in the parish' the custom of working on feast-days.[214]

Aware of the insistence of the Church on religious observance, historians have too readily assumed that in Spain it fostered an anti-work ethic. This has generated facile and now discredited conclusions about 'decline' and economic incapacity in the Mediterranean. Quite apart from their determination to enforce the discipline of religious time, clergy in early modern Spain were divided among themselves over the proper exploitation of secular time. A respectable body of clerical opinion stressed firmly and consistently that work and profit, when directed to the common good, were desirable. Well before the famous memorial of Luis Ortíz to Philip II in 1558, in which the author pleaded that nobles should be trained in the productive arts, Bernal Díaz de Luco was urging parish priests to instil the work ethic in their flock, and tell them to labour

> each one according to his ability so that they may maintain themselves, and the women should be advised to be diligent with their hands at home for there are many honest ways of earning a living... And since there are some who cover up their laziness and inadequacy by saying that it is shameful for people of their rank to be working with their hands, they should be advised that what is really shameful is going begging to and bothering family and friends and giving satisfaction to their enemies.

At the same time, Díaz condemned

> a pestilence of the soul which the devil especially in these times has sown and cultivated, persuading the sons of noblemen that it is shameful and demeaning if they are poor to apply themselves to an honest trade; making them instead resort to theft and a dishonourable way of life, living always in a perpetual hatred of peace and justice... and eventually driving them in desperation to live off wars, where vices may be acquired free and hellish habits learned...[215]

The priest, in short, must tell parishioners that work is honourable and must stress 'that natural law obliges man to work, and this cannot be negated by the empty and foolish opinion of people or the human privileges of the nobility'.

Marco Antonio de Camos, prior of the Augustinians in Barcelona, cited the example of Florence as a model of industry: 'when I was in Florence all those who traded in silk and did business in it (as one can see by their main street, which is where the silk merchants live) were well-born and refined people, who in order not to be idle worked in that profession without thereby demeaning themselves'; from which he concluded 'that it is not the profession but its abuse that is normally condemned'.[216]

An entire treatise was dedicated to the topic by a professor of law at Salamanca, Gaspar Gutiérrez de los Rios. In his *General report on the position of the arts* (1600), dedicated to the duke of Lerma and written at a time of self-examination when others such as González de Cellorigo were also probing the reasons for Spain's backwardness, Gutiérrez praised work as the source of 'true and public nobility, and through it one may obtain honour and reputation', and suggested that failure to work was the cause of depopulation in Spain, unlike 'Flanders, Venice and other countries', where men work.[217] He should, perhaps, also have cited Catalonia, where friar Miquel Agustí in the same years preached the virtues of constant work on the land ('men were made to till the fields, not to build cities'), asserting not only that 'the labourer must not stop working for one second and if he loses a second he must lose it on some work' but also that the woman must be there before him at the task.[218]

The sixteenth century, which brought a moderate prosperity to the principality and enabled communities to invest in religious innovation, was accompanied by two serious negative developments which posed problems for the Christian conscience and threatened the security of social order: poverty in the streets and violence in the countryside.

The epoch of price revolution, demographic increase, social change and political crisis, contributed to greater polarisation between rich and poor.[219] In western Europe the increase in vagrancy during the sixteenth century was noted most acutely in the towns, where the authorities struggled to give adequate charitable relief and maintain social order. In Spain the problem was aggravated by a steady immigration of vagrants into the peninsula, attracted by the wealth allegedly pouring in from the New World. One of the earliest writers on the problem, the Franciscan fray Gabriel de Toro, in 1548 published a passionate defence of the poor and the need to allow begging, in which he underlined the contrast between 'rich churches and clergy' and 'the little that is spent on the poor and on charity'.[220] The clergy were soon caught up in the controversy over giving aid to the poor.[221]

Mediaeval poor relief had been organised in Barcelona through a charity known as the Pia Almoina, whose task was made easier with the foundation in 1401 of the Hospital of Holy Cross. In the fifteenth century the parishes in Barcelona were contributing through the *bací* or plate of the poor, whose income came largely from investments (*censals*) settled on the poor of the parish.[222] Catalonia was not exempt from the increase in poor and vagrants. In 1557 Despuig lamented 'the infinite number of poor beggars that there are today in Tortosa, because of the cruel and widespread hunger throughout most of Spain; they fill the streets and it is painful to see them, apart from another legion of local poor who quite simply die of hunger'; but the crunch of the complaint was over the failure of the bishop to give poor relief.[223] Diego Pérez at the turn of the century lamented the lot of the poor in Barcelona: 'Is it not true that we have poor? Do you not see that the Hospital has no rest home? Do you not see that for lack of places and beds the poor lie two by two, or three by three, in one bed? Do you not see that they leave the Hospital naked and discontented and hard times will bring them back?'[224]

From the beginning the reform movement in the Church was concerned to approach the problem of poverty constructively, and the important mid-century controversy in Castile between the views of Domingo de Soto, who supported the traditional tolerance of begging, and Juan de Medina, who supported the alternative of hospitalisation, was evidence of public concern over the issue.[225] It is interesting to note that Medina ended his career in Montserrat (where he died in 1572), but we have no record of his views on the situation in Catalonia. Throughout Spain a parallel system of outdoor relief (largely operated by confraternities) and of occasional hospitalisation continued to be the norm, with pressure from the 1540s for consolidation of small private hospitals into one central municipal hospital. After the reception of Trent in the peninsula in the 1560s, the whole administration of poor relief began to be overhauled, since the Council had ruled that 'pious works' fell within the jurisdiction of bishops, who made firm attempts to regulate the confraternities and hospitals in their dioceses. During the same period the social situation served to revitalise old charities, such as the fourteenth-century Orphans' Hospital, administered since 1554 by the bishop of Barcelona.[226]

Meanwhile a campaign to promote hospitals was carried out by the Catalan cleric Miquel Giginta, canon of Elna and son of a distinguished Perpinyà family, who published in Coimbra during a stay in Portugal his *Treatise on the Relief of the Poor* (1576), which he followed up in 1583 with *Chain of Gold* (Perpinyà), and in 1587 with *Watchtower of Charity* (Saragossa). Giginta's proposals, undoubtedly influenced by Italian models[227] and helped by powerful patronage in the shape of the president of the Royal Council

Antonio de Pazos and cardinal Quiroga of Toledo, converted this Catalan into possibly the most important poor-relief reformer of the period. In 1583 he visited Perpinyà, Tarragona and Barcelona in his attempts to create hospitals. It was in Barcelona that his talks with Diego Pérez found warm support from bishop Dimas Loris and the Consell de Cent, and as a result the Misericordia came into being in 1583. To rally support for the hospital, Dimas Loris arranged for the publication in 1586 of fray Cristóbal Moreno's *Clarity of the Simple*, in which the author criticised the rich for no longer giving adequately to charity and for wanting to spend their money on buying houses: 'not satisfied with one house they purchase another, and another vineyard on top of the other, and more fields on top of the others, in short they wish to get hold of everything and make themselves masters of everything... The result is that the rich are still consuming the poor and sucking their blood'.[228]

In Barcelona, the new Hospital of the Misericordia was financed largely by clerical charity, and in 1590, when licensing preachers to seek alms for it, bishop Dimas Loris observed that 'on occasion there have been over 560 poor' resident in it.[229] Periodic sweeps of the city were made in order to keep the streets clear of the indigent population.[230] Like all hospitals of the time, the Misericordia had a precarious existence, and fray Gaspar Salas wrote a tract in 1636 expressly to ask for alms from the city, the clergy and from testators. Condemning outdoor relief as wasteful and self-defeating – 'to give charity out of doors is more to deceive the world than to please God' – Salas stressed that the new administration of the hospital 'can last forever if the citizens prove to be givers of charity'. According to him, 'already the cities of Gerona and Vic are trying to gather up' the poor.[231] Little is known of rural poor relief, but there is no doubt that the only ongoing system in existence in Catalonia was that practised in each parish, where each church was enjoined to have a special collection (*bací*) for distribution to the poor.

In his instruction to preachers in 1609 the bishop of Barcelona asked them to preach against 'deadly hatreds, cruelties, revenges and homicides; denounce the robbery and thefts in Catalonia; dissuade people from helping robbers; and criticise the little fidelity and loyalty that there is between men in Catalonia'.[232] No wholly convincing explanation has been found for the upsurge of violence in early modern Catalonia, though historians have pointed to the recent civil wars, family rivalries and the inheritance system as possible contributory factors. Contemporary edicts by the viceroy and other authorities point unequivocally to the widespread keeping of small-arms as a primary stimulant to violence. In 1616, a royal official claimed that in the Vall d'Arán 'boys of fourteen to old men aged sixty' were 'carrying *pedrenyals*', 'resulting in twelve years in over forty-six deaths ... and feuds and dissensions';[233] but the criticism of weapons is not wholly convincing, since in practice it was the community of armed citizens that kept the peace, in the absence of any police force. The laws of Catalonia permitted arms but attempted to prohibit their unlawful use, a policy no more successful in that day than in ours. In the *Corts* of Monzón of 1587 a constitution was adopted specifically inviting all communities in Catalonia to arm themselves with arquebuses, but forbidding the use of small firearms, the intention being to arm the population for self-defence in case of the French wars spilling over the frontier, but to disarm them for private quarrels. The city of Perpinyà, which felt itself the most vulnerable, protested at this measure, which it claimed would disarm ordinary people;[234] and in 1589 the Council of Aragon also came out against the prohibition, arguing that it was 'best to allow them to keep pedrenyals proportionate to the number of arquebuses they have'.[235] The practical effect of the law was simply to sanction the keeping of arms, which were in the possession of every significant citizen in the towns[236] and every peasant farmer in the countryside.[237] It followed that the clergy throughout the province were armed, and continued so despite repeated attempts by the bishops to forbid the keeping of weapons.

In 1589 fray Joan de Jesús, provincial of the Discalced Carmelites in Catalonia, presented to the Madrid government a picture of a principality overrun by violence, and when 'preachers have condemned these things from the pulpit they have been warned to keep quiet or it would not go well with them'. The situation seemed so bad that it brought from him and a group of like-minded Catalans the first recorded invitation to the Castilian government to abolish the laws in Catalonia and introduce those of Castile:

> the land is so afflicted and oppressed that it seems to the communities that if it were to occur to Your Majesty to govern them with the laws of Castile they would breathe again and come back to life. This would perhaps be a good opportunity for Your Majesty to get rid of these laws and put this land in a reasonable state, and I say this because there is much need of it, unless one wishes to let enter the pestilence of heresy from France; and fear of this makes me hope that Your Majesty will undertake this task, which would be no small undertaking. Your Majesty will know best how to do it, and with more thought it will perhaps be easier than it seems. I send with this a memorial that some nobles of rank and good Christians, who share my wishes, have given me.[238]

Fortunately Philip II did not have the outlook of Olivares, and if he saw the letter he did not see fit to respond to it.

Because the Church claimed to represent the will of God, it often exercised a determining voice in questions of popular violence; but even the Church could do no more than take note of existing procedures, and in practice it was the will of the community that prevailed rather than the decisions of an external body.[239] Those wishing to solve disputes were always governed by set procedures, which formed a sort of unwritten law and normally justified themselves by appealing directly to God or to the opinion of the community; only if the procedures were violated could an action meet with general disapproval and be regarded as a clear crime. In feudal societies such as Catalonia there was a coexistence of two options: the 'legal', represented by the existence of royal or baronial courts and by a small body of published law, and the 'popular', represented by traditional procedures and by village opinion. The firmness of the Church against duels or challenges (*desafius*) illustrates one aspect of the problem. Private hostilities in mediaeval society were usually resolved at elite levels by the challenge or duel; in Catalonia by the later middle ages the full form of the challenge took the form of a *deseiximent*, in which one person declared in a formal letter to another that he would henceforth be considered a mortal enemy. The procedure, still common in the sixteenth century, usually provoked the flight of the recipient and the evolution of a pattern of clan vengeance that might continue for a long period, with hostilities perpetuating themselves through the violence system of banditry. The letter of challenge, or *cartell de desafiu*, was usually pinned up on the local church door, thus inviting the support of God and of the community. However neither the Church nor the local authorities were happy about private vengeances, and from 1413 the Constitutions of the province had prohibited cartells, one of 1503 forbade revenge against the family or friends of a man committing homicide, and another in 1537 forbade challenges on pain of death. The Council of Trent had been aware of the problems of private conflicts and outlawed the duel. Papal authority put its weight behind the campaign, and in 1577 the bishop of Barcelona issued a bull of Gregory XIII, dated February that year, in which the pope condemned

> those in the realms of Aragon and Valencia and the principality of Catalonia and counties of Rosselló and Cerdanya who have maintained their own private law, and through the evil custom that has persisted there for a long time have continued to claim that this is licit for them specially if they are nobles and wish to defend their honour.[240]

Alleged slights to 'honour', it was recognised, lay behind much of the violence, and the Church correspondingly tried to keep the traditional 'peace of God' by intervening in disputes over honour. In 1577 and 1591 the bishops of Barcelona threatened excommunication against defamers using 'secret writings placed in public places and commonly known as *pasquinades* or *libelles famosos*'; and in 1603 against those in Sabadell who threatened the 'honour and good name' of people by 'singing indecent songs by night and day' against them.[241]

The Church saw itself as the upholder of honour in the community, and attempted to stifle disputes and vendettas before they had a chance of tearing the community apart. A striking aspect of clerical intervention can be seen in the *actes de perdó* (acts of pardon) which some parish priests drew up during this period, and whose genesis is unclear. Records for the seventeenth century in the parish of St Vicenç of Sarrià speak for themselves.[242] As the result of a challenge in March 1635, 'Joan Jordà, *pagès* of Sarrià, laid low on his bed by a mortal wound from a shotgun fired by Joan Duro, likewise pagès of Sarrià, has requested me Joan Baptista Piguillem, priest and rector of Sarrià, and notary of the same, to declare that he pardons the said Duro, so that for this crime neither the secular justice nor any other may pursue and trouble him, even if on his side father or mother or other relative were to demand that the said Duro be punished.' Two witnesses were present at the swearing of the document, which the priest 'ut notarius' formalised; in this way it was hoped to cut directly through the knot of violence, removing from both justices and relatives any excuse for further provocations. Such documents are sad testimony to the constant low-level violence in rural society, with similar cases recorded in the same parish of 'injuries done to each other [by two women] in an argument and quarrel which the said two had had, exchanging defamatory words' (1645), 'some stab-wounds' (1646), 'blows with a stone and a stab-wound and gunshot wounds with loss of blood' (1648). Within small societies hatreds could last for ever without the intervention of a moral arbiter to impose a no doubt unwanted 'pardon'. The need for unequivocal language in the following pardon of May 1644 is easy to understand: 'Margarida Pérez, surviving widow of Domingo Pérez, for the love of God pardons Pere Blanquer the death which he with a gunshot gave to her son Domingo Pérez . . . and promises expressly that hereafter she will not seek nor cause to be sought justice, directly or indirectly, against the said Blanquer, and this is her oath.' Such documents, it is clear, applied only to strictly personal violence and quarrels, and not to criminal violence.

As the predominant moral force in society, the Church was inevitably caught up in the disorder of banditry, which plagued Catalan society from approximately the mid-sixteenth to the mid-seventeenth century.[243] The phenomenon was not exclusively Spanish in origin, since the open frontier encouraged French-based bands to invade Spanish territory, and in 1542 the resident military commander attributed the bulk of banditry in the region to Frenchmen – 'today in Catalonia there are over a thousand men who follow this life and none is Catalan, all are Gascons.'[244] In the very period that the provincial council of 1565 was meeting, the viceroy was pursuing a vigorous campaign against criminal violence in the countryside,[245] and in the spring of 1565 wrote to all the *veguers* informing them that 'most of the evils committed in this territory arise from the presence of many idle vagrants who prefer not to work.'[246] For the Church banditry presented two distinct problems: the infiltration of armed heretics from France, and the disruption of the civil community through violence. As the religious wars developed in France, the facility of movement across a completely open frontier where the mountains afforded ready shelter[247] brought heresy within the experience of Catalans. The more immediate threat within the principality was the collapse of civil order, which put at risk the whole system of ecclesiastical authority. The Catalan bishops issued numerous disciplinary decrees to tackle the crisis and tried to enforce communal peace agreements. Of the latter the most successful seems to have been the Union, attempted from the late sixteenth century, which put peacekeeping into the hands of voluntary levies from the local community.[248] The Union enjoyed the full support of the Church, the bishop of Barcelona in 1609 encouraging his preachers to 'inform the people of the benefits of the Union in Catalonia and how great a service to God, the king and the public good it would be to maintain and continue it'.[249] It was within the context of the Union that one of the heroes of the Catalan Counter Reformation, St Josep Calassanç, carried out his ministry as an official of the diocese of Urgell in the late 1580s, until his permanent departure for Italy in 1591.[250]

Despite itself the Church was drawn into the spiral of violence within the Catalan communities, thanks to its inevitable political role. A notorious case was that of the bishop of Vic, summarised inimitably by the diarist Pujades in 1602:

Saturday the sixteenth of November bishop don Francesch Robuster y Sala left Vic as a result of the troubles in that city between the said bishop and his canons: the clergy support the bishop and the city supports the canons. The *nyerros* support the canons and the *cadells* the bishop. On Friday when he was strolling outside the city three shots were fired at him from the walls. Because of this they put armed guards in his house, the palace is closed and there are over a hundred armed men guarding it. An interdict has been placed on the city and masses are not said. All the priests and canons go armed with two or three pistols . . . It has made a very bad impression in Catalonia.[251]

Forty years after the Council of Trent, the episode illustrates brilliantly the difficult conditions to be encountered in more than one diocese. Pujades made strong judgments of the bishop, whom he accused of direct implication in murder, and commented that 'the cause of it all is his greed; even when he was bishop of Elna he alienated many people by unjust fines and extortions, and he has done the same in Vic.'

Bandits provide interesting evidence of the nature of belief in rural society. Though some, such as Rocaguinarda, were looked upon as folk-heroes because they apparently respected religion and the churches, most were notoriously uncaring of the status of churches, altars and clergy. The Carmelite Joan de Jesús in 1590 cited cases that had occurred in the Pyrenees of those who 'fire arquebuses at the images of Christ at crossroads, mock the mass by standing beside the priest saying vile things to him, mistreat the statues of saints, kidnap clergy, steal from churches and so on'; actions which suggested such people might be heretics though he did not go so far as to say that they were.[252] Clergy were as subject as any others to the violence, and in 1591 the canons of Lérida complained that bandits controlled all the highways and 'we clergy do not dare stir out of our houses'.[253] 'In past years,' a witness testified to viceroy Alburquerque in 1616, 'near Vilafranca del Penedès the reverend bishop of Elna was robbed of his money and other baggage, and three or four months ago in the city of Tortosa a pistol was fired at the bishop through the windows of his palace'.[254] In 1615 the bishop of Vic, Andrés de San Jerónimo, reported that 'this week I have called together the rectors from around here; those from further away do not dare leave their villages, and others have come despite the danger . . . Because in their sermons and in the confessional they do their duty and condemn what is bad, they have been threatened with death and many rectors have left their posts because of this.'[255]

After 1616 banditry was brought under control, thanks in part to the brutal efficiency of viceroy Alburquerque: in the memory of the Jesuits of Barcelona, whose duty it was to accompany condemned bandits to the place of execution, 1616 was the year of mass hangings.[256] The Council of Aragon in 1622 received unanimous reports from throughout the province of the 'peace, tranquillity and safety in this area in the past four or five years' (Tallarn and Pallars), 'thieves punished and eliminated' (Tárrega), 'peace and calm' (Agramunt), 'peace and quiet' (Montblanc), 'many years during which there have been no robberies, no bandits and not a single murder' (Lluçanès), 'total peace and quiet' (Urgell, Vic).[257]

Despite the Church's attempt to conserve the sacred character of its personnel, buildings and property, it was unable to educate or to terrify the population into respecting its position, and sacrilege in varying degrees continued to occur not simply at the hands of bandits but also among the people. In July 1628 the viceroy (who happened to be also bishop of Solsona) wrote to the local officials in the Penedès about the 'robberies in the churches of St Pere de Riudebitlles, Sta Maria del Puig de Esparraguera and Sant Genis de Horta, taking monstrances, chalices, chrism flasks, money and other things of value, profaning and destroying totally the respect due to sacred things used in divine worship'.[258] The notable frequency of sacrilege in a confessional society invites reflection on the extent to which the people accepted the special status of the Church and its sacred symbols. Break-ins – such as that in the church at Bages (Elna) on a Sunday afternoon in 1574 when all the doors were smashed in[259] – and theft were frequent enough to excite the comment of diarists of the time, though only theft seems to have merited the attention of the civil courts.[260] In 1597 the rector of St Llorenç Savall reported to the vicar-general the theft from his church of all the cash, the plate, and drapery.[261] Among the prosecutions undertaken in the diocesan court in Barcelona in 1600 were several against clergy for stealing from their own churches, and one against a trader of the city for stealing silver from the seminary and putting it on the market.[262] Those bandits who sacked churches may have done so for religious reasons. A parish priest in Tortosa explained to the inquisitors in 1621 that the frequent theft of the Sacrament from churches was because many bandits believed that if they wore the sacred wafer round their neck 'their enemies could not hurt them',[263] and as a result bandits could be found who felt that wearing the wafer gave them immunity.

In 1615 Francesc Camprubi, chronicler of the Dominican convent of Santa Catarina in Barcelona, lamented the violence of the thieves – 'and I don't mean bandits, for these are finished, but thieves' – in society:

> The whole of Catalonia is in the grip of thieves, scum thieves worse than Turks and Moors, who kidnap priests and laymen and demand a large ransom to divide among themselves, a novel invention of the devil,

unheard-of, impious and tyrannical ... A judge of the Audiència has told me that there are three thousand such men in Catalonia today, enemies of the king and given to evil ... It is utterly shameful to see the thieves burning houses, clothes, crops, hay, harvests, woods, fields and fruits; capturing children or killing them if their parents do not give the ransom; seizing villages and towns, violating girls, kidnapping priests, rectors and rich men.[264]

The most common motive for violating sacred objects was simply theft. Jeroni Pujades gives details of a gang of professional thieves in Barcelona who over a period of two years, from 1628 to 1630, broke into and robbed several properties, including over twenty churches.[265]

The practice of challenges took on, at the level of the Barcelona street, the form of 'stonings' (*pedrades*), a custom common in many Spanish towns during feast-days and weekends, in which groups of young people in one district would challenge those of another to a battle of slings or catapults.[266] A municipal order of February 1456 in Barcelona that 'young men or other persons may not use slings or any other means to stone nor may they throw stones,'[267] suggests by its dating that the practice formed part of the winter Carnival. In Rosselló the *espedragades*, conducted by youth groups, provoked public authority to ban them.[268] In the sixteenth century the bishops of Barcelona were still energetically forbidding the game, although to little effect. In 1622 the vicar-general of bishop Sentis had the sad duty of conducting an enquiry into a pedrada which took place 'outside the Portal Nou' and 'between the Portal de Jonqueres and the Portal del Angel' as part of the celebrations on 25 July, feast of St James: a young man died in the fight, and as a result arrests were made.[269] The bishops were still condemning the practice in the eighteenth century and as late as 1814 a city police decree ordered 'that boys not go throwing stones in any part of the town'.

CHAPTER FIVE

The Inquisition

The times are such that one should think carefully before writing books.

Antonio de Araoz SJ, 1559

Among the travails suffered by this Inquisition and its officials are the contempt and scorn they face in public and in private.

Inquisitor Andrés Bravo, Barcelona 1632

Every surviving commentary by Spaniards on the sixteenth-century Inquisition mentions it with profound respect, and the Holy Office itself never doubted that it had a unique role to play. The Dominican prior Thomas Ramón, in a work published in Barcelona in 1619, reflected on the institution which was largely in the hands of his own order:

> What power is there like that of this holy tribunal? Non est potestas super terram, quae comparetur ei, it alone governs, disposes, annuls and orders as it wishes, and nobody dares say to it, Cur ista facis? All fear and reverence it, and with reason; and no one dares to say a word against or resist it.[1]

After nearly a century and a half of existence the Holy Office had become part of the established structure of power, but the image it projected conflicted openly, in certain parts of Spain at least, with its real loss of privilege. During its great days at the end of the fifteenth century it had secured its reputation as protector of the Faith by burning thousands of *conversos* at the stake, hounding possibly thousands more out of the country, and building up an organisation with unique privileges and an astonishing capacity to survive even when it had no reliable finances. Those days never recurred: Protestantism made only a glancing impact on the peninsula, heresy never became a serious internal problem, and persecution of the Moriscos declined after their expulsion in 1609. By the end of the sixteenth century the Holy Office was a shadow of its former self; and Thomas Ramón's attempt to present it as the terrible Leviathan was particularly ironic since Barcelona, where his book appeared, was where it enjoyed least power and respect. Why, when there seemed little further need for it, did the Inquisition survive?

Once founded, the institution took on a tenacious life of its own, built up personnel and influence, and despite bitter opposition to many of its actions no effective reasons for abolition were ever put forward by critics. Moreover its claim to be the sentinel of orthodoxy was passively accepted by every leading public figure, no doubt because it had judicial functions in certain spheres, particularly heresy, which no other tribunal could fulfil and none contested.

Philip II's dogged support of it, frequently viewed by historians as religious fanaticism, and his identification of the Inquisition's authority with his own, was in part based on the premise that any compromise would inevitably allow Rome to intervene in his realms. The Inquisition had good reason to be grateful to the Catholic King. Rome, above all in its pursuit of the Carranza case, obviously never accepted the king's point of view, and throughout the long years of tension between papacy and king the officials of the former made statements that should not be accepted at face value. 'The king and his ministers', nuncio Castagna reported to Rome in 1567 over the disputes in Catalonia, 'can exercise over the Catalans almost no authority save through the medium of the Inquisition ... they refuse stubbornly to listen to the Catalans and try to give the greatest possible authority to the Inquisition';[2] and in the same years the Venetian envoys were claiming that the Inquisition, not Philip II, ruled Spain.[3] There is no cause to contradict Castagna's view, since we know that the king felt deeply, and with reason, that the Inquisition could usefully block the entry of heresy through Catalonia; 'if there had been no Inquisition,' he said in a memorable phrase of this time, 'there would be many more heretics.'[4] The king nevertheless misjudged the scope offered for interference through the Inquisition; and Castagna and the Italians totally misunderstood the real situation in Catalonia, where the inquisitors in that year faced one of the most serious upheavals they were ever to undergo.

When the Castilian Inquisition was introduced into Catalonia in the 1480s, it was bitterly opposed by those who saw in it an instrument which king Ferdinand could use to advance royal initiative in the principality. There was no objection in principle, since a papal Inquisition was already in being and provoked no conflict with existing institutions. By the early sixteenth century the Holy Office was firmly implanted in Catalonia, with its seat in Barcelona, where thanks to the generosity of king Ferdinand it occupied the northern wing of the Royal Palace, with a door on to the street beside the cathedral; the upper floor was occupied by the Royal *Audiència*. From this centre the two or three inquisitors, aided by a handful of officials, exercised jurisdiction over the territory of all the Catalan bishoprics except those of Lérida and Tortosa (these were allotted to the Inquisitions of Aragon and Valencia respectively). The whole north-west corner of the principality, however, did not recognise the Holy Office. The Vall d'Arán was ruled over by the king of Spain but fell within the French bishopric of Comminges and was consequently outside inquisitorial jurisdiction: when a merchant in the valley in 1574 successfully claimed immunity from the Inquisition, the angry inquisitors intensified their campaign to have the Arán brought within the see of Urgell.[5] A *comisario* was sent to the valleys in September that year but escaped narrowly with his life and wrote back bitterly to Barcelona that

> I have been told and understand that they are all trouble-making drunkards and it is something we should think about, for I understand that in that territory they will not allow the Holy Office to enter in any way, and I have tried to find out the root reasons for this opposition and been told that they are known to be drunkards and spend all the day in the inn.[6]

Wine, it would appear, rather than heresy, was the basis of opposition to the Inquisition. Andorra posed similar problems, for though within the see of Urgell (whose bishop was its joint ruler together with the French count of Foix) it was independent of Spain. In its valleys, the inquisitors reported in 1542, 'live some five hundred people, all or most of whom speak the Catalan language', but 'it is not known whether the Holy Office has ever visited or exercised any jurisdiction there.'[7] In the north-east the county of Rosselló, subject in the earlier period to the archbishop of Narbonne, also raised continuous problems. In a principality where the variety of jurisdictions caused endless legal disputes, it is not surprising that the Inquisition spent most of its career trying to defend its political privileges.

As a court of justice, it had attracted criticism from its inception, since it was quite independent of the laws of the principality and answerable only to the crown. Conflict over its privileges and procedure was continuous, mainly over the day-to-day immunities claimed by the Holy Office and over precedence at public meetings. Throughout the 1480s and in the early sixteenth century there were unremitting clashes between the city of Barcelona and the Inquisition, with repeated protests to the crown against every aspect of the tribunal's activity, including the memorable statement to king Ferdinand in 1509 that confiscation of goods should be stopped because 'goods are not heretics'.[8] Half a century later the French civil wars shifted the attention of the government to the French frontier in Rosselló, and Philip II seems to have regarded the Inquisition as a major weapon in the defence against heresy; but the change did little more than move the centre of conflict to Perpinyà, where major conflicts arose in 1568 and in 1580. In the latter year the claim by an Inquisition official to immunity from taxes led to a severe clash with the *Diputats* of Catalonia.[9]

The Holy Office would have been powerless without a network of officials to help it, and it was over these – the *familiars* or voluntary lay helpers, and the *comisarios* or local clergy who collected information and acted as notaries – that most conflicts arose.[10] The first compromise made between the Catalans and the Inquisition was at the *Corts* of Monzón on 2 August 1512. This 'concordia' was taken as the basic position by the Corts in 1520 but the Corts of 1553 further ruled that no public official in Catalonia could become a familiar, because of the implicit clash between the two jurisdictions. In 1564, the year that the decrees of Trent were received in Spain, the Corts at Monzón accused the Inquisition of extending its jurisdiction and as a result of clashes the Madrid government appointed cardinal Espinosa to draw up in 1568 a concordia to regulate the matter. This offered a solution to the problem of the structure of the Inquisition and the number of its familiars but was not wholly agreeable to the Diputats, who also had other serious disputes of jurisdiction to complain about, leading the viceroy to report from Barcelona in 1569 that 'this land is more in revolt than ever and all its tribunals, the Consellers, the Diputats and the judicial officials, are determined to lose their lives, families and property'[11] rather than give in to the Inquisition. Finally at the 1585 Corts at Monzón the crown accepted 'that the familiars, officials and ministers of the Holy Office cannot be admitted to offices in private jurisdiction or in public administration'. The ruling had to be observed reluctantly by the Inquisition, which in 1609 outlined the sad consequences:

> In the bigger towns for a long time now people do not seek familiar-
> ships in order not to disqualify themselves from holding posts which
> interest them in those towns and which are more valued than familiar-
> ships. This has put an end to them in this city and there are now only
> fifteen familiars, none of any standing and all artisans; and in Gerona
> there is no familiar, in the Seu d'Urgell only one, in Tarragona two, in
> Montblanc only one and in the town of Cervera three, and in Tárrega

one; and so on in the big towns where there is none. One can well see from experience the notable prejudice caused to the Inquisition by the constitution that no familiar or official can hold office in the towns.[12]

The statement reflects a remarkable fall from the level which the tribunal possessed only nine years before,[13] when Barcelona had nineteen familiars, Gerona nine, and Tarragona four. By 1631 the inquisitors were complaining from Barcelona that 'there are at present in this city only six familiars'; and in 1634 they informed that 'in this city there are only three familiars, of whom two are poor and ordinary persons, because nobody wants to be a familiar so as not to be deprived of offices in the city and realm'.[14] The same phenomenon of decline can be observed elsewhere in the peninsula, but that was in part provoked by the rapid fall in population levels of the early century. In Catalonia there was no population crisis, and if familiars declined it was simply because, as the Inquisition itself maintained, the post was not seen as desirable. It is interesting to observe, however, that though the rule was observed in parts of the province subject to the jurisdiction of the Diputació and the Consellers, in other parts of Catalonia familiars (according to a report by the Inquisition in 1628) occasionally seem to have held office.[15] This did not affect areas of the principality where even by the early seventeenth century the Holy Office had failed to penetrate. In 1622 the inquisitors reported that in the Vall d'Arán 'no one wants to be a familiar even though we go to their houses and beg them,' and in Andorra there were still none though one comisario existed.[16] In the rest of the principality familiars continued to exist from generation to generation, but as a passive presence with no visible role.

The comisario network suffered from a similar manpower problem. In 1567 in the whole of the principality there were only fourteen of them. Three years later the inquisitors reported that nobody wanted the post, and in 1569 there was none in Tarragona, Seu d'Urgell and Gerona. The problem seems to have been permanent, for in 1604 they stated that in Gerona and Urgell 'for a long time we have had no comisarios'.[17] In 1635 a canon of the cathedral of Vic[18] applied for the job, saying that 'for ten years there has been no comisario in this district, and there is much need of one.' The only comisario of particular importance in Catalonia was the one in Perpinyà, who acted as a full-scale deputy for the inquisitors in Barcelona, and coordinated the activities of the familiars in Rosselló and Cerdanya.[19] By 1653 there were apparently almost no comisarios in Catalonia.

Clashes were unavoidable in a province where the multiplicity of jurisdictions made it essential that the tribunal protect its own, but it was also drawn unnecessarily into an endless number of disputes provoked by its officials trying to press their privileges, and there may have been good reason for the Council of Aragon to affirm in 1587, on the basis of information from the Audiència in Barcelona, that 'it is usually the inquisitors who provoke the quarrels.'[20] Quarrels of precedence were particularly galling. As representatives – so they said – of both pope and king, the inquisitors claimed precedence over all others in public ceremonies, which led to some delicate compromises or simply to a refusal by others to attend ceremonies at which the inquisitors were present. In 1560 the inquisitors of Barcelona explained to their central council, the Suprema, that 'neither the viceroy nor the Consellers tend to come to the *autos de fe*' for this reason.[21] One of the best known, and most ludicrous, of such conflicts took place in Barcelona cathedral on Passion Sunday 1561.[22] The Consellers, who were attending mass at the church of Santa Maria del Mar, were informed that the inquisitors had set up two armchairs, each with a carpet before it, at the high altar of the cathedral for the reading of the Edict of Faith.[23] Only royalty were entitled to this privileged seating, and there were immediate reactions. The bishop, Guillem Cassador, sent a message to 'tell the inquisitors to remove the chairs and carpet from the high altar, because they should not be there'. The inquisitors refused, and it was the turn of the Consellers, still at mass in Santa Maria, to send messengers. The drama was made more poignant by the fact that all the messages from the Barcelona authorities were delivered in Catalan while the two inquisitors insisted on using only the imperial language, Castilian. On receiving the demand from the Consellers, reported one of the messengers,

> after the message had been delivered the father inquisitors said in their Castilian tongue, 'Who are you?' The messengers and I replied, 'We are officials of the City.' Then the inquisitors replied, 'Tell the Councillors that we represent His Holiness and this is the service of God and of His Holiness and of His Majesty, and here we stay.' Then the messengers replied, 'The place of the inquisitors is in the choir of the church seated next to the bishop, and they cannot sit at the high altar of the church.' Then the said inquisitors retorted with great vehemence and a certain degree of anger, 'Get out, get out'; and the messengers returned to consult with the honourable Consellers.

Eventually the Consellers were obliged to come from Santa Maria and huddle into the back of the crowded cathedral, from which they sent urgent messages even while the celebrant was saying mass and the two inquisitors were seated at the altar. They were joined by the regent of the Audiència and by the viceroy himself. Repeated attempts by the viceroy to get the inquisitors to come down were unsuccessful, and eventually the angry viceroy ordered his officers to remove the armchairs by force. The stubborn inquisitors, deprived of their seats, remained standing impassively, refused an invitation by the viceroy to come down and kneel beside him in the body of the cathedral, and left in silence when the mass was over. The incident may appear petty, but questions of public etiquette and precedence were of enormous importance; and time and again in subsequent years, public disputes over status – whether, for example, one had a right to a cushion at an auto de fe – were to provoke quarrels.[24]

Two further disputes deserve mention because they illuminate the equivocal position of the Holy Office in Catalonia. One of the most serious quarrels of the entire period occurred when Philip II was at his most nervous, in 1568. The arrest of the Diputats, one of the more absurd episodes of an absurd conflict, moved a councillor of the king, the bishop of Cuenca, to write to the Consellers in March 1570 on the preposterous charges of heresy: 'it is enough to make one laugh, and I did so when I first heard of it.'[25] Though the Inquisition was involved in the whole problem, and significantly the papal nuncio interpreted the matter as one in which the king was using the Holy Office to bully Catalans, it is worth noting that the tribunal of Barcelona was also a victim of events. In July 1568, the same month that the Madrid government and the Suprema agreed the concordia of 1568 regulating the tribunal in the principality, inquisitor general Espinosa handed out one of the most stunning condemnations ever levelled against any tribunal in the history of the Inquisition[26] and sacked all the inquisitors of Barcelona, in circumstances that I mention below.

In 1611 another of the major conflicts of the period broke out: the Inquisition laid an interdict on the city of Barcelona and excommunicated the Consellers; in turn, the Audiència decreed the expulsion of the Inquisition.[27] 'On 20 September 1611,' records a contemporary, 'the inquisitors placed an interdict on all the churches of the city of Barcelona because the royal *veguer* confiscated the sword of a coach-driver of the inquisitor,' and this lasted 'till June 1613',[28] when the king intervened and ordered the raising of the censures.[29]

As the incident of 1561 shows, fundamental to much of the conflict in Catalonia was the inability of Catalans to accept a body alien to their history, customs and language. Catalan was the ordinary working language of the tribunal throughout its first seventy years,[30] since most officials and virtually all accused spoke it. Although inquisitors might be non-Catalan they had perforce to come to terms with the language in which depositions and reports were made by their secretaries. Occasionally a non-Catalan – such as the Valencian Fernando de Loazes, inquisitor in the 1530s – knew the tongue and used it without problems; but by the mid-sixteenth century administrative convenience, and the fact that most inquisitors were non-Catalan, rapidly undermined the appearance of Catalan in the records. In the 1560s an official review of the tribunal of Barcelona pointed out that 'all the reports that the comisarios make are in the Catalan language, which for an inquisitor to learn to read would cost one to two years,' and therefore recommended that 'since Catalans normally understand our language well and most speak it, depositions should be made in the Castilian language, and likewise all trials held in private should be written in it.'[31] From this time most paperwork in the tribunal was done in Castilian. This was a preoccupation of the Diputats of Catalonia when in 1600 they set out their views on the subject.[32] 'Ever since foreigners took over the Inquisition,' they stated, 'there have been many cases of injustice.' A plea should therefore be made to the pope for a separate inquisitor general for the Crown of Aragon (there had been one briefly in 1491), and the inquisitors of Catalonia should remember they 'are obliged to be subject to the constitutions of Catalonia in matters that do not affect faith'. Likewise, 'since they find difficulty in understanding our tongue, grave problems arise in the taking of depositions from prisoners and witnesses, for even if they are Catalans or French and depose in that language the transcript is done in Castilian,' with the clear danger of distortion of rendering; and the situation was not helped by the fact that secretaries in the Inquisition 'for some time now have been people lacking in letters and ignorant of Latin'. It is not surprising that pious Catalans were always equivocal in their views about the Inquisition, Pujades for example commenting on the death of inquisitor Valdés in Barcelona in November 1621 that he was 'a good scholar but a great foe of the liberties of Catalonia'.[33]

After the brief threat of Protestantism in Castile in the late 1550s the Inquisition settled down into a role of educating the population, varying from it only in those parts of Spain where the role was combined with a policy of rigour towards the Moriscos; but those who now bore the brunt of the tribunal's attention did not come from the traditional Jewish or Muslim minorities. Despite serious defects in the reliability of some recent analyses of Inquisition cases,[34] their general burden is incontrovertible: in the epoch of the Counter Reformation, some ninety per cent of the cases tried by the

Inquisition involved Old Christians, that is, people who did not come from the minority faiths. The Inquisition throughout Spain became a conscious arm of the Counter Reformation, chastising offences which touched religion and morals and enforcing cathetical norms among the faithful.[35]

Its role as a bulwark against heresy remained in force, but at least in Catalonia there were practical limits to what it could achieve. The small team of two or three inquisitors in Barcelona was expected to monitor an extensive triangle bordered on one side by open sea and on another by a difficult mountain area that stretched out into a long common frontier with Huguenot-infested territories in France. The inquisitors had neither the contacts nor the officials to be able to operate a successful invigilation, nor were they ever able to stop free and open intercourse between Catalans and French. In the early years of the sixteenth century, before the successes of Calvinism in France and the reverses of the emperor in Germany, the Barcelona inquisitors were fairly sanguine about their control of the situation. An official visiting the tribunal reported in 1549 that 'it is many days and years since anybody was imprisoned in this Inquisition for heresy.'[36] When some measures were taken in later months, the inquisitors were happy to exaggerate their achievements. 'On the seventh of this month', they informed the Suprema in November 1552, 'we held an auto de fe in this Holy Office and though not many people appeared in it since this land has no Moors and not even a memory of Jews, it was a success and gave great satisfaction and edification to the people, so much so that I believe not one Lutheran will be left in all Catalonia.'[37] There were local conflicts of jurisdiction and the first measures of censorship were being taken, but of heresy there was no sign; when inquisitors made visitations into the countryside heresy was conspicuously absent. It would be instructive to learn that in subsequent years heresy began to appear among the natives of the country, but this never happened. As late as 1569 inquisitor Mendoza, praising the faith of the Catalans, could do no more than suggest from Perpinyà that 'an inquisitor is needed here in order to frighten the people from France.'[38] Throughout the period of the Counter Reformation not a single serious case of heresy was discovered among the Catalan population, an astonishing situation when one realises that the principality was completely open to access from the outside world, not only across the open land frontier but also by sea. The comment of the Jesuit Pere Gil in 1600 must therefore be accepted as a realistic appraisal rather than parochial exaggeration: 'In matters of the Catholic faith, the Catalans are such decided enemies of the new inventions of infidels and heretics, that in all these years when we have had as neighbours only forty leagues away the heretics of France, heresy has never penetrated Catalonia nor has a single Catalan been found to have turned heretic.'[39]

Not surprisingly the inquisitors identified heresy exclusively with the neighbouring country, to such an extent that the Diputats in 1575 harshly criticised them for holding 'the whole French nation to be of doubtful faith' when they knew very well that most of the people of France were Catholic.[40] Now and then there were alarms about armed invasion by 'Lutherans', as the Spaniards liked to call all Protestants, but the only concrete action the Holy Office was called upon to take was when Calvinist bandits fell into their hands.[41]

Reluctant admiration of this phenomenon can be seen in the report of inquisitor Mendoza who in 1569, after touring the whole of northern Catalonia from Perpinyà and Salses to Besalú, Gerona and all the northern sea-coast, concluded:

> They are all very Catholic and good Christians ... Their Christianity is such that it is cause for wonder, living as they do next to and among heretics and dealing with them every day. They could very well be deceiving me as a mere man, but at least in appearances and judging from my contact with them I can come to no other conclusion, and I speak as an eyewitness. The fact is that out of twenty-four people we arrested on this visit only one is Catalan ...[42]

The continuing orthodoxy of the Catalans, even in Rosselló and despite the intimate contact with France, perplexed inquisitors, who were well aware that both French ideas and French books were penetrating the country with very little hindrance. When they cast their gaze on the principality, the dissidence they encountered seemed to be not Catalan but French in origin.

Residents of French origin, familiar with the liberty of opinion permitted in France, did not forgo that liberty when they came to the principality. In 1593 a French Capuchin friar apologised for expressing too freely his view that religious should be allowed to marry: 'he spoke with the liberty of conscience that the kings had granted in France, and did not understand that in Spain one could not make use of this liberty.'[43] In practice the liberty did also exist in many parts of Catalan Spain, such as Perpinyà with its large French population. A group of French, chatting outside the church in Vilanova de la Rao (Perpinyà) in 1591, affirmed that 'there is no need for mass or saints or Avemarias or Paternosters, and the Lutherans in France have a better religion than we have';[44] and one can find similar opinions picked up in other parts of the principality, but nearly always expressed by those of French origin, almost never by Catalans. The contagion, if I may term it such, clearly and recognisably had its roots in France. Was it because the French minority in Catalonia looked northwards for its identity, while the native majority rejected both that identity and its ideologies? Whenever we come across anti-dogmatic statements in the records of the Catalan Inquisition, it is virtually certain that the speaker is of French origin. A seventy-year-old priest of Garrigás (Gerona) said to a colleague of his in 1578: 'the mass was not invented by God but by St Gregory, and for that reason the Huguenots do not want it,' 'when asked what he thought about Purgatory he said "How do I know if there is or isn't one, I've never been there"', 'how does St Augustine know if there is a Purgatory, did he happen to go there before he died or died first and then came back to be able to tell us?'[45] It is no surprise to find that he was born in the diocese of Cahors. 'Who knows if there is a heaven or hell, have you been there?', Jaume Potro of Sant Myn (Urgell) said in conversation; he was, of course, French, and the witness testified that 'those who know him all complain that they hold him to be a bad Christian and that he does not go to mass.'[46] The French obviously had no special propensity to heresy, but their experience drew on a different cultural background in which for a generation unorthodox ideas had been circulating; in Catalonia, by contrast, dissent focused not on dogma but on principles of justice and morality.

Few areas of inquisitorial authority have been more misunderstood than that of the censorship of books. As we shall see, the Holy Office had no monopoly in the matter, did not exercise a universal system of control, and usually failed to operate efficiently. Despite this, it has been suggested that the Inquisition destroyed culture in Catalonia.[47] The entry of the Barcelona tribunal into the field[48] dates from October 1551, when inquisitor Arias wrote to the Suprema:

> I received your letter of the sixteenth of last month and the Catalogue of heretical books which was done in Louvain... All you say will be carried out... Edicts will be sent to the cities and main towns in each district and orders will be given for banned books to be brought to this Holy Office or to the comisarios in the district, who will be told to keep them and not give them to anybody until I report everything to you and you give instructions. The edicts will say that Your Reverence revokes all the licences given for having Bibles in any vernacular language and all the other banned books, and the Bibles that you mention will be collected as well as the Roman missals mentioned at the beginning of the Catalogue.[49]

The edicts were probably issued, but there is no evidence that any other steps were taken to enforce the intentions of the Suprema. Three months later, having heard nothing from Barcelona, the Suprema wrote on 12 January 1552 to repeat its instructions; and on 3 April the inquisitors wrote back assuring that 'in the matter of the condemned books we have done and will do what you order, and when we bring in the books from the cities and district towns you will be sent a list of everything.'[50] No such list appears in the surviving documentation. Eight months later, however, there was some movement and the inquisitors reported that 'some prohibited books are now being handed in to this Holy Office'; but no one was very sure what was meant to be prohibited, and the booksellers sent a collective petition for clarification, which was forwarded to the Suprema in Valladolid. Further problems arose with standard classical texts used by students in the university: 'in the said books of classics and others like Terence and Cicero's *De officiis* and *De oratore* and so on, the students have many which are glossed by heretics and they come here to complain about the seizure.'[51] These were early days in the experience of censorship, and complaints and protests at the illogicality of the exercise were common. Was absolutely everything by Erasmus to be prohibited, for example? The inquisitors wrote in 1559, asking whether they were empowered to 'dispense those who have some works of Erasmus and other works glossed by heretics'.[52] Erasmus survived, along with many other authors.[53]

After a momentary alarm in July 1559 over the intrusion into Catalonia of a papal catalogue of prohibited books which was inadvertently licensed by the bishop of Barcelona and which scandalised Catalans by prohibiting the works of Ramon Llull,[54] the inquisitors devoted their energies to carrying out the instructions of the October 1559 Spanish Index of Valdés.[55] As with the previous Index of 1551, there were inevitably objections both to its content and to the way in which it was enforced: the sweeping regulation that 'all and any sermons, letters, treatises, manuscript prayers which touch on sacred scripture or on the sacraments' be handed in to the Holy Office was bitterly criticised by the rector of the Jesuit college in Seville, who reported how he had been informed by the inquisitor of Seville that the order covered Loyola's *Exercises* in Spanish (as yet unpublished, and circulating only in manuscript). 'I collected those we had in the house', he wrote, 'and have just handed them in, today Friday 20 October at six o'clock in the evening ... The pain of this has laid me low in bed with grief.' As a sad afterthought, he added, 'I have seen in this time the prohibition of works which were highly Catholic and beneficial and by Christian authors.'[56] His view was shared by the provincial of Castile, Araoz, who commented that 'the times are such that one should think carefully before writing books.'[57]

Despite the very grave problems created for the Company of Jesus by the 1559 Index, the Jesuits in Barcelona, who still had no permanent base in the province, decided to make themselves useful and father Govierno put himself at the disposal of the inquisitors who 'have made him their comisario in this matter, to be contacted by all the religious orders with lists of their books, so he can advise them which they can keep and which they have to tear up or burn. I arrived at a time when a good part of the burden fell on me... because of the many printed items which were seized and are being seized by the Holy Office.'[58]

Thanks to Jesuit help, the implementation of the 1559 Index was apparently more successful than that of the previous one. In December 1559 a Jesuit confirmed the good work being done by father Govierno, whose manner of censoring books was apparently so gracious

> that no one shows resentment even when he scores through the rare and precious books they have. He has corrected a great number of Bibles, and has found a lot of harmful and poisonous material in books and places other than those mentioned in the Catalogue, and has made a note of everything and advised the gentlemen of the Holy Office to look into it. On seven or eight occasions we have burnt mountains of books here in our house, without counting those set aside until it is decided what to do with them. It has been an outstanding work and given a good name to the Company. It helped to open a door for us to have contact with the religious orders and gave our order more standing. Govierno is being pressed by monasteries outside the city to go and visit their libraries.[59]

In September 1560 another correspondent stated that the inquisitors and the bishop of Barcelona[60] 'have given father Govierno the job of looking at books to be printed, and none is printed unless he sees it first, and this is seen as very beneficial because in this way books which are profane and of bad doctrine will not be printed.'

The role allotted to father Govierno was unique, for normally the controls exercised by the Inquisition and the diocese operated separately and only a sense of crisis would have allowed them to merge their different roles into one.

Over the next quarter of a century the work of censorship continued, slowly but no doubt adequately. A group of censors (*calificadores*) was recruited from the main religious orders, to help with the task of examining specialist books which the inquisitors were not equipped to handle. The job was onerous and there were constant problems provoked by the fact that the open frontier with France made import easy. The inquisitors informed the Suprema in January 1569 that 'the books that enter through this frontier are very numerous and even if we were many inquisitors we would not be sufficient to deal with so many volumes; to entrust the work to friars and experts is not, we think, going to satisfy feelings and annoys the booksellers greatly.'[61]

They requested permission, therefore, 'to appoint two persons to look at the books, and they will be paid by the booksellers for such is their request and wish'. The idea would have saved the tribunal an enormous amount of effort, but seems not to have been acceptable to the Suprema and was not put into practice. In December 1569 they reported that 'books are being confiscated and a list is being made of those that contain additions or anything heretical', and that 'the superiors of some monasteries in this city have come to say that in their libraries are some works by sacred doctors which contain translations by heretics, and they ask for permission to leave the books there but confiscated in the name of the Holy Office.'[62] The major grievance at this period was that a 'prohibited' book could be classified as such merely for containing the name of a heretic or an innocuous text by him, and all owners of books were understandably wary of losing their precious volumes for such a trivial reason.

In July 1569 the inquisitors after a long lapse of time – 'they have not been visited for many years' – made an inspection of the bookshops in Barcelona:

> in the visit we found many prohibited books, though some of them only have prologues by heretics, and others only additions, and others only trifles. We are determined, because of the harm that can be done and is being done in this land, to punish the retailers with the penalties laid down in the Catalogue, though there are some booksellers so poor that they would have nothing with which to pay the full fine.[63]

The popular image of a Spain sealed off from intellectual contact with the outside world must be set beside the reality of a Catalonia into which, as the inquisitors admitted in 1572, 'every day enter books both for Spain and for other parts'.[64] On the principal land route from both Italy and France, Catalonia became a centre for imports. 'Here we have seized some Vatable Bibles brought from France for a bookseller in Salamanca,' reported the inquisitor in 1569; but the books were released on checking with an official in Salamanca that they could enter if corrected.[65] The flow of books was far from being heretical, since booksellers, religious houses and private individuals continued without hindrance to import; and only occasionally were there incidents such as the entry in 1571 of an unidentified book for the monks of Scala Dei which happened to be about Luther, and 'though the author is Catholic, it has caused offence'.[66] When inquisitor Mendoza made an inspection of the bookshops of Perpinyà in November 1569 'nothing was found worth comment'.[67] Likewise, visiting the bookshops of Gerona, 'nothing was found relating to this Holy Office'. His inspection was by no means superficial. He visited all the textile shops to make sure that imported clothing bore no heretical imagery, and in the comb shops of Perpinyà found many combs which had scenes from the lives of saints painted on them, a practice which he ordered to cease. At the same time, he picked up superstitious books: one, which he sent to the Suprema, was 'a book of the miracles of Our Lady of the Rosary, in which there are many unauthorised miracles and some which could mislead the simple'.[68]

A new phase in the experience of censorship opened with the publication of the Index of the Council of Trent in 1564. From this time on it became apparent that the censors should more sensibly ban only sections of books and not books in their entirety, a policy which the 1570 Netherlands Index of Arias Montano, which closely followed the Tridentine Index, followed faithfully.[69] The inquisitors of Barcelona obtained a copy of the Tridentine Index shortly after its issue and began to use it as a guide in their work, resulting in a 'great abundance of banned books';[70] but in June 1568 the Suprema instructed them to keep the Index only as a work of reference and not to act on it until further instructions. This left the tribunal with a large number of books which they could not confiscate, but which they felt they should not return to the owners. The latter, however, pleaded 'insistently' for the return of their volumes, and eventually in December 1574 (six years later, a typical inquisitorial delay) the inquisitors were authorised to expurgate the names of heretics from the books and give them back. The success of the dual policy of prohibition and expurgation encouraged the Suprema to begin preparation of a new Index for the guidance of the inquisitors.[71] No doubt the Barcelona inquisitors kept in mind meanwhile the principles on which the Montano Index of Flanders (on sale for 1s in Barcelona bookshops)[72] had been drawn up.

On 19 October 1584 the inquisitors of Barcelona received from the Suprema twelve volumes of the new Catalogue of Quiroga. A copy was sent to each of the bishoprics in Catalonia, to be dealt with by the resident comisario, who was to 'meet with learned persons to take in the contents of the Catalogue; and the same is being done in this city; and visits are being made to the bookshops where inventories are made of those books which require emendation, and of those which are prohibited so that nothing is sold until the necessary checks have been made'.[73] The newly prohibited books should have caused no problem, since most were in foreign languages and it was unlikely that they would have entered the country. Expurgations, however, were more onerous, and the task of examining and re-examining books took years. If, moreover, no Index were at hand to guide the censor, the work quite simply could not be done, and in July 1586 the inquisitors told the Suprema that 'in this principality there is a great shortage of the Catalogue and the expurgatory Index, and we think that some of those you sent have not arrived, as a result of which there must be a great many books that are not corrected, for every day they bring them to be corrected by the Holy Office.'[74] In principle booksellers were allowed to obtain their own copy of the Index and do their own censoring; but 'no bookseller wants to burden himself with importing these books because they say they are very expensive,' so books remained uncensored because of the excuse that people had to wait in line for access to the copy held by the correctors.

The lack of Catalogues against which to check books that might be banned was cited as an excuse by the booksellers of Barcelona in 1593 when the tribunal sent two experts, one a Jesuit, to visit their premises. The two

> found on their visit that eighteen booksellers had some books to expurgate or to ban, and it was decided to summon them . . . and in the interview they replied that they had no copies of the Catalogue, and some said that the prohibited books found had already been set aside in their bookshops . . . It was decided that all be severely reprimanded and warned for the future, and if they were found guilty they would be severely punished. The most guilty booksellers were fined varying sums, the fines totalling £68, and it was ordered to expurgate the said books and return them to their owners, and the prohibited books were confiscated.[75]

This is the only known case of action against booksellers and there is no record of further disciplinary measures against them in the period.

The inquisitors in the provinces were normally officials with little expertise in the many fields they intervened in, and therefore relied completely on others for more professional advice about literature. Their activity was dictated by the opinions and orders of the Suprema rather than by their own initiative. They also relied on information from the public: apart from books which by definition invited action, such as those by heresiarchs or on disapproved subjects like magic, a great number of works that fell foul of the Inquisition did so because someone had taken the trouble to denounce them. It followed that many writings were never denounced to the Holy Office, and many others were denounced only several years after publication when some scrupulous reader might light on a passage he did not like. There is every reason to apply to Spain the observation made of Italy, that 'the Inquisition's largely futile effort to find and destroy prohibited books depended on denunciations, chance discoveries, and voluntary compliance by the bookmen':[76] the search for books was not the result of active policing.

Denounced books were not automatically condemned. At every stage, whether in the preparation of the Indices or simply in the prohibition of a single book, the Inquisition called upon the advice of its censors; and also took care to see that they came from different religious orders so that it had a balance of opinions. This method, like all censorship, had obvious dangers: the prejudices of the majority of censors carried immense weight, and if all shared the same prejudice the book stood little chance. In Barcelona the censors in the early seventeenth century usually included one Dominican, one Jesuit[77] and one Franciscan, and the average number on the panel was six. However, the political situation in the principality occasionally caused complications: in 1571, for instance, the inquisitors reported[78] that 'in this city there are no theologians we can use, because apart from the fact that there are only one or two of quality these two are and have been great critics of this Holy Office; and so we are using some Castilians.'

Inevitably, there could be sharp differences of opinion among the censors, and the final decision of the inquisitors might be disagreeable to some of its theologians. The censorship system of the Inquisition, therefore, can in some measure be regarded as a consensus of currently prevailing views rather than as the arbitrary imposition of one sole view. But one should remember that many openly disagreed with it, not because they disliked censorship but because (as in the reaction of many to the Index of 1559)[79] they considered the decisions mistaken. The system had some flexibility, since views both of inquisitors and of censors could change, and after the 1560s the prejudice of inquisitor Valdés against vernacular spirituality was dropped, but once a book was condemned it remained condemned, in a typical bureaucratic refusal to admit the possibility of error.

In an effort to make the next Index, which came out in 1612, as thorough as possible, the Suprema embarked on an ambitious programme. First, they attempted to purge all the bookshops in the country. A directive (*carta acordada*) of 5 July 1605 told the Barcelona inquisitors that

> Because it is essential to take great care over the many books that arrive from abroad, as soon as you receive this arrange for all the booksellers, whatever the nature of their material, to draw up within thirty days an inventory of all the books they have in their possession, regardless of language and subject, whether bound or unbound, and any other loose sheets.[80]

The lists were then to be taken to the correctors and checked against the Catalogue of 1584. They took not one month but two to draw up, and were in the hands of the Barcelona inquisitors by the end of October;[81] but there is no evidence whether they served their purpose. Another virtually identical order dated 7 December 1609 required the process to be repeated, but we do not know whether it was complied with.

The second part of the Suprema's programme, put into effect from 1605, was to consult with all the experts in the country on preparing a new up-to-date Index. In February 1606 the Barcelona tribunal received news of the preparation of the new work, and were told to contact all the 'masters in theology and in all the other branches of letters', as well as all 'book specialists'; they were also told to ask each university in their district to set up a committee of theologians, together with some from the faculties of astrology, to make suggestions.[82] Among the responses sent to the Suprema at this time was a fourteen-page memorandum on censorship from the Barcelona Jesuit Joan Corça,[83] in which he commented that many people never bothered to present their books for correction to the Inquisition but carried out their own censorship using the Index as a guide: 'many private persons and booksellers do this', their principal aim being to avoid the crude defacing of pages that often occurred with the approved censors.

When books were added to the list of works disapproved by the Inquisition, the Suprema sent out directives to each tribunal. The records of the Barcelona officials show that between 1586 and 1618 over forty-five further books were ordered seized, among them (in 1599) Francisco de Osuna's *Spiritual ABC*.[84] Some bans were provoked by the arrival of the author's book in the country, some by the intervention of the government: each prohibition had a story and was seldom part of a systematic campaign of repression. An example of government influence was the prohibition of a book by the eminent Jesuit Juan de Mariana: an order for its ban was received by the Barcelona Inquisition on 2 October 1608, and two days later the order was read from the pulpit of the cathedral and subsequent instructions were sent for its reading in the other towns; but there is no evidence of any response to the measures.[85]

When books were totally condemned their normal fate was to be burnt, in a ritual exorcism of the thoughts contained therein. The first evidence of this happening in Catalonia comes with the report of the satisfied Jesuit in 1559, quoted above, that 'we have burnt mountains of them'. Thereafter few such incidents are recorded. The account of the auto de fe held on 21 December 1573 includes expenses 'for burning the books', without specifying which books were affected;[86] and Pujades records one case in April 1609 when 'on Friday the third the father inquisitors ordered the collecting up of some banned books, and burnt them before the gates of the palace of the Inquisition,'[87] a minor symbolic act, and a far cry from the common resort to book-burning in France or the thousands of volumes burnt by the Roman inquisitors in March 1559 and the Venetian inquisitors in 1571.[88]

Because Barcelona was a port, the inquisitors appointed qualified clergy as comisarios to look out for the entry of prohibited material in ships. The peace with England in 1604 and the operation of the 1576 Alba-Cobham agreement gave English ships protection, and in January 1605 the inquisitors of Barcelona received instructions not to visit English or Scottish vessels.[89] In 1611 the comisario made the mistake of seizing a quantity of Bibles from an English ship, and the Inquisition informed the Suprema they had corrected the overzealous man by warning him 'that from then on he should not take used books, for it seems to us that your intention is that only new books should be taken, on the assumption that they are meant for sale'.[90] The peace with England and the Twelve Years' Truce with the United Provinces restored normal trade links but produced correspondingly severe problems for the Inquisition, which was already trying to deal with the inflow of books from other countries and now faced a flood of literature from the Protestant north. In February 1610 the Barcelona inquisitors received a warning to look out for the import of books printed by 'the heretics of Holland, England and Germany', in small format and 'tucked into the folds of cloths, in the drapery, and some in the form of decks of cards':[91] the volumes included Bibles and authors such as Cipriano Valera, James I and William Perkin. In 1616 the Suprema received reliable information that the Dutch had printed a large quantity of heretical books, including a thousand Bibles, for transport to the colonies (it is not clear whether the material was in Spanish or Dutch). In January 1627 the inquisitors of Barcelona were instructed to order the comisarios in Catalan ports 'to take great vigilance and care in their visits to ships and to examine all the trunks, barrels and bales', since books were being imported illegally.[92]

The group of people who gave most trouble to the inquisitors were the booksellers. Booksellers in Catalonia seem to have been neither as committed nor as ingenious as those of the great book centre at Venice, where there was a veritable smuggling network in the 1570s and 1580s, designed to frustrate the vigilance of the Inquisition, and which offered to its customers 'a nearly complete spectrum of banned foreign titles in the 1580s'.[93] However, they were capable of giving problems. In 1627 the Suprema advised the Barcelona inquisitors to send copies of all their edicts to local booksellers so that these could not plead ignorance. They also instructed them to carry out the expurgations stipulated by the recent Index of 1621: 'within six months from the date of publication of the Index all books to be expurgated should be expurgated, and if this is not done all books will be confiscated and the owner will be fined fifty ducats.'[94]

Since there were several licensing authorities in Barcelona it was not too difficult for a printer-bookseller to defy the Inquisition. In August 1619 the tribunal in Madrid had banned publication of a life of Francisco de Yepes by the Carmelite friar José de Velasco; the order for banning it was received in Barcelona exactly (and unaccountably) four years later, and the Barcelona tribunal immediately issued an edict in September 1623 banning the work. By then the Barcelona printer Jeroni Margarit had decided to publish the work, and brought out his edition in 1624. The Suprema were astonished that a book could be published despite their ban, and the Barcelona inquisitors lamely explained that 'the printing was done without licence from this Holy Office, but with that of the bishop, as can be seen in the book and as Margarit admits.'[95] They embargoed his stock of 474 books, but nothing else appears to have happened, in a case which clearly involved two jurisdictions.

The issue of cardinal Zapata's new Index in 1632 was accompanied by an edict giving booksellers and others a fixed period for complying with its terms, but the tribunal reported that to the booksellers of Barcelona 'it seems impossible to be able to carry out the expurgation of the said books within the ninety days set as a limit nor indeed in many more'; and referred to the booksellers as 'disobedient and rebellious'.[96]

It is frequently claimed that the Inquisition had a major role in restricting reading and thinking in Spain,[97] but the actual activity of the Holy Office, as seen through its own documentation, is a far cry from the role it would like to have played or that scholars have attributed to it. The Inquisition's censorship activity in Catalonia achieved a certain efficiency in the 1550s, when the Jesuits directed operations, but its overall role in this field was unremarkable, and it is impossible to accept the idea of a massive system of 'thought control' which 'drained away the basis for intellectual behaviour' and which for nearly three centuries 'fossilised academic culture'.[98] The government and the inquisitors would have been delighted with such a glowing report on their success, but fortunately there is little basis for it, and neither then nor since has a thought-control system been devised capable of crushing a culture for three hundred years.

In the century after the Reformation the frontier with France was a priority concern because of the possible infiltration of heresy, but not until 1552, when six Frenchmen were 'reconciled' for 'Lutheranism' in an auto de fe in Barcelona and one was 'relaxed' or burnt,[99] did the danger become apparent. From that date Catalans, who in previous decades had been punished by the Inquisition largely for suspicion of Judaism, ceased to be a problem and virtually all accusations of heresy were restricted to people of French origin. For the Inquisition it was a welcome development, since it had virtually run out of 'cases of faith' and in the summer of 1560 the bulk of the prosecutions it undertook were disciplinary or 'criminal cases' rather than heresy-related. People were even saying that the tribunal was superfluous. In October 1560 one of the inquisitors suggested to the Suprema that it was time to hold an auto de fe, since there had been none for seven years: 'I feel that it is essential both for the foreigners who enter here as well as for those of this land who vaunting themselves as good Christians all give out that the Inquisition is superfluous here and does nothing nor is there anything to do.'[100]

From this date there would be no doubt as to where the tribunal would find its heretics: among the 'foreigners', in the majority French. In the subsequent generation virtually all people accused of heresy were French, and in some autos de fe most of those appearing were French, even when heresy was not at issue. In the auto of July 1563, out of forty-five penitents thirty-six were French, and in the great auto of February 1564 put on specially for Philip II in the Born, out of thirty-eight penitents thirty-two were French; in that of August 1565, out of forty-seven penitents only nine were Spanish and all the five 'relaxed' were French.[101]

Were the French in the principality the vanguard of an heretical invasion? Since the thirteenth century the Catalan lands had been susceptible to the spread of unorthodox beliefs across the undefined frontier,[102] and southward migration during the sixteenth century, beginning approximately in the 1540s, renewed fears on the issue.

The civil conflicts in France were a principal reason for French immigration, which continued at a high rate into the early decades of the seventeenth century, making a fruitful contribution to the demography and economy of the province, and producing a population profile in which, according to a census of 1637, over one-tenth of the males in the coastal areas were of French origin.[103] The linking of the two populations was not affected by the Pyrenees, which remained a geographic but not a human dividing line. Rosselló and the counties of Cerdanya, frequently disputed by the French crown, were Catalan in sentiment but also had a good working relationship with Languedoc, and there was free movement of population between them. Towards the west, the Vall d'Arán was culturally closer to Gascony than to Spain and had a heavy concentration of French residents (over one-third of the population, according to a report of 1555).[104] In the city of Perpinyà, one-third of the residents in 1542 were French, and by 1625 a report claimed that 'within Perpinyà there are more French than Catalans'.[105] The bishop of Elna commented in 1606 on 'the great number of unlettered people who come from France every day to settle in this land',[106] testimony to the irreversible mix of population in parts of Rosselló. Throughout the period, Catalans lived on close terms with the religious problems affecting France.

In a stimulating survey written over a generation ago, Joan Reglà fixed on the year 1568 as the central axis of a change of direction forced by Philip II on a Catalonia under stress from 'foreign pressure, frontier crisis, and Spanish isolation'.[107] The blow for Catalonia came, he argued, from 'three measures that isolated Catalonia ideologically': the freezing of population movements, restrictions on printing, and restraints on the French minority. In perspective, the evidence for a change of direction is difficult to identify. Population movements were never restricted, because there was no means whereby this could be done, and French immigration continued to increase, with a consequent rise in intermarriage: in the Barcelona parish of Sant Just one-third of marriages in the 1570s and one-quarter in the 1590s, involved Frenchmen.[108] Nor was printing ever restricted, and the system of censorship did not stop the circulation of books.[109] Reglà's observations on the fate of the French remain, however, valid. Given the complete absence of any bureaucracy or system of vigilance with which to control the French population, the Madrid government was forced to appeal to its Church officials for help. In May 1560, as tensions in France began to move towards civil war, Philip II reminded viceroy García de Toledo of 'the danger of that land being harmed by its proximity to France, and all precautions should be taken, among them that the inquisitors should go round the villages of the principality and counties on the frontier where we understand the greatest danger is.'[110]

'Go round the villages'! The astonishing naivety of the suggestion that the three inquisitors of Barcelona, who never in the history of the tribunal had ventured into the distant and inaccessible mountain areas, should now set out and begin to operate as a sort of frontier police (without, it must be noted, any military support) along hundreds of kilometres of the Pyrenees, provokes one to doubt the common sense of the king's advisers. And indeed there is no record that the inquisitors ever put the idea into execution. In November 1561 it was the turn of the clergy: the viceroy was ordered 'that the Church ordinaries [i.e. bishops] and their vicars-general examine with great care in their dioceses the foreigners who come and live in their districts, whether they are good Christians, go to mass and confession and know their prayers and behave as Catholics'.[111] The order seems not to have got further than the viceroy's desk, and in the Barcelona diocese, where the order stood most chance of being put into effect, there is no evidence of any such measures being ordered by the vicar-general. In 1568, certainly, a clear royal order was sent out by the viceroy to all the Catalan bishops, stating that 'for the conservation of the Catholic faith we prohibit any born Frenchmen, of whatever condition, from teaching and catechising children in the principality and counties.'[112] Since most village schoolteachers had to have an episcopal licence before they could teach, it is possible that some may have been affected by the order, though it is unlikely that communities would have appointed foreigners to teach their children; whatever the case, the 1637 census shows virtually no French in liberal professions.[113]

The consequence of official pressure against people of French origin may be imagined. The identification of France with heresy, at once both captious and untrue, gave the Inquisition an excellent opportunity to renew its activity, and allowed ordinary Catalans to victimise and denounce French people they distrusted. Both in the listings of the autos de fe and in the many denunciations which occurred in rural areas, French immigrants occupied a place out of proportion to their numbers. Of a sample of 1735 people prosecuted by the Inquisition in the years 1578–1635, twenty-seven per cent were of French origin, a ratio which would undoubtedly be higher if the two preceding decades were included.[114] The tendency never attained the dimensions of a systematic persecution of the French in the principality, but it was patent enough for upper-class Catalans to feel satisfied that heresy, if it existed in the country at all, involved only foreigners. In 1560 a secretary of the Barcelona Inquisition, who had been in charge of property sequestrations for over forty years, summed up that period by saying that 'all sequestrations done up to today have been of people with very little property, Frenchmen and people from outside these realms, mostly poor.'[115] The secretary of the Consell de Cent, commenting on the auto held in the plaça del Rei in May 1561, noted with satisfaction: 'they brought out twenty-one penitents and among them one woman, the rest were French and a Castilian';[116] the only Catalan was the woman.

To contemporaries, a person was 'French' if perceived to be so, even if his origins were in the distant past: in Catalonia the matter was important, since the constitutions excluded foreigners from the privilege of holding office. The Inquisition also had rules which excluded foreigners, and was careful not to appoint people of French origin to posts unless a dispensation had first been obtained from the Suprema.[117] There was consequently a built-in political prejudice against the French, aggravated further by the normal distrust of outsiders and by the suspicion that they had a different way of thinking in religious matters. Catalan authorities unfailingly protected their rights and security,[118] but by contrast Catalan writers such as Corbera in the early and Feliu de la Penya in the late seventeenth century did not hesitate to put down in print opinions of the French that were openly contemptuous. This arose in part because of status prejudice (virtually all the French resident in Barcelona in 1637 were described as 'poor') and because the immigrants were engaged in lowly service employment.

The French in Barcelona and along the Mediterranean coast may have been somewhat more accepted because they were engaged in professions (trade, transport, domestic service) which fostered daily and common intercourse. But in the countryside and the mountains, where they were fewer, scattered among an exiguous population (in Urgell, Pallars and adjacent areas the density was one Catalan household per square kilometre) and engaged in more menial professions, they found it more difficult to become accepted. Denunciations to the Holy Office usually involved those who were of recent immigration, from the frontier areas, involved in casual labour or otherwise simply transients. The marginalisation practised by the host population was effectively not against the French in principle but against those who had not been sufficiently integrated into the life of the community and who therefore became the victims of the ire, individual or communal, of those who attempted to deflect away from themselves the curiosity of the outsider inquisitors. Among the 'French' denounced in 1597,[119] for example, was one called simply 'the soldier', 'who goes about selling glass in the tierra de Penedès'; another called Pau, a Gascon, 'who goes about selling glass'; one called Miquel Joan, who 'goes around different villages making underwear and comes to the town of Valls'; and one called Vicente, 'a house-builder, who visits the villages of Creixell, Torredembarra y Montornes'; all were unquestionably itinerants, non-resident in their areas and alien to the community which had denounced them. Official pressure against the minority was not exclusively an imposition from above, it was in great measure a reflection of the discrimination already practised by much of the rural population. A special feature of the Inquisition's activity in Catalonia, comparable to the antisemitism or xenophobia to be found elsewhere in the peninsula, was that its pressure fell most heavily not on Catalans but on minority groups.

The offences of which French were most accused before the Inquisition fell into a logical pattern. In a sample of just over a thousand cases some forty-five per cent were accused of 'Lutheranism', a term used to cover anything related to Protestant belief; ten per cent of bigamy, explicable by the facility of moving from one country to another; and six per cent of bestiality, an offence to be identified with transhumant shepherds.[120] The analysis of these alleged offences as though the Inquisition were the accuser is however almost meaningless, for the real accusers in most cases were members of the local community, and only by studying each case in detail would it be possible to understand the degree to which ordinary Catalans absolved themselves by turning the finger of guilt against the French among them.

The prejudice against the French extended to their clergy. French priests were active in the Catalan lands, given that for much of the sixteenth century the frontier areas were under French archdioceses: in the see of Urgell in the early 1500s two-thirds of all functioning priests (ranging from parish clergy to chantry priests) were French.[121] The clergy in the synod of Urgell in 1616 petitioned the bishop that 'because great abuses and problems have arisen from having foreign priests, no French priest should reside in the present diocese'; but the bishop refused to take so sweeping a step and promised to proceed 'according to the condition and circumstances of individuals'.[122] In April 1622 a report from the city council of Urgell claimed that the diocese was still 'full of French priests, who carry out their parish functions through vicars, most of whom are idiots'.[123] The diocesan synod of that year petitioned once again to deprive French priests, and when this failed another synod in 1635 asked that only French clergy resident for ten years be given a cure of souls; this time the bishop agreed.[124] A firm move was made by the provincial council of Tarragona in 1630, which decreed that 'no foreigner may enjoy nor have a church benefice in this principality or the frontiers,'[125] the last word being added no doubt to cover continuing French tenure of benefices in the Pyrenean parishes formerly under the French Church.

By the nineteenth century, a long tradition of popular belief in magic had led to many remote areas in Catalonia being identified with witches and their doings,[126] but though these oral traditions may have been of long standing it is doubtful if they represented a real persistence of magical rites. Rocks and mountain peaks were commonly identified with sorcery: most obviously, the bizarre heights of Montserrat made it into a magic mountain which the Christians sanctified and revered, and sites on the mountain such as the hermitage of Bellmunt continued to exercise a strong pull on the popular imagination. Popular traditions point still to rocks such as the 'witches' rock' at Sabassona, and the *comunidor* or table of witches at Aiguafreda de Dalt;[127] but ironically these sites do not seem to figure in the known cases of witchcraft that came before the courts.

In reality, given the blurred frontier between Christian and popular magic, the campaign against unofficial forms of belief was never clearly defined or systematically put into practice. The Church itself was obliged to tolerate where it had no alternative and where its own personnel usurped the ancient functions of village healers. Pujades in 1610 reports the phenomenon of fray Francisco Canales, ex-monk of Montserrat who joined the local Servite community at Santa Madrona and 'works numberless miraculous cures on people, giving them bread and holy water and curing by touch all the illnesses of those who go with faith, except those with the French disease. On days both of work and of rest the roads to Santa Madrona are full.'[128]

The exercise of magic in the villages seems to have been seldom interfered with, to judge by the scant surviving documentation. In 1424 the authorities in the Vall d'Aneu, in the Pyrenees, threatened death by burning (an unusual punishment, since hanging was more common in secular courts) to anyone found guilty of devil-worship in the mysterious cave of Biterna,[129] but it is not known whether witches were executed. Biterna appears again in Jaume Roig's *Mirror, or Book of Ladies* (1460) where the author says of the witches that

Moltes n'han mortes	Many have died
en foc cremades,	burnt in fire
sentenciades	after condemnation
ab bons processos	in the courts

| per tals excessos | for their crimes |
| en Catalunya. | in Catalonia. |

There appears to have been no obvious tradition of witchcraft persecution in the Catalan lands. In part this may have been because of the firm policy of the modern Inquisition not to proceed in such cases, a position that had emerged from the high-level conference held at Granada in 1526 under the auspices of the royal Council.[130] Thereafter the Inquisition adopted an attitude of frank scepticism over the reality of witchcraft, with the result that for most of this period the Catalan lands were untouched by the 'witch-craze' which some historians have identified in other countries.

The major exception to this in the mid-sixteenth century was the case of the Valencian Juan Mallet, who in 1548, apparently during a period of epidemic, extended his activities as a witchhunter into Catalonia and received the collaboration of many towns, especially Tarragona. Local officials 'took him through the villages and brought out people from their houses so he could look at them and say which were witches, and those he pointed out were arrested without any evidence or proof whatever'.[131] Though the persecution was secular some witches ended up in the cells of the Inquisition. The inquisitor in Barcelona, Diego Sarmiento, was aware of the clear policy of the Suprema, laid down in 1526, and was personally horrified at the arrest without proof of so many innocent people; but he felt obliged to consult with the Catalan authorities, and in June 1548 held a special top-level conference in the palace of the tribunal attended by the bishop of Barcelona, seven judges of the Royal Audiència, and nine leading clergy including the abbot of Montserrat and the provincials of the main religious orders. Sarmiento asked them to rule on whether 'the said witches could travel bodily and appear in the form of animals, as some of them claim and confess': in short, whether the witches' own admissions to flying through the air and lycanthropy could be accepted. Both the theme and the vote recall the Granada 1526 conference. The unanimous conclusion of the participants was that 'their opinion is that these witches can travel bodily because the devil takes them, and they can do the ills and murders they confess and they should be firmly punished.' As a result of this ruling, Sarmiento allowed the Inquisition to burn seven of the accused women as witches early in 1549.

The Suprema was appalled that this should have happened, and in May sent the inquisitor Francisco Vaca to report on the state of the Barcelona tribunal. Vaca was shocked by the illegality of the trials and ordered the immediate release of two witches still in the cells. The report he sent back to the Suprema in Valladolid has escaped the attention of historians and consequently has never received the attention it deserves. Over half a century before the well-known case of the inquisitor Salazar Frias, Vaca produced one of the most damning indictments of witch persecution ever recorded. He sent a typical trial transcript back to Valladolid and commented 'I believe that most of the other cases are as laughable as this one indicates'; women had been arrested on no evidence at all and put into prisons 'where they were questioned in a manner that was both illegal and contrary to the rules of the Holy Office'; and normal procedures were neglected on the grounds that 'since the women confessed without pressure or torture it was not necessary to observe the forms of trial.'[132] His recommendation was that all those arrested be freed immediately and all confiscations be returned. Sarmiento was sacked in 1550 for not having first sent the trial evidence to Valladolid for examination and approval.[133]

After this event, the Inquisition of Catalonia executed no further witches throughout its history, and intervened wherever possible to stop executions. In 1574 the Suprema was informed that officials of the bishop of Urgell had arrested and punished three self-confessed witches; presumably the inquisitors managed to save the women. They were less fortunate with secular jurisdictions: in the same year in the remote jurisdiction of Castellbó 'the governor proceeded against six women', who were tortured and eventually confessed to having adored the devil, and 'finally he hanged them'.[134] The official was summoned to Barcelona and fined for contravening past orders 'in which the royal justices were prohibited from exercising jurisdiction over these cases'. The subsequent policy of the Catalan tribunal was inevitably influenced by the guidelines issued to the Inquisition of Navarre after the famous auto de fe of Logroño in 1610.[135] To reinforce this policy, and to make sure that it was not misunderstood, the Suprema in August 1611 decreed the seizure of all copies of any narratives or publications relating to the said auto de fe.[136]

Despite the attitude of the Inquisition, which in any case had only partial jurisdiction over cases involving magic and witchcraft, prosecutions and executions of witches continued sporadically throughout Spain and also in Catalonia. For the most part they arose out of the common context of community and family tensions. Of the many such cases one may mention that of Catarina Servada of Argelès, interrogated by the comisario of Rosselló in 1606. In her conflicts with her husband and with neighbours Catarina repeatedly made claims to be a witch and issued threats against those who crossed her. This helped to worsen relations with her husband, who regularly beat her because, he said, she was a 'very terrible woman'; but when he beat her she put spells on him and eventually he was one of the several who denounced her to the Holy Office.[137]

The second decade of the seventeenth century, when the controversy provoked by Salazar Frias and the witches of Navarre elicited from leading scholars (notably Pedro de Valencia) their opinions on the matter, also coincided with a serious resurgence of the problem, probably the last major outbreak of modern times in the principality. Harvest failures were followed by the activity of witchfinders who went through the countryside identifying the culprits. Though the Holy Office refused to prosecute the accused, the local secular magistrates were not so coy, and between 1618 and 1622 hanged dozens of so-called witches in the vicinity of Viladrau, the Lluçanés, and the areas of Urgell and Segarra; around Vic in 1618, the city council reported, 'many have been arrested'.[138] Wherever possible, if only to protect its claim to jurisdiction in the matter, the Inquisition tried to cut short the activities of the witch-finders. In 1617 it arrested fifty-one-year-old Cosme Soler, who for a year had pursued a blood-chilling career as witchfinder. In 1616 Soler, with a reputation in such matters, was invited to Aragon by a local seigneur to sniff out witchcraft on his estates. There he carried out his standard method of identifying witches, which was, as the indignant inquisitors reported:

> he would identify the women as witches because they had a mark like a crow's-foot on their left shoulder, and in order to find the mark he would wash and scrub them with holy water, and in this way he went from village to village pointing out those he said were witches, and the justices threw them into prison on his word alone ... and they tortured them until they confessed to killing babies and having contact with the devil, and some were hanged.

The death-toll, as far as the inquisitors could find out, was three women hanged in Aragon, and the following in Catalonia:

> ... in the village of Montclar in the bishopric of Urgell he identified two and they were hanged; and in another village another two were hanged for the same reason; and in Castelló de Farfanya he identified nine more and seven had marks and three were hanged; in Bellpuig he identified three and two had the mark and one was hanged; and in the village of Torregrosa he identified four or five, and one was hanged.[139]

Since there was no direct legal case against Soler, he was able to escape with a mere warning from the inquisitors. They were, on the other hand, much firmer with Laurence Carmell, a young Frenchman of twenty-three residing in Perpinyà who made his living by identifying witches in Rosselló, and was arrested by the Inquisition in 1619.[140] Carmell 'went through many villages in Catalonia identifying witches and in some regions he was accompanied by judicial officials' looking for the tell-tale sign of the crow's-foot on the body and using holy water to discover it. Among towns which collaborated with him was Tuir, whose council in November 1618 decided that 'to remedy the great and notable harm' to the crops they should invite the services of Carmell, 'who is going from village to village'.[141] The cost of his activity was frightening: 'with the declarations that he made before the secular judges,' reported the Inquisition, 'they condemned to death and ordered hanged a large number of people in the counties of Rosselló and Cerdanya and other parts.' There were executions by the secular judges in Sureda, Millars, Palau del Vidre, Banyoles, Ille and Nefiac.[142] Carmell himself admitted that 'he identified as witches about two hundred men and women, and those he declared had the mark of the witch were immediately arrested by the bailiffs and justices, and up to the day he was arrested by the Holy Office about twenty people had been hanged.' His mind seems not to have been quite right, since he confessed to the Inquisition under interrogation (and without torture) that he had had carnal anal intercourse with the devil. The case was referred to the Suprema, and eventually Carmell was ordered to be instructed in the Christian religion and then sent to the galleys for ten years.

In its own subsequent report on the case, in 1621, the royal court of the Audiència added that much of the blame was attributable to 'the ignorance of the judges' who permitted the women 'to be tortured, and since they were almost all old, weak and feeble women, they confessed at once when tortured, and so very many were condemned'. The Audiència had meanwhile denounced all the proceedings as illegal, and wherever it could had tried to revoke all witchcraft cases to its own jurisdiction. For practical reasons it had not managed to intervene in all the cases, but it successfully prosecuted some of the magistrates and particularly one who had condemned a fourteen-year-old boy to death. The Audiència described the atmosphere in the villages,[143] where 'many women were found dead who had been accused of witchcraft and it is assumed that they were killed by their relatives so that they should not fall into the hands of the justices and bring more infamy on their family. And those who were arrested for the alleged crime were so defamed that nobody dared to defend them nor speak up for them, not even husbands and relatives, because the whole village would rise up against them and not let them speak to anybody.' Crop failure in 1618 was the trigger: the Audiència reported that the crime they were accused of was that they had 'caused hailstones to lay waste the fields and grain, and brought mists to destroy the fruit, and had killed children and cattle, and everybody has made complaints against them for the ills that all are suffering, so that there is no town or village which has not appointed officials to make enquiries and find out if there are witches in the *terme* and if so to punish them.'[144]

It was in this climate that in 1619 Pere Gil, rector of the Jesuit College in Barcelona, addressed to the viceroy, the duke of Alburquerque, a memorandum[145] asking for the suspension of the death sentence in witch prosecutions initiated by the secular courts, which were normally subject to the royal jurisdiction exercised by the Audiència. Asserting that 'it is almost certain that some of them are innocent, and if there are guilty they are blinded and deceived by the devil and most of them do not deserve the death penalty,' Gil set out his argument in a brief paper that cautiously did not contradict any established writers and indeed wherever possible cited Martín del Río, well known for his belief in witches, as his main authority. His main arguments were based on the issues of law and evidence. The prosecutions did not follow standard procedure: 'in the denunciations or accusations no evidence of any sort is cited and they are accused contrary to natural, divine and human law, and contrary to the legal procedure in causis criminalibus.' The accused were terrorised: 'when the trials are prepared, since they are weak, feeble and delicate women they are frightened and threatened by some judges and notaries to say what is not true.' Clergy can testify that torture produced false confessions: 'when tortured, they confess what is not true out of fear and pain and on the basis of their confessions are sentenced to death; and confessors who hear their confessions are in some distress since they see signs that the women are innocent.'

Gil also insisted on other relevant points: that at all times real evidence should be found, that the nature of the accused should be considered, and that the ignorance of the population should be recognised. On evidence, he called for proof of 'evident murders and evident heresies'; 'if it cannot be proved', he stressed, 'that the witches really participated in the murder of children and men and women, and if they have not fallen into any obstinate heresy of deed or word, there is little firm basis for them to be condemned to death.' There were cases when 'some judges condemn them to death simply because there are witnesses who heard them say that on such and such a day they caused storms with thunder, lightning and hail.' Storms, Gil insisted, were permitted by God and could not be caused by humans. The accused (whom he describes always as women, a clear reflection of their predominance in the trials) were categorised by him as 'simple-minded women of little intelligence, feeble and timid, most of them poor, untaught in Christian doctrine and easily deceived, especially by the devil'. All their testimony was based on imaginary happenings: 'they think they hear the devil, but he is not speaking, and that they hear certain things, but they do not hear them, and that they see things which they do not see, and that they go through the air but they do not.'

It was the lack of Christian doctrine that Gil pinpointed as the basic problem:

> There is little opposition when the villages and people say of the witches that they do infinite ills and deserve a thousand deaths, and so the judges tend towards hanging them. For since they are poor, exposed, simple-minded, and ignorant in the faith and the Christian religion and keeping of the commandments and good manners, no one takes their side.

The conclusion was not new, but was important in its context of the continuing effort to eradicate superstition among the remote Catalan villages.

The widespread witchcraft prosecutions of the second decade of the century in Catalonia amounted to a minor epidemic and provoked the central government to intervene. The memoir drawn up for the Council of Aragon by the Audiència in 1621 contained two main suggestions: that a general pardon be issued to the witches of Catalonia as the only way to solve the judicial problem, and that in future all witchcraft cases be reserved solely to the Inquisition.[146] In November 1621 the Council sent the proposals for consideration to the viceroy and the bishops of the principality, and received some interesting replies. The bishop of Tortosa, Luis de Tena, was unhappy about the Inquisition intervening where faith seemed not to be at issue, and thought that such cases should be reserved to the bishops. The bishop of Solsona, fray Juan Alvaro, agreed with the proposals and affirmed that all witchcraft was false and an illusion of the devil ('all the secular judges, by wishing to assert their jurisdiction, deceive themselves frequently'), but warned that the question of jurisdiction was not easily resolved since 'there is some danger that the barons will not be happy at being deprived of this jurisdiction, since in this country everyone defends their jurisdiction with arms.' He also reported the case of a witchfinder called Tarragó 'who went around identifying women as witches and taking off their clothes to see if they had a mark, and some women he unclothed simply for the pleasure of himself and his companions'. Tarragó was arrested by officials of the bishop and sent to Barcelona, but he escaped from custody and disappeared.[147]

In contrast to his colleague of Tortosa, the bishop of Vic, Andrés de San Jerónimo, declared that far from being an illusion witchcraft was real: 'I don't deny that some of their things may be dreams and illusions of the devil, but I maintain that most are true.' Though favourable to the idea of a general pardon, he opposed the idea of the Inquisition going through the province pardoning witches, and in fact blamed the tribunal for what had happened:

> This tribunal has in past years been extremely negligent about enquiring into this matter, and consequently the barons and seigneurs of the villages, on seeing the loss of the crops and the clamouring of the people, have supplied a cure for the ills by punishing these women. And the said barons will certainly not like it if they are deprived of jurisdiction in these cases if it affects them.

The bishop of Barcelona, Joan Sentís, who clearly also believed in the reality of witchcraft, opposed a pardon on the grounds that this would set the witches free to do more evil. Against such views, the Council of Aragon also had before it a statement by inquisitor Salazar Frias, dated 1622, which strongly supported the idea of a pardon ('even if some go unpunished who are guilty') and suggested a policy of deliberate inaction if there were accusations. Salazar insisted that nothing said by the villagers should be believed, for they said 'whatever they have a mind to, out of hatred for their neighbours or because they misinterpret what little children say foolishly in their dreams, or because of things they overhear'.[148]

Both the idea of a pardon and that of reinforcing the role of the Inquisition arose out of the thorny problem of jurisdictions. All the executions[149] had taken place in towns which were not under full royal jurisdiction: officials either of Church prelates or of secular lords had been responsible. The Audiència had limited powers of intervention and tried either to hear appeals from the convictions or to revoke the cases to Barcelona, but all with limited success. The pardon issued by the crown would have had the effect of annulling all the judgments passed; and giving powers to the Holy Office would have had the virtue of keeping control in the hands of a royal tribunal. In the event it seems that neither of the proposals was carried out, and the Audiència contented itself by decrees of 22 June 1622 and 20 February 1627,[150] with revoking all cases of witchcraft to itself and ordering all imprisoned witches to be handed to royal officials.

The stand of the Holy Office against popular belief in witchcraft was unremitting. In 1620, when denunciations were still widespread, the Inquisition received fifteen against fourteen-year-old

Aldonça Rossa, from the mountain village of Bellver de Cerdanya. Known locally as the Bruixeta de Bellver, the girl was feared by everyone because she was reputed to be able to cure people and also to make them unwell.[151] The Inquisition dismissed the case, but warned Aldonça through its comisario in Puigcerdà that she must stop her activities or further action would follow. In the following year there was the case of eighteen-year-old Eulàlia Ursola of Caldes de Montbui, unanimously denounced under torture by six elderly women (five of whom were subsequently hanged as witches by the local bailiff, the sixth escaping to France) who claimed to have seen her going regularly to the *sabbat* with her mother (also hanged as a witch) some six years before. The evidence could not have been more damning, and the bailiff confirmed it by torturing Eulàlia as well. At this stage, in 1621, the Inquisition took Eulàlia into custody. It required only a brief interrogation for the inquisitors to be satisfied that the whole thing was nonsense, and she was unconditionally set free.[152]

The local outbreaks against witches went on. Events in 1627 in the village of Tragó, in the region of Ager, illustrate once again the determination of the Inquisition to intervene wherever possible. The bailiff of Ager condemned two elderly sisters to death as witches, but as soon as the inquisitors heard of it they ordered the local comisario to take custody of the accused. Before the comisario could arrive the bailiff released the two women from prison, put them in the custody of his official, an old soldier aged nearly seventy, and instructed him to take them away and carry out the death sentence, which he did on one of the two unfortunates, garrotting her in a field. The Inquisition eventually succeeded in taking custody of the remaining sister and of three other women, all of whom had been tortured by the justices. The accused were told to absent themselves from the district for a number of years, and the inquisitors ordered 'that they not be handed to the secular justice even if it asks'.[153]

After about 1627 there appear to have been no significant outbreaks of rural obsession with witchcraft. It would be difficult to attribute this to an improvement in rural conditions around that time, for the reverse was true: a plague epidemic in 1629 was followed by harvest failures in 1630 (common to all Spain and Europe), and in the spring of 1631 the inquisitors of Barcelona reported that 'along the roads one can find people who have died from pure starvation.'[154] No doubt witches continued to suffer, but the gross practices which had in the previous decade concerned authorities in both Barcelona and Madrid, in all probability became a thing of the past. The Inquisition in the rest of the century continued relentlessly to castigate superstitious practices of every sort, but witches became a protected minority, as the case of Isabel Amada demonstrates. Amada, a widow of Mataró, was denounced in 1665 by shepherds who had refused to give her alms. Within three days, they said, 'two of their mules and thirty sheep died, and the accused claimed she had done it with the help of the devil.' She was set free by the inquisitors.[155] Witchcraft, considered as a reflection of the fears and concerns of rural society, continued to exist, but often as an elite game, as in the case, also of 1665 in Barcelona, when a group of middle-class diabolists – including a priest and a surgeon – was prosecuted for saying black masses, conjuring up devils and beheading a goat.[156]

For the Counter Reformation in Catalonia witchcraft was only a marginal question. Not a single work published in the principality devoted space to it, and from Pere Màrtir Coma onwards the only preoccupation of reformers was with popular ignorance, which commentators such as Pere Gil saw as the real problem. Missionary zeal was certainly in many parts of Europe a major stimulant to the witch persecutions: whether the campaigns were initiated by lay judges or by priests, whether directed against rural ignorance or against suspected heresy, clergy were always in attendance. The Counter Reformation, moreover, by the mere fact that it was directed against superstition and heresy, may have given further stimulation to the witchhunt and to acceptance of the reality of witchcraft. In Spain however and specifically in Catalonia, the Holy Office refused to sanction traditional harsh procedures against witches. Most prosecutions were initiated by secular jurisdictions and not by Church courts. The example of Catalonia does not support the argument that witchcraft accusations formed part of a 'Catholic offensive [which] made use of the mechanism of fear in order to Christianise the rural masses'.[157]

With impressive unanimity, historians have insisted that the Holy Office operated and imposed on the Spanish people a regime of fear. A leading Jewish scholar maintains that 'the institution maintained its hold on the Iberian population through its terrorist methods, the dependence of royal power on its support, and the apparent absence of any alternative to combat heresy,' and that 'practically no one was safe from its grasp.'[158] A recent scholar argues that 'at the height of its power during the Catholic Reformation the Inquisition achieved the ability to reach remote villages and correct the religious beliefs and activities of the most humble shepherd or lofty lord.'[159] In preceding pages we have implicitly suggested that the circumstances of life in early modern

Europe might make it possible for tyrannies to be efficiently imposed on small communities, but that it was difficult for any authority, whether prince, bishop or tribunal, to dictate the destinies of entire provinces and nations. Because the opinion is still to be found that terror and tyranny constituted the role of the Inquisition in Catalonia,[160] we need to look at the points of contact between the tribunal and the people.

Throughout its history in Catalonia the new Inquisition struggled to establish a permanent presence which could be justified by an observed need, but with the disappearance of the *conversos* around 1500 the need never arose. The Holy Office, smarting under the criticism from Catalans that 'it does nothing nor is there anything to do', sought legitimation instead in the threat from France, and from the 1550s, with strong backing from the Suprema in Castile, the inquisitors tried to emphasise the danger from heresy. This was a paper tiger: no heresy entered the principality, and the waves of immigration converted the French into a more or less accepted minority, vulnerable still to prejudice but in no sense a menace to Catalonia. Catalans were therefore invited to denounce themselves, but this was no more acceptable among Catalans than it was in the heartland of Castile,[161] and by the 1620s the inquisitors were facing a situation in which 'there is no Jewish or Moorish heresy' and prosecutions were 'very few'.[162] This significantly reduced the credibility of the tribunal among the people of the province.

When the inquisitors began operations in a district they would first present their credentials to the local Church and secular authorities, without whose cooperation the exercise was virtually impossible, and announce a Sunday or feast-day when all residents would have to go to high mass together with their children and servants to hear the 'edict of faith' read. This was a lengthy document which listed errors and heresies, especially those relating to the Jewish and Islamic faiths, and invited denunciations from anyone who had seen evidence of the errors. It was normally read just prior to a visitation of the rural area in order to prepare the population for the enquiries to be made by the inquisitor, but was also meant to be read regularly in the main centre of the tribunal. In Catalonia its impact was singularly ineffective. Congregations which preferred masses to be over within half an hour would have to sit and listen for an additional thirty or forty minutes to an elaborate text describing exotic heresies, frequently read in Castilian. It has been argued that the edict was a fearful document which terrorised the rural population: 'fear and terror showed on the faces of the peasants'.[163] This may have been true in some areas of Spain but was patently not true of sixteenth-century Catalonia, where in every area they visited the inquisitors faced indifference. 'I arrived at this town of Perpinyà on the fifth of the month,' Dr Rodrigo de Mendoza wrote in December 1569, 'and up to now nothing has happened to inform you of, because although the edicts have been read there have been only six denunciations...I am setting off for the diocese of Gerona, because here there is nothing to do.'[164] That summer the edicts had also been read in Barcelona: 'we have done the visit of this city,' *licenciado* Gasco reported, 'and nothing has transpired from it'.[165] Ten years later, in Vic, the bishop, Pere de Aragó, publicly refused to allow the inquisitor to read the edict in his cathedral, an action which had no consequences beyond infuriating the Holy Office.[166] By the end of the sixteenth century the inquisitors of Catalonia had decided that edicts of faith were a waste of time. In 1623 they explained to the Suprema that edicts were now infrequent because

> few denunciations are made, and this year we are almost decided not to publish the edicts of faith in this city because in the past four years not a single person has come to the tribunal in response to the edicts. And in 1621 we visited the areas of Perpinyà and Gerona and though it was ten years since the last visit and both are large towns, there were only four or five denunciations and two of them of little significance. To read the edicts every year would be to make people lose any fear of or respect for the censures.[167]

Fourteen years later, in 1637, the theme was the same: they continued to read out edicts from time to time, but 'our experience is that nobody comes to denounce'.[168]

The 1498 Instructions of the Inquisition had enjoined inquisitors to go out into towns and villages: in 1517 such visitations were to be once every four months, and by 1581 were required once a year (the Instructions sent to Barcelona in 1581 and repeated in 1589 were that 'at the end of January or the beginning of February every year one should go out on the visit of the district'.)[169] The purpose was to maintain an inquisitorial presence, though in practice most of the effort was devoted to levying fines.[170] In each town the inquisitors were to read the edict of faith and take testimonies; minor offences could be dealt with on the spot, but graver ones required consultation. Visitations were invariably hated by the inquisitors, who had to travel for long periods through difficult countryside and often through territory in private jurisdiction where the authorities were hostile. Bad weather quickly dissuaded them. In April 1603 'because the weather turned to snow and heavy rain, he could not go' on the visitation to Ampurdà, reported one inquisitor; in August 1605 he confessed that he was most reluctant to make the visitation to the area of Urgell, and conveniently waited until October when 'the rain and mountain snows and swollen rivers' enabled him to plead 'that this visit be carried over to next year, and we will do it when the weather is better'.[171] The visitation was eventually commenced in April 1606, but the inquisitor wrote in despair from the Ripollès to say that everything was 'still snowed under and it doesn't stop snowing', and that his visit was full of 'problems, expenses and dangers'.[172] Perhaps the only consolation was that the inquisitor, accompanied usually by a secretary and a guard (*alguacil*), was undertaking real pastoral work. Journeys had to be made in good weather and not in harvest time: the months chosen were therefore normally from February to July and an average visit would last about four months, but this was only an ideal, since in the mid-sixteenth century in Galicia visitations could last eight months, and in the archdiocese of Toledo ten. In the late sixteenth century inquisitors tried to cover as much ground as possible in one visit but this was impracticable; in 1609 the tribunal therefore decided to divide the principality into four distinct areas for the purpose.[173]

Visitations were a vital part of the inquisitorial presence and could take up almost half the time of an inquisitor. The practical advantage was that instead of waiting in the seat of the tribunal for cases to come in, he could go out looking for his material so that, as the inquisitor of Llerena (Extremadura) commented in 1550 'there be no lack of business with which to serve God and maintain the Holy Office'.[174] Most cases would be dealt with out in the villages rather than in the seat of the tribunal, so few formal trials would be recorded for those months. Against the advantages gained by visits could be set the fact that offences were usually petty and trifling, the money raised by fines might not even cover expenses, and business in Barcelona would pile up during absences; inevitably, in many tribunals of the peninsula by the seventeenth century visitations were a rarity as the Inquisition became more urbanised. In 1631 the inquisitors of Barcelona were routinely instructed to go on the visit, but they excused themselves saying that colleagues were not available through illness, and anyway the countryside was suffering from drought and famine.[175] Visitations were by then a thing of the past. The inconvenience of trying to cover the vast areas involved meant that in practice visits were restricted to larger centres of population from which fines might more easily be raised. If to this we add the infrequency of visits and the preference of tribunals for the cities,[176] we end up with a picture of a rural Catalonia, where over ninety per cent of the population lived, largely out of touch with the Inquisition.

The mechanics of the visitation are of peculiar interest because they reveal the operation of an institution which legend even at the time represented as the most terrible face of the Counter Reformation. All tribunals had in their possession detailed instructions on how a visit should be made, but for our purposes we need only consider the actual practice of the inquisitors. Visits were made irregularly in the early sixteenth century, and seem to have been restricted in scope: that of spring 1558 took in only the Penedès and Tarragona area.[177] From 1563 to 1602 inclusive sixteen visits are recorded, or less than one every two and a half years.[178] In each case an attempt was made to cover a broad territory: in 1596 the entire coastal area from Barcelona up to Perpinyà, in 1583 and 1590 the area between Tarragona and Balaguer, in 1595 the north of Catalonia from Vic and Solsona up to the Pyrenees. The time taken for a visit was normally four months: for those made to the north of Catalonia and the Pyrenees the season chosen was from May to September, after the snows and in the season best calculated to avoid the heat of the south; by contrast visits to the south were made from September to December, after the heat and just before the winter.

The visitation of 1583 gives us a guide to the procedure.[179] The inquisitor involved was Antonio de Toledo, whose round took him in September to the towns of Esparraguera, Olesa, Montserrat, Piera, Monistrol, Igualada, Pobla de Claramunt, and La Llacuna; in October to Santa Coloma, Cervera, Guissona, Agramunt, Balaguer, Castelló de Farfanya, Bellpuig and Tárrega; in November to Vallbona, Montblanc, Poblet, Prades, Scala Dei and Cartuxa, Falset, Cambrils, Riudoms, Reus, Selva, Alcover and Valls; December he spent in Tarragona, Vilafranca and Martorell, before returning to Barcelona on the twenty-seventh. Inquisitors took care in their report to list all towns visited 'personally'; and for us the listing is vital evidence not only of the arduous travelling involved but also of the limitations of the inquisitorial presence. In each of these towns the edict of faith was read from the pulpit at Sunday mass after the public in both town and rural areas had been warned the previous week to attend for the occasion; simultaneously copies of the edict were sent out to the available comisarios of the Inquisition in the vicinity, to be read out in local parishes. 'Sunday the twenty-third [October] the edict was published in Balaguer, a lot of people came from the villages.' By the terms of the edict, members of the public were to come and denounce matters contained in the edict; their testimony would be taken and acted upon later, but in smaller matters the inquisitors were given the freedom to take action on the spot, usually through pecuniary fines.

It has been argued that despite visitations the villages and countryside of Galicia never saw the Holy Office,[180] and the same may be said of Catalonia. By visiting only the major towns and never venturing into the villages, the inquisitors failed to make any mark on the Catalan countryside, nor is there any guarantee that the comisarios, who were few and far between, were able to publish the edicts of faith in every rural parish. It goes without saying that the mountains of Catalonia were not visited by the Holy Office until nearly a century after its foundation. 'The bishop of Urgell wrote to me a few days ago,' noted the inquisitor Pedro Villa in 1559, 'saying his bishopric has never been visited.'[181] Not until the late sixteenth century, when Philip II brought about the relevant changes, did the Inquisition think of venturing into the Vall d'Arán, where 'it appears that this Holy Office has never had jurisdiction over matters of faith in that territory.'[182] Areas which the Suprema may have thought were being visited were in fact not visited at all: inquisitor Rodrigo de Mendoza in a report of 1569 described his visitation as being 'to the counties of Rosselló and Cerdanya', but he never entered Cerdanya, and in Rosselló visited only Perpinyà, Elna and Salses.[183] When he made a visitation in 1595 to the north-west of Catalonia (the only visit to this area ever recorded) the inquisitor Francisco de Arévalo de Zuazo limited it to a route that took in the fifteen towns of Vic, Urgell, Manresa, Solsona, Cardona, Pons, Tremp, Sort, Esterri, Tirvia, Andorra, Puigcerdà, Ripoll, Berga and Terrassa; and arranged for comisarios to distribute the edicts to 600 country parishes.[184] The effort sounds impressive, but one doubts whether the parishes ever received the edicts. Mediona and its neighbours in the valleys of the Alt Penedès seem to have received an inquisitor's visit only once in their entire history,[185] and the normally diligent rectors seem never to have mentioned the reading of an edict of faith.

The inquisitors cannot on the whole be accused of neglect, for Catalonia was an extensive, inaccessible country with poor roads and even poorer security. The fact remains that the vast majority of Catalans never saw an inquisitor in their lives or had any contact with the Holy Office. Within a group of 1735 people dealt with by the Inquisition in the half-century from 1578 to 1635,[186] only fifty-seven per cent were Catalans, while twenty-seven per cent were people of French origin, six per cent were Spaniards (including Moriscos) from elsewhere in the peninsula, and ten per cent were foreigners. The figures suggest that because of its inability to locate errors among the Catalan population the tribunal diverted its attention to other groups, representing close to half of its prosecutions in this period. If we limit our attention to the Catalans, 996 of whom were prosecuted over these fifty-four years, the average number of prosecutions per year was eighteen. Projected on to the Catalan population of the principality, an estimated 450,000 people around 1600, this means that less than one in every twenty-five thousand Catalans per year was prosecuted between 1578 and 1635.

The bare figures, as often, tell only half the story. Approximately a quarter of the prosecutions were of Catalans living in the big towns (with Barcelona answering for three-fourths of them), so that the incidence of prosecution in the countryside was considerably lower than we have suggested. A glance over the map confirms that during the peak years of the Counter Reformation the Catalan countryside was virtually undisturbed by the Holy Office. Entire tracts of the principality, especially in the Berguedà, the Solsonès, and the Noguera, remained untouched by the Inquisition; throughout the half-century referred to, not a single person was prosecuted in the Pallars Jussà outside of the town of Tremp, and the entire foothills of the Pyrenees were virtually untouched. Where cases occurred in the interior, they were almost invariably limited to the central town: of the three cases that arose in Lower Cerdanya, two were in Puigcerdà and one in Bellver; of thirteen cases in the Ripollès, seven were in Ripoll itself. The villages were left undisturbed.[187]

The inquisitors were aware of the problem, and when inquisitor Francisco de Ribera made his visitation of the area of Gerona and Elna in 1578 he proudly said that he expected great benefits (that is, denunciations) to come from the trip, 'because we have gone into lands where no inquisitor has ever been thanks to the proximity of France and the rugged terrain'.[188] This pious hope that the extra effort would be amply repaid by villages which precisely because they had never seen an inquisitor would be anxious to denounce heresies in their midst, remained unfulfilled.

The gap between the Holy Office and the people was in effect greater than the mere lack of contact. Even when contact occurred the most serious obstacle the inquisitors faced was the wall of silence with which rural communities defended themselves. In Galicia there was the case of the rector of Santa Maria de Dascos (Lugo) who warned his flock at Sunday mass just before the visitation that 'we should be careful tomorrow when the inquisitor comes on his visit, for the love of God don't betray yourselves or meddle in things touching the Holy Office, for it can cause us much harm'.[189] To some extent the closed mouths may be compared with the silence that greeted diocesan visitors when they visited the parishes and asked after local 'vitia publica'. The response was nearly always negative, and the visitors therefore reported that there were no vices. Even when village enmities could not restrain themselves and denunciations were made, the disciplinary powers of the visitor were limited: when in 1635 a couple in Llavaneres were denounced for living apart the visitor could only exhort them to return to each other.[190] The case of the Inquisition was more serious, for it identified not vice but heresy and its punishments were therefore more severe.

In Catalonia the first sign of local obduracy was the lack of denunciations. Inquisitor Dr Joan Aymar spent June to October visiting Rosselló and Cerdanya in 1579 and came up with a total of four denunciations.[191] Dr Francisco de Ribera made a pioneering visit in 1581 when for the first time in its history the Inquisition appeared in the mountains: 'all these valleys are part of the Pyrenean mountains bordering France which up to now have never been visited by any inquisitor because of their harsh terrain.'[192] His visitation, which started in August, took him to the remote and spectacular fastnesses of Tremp, Pallars, the Vall de Cardós, and the Vall d'Aneu, and reaped a total of no more than fourteen cases, of which four involved priests; the others included offences alleged to have happened eight, ten and twenty years previously. The edicts of faith clearly meant nothing to these people. While in the Vall d'Aneu Ribera enquired of various leading officials what they thought of the Inquisition being introduced there, but received no encouragement. The clergy were especially vociferous in their opposition and he reported that a gang of clergy 'numbering over forty, with red caps and feathers and each with two pistols'[193] kidnapped a priest who was said to be in favour of the Inquisition and took him prisoner to France. On his way back to Barcelona the inquisitor also included the area of Vic in his visitation, but in the whole diocese could work up only one denunciation, directed against an ancient of seventy years.

In other visitations the story was similar. Four months of tireless journeying in 1582 produced a mere seven testimonies. In 1590 five months produced five cases: a monk phrasing himself badly in a sermon, a parish priest who admitted sodomising a woman, a resident of Montblanc for disrespect at mass, two shepherds for bestiality.[194] This was hardly the sort of job a tribunal dedicated to the protection of the Catholic faith should be doing.

No less significant than the lack of denunciations was the nature of offences denounced. There were years in which the visitations managed to produce many cases: in 1596 there were eighty-three, in 1597 eighty-eight; but the figures are deceptive, for analysis shows the cases to be minor ones,[195] the very situation that caused local inquisitors to doubt whether visitations were of any use at all. Moreover time and again denunciations were made against people whom the Inquisition could not possibly locate or identify, reducing the whole process to a comedy in which nothing was really being denounced at all. The visitation made of Barcelona in the Lent of 1572 produced twenty-nine testimonies, but among them featured an unnamed woman in far-off Galicia, a notary who had said 'four or five years ago' that fornication was no sin, and a silversmith (now safely deceased) who had said something 'twenty years ago'.[196]

The phenomenon can be seen in detail in a typical visitation of the period. When the inquisitor Dr Juan Alvarez de Zaldas came back to Barcelona in 1581 after a four-month visitation through the archdiocese of Tarragona, which had not been visited for ten years, he expressed surprise that the number of denunciations was so low. He had visited twenty-three towns, including very large ones such as Tarragona, Vilafranca and Igualada, yet had managed to obtain only fifty-three.[197] It is possible that the absence of heresy gave him cause for satisfaction but we may also wonder at his naivety in believing that an outsider clergyman, a Castilian moreover who spoke no Catalan, could wander at will into the parishes of Catalonia and ask them to yield up their secrets to him. In the event the nature of the fifty-three denunciations is a vivid commentary on the inefficacy of the visitation as a means for attempting social control, and explains why by the early seventeenth century the Inquisition of Barcelona had stopped making them. In the whole of Igualada only one man was denounced, an ancient of eighty years, for swearing; in Cervera one person, a peasant, was denounced for the same offence; in the whole of Tarragona there were only two trifling cases; and everywhere else the denunciations were such that one suspects the denouncers of throwing crumbs to the inquisitor. Five were directed against familiars; another (in Poblet) alleged bestiality 'twelve years ago'; one was against a man for saying ('he said it ten years ago') that fornication was no sin; one involved a woman having said thirty years before (she was now safely dead) that there was no heaven and hell.

The wall of silence induced inquisitor Cristóbal Bernardo de Quiros to report in August 1614 that

I have this year made the normal visit of the Holy Office through the area corresponding to me. These visits would be more fruitful if the anathema were read and if the people of this land were not so intimidated that they do not dare tell the truth, thinking that if they speak they will be killed, as is quite common in other tribunals. And although they are assured that in the Holy Office names of witnesses are kept secret they do not respond; and many times on this visit it has happened to me that the witness states clearly that he has seen an offence committed, but as soon as the secretary takes up the pen to write it down he withdraws the statement. I have been four months on this visit.[198]

Denunciations in the Catalan Inquisition fall into two main categories: those based on suspicion of the outsider, a category instanced clearly by the French minority; and those based on malice or concern deriving from personal or community tensions. The intrusion of the tribunal was obviously deeply resented by many, and we shall have occasion to see how this affected the role of familiars; but it must also have been greeted gladly by those who had a cause or a complaint that no other tribunal could take up. The free-ranging commission of the inquisitors was an open invitation. In a typical case of 1607, when a young woman in Barcelona quarrelled with her husband, a silversmith, out of spite she denounced both him and her mother-in-law to the Inquisition. She was publicly criticised by a young painter who 'told her that if she were a good wife she would not have accused her husband and her mother-in-law before the Inquisition', at which a friend of hers replied 'that if the accusation were not true the Inquisition would punish the accuser', to which the painter replied 'they do favours for everybody', a retort which earned him in turn a denunciation to the Holy Office.[199] The painter was fined £10 for doubting the impartiality of the Inquisition. Meanwhile the silversmith, who had threatened to kill his wife for denouncing his mother, was lightly reprimanded by the inquisitors, who saw some justice in his attitude.[200] They were no doubt perfectly aware of their delicate position and tried to act accordingly. In 1632 they were faced with a long-drawn-out case in the village of La Guàrdia (Montserrat) when a woman had refused to accept the kiss of peace at mass in the church and instead made a scene, 'to the great scandal of the village', which inevitably provoked a denunciation to the Inquisition for blasphemy. The tribunal limited itself to examining the woman to see if she knew her basic prayers, and refused to get drawn into the quarrel.[201] Time and again, in case after case, private, family and community quarrels were the real motive in denunciations which masqueraded as religious. Even outright attacks on the Inquisition were not always what they seemed: in 1632 when a trader of St Pere Pescador (Gerona) shot an official of the tribunal, the inquisitors commented that the whole matter arose from circumstances that were not his fault and that 'the quarrel was born out of causes and conflicts the two had had a long time before.'[202] If Catalans brought their complaints to the Inquisition, it was not because they were terrorised but because the tribunal was a very convenient tool for settling scores.

The judicial conduct of the Inquisition was seldom as arbitrary as depicted in legend. Abuses and errors occurred, as in any court both then and now, but grave abuses were often checked as soon as higher authority could intervene. In the day-to-day practice of its decisions the Catalan tribunal, impinging as it did on the area of other jurisdictions, took care to consult regularly both with the Audiència, for civil and criminal cases, and with the Church courts, for cases involving clergy; in addition, from the early seventeenth century all judgments had to be approved by the Suprema before implementation. In this way three other courts were on hand to help and legitimise verdicts, a cooperation which continued throughout the period and arguably helped to minimise the problems. The use of outside 'consultors' was standard practice[203] and in the Barcelona tribunal at least seems to have been regularly used, with either the bishop or his representative attending, particularly in cases involving clergy. In a typical case in 1539,[204] involving a woman accused of judaising, the judges were the inquisitor (Fernando de Loazes), two judges of the royal Audiència, a doctor of laws, and two abbots including abbot Guillem Cassador (the later bishop). In 1552 the tribunal reported that both in grave cases affecting familiars and in cases of faith 'those in the royal Audiència come to see and vote in the trials held in this Holy Office',[205] not an impracticable procedure since both Audiència and Inquisition resided in the same building. In cases of sodomy it always insisted that its jurisdiction was limited, and recognised that the Audiència had a right to try such cases 'since this crime is *mixti fori* and not mere *eclesiastico* like heresy'; the death penalty was therefore almost never used by the Inquisition here, and those brought before it were given a preliminary sentence and then handed over to the civil authorities.[206] Half a century later in a difficult case of 1633 outside judges were still being used as a matter of course: the trial was of a fifteen-year-old youth from Ripoll accused of raping a seven-year-old boy, at which two judges of the Audiència sat with the two inquisitors of the city. One inquisitor ruled that the accused be tortured, but the other agreed with the judges that the prosecution be dropped, and in view of the disagreement the case was referred to the Suprema, which decreed that the youth be reprimanded and banished from Ripoll for six years.[207]

Wherever it operated the Holy Office relied heavily on the public auto de fe as a symbol of its power not only over the population, who would thereby be edified, but over the ruling classes, who were encouraged to participate in the proceedings: numberless autos in Castile testify to the living force of the Inquisition there.[208] At its most developed in the early seventeenth century, the auto de fe was a grand public spectacle combining all the most solemn components of official religion – processions, vestments, high mass – which were calculated to draw in the crowds and impress them with the power of the Holy Office. The best organised would last for a day or more, and in order to achieve maximum effect the Inquisition would try to accumulate as many prisoners as possible, sometimes delaying their trials deliberately for months so that they could be used in the ceremony. At the proceedings sentences would be handed out and those condemned to the stake would be handed over to the secular authorities to be executed, usually just beyond the city gates. Public dignitaries, sometimes the king himself, would by their presence contribute to the splendour of the occasion.

In Catalonia things were different. Since the administrative elite were not permitted to be employed as familiars, their public participation in proceedings was limited and as a result there were few imposing processions in Barcelona on the scale practised in the rest of Spain. In the early sixteenth century autos were held in the small plaça del Rei in front of the palace of the Inquisition, which limited the scale of proceedings. Moreover, as the inquisitors reminded the Suprema in 1560, 'neither the viceroy nor the Consellers tend to come to the auto', because the Inquisition habitually asked for an oath of loyalty to itself at the commencement of proceedings and all the Catalan authorities refused such oaths as unconstitutional.[209] The position of the viceroy was commented on when some time later the tribunal called the attention of the Suprema to 'the abuse that exists in this land of not wishing to swear on the day of the auto ... The viceroy says that he would happily do so if His Majesty orders him to.'[210] Public indifference to the tribunal in Catalonia was, as the inquisitors emphasised in a letter of 1560 which we have had occasion to quote before, good reason why an auto should be held soon: 'I feel that it is essential both for the foreigners who enter here as well as for those of this land who, vaunting themselves as good Christians, all give out that the Inquisition is superfluous here and does nothing nor is there anything to do.'[211]

What the inquisitors most regretted was the unwillingness of the civic authorities and upper classes to take them seriously. For their part the Catalans saw no reason to have a heresy tribunal in a country without heresy, an attitude that shines through the laconic entries in the official journal of the Consell de Cent. The auto of

16 May 1561 was held in the plaça del Rei, with (observed the secretary to the Consell) only one Catalan woman among the twenty-one accused.[212] In that of 11 July 1563, 'most were French and the rest foreigners from elsewhere'.[213]

The auto of 5 March 1564 was important for a number of reasons. Put on specially for Philip II on his visit to the city for the meeting of the Corts, it was held with splendour in the plaça del Born, the open space near the port on the outer fringe of Barcelona where all public entertainments took place and where the tribunal would in future years hold its larger autos. Even for this special event the tribunal was able to collect no more than thirty-eight accused, of whom (noted the secretary to the Consell) 'most were Lutherans, and foreigners'.[214] On 12 August 1565 another magnificent auto was held, coinciding conveniently with the arrival of delegates for the provincial council of Tarragona to be held in the following month in the city: it took place in the 'presence of the prince and princess, the archbishop of Tarragona, bishops, abbots and other prelates, the Consellers and nobles and citizens of this city, who accompanied the inquisitors from the royal palace to the plaça del Born . . . All the accused were foreigners and poor people from various parts of this realm.'[215] Those of 1564 and 1565 were exceptional events, and after the Lutheran crisis had passed the Inquisition was obliged to put on smaller shows with the occasional presence of the Consellers, or more normally to hold private autos de fe within the walls of the Dominican friary of Santa Catarina. In these years when the French civil wars first raised the spectre of a Protestant France, the Inquisition managed to put one on almost annually through the 1560s and 1570s, until the pace slowed in the 1580s. French formed the vast majority of cases in the 1560s, but by the 1580s had fallen to a trickle.

'Among the many private autos of the Inquisition held in our church at various times', the contemporary chronicler of Santa Catarina singles out that of 11 September 1594 when the viceroy duke of Máqueda wished to be present;[216] it was a small affair, with twelve persons castigated for bigamy and other lesser offences. The auto de fe in Catalonia had, in short, a role in the 1560s and 1570s when it was used against foreigners, but thereafter and during the high tide of the Counter Reformation it was practically moribund. One of its more showy stagings in the entire period was on 8 September 1602, put on at the Born with twenty-seven penitents, when (claimed an enthusiastic participant) 'our procession caused terror in the people';[217] more generally there were no processions. Their rarity was notable. Jeroni Pujades, whose diary begins in 1600, had to wait until 1602 when he was aged thirty-four before he had the excitement of recording his first public auto: 'there had been none for twenty-four years except privately in churches two or three times; the last solemn one was on 19 May 1578'; and then he had to wait another quarter of a century before he could record the next one, on 21 June 1627.[218]

The inquisitors in 1622 explained the position to the Suprema: 'It is as well for you to know that this Inquisition is unique in Spain in that it does not celebrate autos with the same pomp and decency as in other Inquisitions, and that this Inquisition is very poor, so that what used to be done in public autos is now more conveniently done in some church when necessary.'[219]

With good reason did the inquisitors of the seventeenth century look back on the previous generation as a golden age. 'In the days of the blessed memory of Philip the Second', they sighed in 1623, 'the Inquisition experienced great felicity because service and zeal were rewarded; for some time now all this has gone and all that is left are travails and afflictions.' They also explained that 'the cases of faith that we usually have in this Inquisition are very few because here there is no Jewish nor Moorish heresy, and normally there are no more than five or six prisoners in the cells, and we never hold back cases of faith for fiestas but always despatch them as soon as possible.'[220] The auto of June 1627 was, however, cause for satisfaction. 'The auto was celebrated with much solemnity, quiet and peace, and since there had been none for twenty-five years the people (an infinite number) were most edified': the viceroy, Audiència, Diputats and Consellers were all present, and the only complaints were that the bishop did not come ('the Inquisition owes him very little', they commented sourly) and that the nobility did not attend ('only four or five of them came') because they were not given precedence over the cathedral chapter; but virtually all the comisarios and familiars of the Catalan Inquisition participated ('they were close to six hundred, all in uniform and on horse').[221] Only ten penitents were the reason for the display, 'but the great number of people who came', commented a participant, 'is something to think about; nothing like it has ever been seen'.[222] It was the last great auto of the Catalan tribunal.

The activity of the Catalan Inquisition may in part be measured through statistics of the accused, but there are grounds for being cautious about the available figures. The inquisitors drew up indexes of their 'cases of faith' which have usually been taken as the sum total of their work, but these were only a part of their activity, for they also conducted a number of 'civil and criminal cases'[223] which were of importance. We know, for example, that between December 1562 and the spring of 1567 the tribunal held in its cells, according to a detailed account drawn up by the keeper of the cells, a total of 118 persons representing 'civil and criminal prisoners', cases which were normally despatched quickly but in some instances involved detentions lasting eighteen months.[224] None of these appears in the 'faith' listings. Over half a century later their importance was still great enough to merit emphasis by the inquisitors: mentioning the small number of cases of faith, they stated that 'here a great part of the business is in civil and criminal cases, and more in civil than in criminal, and civil cases in this land are immortal.'[225] Moreover, an unverifiable number were dealt with on the spot when inquisitors made their visitations, and never reached the pages of the index of 'cases of faith': for example, of the 103 persons dealt with by inquisitor Alonso Márquez de Prado in 1596 in his visit to the coastal area between Barcelona and Elna, only four seem to have been entered in the listing of cases of faith, and only forty-eight cases are listed for that year;[226] so that omission of the visitation cases completely distorts the 'activity' for that year. The catalogue of cases of faith cannot consequently be used as a reliable guide to the work of the inquisitors and may often represent little more than half their activity.[227]

In broad lines the peak of inquisitorial activity was between the 1560s and the 1630s but had little to do with the Catalans, who figured among the accused less for offences of faith than for general moral discipline, and the level of prosecutions remained high largely thanks to the French. When the number of foreigners accused began to decline the tribunal had cause for worry. Of twenty cases that occurred between December 1583 and December 1584 only six involved foreigners; of twenty-nine in the year 1585, only six involved French.[228] It was therefore a troubled tribunal that kept sending excuses to the Suprema to explain the fall in prosecutions: 'it is not negligence nor slackness on our part that there are not more cases,' they wrote in December 1586; and two years later in 1588 it was the same story, 'We have made every effort possible to punish the offences that have come to our attention, so it is not negligence that there are not more cases.'[229] In this latter year only eighteen prosecutions had been made, of which two involved French.

Struggling to protect its interests against every other jurisdiction, the tribunal of Barcelona was also subject to constant scrutiny from its Supreme Council, which in accord with precedent made official visits to check that all was in order. Though these were infrequent, they could have the unfortunate result of terminating in disaster. The disputes which the inquisitors of Catalonia had in the year 1567 with the Diputació were only part of their worries: it was also the occasion of the official visit made from Madrid[230] by the inquisitor Francisco de Soto Salazar, who that year had already carried out a devastating review of the Inquisition of Valencia. The recorded proceedings show that he began by lengthy interrogation of witnesses over irregularities in the tribunal. He then revised closely several judgments made by the inquisitors, as well as judgments passed in criminal matters. A long list of charges was then drawn up against inquisitor Padilla, to which he was allowed to present a reasoned defence. The matter did not end there, for the whole matter was referred to the inquisitor general Espinosa, who in a judgment of 20 July 1568 issued one of the most damning indictments ever passed by the Suprema against its own officials. The three inquisitors of Barcelona, Mesia, Zorita and Padilla, were sacked and suspended from holding office for three years.[231]

The sackings of 1568 occurred less because the Suprema wished to punish its own officials than as a response to continuous and serious protests from other public bodies in the principality. Hostility to the tribunal reached down into all levels of the population, and the evidence suggests that it was received by most Catalans not with fear but with contempt and distrust. In 1572 Nadal Ferrer of Pra (Tarragona) was arrested for asserting that 'the Holy Office arrested no one but the rich, in order to get their money, and the only thing the Holy Office existed for was to get money.'[232] The view was common throughout Spain, and in Catalonia has its continuity from the protest in 1509 that 'goods are not heretics'. In 1632 the parish priest of Taús (Urgell), accused of shooting at a familiar's son, was summoned before the tribunal in Barcelona but 'replied that he did not wish to come nor would by any means come, and they could summon him before his bishop but he didn't recognise the Inquisition and didn't give a fig for it';[233] fortunately for him, the Inquisition soon recognised that the blame lay with the familiar, whose family were notorious as troublemakers.

Throughout its career in Catalonia the tribunal never ceased to complain of 'the calumnies and other means they use in this land in order to demolish the rights and privileges of this Holy Office and oust its officials'.[234] In 1618 the inquisitors reported that 'in this province they bear ill will to the tribunal of the Holy Office and would destroy it if they could.'[235] In 1627 they concluded that 'all the people of this land, both clergy and laymen, have always shown little sympathy for the Holy Office,' and the following year it was the same story: 'the people of this land are insolent, rebellious and totally opposed to the Inquisition, and make particular efforts to do everything they can against it, and the nobility and other persons attempt to do the same in every way possible.'[236]

These complaints were essentially directed against those in power in the province rather than against the people. If there were attacks against familiars or personnel of the Holy Office, the instigators were almost without exception people in authority, who were in practice beyond the law. A case in point was an incident of 1611 when the baron of Segur, Miquel de Caldes, murdered two familiars of Prats del Rei, but remained beyond reach of the Inquisition 'because this gentleman has many relatives in this land and is always accompanied by bandit types'; moreover, he was friendly with the viceroy and managed to obtain a pardon from the Audiència.[237] In 1620 an inquisitor explained that 'if a case arises that involves a nobleman or person in power, since it is normal for them to use pistols (*pedrenyals*) and kill with facility you will be hard put to find a witness to testify even if he knows what happened,' and cited the recent murder of a familiar in La Bisbal by two nobles, Joan and Francesc Margarit.[238] In 1632 the tribunal complained over the contempt shown to it publicly by three canons of Tarragona, all of them from leading local families. Unable to take any action against them, the inquisitors wrote despairingly to Madrid that, 'Among the travails that this Inquisition and its ministers suffer in this principality because of the freedoms and liberties its people enjoy, the gravest is the contempt and scorn which they have for it in both public and private, on all occasions and in every manner.' The problem, they said, was 'the many liberties that the Catalans have and the little respect they have for the inquisitors'.[239]

It is surprising to find that little attention was paid by the Castilian government to the complaints of the Inquisition in Barcelona. A revealing letter of 1599, sent in the name of Philip III but actually drawn up by the marquis of Denia (the later duke of Lerma), instructed the Council of Aragon not to take seriously the complaints made by the tribunal against Catalans, since often it created its own problems: 'it is important to see that the Inquisition does not meddle in things that are not its concern, since one can see the harm it caused in Saragossa over Antonio Pérez.'[240] From this episode to the disgrace of inquisitor Sanz y Muñoz at the end of the seventeenth century,[241] events demonstrated the determination of the Madrid government to keep the Inquisition in its place.

The prevalence of hostility and distrust did not mean that the tribunal was hated as an oppressor. Catalans, especially conservative Catalans like Jeroni Pujades, were willing to accept both its existence and its role but had no sympathy whatever for its frankly Castilian character. The point can be made precisely by referring to the fate of the tribunal in the Catalan revolution of 1640. Anxious to find money from whatever quarter for the war with France, the Madrid government at the end of 1639 had the bright idea of asking the Inquisition to accept a salary cut of one-third, and to raise a special levy through its familiars and comisarios. A special order was accordingly issued in January 1640 for 'each of the familiars to appear personally before the tribunal'; but the response was obviously disappointing, for the inquisitor Bernardo Luis Cotoner reported to the Suprema ten days later that 'many' (no doubt a softener for 'most') of the officials were reluctant to collaborate.[242] As events developed in Catalonia, the hapless inquisitors found themselves being identified in the popular mind with the hated policies of Olivares: their power crumbled rapidly, and they prepared for flight. On Christmas Eve 1640 there was a riot in front of the Inquisition which left no doubt in their minds about public opinion. The events, as described later by the inquisitors, were as follows:

> On Christmas Eve we were besieged in our house by an infinite number of people of Barcelona claiming that we had hidden in the secret parts of the Inquisition five hundred Castilians who were meant to assault Barcelona if the army of His Majesty were to march against it. They had the presumption and insolence to break down all the doors they found shut, even those of the cells and prisons; they smashed the doors of the office and archive, went in and robbed twenty-five ducats that a poor secretary had on his desk; they tried to break into several other parts of the palace in order to find the hideout where they said the Castilians were. They levelled many insults at us, among them that it would be fitting to hang the inquisitors by their feet and flog them (*darles humo de çapatos viejos*) until they confessed where they had the Castilians hidden.
>
> On Christmas Day they came back and continued the riot. They went through all the files and took away a large quantity of papers of information on *limpieza* which were in a drawer of the desk in the office.[243]

The terrifying events of those days, when the viceroy was murdered and armed groups roamed the streets, were summed up in one brief phrase by a Jesuit witness: 'the whole of Barcelona seemed a Troy'.[244] For the Inquisition the incidents were unique, representing the only occasion in the history of ancien régime Spain that their premises were attacked, and demonstrate clearly on which matter – limpieza proofs – there was the most public resentment. Two prisoners, apparently the only ones in custody, were released, but they were soon returned when it was found that their offences had nothing to do with religion. In February 1641 inquisitor Abbad wrote to the Suprema that 'the first thing I need to report is that I am all alone in this Inquisition. Inquisitor Dr Bernardo Luis Cotoner, who told me that he would stay at my side till death, has decided to go to Mallorca with a passport from the Diputats.'[245]

The impact of the Inquisition on the people of Catalonia during the Counter Reformation will be considered here through the experience of those Catalans who passed through the hands of the tribunal in the fifty or so years between 1578 and 1635.[246] Non-Catalan elements will be excluded on the premise that they were marginal to the history of the Catalans. Foreigners, for example, were obviously a case apart: in 1596 eighteen English sailors from a captured ship were penitenced,[247] but their fate had little to do with the people of Catalonia; nor for that matter did that of the ten Aragonese Moriscos arrested in 1606.[248] The French fell into a special category and we have had occasion to consider them already. The French people habitually denounced fitted into a recognisable group as a suspected minority and their experience had little in common with that of Catalans. The inquisitors were aware of the special status of many accused French, who were specifically described as 'resident' (i.e. temporary resident) of a town rather than a 'native' or a householder (*vecino*) of it: an example in 1597 was the case of 'Pere, a native Frenchman, resident in the village of Lio, denounced by a woman who saw him following a pig with his member erect',[249] a situation in which the combination of strange conduct and being an outsider obviously invited denunciation.

The figures in our sample[250] can be briefly summarised. Of some 1735 persons dealt with by the Inquisition in the stated period, 996 or 57 per cent were Catalans, 475 or 27 per cent were French, 100 or 6 per cent were Spanish (including Moriscos) and 165 or 10 per cent were foreigners. The 996 Catalans came overwhelmingly from the towns: for example, Perpinyà produced some 45 per cent of the cases in Cerdanya and Rosselló, and the city of Barcelona answered for nearly one-fifth of all cases in the principality. The figures leave no doubt that the Holy Office in Catalonia had become restricted to the towns for its impact.

The offences for which Catalans appeared before the Inquisition have been set out in the following seven categories,[251] which relate the work of the tribunal to the context of the Counter Reformation:

Discipline of the clergy	186
Discipline of the laity	133
Superstition	110
Discipline of the Inquisition	203

Moral control	145
Sexual offences	201
Heretical activity	9
Trading horses	9
Total:	996

Some of the categories will be touched on in other sections of this book,[252] but require explanation here. Discipline of the clergy includes 157 cases where clergy were involved with a variety of offences ranging from solicitation in the confessional to dabbling in magic; and twenty-nine cases where sermons were denounced. Discipline of the laity includes 101 cases of verbal statements about the Church, and a few of laymen saying mass; three involving debts to the Church; eighteen cases of theft from churches; three of non-observance of religious duties; and two involving the murder of a priest. The cases of superstition include fifty-two incidents of astrology, cures and money-finding; fifty of witchcraft; and two of false visions. The discipline of the Inquisition covers seventy-seven cases of familiars and comisarios, and 126 of people arrested for impeding the tribunal in its duties. Cases of moral control include 126 people accused of blasphemy and swearing (and the one recorded case of a charivari); ten accused of false testimony, and nine of reading forbidden books. The sexual cases include forty-nine purely verbal offences, chiefly the assertion that marriage was better than chastity; sixty-six of bigamy; eighty-five cases of bestiality and sodomy;[253] and one of indecency with women. The incidents of heresy include five accused of consorting with heretics and four of converting to Islam. Some people were accused of multiple offences, but have been entered here only under what appeared to be the main charge.

It is immediately obvious from the listing that heresy was no problem in Catalonia: not a single Catalan throughout the years covered was accused substantively of any Reformation heresy or of holding to Judaism. Accusations certainly existed: the inquisitors wanted to know why Gabriel Coma, trader of Manresa, had gone to France and participated in a Protestant service, but the initial accusation against him at his arrest in 1624 had been one of sodomy (with a woman), so that the suspicion of heresy was incidental; he was eventually put on show in the auto of 1627, heavily fined and banished from his town for three years.[254] Antonia Cometa, of Sant Martí de Villalonga, was in 1596 suspected of Judaism, but since the inquisitors could not identify her beliefs and the accused had no Jewish background whatever she seems to have had her case dismissed.[255] If Catalans defected from the Catholic faith it was not towards Calvinism but towards Islam,[256] to an extent however so tiny as to be negligible.

The offences coming before a disciplinary tribunal reflect little more than the efficacy of the tribunal and cannot be taken as a mirror of social reality. In the given sample, it is unlikely that only three persons neglected their religious duties, only three owed money to the Church, only ten gave false testimony, and only nine read forbidden books.[257] The figures do not even reflect matters that the Inquisition would have liked to prosecute, for in practice most cases arose out of voluntary denunciations by members of the public, often admittedly in response to a list of offences suggested by the inquisitors in their edicts of faith. Despite drawbacks in the data, our listing offers useful information about areas in which the tribunal chose to intervene during the Counter Reformation. Apart from protecting its own interests (the 203 disciplinary cases which made up 20 per cent of Catalan prosecutions), the tribunal made a substantial contribution to the Counter Reformation in the areas of clerical discipline (18.7 per cent), discipline of the laity and moral control (28 per cent), superstition (11 per cent) and sexual discipline (20 per cent).

The Inquisition in Catalonia never developed into a tool of repression, ready to be used by Church or state for their own ends. In practice it had little part to play in the everyday life of the communities of the principality. The only occasion when some contact might be made with the villages was when a comisario or familiar had to be replaced, and that occurred at lengthy intervals, made more lengthy (possibly a generation) by the practice of handing down familiarships from father to son. Whatever the situation may have been elsewhere in the peninsula,[258] in the principality few clergy wished to collaborate with the Inquisition by becoming comisarios. The post of familiar was in theory more attractive, for it brought certain privileges such as freedom from taxes and the right to bear arms; but in the Catalan countryside, where most people had arms anyway and freedom from royal taxation was of little value if one paid taxes only to a seigneur, its appeal was more limited. Perhaps the most significant advantage was a legal one, in that familiars could claim to be within the jurisdiction of the Inquisition and therefore exempt from other legal authorities. Because of this exemption and the right to bear arms, the tribunal made great efforts to choose only peaceable men as familiars, but in the political framework of Catalonia friction could not be avoided. Secular lords always resented their existence, since by their appointment they put themselves under a rival jurisdiction.

In 1631 the count of Guimerà, seigneur of the town of Oleta, 'complained that the familiars, who were exempt from his juris-diction, were troubling his vassals', but the inquisitors rejected his protest as 'of no importance'.[259] In the same year Francesc Barrufet, waxmaker and familiar of Bellpuig,[260] a town ruled by the duke of Sessa, was imprisoned by the town governor for unlicensed possession of pistols; Barrufet broke out of jail and fled to the inquisitors of Barcelona for redress, but they ruled against him. His dramatic career may be taken as an example of the conduct of many familiars of the time.

The disciplining of familiars was a regular duty of the Inquisition: violence, immorality, and corruption were common offences, but the tribunal seems often to have been excessively lenient. In 1632 the familiar of Crespià (Gerona), with a record of guns, violence, gambling and counterfeiting, was let off with a reprimand; and in 1634 a familiar of Tarragona, suspected of successfully poisoning his wife after two previous attempts, was let off with a fine and temporary banishment.[261] In some communities, resentments would inevitably emerge. In 1618 when a familiar of Oleta went to the village of Juncet to detain a man accused of bigamy, the women of the village set upon him and his two colleagues, and a band of five men set the prisoner free.[262] In 1620 a (no doubt drunken) trader of Cervera said 'in the presence of many people, and shouting a lot, that the Holy Office appointed familiars only from Jews and trash'.[263] In 1631 a peasant of Figueres accused a familiar of arresting someone for reasons unconnected with religion, sought him out on the highway and wounded him with a gun.[264] In such cases, quarrels had less to do with the tribunal than with local ties of kindred or local rivalries. This was recognised by the inquisitors when they examined the case of a familiar in Villars (Rosselló) who had shot at and wounded the local bailiff; they dismissed the testimony against their man, commenting that 'the evidence was weak and came from people who were enemies of the accused and close friends of the contrary party.'[265] The 'contrary party' might include any or all of the different power groups in the local com-munity, whether ecclesiastical or lay. All too often, the parish priest was also an enemy of the familiar, to the extent of blows, wounds and shots; the conflict between the familiar and the priest in Fontcoberta (Gerona) was such that in 1632 the inquisitors warned the familiar of 'the way in which he should treat his parish priest and respect him', and the priest 'was warned of the way in which he should treat the familiar'.[266] Tensions with royal officials are reflected in the statement in 1634 by the legal adviser to the bailiff of Cervera that 'he would prefer to be a hangman than a minister of the Holy Office, only scum could be that.'[267] When each side stood stubbornly on their rights, conflict was inevitable. In 1635 the Inquisition began proceedings against the three town councillors (*paheres*) of Pons (Urgell) because 'they took steps against the familiars and ministers of the Holy Office, depriving them of trade and sustenance, ordering under penalty that no one give them bread, meat or wine, and not allowing them to cook in the bakery nor go in and out of the gates of the town,' all in order to 'force them to pay a certain tax imposed by the town council'.[268]

The evidence we have seen makes it clear that unlike parts of Castile where the status of familiar was honoured and held by members of the highest nobility, in Catalonia the rank was normally despised. An analysis of the social standing of the 849 familiars of Catalonia in 1600[269] shows that 17 per cent were urban traders, 2.5 per cent were notaries, 1 per cent pharmacists, 1 per cent seamen, 5 per cent independent farmers (*pagesos*) and the great majority, 58.6 per cent, small peasants; 12 per cent had no profession or came from a variety of callings. In its own analysis the Inquisition in 1622 concluded that 'in this district of the Inquisition familiarships and posts in the Holy Office are not as esteemed or desired as in Castile, Saragossa and Valencia ... Nobody wants a familiarship or other post unless he be an inn-keeper or publican or person of that type.'[270] The pessimistic analysis was perhaps exaggerated, but it was repeated time and again (the phrasing in 1622 virtually repeats that of an earlier letter in 1618 when the complaint had also been that familiars were 'lowly people and among them inn-keepers and publicans'),[271] and tells us how the Inquisition saw its own situation. 'In this Inquisition', they informed in 1620, 'most familiars cannot sign their name, because most are peasants.'[272] The situation in Catalonia was clearly different from Castile, and the Suprema in Madrid made an attempt to raise standards: in June 1604 the tribunal of Barcelona received instructions that 'from now on you will not admit as familiars any butcher, pastry-cook or cobbler, nor other similar mechanical offices,'[273] a statement which speaks for itself.

In the mid-sixteenth century the Inquisition of Barcelona seems to have allowed people of French origin to become familiars, but the outbreak of religious troubles in France changed the situation and in October 1575 it was instructed not to appoint foreigners – implicitly, French – as familiars,[274] and the rule seems to have been generally followed. Given the ambiguity about who was really 'French', the inquisitors were willing to appoint where the candidate was clearly not a foreigner but merely of French origin; though difficulties would arise when it came to verifying information. In

1634 when Joan Ribot of the town of Oleta (in the Pyrenees) applied for the job, the tribunal were inclined to accept him as a natural successor to his father, who had been familiar before him; but the fact that he had a French wife was used to turn down the application, possibly in part because the seigneur of Oleta was opposed to the proposal, but more likely because the tribunal had instructions not to proceed with cases where foreign origin made it impossible to enquire into purity of blood.[275]

New applicants for familiarships fell exactly into categories defined by the Inquisition itself: 'in the villages our experience is that only two classes of people ask for familiarships: those who want to live quietly at home free of service in posts of justice or on the town council, and those who are vassals of a baron and want to free themselves from his jurisdiction.'[276] In the first category we may identify successful peasants, as well as traders who preferred to devote their time to business rather than to politics. When Bartomeu Botines, aged thirty, farmer of the village of Astor, north of Igualada, applied for a familiarship in 1623, he was the first to do so in that area and clearly thought, rightly or wrongly, that he was taking a step forward in his community of twelve households.[277] When Salvador Feliu of Mataró, a farmer who later in his career becomes better known to historians as a trader, applied in 1628 at the age of forty to become a familiar, he did so in the normal course of family business, since the only other familiar in Mataró was his relative Narcis Portell, notary of the town. Reporting on his application the comisario stated that he had nothing unfavourable to say of Feliu except that he was 'a bit bad-tempered', and that Mataró was a town of about 700 households. Feliu was of humble origins – his father and grandfather were farmworkers and his wife's grandfather was a cobbler of Mataró[278] – so his application confirms the rule that in Catalonia familiars were of humble origin. But we should pay attention to what the familiarship represented to him. He had close family and work links with two other men of similar condition, the notary Portell and Jaume Palau, a trader from nearby Vilanova de Bellpuig, both familiars in their respective communities, so that the common link of the Inquisition, although it brought no significant privileges and had negligible religious significance, gave them a common tie which brought them together and undoubtedly promoted their common business enterprise, for a generation later all three families were part of the busy commercial network of the Catalan coast.[279]

The familiar network, which as we have seen grew smaller with time, survived largely on a generational basis and little new blood entered it. When Joan Santa Ametlla, a labourer of Agramunt

(Urgell), applied for the post in 1628 he stated that 'in the village there are about seventy houses and there has been no familiar since his father died': he was appointed immediately. When an application was made in the same year by Jaume Vilella, priest of Sanahuja, his claim was based on 'his father, who was notary and familiar for over thirty years'; it had been a long wait, for Vilella was already fifty years old. Jaume Vila, labourer of Viver (Solsona) applied in the same year, saying that 'four months ago the bandits killed his father, who was familiar in the village.' Both Vilella and Vila were appointed at once.[280] The expressive application from Narcis Coll of Gerona sums up the pattern in Catalonia. Aged twenty-one and married with children, Narcis explained that his father Joan Font y Coll had been familiar in the city for sixteen years and had just died in July 1632; wherefore he now wished to carry on the family tradition, 'in the same way that Pere Alrra his father-in-law and those who preceded him in the same family of Alrra and a great part of their family and relatives have served and serve as familiars of the Holy Office'.[281]

Attempts of aspirants to free themselves from other jurisdictions was a permanent problem for the Inquisition, for it brought the tribunal directly into a social conflict it did not desire and represented one of the principal reasons for the political opposition it faced in the principality. The issue had been raised in virtually every Corts since the early sixteenth century, and during the 1626 Corts an inquisitor argued that 'the reason why the three *braços* (estates) and in particular the military estate have tried their best to restrict the Holy Office is because this principality has more towns and villages in baronial jurisdiction than other realms have.'[282] The inquisitors recognised that 'in this land those who want to serve the Inquisition do not do it to acquire honour as in Castile, but to free themselves from the long-standing and heavy taxes and contributions that the barons and also the bishops impose on their subjects.'[283] In 1552 they attributed most of the complaints against familiars to 'certain nobles' who objected to familiars in their villages who brought lawsuits against their jurisdiction.[284] In 1575 they faced a protest from don Nofre Doms, lord of the village of Vilallonga in Rosselló, which with only thirty-three households boasted no less than three familiars who wished to 'exempt themselves from my jurisdiction', and 'commit every day against me many acts of disrespect and disobedience'.[285] Quarrels over jurisdiction frequently dragged the tribunal into problems it no doubt wished to avoid, as in the lengthy proceedings in 1582 when it prosecuted the governor of Castellbó and other officials for the murder of 'el Superbo de Querol', who had come to Seu d'Urgell to give evidence to the comisario there but had been arrested and murdered on the governor's orders.[286] When in 1615 the archbishop of Tarragona, who was also seigneur of most of the *vegueria* of Tarragona, including the towns of Tarragona and Reus, complained about the conduct of familiars in those towns, the inquisitors had to bear in mind the ecclesiastical as well as secular eminence of the complainant, and observed that 'we are very careful not to give the archbishop any reason to be dissatisfied with us or with the familiars.'[287] In the 1620s there were several serious problems over familiars in the diocese of Urgell: in 1627 the bishop protested over a vassal of his in Tremp who refused to take an oath of fealty to him on the grounds that he was a familiar and therefore subject to inquisitorial jurisdiction; after further similar conflicts with familiars the bishop in 1629 had one arrested so that the Inquisition should not 'encourage vassals to lose respect for their lords'.[288] In 1632 the viceroy reported to the law officials in Rosselló and Cerdanya 'the great harm done to the royal patrimony from the fact that familiars who owe royal taxes'[289] were hiding behind their privileges in order to avoid paying. The inquisitors reported in 1636 that they had received, as we have seen, protests from the count of Guimerà, Gaspar Galcerà de Urrea y Aragó, 'expressing his anger that his vassals were trying to become familiars and exempt themselves from his jurisdiction' in the town of Oleta.[290] Thanks to the possibility of escaping into other jurisdictions, in some areas the proportion of familiars ironically increased during the early seventeenth century, against the general trend. In 1633 the marquis of Aitona complained 'of the large number of familiars in his estates', with nine in Arenys for a population of 500 households and seven in Canet for a population of 300 households.[291] In 1646 the cathedral of Perpinyà complained that whereas the bishopric normally had no more than five comisarios or familiars, it now had nineteen, a figure it considered unacceptable if only because the majority were 'ecclesiastical persons who live scandalously and have become familiars only for this'.[292]

Central to the appointment of familiars was the requirement that they be *limpios*, free of Jewish or Moorish blood, a rule always taken for granted in the Inquisition but only formalised in 1572. Many other institutions in sixteenth-century Spain insisted on the need for limpieza, on the premise that in an age of heresy those of semitic origin were the most likely to be heretics, but though the practice spread in mid-century it was always strongly opposed at every level and never succeeded in gaining the importance which

has sometimes been attributed to it. Even when the rule was practised it was always contravened, not least by the king himself. As a
young man newly come to power, Philip II in the 1540s seemed
inclined to support discrimination against people of Jewish origin;
but as the decades passed he relaxed the practice while still holding
to the theory, and by the end of his life he had jettisoned the theory
as well. The evolution is well illustrated by the case of Francisco de
Reinoso, whose appointment to the archdeaconate of Toledo by
pope Pius V in 1570 was blocked by the king on the grounds that
the candidate was not limpio; but many years later in 1597 Philip
appointed the very same Reinoso to the see of Córdoba.[293] Well
before that, the king had set up a special commission to look into
the possibility of abolishing or modifying the rules for limpieza.

The move to abolish or at the very least to modify the limpieza
regulations gained force at the highest level in Castile from the
1580s onward,[294] with the explicit support of the king, various
inquisitors general, and leading personalities in Church and state. In
Catalonia the practice had no recognised status and was always
regarded as alien. There can be no more remarkable proof of this
than the case of Diego Pérez, apostle of the Catalan Counter
Reformation, who was not only of converso origin but had spent
months in the cells of the Inquisition of Córdoba, where he was
accused of saying that conversos were better people than non-
conversos and that 'it is a sin to observe the rules of limpieza';[295]
yet emerged to pursue a brilliant career in Barcelona. From the
very commencement of the Inquisition's career the Catalans, in
a province where the Jewish presence even in 1492 had been
negligible, refused to accept that conversos presented any threat to
orthodoxy.[296] Requirements for limpieza existed only in a handful
of institutions of Castilian origin, such as religious orders or the
Inquisition, but the search for Jewish origins among a population
with few or none was clearly a pious farce, and proofs were never
undertaken seriously in Catalonia, so that the reforms of 1623 in
the regulations were ironically a serious nuisance. They limited
enquiries to paternal and maternal fathers and grandfathers,
without going further back in time, but they also required 'twelve
or at least eight witnesses' for each genealogy. Literal observance of
the changes produced the sort of problems that occurred in the
application, mentioned above, of Bertomeu Botines of Astor. A
comisario had to be sent out in August 1623 from Igualada together
with a notary and an assistant. They interviewed fifty-three witnesses and drew up a file of ninety-six closely handwritten pages,
all of which occupied eleven days of work; but the inquisitor in
Barcelona was angry that several of the genealogies had only five or

six witnesses instead of the specified number, and the luckless comisario had to go back to the villages five years later and interview twenty-four more witnesses, so that not until December 1628 was the appointment of Botines confirmed.[297]

The rules were followed again when in the same year (1623) Simon Borràs of Bellpuig applied to be a familiar. The enquiries into genealogy were begun in April 1624 but a complication arose when it turned out that his wife's paternal grandfather had come from France, as a result of which the comisario at Puigcerdà had to be approached and a statement obtained from the rector of Enveig. Since the Inquisition had no jurisdiction in France it was proposed that witnesses be called to the Spanish frontier to give their evidence there. All this praiseworthy conformity to the rules dragged the verification process out for twelve years.[298]

In time the so-called 'proofs of purity' turned into what the religious orders really required, a check on good social antecedents and behaviour, in order to recruit a worthy Counter-Reformation clergy. In the examination of candidates for entry to the Jeronimite monastery of Vall d'Hebró, Barcelona, the formula 'information on purity of blood' was by the end of the sixteenth century more often replaced by the formula 'information on lineage' or 'proofs of genealogy'. What was sought in 'lineage' was quite simply whether the candidate was of legitimate birth, of good family, and in particular that he was 'without known or hidden disease, is a good Christian, and of good reputation, and has no creditors to whom he has any debts... and has not been a thief, robber or murderer, and has committed no serious criminal act, and is not married or betrothed... nor has any other impediment to becoming a religious'.[299]

In all this there was no obsession with the possible Jewish antecedents of the aspirant, and under the apparently racialist formula of limpieza a perfectly normal enquiry was proceeding. The Inquisition, given its own peculiar history of antisemitism, should have been more conscious of the Jewish element, but in Catalonia again the reality was different: 'in this Inquisition these norms are not observed and familiars are appointed without investigating anything,'[300] it was claimed in 1627. The statement is not wholly true. As recently as 1623 the rules for limpieza had been revised in the light of the new policy introduced under Olivares, and as we have seen the Inquisition was fairly diligent in implementing it; but it was difficult to interview the requisite number of witnesses from scattered villages in the inaccessible interior and, since it was pointless to search for Jewish origins, enquiries tended to concentrate on the social acceptability of the applicant.

The tribunal's attempt to perpetuate infamy through the exposure of *sanbenitos* (garments which some penitents were condemned to wear) had always been resented throughout Spain and nowhere more so than in Catalonia, where the tribunal found it impossible to hang them out in public and they had to be kept privately in a cloister of the Dominican friary of Santa Catarina. In May 1600 most of the fifteenth-century garments, decaying and illegible, were renewed, and those decreed since 1568 were added to the collection, giving a total of 538 sanbenitos, without counting others which were totally perished.[301] A generation later, in 1634, the surviving sanbenitos in the convent were again renewed because they were old, tattered and illegible.[302] In 1668 during his journey through Spain Cosimo de' Medici was interested to see them still exposed.[303] By the end of the seventeenth century in Barcelona sanbenitos were virtually a thing of the past: in the whole second half of the century only sixteen were hung up in Santa Catarina, of which eleven concerned people of Catalan origin.[304] Popular hostility to limpieza, the proofs, and the garments can be seen in scattered incidents, such as that of the priest of Cotlliure who in 1603 helped a parishioner destroy the sanbenito of his grandfather exposed in the parish church.[305] Nowhere was it more clearly shown than in 1640, when the first thing that the rioters did in sacking the palace of the Inquisition was to do away with the documents on limpieza.[306]

Yet the system of infamy created by the Inquisition was difficult to shake off. Minor offences for which one appeared before the tribunal did not bring dishonour and it was normal for the accused to ask for a statement of 'rehabilitation' from the Inquisition, saying that they had completed their punishment and could resume their former status without penalty. In 1611 fray Lucas Gil, a Dominican of Vic, testified that he had completed his punishment, and was allowed to resume confessing.[307] Since the vast majority of offences in the Catalan tribunal after about 1540 fell into this category, the activity of the Inquisition in that period was not as socially destructive as it had been when exercised against conversos. A few graver offences, however, had lasting consequences, because they brought shame in the community and inflicted infamy on the whole family. One such was the case of Gabriel Coma, merchant of Manresa, who appeared in the auto de fe of 1627: he had been in prison since 1624, accused by two women of sodomising them, though the Inquisition took more seriously the fact that he had been to France and attended Calvinist services, as a result of which he was made to appear in the auto with a cap and candle, fined and expelled from Catalonia for three years.[308] The same year his worried family wrote to the Inquisition for an assurance that 'the alleged offences will not prejudice his three sons who were born before their father committed' the faults.[309]

The low-level career of the Inquisition in Catalonia did not prevent its making a reasonable contribution to the work of the Counter Reformation, but there were few marginal benefits and it did not even have the comfort of being able to accumulate property and become rich since there were, as we have seen, very few confiscations in the province. However, the survival of the private accounts of a secretary of the tribunal, the Catalan Pau Fuster, who seems to have held the post between at least 1602 and 1613, shows that diligence could reap rewards even out of unpromising circumstances. As the key administrative officer of a network which involved personnel and interests right across the principality, Fuster seems to have diverted to his private use some of the income and property rights of the Holy Office, the cash from which he entered in his own name in the municipal bank (Taula) of Barcelona; certainly the withdrawals from the bank were for exclusively private expenses, such as the £30 taken out in June 1608 to buy towels and a tablecloth, the £10 the same month to buy a hat, the £99 taken out in November 1609 to buy a gold chain or the £26 in October 1611 'to buy twelve lengths of taffeta to make a dress for my lady wife'.[310] Some of his assets may have arisen out of his post in the Inquisition, such as the £196 received in February 1607 from a familiar of Torredembarra; but some may have come also from his second wife Paula, a notary's widow, who brought with her a good dowry and censals and a country house in Vilafranca del Penedès. It may be that all his investment income, from censals and rents, was honestly come by; whatever the case, his diligence is ample evidence that the enforcement of the faith in Counter-Reformation Catalonia could also be a business enterprise.

CHAPTER SIX

The Reshaping of Marriage and Sexuality

Honour and service and possession and ownership of goods and table and clothing and bed, and whatever else pertains to the state of the husband: all of this the wife has equally.
Vicente Mexía, *Salutary instruction on the state of marriage*, 1566

The labour of Catholic reformers in the field of sexual morality was so intense that it is valid to ask whether they were merely curing deficiencies or attempting something more: to introduce new ideals. When writers of the sixteenth century exhorted men not to beat their wives and to treat their children with respect, were they correcting earlier attitudes that had fallen away from the ideal, or were they in reality innovating and fighting against an attitude that had accepted the mistreatment of wives and children as normal? The confessors' manuals offer only a partial answer: since their purpose was to resolve doubts they usually based their conclusions on traditional authority, thereby giving the impression of simply reasserting the eternal morality of Christendom. It is easy as a consequence to fall into the fallacy of believing that Catholic Europe – not only the body of clerical opinion but even more the common practice of the law and the people – had a traditional morality that was commonly accepted and practised, until modified by the Reformation and the Industrial Revolution. The evidence from Spain suggests that there was no clearly established traditional Catholic morality, and that the Counter Reformation was attempting to enter into new areas.

The intervention occurred in two major spheres: there was a juridical attempt to define the nature of marriage, and there was a moral attempt to define the human relationships affecting marriage and the family. In both, the Church was making a positive effort to extend its authority into new fields. The juridical attempt had already been made in detail at the 1215 Lateran Council and may not therefore appear innovatory, but the extensive debates at Trent and the exhaustive manuals written by theologians demonstrate that something new was happening.

The moral issue was unquestionably new. Over a substantial range of issues – birth control, sexual intercourse, marriage – there were significant differences of emphasis among contemporaries, making it difficult to argue for a unique traditional morality. The struggle to impose official norms (such as 'prenuptial' chastity) was so fierce that it is difficult to deny the parallel existence of two moralities: the actual, rooted in popular tradition, and the ideal, formulated by Church reformers. The growth of the important literary genre of confessors' manuals, written to help clergy resolve the doubts of penitents, clarified the discussion of a broad range of issues touching human conduct and helped to create a consensus on points in dispute. The moral theologians in Spain did not proceed from unquestioned principles but based their expositions of social morality on the Bible (invariably the Old Testament) and on the day-to-day practice of the people, and arrived at normative rules on the basis of existing conditions of law, economy and community precept. 'Catholic morality' evolved out of a fusion of traditional Church teaching and contemporary social needs: it was in a constant process of change, with each new position being presented as the abiding standard. The reformers claimed not to be innovating, on the grounds that they were merely presenting old rules within the new context of a society threatened by heresy. In reality, in every direction they were pushing forward the frontiers of substantially new norms and vigorously confronting old standards which had in their day seemed to be tolerated within the Catholic system.

The sources for studying changes in moral discipline are mainly the documentation of the Church courts, whose role in Spain has seldom been examined. After the Reformation the Protestant countries were quick to take over the courts, which proved invaluable in enforcing change and controlling discipline over a broad range of activities.[1] It is plausible to argue that the post-Reformation courts, which unified in one tribunal powers which the clergy had shared more broadly, were at once more effective and more oppressive than the Catholic system, which trundled on at its old ineffective level.[2] In Catalonia, the diocesan court in the sixteenth century was a passive rather than an active body, content to let secular misdemeanours come before the criminal courts and problems of conduct before the tribunal of the Inquisition; only, it seems, when directly appealed to did the bishop's court stir into life. Possibly three-fourths of the cases coming before the Barcelona diocesan officials in this period concerned financial claims and contracts;[3] the one moral question in which it was nevertheless obliged to interfere was that of marriage.

The point at which one's life might have seemed most private, in the act of marriage, was also that at which both Church and state tried vigorously to intervene.[4] Marriage tied two people together in a lifelong relationship, but it normally also involved the participation of two groups of relations and the settlement of property on the partners, so that any public act of marriage became both a community and a legal event, with repercussions far beyond the contractants themselves. Although marriage was the basic relationship of pre-industrial society, in Spain there was also a significant proportion of those who did not marry, thanks to the operation of religious ideals.

The need for a juridical definition of marriage was provoked in part by the long-standing problem of clandestine marriage, which emerged as a major concern in the early sixteenth century. The words 'clandestine' or 'illicit' were applied loosely to all marriages that the authorities (of both Church and state) regarded as undesirable because not performed before witnesses. In early mediaeval times in western Europe 'marriage' had been simply the binding promise (or *verba de futuro*) given by a man and a woman to each other, possibly before witnesses; no church ceremony was required and usually no written record, except where property agreements were involved. The eventual completion (*verba de praesenti*) of the promise might be made at a wedding ceremony (not necessarily in church), but its essential component was the bodily union (*copula carnalis*), which in some cases might accompany the verba de futuro and would thus complete the marriage without any need to proceed to verba de praesenti and a formal wedding. Not until the tenth century did the Church begin to require that a religious rite be performed, and not until the eleventh do we find a marriage service coming into existence.[5] Even so, the vast majority of all marriages continued to take place outside church, accompanied in public by family and communal celebrations, with the use of symbols such as the wedding ring (known since the ninth century) or a kiss (practised in fourteenth-century Hungary). In fifteenth-century Florence the marriage ceremony was primarily performed in the home and a formal religious blessing was virtually unknown: the verba de futuro were usually made before family friends in front of a notary, then at the next stage symbols of the union – most commonly, a ring – were exchanged, then finally festivities were held which showed to all and sundry that the marriage had been completed.[6]

It can be seen that there was no formal betrothal process, for the verba de futuro could be both betrothal and marriage, nor were the vast majority of unions 'clandestine', since the promises given were invariably public. However the informality of marriage meant that it was easy to abuse the process, to abandon spouses and to deny the validity of a relationship for which no written evidence or publicity might exist. The protection of social order and morality made it desirable that some form of control be imposed. From about the thirteenth century many countries required the certification of a notary as proof of marriage, and after the Lateran Council of 1215 the Church also required that 'banns' be published. By the fifteenth century in many regions the Church authorities specified that a wedding ceremony must follow within forty days of the verba de futuro, thus creating a sort of 'betrothal' period.

None of this had much impact and problems caused by 'clandestinity' continued to be general. The issue was not in effect one of 'marriage' but of clearer definition of the implications of the verba de futuro: in Champagne in the late fifteenth century of 800 cases that came before the Church courts the majority concerned the making and breaking of promises to marry (*verba*).[7] The most common scenario, as the documents attest, was for a young man to pledge himself to a girl (thus formalising the 'marriage'), have his way with her, and then leave her with the claim that no marriage had taken place. Canon law was explicit that the promise and subsequent physical union constituted a valid marriage, so that all clandestine marriages were by definition valid. But how could the validity be demonstrated? Moreover canon law also specified that those over the age of reason and not bound by other obligations, could marry without the consent of their parents, on the principle that only the consenting parties were involved in the contract. Clandestine unions continued to abound therefore for a wide variety of reasons: the case of Romeo and Juliet was perfectly typical of their age. Given the hidden impediments that might occur in such unions (such as consanguinity) pleas for divorce and nullity were bound to occur. By the sixteenth century the institution of marriage appeared to be in a state of confusion.

Both state and Church were anxious to regulate the problem, but for different reasons. The disposition of property was a concern that remained uppermost in the minds of the ruling elite, since the consent of parents was not deemed essential by the Church. In France in 1556 a law allowed parents to disinherit sons under the age of thirty and daughters under twenty-five who married without their consent. At Trent in 1563 the French bishops pressed vigorously for similar legislation to be adopted by the Church, but the Mediterranean clergy opposed them, and the final decree stated merely that marriages without consent were legal although 'prohibited', and no mention was made of ages. The inability of the Church to be precise on the question obliged the French state, by edicts of 1576 and 1629, to lay down penalties for disapproved marriages, but the problem continued well into the eighteenth century.[8] In Spain repeated Church synod decrees of the fifteenth century had attempted to stop the 'abuse' of clandestine unions. The *Cortes* of Castile in 1555, 1558 and 1560 petitioned the crown that children not be permitted to marry without the permission of their parents.[9] The notion of parental consent was repeatedly stressed in laws but difficult to maintain in practice, for the Church always held that contractants were free. In Catalonia the legal experts were adamant that marriage was a free and voluntary contract. The laws allowed disinheritance but under very strict conditions, and noble families found it difficult to cut off heirs who married against parental consent: in 1577 the Requesens family had to pay a dowry even though the daughter had married without consent, and in 1618 a daughter was given her legacy despite marrying against her father's will.[10]

For the Church the regulation of marriage was an even more fundamental issue. In a society where marriage did not necessarily take place in church, did not require the presence of a priest, relied on a notary for validation, and could be dissolved by secular judges (frequent in Italy), the role of the Church was becoming redundant. The fathers at Trent were accordingly concerned not merely to sort out the problems implicit in clandestinity, but to reclaim for the Church a role that the Lateran Council had tried to sustain. There were also many social dimensions to the question. Juan de Avila in 1551 outlined to archbishop Guerrero of Granada the problems that there had been in his experience with clandestine unions:

they estrange fathers and sons... and often disrupt villages with violence and killings. A girl will marry a man secretly and then not dare to publicise it for fear of her father; or if she confesses it, she is not believed; and not daring to contradict her father's will agrees to marry another in facie Ecclesiae; and so they live in sin, since the first marriage was valid and frequently consummated. What can this unhappy woman do, who cannot take her first husband nor leave her second? We know cases where the girls have hanged themselves... Item: an infinite number of maidens have been deceived and undone, sinning with men and trusting in the promise of marriage made to them; and some have left their parents' house and gone to their perdition...

'It is vital', concluded Juan de Avila, in the hope that Guerrero would bring up the matter at Trent, 'to invalidate all marriages where there is no witness.'[11]

Trent did not legislate on the question until 1563, when on 11

November the famous decree Tametsi was issued, against the votes of a strong minority, including Diego Laínez and the pope's representative cardinal Simonetta, who felt that the Church had no authority to invalidate clandestine unions.[12] Tametsi compromised to the extent of recognising all existing unions, but ruled that for the future a marriage would be valid only if performed by the parish priest and in the presence of at least two witnesses; parental consent was declared to be desirable but not obligatory, and banns had to be published. The essential principle that marriage had to be 'public' to be valid was established. It was a revolutionary move (justified by Guerrero in the Council on the grounds that the Church had the right to alter human laws) which unequivocally claimed for the Church sole control of the validity of marriages. Given its novelty and the fact that it went against common custom and local law throughout much of the Catholic world, the decree had little impact for over a generation, despite very clear rulings such as that of the Franciscan fray Antonio de Córdoba in his *Treatise on cases of conscience* (1573) that since Trent there could be no further doubts about what constituted a valid marriage, 'because there it was laid down that no marriage is valid unless performed before a priest and with two or three witnesses'.[13] Controversy continued among theologians over the role of the priest, the majority arguing that despite attempts of Trent to inflate his role he was not the minister of the sacrament but simply officiated at it, the true ministers being the contractants. The delicate confusions into which theologians could fall is illustrated by the case of Catalonia's best-selling manual, the *Directory of Curates* of Pere Màrtir Comas, bishop of Elna. In 1601, after the book had been published in Castilian, the Inquisition ordered the expurgation from the book of the phrases, 'the minister of this sacrament [marriage] is the parish priest or another priest', and 'after the Council of Trent no marriage is valid that is performed against the wishes of the bishop';[14] phrases which were erroneous according to the current doctrine but which had apparently been accepted without comment by the clergy of Catalonia for half a century.

In Catalonia the provincial council of Tarragona as early as 1129 had outlawed clandestine unions,[15] but deep-rooted practice and attitudes were difficult to displace. Many must have shared the opinion of the priest of Sant Joan de les Abadesses who affirmed stubbornly in 1585 (he was reprimanded for it by the Inquisition) that 'clandestine marriage is true marriage despite the Council of Trent saying the contrary';[16] but the changes filtered in nevertheless. In areas such as Champagne verbal commitments, which constituted the form of pre-Tridentine marriage, had disappeared by the end of the seventeenth century,[17] and the same seems to be true of Barcelona, for there is little or no mention of them in the diocesan courts after the 1670s, which suggests that a century after Trent the reforms had come to stay. If clandestinity had indeed vanished in Catalan marriages by the third quarter of the seventeenth century, the process helps to explain the simultaneous stabilisation of marriages at all social levels through the mechanism of the 'marriage clauses' which in the seventeenth but more particularly in the eighteenth century became the hallmark of Catalan property arrangements.[18] The picture however was more complex than this, as we shall see.

The new trend was towards marriage within church rather than out of it: other countries already accepted the practice, for at the same period in Elizabethan England when people spoke of marriage they usually meant marriage in church.[19] In both Protestant and Catholic Europe the drive to make marriage into a religious rite subject to the rules of the Church authorities seems to have been successful. The nature of marriage was also redefined: for the Jesuit Astete in 1598 'marriage is not only a sacrament' (its first nature) 'it is also a natural contract' (its secondary nature), a reversing of the old view in which marriage had been a human contract to which the Church merely added its blessing.[20]

One of the major related problems that the Counter Reformation attempted to deal with was what we shall call 'unsacramental marriage', sometimes (mistakenly) presented by historians as a question of engaged couples living together before marriage. Traditionally in western Europe the exchange of verba de futuro was in practice considered to be the 'marriage', with the subsequent carnal union sealing the process. In Franconia (Germany), even after the Lutheran Reformation 'local custom continued to sanction sex before the public wedding';[21] and it was the same in many parts of Catholic Spain. Only in the case of child betrothals (the minimum canonical age for this was seven years), in use especially when dynastic and property interests were involved, did the distinction between de futuro and de praesenti have obvious meaning, since the copula would have to wait for several years. In the countryside, 'marriage' was deemed to be completed after the verba de futuro and the subsequent sexual union.

For the Catholic reformers, especially after the Tridentine regulations, this was illegal cohabitation; but it seems to have been the common practice in Catalonia. Community use accepted such marriages, with many couples living together under the parental roof until their economic circumstances might allow them to set up a separate family unit. In the marquisate of Cenete (Andalusia) in 1591 the Jesuits claimed to have brought about 'reformation in many things and particularly in one great abuse, which was that couples waited two, three, four and more years without marrying, waiting now for a good harvest, or for another, or for other things before marrying, and by then they were burdened with children and in mortal sin'.[22] The partial concessions of the moralists – Azpilcueta permitting that 'betrothed may not only see and talk to each other but also kiss, embrace and touch each other',[23] and Francisco Ortiz Lucio in his *Compendium of all the Summas* (Barcelona 1598) generously allowing that 'betrothed may kiss each other if they do not put themselves in danger of copula'[24] – were clearly wasted in a context where 'betrothed' couples not only did make love but actually lived together as husband and wife. In 1598 the dean of Lérida cathedral during a visit to parishes in Monzón denounced 'the abuse in this town by those who live together before celebrating marriage by verba de praesenti and in the form laid down by the Council of Trent'.[25] The efforts of the Church to reform the standards of marriage and of personal relationships were untiring, but their efficacy was not to be guaranteed. In Mediona in 1578 the diocesan visitor issued an order, which was clearly being issued throughout the diocese, that 'no sponsus by verba de futuro may go to the house of the sponsa or to any other place to have dealings with her, unless they are first married by verba de praesenti.'[26] As late as 1687 in the Valencian countryside pastoral visits by the bishop found that 'in some places when some persons agree to marry with verba de futuro, they take such liberty and deal with each other with such freedom that they may live in the same house or enter into the house of the other,'[27] and the situation continued into the eighteenth century.

Before we imagine that an outbreak of immorality had taken place in the Spanish countryside, it is crucial to sort out what was really happening. Two distinct questions were involved. On the one hand the Church was unhappy about the ambiguity in everyday use of the verba de futuro, popularly taken to be equivalent to marriage to the detriment of the verba de praesenti.[28] On the other hand, the Church objected even to verba de praesenti unless they were made in church, before a priest, and to the accompaniment of a nuptial mass. On both counts the Church was objecting to the secular and unsacramental nature of marriage bonds before Trent, and was trying to insist that only ecclesiastical marriage was valid, a claim which went against the common practice of the people of Spain. In the battle to sacramentalise marriage, language played a central role. The common verbs for marrying were *desposar* or *esposar*, and *casar*, in both Castilian and Catalan; but Catholic writers began to reserve the verb desposar for the verba de futuro, thus making the verb equivalent to the concept of betrothal or engagement, and preferred the verb casar for church marriages. These verbal distinctions were innovatory, and could not be justified by the day-to-day practice of, for example, the clergy in Mediona.

In Santa Maria de Mediona throughout the sixteenth and seventeenth centuries the verb to marry was *desposar* or *sposar*, and the act of marriage was to *fer sposalles*, or *fer matrimoni desposalles* in the presence of the notary/priest. At least from the 1570s all such marriages were made with verba de praesenti, so that the confusion of the verba de futuro did not normally exist. In the full tide of the Counter Reformation, marriage in Mediona remained secular in tone: we have seen that only twenty-eight per cent of marriages in the period 1575–1630 were performed in church. People were nevertheless conscious of the claims of the Church, and of the distinction between a secular marriage and an ecclesiastical one, the latter being referred to in the documents as *les noces* or *les bodes*. Matrimonial clauses of 1513 for a couple in the *terme* specify that 'in fulfilment of the present marriage the aforesaid parties agree that the *sposalles* be celebrated now *de present*, and that the *benedictio* in the face of Holy Mother Church to *fer noces* be done in the coming month of January.'[29] A century later, in 1601, contractants in marriage clauses preserved the same distinction: they promised to pay the dowry 'half on the day of the *sposalles* and the other half on the day of the *bodes*'.[30] It became more frequent however, thanks to Church pressure, for couples to follow up the secular sposalles with the formal Church blessing (benedictio), consisting essentially of a nuptial mass.

Because the church ceremony was in the eyes of the bishops the authentic one, the sposalles were often treated as a mere betrothal, even if performed with verba de praesenti, and the marriage clauses (discussed below) tended to insist that sposalles should be followed within a fixed time by the benedictio. By extension, couples were expected to abstain from intercourse until they had been to church, and many moralists presented to their readers the ideal Biblical paradigm of Tobias, who was saved because instead of going immediately to bed he spent the nights in prayer jointly with his spouse. 'If you read the whole Bible from the first chapter to the last,' was the view of fray Jerónimo de Lemos in 1583, 'you will not find in it another story more profitable for a bridegroom.'[31] It was within this context that the clergy denounced the practice of bedding before the 'wedding'. When the bishop of Barcelona,

Guillem Cassador, issued the Tridentine regulations in the diocese on 11 May 1565,[32] he emphasised that 'those desposats by verba de praesenti may not live together in the same house until they have received ecclesiastical blessing in the church.' It was the start of a long campaign to replace secular marriage with church marriage, but success was not easy to come by. Four generations later, a best-selling manual for priests, Noydens' *Practice for Curates*, written against the background of the archdiocese of Toledo, concluded that 'many habitually consummate the marriage before receiving the blessing.'[33] In the Barcelona diocese there were continuous decrees condemning the cohabitation of couples who had been married by marriage clauses (*encartats*) or who had gone through the civil marriage of verba de praesenti. At Easter 1600 bishop Coloma stated that 'the abuses and sins to be found among the encartats and who are promised to marry, oblige us to apply an effective remedy';[34] in 1604 bishop Rovirola condemned 'encartats or engaged men who enter the houses of their betrothed'[35] and in 1608 he ordered 'that those esposats by verba de praesenti not live together before celebrating the nuptial mass'.[36] In May 1620 the vicar-general of the diocese, Pau Plà, was obliged to issue a 'Letter to engaged couples', which spoke of 'many great abuses among the encartats and engaged couples, in entering the houses of their engaged partners before being married, committing many great and enormous sins and furthermore with even greater risk of ills, such as abandoning the engaged girls after seducing them, and entering their houses to the great scandal of the neighbourhood; and because of these abuses rectors, vicars and curates may not marry them unless they receive permission'.[37] On pain of a fine of ten ducats, the vicar-general forbade clergy to marry men 'who have entered the houses of their betrothed partners (for which information should be taken from neighbours)', unless written permission had been given by him or another vicar-general.

In the diocese of Urgell the situation was the same. The synod there in 1610 condemned 'the great abuse in the present diocese of encartats who live together before celebrating the marriage', and in 1616 insisted that 'those who are married [sposats] by verba de praesenti must receive the nuptial blessing within two months.'[38] In the 1660s the diocese had accepted that cohabitation after verba de praesenti would continue, and imposed a fine of £10 for those who failed to proceed to a church marriage, though the fine was to be graduated for those too poor to pay it. Nothing had changed by 1689, when the bishop complained that even the fine was no longer levied and that 'there is little improvement in the matter of the encartats, to the great peril of their souls.'[39]

It became a standard stipulation in Catalonia from the end of the sixteenth century that those who had contracted *matrimonium* must hear a mass of benediction within at least two months, sometimes more.[40] Like other directives, this was seldom observed. In Mediona, though most couples by the early seventeenth century tended to have a mass, they waited a long time before doing so, delays of one and two years being common: when Joana Vic of Sobiranes married a Tort of St Quintí in October 1586 (in the *mas* and not in church), the couple waited until June 1588 before going to the parish church to receive the blessing.[41] We may assume that they did not wait two years to seal the nuptial bond. Aware of the tenacity with which not simply young couples but also 'parents, guardians and relatives' clung to their traditional practice of marriage, to such an extent that 'the chief prosecutor of our tribunal has drawn up a report saying that many after being esposats live with their wives and let many months pass before receiving the nuptial blessing,' the bishop of Vic in 1628 issued a long six-page edict on the question, insisting that 'even though by reason of the exchange of promises and signing of marriage clauses the betrothed parties must marry within the stipulated time, until they are married in the face of Holy Mother Church it is in no way licit for them to have carnal relations.'[42] The inefficacy of the directives is shown by the fact that a generation later in the diocese of Barcelona, over one century after the closure of Trent, the synod of 1669 was still having to rule 'that those who have contracted marriage by verba de praesenti not live together nor consummate unless they first receive a solemn nuptial blessing, or should receive it within two months'.[43]

The imposition of ecclesiastical marriage had far-reaching and contradictory consequences. While insisting that only church marriage validated sex, the Church continued to maintain the traditional norms: the Vic decrees of 1628, for example, repeated that verba de futuro contracts were legitimate and could not be dissolved without application to the vicar-general of the diocese.[44]

The apparent contradiction between the validity of secular marriage and that of church marriage inevitably raised the problem of what the Church regarded as premarital intercourse and premarital pregnancy. Speedy pregnancies were much desired in peasant communities, as a guarantee that the family would have a succession, and the long wait before nuptial mass must have meant that many girls approached the altar pregnant. Premarital intercourse can, on the evidence available, be considered the norm rather than the exception,[45] but only among couples already tied together by some sort of verbal bond: casual sex among the young was exceptional. Prenuptial pregnancy was therefore common, but the notion suffers from the difficulty of assuming that the church marriage (that is, the 'blessing' noted in the church register) was the effective marriage, and that conceptions pre-dating this were the fruit of lax morality. In practice, as we have seen for Mediona, in most cases the effective marriage took place long before the coming to church; so that data for prenuptial conceptions are not sufficient evidence of liberal sexual contact between young people. Against this, admittedly, we must set the fact that in some early modern societies bridal pregnancies were high – for England the figure is one-fifth of all church marriages[46] – and may be attributed more to incontinence than to pre-church cohabitation, a practice apparently almost unknown in England. Incontinence, no doubt, was the target in 1593 of the bishop of Urgell who, in a clear comment on his own flock, praised the example of a woman saint who 'came into her husband's power with her honour intact, not like many who first lose it in hidden places'.[47]

Another of the instructions of this period arising from Trent was that those about to be married receive adequate instruction in the faith, without which the parish priest was not authorised to marry them. The requirement proved to be optimistic and self-defeating. In the diocesan synod of Barcelona held in April 1574, one of the petitions of the clergy to the bishop was that 'his Reverence be pleased to modify the edict ordering that those who do not know the Christian doctrine cannot be married, in view of the considerable difficulty of many people in learning it, and the experience that in the archdiocese of Tarragona and in the present diocese the rectors have seen and encountered great resentment in the attitude of those who wish to marry'; the bishop accepted this, and left the enforcement of the rules to the judgment of the parish clergy.[48] In Mediona no attempt seems to have been made to enforce the Christian instruction of betrothed until the early seventeenth century. Only at the beginning of 1612, when Jaume Ferrer of Igualada arrived as one of the vicars of Santa Maria, does the record state clearly of the young man from St Pere de Riudebitlles who married a Mediona girl, that 'they were examined in Christian doctrine and found satisfactory and were married by me, Jaume Ferrer.' For the next few months, candidates for marriage were examined and their sufficiency in doctrine noted. However, Jaume Ferrer died in February 1613, and the practice immediately ceased; the new vicar, Magi Fons, seems not to have bothered. Local clergy were apparently a law unto themselves in their application of directives. There is, for example, no record of banns being read out for marriages in Santa Maria until the new vicar in 1621, Vicenç Perere, began the practice.[49]

Although the diocesan court in Barcelona reserved to itself the right to rule on the validity of marriages based on the old concept of verba de futuro, in practice it had to deal with confusions over the matter for up to a century after. The long time that it took for the Tridentine rules to be accepted among the people may be seen in the case of Jerónima Reventos and Pere Joan Olivella, both of Barcelona. In May 1600 Jerónima brought before the diocesan court a plea for separation. It was, in effect, a test case. One year after her previous husband's death, she stated, 'influenced by Pere Joan Olivella, master builder of this city, that they should become man and wife, and believing that they in fact were, she has been with the said Olivella for seven or eight years living with him as man and wife; but finally understanding that they were not married in accordance with the rules of the holy canons and having been misled in her ignorance by the said Olivella, and because of the bad treatment she has received from him in that time as well as because she does not wish to live any longer with him in sin but rather be set free', she now asked the court to declare that she was truly not married and therefore free. The marriage had been in 1588, which meant that they had not been living together for some four years, and she now apparently wanted to marry someone else.

Olivella's case, as put forward by his lawyer, was a direct presentation of the old pre-Trent attitude. He expressed surprise at the terms of the petition, since there was no doubt that he was married. 'They were married by the reverend vicar of the church of the Pi, in the house of Angela Olivella, living in the street Carme and mother of the aforesaid', he stated; 'when the said sposalles were celebrated they were done with such publicity that there were three days of fiestas with parties and dancing, and it is clearly false and most ill done and in great disrespect of the sacrament of Holy Matrimony to say that it was not consummated in the face of Holy Mother Church.' The essential steps of a verbal promise, witnesses, and the presence of a priest had all been taken, though we may note in passing that the marriage had been performed in a house and not in church. The two had shared a house together, she had taken his surname, and they had had three daughters together: 'and all this is publicly known and all the neighbours have understood that they were husband and wife and that the said girls were born of a legitimate marriage.' It is true that there was no written evidence of the betrothal, but that was because records at the Pi only began to be kept properly after the big epidemic of 1589; before that date 'there was no specific marriage register, and marriages were recorded on loose sheets which were easy to lose.' In brief, the marriage was legitimate because according to the principles of canon law 'the contract of marriage is fulfilled by mere consent.'

It was a convincing case: no church ceremony had taken place, but custom, canon law and public opinion all combined to demonstrate that it was a true marriage. Jerónima's lawyer, however, stuck on one single point which in effect was his sole argument: the opposing case was necessarily mere 'mockery', since 'in this case the only valid proof of marriage is the register that the rector of the parish is obliged to keep, and no other proof is valid, according to the rules of the Council' of Trent. The judgment given was brutally simple: no proof of marriage according to the rules of Trent existed, therefore no marriage had taken place, and each party was therefore free to remarry. No doubt such judgments also continued to be made after this date; there can be little doubt that well over a generation after the new rules had been introduced, lawyers were having to sort out what in the Church's eyes constituted a valid marriage.[50]

A comparable case occurred in 1626, again in the parish of the Pi. Jeroni Soler, an exchange broker of Barcelona, had undergone a similar ceremony in the house of Mariana Torre: 'the said Soler obtained a licence from the vicar-general to get married without banns, and so last October the reverend rector of the parish church of the Pi was called, and before him and other witnesses the said Soler stated and declared that he took to wife the said Mariana Torre'; the witnesses included friends and Mariana's parents. But shortly afterwards Soler changed his mind about her and 'refused to treat her as his legitimate wife and refused to live with her and support her'. He seems to have used as his excuse some defect in the procedure (his statement is not in the record), for Mariana pleaded to the vicar-general 'that your reverence declare that between the two there is a legitimate and true marriage contracted by verba de praesenti, and even if that were not so, that there was a sposalles by verba de futuro, in such a manner that the said Soler be compelled and forced to celebrate it now in the face of Holy Mother Church'. A simple but fundamental confusion had arisen in this case: Mariana had assumed the ceremony was of de praesenti and therefore binding, but Soler decided it was only of de futuro, which left him free to desert her legally, leaving her with the legally weak plea that the ceremony 'was a true sposalles de futuro and as such obligates him to have to contract marriage by verba de praesenti'. There is no record of the outcome of the case, which presumably went against Mariana, since she was clinging on to a traditional reading of the rites of marriage which the Church for over half a century had ruled obsolete. The case is vivid evidence that despite the official change in rules, both people and clergy were continuing with the old way of doing things, and appealed for official intervention only when things went wrong.[51]

Presumably cases like these continued to arise frequently but by 1670, one century after Trent, they no longer appear in the documentation of the diocesan court in Barcelona and it seems fair to conclude that by then most marriages were following the official procedure. The cases of that period refer only to marriage being 'contracted', and 'in the face of Holy Mother Church', meaning that the ceremony was within a church building. The old concept of verba de futuro lingered on in questions of jilting, which naturally hinged on the issue of broken promises. Catalan law stated clearly that the man who dishonoured a girl had to marry her or pay her ('endow' her, or pay for her marriage).[52] In 1626 Ana Morera of La Llacuna gave her virginity to Pere Marges of the same parish, and as a result gave birth to a daughter. This may not have been serious since Marges continued to be her lover and 'many times thereafter gave his word that he would marry her'. Eventually however it became clear that he had no such intention, so Ana went to Barcelona to complain to the vicar-general that 'up to today he has not fulfilled his promise', and asked them to 'order, compel and force the said Pere Marges to marry or endow her'. To drive the point home, she made a formal complaint of rape, that he 'carnally knew her with violence and force'. As a result Marges was arrested and kept in the episcopal prisons, and the eventual agreement was that he pay her 200 ducats, a large sum, and that she release him from further responsibility.[53]

A comparable case of broken promises came up in the diocesan court in 1636. When Maria Ferrer, at mass in her Barcelona parish of Saints Just and Pastor, heard banns being read for a proposed marriage between the French trader Joan Cartan and the widow Luisa Roca, she went to the vicar-general and denounced Cartan, saying that 'he had first promised to marry her, and by holding to the promise she had lost other chances of getting married,' and that they had had sex 'as if man and wife, taking her virginity'; all circumstances creating a valid marriage according to the old rules. She also produced a promise to marry her, written by Cartan in Catalan.[54] Subsequently a licence was issued for him to marry Ferrer, but there is no record that he did.

Although the nuclear family (man, wife and children) was the predominant unit in Spanish households, the extended family was the unit more readily recognised by legal systems: in Castile a law manual of 1553 defined the family as 'the man and his wife and all who live under him subject to him, such as sons, grandsons, dependants and servants', and the standard dictionary of Covarrubias (1611) stated a family was 'the people whom a man maintains within his house', or more specifically 'the man and his wife and those under his control such as children and servants'.[55] In Spain as elsewhere the word 'family' also retained its older usage of the linear family, or those sharing a common line of descent. In treating of the family Counter-Reformation writers tended to take an ample perspective of family relations and did not limit themselves exclusively to the links between parents and children. They also wrote for a wide public and consequently used the most suitable idiom, Castilian: there are no early modern works that focus specifically on the Catalan family.

Yet the Catalan family had characteristics which set it apart juridically from the family in other parts of Spain.[56] In an agrarian society where the land was dominated by the family house (*casa pairal*), which was the typical social unit in the greater part of Catalonia and northwards across the Pyrenees,[57] the concern to preserve property holdings intact led to a stress on primogeniture, in which the marriage of the heir took precedence over the marriage needs of the rest of the family. Such a system could work only if firm discipline were exercised in the kinship group, and if other members of the family accepted their secondary role passively. However, in Catalonia as elsewhere,[58] if there were rules they were frequently broken. In the early modern period the complex inheritance customs of Catalonia tended to settle down into a fixed series of rules governing family and property. Virtually all marriages, even where little property was involved, were regulated by marriage clauses (*capítols*) agreed between the contractants and their families. Young people retained the theoretical freedom to marry without the consent of their parents, but in that case they could (as we have seen they did not always) forfeit their property and other rights. The system tended more and more to favour a matrimonial system in which, although the principle of liberty was guaranteed, the disposition of property was kept safely in the hands of the parents until it could be handed over. In the marriage contract the bride would receive a dowry from her parents or guardians, which might vary in value from about £25 to £50 among *pagesos* to about £2000 among the nobility and *ciutadans honrats*. In rural Mediona the normal dowry between 1570 and 1620 among pagesos was about £100, with a bottom level of £50 and a top of £150 among the few exceptions.[59] The dowry remained the property of the bride (in reality, of her parents) during marriage but was administered by the husband, and in the case of his death she had the right to reclaim it from him after the first year of mourning. She could also claim the *tenuta*, the right as widow to be supported by her husband's goods. In principle, then, the Catalan wife retained property rights and her marriage did not represent a loss for her parents. If as a widow she married again she forfeited half the dowry, which went either to her parents, if living, or to the children of the previous marriage.

The husband brought to the marriage an *escreix*, or gift proportional to the dowry, its value varying according to region and status: this remained the property of the wife unless she remarried. In the diocese of Barcelona and in Mediona the escreix was as a rule half the value of the dowry.[60] The system, by protecting the inheritance of the woman and her children, was concerned to obtain the maximum of stability with the minimum of property mobility. This objective was achieved primarily through the principle of primogeniture, central to classic Catalan society. One child (not necessarily the eldest) became the sole 'heir' (*hereu* if male, *pubilla* if female); and all the others were provided with the basics of inheritance (in the case of girls, their future dowry was guaranteed), and with the right to continue living under the family roof. The family home, which is what the mas was throughout the Catalan countryside, became in this way a centre of stability of lineage and property, inhabited by large families consisting of the parents, the hereu, and the *fadristerns* or propertyless brothers of the hereu.

The marriage clauses which regulated this system have been looked upon, rightly, as a clue to the apparent stability of property relationships in rural Catalonia.[61] Little attention however has been paid to the fact that it was the Counter-Reformation Church which played a key role in this process, not indeed in the disposing of property, which followed precedents laid down carefully by the legists of the period and particularly those of the seventeenth century, but in the consolidation of the process of marriage, which after all was what the clauses were meant to do. The change in the terminology of the clauses, a change so important that it can only be described as revolutionary, may be followed in detail in the diocese of Barcelona and the marriage clauses of rural Mediona.

In the fifteenth century the clauses accepted the pre-Tridentine norm, touched on above, that marriage or espousal (esposalles) took place definitively with verba de praesenti. These verba could be given either at the moment of signing the clauses (we find some in 1400 stating that 'the said marriage will be carried out and fulfilled by verba de praesenti or sposalles during today')[62] or at a specified future date. The clauses normally stated that the marriage, a secular ceremony when vows and rings were exchanged in the presence of a notary, would be followed at a future date by the nuptial rites, usually called a benedictio,[63] which consisted of mass with communion. There was never any doubt that the first ceremony was a full marriage, as we can see by the terms of marriage clauses in Mediona. In November 1513 the clauses for Sebastià Sants of Puig Gomar and Joanna Torrens of Mas del Agullons specified a dowry of £25 and an escreix from Torrens of £12. Moreover, 'the said Sebastià Sants takes the said Joanna as his loyal wife, giving himself to her as loyal husband by verba de praesenti as the law of God demands,' and in turn 'the said Joanna, with the advice and express consent of her father and mother and friends gives herself with the dowry to the said Sebastià Sants as loyal wife and takes him as her loyal husband by verba de praesenti as God and Holy Mother Church demand.'[64] The carefully phrased terms established an immediate marriage through the signing of the clauses, with the consent of the contractants, parents and community ('friends'). The clauses of March 1525 which bound together Llorenç Tort of St Quintí and Magdalena Vic of Mas Sobiranes, also gave a dowry of £25 and had similar conditions. Tort 'with the consent and express will of his family takes the said Magdalena as his loyal wife', while she 'takes the said for her loyal husband, giving herself to him as loyal wife, according to the law of God and as Holy Mother Church has ordained'.[65] However, 'to fulfil the present marriage, they agree that the esposalles be celebrated now de praesenti, and that the blessing be received in the face of Holy Mother Church during the coming month of June'; so that the couple bound themselves to a nuptial mass three months after the marriage. What these and similar clauses of the period conveyed, in short, was a more or less immediate[66] secular marriage, with the possibility of a church ceremony at some time in the future.

None of this suited the Catholic reformers, for whom the partners bound by the clauses were merely 'contracted' (encartats) or 'engaged' (promesos) rather than truly married, even if they had exchanged verba de praesenti. Nor did the clergy consider it acceptable that such couples should immediately live together as husband and wife, a practice clearly sanctioned by the clauses (which spoke of 'husband' and 'wife') and therefore common throughout Catalonia. At Trent the view which won the day was that a marriage must consist of two parts, the contract and the blessing, and couples had no right to set up as spouses if they had not first obtained the nuptial mass.[67] The contract, in their view, was not a marriage but merely an engagement. This view, which undermined an assumption common to the marriage clauses in Catalonia, was pressed home vigorously by every bishop from the late sixteenth century onwards, as we have seen from the 1628 instruction issued by the bishop of Vic. It is clear that for the bishops the old form of secular marriage sanctioned in the clauses was unacceptable unless a nuptial mass was celebrated, and that those who only performed the first ceremony were, although legally married, living in sin. It was a major attempt by the Church to arrogate to itself a jurisdiction over marriage which it had never effectively possessed but which it now wished to affirm, despite the fact that it went against the common custom of Catalonia.

The slow but fundamental change that took place in marriage clauses is evidence of the seriousness of the Church campaign. Before Trent the wording stated unequivocally that the contractants were 'wife' and 'husband', but after Trent the wording was slowly changed so as to eliminate this description. In the clauses drawn up in April 1600 for Antoni Busquet of St Quintí and Mariana Palles of Capellades, the term 'wife' was now 'wife to be', and the 'husband' a 'husband to be', while both parties undertook to 'carry out and fulfil the present marriage by verba de praesenti and ecclesiastical blessing' in June, unequivocally linking together the verba de praesenti with the nuptial mass.[68] Another comparable formula, common to some clauses in Mediona after about 1600, can be found in those drawn up in May 1601 for Quintí Mallofre of Mas de les Parellades and Eulàlia Poca of St Quintí. The dowry in this case was an exceptional £220, and the two promised 'to carry out and fulfil the present marriage by verba de praesenti suitable and sufficient to contract a marriage of esposalles and receive ecclesiastical blessing', a wording which linked the verba, the esposalles and the blessing into one act.[69]

The intricacies of the marriage contract would continue to cause confusion and there was always resistance to the imposition of Church control over sexual behaviour, but in the case of the marriage clauses the bishops had a vital weapon which they did not hesitate to use: the power to appoint notaries, who dictated the wording of the clauses. As we have seen,[70] in most dioceses the rural notaries tended to be appointed by the bishop, who issued standard formulations of clauses for their guidance: in 1600 bishop Coloma of Barcelona supplied three different formulations to cater for different categories of marriage.[71] By the early seventeenth century in Mediona marriage clauses were normally Tridentine in form, and the tendency was growing for ceremonies (esposalles) to be carried out in church together with a nuptial mass.[72] The situation was still not wholly satisfactory: half of the forty-four marriages performed in the parish of Santa Maria in the ten years 1620–30 were accompanied by nuptial mass, but though all the others also went to church for a blessing eventually there were couples who waited for four, six and in one case eighteen months before doing so. However, there were no longer cases like the marriage in February 1584 of the daughter of Montserrat Martí; the ceremony was carried out in his mas of Casa Nova in Agullàdolç, and the couple did not bother to have a nuptial mass until July 1586.

If historians are right to point to 'the tenacity of the belief that people could regulate their own matrimonial affairs without the assistance or interference of the Church',[73] then the Counter Reformation may have had little or no effect on the sturdy independence of the Catalan mas. But we know that ideas on marriage were changing in Spain, and should therefore take note of some views current in the peninsula, in books that were published in Barcelona or sold in the city and to be found in the libraries of contemporary Catalans.

Although several Spanish writers of the early sixteenth century had addressed themselves to the theme of married life, the first one to claim to be devoting himself explicitly to the subject was Francisco de Osuna, whose *Pole Star for all Conditions* (1531)[74] appeared shortly before the first sessions of Trent. During the Trent period, perhaps the most substantial treatment of the subject came from Pedro de Luján in his *Matrimonial Colloquies* (1550), a dialogue in which advice on the married way of life was offered by a married woman to the young maiden Eulàlia. Among the most important tracts on marriage to appear in the period was fray Vicente Mexía's *Salutary Instruction on the State of Marriage* (Córdoba 1566). In his old age, when his failing voice no longer served to deliver discourses from the pulpit, the Dominican preacher explained that 'seeing the clear need that everybody has to know as Christians what pertains to matrimony, I put my mind to writing the present work, which I think contains all or almost all that touches married persons.' He was echoed by fray Martín Cano, who observed in the preface that 'nothing I have seen so far has satisfied the long-standing wish to see a book written expressly to inform married people.' The Córdoba Dominicans were conscious that the work broke new ground, and indeed Mexía's tract, written in simple and lucid Castilian ('this is written for people untrained in letters'), departed completely from the older courtly tradition and dealt with the moral problems of the average family. The author himself confessed that his first aim had been to write for 'married women of rank and position', but that he later thought it more useful 'to give general guidance to all ranks of people in the state of matrimony'. His work, in both its approach and its style, was a radical break from the type of presentation given by Osuna, who had made clear in 1531 that virginity rather than marriage was the highest of all states for the Christian. Writing immediately after Trent, Mexía none the less seems not consciously to reflect the attitudes of the Counter Reformation, and he nowhere cites any of the sessions of Trent; by contrast, though he regularly cites Aquinas, throughout he relies almost exclusively on the Bible as the basis of all his conclusions. The work may be taken to reflect traditional moral practice as seen through the eyes of reformist Dominicans, a mingling in short of old and new.

Seeing in the relationship between husband and wife the basis of marriage, Mexía inevitably spent much space on defining it. Condemning those many who 'dare to treat their wives as slaves, saying that they have to be subject and obedient as to a lord', he said that 'those who presume to do this offend greatly against God and justice and the natural order.' The man is certainly superior to the woman in matrimony, and the woman is subject to the man, but having affirmed that this is the relationship as laid down by God Mexía hastened to clarify the situation. The subjection of the woman, he reminded men, 'is quite different from all other types of subjection'; for though the husband governs as the head governs the body, 'yet in all else the relation is not one of greater and lesser but of equals in everything ... equals in honour and service and reverence and possession and ownership of goods and table and clothing and bed and whatever else pertains to the state of the husband: all of this the wife has equally and without distinction.'[75] Without using the concept of love, a word which does not emerge consciously in these pages, the author preferred to explain the contract between man and wife in more concrete terms. As in a political community, where power is conceded voluntarily, Mexía explained, so in marriage the power of a man over his wife is granted voluntarily by the wife, but the wife still retains all her rights and must be treated 'not as a slave or servant but as a free woman, lady of the house and estate and goods and whatever else he has, with the one obligation of obeying him'. Even this obligation does not hurt the wife's rights, and in certain circumstances (notorious adultery is the example cited) the wife may reclaim her freedom from her husband.

In a summary of his position Mexía stresses once again his emphasis on the liberty of the partners within marriage:

In everything said so far the main point is to show that the married woman though subject to the governance of her husband does not lose her liberty as lady of the house and of everything that belongs to the husband. And to summarise it in a few words it can be reduced to two main considerations that the husband must keep before him in order to avoid any excess in governance of his wife. One is, to take care not to offend against the respect due to her as mistress of the house. The other is, not to harm her by wishing without reason to take from her what she is in justice due, namely the liberty which she as his wife must have and enjoy in everything.[76]

It goes without saying that Mexía throughout the book insisted on the contractual nature of marriage and therefore on the mutual obligation of both man and wife; the wife is adjured to serve the husband well just as the husband is urged to serve his wife well: 'husbands must guard against injuring wives by word or mistreating them in deed ... they must be treated lovingly, and provided adequately with what they need.'

Most writers were agreed on the unacceptability of violence within marriage:[77] Juan de Dueñas in his *Mirror to Console the Sad* (1582) lamented that 'many husbands treat their wives not as wives nor even as servants but as slaves; dishonouring them with ugly and bad words, or with evil deeds, laying hands on them, beating them, pulling them by the hair, bruising them ... Making their life more properly a death than a life.'[78] The mutual duties of husband and wife were similarly emphasised by the Franciscan fray Antonio Alvarez in his *Sylva Spiritual* (Saragossa 1590). Addressing himself to the husband, Alvarez said:

Now tell me, brother, how often you have discussed with your wife matters of the house and family, consulted her on affairs and business and investments, over helping your children and giving them a good settlement according to their rank, and other such matters? Have you ever discussed what you will do with your life and hers to build a common ladder hand in hand to heaven? I would not be surprised if you told me the truth and said Never. O unforgivable omission, worthy of punishment! Take this to heart, that the first step on the way to heaven is this common link and bond that good married couples should have, husband and wife going jointly in all their business and dealings hand in hand on the way to heaven.[79]

Marco Antonio de Camos' *Microcosmia* (Barcelona 1592) was typical of the growing literature that attempted to present a Christian view of marriage and is certainly the most appealing of all such works published in Catalonia. One of the interlocutors in his dialogue, Turritano, attacked the institution of marriage in these words: 'Who wishes to marry? Truly, woman has I don't know what in her nature that makes her uncontrollable... which is why when Simonides was asked what woman represented for man, replied: shipwreck, a storm in his house, a troubler of his peace, servitude of his life, a continuous hurt, a constant quarrel; a room containing a tiger, a rabid dog in disguise, in fine a necessary evil which we have to suffer. Happy he who is free of woman, says Hesiod.' To this Valdiglesia, who represents the views of the author, responds, 'I am sure you would not talk like this if you were in the presence of one... All you say is to be understood of the bad woman....' He then goes on to praise women and their achievements, and to explain that their subjection 'is not one of slavery but, as St Paul says, honest and conjugal subjection'. The praises are bestowed on all the famous women of classical and Biblical times, and it is significant that among those who merit them is Isabella the Catholic. When Turritano at a later stage complains that he has 'decided not to marry', and that 'the married man is no longer master of himself and cannot give himself to the study of letters or other matters, since he has to bear the heavy burden of the wife,' whereas a servant would be more reliable in the house, the same emphasis is given to the benefits of marriage. Above all, says Camos, husband and wife must tolerate each other, with 'the constancy and patience of tolerating each other, and pardoning injuries with charity', and the woman must respect her man if she herself wishes respect, 'for it would be a miracle to find a woman respected as lady who does not respect her husband as lord'. Turritano objects that St Paul says women must fear their husbands, which makes Valdiglesia explain that 'the fear that the apostle says woman must have of their husbands is not to be understood as a servile fear but as an upright conjugal fear, such as a son has for a father... it is a fear based on love.' As for the man, he must realise the great travails the woman goes through for his sake: 'Will you, ungrateful man, not suffer the woman who bears and gives you children of your own flesh and blood, bearing them nine months at the risk of her health, giving birth to them in pain and peril of her life, and rearing them with such patience?' In sum, says Camos, the wife is 'neither superior nor inferior but equal in love and companionship'.[80]

The insistence on equality and freedom, however, must be placed within context: from the earliest writers onwards, there was a general agreement that the woman's role was primarily domestic. Not all, perhaps, would have reduced the matter to the terse phrase of a writer of 1589 – 'few woman friends and few outings from the house'[81] – but an inevitable male outlook fashioned the opinion of most writers, beginning with Luján's apothegm, directed to Eulàlia, on what most befitted a woman: 'a distaff in her belt as a man wears a sword'. For some of these writers – and one understands readily why commentators such as Astete (see below) placed such emphasis on freedom – the wife was a virtual slave in the house, attending to every task both great and small, waiting upon husband and children at every moment of the day, going to bed the last (in a phrase common to more than one writer) and getting up the first.[82]

Though much of the literature insisted on the nature of the husband/wife relationship, this should not be taken to mean that the mutual relationship existed independently of other obligations. The 'couple' of modern bourgeois life was unknown in pre-industrial Catalonia; in practice, husband and wife existed as realities only because other obligations brought them together: family, children, household, work. As has been said of the French peasant family of a later period, 'the couple did not exist, because it had no space dedicated to it,'[83] all household space, even the bed, being communal. The notion of shared duties and of mutual help was central to the change in attitude which some writers of the Counter Reformation tried to inculcate.

The most complete treatment of marriage within the context of the Counter Reformation came from the Jesuit Gaspar Astete's *The Government of the Family and the State of Marriage* (Valladolid 1598). Though writing with the full weight of Trent behind him, Astete in no way limited himself to the ecclesiastical dimensions of marriage, and his manual was a remarkable blend of official advice, homely counsel, and good humour directed to the ordinary reader. 'The state of matrimony', he said, 'is one of the states of the Church, and the first and oldest,' taking precedence over all the other conditions in the Church, whether secular or priestly. It is a profession, and 'just as any other workman wishes to be perfect in his art and calling, so with more reason should the married person be perfect in his state.' The husband and wife must love and respect each other; the husband in particular 'must trust in his wife and esteem her and praise her things and speak well of her when she is and when she is not there'. Beginning with the principle that 'married couples have to share the burdens of marriage', Astete went beyond it and argued for considerable autonomy for the wife. 'Husbands', he said, 'must leave some things to the will of the wives,' leaving them to spend cash in the way they think best, dress as is befitting, go to mass frequently if they wish. When talking of cash, indeed, Astete was almost unique among writers of the period in calling for full autonomy for the wife: 'I affirm that if the husband is generally satisfied with his wife he should hand her either all the money or at least what is sufficient for the household to be well provided for'; and cited his own personal experience of 'a man I knew who would hand to his wife everything he had, saying: Señora, give me my meals and let me not go without clothing and the rest, and after do your own duties,' adding by way of comment that 'commonly women are less prodigal in expenses that harm the household than husbands.'[84]

The information supplied by these writers allowed a substantial treatment of marriage to appear in the *Summa of Cases of Conscience* of the Portuguese Franciscan Manuel Rodríguez. Written as a guide for confessors, and therefore couched exclusively in the standard terminology of what was and what was not sinful, Rodríguez' manual was published first in Lisbon in 1593 and then issued in Salamanca, Saragossa and Barcelona. It was particularly successful in Barcelona, where the 1596 edition was followed by a second in 1597 and another in 1607. Though basing himself very strongly on Trent, Rodríguez like other authors of the same genre felt himself free to disagree with received opinion on many issues. On the matter of the conflict between rights of marriage and the decree Tametsi, he was adamant that 'the son or daughter who marries against the wishes of the father sins mortally. For although the Council of Trent may say that such a marriage is valid it does not remove from children the duty of consulting the father . . . and so fathers may prevent children from marrying, nor do they thereby incur the penalties of the Council.' Rodríguez' volume, one of the most widely used in the period of the Counter Reformation, was on the whole harsh in its judgments. For example, he asserted that 'the husband sins if he severely whips or harshly punishes his wife,' but then went on to say that 'he may however punish and whip her if he suspects infidelity.'[85] The full Counter-Reformation doctrine of marriage did not emerge in print until the Jesuit Tomás Sánchez brought out his magisterial *De Sancto Matrimonii Sacramento*. Issued in two volumes, in Genoa in 1602 and then in Madrid in 1605, the work was destined to remain the standard corpus of thought on Catholic marriage. Its publication abroad, and in Latin, demonstrates that it was written for the learned world and not in the first instance meant as a contribution to the educational process taking place in Spain.

The existence of romantic love in early modern Europe remains a matter of debate, for love assumes the freedom to choose and choice, as has been suggested for England,[86] was normally restricted to a small section of the elite. There is no definitive proof that love was generally accepted as a precondition of marriage, and though Don Quixote in the early seventeenth century opined that 'for lovers to get married is the happiest of endings'[87] no commentator seems to have insisted that love ought to precede wedlock. On the other hand, all in greater or lesser degree insisted that love must exist within marriage, without making any effort to resolve the possible contradictions between the notion of love and the reality of servitude. Luján, who insisted firmly on the servitude of the wife, insisted no less that 'if love is lacking in the marriage, everything is lacking.'[88] The Counter Reformation did not innovate on the basic ideas of the relation between man and wife and contributed no new perception of love; but after mid-century there was a much greater emphasis, unknown in previous writings, on the duties of the husband within marriage, and a clearer recognition that the wife's role was not merely to accept a position of servitude.[89]

Jerónimo de Lemos' *Tower of David* (1567) was one of the first works of the post-Tridentine period in Spain to consider 'love' not simply as the obedience owed by the wife but also as the respect owed by the husband. His section headings stated unequivocally that 'the sauce of marriage is love,' that 'love between couples achieves much,' and that 'the strengths of love are many.' Inevitably, the definition of love was derived heavily from the Bible. Lemos says for example: 'What would one not do for love? It has been well said that love conquers all. And no wonder, for God himself through love for the human race gave his son for our redemption.' But the entire context of the repeated references to 'love' demonstrates that the concept was considered concretely within the theme of marriage, as a sentiment which though related to its divine origins governed and modified the relationship between a man and a woman. The married interlocutor of the dialogue, Tranquilo, gives the following advice on treating one's wife:

> Keep yourself from three things as from the fire . . . First, never lay your hands on her. Things are in a serious state at home if they have come to this, for it is something done only by low, rude and vulgar people . . . An honourable man may not mistreat or harm his wife, for she is his companion not his slave. The second thing to guard from, is not to offend your wife before anybody else . . . And the third thing, is not to go through the town and to the neighbours complaining of your wife and listing her defects.[90]

None of these writers dared to specify the precise role of sexuality within love, and though many, such as Tomás Sánchez, allowed that sex is an expression of love, a view enunciated before them by

Aquinas, they all identified the function of sex with the classic Christian concept of the *debitum*, the marital duty, implying moreover that anything which went beyond the duty and involved simple pleasure was sinful. None of the writers, inevitably, dared to say that sexual love can lead to marriage. The continued assertion by so many works of an ideal of love from which sexuality was carefully censored perpetuated in society a clearly double standard, in which the reality of sexual mores among the people was suppressed on the grounds that the authentic morality was in effect the official aspiration towards non-carnal affection.

The most explicit statement of love as the basis of marriage comes in the beautiful dialogue by Marco Antonio de Camos, *Microcosmia and Universal Government of the Christian Man* (1592). Camos was prior of the Augustinian friary in Barcelona, and in many respects his book represents the most liberal thought of the period. Speaking of matrimony, the dialogue claims:

> This is its principal aim: union through love, so that love may grow in them and extend to the children and family. Even if there were no other aim to it, this in itself is to be desired and is of great benefit. And how much more of benefit is faith, understood here as the loyalty and fidelity that the wife owes to the husband and the husband to the wife.[91]

By this date the use of the word love to signify the basic relation in marriage was standard: Manuel Rodríguez titles one of his chapters, for example, 'Of the love of married persons'. By the mid-seventeenth century the appearance of the *Letter-Guide to the Married* (Lisbon 1651), by Francisco de Mello, author of the well-known work on the Catalan revolt, was good evidence of the acceptance of high marriage ideals among the elite. Mello's small tract, written for a friend who was about to get married, was simply a paean of praise to the delights of a happy marriage, while emphasising the mutual obligations of husband and wife.

There is every reason for concluding that love was a normal and respected sentiment in Catalonia. The testaments drawn up in Mediona at the end of the sixteenth century are clear witness: in the careful provisions made by Pere Esteve, pagès of Mas de Prades, for his wife in 1598; in the special provisions by Sebastià Torrens, pagès, in 1599, for his wife 'for the love and good service she has given me'; in the will of Joan Ruis, pagès, of St Joan de Conilles, leaving all his property to 'Eulàlia, my beloved wife'.[92]

A quite different tendency, among writers who felt that the concept of love was undermining the nature of marriage, can be found in the Jesuit Luis de la Puente, who in his *On the Perfection of the Christian* (Valladolid 1613) emphasised the great need for wives to be subject to their husbands, and devoted much space to 'the importance of this subjection'. He criticised, for example, 'the excessive love shown them by their husbands' to the extent that men end up being dominated by their spouses. 'The perfect married man', was his verdict, 'should not normally speak to his wife with words of excessive tenderness that show too much softness and love, but with suitable authority and gravity.'[93]

Love in western Europe had always implied freedom, and the courtly love of the late mediaeval Mediterranean had specifically adopted an ideal of a love not tied down by marriage or by family. The recognition of love and the existence of illicit marriages implied that there was some freedom to choose one's partner, though as elsewhere in Europe there were inevitably practical restrictions. The view that 'popular marriage in former times was usually affectionless, held together by considerations of property and lineage,'[94] has now long been superseded by the recognition that affection has a part to play in the making of marriage bonds. Similarly, the view that there was a highly oppressive 'stability' in the rural community[95] which restricted movement and therefore choice of marriage partners, was incontestably true of many societies down to modern times but cannot be taken as a general rule. The evidence available for Catalonia suggests a fluid society which offered considerable choice. Two notable factors contributed to fluidity in this period: the immigration of French males into towns and villages, and the drift of the labour force towards the Mediterranean coast. Mediona offers a tiny example of both these developments. It has been stated that some two-thirds of the marriages celebrated in the period 1575–1630 involved partners from outside the terme, usually from the ten-kilometre radius around the region. Apart from about ten instances where the outsider was female, the contribution of outsiders to marriages in the terme was overwhelmingly male, confirming a rule general to communities in western Europe.[96] The 'strangers' tended to be men working in the terme, and were easily absorbed into the community, where their presence offered the women a choice but did not threaten the stability of society.

Clandestine marriages had been a prominent example of the exercise of freedom of choice, and we have seen that the Counter Reformation was a powerful influence in outlawing them. The perennial conflict between the wishes of contractants and the will of parents was, however, never satisfactorily resolved. The leading Catalan jurists all emphasised that freedom was basic to marriage, and that no marriage contract was valid unless agreed to voluntarily by the parties; even when contracts were made by agents authorised by the parties, they had no force until actually signed by the parties without duress.[97] In practice the jurists were compelled to recognise that parents had obvious rights. Among the upper classes, for whom property was a central issue in marriage, the will of parents tended to preponderate and as a result all the moralists gave priority to parental choice, the Jesuit Andrade stating that 'God will punish those who marry against the wishes of their parents.'[98] The Church tended to decide the issue in favour of parents and property but always reserved the right to change its emphasis. The instructions given to the clergy of Vic in 1628, for example, specified that the consent of parents or guardians must be obtained before any marriage, not because such consent was necessary but simply because it avoided complications.[99] It is not surprising to find that most marriage clauses of the period, their text inevitably influenced by the bishops, included a reference to the consent of parents.

Love was recognised less as a prelude to marriage than as a desirable relationship within it, and at no stage could it be cited as a reason for making a choice of partner against accepted norms; but freedom to choose one's partner, or to approve of one's partner if the choice was made by someone else, was recognised as a paramount right throughout Spain.[100] Among the lower classes, where property had little role, this right operated in practice; and the general work mobility of young people, together with the fact that low expectation of life usually left only one parent to try to exercise control,[101] gave a practical freedom of which strict families might disapprove. Ironically, among wealthy families there was consequently less freedom of choice, and liberty became rather a prerogative of the lower classes. An interesting case before the diocesan court at Barcelona in 1625 throws light on the relationship between courting and freedom of choice. A young weaver, Jaume Mansa, was accused by Maria Ferreron of breaking a promise to marry her, and since the existence or otherwise of the promise was impossible to prove Mansa was driven back on two defences: first, that courtship of a girl did not always imply an intention to marry, second that Maria was not in any case the type of girl a nice boy would marry. Witnesses did not deny that the two had been keeping each other's company a great deal but, said a friend of Mansa, 'he does not know if they did it with a view to marriage or just to pass the time.' As for himself, the friend went on, 'he has courted many times but has never married the girl he was courting, and he understands that the same is true of all the other young men, that not all those who go courting marry the girls they have courted: for marriages ought to be of one's free will and not forced,'[102] unique testimony from a member of the younger generation in Barcelona who used to enjoy paying compliments to girls while 'strolling down the Rambla'. Mansa's own declaration said explicitly that 'it is common and habitual practice among young men and young women to court only for pleasure and in order to pass the time, with no intention of getting married,' a liberty which apparently could be found in Barcelona but was unlikely to have existed in the Catalan countryside. Nor, indeed, did the liberty exist for girls on the same scale: Maria's name was systematically blackened by several witnesses, not least by Mansa himself, claiming that she 'has lived very freely and loosely and not very honestly, for she has been seen going alone after young men outside the city'.

In rural communities – unlike cities with their high mobility and exogamy – choice was restricted by the number of partners available, but the evidence for Catalonia does not suggest that this was a major hindrance, given the mobility among some communities and the peculiar factor of French immigration. Some country parishes might have a high degree of endogamy,[103] but Mediona is proof that contact between parishes could supply an ample range of choice. Introduction of new blood was never enough to solve a fundamental problem of all self-sufficient communities in Europe: the high degree of consanguinity among young people. When in 1616 the Spanish government attempted to reform the political structure of the Vall d'Arán, it focused particularly on the presumed level of incest among the inhabitants;[104] but the problem was general in Catalonia, and affected a number of issues beyond the central one of marriage.

All societies have a taboo over marriage unions between close relatives, but in late mediaeval Europe such family relationships were difficult to identify, and in small towns and villages with high endogamy the problem could be acute, so that it was common for couples to seek dispensation (available only from Rome) from the rules prohibiting marriage within the forbidden degrees, specified since the Lateran Council of 1215 as being everyone within the fourth degree.[105] In Mediona in 1596, for example, Joan Pino of Sta Margarida was given a dispensation, issued in Rome in 1595, setting aside his consanguinity with Candia Pino of Moja; and in the same year two cousins 'tertio consanguinitatis gradu' of Masquefa were likewise permitted to marry.[106] In the Pyrenean valleys the problem was known to be acute. In 1625 Antoni Babot and Maria Joana Martí, cousins from Andorra, argued that they needed a dispensation because 'they could not and in fact cannot contract marriage in the valleys of Andorra more suitably and with less consanguinity than they have, et hoc propter angustia of the Andorra valleys'.[107] The word *angustia*, as used in the Catalan of that time, referred to the smallness of the communities. In 1662

Pere Pau Bellera and Mariangela Feliu of the adjacent villages of Claverol and Figuerola in Urgell pleaded for dispensations and the latter stated that 'because of the angustia and smallness of the villages, even if they went from one village to the next they would not find anybody with whom they could contract marriage, of their own rank and condition, who was not related to them by blood'.[108] Though the testimonies point to a common phenomenon, it is likely that the problem was solved naturally by emigration rather than by incest; in any case, the surviving documentation suggests that very few dispensations were applied for (in the diocese of Urgell, as few as one application a year). Applications went through the vicar-general of the diocese, who would normally establish the nature of the blood relationship by testimonies from three of the oldest inhabitants in the community, and would then issue a permission in the name of the pope. In practice, many considerations entered into whether a dispensation could be issued. When Antoni Vidal and Susana Vilana, both of Oliana, were allowed by the vicar-general of Urgell in 1601 to marry despite their consanguinity, witnesses were asked 'if the said Susana has sufficient dowry to marry a man of her condition who is not related to her' (to which the answer given was 'No'), and 'if Antoni has stolen Susana away and has her in his power' (to which the answer was 'Yes'); so that the further evidence of limited choice influenced the giving of a dispensation.[109] In the diocese of Urgell, from which these cases come, the most common tactic used by those wanting a dispensation was to force the issue by claiming that they had had sex together and that permission was necessary so that the girl would not be defamed; in 1627 Esteve Prat and Eulàlia Viladomar confessed significantly that 'they have had bodily copula, but not so that His Holiness would more easily grant a dispensation for them to marry, but out of fragility,' that is, from weakness of the flesh.

The possible links within a community could also be aggravated by the custom of giving godparents, who by taking on the role (to all appearances a spiritual one) were deemed also to fall within the forbidden degrees; and since in some parts of Spain it was possible to have as many as ten godparents at a baptism[110] the creation of yet more family links raised still higher the risks of 'consanguinity'. The Council of Trent was adamant that godparents be restricted in number to only one male and one female, a regulation which was among the few of the Council to have taken effect in the Spanish parishes, where from the mid-sixteenth century the practice of multiple godparents seems to have vanished immediately. Yet the system of godparents continued to be of great significance in the communities, for it was fundamentally what gave substance to the rite of baptism. Baptism was the rite of passage by which one entered into the family and community (the notion of entering into the Church was only one aspect of the whole), and the record of baptism was in an absolute sense the only proof that one existed at all. Entry into the Christian community had to be protected and guaranteed by guardians, preferably guardians of power and status who would ensure the infant's role in subsequent years, though in poorer communities with little property godparents might be selected at random from family and friends.[111] Baptism initiated the infant into a system of relationships which affected his social position and also his eventual choice of a marriage partner. It was still, as it had been in the west since at least Roman times,[112] a kinship rite rather than a sacrament, and it was consequently the kinship emphasis that both Luther and the Counter Reformation attempted to minimise or abolish, not only because it created more and more forbidden degrees and therefore impediments to marriage but also because it obscured entirely the theological concept of the ceremony. In Santa Maria de Mediona the community nature of baptism was emphasised by the fact that the ceremony was carried out almost exclusively in the mas rather than in the church, despite continuous episcopal directives to the contrary: of the 112 baptisms performed by the vicars between 1587 and 1593, only two were in a church building.[113] The practice had been banned in the province of Tarragona since the provincial council of 1429,[114] and continued to be prohibited by synods throughout the period[115] but it is likely that rural parishes ignored the ruling.

The question of marital fidelity, in a society which did not allow divorce, centred on the action that might be taken against the offending party. Surviving customary laws in much of western Europe allowed the husband to take extreme sanctions against his wife, and though moral theologians had to accept this in practice, they were adamant that there was a real conflict between such laws and the laws of God. Astete followed standard thought in condemning outright as murder the frequently used right to kill an unfaithful wife in flagrante delicto: 'it is a serious and outrageous crime, because though the laws do not punish the man he sins mortally and whoever kills his wife on his own authority is a murderer.'[116] Wife-murders went on periodically despite such condemnations – we have noted a case in the terme of Mediona, and Pujades in 1602 noted one in Barcelona[117] – and the Church tended to impose temporary sanctions on the offender but could never actually overcome popular approval of the action. Juan de Pedraza's *Summa of Cases of Conscience*, published in Barcelona in 1566 and then because of its success published in Catalan in 1571 and in 1588, admitted that 'the common people take it as accepted that if one finds one's wife with another man one may kill them without blame,' but went on immediately to say that the killer 'sins mortally'.[118]

The act of sexual infidelity in itself was seldom regarded as fundamental, since it was a sin and an offence against the contract of marriage of dimensions similar to, say, bad treatment, but did not necessarily destroy the marriage. When in Barcelona in 1621 Sperança Font brought in a plea for separation from her husband, little reliance could be put on her claim that he had brought in a woman to sleep in bed with them, and she had to resort to the more cogent plea of a threat to her life.[119] The moralists did not condone any 'double standard', Astete stating clearly that 'the adulterous man sins more than the woman', 'although' (he adds) 'on the woman's side there is more risk and harm'.[120] The distinction was a purely practical one: an adulterous woman getting pregnant by another man was implicitly destroying the basis of the marriage, which was to have and rear the children of her husband; and she was therefore creating a public offence. Getting pregnant therefore made her offence immediately graver than the man's, for it created public dishonour. In the same way, if the husband offended against the wife in a way that compromised her honour, she had a right to plead for separation; as Mexía says,

> in such a case if the fact were public and demonstrable and there were no way of remedy nor possibility of pardoning him, the wife could get a Church ruling to separate from her husband and not live with him. She would consequently be free of any subjection to him, and of the obligation to obey him, but not of the matrimonial bond whereby she cannot remarry while he lives.[121]

Dishonour rather than adultery was the primary offence; women, too, had honour, and were entitled to defend it. It may be that thanks to the concept of honour the double standard had less force in early modern Spain, but there is no clear evidence of this and against it one must take into account the notorious chauvinism of some Mediterranean societies.

By the same token, in cases where the step of separation had not been taken, Mexía discussed the position of a wife whose husband is a known adulterer, and whether the wife had the right to refuse to have sex with him. The position, as accepted by Rodríguez in 1593, was that 'the husband may legitimately refuse to have intercourse with his adulterous wife ... but note that the wife also has this liberty';[122] the right, however, does not exist if both are guilty. Unable to protect the marriage unit solely by pressure on the male, the Church attempted to vindicate the rights of the female.

The instability of love and marriage in our day was already a problem in early modern times: 'it is no surprise', commented Diego Pérez in Catalonia in 1588, 'that in our time there is such unhappiness in marriages, because they are agreed and practised without the spirit of God.'[123] Astete in 1598 condemned the high incidence of adultery: 'there is such evil in the world today on this matter that it is a disgrace to see how openly and unashamedly and godlessly so many adulteries are committed, and with no penalty or punishment.'[124] Such comments are nevertheless misleading, since they start with the unspoken premise, implicit in the approach of Catholic moralists of the time, that stability of marriage was the norm; when there is considerable evidence to suggest that stability was the desired ideal rather than the daily reality. In late mediaeval Flanders, broken marriages and separation by mutual consent were commonplace.[125] In post-Reformation Germany, the attempt to stabilise marriage discipline was a constant challenge, with the Lutheran church courts particularly active precisely in the mid-sixteenth century.[126] There is every reason to think that Spain was no different. At every social level the security of the conjugal pair might be threatened by emotional and sexual tensions, family and property interests, subsistence crises and mortality: broken marriages were in pre-industrial times a commonplace, and a happy old age was the lot of the single rather than the espoused.

Instability through mortality was the most common of all the factors that threatened marriage. In the seventeenth century in Sant Feliu de Llobregat the average length of marriages before the death of one partner was as low as 13.2 years, though elsewhere in the interior the average could rise to just over 20 years. By the time that most young people got themselves married,[127] one of their parents was no longer alive.

Mediaeval marriage in the west did not always accept that the marriage bond was indissoluble,[128] and among the upper classes marriage was often, as a secular contract, annulled if certain conditions, such as an heir or the payment of a dowry, were not fulfilled. Only gradually did the Church manage to introduce and impose its own principles of indissolubility, but well into the sixteenth century, as we have seen, marriage subsisted as a secular rather than a sacramental union. Civil marriage, whatever its honest intentions, carried no implied or spoken promise of permanence, and it is not surprising that throughout many rural communities in the west the breaking of the bonds by separation or bigamy was to be found. The man punished by the Inquisition of Toledo in 1694 for claiming that marriage was merely a renewable contract, was typical of a body of opinion in Spain that seldom surfaces in the documentation.[129]

In its turn the Church had to recognise that there could be practical obstacles to continuing a union, and the need for 'divorce' (or 'separation' as it should properly be called since complete divorce was not recognised by the Church) was accepted by all authorities on the subject, leading to its rapid acceptance in principle by some Protestants.[130] 'Although divorce is allowed,' notes Astete, 'it is not to be undertaken lightly or on mere suspicion without proof, for experience shows that it causes infinite harm to both body and soul.' 'Divorce cannot be carried out on one's own authority' – a clear indication that couples separated voluntarily – 'but on the decision of the Church, and with much mature reflection.'[131] As these comments might lead us to suspect, separation in the Spanish Church was very rarely granted. Rodríguez followed Church practice in allowing cruelty as the major reason for divorce: 'the wife may ask for a divorce from her husband on grounds of cruelty, and the judge must not permit her to return and live with him even if he swears he will not mistreat her, unless there are adequate guarantees.'[132] Its availability, none the less, always provoked a number of petitions for divorce, as the evidence from the episcopal authorities at Barcelona shows clearly.

'Divorce' in a Catholic country consisted of legal separation sanctioned by the Church courts, normally the diocesan court. In the diocese of Barcelona during the sixteenth and seventeenth centuries as few as two or three petitions for divorce might be made in a year, an insignificant number given the size of the diocese. Since separation of spouses was fairly common among the population, the divorce figures are no guide at all to the real situation. Why then did some bother to seek a legal separation? At no time, one should observe in view of the twentieth-century approach to the question, was infidelity, whether of husband or of wife, ever taken as adequate grounds for breaking the contract of marriage. In all cases the motive cited was unequivocal: to preserve the threefold security of person, property and honour, avoiding any further threats of physical violence, theft of domestic goods, or harm to personal reputation; and only those cases would come to court where these could no longer be assured. The property issue was often crucial. In his standard *Curia Eclesiastica*, the authoritative Ortiz de Salzedo demonstrated that the dowry figured in the divorce ruling in Castile;[133] and in Catalonia the husband had to return the dowry in case of separation.[134]

The procedure for divorce, as it functioned in the diocese of

Barcelona, was not complicated. A plaintiff would present a request through a notary to the vicar-general of the diocese, whose task it would be to get corroborating testimonies. Once the testimonies were received the diocesan official would normally grant a temporary separation, which meant that the plaintiff could live apart and not be molested by the partner. On 10 February 1622, for instance, Paula Torres, wife of a transporter of Barcelona, presented a complaint of her husband 'striking and hitting her and continually threatening her with a dagger and trying to kill her, to the great scandal of all the neighbours', and the order permitting separation was granted the very next day.[135] At this stage it was not necessary to obtain any statement from the partner. Given their socially inferior role, women normally tended to be the plaintiffs.[136] As in all divorce cases, the allegations were not necessarily true. It is legitimate to suspect that because infidelity could not normally be cited as grounds,[137] the plaintiff might often invent a danger to life and limb, and most petitions were directed to demonstrating that a severe risk to security existed. To cite the petitions made in 1660, the wife of a master-builder of Sitges claimed that 'she is mistreated by her husband who threatens to kill her and beats her with his fists and objects, and kicks her'; the wife of a merchant of Barcelona denounced 'the many attempts her husband has made to try to kill her by various means'; the wife of a ciutadà honrat denounced 'death threats'; and the wife of a weaver of Barcelona said that 'he put a dagger to her chest and in particular on one day he took her by the throat and tried to strangle her.'[138] The complaints may have been true, but in principle must be treated with the scepticism due to all such allegations made in the courts, the danger of death being an effective way to pressurise the authorities to grant separation. The major type of cruelty cited in petitions was not physical mistreatment so much as a threat to life by privation of sustenance, an allegation common among those of lesser social standing: the wife of the master-builder alleged that 'her husband refuses to work and to give her the necessary maintenance,' and the wife of the weaver claimed that 'worst of all, he refuses to give her food or anything else.'[139] Husbands, on the other hand, could not in honour claim that they had suffered violence at the hands of their wives, and their accusations normally focused on habitual infidelity, theft and dereliction of duty. Joan Bonet, weaver of Barcelona, whose wife in 1599 was pressing charges against him, stated in his turn that she 'is an adulteress and has committed adultery many times and therefore in law she has no right to press a claim for divorce'; he also claimed that she had left him eighteen months before, taking with her all the money and many of the clothes in the house.[140] Joan Prats, of

Palau, fell back by contrast on the threat of violence: he claimed in 1601 that his wife Eulàlia had tried to poison him two weeks after their marriage in 1585, and that shortly after he fled for his own safety.[141]

Behind the allegations and counter-allegations lurks stray evidence which often puts the cases into their real context. One may for instance question why couples like Joan and Eulàlia Prats who had not lived together for over fifteen years only now decided to ask for separation. In their case the pleas for a divorce were precipitated by a Church order requiring them to live together again. In the case of Joan Pons, farmer of Premià, who in 1597 accused his wife Paula Ponsa of continual adultery, he had hesitated for seven years because (he said) his wife's brothers had threatened him if he did anything against her honour.[142] The 1600 petition for divorce by Miguel Brunet, sculptor of Barcelona, had curious aspects. He married a widow, Anna Vinyals, in 1580, and thereafter they lived together for some five (his figure) or ten (her figure) years, so that by the time of the petition they had been separated for possibly up to fifteen years. According to Anna, whose previous husband was presumed to have perished in the wars in Flanders, they had been together 'until the said Brunet became friendly with the woman-friend he today keeps publicly in his house, from which he has thrown his wife out . . . and in order to be able to marry her he has diabolically invented the story that Antich Vinyals is alive, when in fact he has been dead for over twenty-five years.' Brunet, in effect, was seeking a full annulment of his marriage on the grounds that Anna's husband was still alive and that he had been tricked into marrying her; his motive, it would appear, was the wish to marry his current woman. No firm evidence was produced that Vinyals was still alive, but ironically witnesses testified to having seen him alive and well in Naples shortly after Anna's remarriage, so on this slender evidence the marriage was annulled.[143] These examples demonstrate that the cases which reached the diocesan court tended to arise from exceptional circumstances and prove little either by their nature or by their frequency about the fragility of marriage bonds in Catalonia.

Church courts no doubt often made the wrong decision, working as they did in an ill-defined area, where usually the only evidence was verbal and misleading, but they perhaps deserve some sympathy for being used frequently as instruments in an elaborate game of human emotions. In 1596, for example, the vicar-general of Barcelona dissolved the marriage of Marianna and Joan Maganya on the grounds of the latter's impotence at the time of marriage, and the evidence showed that at the time of the petition Joan was sexually inactive because of a severe urine infection; but we may well find reasonable his argument that there must be some external explanation for the petition by his wife, since 'they have lived together as man and wife, in one bed and living in the same house, for over ten years,' and that she was demonstrably not a virgin, and had conceived once but without giving birth, and that all of this contradicted the claim that he had been impotent.[144]

Second marriages, which in Catalonia in the seventeenth century often made up a quarter to a third of all marriages,[145] may have run a high risk of failure, but the only conclusion possible from the small sample from Barcelona (five second marriages in a sample of thirty divorces consulted) is that they were no more stable than first marriages.[146] Witnesses in 1621 claimed that Pau Sabater, a carder of Barcelona, had lived 'in great peace and quiet' with his first wife, but that his second, Eulàlia, abused him verbally and threatened him with a knife.[147] The noble lady Paula Major married as her second husband in 1622 a merchant of Barcelona, but in 1625 put in a plea for divorce on the grounds that he beat her and spent her money 'dishonestly'; a witness claimed to have seen her 'face covered with blood and she was unable to go out for several days'.[148] Interesting for this and other aspects is the petition by Anna Maria Mir in 1670 for separation from her husband Joan Costa, locksmith of Barcelona. She was his second wife, but only four months later was asking for divorce on the grounds of his violence, and a neighbour who had lived opposite Costa for three years claimed that his previous wife had died from blows to the body. Mir's initial petition cited as grounds that 'he refuses to give her any maintenance for living,' but six months later the court ordered her to return to her spouse, since he had made an undertaking not to mistreat her.[149]

The relatively small number of divorce applications may in part have been influenced by the costs involved, but the procedure seems to have been simple and relatively quick. It is unusual to find a case such as that of Francesca Pallarols, whose petition for separation, initiated in 1596, had still not been decided or conceded in 1610.[150] The numbers for divorce cannot be regarded as a real reflection of the matrimonial problem in Catalonia, since in practice the most common solution, adopted it seems by all social classes, was simply to separate. The bishops were actively aware of the problem, Alonso Coloma in April 1600 for example exhorting his clergy to attend to 'the harm that follows from couples living apart'.[151] A constant theme of pastoral visits was the concern over separated couples: in Solsona in 1668 and in Barcelona in 1669 the synodal decrees urged parishioners living apart to return to their 'conjugal life'.[152]

The fact that most divorce applications were from the city of Barcelona suggests, moreover, that distance from the diocesan court obviously created problems. The Church, by controlling the incidence of divorce, attempted to maintain official norms about the permanence of marriage; but there is no secure evidence that this worked any more in the early modern period than it has done in the twentieth century. Moreover the obligation to live together was pursued in the face of clear perils to life and limb, as in the case of Joana Ramoneda of Terrassa, who left her husband in 1594 after a year of marriage, specifically because he had stabbed her nigh-fatally (there were three deep wounds in her ribs), but was in 1596 ordered to return to him, while he was fined £300 by the episcopal court for the violence done to her.[153] It is significant of the Barcelona divorces that virtually none ended in voluntary reconciliation. Permanent marriage, as we now recognise, was in any case a relative thing in early modern Europe, where the early demise of one partner meant that on average few couples were together for more than twenty years.[154]

Social shame was frequently used as grounds for divorce. Sexual inadequacy (in all cases, male) invited applications for divorce and nullity since it brought shame on the woman in her community because of the failure to bear children. When Joana Sabatera of Cardadeu brought a plaint against her husband Pere Jovany in 1596, saying that 'she has lived with him for over six months in which time there has never been copula between them, and she is today as virgin as when she married,' a priest of the parish volunteered the information that everybody in the village knew of Pere's problem: 'he has heard people say many times in Cardadeu that the said Pere Jovany didn't have much of a member and that he was impotent.'[155] Accusations of impotence were often difficult to prove, and in a case of 1596 by Mariana Comelles against her husband in Barcelona, the official seems to have given the wife the benefit of the doubt, for her marriage was dissolved despite the husband's plea that they had had a normal sexual life together 'for over ten years until now, when by the influence of some evil spirit she has begun the present case'.[156] In 1671 Maria Vigo of Barcelona stated that when she married her husband, a notary, 'they lived together for twenty or more days but in that time she found that the said Vigo because of impotence could not consummate carnally, and since she is today still an intact virgin' she pleaded for nullity.[157] Anna Feixes, wife of a house-painter of Barcelona, added contamination by 'the French disease', abandonment, and the death of her child through lack of maintenance to the accusations of violence levelled against her husband in 1622.[158]

Despite its notorious prejudice against women,[159] one it shared with the laws and attitudes of contemporary society, the Church seems to have dealt fairly with women plaintiffs, who were for example invariably allowed to live apart from their spouses until they could prove their allegations. Over and above the testimony of the parties to each case, the officials in Barcelona were always concerned to uphold the community values that might be involved, and to maintain marriages not simply because marriage was indissoluble but more cogently because public scandal (that is, the injuring of community norms) might occur.

Since divorce did not exist, bigamy became the alternative, and it was not a novel one. Already in the fourteenth century the bishop of Elna was complaining of 'many in our diocese' who resorted to it,[160] and though it is difficult to identify an offence which by definition was occult it seems that very many, both men and women, made use of this escape route. Since a precondition of bigamy is that it can usually be done only in a society quite distant from that in which one's first spouse lives, the diocesan authorities normally did not have the means to pursue enquiries, and the Inquisition became the ideal tribunal for the purpose. In Catalonia since 1512 it had been laid down that cases of bigamy were reserved for civil and episcopal courts unless heresy was involved,[161] a position the Inquisition accepted when it stated in 1610 that 'it is the task of the civil government to judge the issue of two marriages, and the Holy Office is there only to punish the offence'[162] of heresy; but in practice the distinction was seldom respected by the officials of the tribunal, and in 1610 the Suprema in Madrid had to remind the Barcelona inquisitors of the fact and dismissed the three prosecutions initiated that year against bigamists. Particularly in the mid-sixteenth century the Inquisition was remarkably active, with bigamists featuring as between five and ten per cent of all those arrested in the tribunals of the peninsula.[163] In Counter-Reformation Catalonia the records of the Inquisition show that between the years 1578 and 1635 some sixty-six people were prosecuted, accounting for about seven per cent of the prosecutions brought by the tribunal in that period; but since, as we have noted, the Holy Office was not the primary court for the offence, the real incidence of bigamy was certainly much higher than the figures suggest. The normal punishment meted out to bigamists by the Inquisition in the 1580s was one hundred lashes in public and a term of three to five years in the galleys for men, while women were banished from the locality; in 1603 there was a variant punishment for men: two hundred lashes, and five years' service in the municipal hospital.[164]

The only way bishops could try to control the phenomenon was through the vigilance of parish priests: the 1669 synodal constitutions of Barcelona, for example, report that 'some men and women, because they cannot live with the licence they wish in towns and villages where they are known, go to live in villages' far from their normal residence. Rectors were therefore ordered that 'when outsiders arrive to live in their villages and are not known, they should be asked to show the original proof of their marriage.'[165]

In claiming control over the rites of marriage the Church attempted to eliminate certain practices which had existed in the old secular context. In traditional society any divergences from the communally accepted pattern of marriage were looked upon as disorders which had to be righted. One typical disorder was the henpecked husband, a theme classic in its origins but of concern equally to contemporaries because it threatened the family by reversing the order of obedience between man and wife. Every writer without exception enjoined the subjection of the woman to the man; husbands, stated Tomás Ramón in his *New Decree of Reformation*, 'should not permit them to rule the house', and painted an exaggerated image of some wives who ruined their husbands by their excessive material demands.[166] Henpecked husbands, like other disorders, invited, from the rest of the community, criticisms and satire which were sometimes meant to correct the disorder and can be regarded as penal in form, but very frequently also formed part of community celebrations and can be described as festive in nature.[167] Other aspects of marriage were also affected by community vigilance, perhaps the most significant being the second marriage, frowned on in many societies and decidedly discriminated against in traditional Catalan law, which deprived widows of considerable property rights if they married again.[168]

The community ritual used against such marriage disorders was known commonly in western Europe as the charivari and had a long history in the peninsula. Etymologically the word refers only to the making of a discordant noise or 'rough music', and in Spain can be associated with the Castilian word *cencerrada* or the Catalan word *esquellotada*. The Catalan form derives from a word for 'little bells' but is not restricted to the use of bells. In social practice, discordant noise and associated customs were resorted to in many different contexts, the only common factor being that they tended to affect the marriage ritual and the married couple. The general

custom in use over broad areas of western Europe was that when a
widow or widower remarried the relatives would make an intolerable noise and nuisance in the church during the wedding. The logic
of the practice is obscure, but it has been suggested that in Spain, as
in France,[169] it partly reflected traditional disapproval of second
marriages, particularly since widowers remarrying tended to be
much older than their new spouses.[170] The element of disapproval
was fundamental, making it possible to view some charivaris as an
explicit rite inversion, with rough music being used instead of
sweet, noise and laughter instead of silence, unpleasant odours
instead of perfume and incense. However, the disapproval was
carried out almost exclusively by village youths,[171] so that the
whole proceedings seem to have reflected also the ritual of power
within the village, where male confraternities were given the role of
protecting the marriage norms acceptable to the community. In
1643 in France a young man defended the custom, saying that 'it
has been observed since a long time ago in this realm, to do a
chalibaly to young men who marry widows or girls who marry
widowers, and to observe the good and honourable custom of the
chalibaly without causing any scandal.'[172]

Church criticisms of the practice were of long standing and can
be found throughout western Europe: in Spain as early as 1410 the
diocesan synod of Salamanca ordered that marriages not be celebrated 'with laughter and play'. In 1547 the diocesan visitor to the
parish of San Vicente in San Sebastián forbade for the future the
custom 'when some are getting married in the church and are
attending mass, for people to come and make a noise and ring bells
and shout and yell in the church and at the altar ... in great derision,
mockery and ridicule of the holy sacrament of matrimony'.[173] The
Counter Reformation was sharply critical of the charivari, since it
also represented a danger to the survival of Christian standards in
marriage. Though noise-making can be found in other historical
contexts, there is little doubt of its direct relationship to second
marriages, which the Church was concerned to validate as legitimate
unions. In June 1566 the diocesan synod of Segorbe forbade any
noise-making at second marriages, 'nor the blowing of horns nor
the ringing of bells', but when canon Villanueva visited the diocese
in the early nineteenth century he said the tradition 'still exists, of
ridiculing through the night those who contract second and third
marriages'.[174]

The customs are testimony to continued community vigilance of
the rites of marriage, which was deemed to affect not merely the
couple but the whole parish. On the French side of the Pyrenees,[175]
the standards set by the parish were enforced by the youth con-

fraternity known as the 'garçons de la paroisse', who intervened in the steps leading up to marriage and for a year after the ceremony continued to supervise the progress made, watching to see that the husband maintained his proper role or that the wife had duly become pregnant, resorting otherwise to the charivari. In Catalonia the noise-making or *esquellots* tended to be a privilege of the confraternities, which demanded payments from the groom through the 'king' or 'abbot' of the youth-group (the charivari was therefore sometimes called the *visclabat*, and in the village of Llofriu his role was to 'play the abbot', 'fer l'abat'). In Monistrol de Montserrat the confraternity of St Sebastian used the money to finance feast days. In Santa Coloma de Queralt an ordinance of the confraternity of St Esteve said: 'If a widow and widower remarry the "king" and "bailiff" may make them pay a pound of wax for our confraternity, and if they refuse to pay then three days of noise and esquellots will be done in the town, as is the custom.'[176]

In the Vallespir an outsider marrying into the community had to pay a fee to the confraternity head, the 'king of the youth', and if he failed to do so could be subjected to the charivari.[177] The bothering of the bridegroom could take several forms, depending on the traditions of the local community. In some areas it was the custom to *fer fum* (smoke out the house of the couple), or to poke fun by parading asses or performing farces. In Aiguafreda the proceedings were organised by a 'General of the esquellots'. In parts of Rosselló the more recognisable form *xerbelli* was given to the custom.[178]

Despite the clear disrespect to sacred things that the charivari might imply, only once in the period 1578–1635 did the Inquisition of Catalonia intervene in the matter. In 1610 eight young men from the village of Cabanabona went

in procession through the village street carrying in a coffin an ass's spine; four of them carried the coffin with their heads covered and two went in front carrying some asses' heads as if they were bearing candles, and all went chanting responses as though for the dead, and they made three stops, and at each they said Kyrie Eleyson Criste Eleyson Kyrie Eleyson Criste Eleyson Kyrie Eleyson Criste Eleyson, and then one of them said the Paternoster and Requiem eternam dona eis domine.

When asked to explain their conduct, the men 'said that in the village it was the custom that when widowers remarried they had to pay some money to the church and if they did not then that affront was done to them and the bones and skulls were left at their doors; and they did it because the man who married did not pay what was the customary amount,' an explanation which the inquisitors accepted, since they dropped the case after reprimanding the men and ordering that they pay the costs involved.[179] The Cabanabona case reminds us that an extension to the charivari custom was the demand that payment be made for marriage. This practice could be found in parts of France, where if an outsider married a girl from the village he was expected to pay a nominal sum for the privilege to groups of noise-making youths.[180] In Catalonia in some villages the young couple on their way to be married would find entrance to the church barred until they paid a nominal sum to the Confraternity of the Rosary; if no payment was made, a village girl would grab the reins of the animal on which the bridal pair were riding and lead it round the town to shame them for not paying. The wedding ceremony was required to have the full sanction of the community, and the groom or the couple were penalised if they failed to respect community wishes. A variation in the villages of Urgell was that those marrying outside the community had to pay a fine when they brought their brides back to the village.[181]

Despite Church opposition, community customs relating to marriage seem to have survived through the Counter Reformation, and bishops attempted in vain to impose their control. In 1670 the diocesan visitor to the parish of Bages (Rosselló) ordered 'that during the celebration of weddings those who attend not say dishonest, injurious or ill-sounding words inside or outside the church'.[182] Continuous criticism by the authorities in Spain culminated with a law in 1765 banning the practice of the charivari[183] but this did not stop it.

The sacramentalisation and regulation of marriage by the Counter-Reformation Church was accompanied by attempts to change attitudes to sexuality. For the Church, sex could take place only within marriage and even then in moderation. By contrast, in the communities of early modern Europe sex had never been restricted to the state of matrimony. It was a common presumption, found throughout Spain and no less in Catalonia, that sex between unmarried adults was neither wrong nor sinful;[184] and the sentiment was not limited to Spaniards.[185] The conviction was apparently so deep-rooted in Castilian society that a canon of Salamanca, Francisco Farfán, in 1585 dedicated a volume of one thousand pages to the theme.[186] The majority of those penanced in autos de fe, he stated, 'are those who fall into this error, against which neither punishments nor threats avail, nor sermons, examples and advice serve, since every day we see further shoots growing forth from this plant';[187] and indeed an analysis of offences shows that propositions regarding sex were far and away the most prosecuted by the Inquisition in this period of the Counter Reformation. Farfán felt that those who held fornication to be natural 'are for the most part rustics and uninstructed'.[188] The prevalence of the belief in fornication was usually related to the existence of prostitution and did not imply any practice of free love: as elsewhere in Europe the availability of publicly licensed sex encouraged the view that it did no harm.[189] 'The greater part of the common people', Farfán explained, justified their views on two counts: that brothels existed by public licence and therefore what took place in brothels was not illegal; and that such intercourse always took the form of a contract, with payment for services rendered, so that once again it was quite legal.[190] By way of refutation, Farfán inevitably had to argue that what was legal was not necessarily right.

Moralising alone was not enough and a report of 1620 ruefully admitted that 'many here believe [the reference is to Castile] that simple fornication is permitted.'[191] As clergy became more conscious of the sexual licence in their midst they took steps to repress it. Though action had been taken against the opinion in previous decades, in November 1573 the Suprema of the Inquisition sent all tribunals instructions to take the problem more seriously and to 'proceed against those who hold this error as though they were heretics'. In January 1575 the Inquisition of Barcelona informed the Suprema that 'we have published the edicts (of faith) in this city and sent others to the comisarios to publish them, and have called together the leaders of the religious orders to inform them of what should be preached and taught on this matter, as you order, and throughout the district we are ordering the comisarios to do the same with preachers as well as with parish priests.'[192] Seeing the seriousness with which the Suprema was taking the offence, the inquisitors asked whether the implication of heresy called for the use of torture, or whether the penalties hitherto used – abjuration and one hundred lashes – would be sufficient.

Many were puzzled over why the Church disapproved of something which seemed natural, and in 1628 a rural labourer in the village of Lluçàs (Urgell) was rigorously castigated by the Inquisition for suggesting that 'Christ our Lord at the time that he was in the world must also have fornicated.'[193] The presumption could also be found among religious, both male and female, who were thereupon punished by the Inquisition, not for the simple resort to sex but for the more heretical stance, identified as an *alumbrado* belief, that carnal love was not sinful. In 1627 two nuns aged thirty and forty from the convent of Minims in Barcelona were accused of sexual relations with a preacher from the Mercedarian friary and of assuring him that he was doing no wrong; in the same year a priest of

Barcelona was denounced for forming a group to practise free love.[194]

It was among the common people of Catalonia that the attitude was most deeply ingrained, as we see from the records of the Inquisition, the only tribunal with the resources to enquire into the offence. A twenty-eight-year-old farmworker of Barcelona was in 1591 banished from his parish for a year (the penalty usually imposed by the Inquisition in Catalonia) for asserting that 'I do not believe that anyone will go to hell just for screwing.'[195] In 1594 a thirty-year-old farmworker of Falset was denounced for similar sentiments, but interestingly the inquisitors dismissed the charge on the grounds that he was a happily married family man and besides, they said, the proposition 'is not found much in this part of the country.'[196] By contrast, the statement by a parish priest to a woman in 1597 that 'fornication is no sin'[197] was clearly little more than an attempt to have his way with her. In 1599 a native of Puigcerdà resident in Castelldefels was banished for a year for claiming that 'to screw' was not a sin.[198] A basic premise, that sex between consenting adults was not offensive to man and therefore not to God, was stated explicitly by the young prostitute in Barcelona in 1599 who when warned by a customer that what she did was a sin replied 'that it is no sin since we are both unmarried'; whereupon he inexplicably denounced her to the Inquisition which, true to its idea that the whole question arose from deficiency of dogma, exhorted her 'to learn the catechism and come to the Inquisition every two weeks until she has learnt it'.[199] Certainly the eighty-year-old man banished for a year from his parish in La Guàrdia (Urgell) for holding that 'having carnal intercourse with a woman when she is willing is not a sin' was castigated more for his belief than for his capacity.[200] In 1629 a farmworker from Besalú living in Barcelona held that 'to have carnal relations with a woman and pay her for it is no sin'; and the same year one in Reus had formally to retract his statement that 'simple fornication is no sin.'[201]

The widespread acceptance of sexuality in the form of prostitution seemed intolerable to the clergy. For many people fornication seemed licit specifically because of the contractual nature of prostitution, licensed in Spain by public authority. Under Ferdinand and Isabella some aspects of the commerce were put under state control so that the brothels could be taxed. From the early sixteenth century the tendency of legislation was to restrict and control, although the moral permission to allow it in principle remained constant, Rodríguez affirming, for example, that 'it is legitimate for the authorities to allow bad women in a certain part of the city, and it is legitimate to allow these women to have clients.'[202] Perhaps the most important measures of relevance in Castile were the Ordinances of 1570, which imposed regulations on every brothel, insisting that the controller of each (the word used was *arrendador*, signifying one who paid taxes on it) should be answerable to the municipality or the *corregidor*; but as in so many other things the laws were never observed, leading to further regulations in later years. The sending of Alba's army to Flanders, we are told, encouraged a horde of camp-followers: 'with the army that went to Flanders went four hundred prostitutes on horse for the captains and clergy; and behind these lovely and valiant princesses went eight hundred wretched prostitutes for the soldiery.'[203]

In Catholic tradition the various types of prostitution had always been tolerated as the lesser of evils, a mechanism used by male society to purge itself of pressures; but not all men were in principle permitted to resort to the brothels, married men and clergy being expressly forbidden.[204] At the Reformation the general trend was for the Protestant reformers to close brothels, in line with the view that sex was sin. Counter-Reformation clergy in principle looked on prostitution as unacceptable but seemed in practice to offer no objections. Juan de Avila, writing in 1565 to the archbishop of Granada, almost apologetically asked whether brothels in Andalusia could not be closed at least during the hour of Sunday high mass, 'since it is so short a while'.[205] On feast days, Pedro de León observed sadly of Andalusia, 'it is very common for many bad women to come to Seville on fixed days such as Corpus Christi, Easter and feasts of Our Lady...The young men go to see what they have never seen before, and learn their lessons from those who have tasted of the sweetness of the venom...Most of them are artisans and country labourers, who on days when their bodies are resting put their unhappy souls in travail.'[206] The Jesuits made fervent afforts to eliminate the practice at its root, namely by converting the women: in 1609 in Barcelona 'one of the fathers preaching in Lent converted ten bad women.'[207] In Spain the policy was followed not of closing brothels but of attempting to change people's attitude and achieve closure that way. The frequent spectacle of Jesuits waiting outside brothels to enter into earnest conversation with both clients and women as they went in or out, coincides with an evangelical practice that continues down to our own day.

The problem of 'fornication' was not, however, limited to prostitution. Many couples lived together without marrying and their fornication was consequently of much graver import, a clear disrespect to the sacramental norms the Church wished to impose.

It is impossible to judge the extent of cohabitation. Certainly the bishop of Barcelona in 1593 considered it the most serious problem in his diocese; way ahead of all the other sins in a fairly comprehensive list, he placed 'living dishonestly in sin or husbands living separately from their wives without licence', and warned his clergy that cohabitation was 'one of the most important matters in the present Memorial', because 'many men dwell within their homes living for many years with their slaves, their servants and with relatives', the last being a brief reference to consanguinity.[208] Concubinage was also a civil offence when it caused scandal, and in 1573 the viceroy had to complain to the bailiff of Vilafranca del Penedès 'that in that town many live in such public concubinage that they scandalise not only the inhabitants but also those living round about'.[209]

Despite all its deficiencies the institution of marriage remained the bedrock of society and was solemnly upheld by the Church. It is consequently ironic that the Church should have had to censure the opinion of those who held that marriage was a better civil state than the celibate status of the clergy. The formal Church view was that both being sacraments, the one of matrimony and the other of holy orders, neither could be held to be superior. In practice the opinion that marriage was better was seen to be highly subversive,[210] for it suggested that abstention from sex was unnatural and coincided with the Protestant view that clergy should be allowed to marry. When the Inquisition censured the opinion, therefore, it took the view that heresy was implied, though in practice it was usually treated leniently. In 1584 a weaver of Barcelona was given the severe punishment of banishment for two years from the principality for maintaining that 'the state of matrimony is more perfect' than that of holy orders.[211] In 1596 a woman of St Pere de Pineda (Gerona) was, by contrast, merely told to recite the rosary as penance for saying that 'the married man is in a better state than friars and priests';[212] and a blacksmith of Torredembarra was in 1595 fined for asserting that 'the married state is better and more worthwhile than that of the priests.'[213] The impressive hold of this opinion among all sectors of the population emerges in the results of the visitation made by the inquisitor Diego Fernández de Heredía to lower Catalonia in 1597. The Inquisition did not seek the offence, it merely sought denunciations, and the population duly fed in reports of an offence which could safely be denounced since it normally carried little penalty: the inquisitor pardoned all eleven cases denounced to him in the villages of Escornalbou, Montbrio, Vimbodi, Espluga, Calva, Barberà, Maldà, Montblanc, and Ruidecanas; in Montblanc it was a priest who claimed that 'if the state of being a friar were better Our Lord would have said so.'[214] The visit that year marked the high tide of attempts by the Inquisition to repress the opinion. There is no reason to believe that any impact was made. In 1629 a priest of Vilafranca del Penedès was prosecuted for the same proposition.[215]

War against the flesh typified most Counter-Reformation literature. Typical is the aptly titled *Miseries of Man* (1597) of the Barcelona Dominican Tomás de Truxillo, who considered sex to be one of the major miseries of mankind, permissible within marriage only because the sacrament of matrimony allowed it, but otherwise a plague that brought with it disease, blindness and death. The extreme puritanical position to be found among some Jesuits is reflected in Francisco Arias, whose *Spiritual progress* (Madrid 1603) took a grim view of all fleshly delights; the book was in effect an unbridled attack on all the human senses and the sins they cause, the only real delight being necessarily spiritual. In particular Arias seems to have felt a real terror of woman, the very sight of whom, he says clearly, invites to concupiscence. The eyes, above all, are guilty: 'from this disordered hunger for passing the eyes over all sensual delights is born the desire and concern to see spectacles that delight the eye such as games, dances, balls, parties, masques, bull-fights, farces and plays.' Women obviously must be excluded from acting: 'another abuse of these times is that women act in comedies together with men. Holy Scripture warns us that the sight of a woman dressed up scandalises and slays the hearts of many.' Nor should women be allowed to speak in a public role: 'the apostle St Paul says that however wise a woman may be she should not be permitted to teach in a public place where men might hear her. And St Anselm tells us why, saying: That when a woman speaks she incites those who see and hear her to dishonest thoughts of love.' It goes without saying that all dances are to be forbidden 'especially between men and women, for it is a great occasion for sin'.[216]

A long Christian tradition, reflected in the confessors' manuals of late mediaeval Europe,[217] treated as shameful and sinful all functions of the sexual organs, castigated all sensual pleasure as diabolic, and looked with horror on bodily fluids, whether semen or menstrual or the blood of childbirth. It is no surprise to find that zealous clergy reverted to the theme, sometimes displaying an obsessive anti-sexuality. José Gavarri in the late seventeenth century advised young clergy that of all sins sensuality was the one that must be most attacked: 'this vice needs to be most attacked in all sermons, because it is the most common and the most damnable';[218] and when discussing countries where men and women had the custom of greeting each other with a kiss on the face he said categorically that 'in Spain there is no such custom', reporting with satisfaction that 'the custom of kissing each other was condemned as a mortal sin in France in 1637, and they have now got rid of the practice.'[219] We may well doubt the information that French people had ceased kissing each other in public, or that Spaniards had no such custom. Confessors' manuals (written primarily for clergy) devoted considerable space to sexual difficulties, and in particular to the sexual problems of clergy. Arias, for example, warned men that 'they must guard their eyes not only from too much looking at women, but should also take care not to look with liberty at the beauty of boys of a tender age.'[220] Though bishops made an attempt to enforce rules about the age of priests' housekeepers there is no sign that clerical sexuality was ever seriously curtailed, and the Inquisition gave continuous attention to the matter throughout the period. The moralists, like Francisco Ortiz Lucio (incidentally, a violent woman-hater), who published his manual in Barcelona in 1598, were willing to overlook the pressures on a celibate clergy: 'the priest who while hearing confession hears vile things and because of this suffers a natural emission of semen, does not sin if it is involuntary . . . If he has an emission while sleeping and then awakes, that is quite natural.'[221]

Tridentine repression was one stage in the long struggle of the Church against the satisfaction that clergy through the ages had found in sexual activity. It is significant that the largest number of constitutions passed by the provincial councils of Tarragona in the later middle ages on a single theme, a total of twenty-four, was on the subject of clerical concubinage.[222] In the two years 1561–2 the vicar-general of Barcelona had to issue fifty-seven warnings to clergy of the diocese over their concubines.[223] A Jesuit report on public vice in Valencia in 1566 referred to six university teachers with mistresses, one 'who is called la Catalana', and eleven canons of the cathedral with the same failing.[224] In what may be the figures for a single year, 1613, the Inquisition of Catalonia disciplined seventy-seven of its familiars and comisarios (the latter were clergy) for various offences: all the thirty-eight comisarios had one offence in common, 'to do with women', for which thirty-one were disciplined and seven warned.[225] Despite this, the irrepressible tradition of the monks of Benediktbeuern, the wandering scholars,[226] and of Rabelais, continued to persist in the practice of the Catalan countryside. Mossèn Miquel Vinyals, beneficed priest of the church of St Joan in Perpinyà, who lived with a woman and had a daughter by her, believed in 1539 that 'clergy may in good conscience marry even if they are priests,' and that 'the sin of lust, that is simple fornication, is not a mortal sin.'[227] The devotion of clergy to carnal love passed into the folklore of Catalonia, and one of the most famous of all local songs dedicated to the splendour of the mountains of Canigó, the 'Muntanyes regalades', also celebrated the pleasures of pastoral life:[228]

Penses que en dormi sola	You think that I sleep alone
No en dormi sola, no:	But sleep alone I do not:
Una nit ab lo vicari	One night I spend with the vicar,
I l'altra ab lo rector . . .	The next with the rector . . .
Dau-me l'amor, minyona	Give me all your love, my girl
Dau-me lo vostre amor	Give me your love
Dau-me l'amor, minyona	Give me all your love, my girl
Consuelo del meu cor.	Solace of my heart.

The Church courts intervened continuously in cases involving their diocesan clergy. In the parish of Premià (Barcelona) in 1597, the secular jurisdiction, with the bishop's representative present, had to hold court over the case of a local farmer's young wife who within a year after her marriage in 1589 began a career of provocation in the village, 'giving herself now to some now to others and also to the priests and vicars of the present parish'. 'She cannot', her long-suffering husband affirmed, 'deny her body to anyone who asks for it, and that is openly and publicly known in the parish.' One witness declared: 'I have several times seen a vicar of the parish called mossèn Agustí in the woods in a hut, and I have seen Paula Ponsa enter the wood afterwards in pursuit of the vicar.' The local tailor's wife testified of the parish priest mossèn Mores that 'it is publicly known in all Premià that mossèn Mores did what he wished with Paula Ponsa and was her lover'.[229] It is significant of village attitudes that criticism was directed less against the clergy than against the woman, and no action seems to have been taken against the priests. Popular tradition accepted that clergy would have affairs. In August 1599 the widow Catherina Puig denounced the parish priest of Barberà for getting her pregnant and then refusing to pay her off until he could see that a child had been born.[230] Other clergy were more canny: the rector of Peralta de la Sal (Urgell), having got a girl pregnant, promised the cobbler of the neighbouring village of Estanye a large sum of 100 ducats if he married her; after the wedding, however, he refused to pay the money and made life extremely difficult for the couple, apparently because they refused to let him continue the relationship.[231]

The tortuous and tense relations provoked in a village by such situations can be seen in 1609 in the case of Galderic Gerri, a farmer of Tallet (Perpinyà), who was denounced to the Inquisition by his parish priest for some statements, but speedily exonerated when the inquisitors found that the priest was his wife's lover and hence motivated by malice.[232] Such cases never surfaced during the bishop's visitations, when a conspiracy of silence usually prevailed. It was only when some conflictive situation arose within the community, such as the obvious tension between Paula Ponsa and other women in the village, that someone might eventually leak a rumour to the authorities. It was, for example, a quarrel with his fellow priest which eventually stirred up a storm of denunciations against mossèn Anthoni Castellar, rector of Palautordera, in 1599, but even then it took a report to the vicar-general by a passing surgeon to bring out into the open a situation the community resented but preferred to live with.[233] The surgeon, from Saragossa, stated that 'I spent some days in the parish of Palautordera attending to a patient and while I was there I heard such scandal about the rector of the parish living in concubinage that I was alarmed.' When he reproached the rector directly, which as an outsider he felt free to do, the rector told him 'that in conscience he could not do anything about it because he had lived with her for so long that to leave her now would destroy her', and that in the same parish 'a vicar of his also had a relationship with a woman.' The vicar, mossèn Miquel, had in fact run off two years before with the wife of a parishioner.[234] Numerous other cases prove that little effective change had been brought about by the reforms of the Counter Reformation. In 1597 the rector of Arbós was denounced by the *jurats* of the town for sexual relations with the widow Sardana, whom they had tried to drive from the town but who was protected by him; and within the same period the vicar-general received a denunciation of a priest in Barcelona who 'has been living for three or four years with a young woman called Marianna and they live together in a house as man and wife and have three children, to the scandal of the whole neighbourhood'.[235] In 1600 in St Esteve del Coll witnesses said it was 'publicly known' that the rector was 'living with' a certain Padrona; and that 'the husband of the said Padrona works in the house of the rector and the said Padrona enters often into the house of the rector.'[236] Down to modern times, the propensity of some clergy to cohabit with the women of the parish has remained a stock theme of rural folklore and songs.

The Inquisition shared with Church courts the overview of sexual misdemeanours, which formed by far the biggest category of prosecutions but were still no more than the tip of the iceberg.[237] Solicitation in the confessional remained the most common clerical offence, but for fear of publicity was not always denounced by those solicited, and even then considerable credit was given to the accused, as when a parish priest in Tarragona, Francesc Vidal, claimed in 1635 that the accusations were motivated by immoral women to whom he had refused communion, a defence the Inquisition accepted.[238] Provocative statements, such as that by a priest of Banyoles in 1631 that 'priests should be able to say mass stark naked so as to show off their private parts to the women,'[239] were let off with a reprimand. In theory the new confessional was intended to be a protection for the public, but many continued to have curtains rather than a grille to separate priest and penitent, so that solicitation continued as a regular offence: in 1609 the vicar of Conesa was accused of molesting a number of teenage girls,[240] but his case was no more than typical of a continuing problem. Comparable in frequency was the offence of sodomy, located principally in monasteries and among schoolteachers: in 1607 a twenty-six-year-old schoolmaster-priest of Vic was accused of offences against his boys; and in 1617 boys aged nine were among those who testified against a cleric of Castelló.[241] There were variants on the theme such as the case, in a Perpinyà religious house in 1616, of the friar accused of soliciting males in the confessional.[242] In some measure, then, the anti-sexuality of many books written by clergy can fairly be seen as an attempt to conjure away a problem which was very much also a clerical one.

Hostility to sex was projected on to the faithful and repression of sexuality was encouraged. It is not surprising to find a theologian suggesting that for a married couple to make love might inhabilitate them from taking communion,[243] thereby equating sex with sin. There were shades of opinion on the question, but the exposition by Rodríguez seems to have been the common view:[244] 'after a wet dream or after marital copula it is not allowed to go to communion the next day ... Angles says that to give communion to the married person the day after having had copula is allowed, since the act is not sinful and can even be meritorious; I concede that it is meritorious, but it also has in it some indecency.'

For centuries the Catholic clergy had struggled against the role of the body in the scheme of things, and had attempted to liberate the spirit from carnal and sexual chains,[245] and more particularly from the lures of woman, whose only permitted representative was an idealised and asexual figure of the Virgin Mary. Few religious writers were free from the ritual and unrestrained condemnation of womanly beauty, which they saw as a corruption introduced into the modern world. Developing the theme in 1617, the Augustinian friar Antonio Marques expressed himself in terms that suggest an attempt to exorcise the daily presence of women at mass. Condemning the vogue for make-up, for 'white teeth and fair hair',

'I judge, ladies,' he said, 'that your time would be better employed whitening your souls with chastity and making them fair with charity'; and that women 'should have their head covered in church and with the gown covering the breasts', so as not to distract the clergy from the performance of their office; for all beauty was perdition and transitory.[246]

From these writers it is a change to turn to fray Martín de la Vera, monk of the Escorial, who in 1630 published a guide for clergy which was not only the fruit of a broad culture (Tertullian, Hugo of St Victor, Herp and Gerson are among his preferred sources) but which expressly praised the body as the only vehicle through which the soul could work, and which went so far as to devote an entire chapter to the benefits of kissing, including the kiss of peace at mass.[247]

Though clergy could not partake of the failings of the flesh they did not have to shut their eyes to the pleasure of others: when in 1665 Honorat Ciuro assisted at the wedding ceremonies for his nephew, the hereu of the family at Cameles (Rosselló), he and a fellow-priest drank their way through the night but in order to get the wine had to pass by the wedding chamber, and 'on the way to get the wine, which was several times during the night, they could not fail to hear many dishonest words and cries.'[248] The delights of this world were not per se sinful, as Catalan clergy knew if they had worked their way through the thousand pages of the most famous confessors' manual of its day, published in Barcelona in 1567, the year after the council of Tarragona: Azpilcueta ruled that 'it is not even a venial sin to take delight in and wish to enjoy looking at and talking to a beautiful creature, and seeing her new, rich and splendid clothes; as long as there is no bad intention.'[249]

One cannot fail to mention a priest and poet of the Counter Reformation in Catalonia whose Renaissance outlook takes us into a sensual world of gallant clergy:

> ...*mossèn Joan de la Cabanya,*
> *Fadrí de gran ventura i poca manya,*
> *Fiador de casades i donzelles* –

> ...mossèn Joan de la Cabanya,
> young man of daring and dexterity,
> gallant to married women and damsels –

and unattainable maidens –

> *Si negar-me ta gràcia determines* ...

> If you deny me your favour ...

Penjaré la sotana i em faré	I'll hang up my cassock and
sastre —	turn tailor -

and, above all, of the beautiful young nun he saw praying in his own parish church:[250]

En lo cor de la Iglésia de	In the choir of the church at
Vallbona	Vallbona
Un matí agenollada sor	Sister Maria at prayers one
Maria . . .	morning . . .
Alça's tot de puntetes lo	The vicar tiptoes towards her,
vicari,	
Rendit a la triunfant, postrada	triumphant even as she
en terra,	supplicates
Que ab llavis de coral lo altar	the altar with lips of coral.
rosega.	
'O dolça boca – diu – de	'O sweet mouth, sweet
efectes varii.	poison,
Mentres aplaca el cel, al món	that, storming both heaven
fa guerra	and the world,
I los vius mata quan per los	slays the living in praying for
morts prega.'	the dead'.

The disciplining of sex in Catalonia did not take the form it often took in Reformation Europe, where indulgence became a social crime and not merely a private offence.[251] The Counter Reformation, by contrast, did not bring sexual discipline before any special courts, and left it almost exclusively to the sanction of the confessional. The only courts that appeared to discipline behaviour were the civil ones, where public order and honour were involved,[252] or the Inquisition, which however prosecuted propositions rather than sexual offences, and did so on a negligible scale in Catalonia compared to the frequent prosecutions to be found in other Inquisitions of the peninsula.[253] Where the Reformation replaced the notion of private sin by that of social responsibility, the Counter Reformation, which was no less conscious of the wickedness of sexuality and particularly of female sexuality, sought a solution in the traditional system of private penitence. The often shrill moralising of clergy was proof of a more demanding official attitude in the Church, but the evidence for a real moral change among the people is much harder to come by. In any case, the toleration of prostitution and brothels showed that the Church admitted that sexuality could not be disciplined and required an outlet, one available for men but not for women.

In traditional Europe and no less in Catalonia the role of the individual in society was determined by status and function alone; the laws recognised no rights to the person apart from those which pertained to his or her role, and by implication the laws did not discriminate between the sexes, so that a woman who fulfilled a recognised role was received on equal terms. Since property was the main determinant of status, women with property had a recognised role to play in Catalan society: they were known to attend the assemblies of the rural community, and on rare occasions sat in the Corts.[254] Their property rights were, indeed, the main avenue to an active social role, and the dowry brought by a bride was the single most important and contentious problem affecting women in early modern Catalonia.

Treatises of the early sixteenth century on the subject dealt mainly of noble and gentlewomen, and formed part of the corpus of Renaissance courtly writing. Secular literature followed the troubadour tradition and presented, mainly in the novels of chivalry, pastoral images of highly idealised women. The transition to a more serious perspective can be seen particularly in the writings of Juan Luis Vives and Antonio de Guevara, whose humanism opened the way to a more positive attitude; as the translator of Vives noted (Valencia 1528), previous writers on the subject 'instead of extending a hand to women gave them the foot, neither instructing nor teaching them but criticising and reviling them.'[255]

In the course of the sixteenth century religious reformers (all of them male, with the significant exception of Teresa of Avila) were compelled to examine the role of women and to move beyond the mere consideration (central to many of the ideas in Erasmus and Vives) of their education. In doing so, many found it impossible to shake off the immense burden of centuries of virulent anti-feminism in the Church and therefore tended to move within the confines of traditional moral ideas; few ventured into offering woman an independent role. Works such as Luis de León's *The perfect wife* (1583) were not innovative but rather in line with the evolution of other attitudes in the period.[256] More idealistic were books on the emulation of Biblical women, a fairly unexciting genre well represented by Martín Carrillo, abbot of Montearagon, whose *Praise of famous women of the Old Testament*, published at Huesca in 1627, took all the famous women of the Bible as paradigms of virtues and did not omit to learn from the vicious women either, a point the author took over from the contemporary Italian writer Cesar Capacio, author of *Illustrium mulierum Elogia*, who had suggested that the great whores might also be used to point the way to virtue. The genre of praising women in everyday life was represented by Juan de Spinosa, author of *Dialogue in praise of women* (Milan 1580); and by Cristóbal Acosta Africano, whose *Treatise in praise of women* was written in Valladolid in 1585 and published in Venice in 1592. Praising matrimony as 'the greatest and most natural good, satisfaction and felicity that there is among earthly things', Acosta reminded his reader that the duty of a man was to 'honour women and never speak ill of them; employ the eyes in looking on her, the hands in serving her, the property in giving her gifts, the heart in making her happy'. Quarrels within marriage were bad: 'there can be no greater scandal to neighbours than seeing and hearing quarrels between husband and wife.' Acosta denounced men who 'in their homes are demons and mistreat their wives', and said that to speak ill of women 'was the natural conduct of vulgar and common people'.[257]

The Counter-Reformation moralists considered that woman had three principal roles: her duties and obligations prior to marriage; the place of a mature woman in the context of the family; and the duties of a woman dedicated to religion. In all three respects there was an unspoken assumption that security of property and stability of status were the twin pillars upholding a society which for all practical purposes was patriarchal in discipline. Women were seen as an important but subordinate element in a male power structure, and writers attempted to describe their role within this structure. However, Spain (and within Spain Catalonia) disposed of economic and legal traditions which gave women a more independent role than is often supposed, and which militated against the apparently exclusive domination of the male sex. Counter-Reformation thought did not always take this into account, and often wilfully refused to recognise it.

Since we know nothing about women's roles in pre-sixteenth-century Catalonia it is difficult to measure changes that may have come with the Counter Reformation. In the urban context of sixteenth-century Augsburg, it has been argued that the Reformation tended to insist 'on a vision of women's incorporation within the household under the leadership of their husbands', with a broader and growing preoccupation with the disciplining of 'sin';[258] but this basically bourgeois role was certainly not central to the experience of Catalonia, where the initial concern seems to have been rather the disciplining of marriage. As we have seen, young women in the epoch of Trent were firmly dissuaded from illicit marriages, from marrying without permission, and in general from taking any sexual initiative. The attitude reflected old prejudices, to be found even in humanistic writers, that women should accept a cloistered role and that they were incapable of any other. Huarte de

San Juan, in his *Examen de ingenios* (Barcelona 1607), suggested a biological explanation for his theory that women had no intellectual capacity.[259] Few went as far as this, but in general a strongly restrictive hand on the young maiden was the general line taken by moralists. Gaspar de Astete, for example, believed that young women might be taught to read, but not learn to write, since that might enable them to write notes to illicit lovers. Astete, indeed, favoured a thorough cloistering: the maiden 'should not go out to see other women, should not dance, should not play mocking games, should not go to public parties, should not drink wine and should not stir from the house'.[260] It is evident, however, that this advice applied only to a young lady of the upper classes, and reliance on such sources can give a misleading idea of other social levels. Though many elite girls were necessarily restricted to the house, taught only by private tutors, and in the end compelled to accept spouses chosen by their parents, the greater mass of the population, in Spain as in most of western Europe, enjoyed a practical freedom which cannot be discounted. The restrictions placed on rich young girls arose in part out of consideration for the property and inheritance interests involved, in part out of the presumption that they should give an example to the rest of society.

The moralists inveighed repeatedly against the mobility available to the normal unmarried girl, and their attacks are excellent testimony to the existence of the freedom they wished to deny. Vives, early on, identified it as a popular (he cites the 'common people') view that 'in order to get married young girls should go out, dress themselves up, chat to each other, dance and sing and even, if possible, chat to the young men they are to marry.'[261] The Jesuit Escrivá in 1613 complained that 'it seems to many now that young girls who are of marriageable age should be allowed to go out, stroll around and be seen . . . A pestilential abuse, introduced by the devil.'[262] Gavarri in 1673 preferred that women not leave their houses, that men should 'flee from the sensuality and contact and sight of women', and that women should conduct themselves just like 'tortoises [who] when seen in public immediately hide in their shells so as not to be seen.'[263] The constant determination to cloister women is clear evidence of the continuing freedom available to many. Galindo in Castile reported in 1682 that girls looked for marriage partners 'without missing fiesta or dance, street or doorway or window at all times and hours'.[264] Freedom of movement did not imply that the choice of a husband was free, but it clearly made sexual freedom more possible.

Ironically, the greater dedication to religion demanded by the Church afforded greater sexual freedom to women of all ages. We have seen that the authorities quickly recognised the capacity for harm in the promiscuous mixing of sexes during religious festivities, and attempted to curtail *romerías* and other celebrations. One freedom they could not take away was the simple freedom of going to church. Some early writers had extended the principle of cloister to the extent of disallowing young women from going to mass, but by the time of the Counter Reformation mass was accepted as a universal obligation and confessors' manuals insisted on the duty of the husband to allow his wife out to devotions, while conceding also that the civil position of a husband meant his wife must obey if he forbade her going to church. The church, and religious attendance in general, became a means whereby women, unmarried and married and even those in religious orders, liberated themselves from the cloister of their normal lives and made illicit contact with others in the world outside. 'In few places', observed Azpilcueta, 'are more contacts and distractions made than in church'.[265]

The wholly anti-feminist clerical tradition may be found in the writings of the Franciscan Francisco Ortiz Lucio, whose *Garden of holy loves* (Alcalá 1589) began with the proposition 'the love of women is perilous', and continued for several pages with a bitter anti-woman invective that is worthy of attention simply because it was unusual among the clerical writers of the time.[266] Though the strain of thought was fundamentally irrational (the Virgin Mary seems not to have been considered in the category of woman), and often patently influenced by sexual defensiveness, it was impossible to escape from because it formed a fundamental element of historic Christianity and writers quoting from the fathers could not escape quoting the descriptions of woman given by St Ambrose ('ianua Diaboli, via iniquitatis') or St Maximus ('viri naufragium, domus tempestas, quietis impedimentum'),[267] among many others. The prejudice existed only among a restricted range of writers, however, and there is ample evidence of a more realistic and practical attitude to women among other moralists, clergy included.

Many authors recognised that religious practice and the life of the Church depended largely on women, who made up the majority of active worshippers. Innumerable parish priests accepted that without their help their work would be insupportable, and throughout Catalonia women were accepted into confraternities together with men and many women's guilds fulfilled a crucial role in the parish. Their participation was at best only partial: confraternities with women members, for example, normally did not allow them to hold office nor were they given the right to vote. When women stepped outside these limits, as at Olesa de Montserrat in 1771, the diocesan visitor was scandalised, terming 'execrable corruption and abominable abuse' the parish practice of 'four women known as administrators going with candles before the priest and attendants of the Tabernacle or Bed of Our Lady, in the procession on the day of the Assumption'.[268]

To a considerable extent work could also liberate women from their assigned cloister role, but this appears to have had a limited importance in the Catalan lands. In the rainier climates of the Basque lands and northern France, women were an important element in agriculture; but in the Mediterranean area they appear to have been discouraged from working in the fields, as this was held to endanger the man's honour. They were nevertheless allotted a large share of all work: fray Miquel Agustí, writing in 1617 for Catalan farmers, reflected classic attitudes rather than his own views when he stated that 'the woman has to be the first to start work and the last to leave off, the first to get up from the bed and the last to lie down in it,' hardly words of comfort for the Catalan peasant wife.[269]

Though writers of the Counter Reformation were strong advocates of the right of women to fulfil their domestic and public roles with the maximum of dignity and liberty, they seemed to present another face when it came to defining the role of women within the all-male enclave of the Church itself. In the course of the sixteenth century pressure from above tended to exclude them from any part of the public liturgy or from helping in the sacerdotal area of the sacristy and altar. Women's confraternities were reduced to simple duties of cleaning and decorating. Within the body of the church during devotions the separation of men and women became mandatory and persisted into the present century among rural Christian communities. As with other changes, separation was no novelty in Spain. The diocesan synod of Tuy (Galicia) in 1528 had ruled 'that in the churches there be a line beyond which women may not cross nor mix with the men, and the men are to be in front, before the altar', and a similar ruling had been made in the diocese of León in 1526;[270] but there is little evidence of its being widespread practice. Many clergy strongly believed that in all aspects of public life women must be pushed back into a secluded and separate role, and in the mid-sixteenth century a memorandum to the king's Council complained 'that in the theatres there is no separate place for the women and the men, nor are there separate doors and they come in and leave by the same door'.[271] The same pressure group continued for many years to demand that women be excluded from the stage. By the 1590s, when the controversy over women in the theatre reached its climax, Marco Antonio Camos commented in Barcelona that 'it seems to me just that men be separated from women and that they enter by different doors.'[272] As precedent, he cited the common custom of churches in Rome, and more particularly the practice in Borromeo's cathedral of Milan. From this it seems clear that the reformers were wishing to impose on Spaniards a custom which, though it had some precedents in the peninsula, was consciously imported from Italy. Virtually all episcopal directives of the post-Tridentine period direct that men be separated from women in the churches, and there were many good reasons why they should have done so, if only to protect women from the uninvited attentions of the men. The diocesan visitor to the parish of Bescaran (Urgell) in 1575 ordered that 'women not dare to seat themselves on the benches where the men are, but instead from the entrance of the church downwards, so that they not mix with the men'.[273] The clamorous tone of those calling for separation is a good indication that the practice was difficult to impose; and though separation may have come to be accepted in many churches, there is also clear evidence that it failed in much of the country. In an apparently unpublished tract written in Catalonia in 1617, the Augustinian friar Antonio Marques commented that because of the provocative dresses of women at mass 'the holy fathers [i.e. of Trent] ordered that in the church men be separated from women, as practised in Italy.' However, Marques went on, it proved very difficult to introduce this new custom into the country, and so 'since we cannot achieve this in Spain, one should order women to cover themselves' so as not to distract the clergy.[274]

In many churches, efforts continued to be made to enforce separation. The vicar-general of Barcelona in 1590 repeated the rules governing sexes in the cathedral, and warned that if men dared to trespass into the area reserved for women, the cathedral bell would be rung.[275] The lack of success in this area, confirming Marques' conclusion of 1617, can be seen in the 1750s when the diocesan visitor to Llinàs (Llobregat), ordered the separation of sexes in church; and in the Penedès, in Mediona's neighbour village of La Llacuna, he ordered that in future 'women be separated from men, and on no account may men and women sit together'.[276] Separation of sexes was also enforced in northern Europe by the Protestant churches,[277] but little is known of its success.

The attempted relegation of women to a secondary role in religious matters could conflict with community traditions, which often allotted them a recognised role. We have noted that the Church sometimes disapproved of their holding office in confraternities. There were also folk customs which conceded a role to women. In southern Catalonia the feast of St Agatha (5 February) was celebrated as the feast of women, with ritual rite inversion in which a woman was elected as mayor for a day or the fiesta was organised by women or they were given the initiative in asking men to dance. The Church probably had to accommodate these rituals and in so doing allowed women a status which the clergy were normally reluctant to concede.

Marginalisation of woman in religious life was most acute in the convents. The Counter Reformation by no means diminished woman's role (the well-known activity of St Teresa at the end of the sixteenth century is proof that it did not),[278] but by attempting to discipline female religion it consciously imposed a male dominance not always congenial to the Spanish tradition, where the role of the female contemplative (the *beata*) had always been recognised as significant. Convents of the period have been described as a 'parking-lot for women',[279] being 'in part centres of religious life, in part boarding-schools for girls, in part a place for spinsters, in part refuges for widows and elderly'. The imposition of the cloister on convents in post-Tridentine Catalonia – where the rules had never stipulated it – provides an interesting commentary not only on the hesitant progress of the Counter Reformation, but also on the relative roles of men and women in the religious life of the period.

In early sixteenth-century Catalonia most women's convents resembled religious hostels rather than enclosed institutions; rural convents were rare, all the thriving houses being located fairly close to population centres which financed them. Each convent had a core of professed nuns, but normally also took in two other major categories: young women of good family who observed part of the rule but in general used the place as a finishing-school, and older women and widows who were religiously inclined but used the place as a retirement home. In the better endowed convents virtually all nuns were from the upper classes, given that all had to pay the entry fee or 'dowry' (which in mid-century in the aristocratic convent of Junqueres was £150). In view of the heterogeneous character of the women it was not possible to impose any strict control, and male visitors came and went freely, guests stayed overnight, 'nuns' went home at will to live with their families. To the male reformers of the period, all this was utterly scandalous. We may observe the progress of reform attempts through the example of the rich Barcelona convent of Santa Maria de Junqueres, founded in the thirteenth century for noblewomen and under the rule of the Castilian Order of Santiago, whose head was the crown itself.

In 1495 as part of the movement for reform originating in Castile visitors were sent to reform Junqueres, and ordered a radical imposition of the cloister rules, prohibiting men from entering, ordering confession to be through a grille in the wall, and imposing a community life on the twenty-one nuns there. When the next visit was made, in 1501, it was found that none of the previous orders had been complied with; the visitors accordingly repeated all the injunctions, and insisted that when the nuns made their vows they should 'take vows of Obedience, Chastity and Poverty, since it is understood they only have vows of Obedience', a concession made by the order of Santiago in 1480. In 1504 the visitors found that of all the reforms enjoined in 1495 only the construction of a dormitory had been done; and that the nuns were failing to go to confession and communion. Matters were not helped by the fact that the prioress and nuns claimed they could not read the rules of the order, which were in Castilian; in 1529, accordingly, permission was given for the rules to be translated. The gradual filtration of Castilian influences is shown by the introduction for the first time, in 1549, of limpieza proofs, undoubtedly a consequence of their introduction in Toledo in 1547.

Not until the visit of 1560 was a serious attempt made to make the nuns observe the rule. The visitors read to the assembled convent a long list of extremely strict regulations, at the end of which (as the visitor reported) 'Doña Magdalena De Mallo, the prioress elect, and all the other nuns of the convent said that they were appealing and did appeal to His Majesty against the mandates and all the other measures that we had done.'[280] The visitors denied them the right to appeal, but the chapter general heard their appeal in 1561 and inevitably rejected it. The visitors then expelled seven leading protesters from the convent, ordered the remainder to observe the new rules, and introduced ten docile new nuns. In 1576 further changes were introduced when for the first time the use of the Tridentine Roman rite was imposed.

The problems of the female cloister at Junqueres, however, were less religious than social. The nuns in 1560 were all from elite families (one was a marquesa), and as long as recruitment for the convents was restricted to the upper classes, the individualistic daughters of the rich would continue to question why they should suffer deprivation of the normal courtesies of daily life. Nor did the Counter Reformation manage to alter the social bias, which continued as strongly as ever. The imposition of limpieza proofs in 1549 and again in 1561 was a trend towards exclusivity, accentuated further by the steady raising of the cost of a dowry: between 1561 and 1600 the dowry at Junqueres rose from £150 to £300. Despite half a century of attempted reforms the convent continued its role as a finishing-school: in 1605 the superior reported the recent marriage of sixteen girls, with impeccably elite surnames such as Sentmenat, Doms, Guimerà, Eril and Alentorn. When the visitors in

1605 attempted to visit the main centres of communal life in the convent (strictly required in the reforms ever since 1495), these were found not to exist: 'we could not visit the kitchen, because there is no common kitchen,' 'we tried to visit the dormitory and found that there is no common dormitory, because each of the nuns sleeps in a private house she has within the convent.'[281] The visitors, astonishingly, did nothing to alter this state of things: within the ample grounds of the rich convent, therefore, each elite family continued to maintain its own 'house' in which the family members, technically nuns or postulates, maintained servants and lived and ate separately, the only centre for common activity being the chapel. The aristocratic character of some women's convents seems to have prevailed mainly within the Barcelona area, where the elite used the houses as residences for their women. The situation in houses such as the prominent convent of Santa Clara at Pedralbes, of which the Council of Aragon noted in 1670 that the nuns were 'all persons of rank, daughters of noble families',[282] was simply a continuation of something which had preceded the reform period and never been altered.

Reform of the women's convents in Catalonia was a long-term struggle, in which a decidedly masculine Church attempted to impose on convents restrictions they had never known. The Cistercian convent at Vallbona, a dependency of the monastery at Santes Creus, continued successfully for over twenty years to defy the royal and papal commissioners. After the first moves had been made against the convent, in 1580 the nuns obtained a papal brief protecting them from accepting the cloister, which they claimed had not been in their constitutions. In 1601 the bishop of Lérida rejected this defence as 'irrelevant' and enclosed the convent, setting in train works to bring it into effect, such as walls, grilles, and bars. Eventually in 1603 several nuns were expelled from the convent and the new regime imposed.[283] A similar story occurred over the same period with several other foundations, with no quarter given the nuns: some Benedictine nuns were accused in 1610, for instance, that 'for many years they have lived vilely and dishonestly, living with men and most of them with children.'[284]

The evidence from Catalonia suggests that the Counter Reformation had an ambivalent impact on the role of women in religion. On one hand, it vindicated their role relative to the practice of the sacraments: they were to be treated with respect within matrimony, they were to be allowed to go to church and participate in religious observances. On the other hand, by elevating the male priesthood above them, by separating them from men in church, by excluding them from the sacristy and the altar and from church administration, by insisting on the cloister, it re-imposed a male dominance that had not always been traditional. It has been argued that the Catholic reforms were fundamentally misogynistic, and that feminine sainthood in the period was founded on penitence and self-abasement, with even the most notable female saints presented as weak vessels rather than as heroes.[285] The conclusion has some merits; but the chauvinistic outlook of the Church was modified in part by the social reality within which the male clergy worked, and also by the efforts of individual priests to rethink the terms on which men and women lived together within the Christian community. The alternative view that 'the growth of the cults of the Holy Family and of the Infant Jesus, and the proliferation of associated confraternities, afforded a widespread sanctification of the role of women and of children within the family,'[286] is more difficult to sustain and supported by little historical evidence; nor is it clear that in its daily social activity 'the Church consistently favoured women above men,'[287] at least in Catalonia. In practical terms the Church made no conscious decisions about the roles of the sexes, and its attitude was determined exclusively by the norms of the society in which it found itself.

CHAPTER SEVEN

Taking the Message to the People

The clergy of Spain are the nerve of all Christendom.
                                St Carlo Borromeo, August 1565

*I wished to write this book in the Catalan tongue because it is my
own tongue, and because I wished to do this service to the
Catalan nation.*

                                Pere Font, *Spiritual Exercise*, 1608

A central aspiration of the reform movement, to produce a new breed of dynamic, educated clergy,
proved more difficult to achieve than many had realised. Well
before the Reformation there had been moves to improve the
quality of higher clergy and religious but the institutional base for
a concerted programme was lacking. Reform of the religious orders had already been attempted from the end of the fifteenth
century, with varying results: whether reformed or not, they entered
into a period of great vigour and played a prominent role in the
evangelisation of America. From 1493 to about 1820, over 15,000
religious crossed to America under government auspices, their peak
emigration occurring precisely in the golden age of Trent, from
about 1560 to around 1610.[1] The figures underscore the fact that
Spain's ecclesiastical strength lay with the religious orders, not
with the secular clergy, who were the most urgently in need of
renovation.

Prior to the 1563 Tridentine decree 'Pro Seminariis', clergy in the
Spanish realms had access to any of forty-five colleges of higher
education in the peninsula, which included the famous university
colegios mayores, but only seventeen of these were expressly devoted
to clerical training, with the attendant specialised curricula. Of the
seventeen, one was located in Lérida (1371) and one in Valencia
(1550); all the rest were in the Crown of Castile, with a heavy
concentration in Salamanca (six colleges), and were founded between 1476 and 1554, indicating the active interest of that epoch in
clerical reform.[2] In conformity with its policy of centralising control
on dioceses and parishes, Trent decreed that each diocese should

erect a new seminary of its own to carry out the new educational programme. The plan encountered serious obstacles in the peninsula.

Unlike the older colleges, many dependent on private finance and all based on the classical Spanish College at Bologna, the new 'seminaries' were meant to follow guidelines laid down by Trent: each was to be diocesan-based, controlled fully by the bishop and financed exclusively from diocesan resources; and the curriculum was restricted to six subjects deemed basic to clerical education. Many bishops were understandably enthusiastic about the idea: in Tarragona in 1568 cardinal Cervantes founded one of the earliest new seminaries, which later received the title of 'university'. Elsewhere in Catalonia the pace was slow, with seminaries in Urgell in 1592, and in Barcelona and Gerona in 1598. Throughout the peninsula twenty-three Tridentine seminaries were founded between 1564 and 1610, but only five in the rest of the seventeenth century. The obstacles were the same as elsewhere in Catholic Europe: the opposition of cathedral chapters, which would have had to fund the seminaries; objections from other colleges; episcopal inertia.[3] In Barcelona the bishop had to wait until a suitable site could be found in the shape of the premises of a suppressed Augustinian priory, and the decree of foundation was issued in November 1567;[4] but there were further delays and the inauguration did not take place until 1598, with still more problems in the subsequent century.

Due in part to the lack of adequate seminaries, in Spain there was little significant progress in the reform and training of the secular clergy. When in November 1713 the fiscal general (or chief law officer) of Spain, Melchor de Macanaz, wrote to the bishops of the Crown of Castile to ask whether they would support the founding of training colleges, he did so on the information that among the priesthood 'many do not understand their office and the high ministry to which they have been called, others are given to vice, others to trading, others go round troubling the villages.' Most of the bishops agreed with him, but virtually all felt that the idea was impracticable, partly because of lack of money, partly because unnecessary. Many said they already had good Tridentine seminaries. There was admittedly a continuing problem: 'from my own experience in this bishopric, most have received orders with spurious credentials and a genuine ignorance, and the situation is such that I have suspended many for not even being able to read the canon of the mass ... the ignorance suffered by the villages is severe' (the bishop of Badajoz); 'when I arrived in my diocese I found the clergy to be both numerous and idiots' (bishop of Cartagena); and in Coria the bishop claimed he had recently rejected thirty-eight out of forty candidates for ordination, that his diocese had no Tridentine seminary, and that it was 109 years since the last diocesan synod had been called.[5] A century and a half after Trent, little seemed to have been done.

The clergy in Spain were in as parlous a state as anywhere in the Catholic world. In Valencia where the bishops had held no synod since 1422 the first post-Reformation synod was held by archbishop Tomás Villanueva in June 1548: the bulk of its constitutions affected the clergy's ministry and forms of dress.[6] Everywhere in Europe reformers had put betterment of the clerical estate at the forefront of their programme, but the results were disheartening. In Spain no systematic clerical reform, of the type later undertaken in France with some success,[7] was ever put into effect; and throughout the period in Catalonia there is continuous evidence of the failure of synodal decrees. In Barcelona the synods decreed regular reforms; in Lérida in 1566 Antonio Agustín issued an important edict on the abuses of the clergy;[8] in Vic the epoch of reform included the stipulation of the synod of 1581[9] that clergy not wear secular hats in public but only the bonnet, that they cut their hair every two months, and that they not wear moustaches or goatees. Despite such efforts, it was possible in 1622 for the city council of Urgell to report that the existing vacancy in the see (it had not been occupied for two and a half years) had aggravated the lack of control over the clergy, provoking a spate of violence in which 'many priests have died violently, others have been wounded by pistols and other arms, and in just three months three priests have with their own hands murdered three people.'[10] In 1626, half a century after Trent, one encounters a Catalan parish priest who believed that 'there is glory in this world as in the next,' who heard confessions while dressed in a bright scarlet shirt and a bandit-style cape, who wore his pistols when saying mass, and who was implicated directly in the murder of ten people, one of whom 'after he had stabbed to death he took his blood and put it into the dead man's mouth'.[11]

Thanks to the many structural factors which made clerical reform in Spain as difficult as in other countries – the vested interests of chapters and of lay presentations, the low level of education, the poor disciplinary measures available to bishops – it was difficult to point to any significant gain in the quality of the pastorate.[12] From the mid-sixteenth century there was little change in the nature of complaints. In 1556, when there was no bishop to govern the diocese, the *jurats* of Mallorca claimed that the local clergy were 'well off and live opulently', and that 'they live in such lewdness and licence that we are lost for words to describe their manner of living.'[13] Fray Jerónimo de Lemos, criticising the clergy in 1567 with their 'clothes and dress, silks and expensive attire, fripperies and fancies, their pastimes and entertainments, their words and chatter',[14] was certainly moralising, but there was material to criticise. Ignorance was widespread: in Llucmajor (Mallorca) in 1562 one priest 'can barely read or understand Latin and has a bad reputation', another 'is totally ignorant of the sacraments of the Church',[15] and in the same island's parish of Porreras the clergy understood no Latin.[16] Even in the 1580s, according to the bishop of Oviedo, half his clergy did not understand the (Latin) gospels in the mass, nor did they have the most basic knowledge of how to administer confession.[17] Guillem Evrart, priest of Sant Feliu de Llobregat, was in 1578 suspended from saying mass by the bishop 'until he learns to read';[18] presumably all these years he had been saying it from memory. Long after this, illiterate clergy could be found, such as one denounced in 1599 by the rector of Vilafranca del Penedès, 'mossèn Francesc Alamany, priest of the present town and the most idiotic and barbaric person, who cannot read a word or say mass'.[19] As late as 1690 the episcopal visitor to the Vall d'Aneu judged that 'many of the clergy of the present valley are unworthy to exercise and administer the cure of souls, some because they are illiterate, others because they live dishonestly, others because they are troublemakers, others because they do not set a good example.'[20]

Clergy in Barcelona who bought Francisco Ortiz Lucio's *Compendium of all the Summas*, published there in 1598, would have received an excellent guide to legislation on the clothing they were supposed to wear:

> Clergy must wear their habit closed from top to bottom, and may not wear pigtail or beard, nor wear an open jacket, nor a short cloak, nor any dress of various colours, nor gold and silver embroidery, nor rings and ornaments to display pride and vanity; nor bear arms, nor have birds and dogs for hunting boar; and may not play at dice or cards or chess, nor attend games or comedies or bull-fights . . .[21]

In that same year the clergy of Barcelona also received a reminder from bishop Dimas Loris that according to the rules laid down by the councils of Tarragona 'they may not accompany women nor serve lay-people at table nor be helpers and servants, nor go to see farces nor dress in masks, nor dance nor do any other such low and demeaning things.'[22] Until well into the seventeenth century many secular clergy did not conform to the rules specifying distinctive dress, as we can see from the unequivocal evidence throughout Spain. So-called clerical dress remained in many areas as much of a novelty as it was to the king of France who, riding out one day in

1623 and surprised by the cassock worn by a priest, asked to what new order he belonged.[23]

Non-residence was a permanent, almost incurable, abuse, to be found less in clergy appointed by the bishops than in those, far more numerous, appointed by other jurisdictions. Apart from sheer dereliction of duty, rectors were unable to be resident if they had charge of more than one parish, and if no dwelling was available for them in the parish. Adequate lodging for the rector therefore always appeared as an important feature of diocesan visitations: in the diocese of Urgell in 1575, for instance, the visitor found that the rector of Calvinya had to reside outside the parish for lack of a house, and ordered that 'all the parishioners make a good and decent dwelling for the rector'; the same order had to be made in Hortodo.[24] Beneficed clergy were far and away the biggest category of absentees since their obligation to a church might amount to little more than saying a few masses every year to comply with the terms of the benefice; and many therefore felt free not to live in the area at all. Seventy per cent (or 292) of the *beneficiats* out of a sample of 413 in the Barcelona diocese in 1636 were found by the bishop to be absentees.[25] Unless they formed part of a community of priests, as in many 'collegiate' churches, clergy seemed therefore to be more absent than present. In 1600 bishop Coloma of Barcelona had to issue a decree against 'many and divers persons who obtain rectorates and other benefices in our bishopric of Barcelona' but who 'do not observe or comply with the appointment and remain absent from their rectorates and do not take up residence in them';[26] the order was repeated by the vicar-general in February, and almost simultaneously the bishop ordered the two parish priests of Vilafranca del Penedès to reside in their parish. One generation later in 1636 Vilafranca was still a prime example of the problems in the Church:[27] the parish priests were resident, but of the sixty-six benefices in the church sixty-one were not within the appointment of the bishop, and in twenty-five benefices the incumbent was an absentee. The wilful absence of the rector from Montseny in 1636 made the bishop, in response to a petition from the village, order him to carry out his duties; in the same visitation that year, the visitor observed that in Granollers the thirty-eight benefices were all held by absentees.[28]

It was impossible to control all the clergy when appointments were not in the hands of the bishop. Without strict division of jurisdictions, priests could wander in and out of dioceses, claiming that they had been validly ordained in another, a chaos which led to innumerable abuses, mainly in the administration of confession but also in other areas. In 1606 the Inquisition had to intervene in the case of the rector of Valls, a man of forty years from the Vall d'Arán, who had resided in Catalonia for only nine years and had somehow managed to obtain his post despite the total absence of proof that he had ever been ordained; only the energy of the twenty-six witnesses against him, testifying to his 'bad living and bad example', seduction of women and the use of magic and spells, succeeded in bringing about his expulsion from the area.[29] He was subsequently condemned to five years in the galleys, but returned to roam the province, offering magical cures, and in 1615 was again banished by the Inquisition. As the bishops began to tighten up the rules, new ways of avoiding them were tried. One of the most common was for prospective ordinands to cross over into France, get themselves ordained by a French prelate, and return to Catalonia with apparently valid orders. The books of the Mallorca diocese show at least ten such cases in the last five years of the sixteenth century.[30] Since France, thanks to the civil wars, still had a largely unreformed Catholic Church, there was considerable pressure in Catalonia against accepting the validity of French ordinations.

'Marriage' of the clergy proved as much of a problem in Spain as elsewhere in the pre-Reformation world. It was a standard joke in the Spanish countryside, reflected in popular refrains, that the illegitimate children of the parish were children of the priest; and clerical illegitimacy was a real enough problem, provoking the bishop of Oviedo in 1594 to condemn 'the evil and scandalous custom [among clergy] of keeping the children in the house until they marry'.[31] The problem arose out of the even better-known question of the concubinage of the clergy, but both problems were equally insoluble and there is no evidence that the Counter Reformation ever managed to eliminate one or the other. At the very end of our period, in 1706, the bishop of Lérida complained to the pope of the 'libertinous life of the dean of Lérida, who lives surrounded by his children; and other clergy live as though married in the face of the Church'.[32] Bishops objected in particular to the sons of priests being presented for holy orders, but Rome was not so choosy and regularly issued dispensations for those in breach of the canon law rule prohibiting illegitimates as clergy: in some small measure, the Spanish clergy continued to be self-reproducing in the way that the (reformed) Lutheran clergy in parts of Germany managed to become. The battle to reduce the number of clergy was pursued in some directions, however: it was the stated policy of reformers to restrict and decrease the granting of the tonsure or 'crown', the basic outward symbol of holy orders, and there are indications, in Mallorca for instance,[33] that the policy was effectively pursued.

Of the many vices practised by the clergy, one was constantly denounced but proved to be irreformable: the use of tobacco. Endowed by many writers of the early sixteenth century with a wide range of curative virtues, tobacco was also recognised to be an anti-social habit, and bishops tried to restrict its use. In 1635 Tomás Ramón, a Dominican prior of Barcelona, penned one of the most informative and still relevant essays on the weed. Noting that tobacco was taken in one of two ways, either as snuff or as a cigarette, and referring evidently to its use among the clergy, he said that 'it is used in these two ways in Spain with such frequency that there is almost no moment when it is not applied to nose or to mouth, at all hours and times, between and during meals, when studying, preaching, and even singing in the church; annoying everybody else,' which suggests smoking rather than snuff. He was among the first to observe its habit-forming qualities; 'in Granada I heard an ecclesiastic say that even if the pope ordered him to he would not stop using it,' and in Seville he persuaded some clergy to stop smoking but 'within a day or two after stopping they had returned to using it, and when I asked them why they replied that they couldn't help it.' 'With my own eyes I have seen an infinite number of times in Andalusia how it is used by both laymen and ecclesiastics, even – horrible to say – at the altar.' After citing medical cases of death through tobacco, Ramón asked how man, normally a clean, rational animal, could 'go with noses like sewers, beards filthy with the dust, fingers as though they belonged to tanners, and above all emanating a most disgusting smell'?[34]

As late as 1685, as evidence of the failure of previous prohibitions, in the provincial council of Tarragona a constitution 'prohibits most severely ministering priests in the choir or at the altar from taking tobacco, and excommunicates those who smoke or chew it before saying mass or receiving communion'.[35] Were the bishops aware of the praises of tobacco penned two generations before in Catalonia by the rector of Vallfogona?

Tabac cast, tabac sant, tabac tan fort	Chaste, holy, strong tobacco
Que de ser immortal dubte no té . . .	you will endure forever . . .
Lo que diu mal de tu no sap què és bé,	Critics don't know your worth,
Falta-li enteniment, i fa la sort	in their ignorance they do not
Que no gos del tesor de tu ve!	enjoy the delight you give!

The teaching of doctrine, which in perspective can be seen as the most typical activity of the Counter-Reformation Church, was most desirably done in the language of the people. Because the Protestant Reformation had universally rejected the Latin tongue as inadequate, it is sometimes assumed that the Counter Reformation stuck stubbornly to Latin and thereby lost considerable advantage in the struggle for souls. The reform movement in the Catholic Church was perfectly aware of the importance of the vernacular, and the Council of Trent made a clear recommendation that preaching be done in a language understood by the people. The Church however was also committed to making sure that its pastors could handle the official language of the liturgy, and a dual obligation, both to Latin and to the vernacular, therefore imposed itself.

Literacy levels in Golden Age Spain appear to have been good in comparison with the rest of Europe, with near total literacy among the elite, obvious black spots such as low literacy in the rural areas, and massive illiteracy among most women.[36] A sample of 2843 cases for New Castile shows that some forty-five per cent had the ability to read, write and sign, but of this impressive number only eight persons in the entire time-span 1540–1817 confessed to possessing a book.[37] In Valencia out of a similar sample (2349 cases) the picture was startlingly different, with over three-fourths of professional people possessing books.[38] For Catalonia no adequate surveys exist, but there is no reason to suspect that levels were lower than in Castile. It was inevitable to find mountain communities, such as Escaro in Rosselló, where illiteracy at the end of the seventeenth century was apparently total.[39] In the same period in Perpinyà it appears, on the basis of a sample of 672 confraternity members, that in the very lowest professions eighty per cent could not sign, and in the middling professions (butchers, bakers) sixty; among the noble class all could write.[40] Whatever the situation, the ability of the people to absorb cultural change did not depend on their literacy, and all significant cultural transmission in early modern Spain was oral. In the even less literate society of Reformation Germany,[41] religious change was not restricted by inability to write or read.

The documentation of the Inquisition of Toledo, where knowledge of doctrine on the part of those accused of various offences appears to have improved in the course of the sixteenth century, has sometimes been cited as proof of the success of the Counter Reformation in educating the population.[42] There is nevertheless no clear evidence that literacy improved during the period, and may even have worsened, if recent conclusions for Segovia are applied to all Spain.[43] The teaching of Christian doctrine was oral rather than based on the capacity to read and seems to have been inadequately done when entrusted to the parish rector. Indeed, in the region of Tremp (Urgell), the diocesan visitor in 1575 seems to have scrapped the requirement that everyone over the age of fourteen should know the Pater, Ave, Salve Regina and ten commandments.[44]

The transmission of cultural change did not depend on books. Down to the nineteenth century 'Spaniards did not read books: they talked.'[45] Published literature derived from a spoken culture and was itself diffused orally.[46] Catalonia was no more literate than Spain or Languedoc,[47] and even in public life it was not always necessary to be literate: in 1644 when the town of Tuir sent a mission to Barcelona only one town *cónsol* could go, since 'none of the other cónsols is lettered'.[48] Though of great importance for the successful diffusion of culture, books were not a prerequisite for cultural change, and continued to be scarce in Catalan households. House inventories for the Barcelona area down to 1600[49] show that even obviously literate people like shopkeepers kept manuals of accounts but no books for leisure reading, and there must have been many like the pious lady whose only books were two manuals of piety, whose state was described by the notary in his inventory as 'poor', hastily and more perceptively corrected to 'well used'. At all social levels in Catalonia books were a rarity: no books were owned by Jaume Parrinet, merchant of Barcelona in 1566, nor by Lluis de Vilademany, baron of Vic and seigneur of Taradell and Santa Coloma de Farners in 1573. Clergy were no exception: in 1570 Pere Perelló, rector of Conques (Urgell), possessed seventeen books and Joan Biosquet, priest of Santa Maria del Pi, had the *Letters of Cicero* among his nine books; but by contrast Miquel Mas, of the parish church of Cervera in 1600, had only a missal and breviary, and Joan Spuny, canon of Barcelona in 1587, had only a clutch of missals and breviaries totalling eight books. The prize for non-reading must go to Pau de Bertomeu, canon of Barcelona in 1603, who had no books at all in his house, not even a breviary, and whose study was used solely for stocking corn.[50]

In country parishes the keeping of books was rare. The evidence from forty inventories of *pagesos* in Mediona over the period 1560–1705 shows a total absence of books, with the one exception of Jaume Farrera, of Mas Ginoles, recorded in 1601 as possessing 'a small box with packs of books'.[51] In a bookless society like this, any new message the Counter Reformation might have to offer had to come principally through word of mouth, and this is what indeed happened in the countryside of Catalonia.

Catechesis by the clergy necessarily had to rely on verbal repetition. It was carried out in three main ways: within mass, outside mass, and through the sacraments. Teaching within mass, principally through the sermon but also through the recitation of basic prayers, had the advantage of a captive audience, but was onerous for the clergy and therefore seldom done. Most episcopal visitations after Trent ordered the curate to hold regular classes outside mass hours, after vespers on Sunday afternoon – what Protestants came to know as Sunday school – to educate both children and adults in doctrine. The instructions of the diocesan synod of Barcelona in 1600 are clear: '... after lunch, in the church or near to it, call together the young children and not only teach them some catechism but ask them to explain what they have learnt ... Curates thus have to teach not only at the hour of mass but in addition after lunch.'[52]

This was very difficult to enforce, and from the beginning the attempt to have Sunday schools collapsed before the apparently widespread refusal of the people – specifically, the adults – to attend or allow their children to attend. A farmer of Ager reacted strongly in 1588 to the attempt to hold parish classes in religious doctrine: 'they were talking in the village about catechism having to be taught in the afternoon on feast-days and he said that at that hour his sons were better employed taking the herd to graze than listening to catechism.'[53] Many clergy must have been in the situation of the rector of Sant Feliu del Racó who, asked by the diocesan visitor in 1611 'if he has given out the bishop's edict on teaching catechism', replied 'yes; but since he knows that no one will come to it he teaches catechism only at mass.'[54] In the diocese of Urgell catechism seems not to have been commonly taught even by the end of the seventeenth century. In the synod of 1689 it was noted that 'in many parts of the diocese it is found that the parish priests do not observe the obligation, which is not suited to the poor capacity and lack of comprehension in the villages and among the rustic faithful, and so some priests think that by reciting the catechism at the foot of the altar during solemn high mass they fulfil the said obligation.'[55]

For the recalcitrant, the discipline of the confessional was used. In 1580 the clergy of Barcelona were instructed to this effect by their bishop:[56]

> Then you will ask if he knows his catechism, specifically the Pater Noster, Ave Maria, Credo, articles of faith, the ten commandments of the law of God, and the five of the Church, and all that in vernacular or Latin ... And if he does not know, the confessor will tell him that if he persists in ignorance the next time he will not be absolved.

In the same instructions, the bishop was fully aware that the clergy themselves needed tools with which to teach, and urged them all to be in possession of three books: the Bible, the catechism of Trent, and the catechism (*instructio*) of cardinal Cervantes.

As a last attempt to instruct the young, it had been specified by Trent that couples could not marry without showing that they had an adequate knowledge of doctrine. On this point as well there was considerable opposition, and the clergy in the Barcelona diocese in 1574 tried to get the rule suspended on the grounds that 'we have seen and understood that in the archdiocese of Tarragona and in the present diocese the rectors have found great resentment in the souls of those who wish to marry.'[57] By the end of the century, however, it remained the rule that 'no man or woman may be married unless they first know by heart the Pater Noster and Ave Maria, the Creed, the commandments of the law of God and of the Church, and the Sacraments'.[58] If many parishes were like Mediona, the rule could have been little observed.

Were the people successfully instructed? It is ironic that Catalonia produced one of the great educators of the age, but his work was done in Italy rather than in the principality. Josep Calassanç, a native of Urgell, became vicar-general of the diocese towards the end of the sixteenth century and then went to Rome in 1591 where he devoted his life to teaching children and founded the very successful order known briefly as the Escoles Pies. For Catalonia little or nothing is known of education at this period, nor is there any information about the long-term impact of catechism classes. Catechesis was not done regularly, and it was no accident that the bishops in their visitations always insisted on repeating the directive that classes be held. In Mediona in 1600 the bishop demanded 'that every Sunday after vespers the vicar signal by means of a bell' that the parishioners should come to catechism;[59] the bell may indeed have been sounded, but it would have rung out over an empty valley and there is no evidence that catechism sessions were ever held in the parish. Resistance to classes may be compared to the sad example of Lutheran Germany, where over half a century after the Reformation 'when the catechism is preached the pastor speaks to an empty church,' 'the sexton stands waiting in the empty church until in the end he has to abandon the catechism'; adults were particularly stubborn, and 'in nearly every parish people over eighteen years of age are embarrassed by the catechism and will not attend.'[60]

In Catalonia as in the rest of Spain catechism classes could be given either by the village teacher or under the auspices of the rector. The appointment of a village teacher (*mestre*) was normally a question of status ('it is not good for the town to be without a mestre,' resolved the town of Vinça when appointing theirs in 1608) and most towns of moderate size seem to have had one: in Rosselló the town of Vinça had one from at least 1510, Prada from at least 1580, Prats de Molló from 1584;[61] by the seventeenth century every considerable population had one. In St Quintí de Mediona there is a mention in 1605 of an existing 'schoolmaster', who was to hold classes in the new town hall (Casa del Consell), so we may assume that the post existed since at least the late sixteenth century.[62] Appointed and paid by the local community, the mestre was chosen from any candidate who offered himself, and was often a local beneficed priest looking for spare cash, or might even be a passer-by whom the village thought a good candidate: 'five or six days ago a student arrived in and is still in the town, and if we wish he will stay and be the mestre,' the town council of Vinça reported with satisfaction in the spring of 1609.[63] Village teachers were poorly paid, were never asked for their credentials, and had little dedication: in Prada in 1590, 'because of the negligence of the said mestre, we must find another.' Most important of all from the Church's point of view, the programme of the mestre was not always restricted to the teaching of Latin grammar and might include the teaching of catechism and morals. He might have to 'accompany the children to mass and vespers on Sundays and feast-days and stay with them so that they do not disturb the service'.[64] The programme laid down by bishop Coloma of Barcelona in 1600 was fairly broad;[65] teachers should 'teach the children not only to read well, to write and to count, but also good habits and practices, getting them to hear mass on days of obligation and also the sermon, and to say the Rosary and confess on the main feast-days; and not to swear or fight or blaspheme, and be obedient to their parents . . . and teach them the catechism, and for greater uniformity all should use the catechism of father Ledesma, and instruct them to read good and devout books and not permit books about love and profane things.'

'Local authorities in the sixteenth century regarded public support of educational institutions to be an essential task,' and influential jurists such as Diego de Simancas ruled that 'one of the most important functions of the state must be that children are correctly educated.'[66] It is unlikely, at least in Catalonia, that such education was directed against doctrinal error.[67] Long before there was any perception of a threat from external heresy the village schoolmaster had become a standard feature of the Spanish country-side. Because the mestre might play a crucial role in the formation of children the Counter-Reformation Church made a conscious effort to control his functions, but this interest in education developed surprisingly late, more than a quarter of a century after the end of the Council of Trent. The bishops tried to make sure that the villages got proper instruction and that catechism books were available for the population. They also tried to insist that the mestre, although appointed by the community, receive the approval of the diocesan authorities. For example, a mestre was banned in June 1598 from teaching in the village of Vilanova de Cubells, unless 'he is first examined and approved and admitted to the said post by the reverend bishop or his vicar-general',[68] but this condition had appeared in Catalonia only with the provincial council of Tarragona of 1591, from which year we can date the definitive intervention of the Catalan episcopate in the system of elementary education available in the province.[69]

In practice it seems unlikely that the Church could have imposed its control in a country notorious for its independent jurisdictions, and the evidence suggests that in the bishopric of Elna episcopal approval was never sought for the appointment of teachers.[70] The best that the Church could do was to determine which texts should be used: in Barcelona in 1588 the bishop's directive on the choice of catechism had in mind both the quality of presentation and availability in the vernacular. The directive, dated 13 February and addressed to all teachers in the diocese, 'orders all teachers to make sure that their pupils have the catechism book so as to be able to teach them more easily', and 'in the desire to have conformity and unity among all, we order that the children possess the book of Christian doctrine composed by the reverend doctor father Ledesma of the Company of Jesus, since it is printed in the Catalan tongue and is moreover brief and simple and the most used and accepted throughout Catalonia.'[71] It is interesting that the instructions made Catalan obligatory for all children, even for immigrants, so that the Church cannot be criticised for neglecting the common language of the province. In 1598 bishop Dimas Loris specified that the children should 'every day of the week sing once the catechism in Catalan', and that they use Ledesma.[72]

One reason for the failure of catechism classes, at least in the early period, was that a priest could not possibly teach what he did not himself know. The constant directives to parish clergy by diocesan visitors tried to spell out exactly how instruction of the people should be carried out. In Barcelona at the end of the sixteenth century clergy were reminded that 'every Sunday and holyday of obligation after the offertory of the mass or before it if there is no sermon, they should teach the people in Catalan the Pater Noster, Ave Maria, Credo, Salve Regina, articles of faith and the commandments of the law of God.'[73] Instructions by the bishop of Elna in 1629 specified that the rector should, at mass, 'in order the more easily to offer a remedy for the ignorance of Christian doctrine, in a clear voice and with distinct and intelligible words that the whole congregation can hear and understand, recite out loud three or four sections or themes from the printed summary of Christian doctrine that accompanies the present letter... and the congregation should repeat this quietly to themselves, to fix it more securely in the memory.'[74]

But the documentation leaves no doubt that the principal reason for the failure of catechism classes was the resistance of the people: adults refused to come, and male adults refused absolutely to appear, not because of hostility but because of the presumed loss of face they might suffer within the community. When Honorat Ciuro grew up in the 1620s in Cameles (Rosselló), a village of twenty-one households, he learnt his rudiments of grammar from the only resident mestre, the parish rector, but when his family wished him to have a more solid education they sent him, like his elder brother before him, to the grammar school at the town of Ille. Many years later, when Honorat had pursued a career in holy orders and obtained for himself a benefice at Tuir, he came back to reside near Cameles and offered to take over the duties of the parish priest in the spring and early summer of 1654. In particular he decided to take on the task of instructing the congregation, a task which had apparently never been carried out in the village despite nearly a century of Counter Reformation. Although instruction was also meant to feature in the mass itself, the hour normally set aside by authority for catechism was the period after vespers, early in the afternoon.

> After vespers [he wrote in his memoirs][75] began to teach catechism in the church, with my surplice on for greater decorum and reverence. Quite a few boys and girls, and many men and women stayed behind out of curiosity at the novelty. Explained the sign of the cross and what it was to be a Christian, subjects on which they were completely ignorant. Afterwards recited the rosary with them in the chapel of the Conception, and then the litany. All took part with great devotion. Infinite thanks to the good Jesus. Amen.

The curiosity did not last. He continued teaching every Sunday afternoon for several months, but not with the same success, and had to resort to the trick of handing out little images of saints (he learnt this from the Jesuits in Perpinyà), and as a last resort had to scold the congregation.

> *Sunday, 12 April.* At about two o'clock a recital of catechism in the church, after I tolled the church bells and sent a boy out through the

streets with a little hand-bell. Handed out several little images. Explained
the Creed. Then rosary and litany. Lots of little children, and some
women...
Sunday, 19 April. Sermon at mass, catechism after lunch with rosary
and litany. Explained the Paternoster and handed out small images.
Quite a few children and lots of women, with a few men...
Sunday, 7 June. In the sermon criticised those who gambled rather than
coming to the rosary. In the afternoon, catechism with rosary and
litany. A few more men came, thanks to the sermon.

In Spain there is no evidence of a blind adherence to Latin. The
language had never been widely known and ignorance of it was
widespread among the clergy, not because standards had declined
but because no great emphasis had ever been placed upon it. When
the official visitor of the Cistercian order visited Santes Creus in
1532 he noted the general ignorance of Latin among the monks and
observed that 'all the monks in this monastery handled Latin as
though it were Greek.'[76] Those who lamented the ignorance of
Latin were never in a position to cite some past epoch when Latin
had been widely known, and even in the late seventeenth century,
after a century of reforms, the secretary to the grand duke of
Tuscany gained the impression that Latin was unknown among the
Spanish elite.[77] In Catalonia the use of Latin, though obligatory in
schools and universities, seems never to have become generalised
except among a tiny handful of the elite, and in the course of the
sixteenth and seventeenth centuries its use in notarial acts pro-
gressively decayed.[78] When Despuig wrote his *Colloquies* in 1557
he did so in Catalan, given the lack of knowledge of Latin. By 1628
Andreu Bosch, writing in Catalan, lamented that Latin 'has now
been reduced only to the classes in letters in the schools where it
is taught by the teacher'.[79] In effect, the language retained its
scholarly role but was seldom used for official purposes. Throughout western Europe, 'Latin continued to be a passport to culture
and status, but its importance declined during the early modern
period.'[80]

The new Tridentine rites naturally adopted Latin, the lingua
franca now imposed on the Catholic Church, but its use was limited
to ritual texts – the mass, the breviary – which could be taken
straight from a book. In virtually every other respect the Counter
Reformation witnessed on the Spanish evidence a massive resort to
the vernacular. Book after book was published with the author
declaring clearly the utility of writing in the tongue which now,
with the extension of the monarchy, was the lingua franca of the
western world, and therefore of Spain as well. In the early century

Francisco de Monzón, professor of theology at Coimbra, explained why he was writing his *Mirror of a Christian Prince* (Lisbon 1544) in Castilian: 'it is understood now in most Christian nations and few now dedicate themselves to reading Latin since they haven't studied it.' His view was a considered advance on that of the great Navarrese scholar Martín de Azpilcueta, 'el doctor Navarro', who wrote his celebrated *Manual for Confessors* in Coimbra in 1552 and chose to do so in Latin in order to have a wider readership for, he said, Castilian and Portuguese 'are languages unknown beyond the Pyrenees';[81] a view he modified four years later when with great effort he translated the whole work (some eight hundred pages) into Castilian. Juan de Orozco y Covarrubias in 1591 excused himself for writing not in Latin but in Castilian, 'for our language has spread so much through the world that it is as general as Latin and some even think it is more widespread...And since in other nations serious people write in their own tongue it would be unjust to do any less in our own.'[82] Gaspar Astete in 1598, after stating that Latin was not wholly suitable for the devotions of 'women and other lay-people', also recognised that much of the sprituality of the educated classes was not based on Latin:[83]

> Some serious spiritual persons often feel more devotion when praying in Spanish than in Latin and it is no wonder. Because of this some servants of God have written many meditations and prayers in romance, and translated devout books to accustom people to what is good. Our experience is that some devotional books move more in romance than in Latin, as we see by the book of Thomas à Kempis commonly called *Contemptus mundi*, and by the meditations of St Augustine, St Bonaventura, Luis de Granada and other books of devotion.

Spiritual trends in the early sixteenth century had always placed emphasis on direct communication, most effectively achieved through the common tongue. The Catholic reformers inherited the feeling, shared also by the Protestant Reformation, that Latin could be a stumbling block to the gospel. This mood was strongly expressed by fray Antonio de Valenzuela in his *Christian doctrine for children and the lowly* (Salamanca 1556):[84]

> In those nations of France and Italy the Christian prayers and the precepts of the Church are never taught save in romance. The apostles taught the gospel to each nation according to the language it knew. Yet we although we know Castilian want to speak in Latin...O great blindness of these wretched times...when the layman does not understand the commandments of the Church nor the deacon the gospel nor the priest the mass.

Though valid for their time, Valenzuela's comments were very soon rendered out of date by the rigorous programme undertaken after the 1560s to educate clergy and people in the use of both Latin and vernacular. After mid-century the Church presses began to issue vernacular manuals to help the faithful follow the Latin rites, and efforts were made to help the people follow the mass and coordinate their vernacular piety with the official ritual.

At the same time, concessions were made to the general ignorance of Latin: Azpilcueta in his *Treatise of praise and complaint*, written in 1566, not only took pains to direct himself to the common reader ('since men should speak and write in the tongue they know best or least badly, I am writing this in the Castilian tongue'), but gave an immediate Castilian translation every time he cited from a Latin author. Azpilcueta's method was cited approvingly two generations later by Martin de la Vera, monk of the Escorial, who praised him for realising that to write a handbook in Latin for choristers 'would be like speaking to them in gibberish', and for translating the work into romance.[85] Numerous books of meditations for mass were published: one, by the Jesuit Francisco Arias, stressed that his *Spiritual progress* (1603) was directed to all conditions of people, both learned and humble, and that only for the former had he added footnotes; for the latter, 'I have set out and simplified the doctrine of this book so that it may serve all manner of people in any secular or religious state who wish to make progress in the service of God.'[86]

It has been suggested that in Spain the 'ideologues of the Counter Reformation created a climate hostile to mass education and popular reading',[87] but this can only be sustained if 'popular' is taken to mean 'secular', for there is ample evidence that the ideologues attempted to popularise their message, and the writers we have cited, who were foremost among the publicists of the time, speak in their own defence. Despite their efforts it remained difficult for the Counter Reformation to create any climate at all, since among those who read books the known and traditional preferences continued to prevail. There were priests who kept no books at all, like the parish priest of Sant Pere de les Puel·les in 1599; by contrast the priest Mateu Palau of Barcelona, who kept some, had a standard assortment of nine volumes: the ordinary of the mass, a book of spiritual exercises, a book on administering sacraments, a book on the processions of the year, one of the proverbs of Solomon, the *Light of the Christian Soul* of Meneses, a Summa of the sacraments, the *Directory of Curates* of Pere Màrtir Coma, and a well-used breviary.[88]

The key to communicating the message of the Counter Reformation was the sermon, in some measure a novelty to the ordinary believer. Great preachers had operated in the later middle ages and famous sermons had been preached at court, but the sermon was an exceptional medium of instruction in the countryside. The early sixteenth-century mass in Spain was, as we have seen, a noisy affair in which there was no interval for a sermon. The imposition of sermons as a regular obligation on parish priests therefore met with considerable resistance. They were an unlooked-for burden on priests, who were only too glad either to omit the duty or give it over to wandering preachers. Besides, none had ever been taught how to give one. For generations if not centuries much of the Church in Spain had met sermons only in the form of discourses from wandering clergy: the people in their own churches did not know what the thing was. In the first decades of the sixteenth century Alfonso de Castro, writing against the background of his own experience in the sophisticated world of Paris and contrasting it with the dismal evidence of the rural world in Spain, pointed to the lack of preaching as the principal source of the heresies of his day.[89] Unequivocal testimony to the situation in Spain can be found in the *Bononia* (1555) of the Valencian humanist Fadrique Furió Ceriol. Referring especially to his native province Furió observed:

> There is many a preacher in the cities and the towns with a good population, but in the villages, hamlets and settlements there is such a lack that one cannot mention it for tears ... And what shall I say of the other provinces of Spain? Is there not the same poverty of preachers? ... Thus we see that at times the Church sleeps, and this is to be blamed not on it but on the vices and sloth of its pastors.[90]

Many villages probably heard no more than one sermon a year, according to Furió, and there were places in Valencia which had not heard a sermon since Christianity was introduced.

At the high tide of the reform era, when Pedro de León went on a mission to the Valle de Lecrín in Andalusia in the early seventeenth century, he found villages which 'in over twenty years had not heard a sermon or talk or catechism', and recalled in his memoirs that 'there were some women aged under twenty years who had never heard voices raised in the church and when we raised our voices during the sermon they hid themselves and covered their faces because it appeared that we wished to punish them.'[91]

For the first time in their history many churches now had to erect pulpits. In the Vallès Oriental in Catalonia the late sixteenth century was the period when pulpits first became common, responding to the need for preachers to be visible at a level higher than the congregation;[92] but a pulpit was not always sufficient. Preachers found that thanks to the novelty of the sermon churches could not hold the numbers who came, and the structure of the church building made it impossible to see and be seen by everyone. There were two solutions to the problem; the first and most immediate was to invite the congregation out into the ampler space of the street; the second was to redesign the interior of the church. The early Jesuits were delighted to have to go out of the church into the public square in order to harangue the large crowds they attracted, and street preaching, encouraged also by Borromeo in Italy, continued to be popular among the missionary orders.

A more lasting solution to the problem of large congregations was to open up the interior of the church. Gothic structures such as Barcelona cathedral, where the main body of the building was occupied (as it still is) by a huge enclosed choir, leaving only the small spaces at either end available for preaching, patently hindered the work of the clergy. The Jesuits pioneered the construction of buildings with a single wide nave which brought the altar and the congregation into full view of each other, and thereby also gave the preacher direct access to his listeners. 'Because year-round preaching was seen as the most effective instrument of public reform, and because the previously empty churches began to be filled with crowds of worshippers, the nave also had to become an assembly hall.'[93]

Although clergy are the main witnesses to the alleged popularity of sermons during the period, their testimony is consistent and usually trustworthy. The sermon became both an art form and a feature of the social activity centring around the mass. What became popular however was not the average weekly sermon of the parish clergy (few clergy in fact preached) but the highly elaborate discourses produced by specialised preachers during a mission or other special occasion.

Books began to be written on the art of preaching: some were conspicuously useful, giving texts for each feast-day together with hints on how to elaborate the homily. The science of preaching was based, historically, on the art of rhetoric, but the state of affairs in Spain may be seen from the fact that for nearly a generation after the outbreak of the Reformation no serious writings on rhetoric were published in the peninsula. There seems to be agreement that the first important work of note, the *Rhetoric in the Castilian language*, published at Alcalá in 1541, came from the pen of the Aragonese Jeronimite friar Miguel de Salinas (d.1577).[94] The study of rhetoric, virtually unknown in Spain, developed only during this period, and consequently came to be identified almost exclusively with ecclesiastical rhetoric. As a consequence all the significant writings on the subject are devoted solidly to the art of preaching. In Barcelona a central contribution to the theme was made by Pedro Juan Núñez, whose *Institutions of Rhetoric* was published in 1578; and by the *Sacred Art of Preaching* (1588) of Diego Pérez, who had built up a reputation as the foremost preacher of the city.

At the same time, prelates gave unequivocal guidance to their clergy about the themes to touch on in preaching. The first bishop of Barcelona to issue clear instructions was Rafael de Rovirola, who in 1609 distributed to his clergy his 'Points for Preachers', an interesting summary of current problems as seen by a Counter-Reformation prelate. The preacher must[95]

Declare the letter of the Gospel
Present solid doctrine
Teach well what touches observance of the commandments
Plant virtues
Uproot vices

Put forward the means by which souls may journey to blessedness, such as works of mercy, and exhort people to works of charity in the General Hospital, the Hospital of Mercy, the poor in prison, and also the construction of the Capuchin monastery; frequenting the sacraments, hearing sermons, gaining indulgences, visiting churches, and similar things which lead to heaven

Do not rebuke [people in authority publicly] because rebuking them in this way makes the common people lose their respect towards their superiors

The things to be rebuked in Catalonia are: mortal enmities, cruelties, revenges and murders. Rebuke the thefts and robberies in Catalonia, exhort people not to shelter the thieves; rebuke the counterfeiters and extortioners; the little faith and loyalty among men in Catalonia; false acts and papers, double-dealing and underhand ways now used by men in Catalonia

Rebuke firmly the vice of sensuality, concubinage, women in the streets, and also exhort those who live separated to return to their conjugal life

Rebuke gaming-houses: rebuke the excess in dress of both women and men and specially of gentlemen and of merchants; rebuke farces and comedies as harmful and warn priests and religious not to go to them; rebuke the abuse in Barcelona of wooden-lance battles

And finally there is at present in this city a sin to rebuke, namely the little respect shown by laymen to the churches, chatting, courting and troublemaking in them.

Typical of the lead given by prelates was the fat volume of some six hundred pages published in 1593 by the bishop of Urgell, Andreu Capella. Written for a wholly Catalan population, the volume was a manual for the clergy, since 'many of those with a cure of souls do not have the capacity or time needed to be able to carry out by themselves' the task of composing a sermon. The sermons were set out so that 'they can be preached or read to the people', and since the public was a rural one 'we have tried to put everything in an easy and simple style so that all will be able to understand.'[96]

Fashions in preaching, however, were inevitably beyond the control of the Church authorities, who were only too pleased to receive the help of the Inquisition in clipping the wings of extravagance. Given the crucial importance of the sermon as the principal vehicle of communication and propaganda in the pre-electronic age, it is not surprising to find a large body of writing, both favourable and hostile, devoted to it. The idiocies of preachers were a constant subject of comment. Pedro de Luján in mid-century observed that with many preachers 'it was more play-acting than preaching', and went on to regret 'seeing preachers preach in the way that a rhetorician speaks to the people; on reaching the ear, the words pass through or fail to enter'.[97] In his *Dialogues* (1610), Gaspar Lucas Hidalgo cited the case of a friar 'who preaching on the day of the Annunciation addressed the women thus: How, ladies, do you think the angel found the Virgin when he came with his message? Do you think she was singing sarabands and chaconnes like you? Why no, she was on her knees praying the rosary.'[98] In a fierce attack on flowery sermons and on preachers 'whose aim is not to gain children for God but to win approval, applause and acclamation' the Dominican Tomás Ramón cited the case that 'happened in 1630 in Seville to a preacher who with his flowery sermons used to carry the people away with him spellbound ... The inquisitors ordered him not to preach any more, a holy and just demand; and bishops have a similar obligation not to let such buffoons go up into the pulpit in their churches.'[99]

Improvement of preaching remained a permanent challenge. As late as 1689 the bishop of Tortosa, fray Severo Thomás, was condemning the preachers in his diocese 'for having generally forgotten to fulfil the duty of their ministry, preaching insipid doctrine and impertinent, useless, vain and tortuous speeches ... airy discourses that twist and violate sacred Scripture in order to indulge caprices of fancy'. 'We bishops', he went on, 'have to stop this type of sermon.' Instead, he urged his preachers to concentrate only on the four last things, and to preach 'in the Italian way' with a crucifix in the pulpit, a style which he now ordered to be observed in his diocese. 'Father preachers,' he concluded, 'I beg you to adapt to this method of preaching.'[100] The use of a crucifix was no radical move: preaching in Andalusia in the 1670s, the Franciscan José Gavarri used to bring out a human skull in the pulpit, 'because it has the power to move'.[101]

There was a danger that the emergence into the pulpit of tens and thousands of untrained preachers, speaking freely on an unlimited range of themes, would lead to a terrifying Babel of opinions. There was no way of controlling this chaos other than through the offices of the Inquisition, which consequently tried to assert its control of the pulpit. Censorship of the spoken word was no novelty: in an epoch when the pulpit controlled the masses more than a book could and where it could disseminate both heresy and sedition, the two major political crimes of the age, it would have been astonishing had there been no machinery to intervene. In France as early as 1549 a law had made parish officials answer for their preachers, and in 1596 for example the cathedral chapter of Rheims was made responsible for everything preached in its pulpits; it was not unusual for French congregations to denounce their clergy, and 'hardly would a dissident preacher have stepped down from his pulpit before one of his hearers would be running to the magistrate.'[102] Yet in Spain there was surprisingly little interference with the pulpit or with the often daring incursions of clergy into politics.

In Catalonia intervention of the Holy Office in preaching occurred mainly in the first decades of the seventeenth century. It was concerned more with dogmatic errors than the quality of discourse and depended for information exclusively on sharp-eared members of the congregation, few of whom seem to have bothered, so that an average of no more than one sermon a year appears to have been denounced, a derisory total for a society which has often been depicted as in the grip of ideological control. Those sharp enough to find errors in the words of a preacher were as a rule more often his colleagues than the general public. In 1590 fray Cristóbal de Atiença, prior of the monastery of St Augustine in Cervera, was denounced for having claimed in a sermon that 'if the tyrant had eaten the roasted flesh of St Lawrence it would have had the same effect on him that the Blessed Sacrament has on a soul in mortal sin'; words which scandalised his listeners to the extent that in the afternoon some of the students in the monastery approached him and argued vigorously with him.[103] In 1592 the vicar of Guissona was summoned to explain some statements in a sermon, but was able to demonstrate clearly that every phrase had been taken from orthodox authors, and the case was dismissed.[104] In 1610 a

Carmelite friar in Gerona was ordered to reinterpret some doubtful propositions to his congregation, and the same was enjoined on a priest of the cathedral in Barcelona;[105] this was the procedure most commonly followed in the majority of cases. All too often petty denunciations of fairly innocuous statements had to be looked into, as with a sermon preached in 1611 at St Feliu de Guíxols;[106] but the Inquisition, since it merely received information rather than going round prying into sermons, had to take the rough with the smooth. Occasionally the records show the inquisitors giving advice about preaching: in 1622 they 'gravely' reprimanded Dr Comes, of a church in Perpinyà, for various statements in his sermons, which they felt were more 'proper to the university' than to the pulpit;[107] and a similar criticism was levelled against a Carmelite friar in Vic in 1628, who was warned 'not to preach unusual subtleties which might cause scandal'.[108] Even Jesuits were not immune: their rector in Vic was 'gravely' reprimanded in 1631.[109] No better advice could have been offered than that given in 1632 to the rector of Lladorre, in the Vall de Cardós (Urgell), that he should take care when 'preaching and teaching, especially to ignorant people like peasants and rustics; and in the masses and other ceremonies he should use respectable and courteous language to his flock so as not to cause scandal'.[110] The tenor of all these cases is clear: the Holy Office was making no attempt to control free speech but rather was endeavouring in accord with the outlook of the Counter Reformation to remedy defects in the otherwise uncontrolled use of the pulpit. The need to avoid 'scandal' appears as a priority: rash words from the privileged position of the pulpit might offend local piety and provoke divisions and conflict in the community.

The development of preaching raised problems associated with use of the vernacular. No European country in the mid-sixteenth century had a single common vernacular, and English Protestant reformers who claimed to be giving their people a prayer-book they could understand (in 1549) were quickly reminded that the people (in this case, the Cornish) were apt to reject the imposition of a vernacular not their own. In France, Germany and throughout the continent both Protestant and Catholic missionaries found their efforts at change frustrated by their inability to teach or preach in local dialects. In Spain, though it was possible to preach in Castilian to congregations, for up to a quarter of the population Castilian was not the normal language of daily discourse. Spaniards were uniquely aware of the problems involved, since decades of mission-ary work among the minority Moriscos had obliged many clergy to take the study of languages seriously; and the evangelisation of

America bore fruit in the first grammars ever to be produced for the New World.[111] Early attempts to promote the non-Castilian languages, both in Spain and in America, gave way by the mid-sixteenth century to a more intransigent policy, frankly hostile to the public use of alternative tongues. In 1642, a Portuguese writer commented retrospectively that 'the Castilians permitted use of their language alone, and treated the Portuguese language worse than if it were Greek.'[112] As the Spanish imperial mentality developed, so too did the preference for one official language. The attitude did not however triumph everywhere, and many clergy moved in quite the opposite direction.

In the Basque country it was a period when the native language was actively fostered. Manuals for the clergy such as Sancho de Elso's *Christian Doctrine* (1561) appeared in Basque and Castilian; Gaspar de Astete's *Christian Doctrine*, published in Pamplona in 1608, appeared 'in all the tongues of the diocese', according to the bishop, and remained for one and a half centuries the standard catechism of the Pamplona diocese, though other vernacular catechisms also appeared. Time and again the bishops insisted that all preaching be in Basque; all missions were preached in Basque; and as late as 1727 when the bishop made a pastoral visit he went to 320 parishes and presided in each one in a 'mission in the Basque language'.[113]

Catalonia presented special problems. Like the Basque country and Portugal it was a region where the vernacular tongue was solidly spoken. Provincial councils at Tarragona (notably in 1602) insisted unequivocally that Catalan be the only medium of instruction used in the pulpit and in schools, and the only catechisms made available for school use were in Catalan. Though Castilian continued to be tolerated, the clergy remained in no doubt that the proper language through which to work for the conversion of the people was Catalan. This created difficulties for international religious orders, whose members had to be able to express themselves in Catalan if they wished to preach in public. Most of the early Capuchins in Catalonia, for example, were Castilians and encountered problems when it came to sermons; but several followed the lead of fray Gregorio de Castilla (d.1593) who 'when he saw that preaching in his native tongue produced little fruit among the common people, applied himself with particular effort to learn the Catalan language.' Typical of the tolerance that existed among Catalans on the language issue was the case of the Castilian Jesuit father Pons, who 'began to preach a Lenten mission in Catalan in Gerona; the citizens saw the problem he had in expressing himself and told him to finish the mission in Castilian but he replied that God would demand an account of them and not of him, since Castilian was not understood in Catalonia'.[114] The provincial council of Tarragona in 1591 and 1602 made Catalan the obligatory language for preaching, but the need was also recognised by clergy coming into the province. The provincial chapter of the Discalced Carmelites held at Mataró in October 1598 decided 'that Catalan preachers preach in their own language so that the harvest of souls hoped for through their sermons may be realised', though dispensations were given to friars who came from other regions and could not speak the language. In July 1601 the chapter went further and urged religious to speak the language among themselves: 'we order all the religious in our Province . . . to speak as a matter of course in Catalan. To Catalan preachers we order that in villages away from the cities they preach exclusively in Catalan.'[115]

This last phrase was crucial. In the more cosmopolitan air of Barcelona the combination of extraneous clergy and Castilian fashions made it more common for sermons to be in Spanish rather than Catalan. Moreover for historic reasons the Church in Catalonia did not coincide only with Catalan-speaking areas: a good part of the see of Lérida embraced Aragonese territory, where the population spoke only Castilian, and the southern parts of the diocese of Tortosa also contained people who used Castilian. There were therefore good grounds for allowing preaching in Castilian in some areas, but the general policy adopted by all bishops and diocesan synods in the early seventeenth century was to insist on the need for sermons in Catalan.

The controversy which developed over the relative roles of the two languages was of particular importance. In 1636 at the provincial council of Tarragona the bishop of Tortosa, Justino Antolínez, obtained a decision that all preaching in the principality be normally in Catalan, especially in Advent and Lent, a decision which the bishops, such as that of Elna in 1631,[116] had been practising for years. Over the next few months the debates in and out of the provincial council gave rise to a well-known published controversy in which the merits of the measure were debated. A Catalan canon of Tortosa, Alexandre Ros, writing under the pseudonym 'Dr Juan Gomez Adrin', argued that the wrong decision had been made. Since his arguments and those of his protagonist are seldom explicitly cited, they will be touched on here for the light they shed on the problems facing the Counter Reformation in the province.

Although admitting that there were parts of the country where it was necessary to preach only in Catalan, Adrin argued that Castilian should continue to be freely used, for three main reasons. First, all books printed in the province were in Castilian:

I am astonished that such a sweeping generalisation is made about the ignorance of Castilian in this principality, where all the books that are printed are in this language. Are the frequent editions of books not evidence enough that Castilian is read a lot and that people understand it? The *Flos Sanctorum* which even the common people consult, the spiritual books of Rodríguez, Molina, fray Luis de Granada . . . these and other innumerable books that are printed here and sell rapidly, is it not obvious that they are understood, since they are not to be found? Where are more comedies printed than in Catalonia, leafed through not only by critics but by the vulgar, and found more on the pillows of ladies than in the libraries of the learned?

Second, all the leading prelates and preachers of the time had preached in Castilian. This was clearly the case with the bishops, since 'the majority of the prelates of Catalonia are Castilians.' Moreover,

the many apostles who have preached in Castilian in most of the cities of Catalonia: can one believe they spoke to the wind? It would take long to list the outstanding preachers who to great applause and with evident success have preached in Castilian. The apostle of this principality and disciple of the master Juan de Avila, father Diego Pérez, who converted so many souls, did he not preach in his Castilian tongue? Father Lorenzo de San Juan, apostle of Catalonia, did he not speak this tongue?[117]

Finally and more contentiously Adrin affirmed that Castilian must be used because it was the 'common language of the monarchy of Spain', and that Castilian was 'the language of empire': 'we have to speak not in the language proper to a province but in that which is general and common to the nation, such as Castilian is in the monarchy.'

Adrin's paper was formally addressed to the Church council at Tarragona. There was an immediate reply, addressed however to a different platform, to the *Diputats* of Catalonia, from Dr Diego Cisteller. Cisteller's tract, written in Castilian, started from the simple principle, laid down by Trent, that the people must be preached to in a language they understood. In addition, he posited the basic fact that 'in Catalonia the common people do not understand Castilian.' Outside of Barcelona, there were few Castilians in the province: 'as you can see from Tortosa, Gerona, and Lérida, where a Castilian may be seen only once in two or three days, fleetingly. And what of Manresa, Solsona, Vic and Urgell, where if they see a Castilian it is by a miracle?' Even in Barcelona the use of Castilian was not common: 'even here the common people, who are the majority, do not understand it, as in the poorer quarters, the whole parish of St Pere, great part of the parish of Santa Maria de Pescadors, and Hortelans; and so on for the rest, including a good part of the cathedral itself, where the bishop who is now there has the sermons preached in Catalan.'

Responding to the issue of the books, Cisteller commented:

> First, these books are not to be found in the hands of the common people but of educated people of quality ... Second, in Catalonia they use Castilian books of devotion because there are none in Catalan, through the negligence of past generations and the vanity of the present; for apart from maybe a *Contemptus mundi* in Catalan you will find hardly a work of devotion in this language.

As for the many who had preached in Castilian, 'I reply that father Lorenzo San Juan and father Fons preached in the towns of Catalonia in Catalan, and also in the cities of Urgell, Vic, Solsona, Manresa, Perpinyà; and in Gerona, as witnesses still testify, father Lorenzo San Juan preached a Lenten mission in Catalan for fear of not being understood.' Cisteller also observed that some of the preachers, especially the Jesuits, were from Valencia and consequently 'preach the commandments from the pulpit in Valencian because they think they will not be understood in Castilian'.

Although there was a need to preach in Catalan, some preachers were conscious that it was not a polished language and that Castilian was capable of more refinement. Cisteller seized on this disadvantage as being a veritable advantage. By preaching in Catalan preachers would avoid the ponderous and showy turns of phrase used in Castilian: 'fifty years ago (it is only fifty since Castilian preaching entered Catalonia) Catalan preachers did not embroider the language.'[118]

Cisteller's argument may not have seemed very convincing to those young Catalan clergy, and apparently there were more than a few of them, who went to Castile specifically to learn how to preach in refined Castilian. Camprubi in his chronicle of Sta Catarina sourly narrates the story of one young professed who received permission from the prior to 'go to study in Castile, or rather to learn the Castilian language and preach thereafter in it (a fashion among some Catalans that I won't dare call perverse)'.[119] There was an undeniable snob appeal about speaking the 'language of empire', but it appears that not all Catalans were equally successful in learning the language, for a writer in Perpinyà in 1590 commented that 'though there are many who go with their mouths open to listen to and read Castilian, when it comes to the practice they don't understand half the words.'[120]

Despite the sparring between protagonists of the two languages, in practice most preachers were obliged to use both in their work. The missionary notes made by clergy during these years give useful evidence of how they went about it. The Dominican Joan Guasch, who kept a 'spiritual itinerary' in which he jotted down all his notes for the whole year, used Catalan for all aspects of popular devotion, such as prayers, catechisms and confessions, but for more formal occasions, such as preaching Lenten sermons, he often made notes in Castilian and preached in that language when necessary. More generally, he preached in Catalan. There survive five remarkable volumes of the sermons he preached between about 1576 and 1613 in the remote interior of Catalonia, in the mountainous area around the towns of Ager and Tremp. Written down carefully in a precise hand and methodically divided up among the major feast-days, his notes are splendid testimony to the missionary labour of those who ventured into the semi-Christian interior, using for their medium a simple and direct Catalan which had little to do with fashionable rhetoric.

Guasch would invariably begin his sermons with a quotation in Latin from the gospels, followed immediately by a Catalan translation. He would then enter into a simple discourse, unembroidered by quotations, on the virtues and vices of daily life. When using imagery, he normally resorted to rural parallels: for the feast of St Stephen, his dominant image was of chickens hiding under the wings of their mother hen, just as his audience should seek shelter under the wings of God.[121] His sermon for New Year's Day 1573 began in simple, direct language:

> Let us talk now of New Years. Today we begin the year and this year is new. A New Year, then, demands a new life. Sinner, you have left behind the year 1572. So leave behind the evil life you had in the year 1572, and since you have left the year then also leave the evil life you led. Since you are beginning a new year, begin a new life from today forward such as you have not lived till now. Renew yourself in life, renew yourself in your habits and practices. . . .
>
> Look forward from today, start a new book, start a new life. If you go to the house where the merchants are you will see that at this time at the end of the year they settle their bills and start a new book, and the notaries also have books for each year. So then, Christian, that old book of your conscience, change it, renew it.[122]

The secular clergy, tied to their parishes, did not need to or did not bother to increase their language competence, but the regular clergy made enormous efforts, based as their work was on missions, to learn the language of the people and to preach in it.[123] An outstanding example was the Augustinian Diego López de Andrade, a Portuguese educated in Perpinyà who ended his career as arch-bishop of Otranto. His facility in languages enabled him to preach in Braga in Portuguese, in Santiago in Castilian, in Montserrat in Catalan, and in Rome in Italian and Latin.[124]

Catalan historians have usually blamed Castile for a deliberate policy of linguistic imperialism and have correctly pointed out that although the printing press flourished in Barcelona it was a press which largely restricted itself to books in Castilian. Resentment of Castilian hegemony in language came to a head in 1640, at which time a Catalan writer wrote to Uztarroz, the chronicler of Aragon, urging him to 'disabuse the Castilians, who think that they know everything and have arrogated to themselves the leadership in letters'.[125] The available data for publications seem to bear out the view that the vernacular was on the defensive before the advance of Castilian: in Valencia in the period 1473–1506, 49 books were published in Valencian, the same number in Latin, and only 5 in Castilian; in the years 1510–72, there were 220 in Latin, but also 219 in Castilian, and only 68 in Valencian.[126] Though no study has been done on book production in Catalonia during the period, the catalogue of Aguiló i Fuster and the incomplete holdings of the libraries in Barcelona confirm amply the one point on which both Adrin and Cisteller agreed: the decay of publication in the Catalan language.

However, no pre-industrial culture can be judged exclusively by book output, and it is misleading to assume that the Catalan language decayed because Castilian book production in Barcelona increased. The very same Counter-Reformation Church that was responsible for the majority of the Castilian printed books produced in this period was officially and energetically devoted to the use of the vernacular among all levels of the population and above all in the schools. At the level of popular culture the use of Catalan was encouraged and fostered: possibly the bulk of surviving manuscript sermons is in Catalan and not in Castilian, and the impressive number of *goigs* is testimony to the use of Catalan in the parishes. We must conclude that, contrary to what is often supposed, the oral culture of the Catalan people was encouraged and given new life during the period. The synodal constitutions of the diocese of Barcelona as late as 1669, over a century after Trent, show that every aspect of the religious message was in Catalan: all the essen-tial prayers – the Pater, Ave, creed – were in Catalan alone; the obligatory catechisms were in Catalan; all instruction (as distinct from preaching) had to be in Catalan; and all the constitutions setting this out were printed 'in the common language of our province so that parish priests and preachers may have it as a prompt in which they can conveniently find what they have to teach'.[127] The dominance of Castilian as a literary medium did evident harm to Catalan culture, but the language survived effortlessly.

The appointment of Castilians to Catalan sees evoked unfavourable comment at the time and also merited mention in Cisteller's tract; it has since been assumed that this harmed the regional language. It is clear however from the diocesan papers that the bishops, who tended to work through Catalan officials, always gave priority to Catalan in their directives and reserved Castilian for political correspondence. Moreover, unlike the early half of the sixteenth century when non-Catalans among new appointments outnumbered Catalans by two to one, during the Counter Reformation nearly half of all bishops appointed in the principality were Catalans.[128] Even Catalan bishops, it must be admitted, were by their status part of an administrative structure that tended to be Castile-orientated. Examination of the 175 titles in the personal library of the Catalan Rafel Riffos, bishop of Elna in 1619–20, turns up only one Catalan work, the *Book of the Rosary*; by contrast, apart from the presence of Petrarch and Bellarmine to indicate broader horizons, the notable works are all Castilian: the *Names of Christ* of Luis de León, the *Emblems* of Covarrubias, the *Manual* of Azpilcueta, and the works of fray Juan de los Angeles.[129]

The decline of cultured Catalan was patent. Key books continued to be issued in Catalan but only because authors made a conscious effort. 'Since I am a born Catalan,' observed Geroni Taix when he published his best-selling book on the Rosary in 1597, 'I feared doing harm to my Catalans and to my tongue, so I have made the effort to write in the Catalan language.'[130] Of the thirty-eight known works printed at Lérida in the first two decades of the seventeenth century, twelve were in Latin, the rest in Castilian; none was in Catalan.[131] Spiritual literature continued to be published overwhelmingly in Castilian, cause enough for Pere Font to explain that 'the great need felt by natives of the present principality to have works of devotion printed in the Catalan language, has inspired and almost forced me to make a special effort in writing and composing the present book in my tongue': the work was his *Spiritual Exercise* of 1608,[132] one of the few good manuals of spirituality to be issued in Catalan in the entire Counter Reformation. Licensed by bishop Rovirola of Barcelona and based firmly on the Council of Trent (which is cited on nearly every page), the book is also outstanding for being a faithful reflection of current piety in Catalonia: apart from some standard Church fathers it limits its sources to Scripture, Thomas à Kempis, the Jesuit Francisco Arias, and the Barcelona contemporaries Dimas Loris, Diego Pérez and Pere Gil; Castilian piety is almost wholly absent.

Works of piety continued to appear in Catalan but they were few, and when in 1685 Joan Valls, rector of Alcover and former vicar-general of Tarragona, published his *Directory of the Christian life*, a Castilian Jesuit praised it precisely because it was an exception: 'its usefulness will be all the greater among those who do not well understand Castilian or Latin, in which most spiritual books are printed.'[133]

There remained much room for dissatisfaction, expressed clearly by writers in Rosselló. 'Seeing that nobody bothers to write in our Catalan tongue,' observed fray Miquel Agustí, whose *Book of the Secrets of Agriculture* (1617) was quickly to achieve success in its Castilian translation, 'it has occurred to me to take the trouble to make selections from many serious writers and translate them into our Catalan language.'[134] When Pere Nicolau, comisario of the Inquisition and prior of Espira in Conflent, wrote his *Declaration of the Names of Mary* in 1630, he proudly referred to Catalan as 'our language' and to Catalonia as 'my nation, fatherland and parish'.[135] There was a less subdued reaction from Andreu Bosch, chronicler of Perpinyà, in a famous work of 1628. Castigating the chaotic and barbarous state of the Catalan tongue, he singled out the preaching clergy for blame since they chose to preach in Castilian rather than in their own language. 'As everyone knows from experience', he insisted, the people at mass were made to listen to sermons in a tongue they did not understand; 'and the worst of it is that those in most need, the children, women and the ignorant, only hear the words but do not understand a thing.' Moreover, the preachers chose to preach in a flowery and convoluted 'Castilian, both extraordinary and inappropriate, with an abundance of synonyms and metaphors, as though they were preaching to angels and not to men'. All this was 'deserving of tears of blood', and the root cause was that the constitution of the Council of Tarragona ruling that preaching be in the language of the people was not being observed, a conclusion for which he claimed also to have the authority of 'many famous preachers'. The only drastic solution, Bosch felt, was a special law in the *Corts*. The chronicler's testimony must be respected but clearly presented only one side of a complex picture, for the evidence we have accumulated leaves no doubt that, despite many shortcomings, conscious and extensive efforts were made by the Church to instruct the people in their own tongue. It is significant that the whole controversy of 1637 arose out of an attempt to ban Castilian, not Catalan.

In the middle of the seventeenth century a Carmelite friar of

Perpinyà, Josep Elias Estrugos, summed up the difficulties faced by his language: 'the writing of Catalan has become a serious problem, because those who should learn to speak their native language have studied Castilian instead, attracted by its sound and by the applause of those who fond of wordiness praise chatter rather than cultivated speech; and so through lack of study there are few who know how to speak Catalan and even less write it.'[136]

Within the context of the labours of the reformers we may conclude that the ability of Catalan to survive, even in Rosselló, had two main causes: the primarily oral rather than literary culture of the people, and the use of the language by the majority of the clergy.[137] Despite attempts at a repressive policy by the French government from the 1670s, the clergy in Rosselló continued to use Catalan in sermons, manuals and parish records well into the eighteenth century and not until 1676 was a sermon preached in French in the cathedral at Perpinyà.[138] When Lluis Guilla published his *Manual of Christian Doctrine* in Catalan at Perpinyà in 1669 (with another edition in 1685), he justified the work on the grounds that children in the county did not understand the three official languages – Latin, Spanish and French.[139] During his examination for holy orders by his (French) bishop in 1790, a priest declared that the national language was useless since the people of the Vallespir understood only Catalan.[140]

Pere Gil, rector of the Jesuit college of Betlem in Barcelona at the opening of the seventeenth century, chose to publish his works in Catalan, and criticised as 'a great pity' the fact that 'ecclesiastics who should be using it for preaching and teaching and ministering and aiding the dying, cannot speak it as perfectly as they should.' In his *Contemptus Mundi*, he rejected criticisms that it was unnecessary to publish in Catalan since everyone understood Castilian: 'apart from a few cities such as Barcelona, Vilafranca del Penedès, Cervera, Tárrega, Fraga, Monzón and others which are on main roads, in the other cities, towns and villages the Castilian language is not understood among the common people and no women speak it,' and he had therefore written in Catalan 'so that all manner of people may benefit from it'.[141] Gil's approach clearly contradicts the role sometimes, and erroneously, attributed to the Jesuits of favouring Castilian over Catalan.

Frequently misunderstood, the Jesuits have also been misrepresented over their attitude to the vernacular on the basis of the conflict at Lérida in 1623 when the councillors of the city complained that the Jesuits in the department of Latin grammar were teaching in Castilian and not in Catalan.[142] It is true that the Jesuits were beginning to use Castilian as a preferred medium of instruction at university level, just as they – in common with all religious orders in the peninsula – used Castilian as the normal medium for correspondence. The preference for Castilian in higher education corresponded to an existing demand among the highly Castilianised elite of the principality and explains the Castilian orientation of the Jesuit College of Cordelles in late seventeenth-century Barcelona.[143] But even the slightest familiarity with Jesuit history demonstrates that the Company in the principality took exceptional care both to teach and to preach in Catalan, and were second to none in their use of the vernacular. The Jesuits had been preaching in Catalan for nearly one hundred years before the Castilian tide caught them up. Their missions year after year to the rural areas of Catalonia, to areas such as Penedès, Anoia, Lluçanès, Vallès, Berguedà, Elna, where the people spoke no language but Catalan, would have been meaningless had they not preached in that tongue; and it is significant that the best-selling catechisms used in Catalan during the sixteenth and seventeenth centuries were by Jesuits. Their policy did not change even in Tortosa, where Castilian was more widely spoken. In 1620 when they undertook a mission to Tortosa they had a problem in the town of Ulldecona because 'the parish priest and jurats demanded that the sermons be in Castilian because no other language had ever been preached.' Despite this, 'father Fons insisted that it had to be in Catalan, and so sermons, teaching and catechism were all done in Catalan, and the women and some men said, "At last we can understand the preachers!" '[144] The policy of vernacular preaching was confirmed by a directive from the Italian general of the order in 1637 advising that 'the brothers in the realms of Catalonia, Valencia and Mallorca should preach in the language of the people.'[145]

One of the small triumphs of the Catalan people, indeed, was the survival of their language, but at the cost of their literature; for it was thanks to the lack of literacy and of a written tradition that the villages took refuge in a wholly oral culture. The survival in Catalonia of an autonomous legal system was also a major guarantor of language, and well into the eighteenth century the bulk of the two fundamental documents of Catalan history, the testament and the matrimonial contract, continued to be drawn up in Catalan, not only in the principality but also in the French-occupied counties.

Castilian inevitably took on, as it did in Portugal,[146] the status of an official language, and its use spread for reasons of administrative convenience,[147] but the vernacular continued to be both accepted and taught, especially under Church auspices, and its use was never discouraged before the disappearance of the *furs* in 1714, so that though we may correctly regard the Counter Reformation as a crucial vehicle for the infiltration of Castilian literature there is little evidence of linguistic imperialism. Well into the late eighteenth century, when all state business in the principality was transacted in Castilian, the bishops used Catalan as their principal administrative language. The decay of published Catalan must be analysed within a context far broader than the simplistic image of a repressed language.

For a perspective of the methods of the Catholic reformers in Spain and Catalonia no better example exists than the Society of Jesus.[148] Ignatius Loyola commenced his career in Catalonia, and it is just to pay some attention to the role there of the best-known religious order of the Catholic reform movement. Ignatius' religious conversion occurred in 1521, after which he journeyed to Montserrat in 1522, and stayed until 1523 at Manresa where he wrote most of the *Spiritual Exercises*, in a cave which much later, in 1595, was ordered to be conserved by the bishop of Vic as a record of his sojourn and is now overbuilt by a vast ecclesiastical structure. Ignatius' first visit to Barcelona was in 1523, prior to his journey to Palestine; on his return he resided in the city from Easter 1524 to July 1526. These early years were looked back to with pride by Catalan Jesuits, but it was nearly twenty years before the Company of Jesus formally entered the principality.

The new order, approved in 1540 by the papacy, had few Spanish roots and was essentially a European grouping based in Italy, which is where outstanding young Spaniards like Ribadeneira (1540), Polanco (1541) and Nadal (1545) joined it. The first Jesuit to enter Spain in an individual capacity was Araoz, a kinsman of Ignatius, who came in 1540; thereafter, using Italy and then the college in Coimbra (1541) as a base, further groups entered the country. The first colleges were founded in Valencia in 1544, in Barcelona in 1545, in Castile at Alcalá in 1546 and at Valladolid, the effective capital of the country, in 1547. These were exciting and heady days for the young company which, small enough to provoke little opposition and new enough to attract the curiosity of all, scored notable successes, not only in Spain where their sermons filled the public squares and won applause at court, but also in Germany at the imperial court, where Favre was recruiting young aristocrats to the Ignatian cause.

The Jesuits have with good reason been considered the archetypal Counter-Reformation movement, and this applies equally to their activity in Spain. Their greatest success was the conversion of Francisco Borja and his admittance into the company in 1546:

thereafter Borja seemed to be the ideal vehicle for extending influence among the elites, without whose help it would have been impossible to found new centres. Growth was slow, given the length of the noviciate: by 1547, when the company had seven houses in Spain, the total membership was only forty-one. Precisely from this period, when the Jesuits were achieving a higher profile with the entry of Borja and with the key role of two Spaniards (Laínez and Salmerón) at the new sessions of Trent, the first major confrontations between the company and the Spanish temperament began to emerge. The substance of the conflicts can be briefly summarised. First, there was deep suspicion, among leading clergy who disliked illuminism and related trends, of the spiritual bases of the Ignatian philosophy; we may recall that Ignatius had been before the Inquisition once in 1527 and now there were others who were ready to use the machinery of the Inquisition to attack the *Spiritual Exercises* and the Jesuits themselves. Second, some members of the religious orders, supported by regular clergy, opposed the introduction into their territory of a new group: this appears to have been at the root of the conflicts in Saragossa in 1555. Third, many disliked the Jesuit policy of not discriminating against minority cultural groups such as Moriscos and *conversos*: this was the reason for the hostility of the archbishop of Toledo, Siliceo. The mid-century was a time both of growth and of conflict for the company, when it shared in the general tension between the influx of European ideas and the struggle of the traditional Spanish – one may say, more exactly, Castilian – outlook to maintain itself.

The 1558 crisis was particularly dangerous for them, since the condemnation of Borja by the Inquisition and the discovery of Protestants led to a situation where, as Diego Laínez commented, 'there are some religious here and in the king's court in Flanders who whisper and say that we are heretic *alumbrados* and rejects of Spain.'[149] Another Jesuit complained that 'the father of lies is on the loose,' listing the long chain of accusations against the company, and chiefly that 'the Theatines (as they call us here in this Babel) are the cause of these errors of Luther.'[150] The atmosphere of conflict was only one aspect of the Jesuit experience and probably not the most typical, but it has unfortunately become the best known, beguiling scholars into supporting 'the accepted idea that the society evinced little interest in instructing or indoctrinating the masses, preferring to concentrate their activities on its leaders'.[151] In reality the Jesuits were second to none in their work of popular evangelisation, as we can see by the example of Catalonia.

When their first house opened in Barcelona in September 1545 among its initial problems was that of language, but the Jesuits approached this without prejudice. The first four fathers of the Barcelona foundation were Catalans.[152] Outsiders were accepted even if they spoke no Catalan (it was Father Estrada's preaching, in Spanish, which inspired the city of Gerona to ask for Jesuits in 1551), but every effort was made to communicate in the language of the country: the efforts of Father Pons to speak in Catalan in Gerona have been mentioned above. The problem of winning friends and earning money took much longer to resolve: 'in these first seven years they had no property at all...until 1552 when they bought three little houses and a plot of land on the site where we now are.'[153] It was some years before they began to be accepted: a father wrote of 'the little support we get from the people', of many murmurings 'because they do not understand the constitution of the company', and the very parish in which the Jesuit house was located began a lawsuit against it.[154] Not until 1555 were they able to open their first chapel, with the help of prominent nobles. The very long period involved – ten years between arrival and the first chapel – is clear testimony to the slowness of their impact.

They were fortunate to coincide with reforming bishops who were glad to use the new order for their purposes. In November 1559 father Baptista wrote: 'The bishop [Jaume Cassador] has given me many gifts, I have dined twice with him... The inquisitors are enthusiastic and make use of this college in many ways.'[155] The favourable reception in Barcelona contrasted with the difficult experiences the company was going through at that period in Valladolid, Saragossa and Granada; but bishop and inquisitors alike were badly in need of help and the Jesuits were an ideal instrument. The employment of father Govierno as a censor by the Inquisition was particularly useful: Alfonso Lozano wrote in the following month that 'it has been notable and given a good reputation to the company and has been no less comforting to those who wish us well. With it a door was opened to contact with all the religious orders.'[156]

The Jesuits had much to offer. First, they offered a spiritual fulfilment outside the bounds of the traditional structure: they were not tied to any specific order (Ignatius had been careful to adopt the name of 'company' rather than 'order') or bishop or parish or even nationality, and when they came they were like a fresh wind of regeneration. Second, they offered direct satisfaction based on a return to almost forgotten practices which touched the soul directly: the emotion of sermons, the purgation of confessions, the solace of frequent communion. If we can measure the achievement in Barcelona by their own words, in 1562 they reported that 'recourse to the sacraments had been much forgotten,' but by 1576 the tone was more optimistic: 'through the medium of the fathers of the company frequent recourse to the sacraments has been introduced in this city, to the extent that there are few churches which do not have many people going to confession.'[157] In addition to all their usual duties, they were fortunate from 1557 to be allowed the use of a pulpit in the cathedral, from which they gave daily talks on cases of conscience and made themselves available for consultation afterwards. Third, they used the energies of the young in a way that probably no religious group in Spain had ever done, turning children into active missioners for the faith. Fourth, they used the senses – singing, theatre (examples of either are legion) – in a way completely unprecedented in Spanish practice. 'The Jesuit theatre was entirely a Roman creation,'[158] conceived in the 1560s, but it spread rapidly to Spain, where it was deliberately used as counter-entertainment to the profanities of Carnival: drama formed part of the curriculum in Jesuit colleges and rules for it were drawn up in 1586. Finally, they had an uncanny capacity for success and survival ('we have till now been taken to be exceptional people who wish always to be like oil upon the water,' one Jesuit aptly reported to Acquaviva in 1587)[159] which appealed to many and earned both friends and foes at court, in the Church, in the Inquisition.

Ample proof of the enthusiasm unleashed by the Counter Reformation may be found in the support given not only to the Jesuits but to all the new religious orders, which came late because they were for the most part imported (from Italy) or reformed (and had to await the process of administrative change). The precursor of the new orders and in some sense the apostle[160] of the Counter Reformation in Catalonia was Diego Pérez de Valdivia, whose problems with the Inquisition have been touched on. Pérez came to Barcelona in 1578, intent like many others on going to the Indies, but remained in the city for a fruitful and active decade, dying there in February 1589 just before the outbreak of the devastating plague epidemic. It was precisely during his stay that the leading orders began to enter the province. The groups which penetrated Catalonia included the Observants of St Augustine (1587), the Discalced Carmelites (1588), the Capuchins (1578),[161] and the Franciscan Observants (1616). Perhaps the most successful of the earlier Counter-Reformation orders were the Carmelites, who came at the request of Diego Pérez and in eighteen years founded fourteen houses in Catalonia. Fundamentally the methods used by all the orders were identical, with an emphasis on preaching and the instruction of children.

The primary driving force of all the early patrons of the orders was less the consciousness of participating in a great international

crusade than an urge to develop the order within the local framework, in accordance with civic piety. When St Teresa's new
Discalced Carmelites established their first Catalan base in the
Rambla in Barcelona in 1586, they were greeted by local municipalities which were keen to make the order their 'own'. Mataró
accepted the Carmel in February 1588 and Tárrega in the following
January; by the end of 1589 there were also Carmels in Perpinyà
and Lérida. Patronage, whether by the municipalities for civic
reasons or by rich citizens and nobles for prestige, was the key
to the success and expansion of the orders. The first Carmelite
foundation in Barcelona was financed by the *ciutadà* Joan Dalmau,
and the duchess of Cardona was among the early patrons.[162] The
establishment of one order, the Jesuits, can be followed as an
example of how growth was possible.

From 1545 the Jesuits in Barcelona rented a house opposite the
parish church of the Pi, where they lived until October 1552 when
they bought the cottages and land at the site where their College of
Betlem was eventually built.[163] From this early penniless period the
company slowly began to develop an income. Prior to 1552 they
lived largely off the rents of a house in the Boqueria given to them
by the notary Antoni Gou (who later joined the company). Between
1553 and 1562 they went on to buy a site comprising seven houses,
together with another site with three shops. The progress would
have been more rapid, for several testaments left them property, but
in many cases they refused such gifts to avoid litigation with other
heirs. With the first real estate in hand in 1553 they obtained
permission from the city and began to construct their church in
April that year; in 1562 they began to extend the building in order
to construct a college and in 1567 'a course in Arts began to be
taught in our house'. From the 1560s the gifts of cash and property
grew but sufficed only to cover basic needs and very rarely enabled
them to buy *censals*. 'We lived twenty-eight years in this city of
Barcelona almost without any income, thanks to the help of a few
legacies and some day-to-day charities.' All this changed radically
in 1573. Pope Gregory XIII in that year gave the company outright possession of the old and uninhabited Cluniac monastery of
Sant Pere Casseres, in Osona just north of Vic, together with its
dependent towns of Creixell, Roda and Bera. The towns were
feudatories of the old monastery, so that its residents now became
feudal vassals of the company. In addition, the properties owned
censals in over thirty parishes; and there were rights of presentation to benefices not only in the principality but even in France
(Pamiers). At one stroke, the Jesuits of Catalonia became well-
endowed feudal seigneurs.[164]

Success bred more success. From this decade, precisely when other orders also began to benefit from the surplus wealth of a booming economy, donations from the rich flowed in. We may single out the duke of Cardona, who in 1577 left to the company perpetual enjoyment of the tithes in Mirambell (Vic); Francisco de Clariana, who in 1583 left two houses; and several other gifts from the families of Rocabertí (1588), Manrique de Lara (1588), and Santa Coloma. In particular the donations of Doña María Manrique de Lara (daughter of the duke of Nájera) were so decisive, approaching some 10,000 ducats, that the fathers in the college at Barcelona proposed that she be given the title of 'founder' of the college.[165] By the early seventeenth century the Jesuits were a prosperous business concern, owning and managing censals, houses (by the 1670s they had bought and sold some two dozen lucrative properties), and extensive lands.

The Jesuit story is a reminder that the Counter Reformation had an essential economic infrastructure without which it could not have taken place. In those first twenty-eight years there must have been many moments when the fathers doubted whether they would ever have the means to carry out God's work, despite the exaggerated optimism of their letters to the general in Rome. They and the other orders were aided by the economic growth in the principality, which brought cash their way and permitted the construction of new colleges and churches; by the population growth which made it possible for new parishes to be established; and by the civic piety which encouraged some towns to adopt specific religious orders.

Mission work in Spain involved a conflict of priorities. The Jesuit leadership was anxious not to let zeal for the foreign missions take precedence over the needs of the peninsula, as we have seen from their correspondence in 1564.[166] Too firm an insistence on the same point by Joan de Jesús, superior of the Carmel in Catalonia, who strongly opposed Italian moves to have his clergy sent into the foreign field, earned him removal from his post for ten years and exile from Catalonia. From the early sixteenth century the new religious orders looked on the peninsula as a primary mission area and, as we have seen, it became common to hear parts of Spain being described as 'Indies'. In 1615, a generation after the closing of Trent, a Spanish noble commented to the Jesuit superior in Andalusia, 'I really don't know why the fathers of the company go to Japan and the Philippines to look for lost souls, when we have here so many in the same condition who do not know whether or not they believe in God.'[167] Throughout the period of the

Counter Reformation missionary work became a fundamental part of the enterprise, with the Jesuits in the vanguard in terms both of methodology and manpower. 'For my part I can say that since I began until now in the year 1615 there has not been a year in which I have not gone on some mission, and two and three in some years,'[168] reported Pedro de León from Andalusia.

Because the Jesuits were a tiny group they were called on as occasional help in the same way that travelling friars had always been accepted by the sedentary organisation of the Church; like the friars, they were freely invited to preach, confess and administer communion. Araoz entered Spain in 1540 after the founding of the order, and when he preached in his Basque country the crowd was 'such that a pulpit was set up in the field'. When he preached in Valencia cathedral four years later, February 1544, 'voices were raised that the pulpit should be set up outside, and so it was taken out into the square, where it was so crowded that for me it was very troublesome... And so it was that I preached for more than five hours'.[169] Preaching, certainly, was the reason why the city of Gerona in 1551, after hearing the sermons of Father Estrada, asked Ignatius to send Jesuits there 'because this city is very much in need of doctrine'. In 1545 Juan Bernal Díaz de Luco, bishop of Calahorra, had asked Ignatius for Jesuits to come and 'teach the diocese'.[170] In 1558 Laínez was informed that 'the cardinal of Burgos has asked for eight or more fathers to go to the mountains to preach and teach Christian doctrine and hear confessions, and so they will go this spring.'[171] The mendicant orders had been the true mediaeval pioneers of missions and their work in the Indies confirmed their primacy in the field; but in Spain it was the Jesuits who became the typical missioners of the Counter Reformation.

Consideration of Jesuit missionary methods in the rest of Spain offers a good guide to their practice in Catalonia. In June 1558 the college at Alcalá reported that 'our members have been much sought after to preach in some parishes and villages away from this town, and an effort has been made not only to preach in some villages but also the same fathers have gone on Sundays and feast-days to preach in the prisons and hospitals.'[172] In January 1561 the rector in Salamanca reported that

during the holidays which last here from the eighth of September to the eighteenth of October sixteen of us were sent out on pilgrimage to different places which asked pressingly for them. They went in twos, normally a father with a brother, so as to help each other better, and the fathers preached in some villages and the brothers taught the catechism, and comforted the afflicted and poor in the hospitals. Some went over forty leagues away, others less, depending on their strength; frequently suffering lack of bed and meals and sometimes it was difficult to find bread and they had to put up in some miserable inn, and suffered the rains and great hardship. But all of this was much less than the desire they had to suffer for Christ.[173]

A common practice was to evangelise in the streets. In Granada in 1557 'a father has gone out to the fields to the place where many go to play, and has preached doctrine and tried to persuade the men to give up the evil habit of swearing.'[174] In the same city in 1559 the Jesuits went out 'through the streets, squares and fields' to persuade people to come to mass; and when they came they were organised into 'groups with one of us at the head of each, hands folded, hats off, both young and old, poor and not poor, reciting the catechism with one voice'.[175] In Barcelona the Consellers 'wanted father Govierno to preach to the public women, of whom he converted seven or eight'.[176] Children were taken off the streets and put into the orphanages, which the Jesuits quickly took over as far as instruction was concerned. In Barcelona in 1557 'we have now managed to have the child orphans taught in our house, something we could not do before, and when they are well instructed in doctrine the bishop can make use of them just as the bishop of Gerona does.'[177] When the children were sufficiently instructed, they were immediately turned into little missioners. In Alcalá in 1558

this Lent we have taught the catechism to the children on four days a week. To do it two brothers would go out with a father and ring a bell along the streets, and the number of children collected was large... Afterwards they would go to a church with the young and there teach them the catechism and some devotions and holy songs they could sing in the streets in place of the dishonest ones they usually sing.[178]

In 1561 in Segovia 'the catechism is taught by singing it in the streets.'[179] The emphasis on children was not only to instil principles early; it was also seen as the only practical way of getting through to the adults, and followed a tradition, deriving from the middle ages,[180] in which saintly children were perceived as the corrective to the errors of their parents. The emphasis in this period may well have had the consequence of giving to adolescents a social role they would not otherwise have had. In Córdoba in 1564 a priest recalled one of their pupils, 'not very old, who when he was in a nearby village and saw the people coming out from mass before it had finished, in the bad custom that there is, placed himself at the door and modestly rebuked them and persuaded them to go back and asked the priest to avoid it for the future'.[181] 'When the children go home,' it was reported from Trigueros (near Huelva) in 1564, 'they greet their parents with "Praised be Jesus Christ", kiss their hands and are always careful that nothing indecent is said in the house, and if it is they correct it with much humility, from which there results a greater respect of parents for their children.'[182] The examples reveal the pious naivety of the Jesuits but also confirm the importance they attached to the role of children in evangelisation.

Over the parents the Jesuits had a means of influence that did not depend on children, namely the confessional. A key technique was the 'general confession', in which the penitent confessed not simply immediate faults but the sins of a whole lifetime, thereby going through a complete purge and starting a new life of salvation. In some rural areas the people had fallen out of the habit of confession, but with the new therapy on offer, as in 1561 in Galicia, 'people came from eight or nine leagues to confess in this college.'[183] The fathers were most of all pleased to be able to report the many cases of people who had not confessed for ten or fifteen years and who were now coming forward to use the sacraments of the Church.

For those living three centuries after the Tridentine enterprise it is difficult to envisage the problems posed by missionary work in Spain. The challenge of 'the Indies' implied something more than areas without Christianity, it presented also the travails and extremes of climate and geography, dangerous illnesses and hostile peoples. Yet rural Catalonia had its own perils and interminable distances. Moreover, the missioners had to reckon with the hostility or indifference of the rural communities, the obstacles posed by local clergy and dignitaries, and the refusal of people to adapt their customs to the demands of the preachers.[184]

Missions had been undertaken by Jesuits elsewhere in the peninsula since at least 1557, and in 1559 in Galicia they claimed that 'a great amount of ignorance that there was until now among the clergy has been remedied,' and 'there is so much reformation that they say generally that since the fathers came to this land it has been much amended.'[185] The work in Catalonia commenced slightly later. Direct street preaching was already practised in Barcelona in 1561: 'one father has preached in the seaport where at each sermon he has got together over three thousand souls, because he chose feast-day afternoons when a great part of Barcelona goes there ... Our father provincial began the catechism of children two weeks ago in our church.'[186] The first recorded missions to the mountainous areas appear to have been in 1566, to Lérida, Gerona and Tarragona.[187] No detailed account is available of subsequent years but the society certainly built up a reputation for its work and in 1576 Pere Gil reported that 'they go through different parts of Catalonia, teaching the villages with much success. Frequent recourse to the sacraments has been introduced in the city.'[188] The reputation of the Jesuits was such that when other new orders attempted to enter the mission field they were met with little enthusiasm. The Catalan Carmelites offered in 1590 to serve in the mountains of Urgell, but the bishop rejected the offer on the grounds that they 'are too inexperienced'.[189] The same prelate observed in 1593 that 'experience shows that the mendicant friars achieve little fruit in the mountains because few of them apply themselves to teaching the catechism. The fathers of the company are more often used for this exercise.'[190] Only the Capuchins were able to compete: in Urgell in the 1670s the bishop relied on both Jesuits and Capuchins 'for the spiritual relief of these mountains'.[191]

By the early seventeenth century the society had achieved an enviable monopoly of missionising in Catalonia. Within Barcelona they were called upon regularly to conduct Lenten devotions in the two major parishes of Santa Maria del Mar and the Pi, and were given an exclusive right to minister to the prisons and to accompany prisoners to execution, a macabre duty which was fully documented at the time for Seville by another Jesuit, Pedro de León, but which in Barcelona too had Baroque overtones.[192] It was, however, in the country areas that their main contribution was made. From 1605 onwards they were employed regularly by the bishop of Vic to conduct Lenten missions, mainly in the Maresme and the Vallès; they conducted missions for the bishop of Tortosa; and the bishop of Barcelona from 1606 used them on his pastoral visits, sending them ahead a day or so earlier 'to prepare and move the people and hear their confessions'. In the next decade it became common to send the fathers out on three or four missions a year, some lasting for extended periods: in Manresa in 1612 they stayed six months. They also ventured further afield. The new Jesuit college in Urgell was beginning to care for that difficult area, but the fathers venturing from their base in Barcelona could be found in Solsona (1615), Sanahuja (1619), Bagá (1620), Rosselló (1632), and Ripoll (1638).

Their techniques were similar to those used in Castile, with preaching as their major weapon. In one town of Vic plagued by bandit rivalry in 1610, they invited both bands to come to church and hear doctrine, and both did indeed come, 'almost all with firearms in their hands, when the fathers wanted to teach catechism'. A religious order famous for its sacred drama, they knew how to put on a show: 'in all these places usually at the end of the mission we had a procession of the Sacrament with all the solemnity normal to Corpus, except that we added in front of the procession little boys and girls in file dressed in white with crowns of flowers on their heads and green branches in one hand and a rosary in the other.'[193] Special attention was always paid to confession, with people coming to them after not having confessed for 'twenty, thirty, forty, fifty and sixty years', a cogent commentary on the lack of adequate pastoral help in the rural areas. Special pride was always taken in the number of 'general confessions' achieved, since these were a sign of spiritual conversion: in one town in Vic in 1609 'we heard over six hundred'; in late September 1630 in the mountains of Lluçanès they got 'three thousand communions and one hundred general confessions'; in Hospitalet and Sarrià in 1633 'over eight hundred general confessions were necessary, since people had in previous confessions hidden their sins out of shame for twenty, thirty, forty, fifty and more years'.[194]

The triumphant and deceptively optimistic tone of the Jesuit annalists is occasionally checked by accounts of opposition and hostility: their fierce criticism of sexual 'dishonesty' gave rise to complaints; in one town nobody would receive them and the two fathers had to spend the night outdoors in the rain; in a town just outside Barcelona they were boycotted and nobody came to listen to them.[195] In the pages of the manuscript history virtue eventually triumphed, but the Jesuits knew well enough that success was never permanent and that the missions must go on.

Traditional Catholicism in Catalonia had an ambiguous character: on one hand, with its roots in the monastic centres created by the mediaeval frontier, it gave the impression (like Galician Catholicism) of being securely based in the countryside; on the other, it was clear that this rural religion was ragged and superficial and that organised practice of the faith was limited to the urban areas. Missionaries everywhere in Spain were conscious of the contrast, and their bitter attacks on the old monastic houses were often motivated by the conviction that these had failed in their duty to keep the faith in the areas of their jurisdiction. Can it be said, then, that the missions succeeded, where others had failed, in winning and retaining the rural areas for the Church of the Counter Reformation? Not all prelates used their resources to patronise missions, and Antonio de Torres in his *Manual of the Christian* (1598) lamented the fact: 'O if the bishops would spend one tiny part of their revenues in sending workers through their dioceses to attend simply to this, to preaching Christian doctrine, and teaching people how to go to confession and communion!'[196]

The task facing the first generation of the Counter Reformation was outlined in 1566 by Pere Màrtir Coma, later to become bishop of Elna. Writing just after Trent, he outlined the work done in the Pyrenees of Urgell: a synod of clergy had been held; 'many decrees and edicts of reformation have been published'; many preachers had been invited; catechisms in Catalan had been distributed through the diocese, and were read out every Sunday by the clergy; a manual for priests had been written, in Catalan.[197] The task of reaching the people was difficult for bishops with no human resources at their disposal,[198] and not until the Jesuits came was an effective missionary campaign undertaken. But the Jesuits in their turn possibly over-estimated their own achievement. In his analysis of the work done in Andalusia by himself and other Jesuit missioners in the first two decades of the seventeenth century, Pedro de León claimed that there were five main areas of achievement: the reformation of people's lives, the reconciliation of enmities, the stopping of swearing, the education of children, and the promotion of religious duties such as confession, communion and devotion to the Virgin.[199] This wholly optimistic assessment may be contrasted with the problems that the Jesuits of Catalonia were still encountering, and not simply in the countryside. After a particularly difficult mission in 1633 to the towns of Hospitalet, Sarrià and St Just d'Esvern, all neighbours of Barcelona, they commented that

> one would not readily believe that in villages so close to Barcelona there would be such ignorance of what it is essential to know for eternal salvation, since there were adults who said that in the most holy Trinity there were ten persons, others who said five, with many other intolerable errors; and generally the children and many of the adults knew their prayers and the creed only in Latin. But we took great care to teach catechism every day[200] and to repeat over and over again what had to be learnt, and the said villages have remained well instructed.
>
> We directed the sermons and teaching against all types of vice but specially against those which were known to be most frequent and common among them, and so we expelled a range of superstitions and prayers concocted by the devil for the curing of ills, and divining the good or bad outcome of things to come, such as weddings or births, by the shape taken by rose petals dipped in water, and other similar things.[201]

In that same decade but thousands of miles away, an English priest in Guatemala found the Indians making precisely the same errors about the Trinity, and using similar types of divination, after one hundred years of the Spanish missionary presence.[202] Were the environs of mid-seventeenth-century Barcelona still an Indies, after two generations of the Counter Reformation?

CHAPTER EIGHT

The Encounter with Europe

There are many bookshops and an incredible wealth of books, no less than in Paris, Toulouse and Salamanca, enough to cause wonderment to people from outside.

Dionis de Jorba, *Excellences of Barcelona*, 1589

From the inception of the Habsburg dynasty Catalans were never left in doubt that their destiny was European, even imperial. Barcelona had been the city in which the Catholic Kings were informed of the discovery of America and it was Barcelona whose interests were most closely touched by the Spanish presence in Italy. The route from Barcelona through Genoa was the preferred one of the Emperor[1] in his journeys to and from the peninsula, and as a result the city was, of all those in the Mediterranean, the one most favoured with imperial visits, from the stupendous celebrations of 1519, when representatives of European chivalry assisted at the first Spanish ceremony of the Golden Fleece,[2] to the great armadas of 1535 and 1541 that set their course for Africa. Given the crucial position of the Catalan capital, it became an international crossroads for kings, captains and missionaries, remaining always at the heart of activity and open to the influences of the whole of western Europe; the infrequent visits of Philip II did little to detract from this. It was a role thrust upon, rather than earned by, Barcelona, which in both population and trade, in the number of printing presses and in direct contacts with northern humanism, had in the opening decades of the sixteenth century been eclipsed by its neighbour Valencia.[3] All this changed as it was drawn into the circuit of empire, and demographic increase helped further to stimulate urban expansion: by the time Diego Pérez arrived there in 1578, a city which had hitherto been regarded as merely the launching-ground for soldiers to Europe, ships to Africa and missionaries to America (the intended objective of Pérez), had become in its own right a metropolis.

In the early sixteenth century other ports, notably Seville,[4] had channelled new ways of thought and new books into Spain and had nurtured the spiritual influences associated with Erasmus and the Reformation. In contrast Barcelona seems to have had little direct contact with Erasmus and humanism, and the outstanding Erasmians of the early century were, as in the case of Miquel Mai, regent of the *Audiència* and close adviser to Charles V, more closely attached to the court than to any circle in Catalonia.[5] Though the popularity of Erasmus among Catalans was greater than often thought, as we shall see presently, it would be mistaken to exaggerate the influence of humanism in the city, which in practical terms leapt straight from the period of Renaissance piety into that of Trent. It was substantially through Barcelona that the Counter Reformation entered Spain. Linked closely by tradition to the see of Rome, the Catalans were the first in the peninsula to accept the decrees of Trent and the first to sustain a programme of provincial councils. Geography was a determining factor, since Barcelona was the port with most direct access to Italy; but it is also obvious that the advance in Spain's imperial interests required more, not less, contacts with the outside world; that military, diplomatic and administrative needs created a constant interchange of ideas and personnel between the peninsula and Europe; and that culture participated to some degree in this imperial experience. It is astonishing to find still current the improbable image of a peninsula cut off from the rest of the civilised world. Its persistence can be attributed to the undeniably profound crisis of 1558–9 with which Philip II commenced his reign in Castile and which merits a brief consideration here. Did the crisis and its accompanying *cordon sanitaire* cut Spain off from the western world? Did it impede the flow of people, literature and ideas crucial to the success of change?

The relevant features of the crisis in Spain were the discovery of Protestants in Valladolid and Seville (1557–8), the new censorship laws of 1558, the new Index of the Inquisition (1559), the restrictions on studying abroad (November 1559), and the arrest of archbishop Carranza of Toledo (1559). The internal crisis occurred in the middle of major developments on the international scene, but Philip was allowed a breathing-space by the 1559 peace of Cateau-Cambrésis, and on his return to the peninsula in September that year he gave urgent attention to religious matters. Castilians themselves were stunned and shocked by the turn of events and could scarcely believe that the previous decades of relative tolerance[6] were being overturned by the threat of heresy and rebellion within the very ranks of the elite. 'Before that time,' a Dominican said of the year 1558, 'Spain was wholly untouched by these errors'; others observed that 'there was no need before to be suspicious of anyone,' and that 'we felt it was a different era.'[7] Francisco Borja, who had personal reasons for concern (a member of his family was among the accused), wrote from Valladolid in 1558 that 'they are confiscating from leading ecclesiastical persons the Lutheran books that they had and have. In short, things here are very serious,'[8] a judgment he was soon to suffer in his own person in the form of personal harassment and voluntary exile from Spain. The complacent confidence of the Spanish Church leadership was severely shaken, and a string of emergency measures came from the regent and from the Inquisition.

The crisis continued for perhaps three or four years – the last great *auto de fe* of Protestants was in 1562 – but it was less decisive than often thought, and there is no evidence that Spain closed its frontiers and its mind,[9] or that Spaniards entered a phase of repression in which they were unable even to think freely. No western European country was capable of such repression, however many laws it might pass, and in Spain there was little effective change. The sense of crisis, moreover, struck mainly at the heartland of Castile and in Seville; in the rest of the peninsula it was barely felt and in Catalonia had only a marginal impact. Philip II and his advisers were obsessed with the need to impede the entry of heresy, but although they scored occasional successes they were frustrated by the lack of means to implement their policy.

Despite the crisis no permanent break took place in relations between Spain and the rest of Europe. Though active relations with England and the Dutch were prejudiced by political factors after the 1560s, indirect cultural influences continued; and links with France were never undermined, even in the epoch of the wars of religion. With the rest of Europe the picture was one of uninterrupted and active contacts, albeit often at a low level dictated by lack of interest or the onset of war, but at levels which contributed to the broadening of Spain's experience of the culture of other nations. The most powerful contact of all was military: every year thousands of Spaniards (mainly from Castile) left to join the armies abroad[10] or to seek their fortune; scores of others served in the trading communities of the major ports.[11]

Two areas of culture may have been negatively affected: universities, and the book trade. In neither case were the Spanish decrees out of step with the measures being adopted in other European states, where religion, political policy and concern for security combined to put the interests of the 'nation' before those of international learning. Moreover, in the decrees of 1558–9 the harshest clause – death for unlicensed publishing – was not only typical of European practice but also, in Spain, never put into effect, unlike for example England where the government did not hesitate to act ferociously against the *Marprelate Tracts*. Were the bans effective? Little or nothing is known of the attendance of Spaniards at universities outside the peninsula; most had gone precisely to those which were not forbidden in 1558 (the colleges at Bologna, Rome, Naples and Coimbra) and the restrictions were not therefore a brutal blow except for those who had studied in French institutions, where the growth of heresy operated by itself as a deterrent. The fall in attendance at foreign institutions[12] was significant of the new trend in Europe, where each state tried to restrict its subjects to those universities which were ideologically sound. However, the break between universities could never have been absolute. As late as 1570, when the humanists Arias Montano and Furió Ceriol were in the Netherlands, Spaniards were studying at Louvain and Montano proposed to Philip II a scheme for exchanging students between the two countries.[13]

The book trade was much harder to bring under control. Like other governments in Europe, the Spaniards were quite serious about stopping the entry of unlicensed literature. The intention of the 1558 decrees and the Index of 1559 was clearly to block the entry into Castile of all heretical and disapproved literature. Without exception historians have consequently presented an image of a nation subjected to total control of its literature. The censorship controls of 1558 which put licensing into the hands of the Council of Castile, the ban on studying abroad, the order of 1572 to inspect the books of the university of Salamanca, the instructions that the Inquisition watch the frontiers, and finally the pragmatic of 1610 'that books composed within these realms not be published outside them', all seem part of a huge apparatus of repression.[14]

Fortunately, much of it was an optical illusion. The laws passed in Castile were not applicable outside it, and certainly not in the realms of Aragon, which continued without formal censorship; the rules of the Council of Castile were systematically evaded; the censorship of the Inquisition left (we have seen) much to be desired, and Spaniards continued freely to publish abroad.

The idea that books ceased to enter or leave Spain after 1559 has never had any factual support, and the entire evolution of the Counter Reformation in the country would be inexplicable had there not been, which there clearly was, a continuous trade in printed literature. The commerce had been active since the end of the fifteenth century and the expansion of printing in the peninsula did nothing to diminish it; indeed despite the good output of the presses (some 1300 editions can be traced for the period 1501–20) circulation was low and printers lacked the capital to produce all the books required, so that those who needed texts looked abroad. Around 1520 'the Venetians, and increasingly the Lyonese and the Parisians, provided the majority of books which were needed by scholars in universities and ecclesiastical centres.'[15] Printers in Spain (nearly all the important early printers in the country were not Spaniards but Germans, Burgundians or Italians)[16] were limited to producing mainly small-circulation and vernacular items, and in Barcelona for example faced a constant uphill struggle against costs, possibly their only adequate income coming from bulk orders placed by the dioceses for mass-books. Their task was made no easier by the booksellers, who offered them poor terms and who could import books when they wanted a secure profit. Printers in Spain were unable to expand or diversify, and authors who needed special type-faces or sought a different market consequently preferred to publish abroad, which further depressed production in the peninsula. Official bodies and the government itself followed the trend. When Salamanca university in 1506 sought to print a good Latin edition of the theologian El Tostado, it did so in Venice rather than Spain, and there were always doubts about the ability of Spanish presses: a humanist who printed a text at Saragossa in 1494 conceded with faint praise that 'for a book printed in Spain this edition is of a high quality.'[17] When searching for possible presses in Spain to produce the new Tridentine manuals Philip II was informed in 1572 that Spanish paper was poor and the printers without resources to finance costly machinery or to employ 'educated typesetters and correctors with knowledge of Latin and other languages'.[18] As we have seen, the king had his missals printed in and imported from Antwerp. A century later the situation was unchanged: François Bertaut on his visit to Valladolid in 1659 reported that 'there are no printers in Spain capable of undertaking big books, which are all sent to be printed in Lyon or Antwerp.'[19] There is every reason to agree with a recent assessment that 'by 1650 Spanish printing was possibly the worst in Europe,'[20] and bibliophiles looked to foreign presses for their collections; in Barcelona, booksellers until at least the mid-seventeenth century stocked a high proportion of foreign editions on their shelves.

The importation of books was not merely normal, it was a necessity, since 'Spanish presses did not supply the demand for books in Spain.'[21] After 1559, and despite the measures of 1558–9, the traffic increased, in part because of the Counter Reformation, in part because of Spain's greater imperial role, so that the further measures of control which the Inquisition attempted were logical responses to a more complex situation. Books poured in from the

Antwerp presses; already in 1558 Luis Ortiz had estimated that Castile lost over 200,000 ducats every year paying for the import of books it could have produced internally.[22] The exchange of books between Italy and Spain was unremitting, and virtually never interfered with by the authorities, nor significantly is there any evidence of control barriers operating between the two countries. Private individuals freely sent books from Italy without having to seek special permission: in 1570 and in 1579, for example, we have details of works imported privately by a Spanish diplomat,[23] and well into the seventeenth century and later the merchants of the Mediterranean ports were importing books privately from Italy.[24] The ports of Catalonia indeed were open to every type of trade despite official prohibitions, and books may well have figured among smuggled items. In 1573 the viceroy complained to the *veguer* of Tarragona that 'on that coast of Tarragona and the port of Salou, and also on the shores of Tamarit, Cambrils and other parts of that *vegueria* it is common for vessels to arrive carrying prohibited goods,' and similar complaints continued to be made of other ports.[25] The efficacy of Spain's book control legislation in this period must be approached with the same scepticism that one approaches much government legislation in our own day. There is ample evidence of repressive decrees being passed, but little or no evidence of their ever being enforced. The most remarkable case is colonial America, where controls collapsed completely; 'books entered in abundance and works formally prohibited circulated without much difficulty through the continent ... There was a clear divorce between legislation and reality.'[26] Whatever the internal problems faced by Spanish printers, they were compounded by the apparently unrestricted trade in the import of books printed abroad.

In the peninsula and even more in America readers were able to lay their hands on the books they desired, and despite theoretical import controls there was no serious hindrance to the book trade, which was adversely affected more by economic reality than by government law. In Catalonia the significant barriers to an effective market were: low demand from the numerically small urban elite; the restriction of much reading to the essential sphere of church piety; and the priority accorded among the people to an oral indigenous culture (in Catalan) over a printed foreign (Castilian) culture. These were the very factors which also depressed the few printing presses in the principality.

Not only was there, despite the systems of control, a regular flow of books into the country, but Spanish writers had the choice of working outside the norms imposed within their country and of publishing their works in Italy, France or the Netherlands. The undeniable restraints that existed in the book trade were possibly at their weakest when it came to art, music, theatre and specifically religious areas such as oratory, where there was a fruitful and creative invasion, arguably even an 'invasion dévote',[27] of the peninsula, fostered by the movement of persons and ideas.

Since the early days of printing Spaniards had published outside the country, and they continued to do so long after the restrictive measures of 1558: the fact is crucial but too often forgotten. Why should Spaniards want to publish abroad? In the great formative period up to 1501, some 800 titles had been published within Spain at thirty centres; and from 1501 to 1520 some further 900 titles were published:[28] Valencia and Barcelona, which had presses at work since 1473, share the longest printing history of all Spanish cities. Everything seemed set on a great expansion of printing in the peninsula, especially in the vernacular, for which there would have been little market outside the country. But at this stage a significant turn of events took place. As a recent scholar has demonstrated, 'in the 1540s a major revolution occurs in Spanish publishing: the majority of Spanish books are published outside of Spain, primarily in Antwerp but also in Lyon, Toulouse, Paris, Louvain, Strasbourg, Cologne, Venice, Lisbon and Coimbra.'[29] The trend applied not only to Latin works but also to the vernacular. There were certainly technical reasons why it seemed preferable to find a foreign press, and problems of quality and production which became graver later were already apparent, but there seems little doubt that the internationalisation of the Spanish book was set in motion by the itinerant court of Charles V and the controversies sparked off during the Reformation, and continued into subsequent decades. Peninsular scholars in the early century addressed themselves to the whole of Christendom and did so in Latin, the only tongue that could attract an international readership: Alfonso de Castro issued his great treatises in Paris and Lyon, Pedro de Soto published all his works abroad, in Augsburg, Ingolstadt and Dillingen. But authors were also beginning to find that with the new international role of Spain there was a willingness of European printers to produce books in Castilian. The way was well prepared for foreign hegemony over Spanish publishing.

After the 1560s, when religious issues became heavily nationalised, there was another change in tendency: the trend became to publish in the vernacular and within Spain, and theologians stated that it was a mortal sin to introduce into the country books printed abroad.[30] Pressure to publish within the peninsula was strengthened not by the 1558 decree, which did not broach the issue at all, but by natural factors[31] and most of all by the demands of the reform movement within the peninsula, as we can see clearly from the prefaces of many books published in the period. Ironically Spaniards were not able to publish at home as much as they would have liked, mainly because of the backward state of printing and distribution in Spain.[32] Already in 1523 Francisco de Vergara had complained that 'it is rare to find anyone willing to print a book in Latin,' and in 1549 a Lyon bookseller addressed his Spanish readership thus: 'when I consider all the books of which you are deprived in Spain because of the shortcomings of the presses, I realised how great a service I could render you by sending you beautifully printed and carefully corrected editions.'[33] In the 1580s the Franciscan Juan de Pineda was complaining of the difficulty of publishing unless a patron could be found, with the result that many possible books were lost forever: 'thus the creative work of poor authors is lost and if books are written they rot because they cannot be published'.[34] As the use and understanding of Castilian spread, however, in step with the growth of imperial commitments after 1560, printers could be found who would risk the expense of printing a book in Milan, in Palermo, in Lisbon, in Antwerp, even though its intended public was to be in Spain. If moreover the book was directed principally to an international audience, even the fact of being written in Spanish did not exclude the possibility of publication abroad.

At the same time that printing in Spanish concentrated on the peninsula, therefore, it continued to function abroad, and indeed Spain is the only nation of early modern times to have had possibly as many titles published abroad as at home, a situation caused not by fear of censorship but by simple publishing considerations.[35] There is also no doubt that nearly all the Spanish works published abroad were intended for import into Spain. This may not have been true for the very early sixteenth century,[36] but by the epoch of the Counter Reformation the flow of works into the peninsula was substantial. Scholars who wrote in Latin continued to publish abroad freely: this development was possible because members of the great religious orders, notably the Jesuits, emphasised the international dimensions of the reform and could subject themselves to the censorship of their own order without having to confine themselves to the censorship of their native country.[37] For economic rather more than for security reasons the government occasionally (as with a decree of 15 September 1617)[38] tried to prohibit publishing outside the country; and Martínez de Mata, a leading *arbitrista* of the mid-seventeenth century, lamented the practice of sending books abroad to be printed;[39] but nothing could be done.

Down to the epoch of Trent, Lyon was regularly used for the

printing of liturgical books: the missal and rite-book of Tarragona, for instance, were produced there in 1550. But the city was also the preferred place of publication for a whole generation of Spanish Counter-Reformation authors: in the late sixteenth century about sixty Spaniards had their works published there; in the early seventeenth century some fifty-two leading Spanish writers, including Juan Eusebio Nieremberg, José de Acosta, and Manuel Rodríguez, chose in their own lifetimes to publish their works in the city, which also saw the appearance of the major classics of Spanish thought, by Francisco Suárez, Nebrija, Martín de Azpilcueta, Alfonso de Castro, Luis de Granada and Antonio de Guevara.[40] Antwerp continued to be the magnet for scholars, the quality of the printing outweighing for authors the often tortuous route eventually taken by the book: Andrés de Uztárroz, chronicler of Aragon in the 1640s, published works in the city specifically for sale in Naples, and others sent their works there for distribution both to Italy and to France.[41] The great centre for Spanish publications however was Italy. The need for post-Tridentine breviaries and missals was never met adequately from the Plantin presses, despite Philip II's attempt to set up a lucrative monopoly, and the Church authorities, many of them openly protesting against the privilege put into the hands of the Jeronimites of the Escorial, were glad to contract for printing in Venice. In 1583 the representative of the Giunti press at Philip II's court was owed over 6500 ducats for missals.[42] The more we contemplate the world of Spanish publishing, taken in its global and not merely in its peninsular context, the more it seems to be of a rich and grand diversity which was never seriously impeded by the activities of the inquisitors, who had in any case neither the personnel nor the jurisdiction to control the universe of scholarship explored by Spanish writers. It follows that the volume of books published in the cities of Spain is no guide to the real number of books published by Spaniards at this period.

The mechanics of control over book imports into Catalonia were outlined in the early seventeenth century by the Catalan Jesuit Joan Ferrer (writing under the pseudonym Bisbe y Vidal): 'Books printed in Spain with just the licence of the bishop may be sold so long as they are not specifically prohibited in the [Inquisitorial] Catalogue. Those which come from Germany, France and other countries where there are heretics may not be sold in Spain unless they are first passed by the tribunal of the Holy Inquisition and given a licence to be sold.'[43] Books imported from other parts of the Spanish monarchy (Italy, the southern Netherlands) were subject to prior inspection only if they were to be sold in the shops; books imported privately had to answer to no public authority unless they were clearly in breach of prohibition orders. The remarkable absence in Ferrer's account of any reference to state control is notable. Random controls could be exercised over books coming in ships to the ports, where the chief reason for complaint was not confiscation (the authorities could not confiscate if there was not a prior prohibition) but arbitrary and interminable delays, so that even licensed booksellers attempted to evade the inquisitors. In about 1566 the humanist Bonaventura Vulcanius cited his experience: 'my books have been detained by the inquisitors in a port of Spain called Bilbao for seven whole months nor have I up to today been able to get hold of any of them';[44] and it was the delays in this type of bureaucracy that compelled the Barcelona booksellers to try to arrange a more sensible method of book control in 1569. Impatient with the inefficiency of the Holy Office, they offered to pay for two full-time censors (selected by the inquisitors) who would devote their time simply to the examination and swift processing of imported books;[45] but there is no evidence of the suggestion being adopted. In practice, all attempts at book control were inefficient; and there is no evidence that it ever interrupted the flow of literature into the country, so that throughout the modern period literate Spaniards were able to read foreign books if they were capable of doing so. Vulcanius, referring to the period around 1570, informed Plantin that their mutual book-dealer in Toledo (Bocangelino) used to import both for him and for friends books from Venice and Lyon; and in 1573 Plantin is on record as sending to Bocangelino from Flanders three bales of books including the *Opera omnia* of Ruysbroek and works by Montano, Alfonso de Castro and Pedro de Soto.[46]

The Counter Reformation, far from tightening the restrictions on Spanish writing, helped to loosen them. Although the Holy Office had a brief to interfere in every aspect of the media of communication it patently could not do so since it lacked the means; and in practice it also had to treat with respect licences issued by the bishops and those issued abroad by valid Catholic authorities. The only way in which the Inquisition or the state could interfere with these publications was by seizing them after they had been published or had entered Spain, and then trying to justify the action. Virtually all foreign books were liable to seizure, though the principal casualty among them tended to be unlicensed Bibles.[47] The position of Catalonia within the Spanish system can be understood only by realising that the government of Madrid had no bureaucracy to impose national vigilance over publications, and indeed there was no system of control that covered all Spain.

Reformation Europe was slow to evolve effective censorship: in England the government produced licensing laws in 1538, in France the Sorbonne issued the first index of prohibited books in 1542, and in the 1540s various Italian prelates and city states passed edicts against heretical works; but the problem was always one of enforcement. The establishment of the Roman Inquisition in 1542 gave some hope of enforcing censorship in Italian lands, and in Naples the Spanish authorities were already issuing bans on books in the same decade.[48] The Italians and the papacy were the first to bring out indexes of prohibition: Spaniards came late into the field.

In the Crown of Castile control was theoretically governed by the laws of 1558 and by subsequent decrees issued by the Council of Castile, which were effective only in areas policed by the Castilian authorities; in the Crown of Aragon, as we shall see, there were differences. Given the difficulties of enforcing the law, and the traditional disregard of the law by Spaniards, it would be mistaken to imagine that controls were effective. Rodríguez in the 1590s summarised the position in Castile as follows: 'booksellers and printers sin mortally if in these realms of Castile they print a book or work, of whatever type, in Latin or romance or other language, without first presenting the work to the Council of Castile to be examined by learned persons and obtain a licence signed in the name of His Majesty and sealed by the Council, after due examination and approval.' However, even in Castile there were variations: 'in parts of the realms of Castile where even after the said pragmatic of 1558 things are printed with the approval and licence of the bishop alone, I would not consider it a mortal sin for the printer to publish.'[49] Thus control of censorship in Castile was normally in the hands of the Council and the role of the Inquisition, especially through its Indexes from 1551 onwards, was complementary but subordinate.

Control over printing in Spain was exercised by the Council of Castile, the Inquisition, the Church (as stated by Ferrer) and by the royal high court (in Barcelona this was the Audiència) in the major cities of the Crown of Aragon. An author consequently had the freedom to apply for a licence to print to any one of these authorities if he wanted to escape possible hostility from another; just as he could print abroad if he thought it easier to obtain permission there.[50] The result was an impressive range of alternatives which gave Spanish authors possibly more effective choice than was available to writers of any other nation in western Europe. But writers in the Crown of Aragon had an additional advantage which calls for special attention: they were not subject to the censorship controls decreed in Castile, with the astonishing consequence that until the end of the sixteenth century there was no regular or obligatory system of state censorship in the Aragonese realms.

This simple but fundamental fact is overlooked by every study of censorship in the peninsula. When Ferdinand and Isabella in 1502 brought in the first government control of censorship their law applied only to the Crown of Castile and not to the whole of Spain.[51] In Barcelona there appear to have been no proper government controls over licensing throughout the reigns of Ferdinand and Charles and the first half of the reign of Philip II, so that banned books were free to circulate.[52] The restrictive decrees passed in September 1558 by the regent Juana were limited to Castile,[53] and no specific legal measures were taken by the crown to interfere in the operation of controls in the Crown of Aragon, provoking Philip II to complain to the viceroy of Catalonia in 1568 that 'in that city and others of that principality the printers publish many new books without having our licence whereas it is just that they should obtain it before printing, but they print without permission or paying the necessary tax, and the booksellers who sell ask very excessive prices for their books.'[54] The tone of the letter suggests a preoccupation with price, but we know that at that date the king was more worried about the publication of heresy, and it was no coincidence that he chose in the very same letter to confirm for Catalans, Aragonese and Valencians his 1559 decree prohibiting study abroad at unapproved universities. Scholars have believed until now that the 1559 measure had been applicable to all Spaniards, but the tenor of the king's words to his viceroy in 1568 is unequivocal:[55]

> Some years ago we ordered published in these our realms of Castile by means of a pragmatic, that no one should go to study outside the realms; and since our will is to do the same for those our realms of the Crown of Aragon, we have ordered the enclosed to be sent to you containing substantially the same as the other. You will publish it and take care that it be kept and observed with due attention, and in this way avoid the harm that might result from going to study abroad.

Like much legislation of the period, the restriction seems to have been shortlived. In 1616 we find a Catalan lawyer openly informing the Council of Aragon that he had taken degrees in Barcelona and Salamanca, and then 'to avoid the expense of Spanish universities went to Toulouse in France where he took the degree of doctor, and having registered the degree in the said city of Barcelona has continued his work as a lawyer in the said city'.[56]

Not until 1573 did Philip II find it possible to assert some form of control over books in Catalonia, and then only through the mechanism of licences issued directly by the viceroy. A decree issued in Barcelona by Don Hernando de Toledo and dated 15 April 1573

> notifies and orders all and any printers and booksellers and other persons in the said principality and counties, that henceforward they may not nor presume in any way to print or sell any books, works or poems of whatever type without first presenting to the viceroy the said books, works and poems to be examined and obtain a licence from His Excellency issued by the court, and this under pain of £200.[57]

The very late arrival of licensing in Catalonia was outdone by the kingdom of Valencia, where licences to print were not deemed necessary before the 1580s; and later still were the Aragonese, who waited until 1592 for their *Cortes* to draw up legislation on printing.[58]

Long before this period, however, three factors conspired to bring some order into the chaos: the Church authorities, in accord with papal constitutions of 1515 and 1564, the latter arising out of Trent, attempted to enforce control of publications by clergy; the Castilian authorities, basing themselves on ordinances of 1554 and the famous law of 1558, issued licences to print not only in Castile but through the royal courts (in Catalonia, the Audiència) in the eastern realms of the peninsula; and both authors and printers felt it advisable to avoid problems by seeking one or the other of these licences, if only to secure the vital 'privilege' which in theory protected the book from pirate printers. The 'privilege' and the 'licence' were of course distinct, but in practice it was impossible to obtain the former without having the latter, and so a regime of control slowly imposed itself. It was only a partial solution, for there were many ways to get round the apparent rigidity of the law, and the simplest was to ignore it altogether.

Clergy, as the most educated sector of the elite, were the majority of those who put pen to paper, and the principal obstacle facing any clerical author was the permission of his religious order (whose regional superior could issue licences) and of his bishop; doubts by these authorities could delay or permanently postpone publication, though few such cases are recorded. Given the administrative autonomy of the Church, bishops had a range of control which operated outside the framework of the regulations of the Council of Castile. As we have seen any bishop in Spain could license a book independently of the Council, assuming only that it had not been in any way condemned in the Indexes of the Inquisition.[59] In practice this freedom was seldom used in Castile, where most licences were issued by the Council, but seems to have been common in the Crown of Aragon. In Barcelona the bishop regularly issued licences to print,[60] and also had jurisdiction over aspects of the activity of printers; often, the episcopal licence merely complemented the civil. In 1594 we find the bishop forbidding booksellers from selling a book because of errors in it;[61] and in 1602 he extended to his diocese a ban placed by the pope on a work by Juan de Orozco y Covarrubias.[62] The collaboration of civil and episcopal authorities in the issuing of licences, and the extraordinary importance of episcopal licensing, has been documented for the late seventeenth century in Valencia, where out of 258 works published between 1665 and 1700, 134 were licensed by the bishop, 90 by both bishop and Audiència and 19 by the Audiència alone.[63]

In 1617 the bishop of Barcelona complained to the printers of the city that after he had issued licences to print, 'some things are modified, removed or changed, causing possible harm' – a standard tactic adopted by most printers of the period when they disagreed with the censors – and accordingly ordered that in future no such changes be made.[64] We may well doubt whether the printers bothered to obey his reverence. It was deemed quite normal in the period for books to go through later, augmented or altered, editions while still displaying only the original earlier licence.[65] In this way the intentions of the licensing system were frustrated and the censorship reduced to a mockery. That, certainly, was when the rules were nominally observed, but we also know that the rules were not observed: in late seventeenth-century Valencia, 40 per cent of books published did not bother to obtain any type of authorisation, licence or censorship,[66] a degree of libertarianism which would have been regarded with horror in the more authoritarian Protestant north of Europe. We have seen that a good proportion of the *goigs* circulating in rural Catalonia seem to have been printed without any official licence whatever, and there is no record that any official action was taken against unlicensed ones. It seems superfluous to add that the system of licences depended on accurate, impartial and informed censorship, and there is no evidence that this was available. Certainly in the Crown of Aragon, and more than likely in Castile as well, censorship was highly inefficient, and the intrusion of the Inquisition into the field may fairly be regarded as an almost welcome attempt to introduce some order into a system which was patently no longer under control.

There is the significant case of Onofre Menescal, a priest of Barcelona cathedral, who in 1607 obtained from the bishop a licence to issue a book which he duly published. Almost immediately however the bishop ordered the suspension of the book for three years, since he had in the meantime received unfavourable opinions about the work. Both author and printer were clearly angry at the turn of events and in 1610 Menescal appealed to the Inquisition, which thereupon allowed the book.[67] It is a good example of the confusions that could arise from conflicting systems of censorship. The Inquisition however had its own inadequacies, as we have seen from its role in Catalonia, and was unable to make up for deficiencies in the national system. Spain of the Counter Reformation remained poorly policed in the realm of ideas, a nation with its frontiers vulnerable to the ideology of other European nations and protected only by the small readership and limited circulation of printed matter. There was nothing unusual about this. We can find the same situation during these years in France, where 'book censorship was inefficient,' 'regulation by means of lists of forbidden books never worked,' and 'the full rigour of the law was often inapplicable';[68] which is all the more remarkable since the French system was apparently much harsher, and printers were actually executed, whereas in the whole history of Habsburg Spain not a single bookseller or printer is known to have been put to death for contravening the law.

Since bishops also exercised some powers over religious spectacles (which in many cases coincided with *comedias* or *autos sacramentales*) and over sermons, the two areas of non-printing which most affected public culture and which arguably rendered these media more powerful than the book, it is obvious that the role of the Church must not be underestimated. In the early seventeenth century, according to Alcalá Yáñez in his *Talkative lay-brother* (1624), 'in the kingdom of Aragon no comedy is allowed to be presented without first being censored and corrected by the vicar-general of the diocese.'[69] In the diocese of Barcelona the bishop seems not to have intervened in theatrical questions.

The variety of controls over literary output in Spain inevitably created confusion and frustration among contemporaries; reading their complaints, many modern scholars have assumed that the country was a police state. Yet opinions were not suppressed, as we can see by the continuous debate over political, economic and moral issues, in which the disputants often sank to the level of 'women in the market-place'; though, as the same source also stressed, 'opinions are an open field in which discourses may exercise their free will.'[70] The most vociferous complainants were booksellers, who were concerned merely to sell books and were anxious that the authorities do their job properly. They were concerned above all at the sheer incompetence of the inquisitors. Cargoes of books were held up in transit for months on end because the inquisitors could not find personnel with the qualifications to examine and censor; many books were allowed to slip through the

net and then seized several months later, when the booksellers
had already paid for them; months and years of failure to censor
properly were punctuated by sudden lightning raids in which the
inquisitors hoped to compensate for previous lethargy. The system,
or lack of it, may have been oppressive; it was certainly infuriating.

'The idea of watertight national compartments in Catholic religious
influences does not correspond to the reality,'[71] and every dimension
of the Counter Reformation in Spain was moulded by external
influences. Ideas, aspirations and methods were alike dependent on
contact with other Catholic countries, which contributed to Spain
perhaps even more than they borrowed from it. None of it would
have been possible without the free movement of books, ideas and
men.[72]

In the early sixteenth century there were vigorous links between
the peninsula and Germany (where for example Pedro de Soto
subsequently published all his major works), but they faded after
the imperial epoch of Charles V, and later cultural contacts were
literary[73] rather than spiritual. By the early seventeenth century
the works of Luis de Granada, St Teresa and John of the Cross
were reaching a German public through the medium of a Dutch
translator.[74] From the epoch of Trent all attention was focused on
Italy, but the Italian connection was by no means the only channel
through which change filtered in these years, and the peninsula
continued to be, both before and after 1558, in active contact with
the intellectual life of its other partners in the monarchy. Even
outside this ambit links continued in surprising places: Gilly's impressive study of Hispanic links with the printers of Basel[75] shows a
contact unbroken by the bitter controversies of the Reformation
epoch, with 114 editions of works by Spaniards published between
1527 and 1564, and a further 70 published between 1565 and
1610, including the works of Antonio Agustín in 1576.

French contact with the Iberian market was among the earliest
and the most lasting, since it continued into the eighteenth century.
From the 1520s Lyon booksellers were active in the peninsula, and
as we have seen Spanish authors were published in France. The flow
of books to the peninsula was substantial: one trader, Andrés Ruiz,
during the years 1557–64 brought in 919 bales of books from
Lyon and 103 bales from Paris,[76] so we may assume that the total
introduced through other agents was considerable. With time the
flow became easier, not more difficult, because censors who had in
a previous generation been capable of expurgating Latin were not
now capable of the same with French, a language they usually did
not understand.[77] On the Catalan frontier, as we have seen, the

inquisitors were unable to stop the flow of volumes and did not dare to embargo bales imported by the Barcelona booksellers. By the early seventeenth century there was a virtually free flow of French books into Spain, much of it across the Pyrenees. In the late sixteenth century Italian was almost the only foreign language read by Spaniards, but by the next generation French was making its presence felt, albeit through translations, such as that of Bodin's *République*, published in 1590 in Turin: in 1595 father Ribadeneira complained that 'the works of Juan Bodino pass through the hands of men of state and are read with much interest and are praised as coming from a learned man.'[78] In 1643 Uztarroz wrote to a colleague that 'we very much appreciate the care you take in asking for the books from France'; Spaniards purchased books freely in Paris and brought them home; French merchants brought books to sell together with their other goods.[79] The volume of this flow was never large, given that not many in Spain could read French easily,[80] but few active impediments were put on it, either by the state or by the Inquisition. If the interchange of ideas between intellectuals continued at an unduly low level it was for reasons unconnected with the accessibility of foreign literature.[81]

The French books that found their way into private libraries are testimony to access between the two nations. In the early seventeenth century significant examples include that of the diplomat Lorenzo Ramírez de Prado, whose large collection of over 250 up-to-date French works – in a library totalling 8951 titles – was looked upon with such alarm by his widow that she asked the Inquisition to send an official to look through it.[82] Juan Messia de Castilla, member of the Council of Finance, had a personal library in 1618 of which 307 volumes, 28.5 per cent of the total, were published in Lyon.[83] In 1620 when the abbot of Montearagón was writing his *Annals and Memorials*, he relied heavily for knowledge of European events on the regular arrival of the *Mercure François*, and at one point in his text he comments, 'As I write this I have received five volumes of the *Mercure François*, which contain what has happened in the world from the year 1605 to the year 1620, which is where my narrative reaches, and though I could use the five volumes to amplify these years I shall follow the plan used in preceding pages and only write of what is most important and worthy of note.'[84] Wars and diplomacy clearly fostered interest: one remarkable example is that of the soldier-diplomat Rebolledo, who lived for twelve years in Denmark and there built up a library (which he brought back to Spain in 1660) which included not only banned books but also the works of Théophile Viau and the French *libertins*.[85]

Because of their open frontier in Rosselló, Catalans had direct contact with the French but little evidence has emerged of their acquaintance with the language. A certain demand for French books undoubtedly existed in Barcelona, for in 1561 the bookseller Joan Guardiola stocked a small selection of works whose titles we do not know because the stock-takers did not consider them important; possibly more important, he also stocked 76 copies of a French-Latin grammar published in Lyon, which represents a substantial use by students; and 39 copies of French choral song, in quarto, as well as a selection (nineteen copies) of French and Italian songs.[86] In the same period the Barcelona magistrate Esteve Naves possessed among the 135 titles in his library, which consisted largely of weighty tomes on jurisprudence, three volumes in French, all on law.[87] Joan Busquet, priest of the parish of the Pi in Barcelona, possessed in 1573 a book of French songs; the humanist Pere Vila of Tarragona had in his library in 1586 a French-Latin dictionary and the *De Oficiis* of Cicero in French.[88] By 1667 booksellers in Barcelona were offering the public French-Spanish dictionaries as a matter of course.[89] These random examples confirm what is apparent from other data such as the immigration of French and the visits of French pilgrims to Montserrat, that regular contact kept alive interest in the language. But it was not of course necessary to know French in order to draw on French cultural sources, for the works of French humanists were available in Latin and, more fundamental than any other aspect, the printers of France flooded the Barcelona market with their books. Of the 497 volumes (representing 125 titles) dedicated to medicine in the bookshop of Joan Guardiola in 1561 nearly all came from Lyon. Unfortunately the significance of France for the Counter Reformation in Catalonia was minimal: by the early seventeenth century François de Sales (subsequently much appreciated in Spain) had come out in Spanish, but in Antwerp rather than in the peninsula.[90] On balance, there was considerably more Spanish influence on the developing French Counter Reformation, particularly through the mediating figure of cardinal Bérulle.

Freedom of contact with Italy was at the root of the cultural changes that concern us, for the Counter Reformation in Catalonia as in Spain was fundamentally Italian. It is virtually impossible to talk exclusively of the action of one country on the other since the impact was always mutual. There were broadly four channels for cultural links between the two countries.[91]

First of the channels were the Spaniards resident in Italy and especially in Rome. The influence of the Renaissance papacy, the attraction of the papal court, and the crucial importance of the Spanish college at Bologna for the recruitment of Spain's bureaucracy, meant that any Spaniard who wished to exhibit signs of culture had to show some links with Italian institutions. The increase of Spanish political influence in Italy after 1499 and especially after 1516, bound the fate of Italy irrevocably to that of Spain. From about 1529, when Charles V went to Genoa from Barcelona and devoted some attention to his Italian dominions, leading Spaniards took up residence in Italy: Garcilaso and Juan de Valdés among the men of letters, Diego Hurtado de Mendoza among the soldier-scholars. Throughout the sixteenth and seventeenth centuries Spaniards of every condition lived and served in Italy, published their books there, and when they went home (with their wives, who also contributed to the cultural interchange) took with them key aspects of Italian taste and culture.

A second channel was represented by the Italians resident in Spain. This was particularly important in the early Renaissance, with the residence in the peninsula of men such as Siculo, Anghiera and Castiglione, and much less relevant after the mid-sixteenth century; but Spanish culture still depended heavily on visits by Italian artists and musicians. Indeed, the Catholic Reform was responsible for the wholesale importation of Italian personnel into the peninsula: religious orders (such as the Jesuits and Capuchins), religious music (to teach Gregorian chant), religious art (the artisans of Baroque at the Escorial and Montserrat), and strolling actors.

A third channel was the diffusion of printing. Many Italian printers were active in the peninsula, and Spaniards in turn chose to publish books in Italy, whether for convenience or by preference; few ever fell foul of the Inquisition. To take one example: when a papal decree of 1567 condemned bullfighting it was ill-received in Spain though Philip II did not stop its publication. However, when fray Antonio de Córdoba in 1569 wrote a treatise which touched on the subject and attacked the papal view, he found that he could not obtain a licence to publish within Spain. He accordingly began to publish in Venice, where the pope somehow managed to intervene and obtained the deletion of the section on bulls.[92] The most astonishing testimony to the quantity of Spanish publications in Italy is the impressive catalogue compiled by the Catalan bibliophile Toda i Güell; in five volumes, his compilation is impressive evidence of the thousands of Spanish publications that came out, not in Spain but in Italy. The data, reproduced in Figure 3 in two-year periods, show that the number of items published rose from about twenty every two years in the late 1540s to over forty in the 60s and 70s, reaching a peak of sixty in the first decade of the seventeenth century.[93] Most items were meant for the Spanish

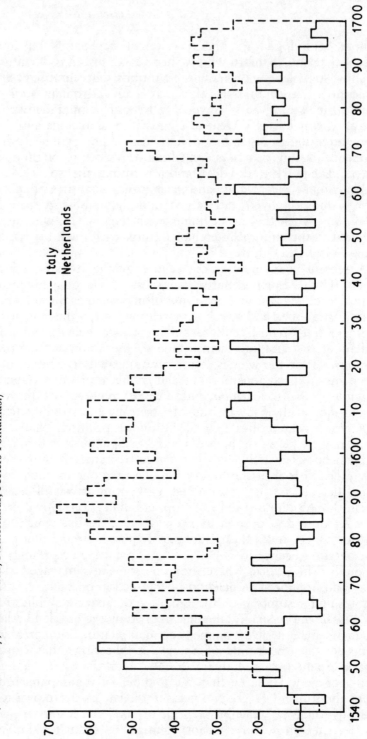

Figure 3 Spanish books published in Italy and the Netherlands 1540–1700.
(Sources: Italy, Toda i Güell; Netherlands, Peeters-Fontainas.)

---- Italy
——— Netherlands

market and cannot be separated from the mainstream of Spanish publishing. Philip II himself paid subsidies for books to be published in Italy which could not be published in Spain for technical reasons.[94]

A fourth channel was the book trade. Several Italian booksellers established themselves in Spain, but it was Spanish demand that invigorated the whole system. Within this category we must mention the growing activity of translators on both sides of the sea, who did a lot to introduce the respective literatures.[95] In the seventeenth century the output of the Venetian presses fell (by 1600 annual production there was only half that of Paris) and that of Rome rose, but the Spanish commitment to publishing books in both cities continued.

Italians were imitated but not admired. Italy was also, notoriously, considered to be the land of licence, an opinion which worked its way through to the common people in Spain, if we may believe the few cases that came before the Inquisition. No Spaniard is on record with any observation approaching that of the French Gabriel Naudé: 'Italy is full of libertines and atheists and people who don't believe anything,' but Spaniards were certainly aware that Italy was a different world, one apparently within the Spanish sphere of influence yet where Jews were still tolerated. At no time did the Spanish authorities make any attempt to restrict contacts. In Catalonia the late sixteenth century was dominated by Italian artists – sculptors, painters – and Italian tastes. Service in Italy familiarised many Catalans with the language, and their books reflect a constant familiarity, while the bookshops had a good supply of Italian literature available. Guardiola in 1561 offered the public some twenty-five titles in Italian, apart from a good selection of Italian songs: the books on sale included the *Orlando Furioso*, Machiavelli's *History of Italy*, Petrarch, Dante and *Il Cortegiano*.[96]

No less important than Italy, particularly in the early sixteenth century, were Netherlandish influences. The links of Spain with the Netherlands were of long standing and possibly more intimate than those with Italy. Of particular importance for Mediterranean spirituality was the export from the Netherlands of mystical thought, with its high tide in the very period that Charles V's accession to the Spanish throne had promoted links between the two countries.[97] To the preceding half-century we can date for example the publication (in Barcelona in 1482) and spread, particularly after Luis de Granada's translation in 1536, of the *Imitation of Christ*; the attempts of García de Cisneros and of the cardinal to introduce Netherlandish thought; and the *Spiritual ABC* of Osuna (1527), which though innocent of direct derivation from the Netherlands was indirectly affected. The crisis of 1559 and the Jesuits' subsequent hostility to northern mysticism was only one side of the picture; within the next generation fray Juan de los Angeles openly diffused the work of the Dutch mystics, Herp in particular.[98] Moreover Netherlands thought was always well received among some of the clergy in the peninsula and by the seventeenth century the previous bias against Netherlands writers was sharply reversed.

There were severe strains on the relationship in the peak years of the Dutch revolt but normality was quickly resumed. Intellectuals of the two nations remained in touch, sharing as they did the common cross of the revolt: the correspondence of Justus Lipsius in the 1590s is a good guide to this interchange. Thanks to the continued military presence, knowledge of the Spanish language remained a general prerequisite in the Netherlands and even in Amsterdam by the late seventeenth century theatres were staging plays in Spanish for the public.[99] Apart from language and marriage (many Spaniards adored the fair complexion and independent spirit of Netherlands women),[100] the peninsula offered the north new dimensions in spiritual literature (St Teresa was an enormous success), and in the diffusion of the picaresque. In turn the Netherlands continued its old fifteenth-century role as an exporter of thought and art to Spain. However, in the more remote areas of the peninsula contact with foreign culture was limited and the barrenness of the intellectual environment was lamented, specifically by the Aragonese poet Lupercio Leonardo de Argensola, writing to Lipsius in 1602, 'Do we honour the muses? Which of them holds sway over us?'[101] It is a question which we may apply to Catalonia.

Northern piety was represented in Catalonia with the writings of García de Cisneros and with the popularity of the *Imitation*; we can see later reflections in the 1557 preface to the Tarragona constitutions.[102] But the omens were not favourable. Barcelona had few direct commercial links with the Netherlands and its military links, despite the role played in the Dutch revolt by Requesens, were probably minimal. The normal passage of cultural influences along these channels could not therefore operate in the case of the principality, and books would certainly have had to come through France rather than by the long sea-route. The lifeline to which many Catalans clung was, as we shall see, Erasmus; but no other significant northern influences can be found in the Catalan Counter Reformation, which orientated itself logically towards the Mediterranean. It follows from this that Castile played a far more decisive part than Catalonia in the exporting of religious influences towards the Netherlands. The process can be followed through the publication of Castilian works at Antwerp. The date 1559, when the inquisitors showed clearly their prejudice against spiritual literature, had a serious impact on all publications. Prior to that date, peninsular writers had been published freely in the Netherlands: works published in Castilian in Antwerp rose from a sprinkling in the 1530s to nine in 1544, seventeen in 1546, twenty-seven in 1550 and twenty-six in 1558; for the next few years there was a sharp fall, and only from 1568, when twelve were published, did the numbers begin to pick up.[103] For roughly a generation after 1570, the religious impact of the Counter Reformation in Castile was extended into the southern Netherlands, with a small but regular stream of spiritual works in Spanish and Latin issuing from the Netherlands presses: a provisional count shows only three such works in Antwerp in 1569, but thereafter the numbers rose to eight a year in the 1590s, and sixteen a year in the first decade of the seventeenth century,[104] a period in which for the first time the works of Gracián de la Madre de Dios and St Teresa (as well as the purely literary works of Lope and Cervantes) invaded the outside world.

Traces of Netherlandish piety can be found in the libraries of Barcelona citizens in the mid- and late-century. Francesc Romeu, a committed humanist and judge of the Audiència, whose large library of over two thousand volumes featuring 542 titles was almost entirely on jurisprudence, included among his non-academic books in 1554 the *Theologia Mystica* of Henry Herp, a work soon to be condemned in the 1559 Inquisitorial Index.[105] The bookseller Guardiola in 1561 offered for sale twenty-one copies of the *Imitation*, each for 2s; and two copies of Johann Tauler's *De Passione Christi*; both titles figure on bookshelves till the end of the century. Authors like Tauler and Herp would have appealed to a tiny audience;[106] of far greater significance was the *Imitation*, stocked in good quantities by all Barcelona booksellers, sometimes in luxury imported editions, and published with equal success in Latin, Castilian and Catalan though it appears not to have attained the rank of a best-seller.[107] The surprising success scored on Barcelona bookshelves was, however, in Erasmian humanism.

The transition from Humanism to Baroque in Spain has frequently been presented in terms of a relapse into inertia and dogmatism, a reversal so complete that some have excluded the seventeenth century from Spain's Golden Age. Recognising that it is impossible to sustain such a picture for the literature of the period, Bataillon has argued for a long-term duration of Erasmianism: 'Spanish Erasmianism was, in great measure, the source of many important books of the Counter Reformation from which thousands of educated Catholics learned to reconcile their adhesion to the Church with the most profound Christian spirit'.[108] His argument implicitly assumes that the prevailing cultural tide of the seventeenth century was reactionary but that a strong undercurrent managed to retain, against official disapproval, traces of consciously disguised Erasmian spirituality; the liberal remnants, in fact, he sees as being so powerful that he strongly rejects the term 'Counter-Reformation',[109] since it implies for him a victory of reaction over the reform movement, the true picture being in his eyes one of an Erasmianism which continued to enrich Spanish thought. For Catalonia the picture usually presented is much bleaker: it has been suggested that Erasmianism disappeared during the early century, that the works even of Luis Vives were 'completely unknown', and that Barcelona began to shut itself off from Europe and became 'every day more provincial and enclosed'.[110]

Bataillon is undoubtedly right to emphasise the continuing appeal of Erasmus in Spain, but our perception of these years suggests that Erasmianism was only one, and not always the most important, of the influences that helped to shape the Spanish mind. There were also immense, new and Europe-wide horizons being opened up by the reform movement. In the process, there was greater intolerance of old ways. Among the earliest foes the Catholic reformers engaged was what they considered the vice of novels of chivalry. In 1567 Jerónimo Lemos criticised the practice whereby 'if someone is depressed because of an illness or because of some misfortune that has happened and wants consolation, he does not take up books of holy comfort but rather an *Amadis of Gaul* or a *Florián*.'[111] The Franciscan fray Francisco Ortiz Lucio in 1589 condemned the genre: 'there is no purpose and little profit in reading the Celestinas, Dianas, Boscans, Amadises, Esplandians and other books full of fanciful lies. The abuse Satan has introduced with these books leads only to the result that the tender maiden and the youth draw from this reading a spur and stimulant to vileness, setting aflame their desires and appetites.'[112] Notwithstanding these and other views, books of chivalry continued to be best-sellers in Barcelona. They formed a substantial part of the stock of the bookseller Damià Bages in 1590, with the *Ruy de Tortosa* selling cheaply at 10d a copy, the *Amadis* more expensively at 7s 6d, and a luxury edition available of the *Orlando Furioso* at £1 10s; his colleague Onofre Gori at the same period had in stock 157 copies of the *Doncella Teodor* at about 4d a copy.[113]

Chivalry thrived in Barcelona. Boosted initially by the jousts which accompanied the ceremonies of the Golden Fleece in 1519 and subsequently by the visits of Philip II who revelled in them, it took on corporate form with the foundation in 1565 of the noble confraternity of the Knights of St George, who periodically put on jousts and tourneys in the Born during the celebration of great feasts.[114] It flourished most at the very time that it was being criticised, and its adepts were not limited to the elite. We can see devotion to it in the treasured book collection of the waxmaker of Barcelona, Egidio Carles. Most likely a veteran of wars in Italy, he had his living room in 1599 lined with twelve religious paintings, including one of Our Lady of the Rosary, and dotted with musical instruments, including a flute, cornets, bagpipe and zither. His books totalled no more than sixteen, but among them the *Orlando Furioso* in Italian, a copy of the *Amadis* in Castilian and another in Italian, the *Tirant lo Blanch* in Catalan, and the *Doncella Teodor*, occupied a special place next to other non-chivalric best-sellers such as a Salamanca edition of the *Guide of Sinners* of Luis de Granada, a volume on the *Corts of Catalonia*, a copy of *Entertainment of Ladies and Gallants*, the *Diana de Montemayor* parts one and two, Pedro de Luján's *Matrimonial colloquies*, part one of the *Flos Sanctorum*, the *Fables* of Aesop in both Latin and Castilian, and a *Dialogue of the Soldier*.[115]

The task was not simply to eliminate the imaginary romances, which were deemed to be incompatible with true religion and learning, but to raise the level of religious literature. A guide to the literature available to Spanish clergy in the opening years of the Counter Reformation is given by Díaz de Luco's *Advice to curates* (1543). An active reformer at Trent and subsequently bishop of Calahorra, Luco put Savonarola, Gerson and other Latin authors at the forefront of his recommended reading; Erasmus – then already under attack – makes no appearance. 'And for those not well instructed in Latin there are nowadays many good books in romance, and many books of confession in romance which I think are beneficial.' It is clear from Díaz de Luco that the capability of reading in Latin was not expected of ordinary clergy, and in Barcelona priests seem to have limited their use of Latin to the basic manuals, preferring the vernacular for other reading: Joan Spuny, canon of the cathedral in 1587, possessed the rite-books ('ordinaris') of Urgell and Barcelona, an old 'much used' Roman missal, a Barcelona missal 'also much used', a book of hours and a Roman missal of the new rite; mossèn Mateu Palau, already referred to above, had a total of nine books in 1600, including the *Directory of Curates* of Coma and Felipe de Meneses' *Light of the Christian soul*.[116] A country priest, the rector of St Sadurní de Conques (Urgell), possessed in 1573 a good stock of seventeen books but virtually all were old breviaries, the exception being a new Roman breviary 'from Antwerp'; he also owned a *Baculus clericalis*, the *Epistles of St Jerome* in Castilian, and the *Book of Ladies*.[117] It goes without saying that a good many literate clergy had impressive Latinity, like Miquel Paret, beneficed priest of the cathedral of Barcelona in 1568, whose collection of 298 titles consisted almost exclusively of Latin theology, the sole exception being a copy of the *Path of the good Christian*.[118]

Ignatius Loyola came to Barcelona in 1524 for his longest and most formative stay. What literature would he have found available in the shops that year, on the eve of the European Reformation?[119] For a city of only some 30,000 people – about the size of Padua, Cologne or Toulouse – the bookshops showed a surprising cosmopolitanism. Although the output of publishing was low, cultural life was fed by an impressive volume of imports, and the riches offered to the public on booksellers' shelves are a clear indication of the discriminating tastes of the reading elite.[120] One possible guide to their tastes may be got from the holdings in that year of the printer-bookseller Joan Bages,[121] whose family continued the business for at least two further generations. His stock of some 570 titles, valued for sale purposes at £217, specialised in classical humanism, most of it apparently imported from Italy, together with Renaissance authors such as Boccaccio and Petrarch. Erasmus was well represented with the *Encomium Moriae*, the *Querela Pacis*,[122] and the *New Testament* (the last at the high price of £2).[123] The survival of Islam as a legal religion in Spain (it was officially suppressed in the Crown of Aragon only from 1526, the year that Ignatius left Barcelona) was shown by the appearance on the shelves of nine copies of the *Koran*. Northern philosophy was represented by the works of Ockham and Hugo of St Victor. There were apparently no books at all in Castilian, and Bages also offered for sale two Bible concordances and a luxury edition of the Bible at £6. Would Ignatius have been edified by this selection?

A generation later, with the Catholic reform movement well under way, our best guide to the type of literature available to the public comes from the holdings of the wealthy printer-bookseller Joan Guardiola, who had his shop in Calceteria street in Barcelona and died in 1561.[124] His stock at that date, two years after the appearance of the Index of Prohibited Books, consisted of some 1854 titles representing the impressive total of 9080 volumes.[125] Apart from 22.3 per cent of the titles which were not classified by subject and described simply as 'bound volumes', those remaining fell into the following subject categories: 19.7 per cent on law, 25 per cent on theology, 4.5 per cent on philosophy, 15.7 per cent on humanities, o.9 per cent on astrology, 6.7 per cent on medicine and 1.9 per cent on music. There was also a small group of 3.3 per cent described as being 'in Castilian', when in fact only about two-thirds were, the rest being in Italian and French. These figures reflect only titles, and a more accurate picture of public demand may be got from the quantities of books, well over half of which were in humanities, with theology representing about a quarter and law just over 10 per cent.

Guardiola was an outlet for books published in France, and about 90 per cent of his stock came directly from publishers in Lyon, with several from Paris and others from Antwerp and Venice. His major offerings to the public were in classical texts: 800 volumes of Ciceronian texts, 196 of Latin grammar, 104 of Terence, 73 of Lucian, 63 of Juvenal, 60 of Aristophanes, were typical items that Catalan scholars and students obviously required. Scholars of Greek were offered Homer, among other works. Renaissance humanism was fully represented, notably by Luis Vives, of whom he offered 47 copies of the *Colloquia*, one volume of *Opera* valued at £5, eight of the *De Anima* at 3s each, six of the *De Veritate Fidei* at 6s each, four of the *De Disciplinis* at 7s 6d each, four of the *Preparatione Animi* at 2s each, two of the *De subventione pauperum* at 1s 6d each, and one each of the *De concordia et discordia*, the *De exhilaratio animi*, and the *Opuscula*.

One author for whom there was a continuing demand in Barcelona in the mid-sixteenth century was Erasmus, if we are to be guided by the holdings of this bookshop. The preference was possibly for his literary works rather than for Erasmian spirituality. Guardiola stocked seventeen copies of the *De copia verborum*, as well as 112 copies of an *Enchiridion ad verborum copia* and one *Epitome copia verborum*; three copies of the *Apophthegmata*, six of *Apologiae*; twenty copies of the *De pueris instituendis*, four volumes of *Epistolae* and four of the *Paraphrases*. The *Enchiridion militis christiani*, which we know was in several private libraries in the city, was either not stocked or had sold out. Biblical scholarship was represented by four Lyon Bibles valued at about £2 each, two Louvain Bibles at £3 10s each, five New Testaments (three in Latin, two in Greek), and one Bible Lexicon published in Cologne. The riches on Guardiola's shelves – in Greek, Latin, French, Italian and Castilian; covering theology, humanities, law, medicine and poetry; imported from Rome, Antwerp, Toulouse, Cologne and Lyon; and ranging in contemporary authors from Alfonso de Castro to François Vatable – are a clear refutation of any idea that Barcelona by mid-century had turned its back on Europe and on humanism and was retreating into provincial insularity.

The popular side of printing was not neglected in the bookshop, which stocked thousands of prints (*stampades*), or fly-sheets containing text and in some cases an illustration: he offered, for example, 1004 grammar-sheets at a penny each, 1260 mass-sheets at twopence each and, for those with more specialised demands, booklets of Aesop's fables at just over 3s each and almanacs at just over 1s each. The range of choice on his shelves was impressive by any standards, and a credit to the Catalan public who bought his wares and contributed to the wealth that he managed to accumulate.

In 1561 the authorities in Castile were still in the grip of the Protestant scare, and in Barcelona the Inquisition had been attempting for two years to implement the 1559 Index of Prohibited Books. Contemplating the bookshelves of Guardiola, the crisis seems remote. Erasmus was on the decline in Castile, which suffered 'the slow disappearance of his name';[126] but in Barcelona his works were still on sale. In Castile Bibles were being rounded up and Lyon and Antwerp Bibles had been under suspicion since 1559; in Barcelona they were still available. With twenty-one copies of the *Imitation of Christ* available in Latin, and twenty-four of the *Cortegiano* in Italian, Guardiola's shop represents the continued survival in Catalonia of Netherlands spirituality and Italian humanism, both soon to be superseded (though not eliminated) by the civilisation of post-Tridentine Catholicism.

The transition to Counter-Reformation publishing in Europe can be measured by one simple index: a rise in output of religious books. Among the new titles licensed at Venice, religious works rose from a proportion of about 16 per cent in 1551–5 to 35 per cent in 1605–7; in all other areas except for law the proportions fell. The tendency is confirmed by figures for the Giolito press at Venice, where religious titles represented some 7 per cent of output in 1541–50, but over 57 per cent in 1581–90.[127] For Spain no such analysis is at present possible, but an examination of the entries in the vast compilation of Nicolás Antonio, the seventeenth-century bibliophile who dedicated himself from his base at Rome to cataloguing the known output of books published by Spaniards, a term in which he also included Catalans and Portuguese, offers a fair impression of trends.[128]

Within the incomplete listing supplied by Antonio, the great rise in output during the peak years of the Counter Reformation stands out clearly. In works relating to doctrine (such as catechisms), he lists 61 titles published between 1526 and 1678: of these only 3 appeared before 1550, but 38 in the half-century 1551–1600, and 19 more in the subsequent half-century 1601–50. For the art of preaching Antonio lists 54 titles published between 1543 and 1674; of these one was published prior to 1563, 21 appeared between 1563 and 1600, and 28 between 1601 and 1650. In this swell of religious books, foreign publishing played a crucial role: of the 38 works on doctrine in the half-century 1551–1600, 8 (21 per cent) were published abroad; of the 49 works on preaching in the period 1563–1650, 14 (28 per cent) came from foreign presses.

The largest number of works on a particular theme was dedicated to what Nicolás Antonio classified as 'moral theology'. He listed 692 titles published by Spanish scholars in the period 1500–1670; if this is broken down into thirty-year periods, the epoch of highest output emerges clearly:

Period	Titles
1500–29	15
1530–59	72
1560–89	115
1590–1619	199
1620–49	204
1650–70	86

Of these titles some 25 per cent in the years 1590–1619 were published outside the country, with Lyon emerging in the seventeenth century as the most favoured foreign city for Spanish theologians to publish their works.[129] From these data it would not be rash to suggest that about a quarter of the religious works published by Spaniards during the Counter Reformation came from foreign presses.

Within this context of a growth in publishing the Catalans played a very modest role, rendered more so by the fact that the explosion of literary output was in the Castilian language. Some stimulus was nevertheless given to Catalan publishing, as may be seen by the chronology of nearly five hundred licences granted by the crown to Barcelona publishers.[130] Of these, 19 were in the 36 years 1519–55, with a significant rise in subsequent twenty-year periods: 67 in 1556–76, 100 in 1577–97, 132 in 1598–1618; and then a falling away in the seventeenth century, with 55 in 1619–39, 27 in 1640–60, and 32 in 1661–81. Over two-thirds (some 68 per cent) of licences were for books on religion, theology and scripture; the only other large categories were 9.7 per cent for history and 8.7 per cent for grammar.

The part played by Catalan publishing in the explosion of religious literature has two distinct aspects:[131] on the one hand, books written in Catalan came to enjoy a popularity unprecedented in the history of the principality; on the other, Catalan printers kept their industry alive by producing Castilian works on a scale not before possible.

Four categories of works in Catalan enjoyed an enduring success. First came those which won an immediate readership within their cultural area because they were pioneering handbooks which responded to a need. Typical of these within the secular area was fray Miquel Agustí's *Book of the Secrets of Agriculture*; but the runaway winner in the religious field was by Pere Màrtir Coma, whose *Directory* (1566) became the one essential manual for Catalan rural clergy for at least a century, was translated into Castilian in 1572, and could be found in every bookshop in Barcelona and in the possession of many a rector throughout the province.[132] In a different class and closely rivalling the *Directory*, was Coma's *Doctrina Christiana* (1569), which even in 1667 was probably the chief catechism used in Catalonia.[133] Other manuals by Catalans, whose popularity is harder to judge for lack of information, included catechisms such as the *Instructio* (1588) by Pere Caldes and the *Christian Doctrine* (1595) by Gaspar Punter. A second category within the same field of devotion and practice was represented by translations of non-Catalan authors. Catechisms in Catalan led the way in simple terms of sales, with the notable examples of the *Doctrine* (1579, published by Jaume Cendrat) of Peter Canisius; and those by Nieremberg, Ledesma, and Bellarmine. Ledesma remained for over a century the officially recommended school textbook in the principality. In a third category came ecclesiastical publications and guides used by every parish priest, such as the volumes of *Mandates* issued by Dimas Loris (1598) and Cassador (1593), or sermon guides such as that by Capella (1593). Finally, there were popular works in demand by confraternities and re-edited generation after generation, among them the best-selling work by Geroni Taix on the Rosary.

Most of these works by their nature would have reached a far broader audience than we might imagine if we think of a book as an object bought by óne person, read only by him, and deposited in his library. With this in view, analysis of private libraries becomes a misleading exercise, for one is dealing not with the private culture of the literate elite but with the capacity of a single book to reach hundreds. The presence of only two Catalan books in a village – a guide to preaching for the rector, a catechism for the school – might have cultural consequences of permanent importance for the community.

Though a long-term disservice to the culture of Catalonia, the ability of printers to publish Castilian works was of inestimable importance to the reshaping of religious reading habits in the principality. The publication of Martín de Azpilcueta's *Manual of Confessors* by Bornat in 1567 was perhaps the first important step in introducing a Catalan public to the religious classics being produced elsewhere in the peninsula. A major contribution was made by Damià Bages, who in 1588 issued the *Guide of Sinners* and the *Book of Prayer* of Luis de Granada; the volumes were not cheap, retailing at £1 10s for a *Guide*. In 1589 Hubert Gotard brought out the *Creed* (*Introducción del Símbolo de la Fe*) of Granada, which seems to have retailed for 13s 6d. These and similar classics were the vanguard of the 'devout invasion' which helped to give Catalans and Castilians a common background in their religious aspirations: the process is fairly easy to follow in terms of bibliography, but does not form part of our theme here.

The appearance of Catalan religious books raises again the theme of the so-called 'decadence' of Catalan literature. 'The fact of decadence', it has been pointed out,[134] 'does not depend on the number of writers in Catalan nor on the number of books written ... What decayed was the literary impulse.' There can be no dispute over this conclusion. Counter-Reformation literature in Catalonia had no creative or artistic impulse: it was directed to what it saw as a greater glory, the saving of souls for God. In the process, however, it helped to keep alive the language of the people and conserved for Catalans a religious individuality and identity which might otherwise have been swamped by the cultural imperialism of Castile. The Counter Reformation contributed to the preservation of the indigenous language because it shied away from literary brilliance and elite culture, areas in which it could not compete with Castilians, and concentrated on direct communication with the people through the media of the spoken word and popular tracts. 'Decadence', consequently, becomes a question of perspective. As a scholar has acutely observed, 'underneath every decadence there is still a people, and the moments of decadence of a literature do not always coincide with a decline in the vitality of the people.'[135] Moreover, among this people there was a continuous circulation of printed works which, like Taix's book on the Rosary, have been rejected with scorn by professional scholars but which kept alive for generations the contact between the spoken and the printed word.

Though Catalonia was a society with a primarily oral and visual culture the effort of the reformers was not restricted to these media, and considerable emphasis was placed on the printed word when it came to propaganda. Perhaps the most extensively used of fly-sheets was the goig, but as we have seen this was a product of the local community rather than of the missionary clergy and was in any case notable for the poverty of its visual images.[136] On balance the Catholic preference was for attracting people to the public liturgy, where the oral interest of the sermon and the sensual appeal of music and the altar tended to make the world of the book super-fluous. Indeed, it may be argued that one great advantage of the Church in the post-Reformation period was that it continued to control all the cultural images that predominated in late mediaeval society and therefore did not need to invent new forms: traditional symbols such as the relic of a saint or the Christmas crib were (as they were termed in fifteenth-century England) 'books of the common man', and served perfectly to communicate the message.

The culture of the Counter Reformation in Barcelona during its first generation continued to be infused by Erasmus. Long after the Dutch scholar had fallen into disfavour in the court of Spain, his books could be found on the Mediterranean coast. In 1558 the Roman Index had condemned all his works; in 1559 the Spanish Index condemned a handful, including the *Enchiridion* and the *Colloquies*, but left the *Adages*, the *Commentary on the New Testament*, and others. In the 1583 Index the *Adages* (unless expurgated) were added to the forbidden list and that of 1612 further extended the expurgations, but by then, Bataillon reminds us, 'Erasmianism was no more than a memory'.[137] Occasional authors in Castile, such as the Franciscan Juan de Pineda,[138] could be found citing Erasmus well into the last years of the century, but such cases were rare. If Erasmus faded away, it was not only because of the efficacy of the Inquisition but also because of the very fragile roots of northern humanism in the peninsula. In Barcelona, by contrast, the Inquisition was far less effective, and Erasmus survived to a degree unknown elsewhere in the peninsula.

In 1568, ten years after the Castilian crisis of 1558–9, the protonotary royal (that is, legal secretary) of the Council of Aragon, Miquel Amat, returned from Madrid to die in his native Barcelona. The small number of some twenty works which he kept in a wooden cabinet at his home were the titles he most treasured, and drew admiration for their beauty from the notary who inventoried them.[139] They included the *Spiritual ABC* of Francisco de Osuna, the fundamental spiritual treatise of the early century, in five volumes; the *Works* of Lucian of Samosata, possibly in the Venice 1522 edition (in Greek); titles in Latin including four volumes of the works of Cicero, 'in a hard cover, well printed and in very good condition', the *Decades* of Livy, 'very well printed', and a volume of Pliny; a *Cornucopia latinae linguae*; three volumes of the *Summa artis notariae* of the thirteenth-century authority Rolandino, 'covered in blue leather, with gold leaf, very well bound'; and the *Annotations on the New Testament* of Desiderius Erasmus, 'very well printed'. They obviously represented the jewels of Amat's collection. At the same time he kept in a trunk at a little country house he owned just outside Barcelona, at Mas de Salas, fourteen titles which included the *Vocabulary* of Nebrija, a Latin thesaurus in three volumes, the decrees of the Council of Trent, the chronicle (in Catalan) of Ramon Muntaner, the *Variae* of Magnus Aurelius Cassiodorus, almost certainly in the Augsburg 1533 edition, and the works of Dr López de Villalobos. There can be no finer evidence of the survival of humanism at the highest level in mid-century Barcelona than the books of the protonotary.

His son, Miquel Joan Amat, who became protonotary of the viceroy in Barcelona and archivist of the Royal Archive in the city,[140] died in 1619. He kept a personal library which by then had grown to fifty titles, but the core of the collection was still his father's treasured books, and Cicero, Livy and Erasmus continued to lie side by side in the cabinet with the new editions, which included Luis de Granada's *Creed*, Meneses's *Light of the soul*, Francisco Solsona's *Lucerna Laudemiorum* (published in Barcelona in 1556), two volumes in octavo of Juan Luis Vives, and volumes of Horace and Suetonius.[141]

A parallel case is that of Dr Francesc Romeu, judge of the Audiència of Catalonia, whose library, according to the inventory made at his death in Barcelona in 1554, contained some 542 titles representing well over two thousand volumes,[142] with not a single volume in Castilian. Although the vast bulk of his books were legal studies, Romeu also possessed a *Theologia Mística* by Henry Herp and a volume of Denis the Carthusian (both soon to be condemned in the Index of 1559), the *Imitation of Christ*, three Bibles of unstated provenance, a New Testament, the *Modus orandi Deum* and the *Enchiridion militis Christiani* 'Erasmi' (both also to be condemned in the 1559 Index), and an 'Erasmus *De contemptu mundi*'.[143] Possession of the books, in such a large library, tells us little about Romeu's real views, but it is significant that the works of Netherlandish piety figure prominently among the small number of volumes which were not on law. It was by no means exceptional among the educated elite to have Erasmus, who figured also in the library of Diego Pérez.[144] Those who had the volumes, kept them; the over-scrupulous canon of the cathedral, Serafí Masdovelles, who handed over his copy of Erasmus's *Colloquies* to the Inquisition in 1540,[145] was entirely exceptional. As late as 1586, when the noble Pere Vila of Tarragona died, his inventory of books[146] included three Bibles, and the following works of Erasmus: the *Apophthegmata* (in Castilian), *Annotationes in Novum Testamentum* (two copies, one apparently in Catalan),[147] *Lingua, Enchiridion militis christiani*, the *Adagia*, and the *Paraphrases*, all of them forming easily the most impressive holding of Erasmus so far known in Catalonia. Vila's undoubted humanist leanings may be judged in part by his library, which consisted of 300 titles adding up to some 600 volumes, most on classics and philosophy, including three Greek-Latin dictionaries and a French-Latin dictionary (he had, for example, the *De Oficiis* of Cicero in French); and in part by his international interests, with editions by François Bauduoin (on Justinian) and Pierre Ramée (on Cicero) jostling for space with Bembo, Valla, Sadoleto, Contarini and Scaliger. Like Romeu, he appears to have had almost nothing in Castilian apart from the Erasmus volume.

It would be wrong to suppose that disapproved books disappeared when the inquisitors began their searches, which we have already judged to be inefficient. Just as his works had featured with impunity in Catalan bookshops and private libraries in mid-century despite the reaction in Castile, Erasmus continued to be openly on sale in more than one Barcelona bookshop well into the last years of the reign of Philip II, and his *Colloquies*, banned in 1559, were published in Barcelona in 1568 by the printer Claude Bornat.[148] The printer-bookseller Pau Cortey in 1572 offered for sale the *Apophthegmata* of Erasmus, two copies of the *Paraphrases* 'Erasmi', and nine copies of the *Copia verborum*,[149] together with Hebrew grammars and several books in Greek in addition to the normal stock in Latin. Antoni Oliver was one of the city's prominent printer-booksellers, and in 1585 published a Catalan version of Nebrija's *Grammar*.[150] On his shelves in 1590 were a bound copy of the *Adagia* of Erasmus (banned in the Index of 1583), assessed at a trade price of 9s; an unbound copy of the same, in folio, assessed at the remarkable price of £4 10s and therefore presumably still in demand;[151] Erasmus' *Commentary on the New Testament*; twenty-four copies of Erasmus's *Copia verborum*; twenty inexpensive copies of the *Colloquies* of Luis Vives at 2s each and eight luxury copies at 9s 3d each.[152] Whatever his fate in other bookshops of the peninsula, in Barcelona Erasmus was still on sale. In Perpinyà in the same period the registers for course texts at the university (the Studi General) show that the *Colloquies* in the Virués version were a set-book together with Virgil, Cicero, Terence and Cato.[153]

Thanks to the inefficacy of systems of control, the book trade in Barcelona seems to have been flourishing long after the imposition of censorship. Though a high proportion of works was imported, the booksellers managed to continue a modest level of production in the three languages Catalan, Latin and Castilian. In part this was because they would when necessary pool resources: we have for example the contract drawn up in August 1566 between ten printer-booksellers of Barcelona, among them Damià Bages, forming a small limited company (for three years) to 'print and sell books'; and in 1572 the printer Claude Bornat also signed a five-year agreement with a colleague to print books.[154] The inventoried household effects of the booksellers leave an impression of economic well-being and in some cases of wealth, allowing us to suppose that it was not a decaying profession. A glance at the holdings of four booksellers of the 1590s, when the major policies of both Church and state would have had a generation to take effect, will give us a fair impression of what was and was not available to the public in Counter-Reformation Barcelona, and what the booksellers themselves thought worth offering for sale. The sample is fairly large, some 3000 listed titles representing a combined total of about 12,500 volumes which, since the stock of all four certainly over-lapped in many areas, may have amounted in practice to between 1500 and 2000 titles.

The printer-bookseller Onofre Gori at his death in 1595 left a stock of some 358 titles adding up to well over a thousand volumes, which were bought by a colleague for £458.[155] The works stocked by Gori in large quantity may safely be taken as a guide to their popularity in their respective fields: in business, 223 copies of the *Book of the Consolat del Mar*; in public health, 551 copies of Bruguera's *De Peste*; in education, 47 copies of Ledesma's *Grammar*; in light reading, 157 copies of the *Doncella Teodor* and 16 of the *Fables* of Aesop. By far the biggest category was religious books, with the front-runners being the 51 copies of the first part of the *Flos Sanctorum* (one of the hidden best-sellers of the age); 129 copies of the *Rosary* of Bosch; 288 of the works of fray (soon to be canonised) Pedro de Alcántara; thirty-three of the *Imitation of Christ*; thirty-four of the *Art of serving God*; forty-four of Jaume Montanyes' *Aid for Dying* (1577) in Castilian; fifty-five of the *Colloquies* of Vives; and 149 of the *Confessionary* by Victoria.

With a broad range of stock covering music, education, military science and medicine in addition to the larger categories, Gori's shop was a treasure-house for bibliophiles. We may pick out two new trends. Though religious literature of the previous age was still in demand, with the continuing popularity of Luis Vives – three copies of his *Opuscula* and two of his *Veritate fidei* were on offer, in addition to the *Colloquies* – there was a firm presence of

Counter-Reformation books, notably Coma's *Directory*, and Diego Pérez' *Salutary Documents* and his *Art of Preaching*. The second trend was the entry of books in Castilian, even to the extent of offering Muntanyes in that language.

As in the case of Gori, the holdings of the printer and bookseller Damià Bages give us a good view of items available in Barcelona a generation after the Council of Trent. In 1590, at his death, the stock was valued by two colleagues at £1531, the trade price rather than the value of the books to the public.[156] The shop contained some 597 titles adding up to over 2000 volumes. Well under half the volumes were in Latin, with books on theology, law and medicine dominating the subject matter in this language: foreign titles included several liturgical books printed in Venice; four Lyon Bibles by Guillaume Rouillé dated 1581, ten breviaries by the same, and two Bibles annotated by Vatable.[157] His stock also included four unidentified *Enchiridion* in 16e published by Eguía (the publisher of Erasmus' *Enchiridion*), and a copy of Luis Vives' *De disciplinis*. The bulk stock was all in Castilian: thirty-nine copies of the *Lazarillo de Tormes*, seventy-two copies of Boscán, and a large selection of works on chivalry, all in Castilian, including eight copies of the *Amadis*. The channels through which Castilian began to undermine Catalan among the reading public are evident from this range of books. Like some other dealers, Bages specialised in producing prints (*stampades*). As a printer of books perhaps his best-known publication was the Barcelona edition of Luis de Granada's *Guide of Sinners*, valued in the inventory at £1 10s a copy; but his biggest investment was in printing *pontificals* or diocesan guides, of which his shop stocked 171, valued at £1 10s each.

The holdings of the bookseller Antoni Oliver amounted at his death in 1590 to 254 bound titles representing 760 volumes, and 463 unbound titles adding up to 3665 volumes. He had books from the major foreign presses, Italy obviously, but also the Antwerp presses of Plantin (two copies of Kempis, one of 'Enchiridion Psalmorum', and a *Summa of St Thomas* priced at £9) and items from Paris (a breviary, and two *Histories* by Herodian of 1588 at the steep price of £13). There were also numerous liturgical items which – apart from the works by Erasmus noted above – may have fallen within the category of 'prohibited books': four Bibles, priced between £1 and £2, one of them a 'Honorati', and presumably therefore from Sébastien Honorat at Lyon, and one 'cum figuris'; a 'New Testament', apparently in Catalan;[158] and four Roman missals by Guillaume Rouillé of Lyon, one valued at £5, the others at £1 15s each (the Index of 1559 had condemned the edition of

1550).[159] Apart from a big stock of 845 'unbound vocabularies', of which Oliver himself may have been the publisher, the major items held were all related to aspects of Counter-Reformation piety and education: ten copies of Coma's *Directory of Curates*, ten *Books of the Rosary*, thirteen of the *Imitation of Christ* (not including the two Plantin copies, which cost 12s each compared to the 3s of the Spanish editions), 23 bound *Catechisms* of Canisius and 280 unbound (the former costing 2s each, the latter 6d), 120 confessionaries of Polanco, 102 copies of the *Brief Art* of Ramon Llull, 23 Barcelona editions of the Council of Trent, and 300 confessionaries of Martín de Ayala (issued in Catalan in Barcelona in 1579).

Our fourth and final example is the printer and 'book-merchant' Nadal (or Noel) Barassó, who lived off the plaça del Rei and had a printing press which at the time of his death in 1594 was actively producing several books, with the *Flos Sanctorum* and the *Psalms* waiting in their frames for publication. His stock contained 1333 titles which, with the bulk copies he stored, represented a total of some 5000 volumes.[160] This massive quantity of books covered the four major areas of religion, law, the humanities and medicine, with a stock of 120 *romanceros* featuring prominently among the popular literature. As a printer of the work, Barassó held over a hundred copies of the *Flos Sanctorum*. Greek humanism survived in the form of ten titles dealing with the language, and Luis Vives was well represented with his *Works*, the *De disciplinis*, and the *Instruction of a Christian woman*. The Counter Reformation inevitably determined, as with the other booksellers, the type of manual most in demand: he had a hundred copies of the *Catechism* of Ledesma in Catalan, 214 copies of the Roman breviary, sixty-eight of Alonso de Madrid's *Art of serving God* (three-quarters of a century after its publication – Seville 1521 – still a seller), and one of the *Salutary Documents* of Diego Pérez. The most surprising aspect of Barassó's stock were the fourteen Bibles on his shelves: four were the Plantin Bible of Philip II, but at least three others were on the Inquisition's prohibited list: the Vatable Bible published at Paris; a Lyon Bible, possibly that of 1551, since it is described as being 'with plates', which in that edition were by Holbein; and a Torneso Bible, known to have been issued at Lyon in 1567 and featuring in the 1583 Index of the Inquisition. In addition he had a New Testament, very likely also prohibited, since it is inventoried as being 'incogniti', by an unknown publisher.

Though it is impossible to identify satisfactorily the bulk of the books on sale, the stock of these booksellers in the last decade of the sixteenth century[161] belies any image we may have of intellectual poverty in Catalonia. To offer works for which there was no market would have been commercial suicide, and there is no sign that Barcelona traders lacked acumen: they faithfully met the demand for Latin textbooks in law, humanities and medicine, and at the same time filled their shelves with the religious manuals which were probably their chief source of income.

What changes, if any, took place in reading during the first generation of the Counter Reformation? Our most direct guide is to compare the holdings of Guardiola in mid-century (even though they were largely foreign in origin) with those of the four traders at the end of the century. There were obvious elements of continuity. First, the book trade in Barcelona did not shrink and continued to supply clients with a full range of titles, of which a high proportion continued to be drawn from outside the peninsula. Nor was the stock old, since Oliver had a volume from Paris dated 1588 and Bages had four Rouillé Bibles from Lyon dated 1581. Second, censorship was either ineffective or, more likely, was frankly ignored by both sellers and buyers of books, and none of the authors to be found in mid-century, including Erasmus, was absent from the shelves in the 1590s. Nor is there any record of booksellers in Barcelona being punished by the authorities for their insubordination apart from the single occasion in 1593 referred to above.[162] Third, the international nature of the book trade was uninterrupted: the major works of foreign legists and theologians who wrote in Latin were readily available, and the publishing houses of Italy (especially Venice), Antwerp, Cologne, Lyon and Paris managed to get their wares sold in Barcelona with no apparent difficulty.

But there were also significant changes. For a Catalan public the first and most obvious novelty was the big increase in Castilian literature. Of Guardiola's entire stock of 9080 volumes in mid-century, only about 65, or 0.7 per cent, were in Castilian, and even of those many had been published abroad, such as the *Cancionero General*, published in Antwerp, or the *Orlando Furioso*, in Lyon, with the only important native edition being the works of Boscán, published in Barcelona (1543). In the 1550s books in Barcelona were principally in Latin, with a few Catalan items either in manuscript (Dr Francesc Romeu had a 'handwritten' confession manual) or, more rarely, printed (Romeu had the Barcelona 1482 edition of Josephus in Catalan). Fifty years later a major transformation had taken place. Though Latin books were still in front, since all the leading works in theology and the professions were normally published in that language, the proportion of Castilian had risen appreciably: some 18 per cent of the stock of Bages, measured either in titles or in quantity, was in Castilian. Much of this increase was brought about by the Counter Reformation, but Bages' stock indicates also a steady infiltration of non-religious items, principally the chivalric type of literature represented by the *Amadis*, the *Ruy de Tortosa*, and the *Coplas* of Jorge Manrique. On the religious front, as we have noted in the preceding chapter, the Castilian offensive was decisive: though the Counter Reformation gave a powerful boost to the use of Catalan (the popularity of Coma, Ledesma and Ayala is evident), it also opened the floodgates to Spain's majority language, with Azpilcueta (of whom Barassó had no less than thirteen titles), Luis de León and Luis de Granada prominent among the volumes on the shelves. Nor should this be misunderstood as an invasion fomented by outsiders. On the contrary it was the booksellers of Barcelona who promoted the explosion of Castilian.

A second major change between the 1550s and the 1600s, one associated directly with the Counter Reformation, was the rise of the popular best-seller. The popular content of Guardiola's stock had consisted of fly-sheets such as the grammar leaflets or the almanacs, usually printed in Catalan, which cost one or two pennies. From this there was an enormous jump, both in cost and in culture, to the elite literature of the same epoch, normally published in Latin. The *Flos Sanctorum*, which by its own standards was a best-seller of that period and featured in nearly every private library, cost over £1 and was clearly out of the reach of the general public. By the end of the century the didactic needs of the Counter Reformation had called into existence a wholly new (for Spain) and cheap religious literature: for example, in Oliver's stock the Polanco confessionaries cost a halfpenny, the Ayala confessionaries 1s, the Canisius catechisms 7d, and the *Brief Art* of Llull 1s. For comparison, we should note that at this period a chicken in the market or a man's cap might cost between 1s and 2s. Clergy with few means would still have found Coma's *Directory* at 5s from Oliver a convenient buy (Gori offered the same book for 2s). One of the reasons why fray Pedro de Alcántara was popular was the price: Gori sold his copies for under 1s, Bages for just over. The *Confessionary* of Victoria was offered by Gori at 2d, the *Instruction for hearing Mass* at 3d. It was still no doubt a society that did not buy books, but the multiplication of cheap booklets, whether in Castilian or in Catalan, must have contributed significantly to the instruction of the population, with manuals such as the Catalan *Method for learning grammar*, at 1s a copy (in Gori's shop), helping to spread the basics of language.

This cheap literature was supplemented by the fly-sheets which had already been popular but which during this period were further adapted to the demands of the public. Often richer in their illustrated content than the goigs, the fly-sheets might use popular melodies to spread a didactic message. A typical example is the *Fifteen Mysteries of Our Lady of the Rosary*, a two-leaf sheet issued by Sebastià de Cormellas in 1592 and 1603, which had on the first page an attractive engraving to accompany the chain of pious verses.[163]

Three generations after the provincial council of Tarragona of 1565, literary Barcelona had been fully absorbed into the Hispanic world, which by extension also included the Italian world. The personal library of Domingo Cros, priest of Sta Maria del Mar, included among its thirty-seven titles in 1634 a volume of Bellarmine and a copy of Ribadeneira on *The Schism of England*, along with more standard evidence of culture such as Virgil, Terence, Valla, Arias Montano and Agustí's work on agriculture. That of the merchant Luis Miralles in 1647 (a total of eight books) included a life of Carlo Borromeo.[164] By far the best guide available to the literary world of Barcelona at this epoch, however, is the bookshop of Sebastià de Cormellas, who died in 1667.[165] One of the most successful printers of seventeenth-century Barcelona,[166] Cormellas published at least twenty-seven known titles in Catalan and owned in the street called the Call a highly professional press which boasted a wide range of type-face, including fount for Greek, Hebrew and music. His study-room reflected the age: it was covered with about thirty paintings, including a picture of the Escorial and oils of the archetypal Counter-Reformation saints Francis Xavier and Carlo Borromeo. He also managed a bookshop which on its shelves stocked 793 titles, some 3000 volumes which took the notary four days to inventory, leaving us in the process a perspective of one of the most remarkable book collections of Golden Age Spain.

Cormellas' shop was in effect a repository of the entire achievement of Spain's great age of literary creation. Specialising in three main areas – history, literature and religion – with very little in Latin and humanities and law, his shelves stocked both early literature and the very latest works. Inevitably the bulk of his volumes were in Castilian, and a prospective buyer would have been able to choose items such as Calvete on Philip II's journeys, Méndez Silva on population, the Inca Garcilaso de la Vega, Tomás Mercado on trade, the *Romancero General*, the novels of María de Zayas, the *Enterprises* of Saavedra Fajardo, Las Casas on the *Destruction of the Indies* (a work prohibited by the Inquisition just seven years before), the collected works of Lope in some eighty volumes, and the works of Quevedo, Cervantes and Góngora. Catalans could find Bosch's *Titles*, Roig's *Book of Ladies* and Agustí's *Agriculture* among the many offerings. An earlier spirituality was still available with the *Imitation of Christ*, Meneses' *Light of the Soul* and a *Mental Prayer* of Llull, while the impact of the Counter Reformation could be found in the numerous works on sale by Luis de Granada, Philip Neri, Luis de León, St Teresa (her letters in two volumes), Nieremberg and others. The persistence of chivalry could be seen in the appearance of the *Orlando Furioso*, and an intriguing (because banned by the Inquisition) item was the *Works* of Antonio Pérez. Although there was ample recognition of non-Castilians, particularly with the offer of Latin-Spanish and French-Spanish dictionaries and one of French-Spanish-Catalan, together with occasional books in other languages, the overwhelming first impression to be obtained from contemplating Cormellas' stock is of a juggernaut of Castilian literature crushing all else in its way. Many of the books on sale were certainly printed abroad – Nieremberg, for example, tended to be published in Lyon – but distinctively foreign culture was prominent by its absence; and the role assigned to Catalans was very small indeed.[167]

However, in addition to this rich collection of offerings Cormellas had in his underground storeroom a total of over one thousand titles, 15 per cent of them full size, 32 per cent in quarto, and 53 per cent in small format, adding up to several thousand copies. The small-format collection, equivalent to the pocket-size works of the twentieth century, offers a somewhat different impression from that gained by looking only at the main bookshop, and gives a truer guide to popular demand in seventeenth-century Barcelona. Though most of the titles were stocked in small quantity there were others whose appearance in multiple copies obviously reflected demand: twenty copies of the Guzmán de Alfarache, fifty-two of the novels of María de Zayas, fifty-five of *The lame Devil* of Vélez de Guevara, eighty-one of the *Flower of Lovers*, 128 of the *Triumph of the Faith* of Lope de Vega. The demand for Cicero – easily the most read Latin author in early modern Catalonia – was reflected in 141 copies of his *Letters* and 101 of *Sentences*. The continuing popularity of Luis Vives could be seen in the '243 Luis Vives' entered in the inventory, almost certainly the *Colloquies*, which Cormellas also stocked in normal format in the main bookshop. Items in Catalan were without doubt the most impressive in terms of quantity, from the one hundred Bellarmine catechisms and the 266 of Pere Màrtir Coma to the 329 almanacs, the 68 leaflets on Sta Eulàlia, the 913 *Hours of Our Lady*, the 1304 leaflets on St Antony and the 1053 *Booklets of the Rosary*. The figures leave no doubt that at a popular level in the 1660s Catalan was still actively read in Barcelona.

A past generation of scholars, accepting too easily the traditional pessimistic picture of a principality overwhelmed by the elite culture and the weapons of war of Castile, saw only provincialism and decadence in seventeenth-century Barcelona, but the bookstore of Cormellas presents to us a quite different reality, of a city which had long since cast aside its small-town mentality and had entered into the more cosmopolitan world of the Habsburg empire, taking on board the expansion of Castilian creativity while still conserving for the Catalan public their well-known classics and the popular fly-sheets which were the main vehicle of piety in the principality.

CHAPTER NINE

Conclusion: A Christian Society?

If my sources have not told me the truth then I have not written it either, and he who wishes to be well informed will go to those who know better than I. Farewell.

mossèn Pere Santacana, rector of Mediona, 1603

The reshaping of faith and culture in Catalonia was a long, slow process of which the protagonists themselves were barely conscious, particularly away from the big towns in rural communities such as Mediona. After the opening years of the seventeenth century few significant changes were made in the churches of Mediona, and rural piety followed the lines laid down in the half century after the council of Tarragona. Testaments continued however to rely on the security offered by the masses of St Amador, and anniversary masses remained the exception rather than the rule.[1] The wishes of testators reflected only one major change, the growth of devotion to the Sant Crist of Mediona, a frequent beneficiary of legacies and perhaps the major theme of the local *goigs* in the seventeenth century; otherwise, the transition from old piety to new was almost imperceptible.

Everyday life in the *terme* began to betray stresses which in their turn affected local devotions. 'As is the custom since time immemorial' (the phrase is from 1657), the chief citizens of both St Quintí and Santa Maria met in the cold air of the castle ruins every January seventeenth, the feast of St Antoni Abat, to elect their *jurats* and to treat of community matters. But their deliberations reflected the onset of economic problems in the principality. In October 1625 the *consell* of St Quintí recognised that there was a recession:

In view of the misfortunes of the town and the problems it has today in meeting back-payments and present payments, and since as everyone knows no reductions can be made in them, it is proposed we approach His Excellency our lord the duke of Cardona and request him to grant, in view of the many problems of the town over past years and the lack of receipts to deal with them, that we may contract out the inn, the bakery, and the sales of oil and fish for a fixed period with the aim of paying off the *censals* and other burdens the town has to meet every year.[2]

The times were getting bad, the harvests poor. From 1625 Mediona began to suffer from the long period of crisis that reached its peak in the 1630s and affected the whole principality.[3] The *pagesos* turned their eyes to heaven. In May 1626 'the Consell of the Universitat of the town of St Quintí assembled in the town hall ... all unanimously and in conformity swore that they and their successors would observe as a feast the day of the glorious St Isidore on the fifteenth of May every year as long as the world shall last (mentres que mon sera mon).'[4] The adoption of St Isidore was only incidentally a question of the extension of Castilian influence; more fundamentally, it was a desperate move made throughout many communities of Catalonia to find another intercessor where the old saints seemed to have failed. The drought of 1626 brought another solemn vow. In March the consell of St Quintí decided that

> since we have the figure of the glorious Sta Madrona in the priory church and she has no obligatory feast day and since she is the most appropriate for obtaining rain in times of drought, all as one have sworn that they and theirs will observe the feast on the Sunday nearest the fifteenth of March, when every year a procession will be made to the chapel of Sta Anna.[5]

It was within these years and most probably in the disastrous year 1630 (of which a Barcelona chronicler commented that 'we feel that the end of the world has come')[6] that heaven came to the rescue of Santa Maria. Out in the fields one day a farmer at the plough struck a buried object which turned out to be an old crucifix; recovered and cleaned, and with the wound from the plough still on it, the crucifix was taken in triumph by vicar and people to the church, where it is venerated even today as the Sant Crist of Mediona.[7]

The needs and crises of the terme determined its devotions, and the century continued to produce crises. In 1638 Santa Maria petitioned the duchess of Cardona against St Quintí, since the town had decided to lease out the inn and bakery 'without the agreement of the whole terme' and 'to the prejudice of poor people'. The internal dispute in the terme was rapidly overtaken by the outbreak of war with France, when the jurats of Santa Maria, meeting in the castle, 'decided that they had to buy arms, namely arquebuses, swords and pikes, on the order of the king because of the outbreak of wars in Catalonia'.[8] The secession of Catalonia from Spain in 1641 cost the people of Mediona dear. The parish manual of St Quintí ruefully lists the damage caused to private houses by French troops 'billeted in the terme of Mediona from 24 August 1649 to the end of September of the same year'.[9] The soldiers of Castile in their turn wreaked even greater damage on St Quintí: in January 1651 soldiers 'sacked the town, burnt the sacristy and the parish church of the town, and among other things the public documents and registers of deaths, marriages and baptisms'.[10] Meanwhile the plague was closing in. 'As of today,' the vicar of Santa Maria noted in the margin of his manual, 'there is plague in Vilafranca, in St Pere de Riudebitlles, in Piera, in Vallbona, in Capellades, in La Pobla, in Carme, in St Quintí and in many other places. May God help and protect us.' In June 1652 the bailiff, jurats and other heads of household met in the parish church and undertook the last solemn vow noted in the records that century:

> The greater part of the men of Mediona assembled in the parish church, all with one voice and with much devotion have sworn to observe the feast of the glorious St Antony of Padua and take the saint as intercessor against the plague, trusting that by the favour of the Mother of God, patroness of the terme, and of Saints Sebastian and Roc, and of St Antony of Padua, they will be protected against this misfortune ... On the same day and year they have sworn that on the feast-day of St Roc, which they have also sworn to observe, all will come to morning high mass in the church of Mediona.[11]

After the recovery of Catalonia for Philip IV in 1654, St Quintí and Santa Maria were forced to billet a troop detachment consisting of a lieutenant and six soldiers, and the community protested that 'the terme is exhausted by so many billetings and so many taxes and it is impossible every month to manage to pay £243',[12] a truly monstrous sum for so few inhabitants. In 1657 the consells of both St Quintí and Santa Maria met in emergency session and voted 'unanimously, that lieutenant Don Pedro Planella leave the terme' and voted to pay his expenses.[13] Just over a generation later the War of Succession intruded decisively, with peasant resistance to the royalists centring on St Quintí, sacked by the Bourbon commander in January 1714;[14] but the abolition of the constitutions of Catalonia made little difference, since the jurisdiction of the duke of Cardona was confirmed.

The population expansion of the eighteenth century made its mark on Santa Maria, whose parishioners increased from the 278 souls of communion in 1577 to 400 in 1758 and 638 in 1772;[15] St Quintí at these last two dates had 550 and 650 souls respectively.

On his diocesan visit in 1772 the bishop was moved to find himself
among the simple Christian people of the countryside; he expressed
his joy at visiting 'the smallest villages and meeting those who with
the labour of their hands and the sweat of their brow work to earn
their living'.[16] Two centuries had passed since the instauration of
the Counter Reformation and Mediona seemed to be a Christian
society within a Christian nation. Little appeared to have changed,
least of all the personnel: the parishes were still served by priests
from the *masies*, the vicar of Santa Maria in 1747 being Jaume
Gostems, from the family which had lived in Puigmoltó for over
two hundred years.

A recent study of religious practice at this time in the central
Pyrenees concludes that no qualitative change occurred and that
'the Catholic drive took on here the form of a return to the old
order'; moreover 'for the popular classes the renewal was for
the most part limited to a simple return to old practices and
devotions.'[17] In neighbouring Catalonia the feeling of change is also
at times almost imperceptible, but the conclusion would be misleading. As often before the official Church claimed that it was not
changing and that its innovations were merely reforms or a return
to primitive practice; Church literature itself attempted to disguise
the reality and to maintain the illusion of continuity. The practice of
frequent communion, which provoked an often bitter controversy
in the peninsula and carried over into France with the Jansenist
debates, was presented in manuals as though it were little more
than a long-overdue return to the usage of the primitive Church;
and so with change after change: each was presented not as an
innovation but as a return to normality after decades of neglect.
Whether they were true innovations or not, their cumulative effect
amounted to an attempt to introduce change at every level –
liturgical, social and personal – and the Counter Reformation
can consequently be identified as a true historical event within
the consciousness of Spaniards and of Catalans. Whatever their
criticism of its implications Catholic Catalans clung to the ideal of
Trent, and when in 1641 they transferred their allegiance to the
crown of France they took care to demand of their new masters
'that the sacred Council of Trent be observed in Catalonia completely and integrally as it has been until now'.[18]
    Trent, however, had always been a myth, an ideal to which the
Church aspired but to which the Catholic people paid little more
than lip-service. Even among the clergy there was little satisfaction
with the achievement of Trent, which seemed to have left much
unsolved and moreover created new wounds. Immediately after the

Council's closure a Jesuit in Spain sounded out the reactions of the returning prelates and reported to his general, Laínez, that

> we have learnt from several bishops who were in Trent that they do not come back as pleased with us as we would hope, because of the way we opposed them there, especially over the reformation of the papal Curia, the residence of bishops, and the problem of clandestine marriages; and in general they say that many things which could have been beneficial to the Church were left out because of our opposition.[19]

The sharply differing views over what needed to be done after Trent contrast with the complacent orthodoxy later to be adopted by Catholic writers, who presented the Council as a definitive solution to the problems of the time. The utility of the Council was that it offered clear formulae which could be repeated in provincial assemblies and later in confessors' manuals, but in the daily life of a Catholic nation such as Catalonia the only immediate impact was made by the changes in public liturgy, whereas in every other area generations were to pass before the aspirations of Trent could be implemented, if indeed they were ever put into practice.

The external structure of Catholicism continued untouched, since reform involved no alteration of religion or the social order, and those who directed the process claimed that there had not been any sharp break with the past. Some modern scholars, by contrast, suggest that change was both extensive and radical, arguing that the Catholic reform and its agents were dedicated to the imposition of a novel culture on the traditionalist peoples of Europe, a process which has been termed an 'acculturation of the rural and urban masses'. The court judges set about 'inculcating a new definition of the sacred in the polytheist and animist masses, a new definition of authority and obedience; they took an active part in the vast offensive led by the elites against popular culture'.[20] The argument is one of cultural collision: 'two very different worlds joined and interpenetrated, with traumatic effects,' particularly at the level of popular superstition, where 'the Counter Reformation...was threatening to destroy the ties...that had held society together since the Middle Ages,'[21] and in the process provoked outbursts of witchcraft. In more attenuated form, the view is expressed in the affirmation that 'the militant clergy sought to impose on the masses what was essentially an elite pattern of religion.'[22] This dramatic presentation has little relevance in Catalonia, where imposition of some externals was attempted but took generations to filter down and provoked no traumatic collision, since the nerve centre of everyday religion – the local community – was capable of maintaining its own identity while at the same time absorbing and adapting or rejecting what was offered by the reforms, with the result that some of the most typical of the new developments, such as the Rosary and the confraternities, took root in popular culture and were not destructive of it.

What is certain is that there was change. An older historiography, unsupported by evidence, presented an image of an unchanging Catholic Spain which served as the source of reaction. 'In Iberia the cause of Catholicism and of civilization had become one. Not only was Hispanic Christianity immune to alternatives, but it became a central resource for the renewal of Catholicism and its counter-attack against the north. The soldiers and saints of Iberia ... made Hispanic Catholicism the wellspring of Counter Reformation piety.'[23] The peninsula was presented as a 'fortress' Spain, a 'citadel barred against the outside world',[24] drawing on its great internal resources to fight the heresy outside. The militant images are a mere fraction of the truth: Spanish society was not 'barred against the outside' nor 'immune to alternatives', nor was its piety exclusively Hispanic. If the Catalan experience is in any way representative of what happened in the rest of the peninsula, Spain was too pre-occupied with its own internal deficiencies to wish to export orthodoxy to the other peoples of Europe.

At the opposite pole to the untenable image of a 'fortress' society is the equally unconvincing image of a basically non-Catholic population whose only real dedication was to natural religion, superstition and magic. These forces inevitably played a part in everyday religion (as the missionaries of the time were the first to point out) but seldom if ever intruded into the rites of passage which signposted the progress from birth to death. Clergy in Catalonia never went out to battle against the forces of the night nor were they specifically committed to a campaign against 'popular' culture.[25] The fundamental challenge for them was the contrast between the pre-Tridentine and the post-Tridentine world, between a formal but basically non-clerical and non-sacramental Catholicism in pre-Reformation times, a Catholicism rooted in community norms and agrarian ritual, and the post-Tridentine practice of a religion rigorously defined in terms of clerical privilege, sacramental duty and performance of social obligations.[26]

Put another way, Catalans before the Reformation adhered to the Church as a way of life and used their clergy as ministers of the rites of passage, but they had no effective contact with the sacraments: baptism was primarily a community not a Church rite, confirmation was virtually unknown, confession and communion might at best be attempted once a year, matrimony did not require the Church, and the last rites, as the ultimate entry to another existence, were possibly the only stage at which they might begin to take the role of the Church seriously.[27] The striking absence of a sacramental magic of the Church allowed believers to resort to alternative folk practices which compensated for the inadequacies of the official faith and which in any case seemed not to contradict it. Pre-Reformation religion was at one and the same time both 'Catholic' and 'natural'. The Counter Reformation notoriously succeeded in tidying up this 'Catholic' world: the liturgical calendar was clarified, the prayerbooks were standardised, churches were clean and altars dust-free, the glory of Palestrina and Xurriguera filled the nave with splendour and gold. But was everyday religion effectively reshaped?

A possible parallel may be found in Lutheran Germany, where over half a century after the Reformation the visitation reports still complained of 'godlessness, open scorn for God's word, the gospel and the sacraments, contempt for pastors, gross incivility, not to mention fornication, adultery and every other sort of vice'.[28] The environment and culture of the German lands may have been like that even before the Reformation, but the core issue – the apparent failure of reform – is obvious enough to warrant our broaching it also in the case of Catalonia. In Catalonia the campaign of the Church against traditional subcultures and communal practices which had always formed part of traditional religion, seems largely to have failed because no radical change took place in the social framework within which those practices existed; and the Church had to content itself with a slow assertion of external discipline from above, in the areas it could most directly control or where it could count on the collaboration of secular authority. Within the time-scale of the present book, we can summarise the discipline as falling under three heads: the reform of order, the assertion of the sacraments, and the integration of local with universal Catholicism. All three were fundamentally social rather than religious developments.

The reform of order, barely achieved by the end of the seventeenth century in Catalonia, implied the winning of greater initiative over public matters such as feasts, processions and carnivals, morality, violence and sacrilege; it also implied the power to control members of the clergy.

Assertion of the sacraments, primarily that of penance, had the intended effect of clericalising the Church by making the laity resort to priests with a frequency and respect unknown before; and the role of the priest was further enhanced by the insistence on frequent communion and by the multiplication of anniversary masses. It was the sacrament of matrimony which in Catalonia went through the most substantial change, with far-reaching consequences for Catalan society.

Finally, the acceptance of universal Catholicism at the local level was an almost painless process. It has been suggested that in New Castile there was a persistence of local religion from the mid-sixteenth to the late eighteenth century, and that the piety of the universal Church was adopted and domesticated for local use, with a corresponding decline of devotion to local saints and a remarkable increase in devotion to images of Christ.[29] The process was identical in Catalonia, where as we have seen the villages were happy to absorb new saints and devotions without expressly forgoing the old, though the integration had clear limits: devotions consonant with local piety were acceptable, even where foreign saints such as St Isidore were concerned, provided they conformed to and served the needs of the community. The evolution of the goigs, however, shows that devotions were readily changed, and it was perhaps the unreliability of the lesser saints which encouraged the emergence of what in the end became (apart from devotion to the Virgin) the dominant cult, that of the crucifix or Sant Crist.

Though cities[30] continued to dictate the forms of culture, and the civic piety of Barcelona used the canonisation of Ramon de Penyafort to reassert its hegemony over the principality, the countryside had a continuing and profound role to play in the shaping of belief, and local cults retained their autonomy despite the vigorous attempts of urban missionaries to draw them into a uniformity they invariably refused to accept. The balance between the community and a clericalised religion after Trent is difficult to define. It has been suggested that 'the Baroque age witnessed an unprecedented extension of clerical control over lay piety,'[31] and that a distinction grew up between private and communal religion, with the result that 'piety left the streets for the sheltered altars of parish churches.' The view seems to be based on the urban environment of Zamora, but cannot be applied to Catalonia, where popular piety continued on a firm communal basis. One case history of this may be followed in the development of confraternities of the Blood, for which Perpinyà was notably famous but which extended themselves throughout the principality. In time the confraternities, with their lugubrious flagellation rites, occupied a central part in the foreign image of peninsular religion, and French tourists such as Madame d'Aulnoy supplied with relish bizarre descriptions of the flagellants.

The practice was apparently not Spanish in origin but imported into the peninsula from Italy in the early Renaissance; and the flagellant brotherhoods, normally formed as confraternities of the Cross or of the Blood of Christ, were usually pre-Counter

Reformation in origin. Considerable stimulus was given to it by the Jesuits who, after being initially criticised for not practising 'discipline',[32] went on to become the leading practitioners and could report from their Córdoba college in 1564 that 'our students number 450; even the youngest have their whips (*disciplinas*).'[33] In Barcelona the Confraternity of the Blood appears not to have practised whipping before 1560, but by 1570 its inventory included 'twenty-five sponges' for both men and women, and in 1586 it had 'sixty-six whips'.[34] The 'holy discipline' became generally used in Catalonia during the Jesuit missions.[35] The practice was restricted to men, who were invited to volunteer for the penitential exercise, and the self-flagellation, on a naked body, was always done in a side-room of the church. In one town near Tortosa in 1620 the groans of the flagellants were such that the congregation could barely hear the preacher at mass. In a town near Barcelona in 1633 there were so many volunteers that the Jesuits took over the church for daily whippings; the groans of the penitents were so loud that 'the women, who could not enter inside the church, remained outside on their knees during it, their hands clasped and weeping all through the holy exercise.'[36]

This form of Baroque piety, which northern Europeans always regarded with horror, put down deep communal roots. In the late seventeenth century we find it active in the communities of the Penedès, quite possibly in Mediona but most notably in Vilafranca. As a climax to the Lenten mission by the Jesuits in this town in 1653, the year after the plague:

> the high point was a procession of penitence in which eighty penitents went whipping blood and preceded by over a hundred barefoot young girls dressed in white, their faces covered with black veils. The procession closed with a giant crucifix held by the clergy of the town, who in low and mournful tones sang the psalm Miserere in chorus, followed by all the townspeople reciting the rosary.[37]

When the fathers made another mission to the area in 1671, visiting Capellades and St Quintí among other towns, they found that the drought that year supplied ideal conditions for another penitential procession in Vilafranca:

> many young boys and girls dressed in white ... followed by a great number of penitents, some with iron bars and dragging chains, others with whips of blood, which they shed so copiously that they watered the earth. All the clergy in funereal and devout tones chanting the Miserere, and behind them an infinite number of the people, most of them barefoot.[38]

The procession was repeated when the Jesuits made their next mission to the town in 1679. There is a striking difference between this description and what we know of pre-Counter-Reformation flagellation; in previous epochs the penitents had been a small group, virtually a sect, now they took on the sins of all the community and were supported by the whole community and clergy. The development was a typical one, with the community playing an undiminished role. Religion in Catalonia remained where it had always been, in the community rather than in the church.

Did such impressive communal participation mean that the people were Christianised? Over a century had passed since Trent, and major religious changes had taken place. When the Jesuit fathers Compter and Alegre visited St Quintí in 1681 they were gratified by the attendance at their preaching, and they found the same in neighbouring St Sadurní and St Pere de Riudebitlles: 'in all these places although they are small villages the audiences were big. Much fruit was harvested and many general confessions were made.'[39] But there were still Indies in Catalonia, as the Jesuits themselves testified, not only in the mountains but also in the cities. Their frustration in 1670 with the town of Sarrià (today a suburb of Barcelona) was particularly intense:

> There is no way to explain the ignorance of doctrine to be found continually in the people of that town, and although catechism is taught every Sunday in the parish church as laid down by the sacred Council of Trent, it is usually with little fruit because of the haste of the parish priests and the lack of attention by parishioners; and very few from Sarrià go to hear mass in the parish church, so that there are few on Sundays to listen to the catechism.[40]

In the Pyrenees it was still as though no missionaries had ever been. Preaching in 1675 in the towns of Sirvia, Gurb, Vallferrara and Valleardós, they observed that 'there was a very great need there to teach doctrine, because even the most adult were like children in their knowledge and were ignorant of the most fundamental things... Nearly everyone made a general confession.'[41]

The pace of change was slow, but at no time was it possible to bully the Catalans into accepting new ways. The Inquisition, it has been argued,[42] had the power to affect the beliefs of all Spaniards; but the evidence is incontrovertible that in Catalonia (and possibly in much of Spain as well)[43] the tribunal as a tool of the Counter Reformation had only a minor role. In over ninety per cent of the towns and villages of the principality, during more than three centuries of existence, the Holy Office never once intruded. In sixty per cent of the towns where inquisitorial cases occurred, only one person was cited in more than three hundred years; and in eighty-nine per cent of the towns the number of cases did not exceed three, a maximum of one every century.[44]

The largely marginal role of the Holy Office in Catalonia may be considered from another perspective, through the life of the villages it flitted through. In 1597 the inquisitor Diego Fernández de Heredía took in part of the Penedès during his visitation, and was fortunate to encounter a case in St Pere de Riudebitlles. Anna Fontanelles was denounced to Heredía because when another woman in the village had called her a whore she had replied that 'as such I serve God very well'.[45] The case was dismissed, and the area did not merit the attentions of the Inquisition until ten years later, when Marianna Poch, daughter of a pagès of St Quintí de Mediona and a full-time *beata*, was denounced by nine people for claiming to have had visions of the Virgin Mary and other saints. The inquisitor questioned her, warned her and dismissed the case into the care of the rector; he also advised 'that her fathers set her to work and not let her laze about',[46] no doubt sensible advice. For the villages it was their only recorded contact with the Inquisition in their entire history, and in the case of St Quintí merited no mention in the parish records. Only once again did the area appear, albeit indirectly, in the documentation: Magdalena Monserrada, of the terme of Mediona, was dealt with severely by the Inquisition in 1634 for maintaining that the state of marriage was more perfect than that of the clergy; she was made to abjure her errors in Barcelona, where she apparently lived, and fined £10.[47]

In the brief appearances of the Inquisition in Mediona no part whatsoever was played by the *familiars*. St Quintí in 1600 had two *familiars*, Bartomeu Carmona, then aged fifty-six, and Miguel Salmell, aged thirty: both were farmers from families well established in the town, but played no exceptional role in the life of the community. Nearly every village had a familiar, even tiny settlements such as La Vid, Santa Fe and Plà del Penedès, but they were symbols of a presence which never made itself felt. It is significant that the case in St Pere de Riudebitlles was reported not by the familiar, the sixty-seven-year-old carpenter of the village Jaume Santacana, but by a shrewish woman intent on vengeance.[48]

After its allotted lifespan the impetus of the Counter Reformation decayed. Its rise had been made possible by favourable economic circumstances: a period of economic growth, population expansion, booming trade, and the opening of frontiers into Europe and America. Without the financial resources generated by the expansion most towns would have been unable to construct new churches, endow new religious orders and embellish altarpieces. For Catalonia it was a boom period made even more favourable by its location at the heart of the European imperial system; and when the crisis began to engulf Castile during the early seventeenth century the principality was still in a position to carry on. Nevertheless the reform movement in Spain, like that in France, was in evident disarray by the later seventeenth century. Already in 1633 the city council of Barcelona had decided that there were enough religious foundations to serve the needs of the population,[49] though their reasoning was based on the wholly secular consideration that the city could not service more begging clergy. A look at the problems of the Carmelites suggests further causes peculiar to Catalonia. The conflict of 1641–52 left a permanent mark on this order, in the judgment of its own historian, writing in 1689.[50] In 1600 the order had a total of 106 religious in Catalonia, of whom 92 were native Catalans; in contrast, by about 1660 there was a falling-off in vocations and a particularly notable shortage of Catalans. In addition, commented the chapter-general of 1678, 'the convents are unable to collect the little income that they have, and are getting poorer every day'; the chapter held at Reus in 1681 reported that 'the convents are accumulating debts'. It was clear that the time of expansion had effectively ended, and the chapter of 1678 considered that the peak had been reached in the 1620s ('over fifty years ago').

By the early eighteenth century in the Alt Penedès even some of the most typical devotions of the Counter Reformation were falling into decay. When the bishop visited St Sadurni d'Anoia in 1728 he instructed the rector to 'encourage his parishioners to have devotion to the Blessed Sacrament and become members of the confraternity; and also since he is prior of the confraternity of the Rosary he must try to renew it since it has almost wholly disappeared, and he must exhort them to have devotion to Our Lady.' It was a decay that affected the whole region. In La Vid, 'we have found that the confraternity of Our Lady of the Rosary has almost disappeared; the rector must promote among his parishioners devotion to the Rosary of Our Lady.' In Moja, 'we order the rector to stimulate in his parishioners devotion to the Rosary and attempt to renew the confraternity of the Rosary which we have found totally in oblivion.'[51] The decay was no sign of irreligion, for the communities in these years had moved to other devotions, notably those of the Sant Crist. Nevertheless it was clear that though the reform movement may have changed much, in many parts of the diocese it had not succeeded in uprooting communal traditions. In 1756 in Llinàs the bishop found 'that those getting married do not bother to have a nuptial mass, and there are many who despite repeated requests continue in their neglect'; in La Llacuna in 1758 he had to repeat 'that women be separated from men and on no account sit together'; in Sitges he denounced 'the abuse of dancing in front of the chapels'; and so on through the parishes of the Penedès and Llobregat.[52]

The difficulties of imposing the new Catholicism were pointers to what was happening elsewhere. Braudel has commented that 'the marginal regions of the Mediterranean are the best place to view and possibly to decipher its destiny,'[53] and in Catalonia the cultural changes which brought the people into the post-Tridentine world give us a good guide to the problems faced by Spaniards and Italians. Though many of the innovations of Trent failed to make their mark, over those generations the impact of change helped slowly to reshape traditional society.

The Alt Penedès continued to develop over the next two centuries. St Quintí flourished and overtook Santa Maria: in 1860 the former had 2297 inhabitants, the latter only 463. At the core of the expansion was the great boom in viticulture, which still dominates the culture of the slopes of Mediona. Then the great phylloxera blight hit the vineyards and the whole terme crumbled: St Quintí shrank to half its size and within Mediona the church of St Joan de Conilles, formerly a mere outpost of the parish, in a settlement which had only two houses in the 1820s but thirty in 1848, grew to become the town known today as 'Mediona' but still called simply 'St Joan' by the people. Santa Maria ceased to function as the mother church, its last act in history being the destruction it suffered in 1936 at the hands of some of the population to whom it had for so long ministered the elements of the Christian religion.[54] Today the little church on the mountain, used now only by campers and for occasional religious gatherings, continues as it did throughout the epoch of the Counter Reformation to stand sentinel over the silent, forested valley.

Notes

References and Abbreviations

References to the four listings of Sources are made as follows:

References to the **Select Bibliography** are limited to surnames of authors; where more than one work is involved, dates are given, e.g. Amades, 1948; if more than one work appears for the year, a short title is given as well.

Reference to **Early Printed Books** is also limited to the surname of the author, who is always cited with the date of the edition consulted, which is not always the date of first publication; where a modern edition is used the date is given in parentheses, e.g. Castañega, 1529 (1946).

References to **Archival Sources** follow the abbreviations given in that section. Document abbreviations used are lib. = libro (book), leg. = legajo (bundle), and reg. = registro (register).

References beginning with 'MSS.' are identified in the list of **Contemporary Manuscripts**. This listing is given in order to identify a few original sources which were awkward to place in other listings.

Published works cited incidentally are referenced in full in the notes.

All quotations and most book titles are given in English; specialists requiring the original texts will find them in the Spanish and Catalan editions of this book. All Catalan place names, including those in Rosselló, are given in Catalan with a few exceptions for well-known towns e.g. Lérida, not Lleida. The main units of account (the Catalan lliura, sou, and diner) are expressed with the symbols for English pounds (£), shillings (s) and pence (d). Most Castilian or Catalan words used are explained in the Glossary. Since many occur frequently within one chapter in the text (e.g. *auto de fe, comisario, familiar, goig, jurat, mas, pages, terme*), only the first usage of each in each chapter is italicised. Castilian/Catalan words which are used only occasionally are italicised and explained where they appear in the text.

With many proper names I have followed the form adopted by contemporaries (e.g. both Geroni and Jeroni are used).

Preface

1. Martí Piles, in his introduction to Narcis Feliu de la Penya, *Fénix de Cataluña* (Barcelona, 1683), reprinted with an introduction by H. Kamen in 1983.
2. Josep Elias Estrugos, *Fénix català* (Perpinyà, 1644).
3. Feliu de la Penya, *Fénix*, pp. 7, 52.
4. J. Bossy, in Times Literary Supplement, 6 September 1985.
5. Christian, *Local*, 1981, pp. 147, 179.
6. Camos, 1657; Roig, 1678; Sigismund in MSS. BUB MS. 992 f.4.
7. Azpilcueta, 1572, p.39.

Chapter One

1. Pere Gil in 1600, edited by Iglésies, 1949.
2. MSS. BUB MS. 992 f. 44.
3. ADB: V vol. 86 f. 118.
4. ADB: AP Santa Maria vol. 72.
5. In Catalonia it was common for public notaries to be appointed by the bishop, and in the dioceses of Tarragona and Urgell virtually all notaries were of episcopal appointment; where other secular lords had jurisdiction, they too appointed: see Bono, I/2, p. 136. In small communities the bishop appointed the parish priest as notary. Since clerical notaries were not professionals, they usually followed notarial formulae laid down by the diocese, and published synodal constitutions of the period often included an appendix guide to drawing up legal documents: cf. the 'Formulari y breu instrucció per los rectors o curats que han de exercir lo Art de Notaria en sas parroquias' in *Synodi Barcinonensis*, 1600, p. 190;

Constitutiones Barcinonen, 1673, pp. 337–424; and *Constitutiones Solsona*, 1671, pp. 117–48.
6. ADB: AP Santa Maria vol. 22. Three canons, one of them Onofre Reart, later bishop of Gerona, came to formalise the transfer on 28 November.
7. The castle of Mediona passed from the Order of Templars to the Folc de Cardona family in 1242: see M. del Carmen Alvarez Márquez, *La Baronía de la Conca d'Odena* (Barcelona, 1990), p. 223.
8. A discussion of all the major roads of Catalonia in 1685 by a general of Charles II (MSS. BCC MS. 2371, 'Discurso General hecho por el Mre de Campo D. Ambrosio Borsano') omits mention of the road through Mediona, and later travellers never mention it; yet, as we shall see, both Jesuit missionaries and invading armies used it.
9. The crops are listed in the census of 1717, and the animals in the terme in 1720 are listed in ADB: AP Santa Maria vol. 72. Cereals in 1717 represented 92 per cent of cultures, vines 7 per cent: E. Giralt, 'Evolució de l'agricultura del Penedès', in Iª *Asamblea Intercomarcal de Investigadores del Penedès* (Martorell, 1950).
10. Braudel 1973, I, p. 55.
11. There is a fifteenth-century census of heads of households in AHPB, notary Pedro Pellicer, manual May 1420–May 1422, ff. 78–88. The census of 1553 is published in full in Iglésies, 1979.
12. Cf. Simón Tarrés, p. 75.
13. Iglésies 1979, I, p. 416 gives the hearth population; and the confession lists in ADB: AP Santa Maria vol. 19 give the names of each resident in the parish. A multiplier of seven persons

per household is used, since Conques, for example, features in the census as one household, but there were twelve persons in it, Orpinell features as two households but they totalled twenty persons.

14. In this book the name Mediona will be applied to the whole area called at the time 'vila de St Quintí i terme de Mediona'; the two component parishes will be referred to by their names.

15. 'Die 17 Januarii in castro de Mediona', ADB: AP MP/SM vol. 17 f. 134.

16. The workings of the general council are compiled from the minutes of the same in ADB: AP MP/SQ vol. 13 ff. 9, 157, 286.

17. MSS. Mas vol. XXIII f. 53.

18. In 1267 a Cardona gave the castellanship to Bernat de Barberà as part payment for a steed: Alvarez Márquez, cited p. 223.

19. Decision to erect mill, in ADB: AP MP/SQ vol. 13 f. 2; contracts for butchery e.g. in *ibid.* f. 344.

20. ADB: V vol. 66 f. 6.

21. ADB: AP Santa Maria vol. 2, baptismes 1587–1703.

22. ADB: AP St Quintí, censals, leg. 45.

23. The obligation was laid down by rules of the archdiocese since the year 1329: *Constitutiones Tarraconensium*, 1557, p. 144.

24. ADB: AP Santa Maria, vol. 19. The confession records cover the years 1551 to 1585. The return for 1551 begins 'Hi qui sequuntur sunt qui confessi sunt in ecclesia Beate Marie de Mediona in anno Dom. MDLI' and ends 'The aforementioned are those who in the year 1551 confessed in the part of Mediona, and those of St Quintí are in another account', but the return for St Quintí is not there. The return for 1577 is particularly

detailed: 'Here follow the names of those who confessed in the present parish of the parish church of Our Lady of the castle of Mediona, including heads of households as well as sons and daughters and servants living in the present parish, as follows.'

25. ADB: AP Santa Maria, Llibre de Obits, vol. 22, at 2 June 1621.

26. ADB: V vol. 72.

27. A more extended discussion, centred on Mediona, is given in Chapter Six.

28. The data that follow come from ADB: AP Santa Maria, vol. 9, Matrimonis 1575–1777.

29. The husbands came from Selma, Pobla de Claramunt, Tous, Odena, Armentera, Castelloli, Vallbona and La Llacuna.

30. These were the ages during the seventeenth century in neighbouring St Pere de Riudebitlles, cited Simón Tarrés, p. 79.

31. Decision made in a *Consell General* of St Quintí, 6 November 1599: ADB: AP MP/SM vol. 13 f. 157. See below.

32. ADB: AP MP/SM vol. 15 f. 1.

33. Simón Tarrés, p. 82, suggests that in Catalonia possibly one out of every two births died in infancy, but this figure seems unacceptably high.

34. ADB: AP Santa Maria, Llibre de Obits 1573–1704, vol. 22. The parish records from 1573 to 1587 use the term 'infant', but some 'children' must have been among them. By contrast, after that date the term *albat* is used indifferently for infants and children. From the evidence in Mediona, an albat was any child incapable of receiving the sacraments, and therefore precisely was any baptised female aged under twelve or male under fourteen. In 1613 the vicar severely criticised the Torrens family in Mas dels Agullons for

deliberately letting their son, just aged fourteen, die as an albat ('it has never been known to happen in the parish') in order to save funeral costs (the ecclesiastical charges were about 1s to bury an albat, and over £2 to bury an adult).

35. Such as some rebellious members of the Totasans family in St Joan de Conilles, who both in 1621 and 1623 refused to advise the priest of their condition.

36. A common formula used after about 1600 in St Quintí was: 'In the name of Our Lord, etc. Wherefore I... laid low in bed by a bodily illness from which I fear I may die...'

37. These masses are discussed fully in Chapter Three.

38. ADB: AP St Quintí, leg. 45.

39. ADB: AP St Quintí, leg. 45.

40. The entries logged in the 'llibre de obits' specifically used the word 'record'.

41. 'Purgatory is not mentioned until the seventeenth century; it does not belong to familiar piety... After the Counter Reformation it will become a normal and necessary stage in the migration of the soul': Ariès, 1981, p. 463.

42. ADB: AP MP/SM vol. 13 f. 280.

43. ADB: AP MP/SM vol. 15 ff. 7, 120.

44. All cases from ADB: AP Santa Maria, Llibre de Obits 1573–1704, vol. 22.

45. *Ibid.*

46. MSS. Mas, vol. XXIII f. 223.

47. All cases from ADB: AP Santa Maria, Llibre de Obits 1573–1704, vol. 22.

48. ADB: AP MP/SM vol. 13 f. 79.

49. *Ibid.* f. 171.

50. ADB: AP MP/SM vol. 15 f. 49v.

51. Contemplating the cold and snow around him, *mossèn* Santacana noted: 'Many animals and shepherds must have died in Urgell... I have never been to Urgell nor do I have any wish to go there, they seem to have suffered grave hardship.'

52. *Ibid.* f. 237. Every entry in Santacana's manual was carefully verified by his own direct experience. If he reported an extraneous event he was careful to state his sources. On the news from Barcelona he says: 'I have heard these things from many people and hold them to be reliable, I myself did not see it.' The riot against the Conseller, Hernández, is detailed in *Dietari*, VIII, p. 146.

53. ADB: AP MP/SM vol. 15 f. 308. *Cf.* Vilar, II, p. 326: 'In 1604–6 dearth stalked the countryside.'

54. ADB: AP MP/SM vol. 15 f. 377. A *carga* (load) of wheat cost 30s in 1601, 40s in 1602, in 1606 'it is at £3 10s'.

55. ADB: AP MP/SM 13 f. 79.

56. *Cf.* ACA: RC reg. 4757 ff. 67, 71, 171, for letters from the viceroy to local bailiff. Among the few recorded successes was the *sometent* raised from Igualada and the towns of the Conca d'Odena in 1573 to capture the bandit gang of Moreu Palau. In the song composed to celebrate the action (*Cobles novament fetes*, Barcelona, 1573), due praise was given to Mediona:

Sanct Quintí y Mediona
St Quintí and Mediona

son llochs molt asenyalats
are very famous places

aqui feneix la Conca d'Odena
where the Conca d'Odena ends;

y tots foren avisats
everybody was called out

molt soptadament partiren
and they left immediately

dient a tots 'a Déu siau,
saying to all 'Farewell,

muyren tots en nostra Conca
death in our Conca

los lladres ab Moreu Palau!'
to the bandits of Moreu Palau!'

57.   ADB: AP MP/SM vol. 13 f. 79; vol. 15 ff. 130, 308.

58.   MSS. Mas, vol. XXIII f. 193. Mossèn Mas devoted his leisure to collecting a vast amount of notes on the parishes of the diocese of Barcelona, which he kept in huge volumes now deposited in the Institut Municipal. In the case of St Quintí he diligently copied out information from parish manuals which later disappeared in the war of 1936–9, making his notes a unique source.

59.   ADB: V vol. 34 ff. 73, 75.

60.   The chapels in the terme of Mediona were at Sta Anna, St Joan de Conilles, Santa Maria de Orpinell, St Elies, Sta Margarida, St Pere Sacarrera, and St Salvador de Pareres. All the sites exist today (*see map*, p. 3). In the seventeenth century Ginoles also got its own chapel (to St Quintí), 'built in the house of Jacinto Gili, parish of Santa Maria' (MSS. Mas, vol. XXIV f. 65).

61.   The price for both was £68 12s 6d: MSS. Mas, vol. XXIII.

62.   Contract with Gil Oroge de la Mozas of Flanders, and Miguel López of Huesca, for a total fee of £46: MSS. Mas, vol. XXIII.

63.   The builders were Bernat Marconi and Antoni Colent: MSS. Mas, vol. XXIII.

64.   The statue cost £11 3s 6d: MSS. Mas, vol. XXIII.

65.   The bell cost £35: MSS. Mas, vol. XXIII.

66.   Both visits in ADB: V vol. 40 ff. 128v, 259v.

67.   'In the year 1566 there was a great drought, it did not rain for a year,' Perot de Vilanova, 'Memòries per a sempre', MSS. BCC MS. 501 f. 171.

68.   MP/SQ 1565–7 ff. 261, 267; MP/SQ 1567–8 ff. 63, 212: in

MSS. Mas, vol. XXIII. The basic contract with Terrassa was that the town would supply all materials and pay £200; the work of Oriol was agreed at £57.

69.   ADB: AP MP/SM vol. 11 f. 248.

70.   Martínez del Villar was a canon lawyer from Castile. His private library is inventoried in AHPB notary Pau Calopa, leg. 13.

71.   ADB: V vol. 44 f. 4. For the Council of Tarragona, see Chapter Two.

72.   ADB: V vol. 45 ff. 284, 282.

73.   See Chapter Six, p. 275, for the context of this order.

74.   ADB: V vol. 45 f. 306.

75.   MP/SQ 1585–7 ff. 85, 216: in MSS. Mas, vol. XXIII. In fact the money ran out on Sta Anna, and the work was re-contracted in 1595 to Guillem Sala, builder of Vilafranca: MP/SQ 1593–8 f. 96: MSS. Mas, vol. XXIII. It was re-contracted in 1598, and not consecrated until July 1605: ADB: AP MP/SQ vol. 15 f. 278.

76.   ADB: AP Santa Maria vol. 71.

77.   The cost was £86 18s. MP/SQ 1590–8 f. 338: in MSS. Mas, vol. XXIII.

78.   MP/SQ 1593–8 f. 105: in MSS. Mas, vol. XXIII.

79.   ADB: AP MP/SM vol. 13 f. 56.

80.   MP/SQ 1588–90 f. 223: in MSS. Mas, vol. XXIII.

81.   Founded 'at the instance of the jurats and individuals of St Quintí', constitution in ADB: C vol. 70 f. 92.

82.   MP/SQ 1590–8 f. 340: in MSS. Mas, vol. XXIII.

83.   Agreement signed in castle by Puigdengoles of Conques, Torrens of Mas dels Agullons, Marques of St Joan and Esteve of La Guixera, 6 June 1599: ADB: AP MP/SM vol. 12 f. 20v.

84.   ADB: AP MP/SQ vol. 12 f. 118.

85.   'Adiudicatio del retaula de la capella de Nra Sra del Roser',

ADB: AP MP/SQ vol. 13 f. 286–7.

86. ADB: AP MP/SQ vol. 13 f. 229–30.

87. Details from ADB: V vol. 58 ff. 491, 497.

88. 'Com se han de fer los administradors de las capellas', ADB: AP MP/SM 13 f. 157.

89. Visit of 1609 in ADB: V vol. 66 f. 1–2; bishop Manrique made a visitation on 20 April 1636: *ibid.* vol. 71 f. 239.

90. ADB: AP MP/SM vol. 14 f. 51, September 1602 'Concordia feta per a daurar lo retaula del Roser', sanctioned by sixteen representatives of the masies, 'comprenent la major part del Consell de dit terme de Mediona'. In 1604 Gomar also contracted to paint the altarpiece at Orpinell: *ibid.* f. 158.

91. ADB: AP MP/SQ vol. 15 f. 336.

92. ADB: AP MP/SM vol. 19 f. 185.

93. MP/SQ 1622–5 f. 128; and MP/SQ 1627–9 f. 79: both in MSS. Mas, vol. XXIII.

94. ADB: V vol. 66, f. 79, visit of 10 November 1683. The only vice the visitor thought worth mentioning in St Quintí was the 'the indecency and grave abuse in that parish whereby the men go to church to hear mass with their hair tied into a tail and plaited, which is to want to imitate the Jews who crucified Christ Our Lord'; the style, he commented, 'causat magnam irrisionem'.

95. *Cf.* the 'Inventari de la plata y roba de la iglesia de Mediona', in ADB: AP MP/SM vol. 26 f. 162.

96. Young, II pp. 317–18.

97. *Cf.* Terradas.

98. Andrés Palma, pp 62–3, gives a full list.

99. ADB: AP MP/SM vol. 26 f. 160, lease of May 1665.

100. Vilà Valentí, p. 70.

101. MSS. BCC MS. 313.

102. G. Gavignaud, 'L'organisation économique traditionelle communautaire dans les hauts pays catalans', in *Conflent, Vallespir.*

103. Cavaillès, *passim.*

104. *Cf.* Gutton, 1979, p. 22.

105. J. M. Font i Rius, 'Evolución jurídico-público de una comunidad local en el Pirineo catalán: Ager', in Font i Rius, *Estudis sobre els drets i institucions locals en la Catalunya medieval* (Barcelona, 1985).

106. For the European background, see J. Blum, 'The Internal Structure and Policy of the European Village Community', *Journal of Modern History*, 43, 1971; also Gutton; and Le Bras. In the Camp of Tarragona, south from Mediona, the late mediaeval community which included the towns of Valls, La Selva, Reus, Riudoms and Alcover, was still continuing to meet at least twice a year in this period: see Fort i Cogul.

107. *Cf.* Brutails, discussing Rosselló.

108. ADPO, AC Egat 1, 2.

109. *Cf.* Bushaway, Chapter 2, 'The community and its calendars'.

110. 'Geografia de Catalunya', in Iglésies, 1949, p. 155.

111. Curiously, the most important Catalan agricultural manual of the period, written by a friar, Miquel Agustí, uses no references from the liturgical calendar and instead works entirely from the secular calendar of the moon's phases.

112. The diary of Joan Guàrdia, in Pladevall and Simon, p. 99. '*Ninou*' is the old Catalan name for New Year's.

113. What Victor Turner, *The Ritual Process* (London, 1969), refers to as 'liminality'.

114. Turner, in Babcock, 1978, p. 277.

115. Van Gennep, 1960, *passim.*

116. Christian, *Local*, 1981.

117. Vilà Valentí, pp. 110–13; *cf.* Chauvet, 1947, p. 187, 'La religion de cette terre fut pastorale'.

118. See, in general, Bercé. For Catalonia, Capmany, 1951; and Amades, 1958.

119. The more normal form of this ritual, the charivari, is discussed in Chapter Six.

120. Amades, 1958, pp. 26, 28.

121. Rafael d'Amat, 1987.

122. Rafael d'Amat, *Calaix*, 1987, I, p. 150.

123. Amades, 1954.

124. Phythian-Adams.

125. Phythian-Adams, p. 69.

126. Cited Delumeau, p. 112.

127. Rafael d'Amat, 1987.

128. *Cf.* Muchembled.

129. Pladevall and Simon.

130. Noydens, 1675, p. 119.

131. Ciruelo, 1628, chap. X, p. 209, 'Disputa contra los que descomulgan la langosta'.

132. Delumeau, p. 61–9.

133. Christian, 1981, *Local*, p. 29–31.

134. Noydens, 1675, p. 126.

135. ADB: AP MP/SM 13 f. 222. 'The rivers overflowed, something no one had ever seen; the river Anoia carried away the bridge at Martorell': a scenario repeated within living memory this century.

136. Christian, 1981, *Local*, p. 249 n. 65; Villanueva, II, p. 60.

137. 'Instructio pera Visitadors' of bishop Moncada, 1611, ADB: C vol. 75 f. 158.

138. Consellers to monks, 19 February 1608, IMH Consellers C. XVIII-2.

139. *Dietari*, IV, p. 389.

140. Pujades, IV, p. 130–1.

141. See p. 138 for the *mà armada* of 1612.

142. MSS. BMP MS. 84.

143. 'Dotzena de St Galderich acerca de anar a cercar la reliquia', ADPO, H 155.

144. 'Apocha de la reliquia del glorios St Galderich y promesa de restituir aquella, 1698', ADPO, H 155.

145. *Goigs* were fly-sheets devoted to saints; see Chapter Three.

146. *Diary of Guàrdia*, ed. Pladevall and Simón.

147. Christian, 1981, *Local*, pp. 46, 239–40.

148. M. Mirabet i Cucala, 'Pregàries públiques a la Barcelona del segle XVIII', in *I Congrés*, II, pp. 487–93; Puigvert Solà, 'El calendari festiu d'una comunitat pagesa', *ibid.*, II, pp. 417–27.

149. Myrtille Gonzalbo, p. 52.

150. ADPO, BB 34 f. 96.

151. 'Concell y sindicat fet p la universitat de la vila de Prada p fer baixar la reliquia de Sanct Galderich p las malaltias y ha en Prada, 1639', ADPO, H 155.

152. Durán i Sanpere, I, p. 467–8.

153. For a summary of the developments of this period, see Kamen, *Spain 1469–1714. A Society of Conflict* (London, 1991)

154. Nadal & Giralt. Economic distress and the civil wars were contributors to the immigration.

155. *Cf.* Serra, pp. 205–6; Vilar, II, pp. 325–8.

156. Despuig (1981), p. 133. He was writing in 1557.

157. Letter of town to bishop, 1611, ADB: C vol. 75 f. 200.

158. Figures for number of foundations in Basili de Rubi, Chapter XVII.

159. 'Geografia de Catalunya', in Iglésies, 1949, pp. 274–5.

160. V. Cárcel Ortí, *Historia de la Iglesia en Valencia*, 2 vols (Valencia, 1986), I, pp. 188–9.

161. Iglésies, 1949, p. 294.

162. See, despite his narrow focus, Evenett.

163. Batllori: 'the history of the Counter Reformation was centred, both as objective and as source, on this Council': *I*

Congrés, II, p. 376.

164. Batllori, 'Temes i problemes', 1984, p. 377.
165. Narcis Feliu de la Penya, *Fénix de Cataluña* (Barcelona, 1680), p. 7.
166. *Constitutiones Tarraconensium*, 1557, p. 212 ff.
167. *Cf.* Batllori, 1983, p. 64–5.
168. For a guide to Germany, see Scribner. A good study of the Counter Reformation in an urban setting is Lottin, 1984.
169. See Chapter Four.
170. This is my only, slight, dissent from the emphasis placed by Christian on the 'local' in local religion: *Cf.* his *Local*, 1981, pp. 175–80.

Chapter Two

1. ACA: RC reg. 4351 f. 201.
2. 'The prince was in Barcelona three days', reports the Catalan Calvete de Estrella in his splendid *El felicissimo viaje*, and all was 'feasts and costumes': Calvete, p. 3. Philip took ship from the bay of Roses for Genoa.
3. *Llibre de les Solemnitats*, ed. Durán i Sanpere & Sanabre, II, p. 5.
4. Perot de Vilanova, 'Memòries', MSS. BCC MS. 501 f. 165.
5. *Ibid.* f. 167.
6. Pedro Arellano y Sada, *Catálogo de la exposición bibliográfica del Concilio de Trento* (Barcelona, 1947), p. 158. The return of other bishops is detailed in Gutiérrez, 1951.
7. 'Descripcio', MSS. BCC MS. 313.
8. J. M. Torras i Ribé, 'Aproximació a l'estudi del domini baronial del monestir de Ripoll (1266–1719)', in *I Congrés*, I, pp. 203–9.

9. 'Descripcio', MSS. BCC MS. 313.
10. Cited in R. García Cárcel, *Historia de Cataluña, siglos XVI–XVII*, 2 vols (Barcelona, 1985), I, pp. 236–7.
11. Bishop of Solsona, 23 July 1603, to Council of Aragon, ACA: CA leg. 345. This bundle is also the source for the incomes of Tarragona and Barcelona. The income of Solsona, in the late seventeenth century, is from ACA: CA leg. 474. The incomes of Lérida, Urgell and Tortosa in the mid-seventeenth century are detailed in ACA: CA leg. 547. No statement of income of the sees for this period is reliable; for one survey, see Barrio.
12. For the ecclesiastical history of this period, and the role of the *Observance*, see the useful survey, with a full bibliography, edited by R. García-Villoslada. Unfortunately, there is no history of the Church in Catalonia.
13. Consulta of 18 November 1653, and bishop's report of 10 September 1661, both in ACA: CA leg. 547.
14. See Chapter Nine, p. 431.
15. Christian Hermann, pp. 81–2.
16. E.g.: 'Cisneros helped give the Spanish Church a new strength and vigour at the very moment when the Church was everywhere under attack. The rulers of Spain personally sponsored reform at home, thus simultaneously removing some of the worst sources of complaint and keeping firm control over a movement which might have got out of hand', J.H. Elliott, *Imperial Spain* (Harmondsworth, 1970), p. 105.
17. Borja to Ignatius Loyola, 7 June 1546, in *MHSI Borgia*, vol. II, p. 520; the official, cited in Kamen, 1984, p. 57.
18. For some comments, see Kamen

in Scribner, ed., 1993.

19. For the early Reformation in Spain, see, in particular, Bataillon.

20. Dr Ortiz to Suprema, letters of August and September 1541, AHN Inq lib. 736 ff. 11–12. Nine years before, in the same city, the problem had been Servet (see Bataillon article cited Bataillon, p. 427, n. 6) but Servet never fell into the hands of the Inquisition.

21. E.g. the 'Memorial de lo que debe proponerse al Concilio Tridentino, hecho por el Cabildo de Lérida', probably of about 1540, which reiterates firmly the rights of the cathedral chapter against its bishop, and asks specifically that papal and other taxes be reduced: ACL.

22. Avila's proposals mentioned in Marin Ocete, I, pp. 182–3; Tejada y Ramiro, vol. IV, pp. 687–92. The bishops demanded a reduction in feast-days, control over false relics, the teaching of catechism, and other changes.

23. Pons, 1968, p. 215, 'omnes fere ad laicas personas'.

24. Bishop of Pamplona to D. Lorenzo de Vivanco, 4 January 1714, AHN Consejos lib. 7294 no. 3.

25. Goñi Gaztambide, 1947, p. 136.

26. González Novalín, p. 247.

27. Bada, 1988, p. 211.

28. Serra, pp. 121–2.

29. ACU, Sinodos, ff. 13, 22.

30. Goñi, 1947, p. 136.

31. This was the aspiration of the friar Jerónimo de Mendieta: see J.L. Phelan, *The Millennial Kingdom of the Franciscans in the New World* (Berkeley, 1970).

32. Tejada y Ramiro, vol. V, p. 371.

33. ACA: RC reg. 4352 f. 141.

34. Zaragoza Pascual, 1981, p. 123.

35. Salmerón to Laínez, 22 July 1559, cited Pérez Martínez, 1958, p. 134.

36. Letter of 18 April 1562, cited Tejada y Ramiro, IV, p. 565. The participation of Spaniards in Trent has been examined exhaustively, but usually from a conservative and clerical point of view.

37. See Pastor, vols XVII–XIX.

38. López Martín, p. 30.

39. Philip took a profound interest in doctrine and liturgy, and wrote a long (unpublished) essay on the reforms of Trent. His opposition to the religious concessions in Germany also seems to have been personal rather than due to his advisers.

40. John Lynch, 'Philip II and the Papacy', *Transactions of the Royal Historical Society*, ii, 1961, gives a useful summary.

41. See Bada, 1970, p. 181. The following section is drawn from Bada's text.

42. Bada, 1970, pp. 183–6.

43. See Serrano, vol. I.

44. AGS Estado leg. 148.

45. Tejada IV, pp. 663–4.

46. AHAT, Concilio provincial 1564–6 f. 226. *Cf.* also a good summary in Bada, 1970, pp. 189–211.

47. The national assemblies called by the Emperor in Germany and by Catherine de Medici in France were termed 'colloquies'.

48. Tarsicio de Azcona, in García-Villoslada, vol. III–1, p. 176.

49. García y García.

50. Villanueva, I, p. 76.

51. López Martín, p. 109. For the proceedings of the Granada council, AGS Estado 148 f. 133.

52. Given in Bada, 1970, p. 198.

53. Serrano, vol. I, p. 157.

54. López Martín, p. 133; *cf.* AGS Estado leg. 148 f. 146.

55. Carranza had been arrested by the Inquisition in 1559: see Kamen 1985, pp. 155–60. The definitive account is by J. I. Tellechea, *El arzobispo Carranza*

y su tiempo, 2 vols (Madrid, 1968).

56. Pastor XVII, pp. 12–18.
57. The reference was to the decrees of 29 August and 6 October; see Serrano, I, p. 31.
58. Serrano, I, p. 443.
59. Pastor, XVII, p. 179.
60. Serrano, I, p. 160.
61. Serrano, I, p. 285.
62. Even the seating plan of the councils was laid down: see sketch in ACA: RC reg. 4352 f. 147.
63. The fundamental account is Santos Diez.
64. AGS Estado leg. 146 f. 29.
65. AGS Patronato leg. 22 f. 48.
66. For what follows, Tejada y Ramiro, vol. V.
67. Details and correspondence in AGS Estado leg. 48; and in López Martín, pp. 96–152.
68. López Martín, pp. 88–95.
69. AGS Estado leg. 146 f. 45.
70. Santos Diez, pp. 294–6.
71. Goñi, 1947, p. 182.
72. Tejada y Ramiro, V, p. 400.
73. Villanueva, III, p. 129.
74. See the contributions by Tarsicio de Azcona and José Garcia Oro in García-Villoslada, vol. III–1.
75. Azcona, 1967.
76. Cocheril, pp. 23, 26.
77. *MHSI Borgia*, II, pp. 22, 596.
78. González Novalin, p. 235.
79. Garcia Oro, in García-Villoslada, III–1, p. 321.
80. Garcia Oro, *ibid*. pp. 324–5.
81. *Ibid*. p. 325.
82. Goñi Gaztambide, 1960, p. 5.
83. *MHSI Borgia*, II, p. 520.
84. Letter to the bishops dated 27 March 1567, ACA: RC reg. 4351 f. 143–4. The letters to the Franciscans, dated 17 April, were sent to the male houses in Barcelona, Lérida, Tortosa, Gerona, Tárrega, Cervera, Vic, Vilafranca, Montblanc, Tarragona, Puigcerdà, Berga, Vilafranca de Conflent, and Urgell; and to the female convents of Santa Clara in Lérida, Tortosa, Balaguer, Manresa, Cervera, Vic, Montblanc, Conca d'Orcau, Tárrega and Vilafranca.
85. ACA: RC reg. 4351 ff. 149–53.
86. *Ibid*. ff. 170–6. The Observant provincial was fray Augustí Vinyes.
87. *Ibid*. ff. 201–6, letters of 6 September 1567.
88. Letters of 30 November 1567 to viceroy and to bishop of Urgell, *ibid*. ff. 233–4.
89. Philip II to viceroy, 27 June 1568, *ibid*. ff. 126–9.
90. ACA: RC reg. 4351 f. 149, reg. 4352 f. 15.
91. *Ibid*. reg. 4352 f. 127v.
92. *Ibid*. reg. 4352 ff. 118v–121.
93. Philip to viceroy, 11 October 1567, *ibid*. reg. 4351 f. 219v.
94. Sanahuja, p. 339.
95. For aspects of reform in women's convents in Catalonia, see Chapter Six.
96. Zaragoza Pascual 1977.
97. Letter of 28 March 1592, ACA: CA leg. 477.
98. 'Informe del estado de los monasterios de benedictinos', in Zaragoza Pascual 1981, pp. 84–130.
99. Fray Joan de Jesús to Philip II, 12 October 1590, ACA: CA leg. 342.
100. 'Originale processus visita de Convento et Religiosos BVM de Belpuig', ADU Procesos de Visita 1611, 1662–99.
101. E. Corredera, 'Una visita pastoral en el monasterio de Bellpuig de las Avellanas', *Analecta Sacra Tarraconensis*, 53–4 (1980–1), p. 115.
102. Consulta of Council of Aragon, 12 October 1584, ACA: CA leg. 261 f. 95.
103. Pujades IV, p. 123.
104. See Chapter Three.
105. For detail on what follows, see García-Villoslada, vol. III–1,

pp. 13–21.
106. Llorens i Solé, I p. 392.
107. ACA: CA leg. 266 f. 148.
108. Torreilles, 1905.
109. All documents in ACA: CA leg. 342.
110. Consulta of Council, 3 January 1583, Lisbon, ACA: CA leg. 261 f. 45.
111. Agreement in ADPO, G 54.
112. For details, see García-Villoslada, vol. III–1.
113. Garcia Oro in García-Villoslada, vol. III–1, p. 317.
114. Philip to ambassador, 30 September 1569, ACA: RC reg. 4353 f. 77.
115. García-Villoslada, vol. III–1, p. 318.
116. Goñi Gaztambide, 1960, p. 83.
117. Bada, 1982. Deliberate Castilianisation was, of course, taken further after 1715. Bada shows that seventy-three out of eighty-five appointments in 1715–1851 were non-Catalan.
118. Vicecanciller of Aragon, in ACA: CA leg. 264.
119. Pujades, II, p. 153; III, p. 117.
120. *Cónsols* to king, 14 January 1616, ACA: CA leg. 358.
121. 'Relacion de lo q ha pasado en Perpiñan', ACA: CA leg. 342.
122. Tejada y Ramiro, VI, 115–16. A guide to the decrees of the councils is Costa y Borrás.
123. *Constitutiones Tarraconensium*, pp. 1, 47, 124, 144.
124. *Ibid.*, p. 114.
125. Sanabre, 1956, pp. 16–18.
126. ADB: C vol. 65 ff. 14–60. Other synods of the century are given in detail in ADB Acta Synodalia vol. 1.
127. ACU, Synods, 1610–1635, and 1585–1696.
128. All figures are those of Henry Cock's narrative of that year, pp. 125, 130. In 1588, however, only fifty-one professional confraternities are listed: Durán & Sanabre, II, p. 77.

129. Durán & Sanabre, II, p. 42.
130. Cock, p. 128.
131. Cock, p. 145. Catalina's early death in 1597 devastated Philip. On 14 June the king left to go to Monzón for the Corts which opened on 28 June.
132. Pérez de Valdivia, 1618, f. 32v.
133. For Montserrat, see pp. 154–56.

Chapter Three

1. For some discussions, see e.g. Geertz.
2. For a good short survey of the religion of the people in mid-sixteenth-century Castile, see Redondo, 'Religion populaire' 1986.
3. Thomas, p. 36. This is a small disagreement with a rich and magisterial work.
4. Hoffman, p. 84.
5. Thomas, p. 51.
6. Ciruelo, 1628, p. 25.
7. For example, he explains that women rather than men tended to be witches because, among other reasons, 'they chatter more than men and cannot keep secrets': Castañega, 1529 (1946), p. 37.
8. Castañega, 1529, pp. 20, 39, 89, 117.
9. Rodríguez, 1600, pp. 13–15.
10. Noydens, 1681, p. 10.
11. Tejada y Ramiro, V, p. 67.
12. *Cf.* R. Ricard, *The Spiritual Conquest of Mexico* (University of California Press, 1966); Phelan, cited p. 448 n. 31.
13. On missions to the Islamic population of Spain, see García-Villoslada, vol. IV.
14. Jiménez to Laínez, 4 May 1561, and Francisco de Lara to same, 7 January 1561, both from Monterrey: ARSI Epist Hisp vol. 98 ff. 183, 21.

15. Letter of 28 May 1564, ARSI Epist Hisp vol. 101 f. 179.
16. Cited by González Novalin, in García-Villoslada, vol. III–1, p. 369.
17. 'Dubia quae in causa', AHN Inq lib. 1231 ff. 634–7. *Cf.* Kamen, 1985, p. 210–11.
18. Cited in Redondo, 'Religion populaire', 1986, p. 337.
19. Philip II to bishop of Barcelona, 20 March 1581, ACA: CA leg. 78 f. 131.
20. 'Memorial para el asiento de las montañas de Ribagorza y Perineos', ACA: CA leg. 78, f. 161.
21. 'Por el Provincial de los Descalços Carmelitas de Cataluña. A 3 de Agosto de 1590', *ibid.* unfolioed; Joan de Jesús to Philip II, 12 October 1590, *ibid.* leg. 342.
22. Memoir of Conde de Sástago, 1594, ACA: CA leg. 78 f. 191.
23. Pedro de León, pp. 103, 149.
24. Díaz de Luco, 1543, p. 75.
25. Meneses, 1554 (1978), pp. 317, 321.
26. Meneses, 1554 (1978), pp. 371–2.
27. See Kamen, 1988. John Foxe reported that Castro 'did earnestly inveigh against the bishops for burning of men, saying plainly that they learned it not in scripture, to burn any for conscience sake': *Acts and Monuments* (London, 1838), p. 737.
28. Coma, 1566, pp. x–xi.
29. Bishop of Urgell to archbishop of Saragossa, 21 November 1593, ACA: CA leg. 78 f. 195.
30. Juan de San José, 'Annales', p. 54: MSS. BUB MS. 991.
31. Lucien Febvre, *Le problème de l'incroyance au XVIe siècle. La religion de Rabelais* (Paris, 1947).
32. Cited in François Lebrun, ed., *Histoire des Catholiques en France* (Paris, 1980).
33. René Pintard, *Le libertinage érudit dans la première moitié du XVIIe siècle*, 2 vols (Paris, 1943); Thomas, pp. 198–206.
34. *Cf.* Ingram 1987, pp. 93–8; also Hunter.
35. See Chapter Six.
36. A. Redondo, 'Le discours d'opposition des groupes ruraux face au pouvoir ecclésiastique', in Redondo, 1986; the priest, in AHN Inq lib. 732 f. 478.
37. Prades, 1597, p. 447.
38. AHN Inq lib. 730 ff. 399, 414.
39. *Ibid.* lib. 731 f. 417v.
40. *Ibid.* lib. 730 ff. 415, 431.
41. *Ibid.* lib. 731 f. 173.
42. *Ibid.* lib. 731 f. 400v.
43. *Ibid.* lib. 731 f. 494.
44. *Ibid.* lib. 731 f. 253.
45. *Ibid.* lib. 731, *visita* of 1598.
46. *Ibid.* lib. 731 f. 176v.
47. *Ibid.* lib. 731 f. 202.
48. *Ibid.* lib. 731 f. 252.
49. *Ibid.* lib. 732 f. 225.
50. *Ibid.* lib. 733 f. 352.
51. IMH Consellers C. XVIII vol. 8 ff. 95–161.
52. *Ibid.* vol. 7, f. 42.
53. *Ibid.* vol. 7.
54. *Ibid.*
55. ADU, libro de visita vol. 32 ff. 99, 102v, 103.
56. See the colloquy published as *Liturgie et musique (IXe–XIVe s.)*, Toulouse 1982, in the series *Cahiers de Janjeaux*, vol. 17. This has a full bibliography.
57. González Gil to Laínez, 1564, ARSI Epist Hisp vol. 102 f. 70.
58. Cited Kamen, 1984, 'La Contrarreforma'.
59. Ruiz Alcoholado, 1584, prologue, p. 12. His manual for the missal is Ruiz Alcoholado, 1589.
60. AHPB, notary Lluis Rufet, leg. 26, Inventarios sueltos, 1553–1580 (1).
61. Péligry, 1977.
62. Between 1571 and 1575 Plantin 'shipped some 15,505 breviaries'

to Spain, representing just one-third by value of the total of liturgical books he sent to Spain in those years: Kingdon, p. 146.

63. ADB: V leg. 45.
64. AHPB, notary G.F. Devesa, leg. 13, Pliego de Inventarios, 1591–8.
65. Goñi, 'La adopción', p. 8.
66. Villanueva, XII, pp. 130–206.
67. *Ibid*. XIV, p. 91.
68. *Ibid*. XVII, pp. 68–70, 284.
69. *Ibid*. XVIII, p. 149.
70. Tejada y Ramiro, V, p. 24.
71. For rite inversion and fools, see Chapter Four.
72. Donovan.
73. Cited Vila, 1983, p. 24.
74. Villanueva, XVI, p. 93.
75. Welsford, p. 200.
76. Villanueva, XII, pp. 341–2.
77. *Bisbetó, Sermó del* (no date).
78. Vila, 1983, pp. 26, 123.
79. Tejada y Ramiro, V, p. 240.
80. Tomás Avila, pp. 28–33.
81. ADB: V vol. 84 f. 418.
82. Vila, 1983, p. 54.
83. Villanueva, XII, pp. 205, 195.
84. Donovan.
85. Tomás Avila, p. 24.
86. Baucells. The 'Book of Generations' recited the genealogy of Christ.
87. Pérez Martínez, 1963, I, p. lxxiii.
88. Goñi Gaztambide, 1947.
89. Pérez Martínez, 1963, II pp. 59–94.
90. APP Comunidad: Determinacions, letra C, 1575–1606, f. 43v.
91. Pons, 1968, p. 222.
92. For this dance, see also Chapter Four, p. 192.
93. ADB: V vol. 44 ff. 6, 134; vol. 45 ff. 238–9, 319, 358–9.
94. Costa y Borrás, II, p. 22.
95. ADB Acta Synodalia, vol. 1 (1571–1669), f. 263.
96. Lemos, 1583, p. 360v. Lemos, as a Jeronimite, may well have been simply echoing the opinion of fray José de Sigüenza in his history of the order.

97. For some aspects of the Castilian episcopate by the seventeenth century, see H. E. Rawlings, 'The secularisation of Castilian episcopal office under the Habsburgs, *c*. 1516–1700', *Journal of Ecclesiastical History*, 38, no. 1, Jan 1987.
98. Pérez Martínez, 1963, I, p. xvii.
99. Cited in Pérez Martínez, 1963, I, p. xvii.
100. Goñi Gaztambide, 1947, p. 136.
101. MSS. BCC MS. 90.
102. For listings of Castilian and Valencian *ad limina*, and reference to a general essay on the subject, see the contribution by Milagros Carcel Orti in *Homenatge García Martínez*, 3 vols (Valencia, 1988), vol. I, p. 447ff.
103. These are the relevant dates in the records kept in the Vatican archives.
104. ASV Visitas ad limina 869A, relatio 9 March 1668 of bishop of Vic.
105. Moliné Coll, 1980, p. 424.
106. Printed in Moliné Coll, 1981, pp. 480–95.
107. ASV Visitas ad limina vol. 399A, Lérida.
108. Sobrino Chomon, p. 131.
109. MSS. BCC MS. 90 f. 331.
110. Pérez Martínez, 1963, I, pp. xcix–ci.
111. V. Soladana, *El Venerable Don Juan de Palafox* (Soria, 1982).
112. ASV Visitas ad limina vol. 212, Solsona, f. 28.
113. *Ibid*. vol. 212 ff. 36, 52.
114. *Ibid*. vol. 441, Léon.
115. *Ibid*. vol. 785A, Tarragona.
116. *Ibid*. vol. 399A, Lérida.
117. ASV Visitas ad limina, vol. 399A, Lérida.
118. The situation had been common throughout the Catholic world. *Cf*. Toussaert, p. 103, on confirmation as 'totalement inaperçue' in late mediaeval Flanders.
119. ACA: RC reg. 4352 f. 24.

120. Moliné Coll, 1980, p. 438; 1982, p. 349.
121. Pérez Martínez, 1963, I, p. lxxvii.
122. Pérez Martínez, 1958.
123. Pujades, II, p. 109.
124. AEV Llibres de visites vol. 1206 (1565–8).
125. *Ibid.* vol. 1207.
126. Visitas parroquiales 1554–1607, Sant Benet de Bages, ACA: CA Monacales, Universidad lib. 9 ff. 87–90. The parish in question was St Jaume de Ferrán.
127. Toussaert, pp. 307–9.
128. Pérez Martínez, 1963, I, p. 262.
129. Pérez Martínez, 1963, I–II.
130. ADB: V vol. 45 f. 274.
131. See discussion in Chapter Four on the parish.
132. Dimas Loris, 1598, p. 3.
133. Durán i Sanpere and Durán.
134. Decree of Alonso Coloma, 12 April 1600, ADB: C vol. 72 f. 65.
135. 1650 'Publicatories de la Semmana Santa', ADB: C vol. 80 f. 66.
136. Mexía, 1566, cited Vigil p. 158.
137. *Constitutiones Synodales Vicenses*, f. 25v.
138. Pérez Martínez, 1963, I, p. 377 (St Nicolas), II, pp. 59–94 (Llucmajor).
139. Córdoba, 1573, p. 44.
140. Mexía, 1566, p. 136v.
141. Ortiz Lucio, 1598, p. 61.
142. Zabaleta, 1654.
143. Quoted in Vigil, p. 161.
144. Cited Marti Bonet, I/1 p. 194. As recently as this generation, the children of Igualada used to buy noise-makers with which they would run round 'going to kill Jews' (testimony by Eulàlia Vilà).
145. Le Bras, Chapter III, 'Un domaine mixte: le cimetière'.
146. Pérez Martínez, 1963, I p. 301.
147. ADB: V vol. 45 f. 277.
148. MSS. 'Anals del convent de Santa Catarina', by fray Francesc Camprubi OP, BUB MS. 1005 f. 100; the work covers essen-tially the years 1550–1634, and is a splendid first-hand testimony by a writer who promised that 'I shall try to give a long and full and true account without omitting anything, of things which I have experienced and seen with my own eyes, and it will get better as I go on.'
149. Tellechea, 1970.
150. ADB: V vol. 45 ff. 275, 293, 340.
151. *Ibid.* vol. 45 ff. 238, 319, 358.
152. ACL Libro de Visitas vol. 1.
153. Guillermo Pons, p. 218.
154. 'Visitatio totius diocesis Ep. Manrique de año 1635', ADB: V vol. 71.
155. Marín Ocete, II, pp. 362–4. He also gives references to the bibliography on this subject.
156. López Martín, p. 30.
157. Consulta of Aragon, 24 September 1588, ACA: CA leg. 264 f. 129.
158. ACA: CA leg. 264 f. 12/6.
159. ASV Visitas ad limina vol. 399A, Lérida.
160. 'A Lille, comme dans le reste de l'Europe, l'Eglise de la Contre Réforme va promouvoir les sacraments': Lottin, 1984, p. 209.
161. See Chapter Six.
162. Ricardo Saez, 'Parentés réelles et parentés fictives en Espagne aux XVIe et XVIIe siècles' in Redondo, 1987.
163. *Constitutiones Barcinonen*, p. 169.
164. Martí Bonet, vol. I/1, p. 53 states that 'the great majority of baptismal fonts in the Vallès Oriental are of the sixteenth century.'
165. See Ferreres, pp. 379–82.
166. As in mediaeval Flanders, described in Toussaert, pp. 49–50.
167. ADB: C vol. 75 f. 131 ff.
168. Cited in Toussaert, p. 147.
169. Lladonosa, II, p. 68.
170. Cassador, 1593, p. 13.

171. Dimas Loris, 1598, f. 37v. For 'human scruples' see the next note.
172. Rodríguez, 1600, pp. 393–5. This must have been an important and common phenomenon, for the Jesuits in their Lenten sermons in Barcelona used to plead for used clothes 'with which to clothe some persons of honour who for lack of them could not leave the house nor attend mass on feast days': MSS. 'Crónica de Belén', f. 58.
173. Ortiz Lucio, 1598, p. 86.
174. Díaz de Luco, 1543, p. 107.
175. Pérez Martínez, 1963, II p. 111.
176. Caldes, 1588, ff. 152–3.
177. Dimas Loris, 1598, f. 12v.
178. López Martín, p. 92.
179. Agulhon, cited by Le Bras, p. 174.
180. Cited by Smith, p. 10.
181. Tellechea, 1970, p. 39.
182. ADB: V vol. 84 f. 356.
183. Avila to Guerrero, 10 March 1565, in López Martín, p. 92.
184. Amades, *Hostals i tavernes*, 1936. In the whole *terme* of Mediona there was only one tavern, located in St Quintí, licensed by the duke of Cardona and contracted out by the *jurats* of the town.
185. Caldes, 1588, prologue.
186. Font, 1608, f. 97v.
187. Villanueva, I, p. 165. Villanueva comments on the presumed problems if no separation of sexes was practised at the time.
188. Caldes, 1588, f. 141v.
189. Tejada y Ramiro, V, p. 317.
190. *Cf.* the abstention from daily mass practised by St Cyran and other Jansenists.
191. Tejada y Ramiro, IV, p. 690. Tejada seems to give no date for this document.
192. Mexía, 1566, f. 174.
193. Azpilcueta, 1567, pp. 384–5.
194. Cited Marín Ocete, II, p. 398.
195. Farfán, 1592, p. 77.

196. Molina, 1610, p. 297.
197. Diego Pérez de Valdivia, *Tratado de Frecuente Comunion*, cited by Font, 1608, f. 6v.
198. *Cf.* the observation of a Jesuit in Flanders in 1560 that it was 'la coutume du pays' not to go to communion: Lottin, 1984, p. 228.
199. Caldes, 1588, f. 153v.
200. Rodríguez, 1600, p. 204.
201. Gavarri, 1673, p. 230.
202. Ferté, p. 322.
203. AHN Inq leg. 21551.
204. AHN Inq lib. 732 f. 150.
205. Toussaert, p. 121.
206. Tentler, p. 80.
207. Dimas Loris, 1598, f. 36v.
208. Lladonosa, II, p. 68.
209. Dimas Loris, 1598, f. 4v; synod of 1610, ADB Acta Synodalia vol. 1 f. 127.
210. ADB: P year 1599.
211. BUB MS. 967.
212. Dimas Loris, 1598, f. 4. For the parish registers, see Chapter Four.
213. Ramírez to Laínez, 8 August 1561, ARSI Epist Hisp vol. 98 f. 267.
214. Tellechea, 1970, p. li.
215. Dimas Loris, 1598, f. 3.
216. ADB: V vol. 45 ff. 300, 353.
217. ADB: V vol. 82 f. 78v.
218. González Gil to Laínez, 1564, ARSI Epist Hisp vol. 102 f. 70.
219. APP: Visit of 13 August 1607, Llibre de la Rectoria de Santa Maria del Pí, f. 115.
220. See Chapter Seven.
221. ADB: C vol. 67 f. 45.
222. Ciruelo, 1628, p. 226.
223. Cited in Ferreres, p. 365.
224. There was also a *trentenari* of St Gregory, different in form and known in mediaeval England.
225. Missals of Valencia (1528) and of Vic (1547) list thirty-three masses: Ferreres, p. 366. In parts of Castile the priest was not allowed to leave the church precincts on the day he said the

mass: *ibid.* p. 370.

226. *Cf.* ADB: AP St Quintí leg. 44, where the aniversaris (all of the eighteenth century, there being few in the seventeenth) are treated as *censals*, i.e. as capital sums producing enough interest each year to pay for the annual votive mass.

227. O. López, 'La urgència de la salvació. Les misses post mortem mataronines 1690–1700', *I Congrés*, I, p. 475, cites a Mataró merchant of 1694 who founded an aniversari and asked for 2850 masses.

228. Cited in García Cárcel, *Historia de Cataluña*, vol. I, p. 213.

229. Serpi, 1604: this was the second edition. For Purgatory, see Le Goff, 1984, and the key work of Michel Vovelle on Provence.

230. AHN Inq lib. 731 ff. 205–6.

231. ADB: C vol. 65 ff. 14–60.

232. APP Visites pastorals 1402–1918 f. 6v.

233. The phenomenon has also been observed by Lottin, who states that from the 1580s 'la grande croissade de la Réforme catholique pour imposer le silence dans la maison de Dieu est commencée': Lottin, 1984, p. 244.

234. Caldes, 1588, prologue.

235. Font, 1608, f. 97v.

236. Gavarri, 1673, p. 151.

237. *Ibid.* p. 149.

238. The parish priest of St Domingo, Toledo, in AHN Inq leg. 123 no. 16.

239. Cited in Braudel, II, p. 788.

240. Pérez Martínez, 1963, I, p. 213; II pp. 44–58, 59–94.

241. Pérez de Valdivia, 1588, ff. 194, 44.

242. Torres, 1598, f. 114–15.

243. Acosta Africano, 1592, pp. 53, 83.

244. 'The priest,' says an episcopal order to clergy in the Galician see of Mondoñedo, 'when he is at the altar dressed to say mass, must be reverent and silent as befits so high a ministry, and not disturb his parishioners': AHN section Clero, vol. 6374 f. 15.

245. Hoyos and Hoyos, p. 191.

246. Villanueva, II, p. 160.

247. ADB: C vol. 76 f. 224.

248. *Cf.* Brown, 1981; Delumeau, pp. 180–289.

249. Dulac, 1680, p. 153.

250. Domenec, 1630.

251. Peter Burke, 'How to be a Counter Reformation saint', in Greyerz.

252. Villanueva, XII, p. 198.

253. Villanueva, V, p. 109.

254. Christian, 1981, *Local*, p. 40.

255. *Cf. ibid.* pp. 93–105 for an approach that differs from mine.

256. Pérez Martínez, 1963, II, p. 156.

257. Casas Gaspar, p. 291.

258. Pujades, III, p. 156.

259. ADB: C vol. 78 ff. 291, 301, 315.

260. For the same reason his cult spread rapidly through France and into Europe; 'he was probably most venerated in the Tyrol', comments Tapié, p. 154.

261. All cases are from Martí y Bonet, vol. I/2.

262. Pujades, III, p. 156.

263. ADB: V vol. 71 ff. 43–5.

264. ADB: C vol. 73 f. 44.

265. Y. Carbonell, 'Témoignages artistiques de dévotions collectives en Vallespir au XVIIe siècle', in *Conflent, Vallespir*.

266. ADB: V vol. 71 f. 11.

267. A. Fábrega, 'El P. Pedro Gil y sus Vidas de Santos', *Analecta Sacra Tarraconensis*, 31 (1958), pp. 5–25.

268. *Cf.* Pedro Córdoba, 'La place de l'ange dans l'émergence de la famille', in Redondo, 1988; on the Guardian Angel, see Delumeau, pp. 293–339.

269. Villanueva, XVIII, p. 62.

270. Philip II's collection totalled 7422 items, including 12 bodies,

144 heads and 306 complete arms and legs; see Antonio Rotondo, *Descripción del Escorial*, Madrid, 1861, pp. 68–72.

271. *Dietari*, vol. IX, pp. 20–1.
272. Pujades, IV, p. 137.
273. See the useful exposition in Bataillon, pp. 368–88.
274. *Cf.* Lottin's conclusion that the early seventeenth century in Lille was 'l'âge d'or des reliques': Lottin, 1984, p. 271.
275. IHM Consellers C. XVIII–4.
276. There are documents on the *mà armada* in ADPO, and a short discussion in P. Torreilles, 'La mà armada de 1613', *Revue d'histoire et d'archéologie du Roussillon*, 1902, pp. 185–92.
277. Pujades, IV, p. 196.
278. Pujades, III, p. 155.
279. Pujades, II, pp. 96–7; III, p. 197; IV, p. 137.
280. Cited Delumeau, p. 228.
281. AHN Inq lib. 733 f. 355v.
282. *Ibid.* lib. 733 f. 359v. An Oratory of Neri was not founded in Barcelona until May 1673: Feliu de la Penya, vol. III, p. 356.
283. *Ibid.* lib. 730 f. 416.
284. AHN Inq leg. 730 f. 350.
285. Bibliographic details in Courcelles, pp. 18–19.
286. Amades & Colomines; also Batlle.
287. R. W. Scribner, *For the Sake of Simple Folk. Popular Propaganda for the German Reformation* (Cambridge, 1981).
288. Apart from a few examples taken from specialised studies cited hereafter, all the *goigs* cited in the pages that follow are taken from the rich original collections in BCC, Raros, vol. of Gozos no. XVII; and in IMB, secció de Gràfics.
289. *Cf.* Christian, 1981, *Local*, p. 121, where in New Castile 'one in six villages had a shrine to which other villages came'.
290. Batlle, p. 31.
291. AHN Inq lib. 732 f. 506
292. *Ibid.* lib. 731 f. 289.
293. *Ibid.* leg. 15921 no. 5.
294. Amades & Colomines, I, p. 112. The goigs of Rosselló have been studied by Dominique de Courcelles-Lavedrine in a forthcoming book based on her 1980 Paris thesis, 'Les fêtes religieuses en Roussillon du XVe au XVIIIe siècle'.
295. Cited Delumeau, p. 182.
296. Camos, 1657, prologue.
297. My figures differ substantially from those of Christian, 1981, *Apparitions*, pp. 15–21; my analysis of the information also differs slightly.
298. Feliu de la Penya, III, p. 404.
299. Christian, 1981, *Apparitions*, Chapter 2.
300. *Cf.* Christian, 1981, *Local*, p. 90, who judges that 'by the early sixteenth century an apparition was a rather dangerous enterprise'.
301. This analysis is based on Camos 1657 and on the cases reported in Feliu de la Penya, III.
302. Fàbregas.
303. Taix, 1677, pp. 6–8.
304. Serra i Boldú, p. 23.
305. Taix, 1677, p. 154.
306. MSS. Mas XXIII.
307. *Dietari* V, p. 123.
308. Serra i Boldú, p. 46.
309. Martí Bonet, vol. I/2.
310. Sarrète, 1920.
311. ADB: V vol. 71.
312. Martí Bonet, vol. VI/1, pp. 325–8. The Sarrià reredos was by Agustí Pujol.
313. Martí Bonet, vol. I/2, pp. 369, 402, 544, 624.
314. See Chapter Four for the rose-water rites.
315. Serra i Boldú, pp. 74–8.
316. Amades, 1959, p. 135–6.
317. *Ibid.* p. 51.
318. *Ibid.* p. 52.
319. *Ibid.* p. 52; Nelli p. 303. Curiously, the Counter Refor-

mation in Catalonia seems to have produced no Christmas carols: 'we know no carols of the second half of the sixteenth century nor of the seventeenth', Romeu, 1952, p. 24.

320. Romeu, 1952, p. 56. *Neules* are traditional Catalan rolled wafers.

321. For the case of France, see the argument by Eric Baratay.

322. Data gleaned from the volumes of García y García.

323. Tellechea, 1970, p. lxx.

324. Pérez de Valdivia, 1588, p. 252–4.

325. Rubi, pp. 196, 285.

326. MSS. 'Crónica de Belén', f. 31v.

327. Pérez de Valdivia, 1588, p. 82v.

328. The best surveys of the art of the period are by Joan-Ramón Triadó. The best guides to church decoration at this period are the volumes on the bishopric of Barcelona edited by mossèn Martí Bonet.

329. 'The church we now have was begun to be built on 14 April 1553': ACA Monacales: Hacienda, vol. 2568 f. 1.

330. MSS. 'Crónica de Belén', f. 11v. By this date the church of the Gesù in Rome was well advanced and may have begun to dictate the beginnings of a Jesuit style.

331. *Ibid.* f. 122v.

332. *Ibid.* ff. 323–6 gives a full description of the church as it was before the fire; f. 380v notes the new foundation.

333. Durliat, p. 300.

334. Argaiz, 1677, p. 215.

335. For this period, see Argaiz, 1677; Albareda. The alternative came to be used as the standard solution to sectional conflicts; *cf.* its use in the Peruvian Church, Antonine Tibesar, 'The Alternativa: a Study in Spanish–Creole Relations in Seventeenth-Century Peru', *The Americas*, 9 (1955).

336. Consulta of Council of Aragon,

6 August 1582, ACA: CA leg. 261 f. 30; report by bishop of Tortosa, February 1588, ACA: CA leg. 264 f. 15.

337. ACA: CA leg. 269 f. 55; leg. 358, petition of 15 September 1616.

338. Petition of 1613 in Fort i Cogul, p. 189.

339. Regent, Montserrat de Guardiola, to Council, 25 April 1615, ACA: CA leg. 358 .

340. Pujades, III, p. 101.

341. Argaiz, 1677, p. 238.

342. Earlier miracles are recorded in Pedro de Burgos, *Libro de la historia y milagros de nuestra Señora de Montserrate*, written in *c.* 1514 and first published in 1536 in Barcelona.

343. As noted in Chapter One, Montserrat was the regular recipient of charity from testaments in the terme.

Chapter Four

1. Le Bras, 1976. Among many similar studies see the exposition by Wm Christian Jr, *Person and God in a Spanish valley*, Seminar Press, New York, 1972. *Cf.* Martin Ingram's view that 'most of the inhabitants of early modern Europe experienced religion in the context of small rural social systems', in Greyerz.

2. In 1583 the Inquisition punished a priest (of French origin) for criticising excommunication: AHN Inq lib. 730 f. 397.

3. The success of the Sentmenat family in confirming their rights over tithes in the Vallès in 1729 (Serra, p. 132) was symptomatic of the failure of the Church. In Mediona the tithes went to the Cardonas and to the chapter of Barcelona; the local clergy received only *primicies* (first-fruits).

4. *Cf.* Puigvert i Solà; Pladevall and Pons Guri. Both rely on the 'consueta' or statement of church ceremonial.

5. Martí Bonet, VI/1, p. 187.

6. Pérez Martínez, 1963, II, pp. 28–43.

7. Pérez Martínez, 1963, II, pp. 59–94.

8. Another possible role, the priest as agent of the state, did not in this period occur within Spain's traditional society, but was commonplace in America, see Van Oss, p. 154.

9. In Clermont (France), only 79 benefices were in the gift of the bishop, 677 in the hands of other seigneurs. Gutton, 1979, p. 186.

10. ADB Registra Ordinatorum reg. 24.

11. See pp. 163. *Cf.* the reference to 'guerres perpétuelles' in Gutton, 1979, p. 195.

12. Sales, p. 64.

13. Cited in *ibid.* p. 67.

14. Data from ADB Registra Ordinatorum reg. 24. The most common professions of fathers were farmers, and the minor trades (tailors, shopkeepers).

15. *Cf.* Gutton, 1979, p. 188 for eighteenth-century France; also Hoffman.

16. For Lyon, and by extension for France, Hoffman argues that the raising of clerical standards 'cut the priests off from the laity', p. 166, and laid the seeds of modern anti-clericalism.

17. Christian, 1981, *Local*, pp. 166–7.

18. Gil González Dávila, *Historia de Felipe III* (Madrid, 1771), p. 215.

19. ACA: CA leg. 266 f. 155.

20. MSS. BUB MS. 1010 f. 113.

21. *Cf.* Kamen, 1981, p. 344.

22. An opinion shared, it seems, by Jean Vilar, in Redondo, 1985, p. 104.

23. Bada, 1970, pp. 55–6.

24. Bada, 1988.

25. *Ibid.*

26. ADB: V vol. 73 f. 180.

27. AHN Inq lib. 730 f. 349.

28. *Ibid.* lib. 731 f. 3v.

29. *Ibid.* lib. 730 f. 315.

20. *Ibid.* lib. 731 f. 8.

31. *Ibid.* lib. 731 f. 164.

32. *Constitutiones Gerundensis*, p. 310.

33. *Constitutiones Tarraconensium*, p. 114.

34. Pérez Martínez, 1963, I, p. 271.

35. *Synodi Barcinonensis*, p. 163.

36. *Cf.* in Castile the identity of townships with parishes: Luis de Valdeavellano, *Historia de las Instituciones españolas*, (Madrid, 1968), pp. 534–5, 543–4.

37. *Cf.* Lille, where registers of confession and communion were disliked because they seemed to be an 'Inquisition': Lottin, 1984, p. 228.

38. AHN Inq lib. 735 f. 349.

39. Dimas Loris, 1598, p. 13.

40. Pérez de Valdivia, 1588, p. 256.

41. Gutton, 'Confraternities', in Greyerz, p. 203. For confraternities in Counter-Reformation Lyon, see Hoffman, p. 105.

42. MSS. 'Monumentos', BUB MS. 992, p. 151 of report on the convent of Mataró. For the population of Mataró, Joaquim Llovet, *Mataró 1680–1719: el pas de vila a ciutat* (Mataró, 1966), p. 21.

43. ADB: C vol. 70 ff. 60, 166.

44. Christian, 1981, *Local*, p. 166.

45. Flynn, p. 16.

46. Durán i Sanpere and Sanabre, vol. I, p. 398; vol. II, pp. 5, 77. Henry Cock in 1585 estimated the number at sixty: Cock, p. 125.

47. Flynn, p. 119.

48. *Synodi Barcinonensis*, pp. 161, 171.

49. ADPO, AC Nyer 10.

50. Trogno, p. 12.

51. Trogno gives a good analysis and discussion of this confraternity.

52. ADB: C vol. 72 ff. 130, 137v.

53. ADB: C vol. 78 f. 221. For the flagellants, see also Chapter Nine.
54. Trogno.
55. Martorell in 1601, Vilafranca and Sitges in 1602: ADB: C vol. 72 f. 197v, 73 ff. 39, 44.
56. This conclusion is based on registration of confraternities in the diocesan records.
57. Pladevall and Pons Guri, p. 131. *Cf.* my comments above on the perception of Purgatory.
58. M. Ribot i Iglesies, 'La confraria dels Cavallers de Sant Jordi', in *I Congrés*, I, p. 464.
59. See A. Durán i Sanpere, *Els Cavallers de Sant Jordi* (Barcelona, 1964).
60. For Saragossa, see Aurora Egido, 'Las cofradías zaragozanas del siglo XVII y su proyección literaria', in Redondo, 1988.
61. Madurell i Marimon, 1944, p. 135.
62. ADPO reg. GG. 5, in Desplanque.
63. Torreilles and Desplanque, p. 231.
64. Serra i Boldu, 1981, p. 62.
65. ADB: V vol. 67/1 f. 168.
66. See below, p. 210.
67. For the lord of misrule in western Europe, see Welsford, 1935, Chapter IX.
68. See Chapter Six.
69. Statutes of 25 June 1596 in ADB: C vol. 70 f. 163.
70. ADB: V vol. 71 ff. 133, 141, 156; for St Llorenç the reference is from the year 1636. I take the explanation of the 'ous' from Martí Bonet, I/2, p. 432.
71. On Lyon see e.g. N. Z. Davis; on Romans, Le Roy Ladurie.
72. I hope to look in detail at civic piety in Barcelona (not to be confused with the 'civic righteousness' of the German Reformation) on another occasion.
73. The best look at the elite of Barcelona in this period is by Amelang.
74. B. Moeller, *Imperial Cities and the Reformation*, Philadelphia, 1972; T. Brady, *Ruling Class, Regime and Reformation at Strasbourg 1520–55*, Leiden, 1978.
75. Weinstein & Bell, p. 171; William J. Bouwsma, *Venice & the Defense of Republican Liberty: Renaissance Values in the Age of the Counter Reformation* (University of California, 1968). A view of religion in Toledo in Christian 1981, *Local*, pp. 148–53.
76. The basic source, the *Llibre de les Solemnitats*, is edited by Durán i Sanpere and Sanabre.
77. Durán i Sanpere 1964.
78. Raphael Pastor, *A la humildad que tuvo San Raymundo* (Barcelona 1601), no. 15 in *Spanish and Catalan chapbooks*, BL 11450 e. 25.
79. ADB: AP MP/SQ 13 f. 330.
80. Baltasar Calderon, *Alabanças de la insigne ciudad de Barcelona* (Barcelona, 1604), no. 22 in *Spanish and Catalan chapbooks*, BL 11450 e. 25.
81. Of the six only Penyafort was officially canonised at that date; St Oleguer (*d.* 1136) was eventually canonised in 1676.
82. In 1788 immense efforts were made by the *Consell de Cent* to locate the body of St Pere Nolasc, thirteenth-century Catalan founder of the Order of the Mercé, and excavations went on for six months: IHM Consellers C. XVIII-4.
83. *Dietari*, XVI, p. 202; Capmany, 1951, p. 276. The body was transferred from Canigó to Perpinyà after the Revolution, then back to Canigó in 1902.
84. Batlle Prats.
85. *Cónsols* to Philip II, 26 April 1591, ACA: CA leg. 342.
86. Processions are discussed more fully later in this chapter.

87. Christian, 1981, *Local*, p. 174.
88. *Ibid.* p. 175 estimates the same number for the dioceses of New Castile.
89. ADPO, BB 32 ff. 181–2.
90. F. Bravo, *Pronostico y Calendario de todas las fiestas del año que se guardan en el Principado de Cataluña* (Barcelona, 1684): BCC Fullets Bonsoms 4649 bis. In Solsona in 1629 the synodal constitutions list 90 obligatory religious feasts and 27 recommended; in Barcelona in 1669 the count was 92 obligatory feasts: *Constitutiones Solsona*, pp. 25–7; *Constitutiones Barcinonen*, 1673, pp. 275–7.
91. For feasts, see Velasco; Hoyos Saínz; Casas Gaspar; Capmany, 1951; Griera. A useful European perspective is given by Burke.
92. Babcock, 1978.
93. The view of Max Gluckman, cited in Babcock, 1978, p. 22, was that 'rites of reversal obviously include a protest [but] they are intended to preserve and strengthen the established order.'
94. Turner, in Babcock, 1978, p. 280, follows Van Gennep in suggesting that these stages are the transitional (liminal) rites of passage in society.
95. The fool in European literature is sketched in Welsford, 1935.
96. Pérez de Valdivia, 1618, prologue and p. 28.
97. Amades, 1950–6, vol. I, pp. 238–40.
98. Casas Gaspar, p. 188.
99. ADB: V vol. 82 f. 120.
100. Capmany, 1951, p. 53.
101. Borja to Los Cobos, 11 February 1540, *MHSI Borgia*, vol. II, p. 50. One may add that thirteen years later, when a Jesuit in Oñate, Borja was less tolerant of the masques, and set up a counter-procession to undermine the Carnival celebrations: the Jesuits 'organised a procession of children carrying the crucifix in front, and we learnt from many people who were about to go out with masks and other inventions, that they refrained when they saw the procession': Borja to Loyola, 28 February 1553, *MHSI Borgia*, vol. III, p. 135.
102. Amades, 1934, p. 42.
103. Pujades, III, p. 127.
104. An essential fund of information is Amades 1950–6, vol. II, pp. 3–526.
105. Casas Gaspar, pp. 209–14. Other animals ritually killed in Catalonia to symbolise the death of winter were bears, dogs, cats, ducks, pigs and bulls: Amades 1950–6, vol. II, p. 106ff.
106. *Cf.* Le Roy Ladurie, Chapter 12.
107. Parish of Alius, in ADU, 'Procesos de Visita 1611, 1662–99'.
108. Pujades, I, p. 345.
109. Givanel Mas.
110. Pujades, IV, p. 229.
111. 'A Turk came to the carnival and on his return to Constantinople was asked what he had seen in Spain, and he replied that he had seen a marvellous thing in the city of Barcelona, which was that for a week they ran around as though they had all taken leave of their senses, and he thought that they had indeed gone crazy, but then on the day after they went to the churches and some ashes were put on their foreheads, and they all recovered their senses,' Pérez de Valdivia, 1618, p. 46.
112. Villanueva, XIV, p. 101.
113. *Relacion verdadera de las fiestas de Carnestoltes que se han hecho en la Ciudad de Barcelona*, Bodleian Library, Oxford, Arch. Seld. A. I. 14 no. 5.
114. See Kamen, 'Nudité et Contre-Réforme', in Redondo, 1990.
115. Amades, 1934, p. 77.
116. See Chapter One for the division

of processions into those of joy and those of deliverance.

117. ADB Acta Synodalia, vol. 1, f. 241.
118. ADB Acta Synodalia, vol. 2, f. 267.
119. *Cf.* Delumeau, p. 148. For the twenty formal processions in use in the diocese of Barcelona in 1569, see Bada, 1970, p. 84.
120. See for example the violence in the 'pardon' of Marcevol: Sarrète 1902, p. 13.
121. Pladevall and Simón, pp. 104–6.
122. ADB: V vol. 84 f. 100.
123. 'Publicatories de la Semmana Santa per las professons', 8 April 1650, ADB: C vol. 80 ff. 66–8.
124. Decree by bishop Ramon de Sentmenat, 21 March 1657, ADB: C vol. 81 f. 125.
125. See, in particular, Very; Arias.
126. Details in Chia.
127. ADB: C vol. 72 f. 80; vol. 74 f. 73; vol. 75 f. 69.
128. *Ibid.* vol. 73 f. 123. The same decree ordered that one could not 'at the matins of Christmas sing motets in the common tongue, nor use the organ or other instrument, nor mingle lewd and profane words in the chant. Nor on the day of Purification of the Virgin may clergy throw blessed candles. Nor on Maundy Thursday may those at vigil do immodest things. Nor in Holy Week may people dance with bells.'
129. ADB: C vol. 75 ff. 68–9.
130. Pujades, II, p. 158.
131. ADB: C vol. 76 f. 172.
132. MSS. BUB MS. 1005 f. 333.
133. 'Diario de Joseph de Monfar y Sorts', BUB MS. 1765, at 17 June 1683.
134. Villanueva, III, p. 128.
135. Amades, 1954, p. 39.
136. Cited Armengou i Feliu, p. 24.
137. Cited Salvat y Bové, p. 41–2.
138. Armengou i Feliu, p. 24.
139. *Autos sacramentales* are beyond the range of this book, and the reader is referred to Wardropper, Flecniakoska and Arias in the bibliography.
140. Vila, 1983, p. 143. The first modern text of 'Els Pastorets' dates from 1774.
141. *Constitutiones Barcinonen*, p. 159.
142. The subject is authoritatively dealt with by Cotarelo, pp. 9–27. For aspects in Catalonia see A. Sáenz-Rico Urbina, 'La polémica acerca de la licitud de las comedias, especialmente en Barcelona y en Mallorca', *Pedralbes* (Barcelona), 2, 1982.
143. Writing under the pseudonym Bisbe y Vidal, 1618.
144. See Chapter Seven.
145. Geronimo Vidal SJ to Suprema, 6 May 1634, AHN Inq lib. 747 f. 113.
146. Inquisitors to Suprema, 17 June 1634, *ibid.*, f. 115.
147. *Ibid.* lib. 743 f. 419.
148. Serra i Boldú, p. 69 n. 2.
149. See Agustí, 1617; Violant i Simorra, pp. 26–7.
150. Chia, p. 47.
151. ADB Acta Synodalia, vol. 1, f. 37.
152. ADB: C vol. 71 ff. 9, 163.
153. Villanueva, XVI, p. 90. As I write, in March 1991, the Colometa has been reintroduced into the ceremonial of Lérida cathedral.
154. Villanueva, VII, p. 105.
155. ADB: C vol. 73 f. 123, already cited.
156. Backman, p. 45.
157. Capmany, 1930, p. 48.
158. *Ibid.* p. 43.
159. Villanueva, XXII, p. 37.
160. Moreno, 1586, p. 250.
161. Dimas Loris, 1598, 2v.
162. For the dancing Virgin in Spain, see Hoyos Saínz and Hoyos Sancho, p. 333; Casas Gaspar, p. 138.
163. Backman, p. 98.

164. Ortiz Lucio, 1598, p. 115; Moreno, 1586, p. 255.
165. Pedro de León, p. 158.
166. Pérez de Valdivia, 1588, p. 278.
167. Moreno, 1586, p. 255.
168. Camos, 1592, p. 81: 'I do not think it bad for women to go to soirées and dances, or to see jousts, tourneys and other festivities.'
169. Backman, p. 56.
170. Díaz de Luco, 1543, f. 63.
171. Tejada, V, p. 261, session five, art. 5.
172. Chia, p. 87.
173. Villanueva, III, p. 128.
174. Dueñas, 1591, book IV, Chapter 13, p. 74.
175. Noydens, 1681, pp. 106–7.
176. Cited Cotarelo, p. 435. The reference seems to be to the convent of the Descalzas Reales, where until the nineteenth century the nuns danced and sang on the major feasts: Casas Gaspar, p. 187.
177. Llompart, 1974.
178. Capmany, 1930, I, p. 44.
179. *Ibid.*, I, pp. 84–5. The Vic synod stated: 'We forbid under pain of major excommunication the playing by either day or night, in the squares of towns and villages, what are commonly called "sardanas". The same penalty also applies to those who before the celebration of high mass play any type of dance-music.'
180. Rebull.
181. Pastor, *Cobles ara novament fetes* (1602), in *Spanish and Catalan chap-books*, BL 11450 e. 25, no. 20.
182. Jaume Roig, *Relació breu, verdadera y molt gustosa de les famoses festes, balls, faraus, mascares, capuchades, farces y entremesos y altres coses que se acostumen fer en la noble ciutat de Barcelona en lo temps de Carnestoltes* (1616), in *ibid.* BL 11450 e. 24, no. 10.

183. ADB, Acta Synodalia, vol. 1, f. 241.
184. The genius of the folklorists was to convert the sardana into a symbol of national yearnings. One mild September night at the Castillet in Perpignan, I saw a small group of middle-class dancers do the sardana to the strains of the accompanying *cobla*, but to the incomprehension of many French onlookers.
185. Decree by Santos, and constitutions of the synod of 22 October 1641, in *Constitutiones Solsona*, 1671, pp. 115v and 91. For Barcelona, *Constitutiones Barcinonen*, 1673, p. 290.
186. ACU Sinodos, synod of 1689, article 6.
187. V & E Turner, pp. 31–2.
188. *Cf.* Braudel 1988, p. 156: 'Countless individuals left home. It was artisans rather than peasants, men rather than women, the poor rather than the well-to-do, who were tempted to travel or run away.'
189. *Cf.* L. Rothkrug, 'Popular Religion and Holy Shrines', in Obelkevich.
190. Rothkrug, p. 51.
191. For Barcelona, Durán i Sanpere, 1972, I, p. 467; for Perpinyà, Trogno, p. 9.
192. Argaiz, 1677, p. 244.
193. Cited in Toussaert, pp. 275, 734.
194. The classic history of the shrine, based on a fourteenth-century manuscript, was written by Francesc Marès in 1666, *Història de Nostra Senyora de Núria*. I have used the abbreviated edition by Enric Moliné i Coll (Barcelona, 1987).
195. ADB Acta Synodalia, vol. 1, f. 241.
196. Pérez de Valdivia, 1588, pp. 1–10.
197. ADB, Acta Synodalia, vol. 2, f. 267.
198. ACU Sinodos, synod of 1689, f. 14v.

199. Sarrète, 1902.
200. Ariès, p. 286: 'The late sixteenth and early seventeenth centuries saw the rise of a new genre, born out of popular piety... the ex-voto'. Tosti, *passim*, catalogues items from the seventeenth to the nineteenth centuries.
201. Pérez de Valdivia, 1588, f. 4.
202. Pérez de Valdivia, 1588, p. 13–26.
203. Tejada V, p. 67 constn. 10.
204. ADB: C vol. 72 f. 65.
205. ADB: C vol 74 f. 35.
206. ADB Acta Synodalia vol. 1, f. 127.
207. ACU Sinodos, synod of 1610 ff. 13–21, article 24.
208. Synod of 22 October 1641, in *Constitutiones Solsona*, p. 90.
209. ADPO, AC Escaro no. 1 f. 9.
210. *Cf.* E.P. Thompson, *The Making of the English Working Class* (Harmondsworth, 1968), pp. 401–9, describing how religion (Methodism, in this case) reconciled the worker with his work. But Thompson's focus is slightly different, since he is concerned more with work-discipline, whereas the Catholic clergy, in an economy replete with feast-days, were concerned to define religious discipline, or the framework of religious time. See also his suggestive 'Time, work-discipline and industrial capitalism', *Past and Present*, 38, 1967.
211. In England, a bishop lamented that 'the labouring man will take his rest long in the morning... then must he have his breakfast... at noon he must have his sleeping time...', cited in Keith Thomas, 'Work and leisure in pre-industrial society', *Past and Present*, 29, 1964, p. 61.
212. Gavarri, 1673, p. 13v; on p. 87v he refers again to this as 'the great licence that there is in Andalucia over this', thus making a conscious contrast with his native Aragon.
213. ADB: V vol. 82 f. 176v.
214. *Ibid.*, vol. 84 f. 356.
215. Diaz de Luco 1543, f. 114.
216. Camos, 1592, p. 197.
217. Gutiérrez de los Ríos, 1600, pp. 261, 286.
218. Agustí, 1617, pp. 7–8.
219. H. Kamen, *European Society 1500–1700* (London, 1984), p. 168.
220. Toro, 1548, f. 88; the work has an introduction by Alfonso de Castro.
221. *Cf.* B. Pullan, 'Catholics and the poor in early modern Europe', *Transactions of the Royal Historical Society*, 26, 1976.
222. For an introduction see (*La*) *Pobreza*; and Carme Batlle i Gallart, *L'assistència als pobres a la Barcelona medieval* (s. XIII) (Barcelona, 1987).
223. Despuig (1981), p. 79.
224. Pérez de Valdivia, 1618, p. 22v.
225. There is a good summary of the debates in Flynn, and in Martz.
226. E. Serra, 'La Casa dels Infants Orfes de Barcelona 1652–3', in *Siglo XVII. Seminario de Aplicaciones Didácticas* (Tarragona, 1984).
227. *Cf.* Martz, p. 70.
228. Moreno, 1586, pp. 159–65. The work was first published in Valencia in 1571.
229. ADB: C vol. 68 f. 258.
230. 'Crides fetes per los molt Illres Señors Consellers a fi de recullir tots los pobres en lo Hospital de Nostra Señora de Misericordia' (1633), MSS. BUB MS. 1010 f. 119.
231. Salas, 1636, ff. 10v, 20, 49.
232. 'Puncts per a Predicadors', 27 February 1609, ADB: C vol. 74 f. 187.
233. J. F. de Gracia 1616 (1752).
234. Viceroy to Consejo, 29 October 1587 and Cónsols of Perpinyà to same, 17 November 1587: ACA: CA leg. 265 f. 31.
235. Consulta of Council, 25 March 1589, ACA: CA leg. 235 f. 16.

236. Why in 1624 should a tailor of Barcelona, not the most warlike of professions, have had in his possession an arquebus, a shotgun, a *pedrenyal* and two muskets?: Inventory of Miquel Fontana, in AHPB notary Francisco Aquiles menor, leg. 23, Pliego de Inventarios 1612–44.

237. Inventories of the masies of Mediona show that it was normal (as it still is) for all peasant farmers to have guns for self-defence and for hunting.

238. Fray Joan de Jesús to Philip II, 17 September 1587, ACA: CA leg. 265 f. 171.

239. *Cf.* Gatrell, Lenman, etc, pp. 21–28; see also J.A. Sharpe, 'Enforcing the Law in the Seventeenth-Century English Village', in *ibid.*

240. ADB: C vol. 66 f. 173.

241. ADB: C vol. 66 f. 156; vol. 69 f. 55; vol. 73 f. 76v.

242. All examples from Martí Bonet, 1987, pp. 185–7.

243. Joan Reglà, *El bandolerisme català del barroc*, (Barcelona, 1966), is to date the only adequate survey of this complex phenomenon.

244. Cited Nadal and Giralt, p. 92.

245. ACA: RC reg. 4725 f. 165.

246. *Ibid.* reg. 4727 f. 155v.

247. *Cf.* Nadal and Giralt, pp. 102–4.

248. Reglà, 1956, p. 150.

249. ADB: C vol. 75 f. 3.

250. Reglà, 1956, p. 92.

251. Pujades I, p. 217. The *nyerros* and *cadells* were the two feuding groups who were responsible for much of the violence of this generation in Catalonia.

252. ACA: CA leg. 78 unfolioed.

253. *Ibid.* leg. 342.

254. 'Informacion que el Exmo Sr Duque de Alburquerque ha mandado recevir', ACA: CA leg. 358.

255. Bishop to king, 1 May 1615, ACA: CA leg. 269 f. 92.

256. MSS. 'Crónica de Belén', f. 87v.

257. Letters from royal officials (*veguers*) in August 1622, ACA: CA leg. 368.

258. ACA: RC reg. 5518 f. 16. He ordered an enquiry to be made among silversmiths of Barcelona who might have received the stolen goods.

259. 'Denuntiatio contra los qui volien robar lo argent de la yglesia de Bages', ADPO, G 720 no. 27.

260. *Cf.* B. Durand, 'La répression du vol sacrilège', in *Conflent, Vallespir.*

261. Cases in ADB: P caixa 1600.

262. ADB: P year 1597.

263. AHN Inq lib. 743 f. 314, letter of 22 February 1621. Other bandits were more pragmatic. The bishop of Vic in 1615 cited one who 'having heard that anyone wearing a consecrated wafer need not fear bullets took the Sacrament out of the monstrance, placed it on a hat and fired several gunshots at it to test it, and when a bullet passed through the wafer he mocked those who trusted in such a protection against bullets': ACA: CA leg. 269 f. 21.

264. Camprubi, 'Anals de Santa Catarina', MSS. BUB MS. 1005 ff. 285–6.

265. Pujades, IV, p. 250.

266. For the 'lost people of the "apedreaderos" of Seville', lamented by Pedro de León in 1615, see Pedro de León, p. 29.

267. Capmany, 1951, p. 350.

268. Nelli, p. 270.

269. ADB: P year 1622.

Chapter Five

1. Tomás Ramón, 1619, p. 28. On the early history of the Barcelona tribunal, see Carreras i

Candí; Lea; and Blázquez. A full history written by the inquisitors themselves can be found in AHN Inq leg. 2155[1].

2. Serrano, III, p. lxx.
3. *Cf.* Lea vol. IV, p. 514.
4. Serrano, III, pp. ciii–cv.
5. Inquisitors to Suprema, 18 December 1574, AHN Inq lib. 738 f. 3.
6. *Comisario* of Urgell to inquisitors of Barcelona, 14 September 1574, *ibid.* f. 5.
7. Report in AHN Inq lib. 736 f. 19.
8. Petition of *Consellers* to king, IMH Consellers C. XVIII–6. In 1486, the Consellers said, there were two hundred *converso* merchants trading in the city, 'from whom the city and public good drew great benefits'; now there were only 'fifty-seven houses of the said conversos'.
9. 'Relatio del fet entre los Inquisidors y officials de la Generalitat', *ibid.*
10. My presentation differs fundamentally from that given by Jaime Contreras in his articles 'The social infrastructure of the Inquisition', *The Spanish Inquisition and the inquisitorial mind*, ed. A. Alcalá, New Jersey, 1987; and 'El Santo Oficio en el Principado', in *Ier Congrés*, I, pp. 111–24. Contreras presents a Catalan population 'controlled' by an Inquisition which 'extended itself throughout the rural areas', in the hands of *familiars* drawn from 'the middle classes'. My conclusions, as seen below, are diametrically opposed on all these points.
11. AHN Inq leg. 2155[1].
12. Inquisitors to Suprema, 7 May 1609, AHN Inq lib. 741 f. 325.
13. Report to cardinal Guevara, May 1600, AHN Inq leg. 2155[2]. It should be noted that the 1600 figures are themselves a reduction: in 1567 Barcelona had 79 familiars, Gerona 25 and Tarragona 21.
14. To Suprema, 29 March 1632, AHN Inq lib. 746 f. 60; and 4 November 1634, *ibid.* lib. 747 f. 136.
15. AHN Inq leg. 2155[1]. In Talarn in 1628, for example, familiars were nominated to be *cónsols*; when the viceroy heard of it he informed the town that the constitutions of Catalonia forbade it: ACA: RC reg. 5518 f. 132.
16. To Suprema, 8 October 1622, *ibid.* lib. 744 f. 7.
17. AHN Inq lib. 741 f. 46.
18. Inquisitors to Suprema, 26 May 1635, AHN Inq lib. 747 f. 187.
19. 'Manuale curie Sancti Officii Inquisitionis', covering the years 1604–18, in ADPO, G 164, is the personal register of comisario Simon Traurer, canon of Elna, and gives a full record of his activities.
20. Consulta of Council, 22 August 1587, ACA: CA leg. 262 f. 4.
21. Inquisitors to Suprema, 21 November 1560, AHN Inq lib. 730 f. 26.
22. *Dietari*, IV, pp. 390–7.
23. For edicts of faith, see Kamen, 1985, pp. 161–2.
24. In July 1598 a particularly sharp quarrel occurred with the *Consell de Cent* over some butchers' meat: out shopping one day, the inquisitors claimed that they were not being given proper service by a couple of butchers, whom they arrested, thereby clashing with the civil jurisdiction of the city, who did not think that heresy intruded into matters of meat: *Dietari*, vol. VII, pp. 116–18.
25. Reglà, 1956, pp. 188–96.
26. Auto by Espinosa, AHN Inq leg. 1592[1], no. 20.
27. Audiència decree of 20 October 1611 in BUB MS. 1008 ff. 154–6; justification by Inquisition in

AHN Inq lib. 742 f. 11, letter of 29 October 1611.

28. Massot, 1699, p. 91.

29. Royal order dated Escorial 9 August 1613, ACA Monacales, vol. 2079.

30. All the documentation of the tribunal in IMH from the 1480s down to the 1540s is in Catalan.

31. 'Memoria de las cosas en que se de buen poner orden en la Ynqon de Barna', AHN Inq leg. 1592[1], no. 2. *Cf.* also Monter, p. 70. The word 'secreto' is translated here as 'private', to avoid the misunderstanding caused in English by rendering it as 'secret'.

32. 'Copia dels advertiments fets per los señors diputats', IHM Consellers C. XVIII–6.

33. Pujades, III, p. 72.

34. The pioneering essay by J. Contreras and G. Henningsen, 'Forty-four thousand cases of the Spanish Inquisition (1540–1700)', in J. Tedeschi, ed. *The Inquisition in Early Modern Europe* (De Kalb, 1986), is a good starting point but over-optimistic about statistical data. Blázquez demonstrates, I think convincingly, that the Contreras-Henningsen figures are seriously flawed.

35. For how this worked in the diocese of Toledo, see Dedieu, 1989, pp. 287–307.

36. Licenciado Vaca to Suprema, 17 May 1549, AHN Inq lib. 736 f. 148.

37. *Ibid.* lib. 736 f. 229. The text, in an obvious slip, says 'odios' for 'judios'.

38. *Ibid.* lib. 737 f. 64.

39. 'Geografia', Iglésies, p. 273. The claim that no Catalan turned heretic may have had an occasional exception (for example, the Carmelite Jeroni Coromines was said to have gone to France in about 1596 and turned Protestant for a while: AHN Inq lib. 732 f. 131, 136). One should also note cases outside Catalonia, such as the humanist Pere Galdés, who suffered under the Saragossa Inquisition in 1595; and Bernat Ferrer, tried by the Madrid Inquisition in 1624.

40. AHN Inq lib. 738 f. 227.

41. As in 1593: AHN Inq lib. 731 f. 429v.

42. *Ibid.* lib. 737 f. 233.

43. *Ibid.* lib. 731 f. 172.

44. *Ibid.* lib. 731 f. 107.

45. *Ibid.* lib. 730 f. 308.

46. *Ibid.* lib. 731 f. 289.

47. 'The cutback in literary production in Catalan and in Castilian was caused by the presence of the Inquisition': R. García-Cárcel, *Historia de Cataluña. Siglos XVI–XVII*, vol. I, p. 396, an unlikely claim and made with no supporting evidence.

48. For some internal aspects of inquisitorial censorship see V. Pinto Crespo, *Inquisición y control ideológico en la España del siglo XVI* (Madrid, 1983).

49. AHN Inq lib. 736 f. 218.

50. *Ibid.* lib. 736 f. 244.

51. *Ibid.* lib. 736 f. 271.

52. *Ibid.* lib. 736 f. 395.

53. At this early stage, the works of Erasmus were treated generously: *cf.* Bataillon, pp. 718–19, citing decisions by the Suprema in Valladolid not to confiscate books by Erasmus unless they were specifically forbidden. See also Chapter Eight.

54. AHN Inq lib. 736 ff. 398, 458. Papal censorship had no validity in Spain unless sanctioned by both the local bishop and the Inquisition. When the Dominicans of Barcelona attempted to print a notice in 1632 giving effect to a papal ban on the works of a Jesuit, the Inquisition summoned the printer and ordered that no ban be issued: AHN Inq lib. 746

ff. 254–7.

55. For the Spanish background to censorship, see the basic bibliography in V. Pinto Crespo, a book which limits itself only to inquisitorial censorship. See also Kamen, 1985, Chapter 5, for the general context. For the indices of the sixteenth century, see Bujanda.

56. ARSI Epist Hisp vol. 96 f. 44. The Jesuits were particularly aggrieved by the banning of an edition of the *Obras del Cristiano* by Francisco Borja.

57. Araoz to Laínez, 21 September 1559, *ibid*. vol. 96 f. 430.

58. *Ibid*. vol. 96 f. 471.

59. Alfonso Lozano to Laínez, 11 December 1559, ARSI Epist Hisp vol. 96 f. 478. Govierno was a Catalan called Gubern, but seems to have used the Castilian form for convenience.

60. Juan Rubies to Laínez, 1 September 1560, *ibid*. vol. 97 f. 314.

61. AHN Inq leg. 2155[1].

62. Licenciado Gasco to Suprema, 22 December 1569, AHN Inq lib. 737 f. 35.

63. Licenciado Gasco to Suprema, 24 July 1569, *ibid*. lib. 737 ff. 73–4.

64. Licenciado Francisco de Ribera to same, *ibid*. lib. 737 f. 343.

65. Licenciado Gasco to Suprema, 7 November 1569, *ibid*. lib. 737 ff. 7–8.

66. Inquisitor Mendoza to Suprema, 15 May 1571, *ibid*. lib. 737 f. 319.

67. *Ibid*. lib. 737 f. 228.

68. *Ibid*. lib. 737 f. 255.

69. For the impact of the Trent index on the important Venetian presses, see Grendler, p. 145 ff.

70. *Ibid*. lib. 738 f. 99.

71. V. Pinto Crespo, 'El proceso de elaboración y la configuración del Indice expurgatorio de 1583–84', *Hispania Sacra*, xxx,

1977.

72. On sale in the bookshop of Onofre Gori: AHPB notary Galcerà Francesc Devesa, leg. 4, protocolos 7, año 1595.

73. Inquisitors to Suprema, 27 October 1584, AHN Inq lib. 739 f. 282.

74. Inquisitors to Suprema, 28 July 1586, *ibid*. lib. 739 f. 339.

75. *Ibid*. lib. 731 f. 166.

76. Grendler, p. 162.

77. No Jesuit appears to have been appointed until 1605, when Pere Gil became 'the first censor that the Company has had in this tribunal of Catalonia': MSS. 'Crónica de Belén', f. 32. He was at the time rector of the Jesuit college.

78. AHN Inq lib. 737 f. 262.

79. The Jesuit leader Diego Laínez commented that the Index of 1559 'restricted many spirits and pleased few': Mario Scaduto SJ, 'Laínez e l'Indice del 1559', *Archivum Historicum Societatis Iesu*, xxiv, 47, January–June 1955.

80. *Carta* of 5 July 1605, AHN Inq lib. 743 f. 20.

81. *Ibid*. lib. 741 f. 114.

82. *Ibid*. lib. 743.

83. Memo, possibly of early 1606, in *ibid*. lib. 741 ff. 142–56.

84. *Ibid*. lib. 743 f. 3–46; the Osuna ban in lib. 740 f. 182. For the *cartas acordadas* of this period, see Pinto Crespo, cited above.

85. Inquisitors to Suprema, 9 October 1609, AHN Inq lib. 741 f. 289.

86. 'Relacion de lo que se a gastado por el auto de fe se a celebrado en 21 de deziembre 1573', AHN Inq lib. 738 f. 53.

87. Pujades, II, p. 89.

88. Soman, p. 452; Grendler, pp. 120, 165–8.

89. AHN Inq lib. 743.

90. To Suprema, 16 March 1611, AHN Inq lib. 742 f. 33.

91. Carta acordada of 1 December 1609, *ibid.* lib. 743.
92. To Suprema, 30 April 1627: AHN Inq lib. 745 f. 44.
93. Grendler, Chapter VI.
94. To Suprema, 30 April 1627, reporting receipt of letters of 18, 19 and 21 January: AHN Inq lib. 745 ff. 44–7.
95. To Suprema, 12 February 1628, *ibid.* lib. 745 f. 249.
96. Inquisitors to Suprema, 19 February 1632, AHN Inq lib. 746 f. 176.
97. By contrast Nalle, 1989, p. 93, gives a balanced view to be found in few scholars.
98. V. Pinto Crespo in S. Haliczer, ed. *Inquisition and Society in Early Modern Europe* (London, 1986), p. 185.
99. Auto of 17 October 1552, AHN Inq lib. 730.
100. *Ibid.* lib. 730 f. 23.
101. *Ibid.* lib. 730 ff. 55–8, 59–61, 68–70.
102. *Cf.* E. Le Roy Ladurie, *Montaillou* (London, 1978).
103. Nadal and Giralt, p. 62. There is no evidence that these proportions apply to the interior of Catalonia, with the possible exception of the Pyrenean regions.
104. *Ibid.* p. 58 n. 1.
105. *Ibid.* pp. 91–2.
106. Bishop of Elna to Council of Aragon, 10 July 1606, ACA: CA leg. 349.
107. Reglà, 1956, pp. 181–5.
108. Nadal and Giralt, p. 81.
109. See p. 224, and Chapter Eight.
110. Reglà, 1956, p. 76.
111. Reglà, 1956, p. 77.
112. *Ibid.* p. 181, citing ACA: RC reg. 4731 f. 94.
113. 'Relacion de las casas de franceses que ay en la ciudad de Barcelona', ACA: CA leg. 552.
114. For these and related figures, see the analysis below, p. 263.
115. AHN Inq lib. 736 f. 458.

116. *Dietari*, IV, f. 401.
117. It is surprising that Contreras, in *I Congrés* cited above, p. 118, should note the 'extraordinary frequency' of the Inquisition in appointing French as familiars, when the Inquisition in fact tried to avoid appointing them.
118. Nadal and Giralt, p. 50, n. 6: 'unanimement, les autorités catalanes s'élevèrent contre toute mesure défavorable aux Français fixés dans le pays.'
119. AHN Inq leg. 1592[1].
120. J. Blázquez, p. 366.
121. Moliné Coll, 1988–9, p. 372.
122. ACU, Sinodos, synod of 1616 ff. 22–46, clause 12.
123. ACA: CA leg. 367.
124. ACU, Sinodos, 1622 synod, clause 31; Sinodos 1585–1700, doc. 2, 1635 synod.
125. Nadal and Giralt, p. 153.
126. Amades, 1934, *Bruixes*, p. 41. Women in villages such as Vimbodí in the Conca de Barberà, Altafulla in the campo de Tarragona, Vallgorguina in the Maresme, were reputed to be witches by definition.
127. Fàbregas, pp. 66, 71.
128. Pujades, II, p. 186.
129. Violant y Simorra, p. 532.
130. Kamen, 1985, p. 211.
131. 'Instrucciones sobre las Bruxas', AHN Inq lib. 741 ff. 294–300; Sarmiento's report on Mallet, dated 25 October 1548, is in *ibid.* lib. 736 f. 119.
132. Report by Vaca, 5 May 1549, AHN Inq lib. 736 f. 55.
133. Lea, IV, p. 218.
134. Inquisitors to Suprema, 2 August 1574, AHN Inq lib. 738 f. 60.
135. *Ibid.* lib. 741 ff. 294–300 contains a copy of the Navarre instructions sent to Barcelona. For the Navarre cases, see Julio Caro Baroja, *Inquisición, brujería y criptojudaismo* (Barcelona, 1974), pp. 183–315; and G. Henningsen, *The Witches'*

Advocate (Reno, 1980).

136. AHN Inq lib. 743 f. 40.

137. October 1606 interrogations in ADPO, G 160.

138. Pladevall, pp. 26–31. Monter, p. 274, follows Pladevall in giving unacceptably high figures for the number of witches executed.

139. AHN Inq lib. 732 f. 369.

140. *Ibid*. lib. 732 f. 426. Carmell came from a village near Toulouse.

141. ADPO, serie BB1.

142. Chauvet, p. 198.

143. R. Garcia Carrera, *Les bruixes de Caldes de Montbui* (Caldes, 1985), gives some original documents on a dozen executions by bailiffs in this village in 1619–20.

144. ACA: CA leg. 368.

145. 'Memorial que el Padre Pedro Gil dio al Duque de Alburquerque en defensa de las bruxas', manuscript copy in MSS. BUB MS. 1008 ff. 335–7. The memoir is dated 'Deste Collegio de Belen a 10 de Henero de 1619'.

146. The account that follows is based on papers, principally of January 1622, in ACA: CA leg. 368.

147. Bishop of Tortosa to Council, 31 December 1621; bishop of Solsona to *ibid*. 12 January 1622: ACA: CA leg. 368.

148. Report by Alonso de Salazar Frias, but without his name, in ACA: CA leg. 368. The reference to children is clearly based on his experience in the Basque country.

149. There is no evidence for the improbable figure of 400 witches executed, given by Reglà, 1980, p. 65; he also mistakenly dates the Carmell episode to 1627.

150. ACA: RC reg. 5516 f. 145.

151. AHN Inq lib. 732 f. 508.

152. *Ibid*. lib. 733 f. 37v.

153. *Ibid*. lib. 733 ff. 236–43.

154. Inquisitors to Suprema, 17 May 1631, AHN Inq lib. 746 f. 57. For the price rise from 1629 see the graph in Serra, p. 249.

155. AHN Inq lib. 735.

156. The accused were expelled from Barcelona for five years: *ibid*. lib. 735.

157. This is one of the central theses of Muchembled.

158. Salo Baron, XV, p. 174.

159. Nalle, 1987, p. 579, referring to the diocese of Cuenca.

160. The only researched study of Catalonia, by Blázquez, coincides with my reading of the evidence and concludes that the Inquisition did not terrorise.

161. *Cf*. Dedieu, 1989, p. 146, who says that in Toledo Old Christians behaved to the Inquisition as they did to any other jurisdiction.

162. Inquisitors to Suprema, 16 December 1623, AHN Inq lib. 744 f. 146.

163. No documentation is offered to back up this image given by J. Contreras in the collective volume *Historia de la Inquisición de España y América* (Madrid, 1984), p. 755.

164. Dr Mendoza to Suprema, 22 December 1569, AHN Inq lib. 737 ff. 63–4.

165. Gasco to Suprema, 24 July 1569, *ibid*. lib. 737 ff. 73–4.

166. Blázquez, p. 80, citing AHN Inq lib. 739 f. 26.

167. Inquisitors to Suprema, 15 July 1623, AHN Inq leg. 2155[2].

168. *Ibid*. 11 December 1637, *ibid*. lib. 747 f. 394.

169. Cartas acordadas in AHN Inq lib. 743.

170. *Cf*. Kamen, 1985, pp. 165–6.

171. Letters to Suprema of 13 April 1603, AHN Inq lib. 741 f. 9; and of 3 August and 10 October 1605, *ibid*. ff. 102, 107.

172. Inquisitor Oliván to Suprema, 28 April 1606, *ibid*. f. 124.

173. To Suprema, 25 May 1609,

AHN Inq lib. 741 f. 321.

174. AHN Inq leg. 2700.

175. To Suprema, 17 May 1631, AHN Inq lib. 746 f. 57.

176. *Cf.* Dedieu, 1989, p. 261. Inexplicably, Contreras in *Ier Congrés*, p. 117, comes to the conclusion, contradicted by all the evidence, that the Inquisition 'abandoned' the cities.

177. 'Memoria de la visita que ha hecho el licenciado Lagonylla, Inquisidor de Cataluña', AHN Inq lib. 736 ff. 380–1.

178. In 1563, 1564, 1567, 1569, 1571, 1579, 1581, 1582, 1583, 1590, 1593, 1595, 1596, 1598, 1600, and 1602. All details for these visitations come from AHN Inq leg. 1592[1].

179. Visita in *ibid.* leg. 1592[1] no. 15.

180. J. Contreras, *El Santo Oficio de Galicia* (Madrid, 1982), p. 488.

181. Inquisitor to Suprema, 2 November 1559, AHN Inq lib. 736 ff. 394–5.

182. Licenciado Gasco to Suprema, 15 November 1569, *ibid.* lib. 737 f. 11.

183. AHN Inq lib. 737 ff. 227–34.

184. Visita in AHN Inq leg. 1592[1] no. 4.

185. Even this is doubtful. The cases noted in Chapter Nine were apparently cited to Barcelona and not dealt with in the villages.

186. All percentages are rounded. The figures are presented as a sample group rather than a totality, since three years (1579, 1604 and 1605) are omitted; the sources are AHN Inq libs. 730–2, and leg. 1592[1].

187. Blázquez, p. 355, in an exhaustive analysis, concludes that in the three centuries of the Inquisition's existence in Catalonia it acted in only 6.5 per cent of the centres of population, and 'in the immense majority' of them only one accused was affected. His statistics have not been used here in detail, since he classifies all

Catalans as Spaniards, whereas my analysis expressly distinguishes the two.

188. To Suprema, 21 January 1578, AHN Inq leg. 1592[1].

189. J. Contreras, in *Historia de la Inquisición*, p. 757.

190. ADB: V vol. 71 f. 17.

191. 'Relacion de la visita que hizo el Doctor Joan Aymar en los condados de Rossellon y Serdaña', AHN Inq lib. 739 ff. 65–7.

192. 'Relacion de las testificaciones que uvo en la visita que el Inquisidor Francisco de Ribera hizo en el obispado de Urgell', AHN Inq lib. 739 f. 155.

193. Ribera to Suprema, 1 April 1582, *ibid.* lib. 739 f. 176.

194. AHN Inq leg. 1592[1] nos. 6, 8.

195. The eighty-three cases in 1596 included thirty-five French people (nine of them accused of bigamy and virtually all transients), thirteen Catalans whose cases were dismissed, six clergy accused of sexual offences, and twenty-nine other Catalans accused simply of verbal propositions: AHN Inq leg. 1592[1] no. 11.

196. 'Las denunciaciones que se an hecho en la visita que se a hecho esta Quaresma de 1572 en la ciudad de Barcelona', AHN Inq lib. 737 ff. 367–71.

197. 'Memoria de las villas y lugares que visitó el Dr Juan Alvarez de Caldas', AHN Inq leg. 2155[1].

198. To Suprema, 9 August 1614, AHN Inq lib. 742 f. 233.

199. *Ibid.* lib. 732 f. 30v.

200. *Ibid.* lib. 732 f. 329.

201. *Ibid.* lib. 733 f. 367v.

202. *Ibid.* lib. 733 f. 385.

203. Lea, III, pp. 71–5.

204. IHM Consellers C. XVIII–8 f. 65.

205. Inquisitors to Suprema, 30 December 1552, AHN Inq lib. 736 f. 270–1.

206. Consulta of Council of Aragon,

31 December 1583, ACA:CA leg. 261 f. 28. For a recent look at the Barcelona tribunal's attitude to sodomy see Monter, pp. 111–116.

207. AHN Inq lib. 733 f. 408.

208. For an outline, see Kamen, 1985, pp. 189–97.

209. Inquisitors to Suprema, 21 November 1560, AHN Inq lib. 730 f. 26.

210. *Ibid*. 20 May 1569, *ibid*. lib. 730 f. 91.

211. *Ibid*. 23 October 1560, *ibid*. f. 23.

212. Dietari, IV, p. 401; AHN Inq lib. 730 ff. 35–45. The latter account lists forty-two accused, but twenty of these were penanced before the auto.

213. *Dietari* V, p. 11; AHN Inq lib. 730 ff. 55–8. Of the forty-five accused forty-one were non-Catalans; there were nine relaxed in person, none Catalan. Another auto, for which I can find no details, took place on 12 July 1562.

214. *Dietari*, V, p. 25; AHN Inq lib. 730 ff. 59–61. Three of the thirty-eight were Catalans.

215. *Ibid*. lib. 730 ff. 67–70. There were forty-seven accused; all the five relaxed were French.

216. Camprubi, 'Anals de Santa Catarina', MSS. BUB MS 1005 f. 121; *Dietari*, VI, p. 563.

217. Camprubi, 'Anals de Santa Catarina', MSS. BUB MS 1005 f. 209v.

218. Pujades, I, p. 199; IV, p. 93. The public autos of the late sixteenth century are all detailed in AHN Inq lib. 730 ff. 13 onwards.

219. Inquisitors to Suprema, 13 August 1622, AHN Inq leg. 2155[2].

220. *Ibid*. to Suprema, 16 December 1623, AHN lib. 744 f. 146. Few prisoners were kept by the Barcelona Inquisition because it could not afford to maintain them. If its cells were full, as they

happened to be in 1624, the inquisitors were most reluctant to send their prisoners to the city gaol where, they claimed, 'there are over four hundred prisoners who are starving to death and every day they remove three or four dead': to Suprema, 13 September 1624, *ibid*. lib. 744 f. 181.

221. Inquisitors to Suprema, 26 June 1627, AHN Inq lib. 745 f. 225. The bishop of Barcelona was Joan Sentís, who had been viceroy in the previous four years.

222. Camprubi, 'Anals de Santa Catarina', MSS. BUB MS. 1005 f. 341.

223. Inquisitors to Suprema, 2 December 1560, refer to 'all the civil and criminal cases apart from cases of faith': AHN Inq lib. 730 f. 21.

224. 'Los presos que a avido por cosas fuera de fe que an estado en la carcel', AHN Inq leg. 1592[1] ff. 218–22.

225. Inquisitors to Suprema, 16 December 1623, AHN Inq lib. 744 f. 146.

226. 'Relacion de la visita que el Inquisidor licenciado Alonso Marquez de Prado ha hecho... este año de 1596', AHN Inq leg. 1592[1]; cases of faith of 1596 in *ibid*. lib. 731 ff. 252–65.

227. For a more extensive treatment of the problem of statistics, and for a thorough analysis of cases, see Blázquez, pp. 343–63.

228. AHN Inq lib. 730 ff. 402–11, 425–33.

229. Letters of 19 December 1586 and 20 December 1588, *ibid*. lib. 731 ff. 10, 23.

230. 'Visita de la Inq de Barna que hizo el Illo Señor Francisco de Soto Salazar del Consejo de Su Magd', AHN Inq leg. 1592[1] no. 21. Soto, it should be noted, was the inquisitor who assured St Teresa that her work was in

no danger from the Inquisition.
231. Auto of the inquisitor general in *ibid.* no. 20.
232. From auto de fe of 9 March 1572, AHN Inq lib. 730 f. 144.
233. *Ibid.* lib. 733 f. 378.
234. Licenciado Gasco to Suprema, 5 December 1571, *ibid.* lib. 737 f. 288.
235. To Suprema, 7 September 1618, *ibid.* lib. 743 ff. 95–9.
236. To Suprema, 26 June 1627 and 29 January 1628, *ibid.* lib. 745 ff. 226, 254.
237. To Suprema, 23 April 1611, *ibid.* lib. 742 f. 13.
238. Licenciado Muñoz de la Cuesta to Suprema, 24 July 1620, *ibid.* lib. 743 f. 348.
239. Inquisitors Andrés Bravo and Abad to Suprema, 23 February 1632, AHN Inq lib. 746 f. 179.
240. Philip III to Council, 14 August 1599, ACA: CA leg. 264 f. 108.
241. Kamen, 1981, pp. 366–7.
242. AHN Inq lib. 748 ff. 180, 183.
243. Taken from letters of inquisitor Cotoner of 4 March 1641, and inquisitor Abad, 26 February 1641, in *ibid.* ff. 300–3.
244. MSS. 'Crónica de Belén', f. 165.
245. Letter to Suprema, 18 February 1641, *ibid.* f. 282.
246. My original exposition had a detailed analysis with maps and diagrams, but the appearance of Blázquez now makes this superfluous. For the sources see p. 470, n. 186.
247. AHN Inq lib. 731 ff. 254, 265v.
248. *Ibid.* lib. 732 f. 9.
249. *Ibid.* leg. 1592^1.
250. I emphasise the notion of 'sample'. Different ways of counting the cases can lead to widely differing absolute figures.
251. The categories have been elaborated for this study and do not coincide with those adopted by the Inquisition or with those used by other historians of the tribunal.

252. Clerical discipline and sexual offences are mentioned in Chapters Seven and Six respectively; the other categories are, largely touched on in this chapter.
253. The tribunal had only limited powers over bigamy and used its jurisdiction over sodomy rarely, since in Catalonia the secular bailiffs were active in the matter: 'in many towns and villages of this principality the baronial justices have hanged and burned them', inquisitors to Suprema, 19 September 1606, AHN Inq lib. 741 f. 169.
254. *Ibid.* lib. 733 ff. 176, 230.
255. AHN Inq leg. 1592^1 no. 11, case 1.
256. This theme, marginal to our present purposes, is dealt with by Blázquez, pp. 147–57; and by B. Bennassar, *Los cristianos de Alá* (Madrid, 1989).
257. In reality, only one book was at issue, the *Relaciones* of Antonio Pérez.
258. See the convincing presentation for Cuenca by Nalle, 1987.
259. AHN Inq lib. 733 f. 338.
260. *Ibid.* lib. 733 f. 338v. Barrufet appears repeatedly in the documentation, notably in 1633 as the lover of a nun in the convent at Vallbona; the relationship lasted long, despite efforts by the Church authorities to break it up. It is a comment on the state of the convent that Barrufet in 1634 actually moved in to live with her in her cell: AHN Inq lib. 733 f. 439.
261. *Ibid.* lib. 733 ff. 379, 413.
262. *Ibid.* lib. 732 f. 420.
263. *Ibid.* lib. 732 f. 485.
264. *Ibid.* lib. 733 f. 337.
265. *Ibid.* lib. 733 f. 339v.
266. *Ibid.* lib. 733 f. 383v.
267. *Ibid.* lib. 733 f. 432.
268. *Ibid.* lib. 733 f. 483v.
269. Derived from Blázquez, p. 119.
270. To Suprema, 8 October 1622,

AHN Inq lib. 744 f. 7.

271. To Suprema, 7 September 1618, *ibid.* lib. 743 ff. 95−9.

272. 'Inconvenientes que resultaran en el Santo Officio', AHN Inq lib. 744 f. 191.

273. Carta acordada received June 1604, *ibid.* lib. 743 f. 11.

274. To Suprema, 23 November 1575, AHN Inq lib. 738 f. 169.

275. Inquisitors to Suprema, 14 January 1634, AHN Inq lib. 747 f. 122. A similar case of unverifiable French origins is documented for 1632; on that occasion the tribunal allowed the appointment to proceed: *ibid.* lib. 746 f. 243.

276. To Suprema, 8 October 1622, AHN Inq lib. 744 f. 7.

277. 1623 application of Botines in ADB Inq leg. for years 1623−9. The procedure of proving his *limpieza* took five years, and he was appointed in 1628.

278. Full family origins of Feliu given in ADB Inq leg. for 1628.

279. See J. Llovet, *Mataró 1680−1719. El pas de vila a ciutat* (Mataró, 1966); P. Molas i Ribalta, *Comerç i estructura social a Catalunya i València als segles XVII i XVIII* (Barcelona, 1977), Chapter 4.

280. ADB Inq legs for 1623−9 and for 1628.

281. AHN Inq lib. 746 f. 390.

282. 'Papel que escrivio el Dr Juan Rivera, respondiendo a las pretensiones que tenian contra el Sto Oficio los tres brazos', MSS. BUB MS. 967 no. 29.

283. To Suprema, 12 January 1613, AHN Inq lib. 742 ff. 128−9.

284. To Suprema, 30 December 1552, *ibid.* lib. 736 f. 270.

285. *Ibid.* lib. 738 f. 145.

286. El Superbo's fascinating case is detailed in AHN Inq lib. 730 ff. 345, 421, 434, 440. His real name was Guillem Martí.

287. Inquisitors to Suprema, 25 August 1615, *ibid.* lib. 742 f. 254

288. Bishop of Urgell to inquisitors, *ibid.* lib. 745 ff. 312, 367.

289. Duke of Cardona to procurador real, March 1632, ADPO, G 160.

290. To Suprema, 26 January 1636, *ibid.* lib. 747 f. 278.

291. Don Francisco Gregorio to inquisitor general, 30 April 1633, *ibid.* lib. 746 f. 333. The ninth familiar in Arenys had been appointed, against the advice of the comisario, in 1627; his wife was the daughter of a familiar, which kept the business in the family: *ibid.* lib. 745 ff. 120−1.

292. ADPO, G 160.

293. Serrano, IV, p. lvi.

294. Kamen, 1986.

295. Pérez de Valdivia, (1977), pp. 66, 84. The papers on his case are in AHN Inq leg. 2393 and in libs. 578−9; see J. M. Sánchez Gómez, 'Un discípulo del P. Mto. Avila en la Inquisición de Córdoba', *Hispania*, 9 (1949), no. 34; and Madurell i Marimon, 1957.

296. This, at least, was the attitude of the elite, but *cf.* Blázquez's pertinent comments on the willingness of ordinary Catalans to denounce conversos: *op. cit.*, p. 34.

297. ADB Inq leg. for years 1623−9.

298. *Ibid.*

299. ADB, Inq Limpieza de Religiosos, vol. I.

300. AHN Inq lib. 745 f. 223.

301. Inquisitors to Suprema, 9 May 1600, *ibid.* lib. 740.

302. Inquisitors to Suprema, 14 January 1634, AHN Inq lib. 747 f. 8.

303. Cosme de Medicis, *Viaje*, p. 35.

304. Inquisitors to Suprema, 9 February 1692, AHN Inq leg. 21551.

305. AHN Inq lib. 731 f. 499.

306. See p. 262.
307. To Suprema, 7 May 1611, AHN Inq lib. 742 f. 18.
308. 'Relacion de las causas despachadas en el auto publico de fe que se celebro en la Inquisicion en 21 de junio de este presente año de 1627', AHN Inq lib. 733 f. 230.
309. *Ibid.* lib. 745 f. 338.
310. ACA Monacales vol. 4125 ff. 37, 46.

Chapter Six

1. *Cf.* Ingram, 1987, pp. 1–17.
2. In the post-Reformation see of York in 1575, the archbishop's visitation produced 1200 citations to court, in 1636 the figure was 5000 (Ingram, p. 13), figures to which there is no remote parallel in the history of the Catalan Church at this period.
3. This rough estimate is based on about 300 cases for the late sixteenth and early seventeenth centuries.
4. There is no study of marriage in pre-industrial Spain. Gaudemet is essential for a European perspective. Flandrin, 1979, and Flandrin, 1981, give useful surveys based on France.
5. An indispensable guide is Jean Gaudemet.
6. C. Klapisch-Zuber, Chapter 9.
7. Gottlieb, in Wheaton & Hareven. In Xanten (Cologne) at the end of the fifteenth century the diocesan court faced 468 demands for the validation of 'marriages', 351 of them from the female partner; in Canterbury between 1410 and 1420, out of 41 marriage cases, 38 involved 'clandestinity': cited Gaudemet, pp. 234, 236. In Constance at the end of the sixteenth century, out of some 4000 cases where the status of marriage promises was in question, only some 5 per cent of litigants were compelled to proceed to a formal marriage: Safley, 1981.
8. Diefendorf, 1983, pp. 156–70. In France the state was forced to legislate since the decrees of Trent were never registered as law, and were 'received' by the French Church only in 1615.
9. Sempere y Guarinos, p. 59.
10. Maspons, pp. 3, 20. Basing himself on the classic seventeenth-century authorities, Maspons is the essential guide to family law in early modern Catalonia.
11. Avila, in Marín Ocete, I, p. 182.
12. On Trent, marriage and Tametsi, see the full survey by G. Le Bras, 'Mariage' in *Dictionnaire de Théologie Catholique*, vol. 9 (Paris, 1926), pp. 2123–317; brief treatment in Gaudemet, pp. 285–95.
13. Córdoba, 1573, p. 108.
14. AHN Inq lib. 743 f. 11, carta acordada of 19 July 1601.
15. *Constitutiones Synodales Barcinonen*, p. 124.
16. AHN Inq lib. 730 f. 435 and lib. 731 f. 9.
17. Flandrin, 1981, Chapter 4.
18. Piñol Agulló.
19. Ingram, 1987, p. 132.
20. Astete, 1598, p. 75.
21. Robisheaux, p. 114. I take 'public' here to mean 'church'.
22. Pedro de León, p. 125.
23. Azpilcueta, 1567, p. 167.
24. Ortiz Lucio, 1598, pp. 62, 109. The confusion implicit in the use of the word 'betrothed' (*desposados*) should be noted. The authors mean those who have not yet made *verba de praesenti*, but in other usage desposados also meant 'married'.
25. ACL Libros de Visitas 1.
26. ADB: V vol. 45 f. 284.
27. Primitivo J. Pla Alberola, in (La)

Familia, p. 111.

28. *Cf.* Lottin, 1984, p. 220ff, showing that in Flanders as well the verba de futuro were viewed as a full marriage.

29. ADB: AP MP/SM vol. 6 f. 99.

30. ADB: AP MP/SM vol. 13 f. 274.

31. Lemos, 1583, p. 230. The chief devotee of the story of Tobias was fray Vicente Mexía, who dedicated ten chapters of his work (Mexía 1566) to it.

32. ADB: C vol. 65 ff. 1–4.

33. Noydens, 1681, p. 445. This was the Barcelona, 1681 edition, the seventeenth edition since its first publication in Toledo in 1675.

34. ADB: C vol. 72 f. 65.

35. *Ibid.* 74 f. 37.

36. *Ibid.* 74 f. 123.

37. *Ibid.* 78 f. 154.

38. ACU Sinodos, synod of 1610 f. 13, article 26; synod of 1616 f. 22, article 29.

39. ACU Sinodos, synod of 1689, article 13.

40. 'Matrimonium contrahentes intra duos menses benedictionis missam audiant': *Constitutiones Vicenses*, f. 43v; *Constitutiones Gerunden*, pp. 332–3. In Tortosa, on the other hand, the diocesan synod of 1575 specified a period of six months: *Synodus Dertosana*, p. 48.

41. ADB: AP Santa Maria vol. 9, Matrimonis.

42. 'Edictum de matrimonii sacramento', *Constitutiones Vicenses*, ff. 88–94.

43. *Constitutiones Barcinonen*, p. 247.

44. *Ibid.* f. 41v.

45. *Cf.* Anderson, p. 55.

46. Ingram, 1987, pp. 219, 225.

47. Capella, p. 100.

48. ADB Acta Synodalia vol. 1 f. 31.

49. All data in this paragraph are from ADB: AP Santa Maria vol. 9, Matrimonis.

50. ADB: P year 1600, caixa B/1.

51. *Ibid.* year 1626, caixa A/1.

52. Maspons, p. 25.

53. ADB: P caixa for year 1626.

54. ADB: P year 1600, caixa B/2.

55. The 1553 source is Hugo de Celso, cited by Françoise Vigier, in Redondo, 1987, p. 166 n. 38.

56. No modern study exists. For a juridical perspective, see E. Gacto, 'El grupo familiar de la edad moderna en el Mediterráneo hispánico', and for demography A. Simón Tarrés, 'La familia catalana en el antiguo régimen', both in (La) *Familia*, pp. 36–64, 65–93.

57. The classic 'stem family' described by Le Play was based on his observations in the area of the Pyrenees.

58. *Cf.* Duby's outline of primogeniture problems in mediaeval France.

59. The figures are based on about 100 contracts examined in ADB: AP. Among the lower level was a girl from St Pere de Riudebitlles (£40) in 1569, among the top a member of the Torrens family (£170) in 1600: ADB: AP MP/SM vol. 11 f. 124, vol. 12 f. 68.

60. Same sources. The cited examples also offer exceptions to the rule: the groom in St Pere offered an *escreix* of £90 (over twice the dowry), the groom of 1600 offered only £20 (less than one-eighth).

61. 'What they regulate fundamentally', says the best brief introduction to the *capítols* and their legal significance, 'is the economic aspect': Lalinde Abadía, 1963, p. 227. I use the term 'marriage clauses' and not 'marriage contract' because each of the clauses within the document was an independent contract, and the document was therefore not one single contract.

62. Text in Lalinde, p. 257.

63. The clauses of 1400 call it *noces*,

others of a later period call it *nupcias* or *bodes*.

64. ADB: AP MP/SM 6 f. 99. The contracts use the Catalan form *paraules de present* but for simplicity of exposition I use the Latin form throughout.

65. *Ibid.* f. 251.

66. Clauses of April 1527, *ibid.* f. 445, stipulated the esposalles to be within two weeks of the signing of the contract.

67. Manuel Jiménez Fernández, *La institución matrimonial* (Madrid, 1947), p. 218.

68. ADB: AP MP/SM 13 f. 194.

69. *Ibid.* f. 274.

70. See p. 441 n. 5.

71. 'Formulari y breu instructio per als rectors o curats que han de exercir lo art de notaria en ses parrochies', *Synodi Barcinonensis*, pp. 190–247.

72. ADB: AP Santa Maria vol. 9, Matrimonis. Of 48 marriages performed between 1590 and 1603, at least 54 per cent were in the home; of 106 between 1604 and 1630, the proportion had dropped to 24 per cent.

73. Goody, p. 148, citing Helmholz, *Marriage litigation in medieval England*.

74. 'There is so far no book directed to married persons,' prologue.

75. Mexía, 1566, f. 37.

76. *Ibid.* f. 40. These splendid precepts must be seen in context against a quite different social reality.

77. But see the quotation below, p. 299, from Rodríguez, 1600.

78. Dueñas, 1591, book VI, p. 135.

79. Alvarez, 1590, part I, p. 238.

80. Camos, 1592, pp. 58–62, 73–7, 82–5.

81. Cited in Ferreras, II, p. 621.

82. The phrase occurs for example in Miquel Agustí, 1617, f. 8v.

83. Segalen, p. 49.

84. Astete, 1598, pp. 35, 121, 128, 134.

85. Rodríguez, 1600, p. 38.

86. Stone, 1979, p. 81.

87. Quixote, II, Chapter xxii.

88. Luján, 1550, p. 59.

89. For the notion of love in Counter-Reformation France, see Flandrin, 1979, pp. 161–73.

90. Lemos, 1583, pp. 215, 227.

91. Camos, 1592, part II, dialogue 7, p. 71.

92. ADB: AP MP/SM vol. 12 ff. 9,19,22.

93. Puente, 1612, p. 782.

94. Shorter, p. 62.

95. *Ibid.* pp. 52–61, on 'community controls'.

96. ADB: AP Santa Maria vol. 9, Matrimonis. Half the women came from neighbouring La Llacuna.

97. Maspons, pp. 3, 6.

98. Cited in Vigil, p. 80.

99. *Constitutiones Vicenses*, f. 41.

100. Among Castilian dramatists 'one thing they believed in un-animously was woman's *libertad de amar*. Woman should be allowed to follow her natural inclination in the choice of a husband': McKendrick, p. 328.

101. In seventeenth-century Catalonia two-thirds of spouses lacked at least one parent when they married: Simón Tarrés, p. 80.

102. ADB: P year 1625, caixa B/1.

103. Simón Tarrés, p. 84, cites Castelló d'Empúries, where some two-thirds married within the parish.

104. Juan Francisco de Gracia, 1616 (1752), p. 212.

105. *Cf.* Redondo, 'Les empêchements au mariage et leur transgression dans l'Espagne du XVIe siècle', in Redondo, 1985; also Flandrin, 1979, Chapter I.

106. ADB: P year 1596, caixa B/1.

107. Informaciones de Consanguinidad, ADU, capsa 1, anys 1602–63.

108. *Ibid.*

109. Decree of June 1601 by Cosmas

Tárrega, vicar-general of Urgell, in *ibid*. Susana was the daughter of Antoni's second cousin.

110. This was the case in Murcia: see Francisco Chacón, 'Identidad y parentescos ficticios en Murcia', pp. 41–3, in Redondo, 1988. For consanguinity, Goody Chapters 6 and 7; Flandrin, 1979, Chapter I.

111. Sabean, 'Aspects of kinship behaviour', Chapter 4 in Goody, Thirsk & Thompson, shows how in sixteenth-century Württemberg 'the selection of godparents reflected the pyramid of economic relationships', whereas in other areas the choice was casual.

112. *Cf*. Goody, Chapter 9.

113. ADB: AP Santa Maria vol. 2, Baptismes.

114. *Constitutiones Tarraconensium*, p. 112: 'prohibemus ne in domibus privatis sacrum baptisma alicui conferatur'.

115. *Constitutiones Barcinonen*, p. 169: 'Baptisms may not be celebrated in any private house' (1669).

116. Astete, 1598, p. 226.

117. Pujades, I, p. 218.

118. Pedraza, 1571, p. 46. The publisher in 1571 was Claude Bornat, in 1588 Hubert Gotard.

119. ADB: P year 1621, caixa B/2.

120. Astete, 1598, p. 177.

121. Mexía, 1566, f. 39v.

122. Rodríguez, 1600, p. 764.

123. Pérez de Valdivia, 1588, p. 69.

124. Astete, 1598, p. 161.

125. Toussaert, p. 238: 'divortiunt inter se ad sui libitum', text of 1319.

126. For Augsburg, see Roper, Chapter 4; for Hohenlohe, see Robisheaux, pp. 105–15.

127. Cited by Simón Tarrés, p. 79.

128. *Cf*. Philippe Ariès, 'The indissoluble marriage', in Ariès & Béjin.

129. AHN Inq leg. 24 no. 7.

130. Safley, 1981, 1984.

131. Astete, 1598, p. 225–6.

132. Rodríguez, 1600, p. 764.

133. 'We condemn the said husband N to return to the said N his wife within so many days of this notice, the dowry given according to the contract presented and which he received when they married, as well as half of all the goods they acquired in common during the marriage': Ortiz de Salzedo, 1615, p. 69v. Moreover, comments Ortiz, 'whenever a divorce is granted, the costs are met by the husband.'

134. Maspons, p. 57.

135. ADB: P year 1622, caixa A/2.

136. *Cf*. Catholic Lille in the early eighteenth century, where 71 per cent of plaintiffs were women: Lottin, 1975, p. 114.

137. On the other hand, habitual infidelity within a community brought dishonour, and could be cited as grounds.

138. Cases in ADB: P year 1660, caixes A/1 and A/2.

139. *Ibid*.

140. ADB: P year 1599.

141. ADB: P year 1600, caixa A/2.

142. ADB: P year 1600, caixa A/2.

143. ADB: P year 1600, caixa A/1.

144. ADB: P year 1596, caixa A/2.

145. Sources cited in Simón Tarrés, p. 81. *Cf*. Lille, where one-third of petitions for separation were from remarried partners: Lottin, 1975, p. 116.

146. The years for which divorces have been studied here are: 1596, 1597, 1599, 1600, 1601, 1621, 1622, 1625, 1626, 1660, 1670.

147. ADB: P year 1621, caixa B/2.

148. *Ibid*. year 1625, caixa A/1.

149. *Ibid*. year 1670, caixa 3.

150. *Ibid*. year 1596, caixa B/2.

151. ADB: C leg. 72.

152. *Constitutiones Solsona*, f. 116; *ibid. Barcinonen*, p. 304.

153. ADB: P year 1596, caixa A/1.

154. *Cf*. the figures above for

Catalonia; and the observation of Stone that 'modern divorce is little more than a functional substitute for death': Stone, p. 46.

155. Petition of 27 April 1596, ADB: P year 1596, caixa B/1.

156. ADB: P year 1596, caixa A/2.

157. ADB: P caixa 1670/3.

158. *Ibid.* year 1622, caixa A/2.

159. The following comments on marriage by a Dominican of Barcelona in 1597 may be noted: 'a man given to the study of letters should not marry if at all possible, for it is an obstacle to the study of letters since one cannot serve woman and letters at the same time'; 'marriage binds, but is well described as a bond'; 'matrimony is holy but is no less a burden'. Truxillo, 1597, pp. 30, 362v.

160. Brutails, p. 205; the year was 1327.

161. Kamen, 1985, pp. 53, 58.

162. AHN Inq lib. 732 f. 111.

163. See figures of Contreras reproduced in Kamen, 1985, p. 185.

164. AHN Inq lib. 731, cases of 1588, 1589 and 1603.

165. *Constitutiones Barcinonen*, p. 248.

166. Ramón, 1635, p. 149. Astete, 1598, p. 266, gives an anecdote of a henpecked husband: 'there was a man who had an untamed and perverse wife whom he could never master nor control. When he was away one day they brought news that she had drowned in the river, so he went to the river and began to look for her body upstream. People saw him and asked: Brother, why do you look for your wife upstream? The man replied: When she was alive my wife always went the opposite way and did the opposite of what I said, and because of that I am looking for her upstream to see if I can find her this way.'

167. I take the distinction between penal and festive from the valuable discussion on England in Ingram, 1984, p. 92.

168. *Cf.* Simón Tarrés, p. 81.

169. André Burguière, 'The charivari and religious repression in France during the Ancien Régime', in Wheaton & Hareven.

170. Caro Baroja.

171. For the role of youths in a seventeenth-century Lutheran charivari, *cf.* Robisheaux p. 118–19.

172. Cited Bercé.

173. Tellechea, p. xx.

174. Villanueva, III, p. 124.

175. *Cf.* Gutton, 1984, pp. 51–4.

176. Amades, 1982, III, p. 399.

177. B. Bennassar, in Taillefer, p. 223.

178. Amades, 1982, III, p. 409.

179. AHN Inq lib. 732 f. 107.

180. Bercé cites a case of 1655 in Dauphiné.

181. Serra i Boldú, 1981, p. 87.

182. ADPO, G 720 no. 58.

183. Caro Baroja, p. 80.

184. *Cf.* comments in B. Bennassar, *The Spanish Character* (Berkeley, 1979). A useful brief survey in Redondo, 'Les empêchements au mariage', in Redondo, 1985, pp. 38–46.

185. For fornication in England, Ingram, 1987, pp. 267–74.

186. Farfán, 1585.

187. *Ibid.* 'To the Reader'.

188. *Ibid.* p. 756.

189. Johannes Brenz in 1543 complained of German brothels that 'not only single men but also married men go, and say this does no harm', cited in Roper, p. 107.

190. Farfán, 1585, pp. 703, 739.

191. Cited in Cotarelo, p. 217.

192. Inquisitors to Suprema, 11 January 1575, AHN Inq lib. 738 f. 129

193. *Ibid.* lib. 733 f. 265.

194. *Ibid.* lib. 733 ff. 251, 266.

195. *Ibid.* lib. 731 f. 93.
196. *Ibid.* lib. 731 f. 210.
197. *Ibid.* leg. 15921.
198. *Ibid.* lib. 731 f. 366.
199. *Ibid.* lib. 731 f. 368v.
200. *Ibid.* lib. 731 f. 383.
201. *Ibid.* lib. 733 f. 297.
202. Rodríguez, 1600, p. 661.
203. Cited Herrera Puga, 1974.
204. *Cf.* Lutheran Augsburg, in Roper, Chapter 3.
205. López Martín, p. 92.
206. Pedro de León, p. 40.
207. MSS. 'Crónica de Belén', f. 51.
208. Dimas Loris, 1598, f. 40v.
209. Viceroy to bailiff, 6 February 1572, ACA: RC reg. 4737 f. 61.
210. In practice, too, clergy such as Diego Pérez held that the state of the clergy was superior to that of married persons: Pérez, 1587, preface.
211. AHN Inq lib. 730 f. 419.
212. *Ibid.* lib. 731 f. 254.
213. *Ibid.* lib. 731 f. 235.
214. *Ibid.* leg. 1592¹.
215. *Ibid.* lib. 733 f. 298. The priest, Joan Simó, had also commented that when the devil tempted Christ he came in the form of a friar.
216. Arias, 1603, pp. 693–7.
217. *Cf.* Tentler, Chapter IV.
218. Gavarri, 1673, p. 93.
219. *Ibid.* pp. 232–3.
220. Arias, 1603, p. 697.
221. Ortiz Lucio, 1598, p. 109.
222. *Constitutiones Tarraconensium*, 1557, index.
223. Bada, 1970, p. 59.
224. ARSI Epist Hisp vol. 103 f. 43.
225. 'Comisarios castigados por cosas de mugeres y otros delictos', AHN Inq lib. 742 ff. 123–7. 'May be', because the document is unspecific on this point.
226. *Cf.* the eloquent pages of Helen Waddell, *The Wandering Scholars* (Harmondsworth, 1954). A fourteenth-century Council of Tarragona complained of clergy turning *jongleurs*, and the

227. IHM Consellers C. XVIII–8 ff. 217–55.
228. Cited in Gay de Montellà, p. 213. There are various versions of the 'Muntanyes regalades'.
229. ADB: P year 1600, caixa A/2.
230. *Ibid.* year 1599.
231. A case of 1631: AHN Inq lib. 733 f. 336.
232. *Ibid.* lib. 732.
233. ADB: P year 1599.
234. *Ibid.* year 1597.
235. *Ibid.* denunciations vs. the priests Julià Miquel and Sebastià Fabrigues.
236. ADB: P year 1600.
237. The theme is marginal to this book; for detail, see Lea; Kamen, 1985, pp. 205–9.
238. AHN Inq lib. 733 f. 465.
239. AHN Inq lib. 733 f. 314.
240. AHN Inq lib. 732 ff. 78, 320.
241. AHN Inq lib. 732 ff. 339, 350.
242. AHN Inq lib. 732 f. 320v.
243. Sicardo, *Carta Apologética*, p. 21.
244. Rodríguez, 1600, p. 202.
245. Brown, 1989, *passim*.
246. Fray Antonio Marques, 'Afeite y mundo mugeril' (1617), BUB MS. 1017 ff. 25, 49.
247. Vera, 1630, pp. 49–50: 'the whole life of the soul and all its vital functions come from the body.' Chapter VI of the work is devoted to kissing.
248. Cited Pons, 1929, p. 115.
249. Azpilcueta, 1567, p. 166. Written in 1552, the work was first published in 1555.
250. Francesc Vicenç Garcia, *Sonets*, (Barcelona, 1979), pp. 99, 102, 109.
251. *Cf.* L. Roper for Augsburg, pp. 66–7.
252. *Cf.* Lérida, where of the cases tried by the *veguer*'s court in 1604–5 some 44 per cent concerned theft and 25 per cent

Carmina Burana contain elements of the Mediterranean: *ibid.* p. 236.

involved sexual behaviour: Lladonosa, II, p. 449.

253. *Cf.* Toledo, where the Holy Office was considerably more active against sexual propositions: see Dedieu, 1979.

254. Brutails, p. 244.

255. Vigil, p. 19.

256. A good summary of women's roles in Castile at this period is McKendrick, Introduction.

257. Acosta Africano, 1592, pp. 36–9, 76.

258. Roper, pp. 2, 56–88.

259. The work was first published in Baeza in 1575.

260. Astete, 1598, p. 195.

261. Cited Vigil, p. 83.

262. Vigil, p. 80.

263. Gavarri, 1673, pp. 100–102.

264. Cited Vigil, p. 80.

265. But he also argued for greater freedom of going to mass: 'the custom whereby noble girls never go to mass or sermon before they are married, seems to us intolerable,' Azpilcueta, 1567, p. 360.

266. Women, he says, are whores and beasts, Jezebels and Delilahs; 'wine and women have made the wisest apostasise'; 'no one who deals with woman can fail to fall into her jaws'; all vices are at their worst in women: 'Tratado primero' of Ortiz Lucio, 1589.

267. Cited by Navarro, 1631, pp. 32–5.

268. ADB: V vol. 84 f. 265.

269. Agustí, 1617, f. 8v.

270. García y García, I, p. 432; III, p. 334.

271. Cotarelo, p. 45.

272. *Ibid.*, p. 130.

273. ADU, libro de visita vol. 32 f. 10v.

274. BUB MS. 1017.

275. ADB: C vol. 68 f. 280.

276. ADB: V vol. 82 ff. 120, 322, visits of 1756 and 1758.

277. Ingram, 1987, p. 156.

278. On the other hand, the role of women in Spanish religion was minimal compared to their impressive role in the French Counter Reformation.

279. Vigil, p. 215.

280. 'Copia de las visitas generales que en este Real Monasterio de Santa Maria de Junqueras resultan echas. Llibre de Visitas Antiguas', ACA Monacales, Universidad, lib. 168 f. 133.

281. *Ibid.* lib. 169 ff. 72, 102–3. The hotel/finishing-school character of Junqueres was commented upon in 1512 by Guicciardini when he passed through the city: cited Bada, 1970, p. 62.

282. Consulta of Council, 17 May 1670, ACA: CA leg. 218.

283. Details in *ibid.* leg. 266 f. 156, 'Sumario del proceso de la visita de Valbona'.

284. Zaragoza Pascual, 1978–9.

285. Weinstein & Bell, pp. 224–7, 233–4.

286. R. Wheaton, in Wheaton and Hareven, p. 15.

287. The view is of Gutton, 'Confraternities', in Greyerz, p. 210. Hoffman also concludes, for Lyon, that 'women made some significant gains during the Counter Reformation': Hoffman, p. 145.

Chapter Seven

1. Van Oss, p. 6.

2. Francisco Martín Hernández, 1961.

3. For Spain, see F. Martín Hernández, 1964, p. 155 ff.

4. 'Erectio seminarii', ADB: C vol. 65 f. 118.

5. All bishops' reports as well as the correspondence of Macanaz and the Council of Castile, are in AHN Consejos lib. 7294 no. 3.

6. Villanueva, I, p. 74ff.

7. *Cf.* Hoffman, Chapter 3.

8. Villanueva, XVII, pp. 279–81.

9. Villanueva, VII, p. 105.

10. Petition from city of Urgell, ACA: CA leg. 367.

11. AHN Inq lib. 732 f. 478. The document lists his parish as 'Foronsera', which I have been unable to identify.

12. By way of comparison, see I. Testón and M. Santillana, 'El clero cacereño durante los siglos XVI al XVIII', *Historia Moderna. Actas de las II Jornadas de Metodología y Didáctica de la Historia* (Cáceres, 1983), pp. 463–72; and J. Cobos Ruiz, *El clero en el siglo XVII. Estudio de una visita secreta a la ciudad de Córdoba* (Córdoba, 1976). No study exists of the reform of parish clergy in Spain, unlike the excellent study done for Lyon by Hoffman.

13. Pérez Martínez, 1963, I, p. xxvii.

14. Lemos, 1583, p. 354v.

15. Pérez Martínez, 1963, I, p. lx.

16. *Ibid.*, II, p. 169.

17. González Novalín, p. 227.

18. ADB: V vol. 45 f. 258v.

19. ADB: P year 1599.

20. ADU, Procesos de Visita 1611, 1662–99.

21. Ortiz Lucio, 1598, p. 8.

22. Dimas Loris, 1598, f. 2.

23. Cited Ferté, p. 178.

24. ADU, Libro de visita vol. 32, anys 1575–76, ff. 1, 13.

25. ADB: V vol. 71 *passim*.

26. ADB: C vol. 72 ff. 11–13.

27. *Ibid.* vol. 71 ff. 276–82.

28. ADB: C vol. 71 ff. 76, 98.

29. AHN Inq lib. 732 ff. 3, 263.

30. Pons, 1968, p. 224.

31. González Novalín, p. 246–7.

32. ASV Visitas ad limina 399A, relation of 12 January 1706.

33. Pons, 1968, pp. 240–5.

34. Ramón, 1635.

35. Tejada, VI, p. 136.

36. For an excellent general survey, Houston; for Castile see Nalle,

37. Rodríguez and Bennassar.

38. Berger.

39. ADPO, AC Escaro 3. Whenever a marriage was celebrated, the parish priest stated that the parents were giving verbal permission because they could not write.

40. Torreilles and Desplanque, p. 241. The figures are for 1691.

41. Where 'perhaps only four or five per cent could read': R. Scribner, *The German Reformation* (London, 1986), p. 19.

42. Dedieu, 1979.

43. Le Flem in (De l')*Alphabetisation*, 1987.

44. The provision is scored out. 'Liber visitationis Trempi', ADU, libro de visita vol. 32 f. 231+.

45. Raymond Carr, *Spain 1808–1939* (Oxford, 1966), p. 60; he goes on to comment, 'Much of Spain may pass from the pre-book age straight to the television age.'

46. Margit Frenk.

47. For Languedoc, see Castan, Chapter II, on the priority of verbal over written communication.

48. ADPO, register BB2, in Desplanque.

49. This view is based on the inventories drawn up by the notaries Pau Mallol and Joan Terès for the period 1555–1605: AHPB, see Archival Sources.

50. The cited cases are located as follows: Parrinet, Perelló and Biosquet in notary Francesc Pedralbes, leg. 36, pliego de inventarios (1); Vilademany in notary Lluis Rufet, leg. 26, inventarios sueltos 1553–80 (1); Mas and Spuny in *ibid.* inventarios sueltos 1553–80 (2);

Bertomeu in notary Joan Terés, leg. 16, pliego inventarios 1594–1606. All documents from AHPB.

51. ADB: AP MP/SM 12 f. 149v.
52. *Synodi Barcinonensis*, p. 153.
53. AHN Inq lib. 731 f. 47v.
54. Cited Kamen, 1984, p. 60.
55. ACU, Sinodos 1585–1700, synod of 1689, clause 1.
56. ADB: C vol. 67 f. 45.
57. ADB, Acta Synodalia vol. 1 f. 31, article 23.
58. Dimas Loris, 1598, p. 10.
59. ADB: V vol. 58 f. 497.
60. Strauss, pp. 277–9.
61. Torreilles and Desplanque, p. 165
62. ADB: AP MP/SQ 15 f. 242.
63. Torreilles and Desplanque, p. 193.
64. *Ibid.* p. 231.
65. ADB: C vol. 72 f. 65.
66. Kagan, pp. 12, 20.
67. Kagan suggests (p. 11) that as early as 1512, five years before Luther's appearance, this motive was already crucial; but this seems implausible. He goes on (p. 12) to claim that 'for a society as preoccupied with the maintenance of orthodoxy as sixteenth-century Castile, the proper regulation of elementary education was indispensable.'
68. ADB: C vol. 71 f. 134.
69. None of the Tarragona councils from 1551 to 1587 mentions education: *cf.* Torreilles and Desplanque, p. 173.
70. Torreilles and Desplanque, pp. 182 n. 2, 189–90.
71. ADB: C vol. 69 f. 173B.
72. Dimas Loris, 1598, p. 14v.
73. Dimas Loris, 1598, p. 10.
74. ADPO, AC Escaro 1 f. 9.
75. The memoir of Honorat Ciuro (written in Catalan in the mid-seventeenth century) is cited from the French text in Torreilles 1898, pp. 158–9. For Ciuro see also Pons, 1929, p. 115. I

have been unable to locate the present whereabouts of Ciuro's manuscript.
76. Literally, 'as though it were Hebrew'. Cocheril, p. 23.
77. (Viaje de) *Cosme de Médicis*, vol. I, p. xxi.
78. S. Solé, 'La llengua dels documents notarials catalans', *Recerques*, 12, 1982. The statement needs to be modified according to locality.
79. Bosch, 1628.
80. Houston, p. 24.
81. Azpilcueta, 1567, preface 'to the reader'.
82. Horozco y Covarrubias, 1591, p. 10.
83. Astete, 1598, p. 376.
84. Cited in Asensio, p. 52.
85. Vera, 1630, p. 205.
86. Arias, 1603, p. 5.
87. Nalle, 1989, p. 94.
88. Both cases from AHPB, notary Joan Terès, leg. 16, Pliego de Inventarios, 1593–1605.
89. Alfonso de Castro, *De iuxta haereticorum punitione libri tres*, Venice 1549, lib. III.
90. Cited in Antonio Martí.
91. Pedro de León, pp. 103, 117.
92. Martí Bonet, I/1, p. 53.
93. See Ackerman in Wittkower & Jaffe, p. 19.
94. Martí, p. 89.
95. 'Puncts pera Predicadors' of 27 February 1609, slightly modified by me, ADB: C vol. 74 f. 187.
96. Capella, 1593, preface.
97. Cited in Ferreras, II, p. 967.
98. Lucas Hidalgo, 1610, p. 7.
99. Ramón, 1635, pp. 324, 338.
100. Instruction of 15 January 1689, BCC Fullets Bonsoms 5505.
101. Gavarri, 1673, p. 56.
102. Soman, p. 451.
103. Reported in visit of inquisitor Arévalo, AHN Inq leg. 15921.
104. AHN Inq lib. 731 f. 131v.
105. *Ibid.* lib. 732 f. 99.
106. *Ibid.* lib. 732 case 14.
107. *Ibid.* lib. 733 f. 58.

108. *Ibid.* lib. 733 f. 279v.
109. *Ibid.* lib. 733 f. 329.
110. *Ibid.* lib. 733 f. 358 and f. 401.
111. On catechesis of the Moriscos, see García-Villoslada, vol. IV.
112. Edward Glaser, *Estudios Hispano-Portugueses. Relaciones literarias del Siglo de Oro* (Madrid, 1957), p. v–vii.
113. Goñi Gaztambide, 1947, pp. 287–9.
114. Both cases from Basili de Rubi, p. 197.
115. Beltrán, pp. 41–2.
116. ADPO, AC Escaro 1 f. 12.
117. Lorenzo de San Juan, a native of Cati in Valencia, was rector of the Jesuit college in Barcelona from 1607 to 1610: see MSS. 'Crónica de Belén', f. 44.
118. The leaflets by Adrin and by Cisteller are in BCC Fullets Bonsoms 9966 and 5174. There is a good manuscript version in MSS. BUB MS. 1010 ff. 195–205.
119. MSS. BUB MS. 1005.
120. Miquel Llot, cited Pons, 1929, p. 46.
121. MSS. BUB MS. 629 f. 45.
122. *Ibid.* f. 53.
123. This was also true of Guatemala at the same period: Van Oss, pp. 166–70.
124. Massot, 1699, p. 290.
125. Arco y Garay, I, p. 21.
126. Berger, II, p. 396.
127. *Constitutiones Synodales Barcinonen*, p. 52.
128. Bada, 1982.
129. 'Memorial dels llibres del Rmo Senyor Don Fra Raphel Riffos, q Bisbe de Elna', 1622, ADPO, G 50.
130. Taix, 1597, preface.
131. Lladonosa, II, p. 443.
132. Font, 1608, preface.
133. Valls, 1685, preface.
134. Agustí, 1617, preface to the reader.
135. Pons, 1929, p. 48.
136. Estrugos, 1644, preface 'to the reader'.
137. R. García Cárcel, *Historia de Cataluña*, I, pp. 98–9, states that 'the chief agents of Castilianisation were the members of the religious orders,' and that, for example, 'the Capuchins began always with a conviction of the supremacy of Castilian.' Expressed thus, the statements are not true. He also makes the unfounded claim that the Jesuits opposed the use of Catalan.
138. Alice Marcet, 'La résistance à la francisation dans les montagnes catalanes au XVIIe siècle', in *Conflent, Vallespir*, p. 139.
139. *Cf.* Pons, 1929, p. 158.
140. Alice Marcet, *op. cit.*, p. 139.
141. Cited Iglésies, 1949, pp. 59–60.
142. Elies Serra Ràfols, 'La introducció del castellà com a llengua d'ensenyament', an article first published in 1968 and thereafter repeatedly cited as authoritative; it is reproduced in the *Història de Catalunya*, edited by Pierre Vilar, vol. VIII, pp. 174–81.
143. *Cf.* Amelang, pp. 161–2, 193.
144. MSS. 'Crónica de Belén', f. 104.
145. Cited in Vila, 1983, p. 98.
146. For Portugal, see Ricard, 1956; Glaser; and Domingo Garcia Peres.
147. *Cf.* Castan, 1974, for Languedoc, where the total domination of written French had the primary consequence not of destroying Gascon but of dissuading Gascons from literacy; they used French when drunk, or angry, or when addressing outsiders.
148. Despite the large bibliography on the order, much of it derivative biography and polemic, the history of the Jesuits in Europe, and above all their social and economic history, is largely unwritten. On the Jesuits and the Counter Reformation there is no

informed study in English. For Spain the introduction is the worthy but dated Astraín.

149. Laínez to Araoz, Rome 26 September 1559, *MHSI Borgia*, vol. III, p. 853.

150. Joan Baptista from Valladolid to Laínez, 26 May 1558, ARSI Epist Hisp vol. 96 f. 112.

151. The view of Gerald Strauss, p. 381 n. 183, with reference to Germany.

152. Fathers Queralt, Soler, Cerbos and Casellas.

153. ACA Monacales vol. 2568 f. 1.

154. Cited Bada, 1970, p. 124.

155. Joan Baptista to Laínez, 22 November 1559, ARSI Epist Hisp vol. 96 f. 471.

156. Lozano to Laínez, 11 December 1559, *ibid.* f. 478. On Jesuit caution towards the Inquisition, with which they crossed on several occasions, see the later observation by father García to Acquaviva in 1594, 'In Spain we depend a great deal on the Inquisition and we must help it where we can and not provoke them in any way,' ARSI Epist Hisp 138 f. 29, letter of 13 December 1594.

157. Bada, 1970, p. 126; MSS. 'Crónica de Belén' f. 5.

158. Bjurstrom, in Wittkower and Jaffe, p. 100.

159. Pedro Villalba to Acquaviva, Medina del Campo, 31 May 1587, ARSI Epist Hisp vol. 133 f. 115.

160. 'Precursor of the reform in Catalonia' and 'apostle of Catalonia' are titles given to him by a Carmelite historian writing in 1707: MSS. BUB MS. 991 pp. 3, 98. In this work, Pérez' arrival is dated both 1578 and 1580.

161. The study of the Capuchins by Basili de Rubi is a treasury of scholarship.

162. Juan de San José, 'Annales de los Carmelitas Descalços', MSS. BUB MS. 991, pp. 4, 73.

163. What follows is drawn exclusively from the account 'Del principio y progreso deste Collegio quanto a los bienes rayzes', in ACA Monacales vol. 2568.

164. See Borràs, 1985.

165. 'Memorial del Collegio de la Compañia', ARSI Epist Hisp vol. 1 f. 12.

166. See Chapter Three, p. 85.

167. Pedro de León, p. 162.

168. *Ibid.* p. 62.

169. Astraín, I, p. 240.

170. Cited Bataillon, p. 534 n. 14.

171. Pozo to Laínez, 8 February 1558, ARSI Epist Hisp vol. 96 f. 43.

172. Gaspar to *ibid.* 4 June 1558, *ibid.* vol. 96 f. 129.

173. Henrique to *ibid.* 1 January 1561; *ibid.* vol. 98 f. 3.

174. Ruiz to *ibid.* 31 January 1557, *ibid.* vol. 95 f. 39.

175. Sancho to *ibid.* 27 April 1559, *ibid.* vol. 96 f. 319.

176. Gestí to *ibid.* 29 April 1557, *ibid.* vol. 95 f. 96.

177. Gestí to *ibid.* 16 June 1557, *ibid.* vol. 95 f. 114. The collection of children later became common practice. The first constitutions of the Carmel of the Crown of Aragon, drawn up at the first general chapter, held in Tárrega at the end of 1589, affirmed 'that Christian doctrine be taught in the monasteries of this Province ... going and collecting children from the streets, taking them to a church or to the square, and instructing them': Beltrán, p. 32.

178. Andrés Capilla to Laínez, 30 April 1558, ARSI Epist Hisp vol. 96 f. 94. For the use of children as missioners in sixteenth-century Mexico, see Trexler.

179. Torres to Laínez, 28 January 1561, ARSI Epist Hisp vol. 98 f. 74.

180. *Cf.* Weinstein & Bell, p. 67.

181. Pedro Juárez to Laínez, 30 April 1564, ARSI Epist Hisp vol. 101

f. 111.

182. Ortiz to *ibid.* 20 October 1564, *ibid.* vol. 102 f. 13. Testimony to the success of these methods comes from the Jeronimite friar Hieronimo de Lemos, who recalled (Lemos, 1583, p. 201) the case of a confessor who refused to absolve an old man of seventy until he learnt the creed. Ashamed to ask for instruction from a teacher, the old man sat outside his house and every time the boys passed his door on their way home from school he would offer a penny to whomever could recite the creed best; he did this twice a day, at lunch and in the afternoon, and by the time he had spent ten *maravedis* he had learnt not only the creed but also other prayers.

183. Jiménez to Laínez, Monterrey, ARSI Epist Hisp vol. 98 f. 183.

184. *Cf.* Ferté, Chapter III, for the problems of missions in the seventeenth-century Paris countryside.

185. Juan Martínez to Laínez, 22 May 1559, ARSI Epist Hisp vol. 96 f. 340.

186. Jaime Puellas to Laínez, 31 August 1561, *ibid.* vol. 98 f. 283.

187. MSS. 'Crónica de Belén', f. 3.

188. *Ibid.* f. 5. The sixteenth-century portion of this MS history is the work of Gil; see f. 9v, 'father Gil, who is writing this'.

189. ACA: CA leg. 78.

190. ACA: CA leg. 78 ff. 131, 191, 195.

191. MSS. BCC MS. 90 ff. 449–50.

192. In 1593 when there was a crackdown on bandits they assisted at the execution in the city of some forty condemned; in 1616, year of the great slaughter of bandits by the viceroy duke of Alburquerque, they assisted at the deaths of fifty-eight. This was as nothing to the executions of Catalans by the French in 1646, when 'we had much work in accompanying those to be executed, who at this time were many.' MSS. 'Crónica de Belén' ff. 12, 188. For Pedro de León and the Seville prisons, see P. Herrera Puga, *Sociedad y delincuencia en el Siglo de Oro* (Madrid, 1974).

193. MSS. 'Crónica de Belén', ff. 55–6.

194. *Ibid.* ff. 51, 133, 145.

195. *Ibid.* ff. 51v, 144.

196. Torres, 1598, prologue.

197. Coma, 1566, p. xvi.

198. The bishop of Plasencia in the 1540s set aside funds to pay for three preachers to serve his diocese: cited Bataillon, p. 534.

199. Pedro de León, p. 87.

200. That is, in Catalan, the obligatory language for religious instruction in Catalonia.

201. MSS. 'Crónica de Belén', f. 145v.

202. Thomas Gage, 1655, pp. 148–51: 'As for their Religion they are inwardly hard to believe that which is above sense, nature and the visible sight of the eye... If you demand any account of any point of faith they will give you little or none. The mystery of the Trinity, and of the incarnation, is too hard for them... Not all the teaching and preaching of those Priests hath yet well grounded them in principles of faith.'

Chapter Eight

1. His only complaint, as he warned the new viceroy of the principality, Borja, in 1539, was that 'in the city of Barcelona, as you will see for yourself, they make very bad bread, the worst in Catalonia': *MHSI Borgia*, II, p. 593. Fortunately, the bread has improved since then.

2. For the ceremony see J. Ainaud de Lasarte, *El Toisó d'Or a*

Barcelona (Barcelona, 1949), p. 71. There is an incorrect but enthusiastic version in Feliu de la Penya, III, p. 161.

3. Batllori, 1987, p. 18.
4. Griffin, pp. 147–50.
5. On Mai, see Rubió, pp. 91–105, 'Confluències de cultures a Barcelona en temps de l'emperador'; Bataillon, pp. 317–18, records the brief stay of Mai in Barcelona in 1528 in the company of Erasmians there; *cf.* Batllori, 1983, p. 66.
6. *Cf.* Kamen, 1989.
7. Tellechea, 1968, II, pp. 241, 255.
8. *MHSI Borgia*, III, p. 394, Borja to Luis González, 11 August 1558. Select clergy had been allowed to keep Lutheran books in order to study and refute them.
9. *Cf.* the now superseded presentation in R.O. Jones, *The Golden Age: Prose and Poetry* (London, 1971): 'By 1560 the traditionalists had won: the Spain of Philip II remained closed to the new current of ideas beyond its frontiers ... The spiritual fervour and religious uniformity of Golden Age Spain was accompanied by a closing of minds; if indeed, the latter was not a condition of the former. A law of censorship which had existed since 1502 was strengthened in 1558. Before publication, a book now required the censor's *aprobación*. The importation of foreign books without a royal licence was now made a capital offence ... It is futile to speculate how much Spain and Spanish literature were to lose, how many books were to remain unwritten, through such measures.' Every statement here is inaccurate.
10. Thompson's estimate is *c.* 9000 in a normal year, 20,000 in a

crisis year: see I.A.A. Thompson, *War and Government in Habsburg Spain 1560–1620*, (London, 1976).
11. The Spanish emigration to Europe has never been studied.
12. *Cf.* J.M. López Piñero, *Ciencia y técnica en la sociedad española de los siglos XVI y XVII*, (Barcelona, 1979), p. 141–4, who comments on various aspects, including the fall in attendance of Spanish medical students at Montpellier (310 attended between 1503 and 1558, 14 between 1559 and 1566, none after 1574).
13. Cited in B. Rekers, *Benito Arias Montano* (London, 1972), p. 17. For an interesting orientation, see Jan Lechner, 'Estudiantes de orígen hispánico y portugués en la Universidad de Leiden, 1575–1875', in *Estudios Románicos dedicados al Prof. Andrés Soria Ortega*, 2 vols (Granada, 1985), II, pp. 587–603.
14. Which, suggests one scholar, continued in force till the early nineteenth century: Gilly, pp. 138–9. This opinion is the only point on which I differ from the presentation in Gilly's fine book on the Basel presses.
15. Norton, p. 134.
16. True also for Barcelona: see Madurell Marimón and Rubió, p. 57 n. 142.
17. Griffin, p. 4.
18. Moll, 1981, p. 80.
19. Cited in Péligry, 1981, p. 88.
20. Cruikshank, p. 816.
21. Griffin, p. 11.
22. Cited in Griffin, p. 107.
23. Arróniz, p. 19.
24. Kamen, 1981, p. 500, citing the Alicante merchant Moscoso.
25. ACA: RC reg. 4737 f. 158. In 1628 St Feliu de Guíxols was criticised by the viceroy for contravening a ban on trade with France.

26. Hampe Martínez, p. 61.
27. The phrase, of course, belongs to Henri Bremond's great work on spiritual literature in France.
28. Norton, p. 125.
29. Beardsley, p. 30.
30. Rodríguez, 1600, p. 639.
31. Beardsley suggests that Spanish printers had also by now learned to produce more manageable editions in duodecimo, instead of the bulky quartos of previous decades.
32. Moll, 1981, an essential corrective to previous views.
33. Griffin, pp. 12–13.
34. Pineda (1963–4), pp. 5, 20.
35. It is seriously misleading to state that 'the great presses of Antwerp put within the reach of northern and central Europe many books which otherwise, under the censorship of the Inquisition, would have disappeared': Hoffmeister, p. 78.
36. Norton, p. 136.
37. Hugues Vanay lists a total of 1198 titles by Spanish writers published abroad, 775 of them in the sixteenth century; but his listing draws almost exclusively on Baudrier, *Bibliographie lyonnaise*, and on Sommervogel, *Bibliographie des auteurs de la Compagnie de Jésus*; so that the true total is likely to be much larger.
38. Péligry, 1981, p. 91.
39. Francisco Martínez de Mata, *Memoriales y Discursos*, ed. G. Anes (Madrid, 1971), p. 106, citing a petition of the *Cortes* in 1579: 'Spaniards have directed the printing of books to France, and with this have destroyed the guild of printers.'
40. Gutiérrez, pp. 152–4; Georges Tricou, *passim*; and Péligry, 1981, p. 88. See also the diagram in H.J., Martin et R. Chartier, *Histoire de l'Edition française* (Paris, 1982), I, p. 446.

41. Arco y Garay, I, p. 11.
42. Grendler, p. 16.
43. Bisbe y Vidal, 1618, p. 55.
44. Vries de Heekelingen, p. 28.
45. AHN Inq leg. 2155[1].
46. Vries de Heekelingen, pp. 39, 56, 499–508.
47. *Cf.* Tellechea, 1962, referring to a seizure in 1552. Of the 450 Bibles seized, 36 came from Antwerp, 318 from Lyon, 68 from Paris, and 6 from Basel. Monter, p. 238, notes the seizure of 218 Bibles in Saragossa in 1553, 97 per cent of them printed in France, mainly in Lyon.
48. Grendler, pp. 77–80; López, p. 30–1, mentions Spanish edicts of 1544 and 1550.
49. Rodríguez, 1600, I, pp. 639–40.
50. Strictly speaking, the Inquisition was not a licensing authority and had power only to censor; but it had a limited right to license books for its own use, and under this cover several books seem to have received authority for publication.
51. Novísima Recopilación de Leyes de España, lib. VIII tít. XVI ley I and II; printed in Bujanda, pp. 121–2.
52. Madurell Marimón and Rubió, pp. 94–6. See below for examples.
53. The law banned import of Castilian books 'into these realms' even if printed outside them, and included under 'outside' the realms of Aragon, Valencia, Catalonia and Navarre; the text of the law is given by Bujanda, pp. 122–7.
54. Philip II to Diego Hurtado de Mendoza, 25 May 1568, ACA: RC reg. 4352 f. 111.
55. ACA: RC reg. 4352 f. 111 and f. 118.
56. Petition from Dr Geronimo Tamboni, dated 16 April 1616, ACA: CA leg. 358.

57. ACA: RC reg. 4736 f. 343. Licences had also been issued by the Council of Aragon but they simply extended to the Crown of Aragon privileges issued in Castile.

58. García González has an excellent brief discussion.

59. Bisbe y Vidal, 1618, p. 55.

60. There is an example in ADB: C vol. 75 f. 115.

61. The book was by a Dominican, Salvador Pons: ADB: C vol. 70 f. 23. See p. 492 n. 160.

62. Edict of 28 November 1602, ADB: C vol. 73 f. 71.

63. Calculated from F. Aleixandre, p. 171.

64. ADB: C vol. 76 f. 190v.

65. The best survey of the vicissitudes of the book is in Moll, 1979.

66. Aleixandre, p. 171.

67. Pujades, II, pp. 172–3.

68. Soman, pp. 454–7.

69. Cotarelo, p. 52.

70. Bances y Candamo, 1690, in Cotarelo, p. 75.

71. Evennett, p. 18.

72. *Cf.* the excellent outline by Joan-Ramon Triadó on 'La cultura' in *Historia de España Planeta* (Madrid, 1988), vol. 5, El Siglo de Oro, to which reference is recommended.

73. Farinelli catalogues the rise of anti-Spanish sentiment in Germany after the imperial honeymoon, from the 'Dass doch mein liebes Vaterland/ erlöst werd auss der Spanier Hand' of the sixteenth century to the propaganda of the Thirty Years' War.

74. Schneider, p. 1, emphasises the work of Gilles Alberts of Deventer (1560–1620), resident in Munich, who translated some twenty-two Spanish works, including Guevara, Osuna and Ribadeneira. The first Spanish work put into German was the *Celestina* (translated from Italian) in 1520.

75. Gilly, pp. 155–273. In these figures I exclude editions of Dryander but include those of Arnau de Vilanova. Basel was also a centre of anti-Philip II propaganda over the Netherlands issue, notably through Bonaventura Vulcanius, who had left Toledo for Bruges in 1570: *ibid.* pp. 29–32.

76. Péligry, 1981, p. 89.

77. Gutiérrez, 1977, p. 180.

78. Gutiérrez, 1977, p. 244.

79. Arco y Garay, I, pp. 265, 339, 387.

80. Even diplomats such as Saavedra, negotiator of the peace at Westphalia, had no French; and the predominance of Franche-Comtois diplomats in Spain's service is explicable in part by their command of languages. The great Castilian writers – Lope, Góngora, Calderón – were all ignorant of French.

81. Religious ideas were exchanged well enough, as with Bérulle's import of St Teresa and the Carmel into France; or Cornelis Jansen's enthusiastic reception in Spain in 1622, when he was greeted by the students at Alcalá and Salamanca 'as though I had come down from heaven'.

82. Gutiérrez, 1977, pp. 195–206.

83. Péligry, p. 91. Books in French were presumably only a tiny proportion of this. The appearance of French books in libraries of members of the Council of Castile is noted in J. Fayard, *Les membres du Conseil de Castille à l'époque moderne (1621–1746)* (Paris–Geneva, 1979), pp. 502–19.

84. Martín Carrillo, 1620.

85. M.C. Casado Lobato, 'Autores franceses en la biblioteca de un escritor del siglo XVII', in *Livre et Lecture*, pp. 127–37.

86. 'Una sort de libres en francés': 'Memorial dels libres son en casa Joan Gordiola', AHPB notary Lluis Rufet, leg. 26, Inventarios sueltos 1553–80 (1). The French–Latin grammar, in octavo, is described as 'Conjugationes latinas y fransesas'; both books of song were from Lyon.

87. 18 March 1562 'Inventarium de hereditate et bonis magnifici Stephani Naves, militis et juris doctoris', AHPB notary Jeroni Llop, pliego de escrituras de varios años.

88. Busquet in AHPB notary Francesc Pedralbes, leg. 36, pliego de inventarios (1); Vila in AHPB notary Pau Malliol, leg. 18, pliego de inventarios 1555–86.

89. 1667 inventory of bookseller Sebastià Cormellas: AHPB notary Jaume Corbera, leg. 7, Inventariorum liber 1647–86.

90. Peeters-Fontainas; the date was 1618.

91. The following condensed summary deserves a book, but there is no adequate survey of links between Spain and Italy in the sixteenth century.

92. Serrano, IV p. lix; also Grendler, p. 159.

93. Toda. My listing is of Spanish authors published in Italy, in Spanish or Latin; as well as Spanish works put into Italian. I have counted only first editions, and not subsequent re-editions. Some of the books had previously appeared in Spain.

94. Serrano, IV, p. lix.

95. Meregalli, p. 17, gives figures for books published both in translation and in Spanish at Venice:

date	translation	in Spanish	total
1501–50	93	16	109
1551–1600	724	71	195
1601–50	277	28	305

96. AHPB, notary Rufet, leg. 26, Inventarios sueltos 1553–80 (1).

97. Groult, pp. 56–8, 141–4.

98. Groult, p. 186.

99. J. A. van Praag, *La 'comedia' espagnole aux Pays-Bas au XVIIe et au XVIIIe siècle* (Amsterdam, 1922). *Cf.* G. Parker, 'New light on an Old Theme: Spain and the Netherlands 1550–1650', *European History Quarterly*, 15, no. 2, April 1985.

100. E.g. Hieronymo Campos, 1587, p. 26: 'The women of Holland are large-bodied, beautiful and white.'

101. Argensola to Lipsius, Saragossa 1 December 1602, in Ramírez, p. 337.

102. See Chapter One.

103. Peeters-Fontainas.

104. Bibliotheca Catholica Neerlandica.

105. AHPB notary Pau Mallol, leg. 18, pliego de inventarios 1555–86.

106. For the limited success of Netherlandish literature, see Vosters, 1980.

107. A look through some two hundred inventories in the 1590s shows no trace of the *Imitation* in any private library, yet the bookseller Damià Bages in 1590 had 353 unbound copies, selling at 1s each, waiting to be bound and sold. Among expensive editions were the two copies of *Contemptus Mundi* from Antwerp, valued at 12s each, in the bookshop of Antoni Oliver in 1590; cheaper editions cost from 2s to 3s.

108. Bataillon, p. 770.

109. *Ibid.* pp. 795 n. 90, 803 n. 3, 831.

110. Batllori, 1983, pp. 68–9, basing himself on Madurell and Rubió, *Documents*.

111. Lemos, 1583, p. 266.

112. Ortiz Lucio, 1589, prologue. *Cf.* Dante's presentation of Paolo and Francesca in the *Divine*

Comedy.

113. AHPB notary Miquel Cellers menor, leg. 15, 'Inventario de los bienes relictos del librero Damià Bages'. For Gori (1595), AHPB notary Galcerà Francesc Devesa, leg. 4, protocolos 7, año 1595, inventory of books. For the problem of book prices see the note at the end of this chapter.

114. Durán i Sanpere, 1964. See Chapter Four. The Knights ceased to exist after the traumatic events of 1641–52.

115. AHPB notary Joan Teres, leg. 16, pliego de inventarios 1593–1605. The Luján may have been the Seville 1550 edition.

116. Spuny in AHPB notary Lluis Rufet, leg. 26, Inventarios sueltos 1553–1580 (2); Palau in *ibid.* notary Joan Teres, leg. 16, pliego de inventarios 1593–1605.

117. AHPB notary Francesc Pedralbes, leg. 36, pliego de inventarios (1).

118. AHPB notary Varia, pliego de libreros, leg. 4, no. 21, ss. XV–XVI.

119. *Cf.* Batllori, 'Humanisme i Erasmisme a Barcelona (1524–26)', in Batllori, 1983, p. 64.

120. 'The nature of public readership must be judged not by the books which were published but by the surviving inventories of book-shops. No bookseller would risk filling his shop with goods which he knew in advance he could not sell': Rubió, pp. 107–13.

121. Inventory of 17 January 1524 in AHPB, notary Pere Saragossa, leg. 16, pliego de escrituras sueltas, 1521–24.

122. The *Querela* had appeared in a Castilian translation in 1520, but the copy held by Bages was in Latin.

123. This corrects the view of Batllori 1983, p. 68, that the only book by Erasmus on sale in the early century was the *Moria.*

124. 'Memorial dels libres son en casa Jo. Gordiola', October 1561, AHPB, notary Lluis Rufet, leg. 26, Inventarios, 1553–80 (1). The retail value put on his books alone was the huge sum of £3032 16s 7d, Catalan money. Guardiola financed the publishing of Aesop's *Fables* by the printer Carles Amorós in 1550; he also published in Latin the *Extragravatorium* of Jaume Callis, and the *Lucerna Laudemiorum* of Francisco Solsona, both issued in 1556.

125. Even bigger in quantity than his stock of books, and worth almost as much, was his stock of 'prints' (*stampades*), which included 957 missals and 404 'ordinaris' for the diocese of Gerona, valued together at £862; 545 missals, 413 'ordinaris' and 840 diurnals for the diocese of Urgell, valued at £564; and a wealth of pamphlets.

126. Bataillon, p. 723.

127. Grendler, pp. 132–4.

128. Nicolás Antonio, 1672. The arduous collection of this data was done by Eulàlia Vilà.

129. In the table the last period covers only twenty years. After Lyon the most favoured city was Rome, with others such as Antwerp, Naples, Cologne and Paris playing a part. This general analysis applies only to titles in moral theology, and not to the whole output of the Spanish Counter Reformation.

130. The licences, issued by the Council of Aragon, granted privileges for the territories of the Crown of Aragon, and did not represent new books, since most had previously appeared in Castile (and were therefore governed by the censorship regulations of Castile): Madurell i Marimon, 1964–5.

131. Inexplicably, the religious liter-

ature of early modern Catalonia has never been studied.

132. The publisher both times was Claude Bornat. The book had a long publishing history, appearing in three Catalan editions and some seventeen Castilian editions throughout the peninsula (including Lisbon), cited Gutiérrez, 1951, p. 969. For the book's problems with the Inquisition, see Chapter Five.

133. The bookseller Sebastià Cormellas stocked 266 copies of this tiny handbook (in 16^0).

134. Riquer, IV, p. 435.

135. Rubió, p. 156.

136. By contrast, Lutherans developed a remarkably rich visual literature: cf. R. Scribner, *For the sake of Simple Folk. Popular Propaganda for the German Reformation* (Cambridge, 1981). Even in Germany, Catholic visual imagery was poor (*ibid.* Chapter 8).

137. Bataillon, p. 723.

138. Juan de Pineda, 1589 (1963–4), p. xlix.

139. 'Inventario del Protonotario Real Miguel Amat, 8 Marzo 1568', AHPB, notary Lluis Rufet, leg. 26, Inventarios sueltos, 1553–80. A quarter of the books were on notarial practice; in addition the cabinet contained 'several books by various authors and well printed, some in hard binding and others in parchment, nearly all on Latin and humanities'.

140. Papers on the posts held by Amat are in ACA: CA leg. 346. His son Gaspar succeeded to the same posts as his father.

141. Inventory dated 19 March 1619 of Miquel Joan Amat, *militis*, who lived in the street Den Gimnas: AHPB notary Francisco Aquiles (menor), leg. 23, Pliego de Inventarios 1612–44. The library also included volumes on America, China and Persia (this last in Italian), and two small books in Greek.

142. AHPB notary Pau Mallol, leg. 18, Pliego de Inventarios 1555–86. The only vernacular works in the library appear to be in Catalan.

143. This was an edition of the *Imitation of Christ* published, in Spain, with an appendix consisting of the 'Sermon on the child Jesus' by Erasmus; see Bataillon, p. 207 n. 4.

144. Madurell i Marimon, 1957. The two works by Erasmus, the *De conscribendis epistolis* and some *Epistola*, were bequeathed to Pérez by a colleague.

145. Four years before they were first condemned anywhere (at Paris in 1544), and eleven before they were condemned in Spain in the Index of 1551! See Batllori, 1983, p. 68.

146. AHPB notary Pau Mallol, leg. 18, Pliego de Inventarios 1555–86. Vila had a house in Tarragona, facing the archbishop's palace, and a country villa in Hospitalet.

147. The inventory says 'Erasmo, Sobre lo Testament Nou', but I have located no edition of the work in Catalan. The notary read out the titles in the relevant language, so one explanation might be that the spine was written in Catalan.

148. The work was issued with a royal licence, under the title *Colloquia Familiaria et alia quaedam opuscula*, attributed to Francisco Escobar, and without the name of Erasmus on the title page, but at the end of the book (p. 50) Bornat apologises for printing errors and refers clearly to 'editionem huius primae partis Colloquiorum Erasmi'. The work was published together with Erasmus's *De civilitate*

morum puerilium and the *Meditatio in Ciceronis epistolam.* I have consulted the copy in BCC.

149. 'Inventarium hereditatis et bonorum que fuerunt honor. Pauli Cortea', AHPB Varia, Pliego de Libreros, leg. 4, no. 21, ss. XV–XVI.

150. See Aguiló, no. 2061.

151. Obviously a luxury edition of one of the most influential works of the century, and proof of a continuing public. *Cf.* the response of the Jesuits to its condemnation in 1560: 'Here in the college we have burned many works of Erasmus and especially two or three copies of the *Adages*,' cited Bataillon, p. 716 n. 4. The *Adages* also existed in an expurgated form, but there is no way of telling whether Oliver's volumes were these.

152. AHPB, notary Galcerà Francesc Devesa, leg. 13, Pliego de Inventarios, 1591–8, 'Inventari de la botiga de Me Antoni Oliver librater'.

153. Alain Peyro, 'La scolarisation en Catalogne du Nord', maîtrise de sociologie, Université de Paris VIII, 1975, pp. 25–7. For the Virués version, see Bataillon pp. 294–309, and his conclusion that 'these dialogues contributed more than any other book by Erasmus to broadening the spiritual horizons of the public in the peninsula.'

154. 'Companyia feta y fermada per y entre los honorables mossens', 12 August 1566, AHPB, Varia, Pliego de libreros, leg. 4, no. 21, siglos XV–XVI.

155. AHPB, notary Galcerà Francesc Devesa, leg. 4, protocolos 7, year 1595. For a comment on book prices see the note at the end of this chapter. The stock was sold by Gori's widow to fellow bookseller Cristófor Astor.

156. AHPB, notary Miquel Cellers menor, leg. 15, Inventario de los bienes relictos del librero Damiàn Bages, 1590. Bages' household effects were valued at a further £500.

157. And therefore presumably forbidden in Spain, by the 1559 Index: see Bujanda, p. 320. The religious books include one 'Testament Nou' in 16^0 dated 1583.

158. Since inventories usually identified languages clearly, it is interesting that two different stock-lists at this time should identify a Catalan New Testament.

159. Liturgical works from Lyon seem to have been preponderant even in Castile: of the 450 Bibles seized by the Inquisition of Seville in 1552 some 70 per cent (318) were from Lyon: see Tellechea, 1962.

160. AHPB, notary Galcerà Francesc Devesa, leg. 13, Pliego de Inventarios, 1591–8. The text is much perished, and often impossible to decipher. Barassó was of foreign (probably French) origin: his first name is given variously as Noel, Natalis or Nadal, his family name as Boroson or Barassó or Baresson or even Balanzon. In 1593 he is known to have published two books, the *Book of miracles* by Salvador Pons, and the *Sermons for Sundays* of the bishop of Urgell, Andreu Capella, the latter issued at Sanahuja, in the author's diocese.

161. A directive from the bishop of Barcelona to 'all the booksellers of the city' in September 1594 names the following eighteen booksellers: Bernat Cuçana, Lluis Manescal, Joan Malo, Jeroni Genovés, Rafael Vives, Miquel Manescal, Francesc Trinxer, Pere (?)Dotil, Gabriel

Lloberas, Joan Vela, Pere de Turpia, Jeroni Pi, Rafael Nogués, Onofre Gori, Jaume Mico, Aleixandre (?)Canas, G. Sanglés, and Bertran Andreu. ADB: C vol. 70 f. 23.

162. See Chapter Five.

163. *Quinze misteris de Nostra Senyora del Roser, en copla a la tonada de la guilindo.* I have consulted the specimen in the rare book section of the BCC.

164. AHPB, notary Francesc Aguiles menor, leg. 23, Pliego de inventarios, 1612–44.

165. 'Inventarium bonorum omnium que fuerunt Sebastiani de Cormellas quondam mercatoris civis Barcinone', dated 4 February 1667, in AHPB, notary Jaume Corbera, leg. 7, Inventariorum Liber, 1647–86.

166. The family had been in the trade for over a century, and their house was richly appointed: all the tableware and goblets were of silver, all the decoration in the bedroom gilt or gold, with buttons of gold.

167. All book prices quoted in this chapter are those given when inventories of booksellers' stock were made, and therefore represent the value of books to the retailers only. For example, in 1595 Cristófor Astor i Cortey bought the holdings of the late Onofre Gori from his widow, and the valuation then made is the source for prices I quote from the Gori bookshop. The real price to the public would have been a proportion higher.

Chapter Nine

1. The parish manual for 1651–62 shows that in these twelve years only five people founded anniversaries in Santa Maria, though one of the cases was notable: Francesc Castellvi of Mas Pagès founded twelve for his father in 1662: ADB: AP MP/SM vol. 26 f. 76. At this period each anniversary cost £10; the interest from this capital sum went to pay for the annual mass.

2. ADB: AP MP/SQ vol. 21 f. 106.

3. MSS. BCC 502 f. 35; Vilar II, p. 328: 'from the drought of 1626 to the harvest of 1631, the whole principality suffered dearth.'

4. ADB: AP MP/SQ vol. 21 ff. 157–8. The vote was recorded in 'the presence of the venerable mossèn Jaume Tort, one of the priest vicars of the priorate, and of mossèn Miquel Gili priest and also vicar of the priorate'.

5. ADB: AP MP/SQ vol. 21 f. 256.

6. MSS. BUB MS. 1005 f. 352.

7. See the goig, p. 142.

8. ADB: AP MP/SQ vol. 22bis f. 53v, Consell of 10 March 1639.

9. MSS. MP/SQ 1621–43: Mas XXIII, 'Relació de gastos y danys que feren y causaren los soldats francesos'.

10. MSS. Mas XXIII f. 52. The destruction of 1651 was vouched for in sworn statements made in 1675 by two farmers aged sixty-nine and seventy-five respectively.

11. ADB: AP MP/SM vol. 26 ff. 34–5.

12. ADB: AP Mediona, Historia vol. 72.

13. ADB: AP MP/SM vol. 26 f. 88, decisions of 19 and 23 January 1657.

14. All that remained of the old parish church disappeared; St Quintí is probably unique among the towns of the Alt Penedès in having no significant mediaeval survivals in its parish church.

15. ADB: V vols. 82 f. 323; 84 f. 380v.

16. ADB: V vol. 84 f. 378. The bishop gave confirmation to 143 parishioners.
17. Soulet, pp. 352–4.
18. Sanabre 1956, p. 648.
19. Suárez to Laínez, Burgos 18 May 1564, ARSI Epist Hisp vol. 101 f. 174.
20. Muchembled in Greyerz, pp. 64–5.
21. Cited by Wirth, in Greyerz, p. 68; Muchembled, 'The witches of the Cambrésis', in Obelkevich.
22. Obelkevich, in Obelkevich, p. 5. By contrast Hoffman, p. 169, doubts whether the Counter Reformation was imposed.
23. Weinstein & Bell, pp. 191–2.
24. J. H. Elliott, *Imperial Spain* (London, 1970), pp. 230, 246.
25. The campaign against 'popular' culture has not been discussed as such in this book, which has preferred to focus on other perspectives. For some excellent comments, see Hoffman, pp. 87–97. A general approach is given in Burke.
26. The terms require emphasis, for they demonstrate the conservative nature of Tridentine reform, in which faith became a dimension of social discipline. This was the Borromeo ideal, imposed on Milan and later adopted in France, though not identifiably successful in Catalonia. See the comments by J. Bossy in Evennett, pp. 138–9.
27. But the doubt could remain whether these rites of passage were sacraments: in 1619 the rector of Vilatorrada was reprimanded for asserting to a parishioner that extreme unction was not a sacrament: AHN Inq lib. 732 f. 458.
28. Strauss, p. 276.
29. Christian, 1981, *Local*, Chapter 6.
30. 'The Counter Reformation was very much an urban movement': Hoffman, p. 169.
31. Flynn, pp. 135–7.
32. 'They do not fast and do not do penitences, since they have no whips', 'Memorial para la Congregacion de la Compañía', *MHSI Borgia*, vol. III, p. 346.
33. Pedro Juárez to Laínez, 30 April 1564, ARSI Epist Hisp vol. 101 f. 111.
34. 'Inventaris de la Confraria de la Purissima Sang de Jesu Crist', AHPB, notary Pau Mallol, leg. 18, pliego de inventarios 1555–86.
35. The first regular use of 'discipline' by Jesuits in Catalonia is documented for their Lenten missions in the 1620s but must have started very much earlier: MSS. 'Crónica de Belén', f. 101.
36. MSS. 'Crónica de Belén', f. 145.
37. *Ibid.* f. 227.
38. *Ibid.* f. 321. Heavy iron bars, carried to make the suffering real rather than symbolic, had earlier in the century been banned from processions in Barcelona by the bishop.
39. *Ibid.* f. 384.
40. *Ibid.* f. 315v. Poor attendance at mass was in part because parishioners went to other nearby churches.
41. *Ibid.* f. 347v.
42. Nalle, 1987.
43. The evidence for the tribunal of Llerena, which largely coincided with Extremadura, is qualitatively different from Catalonia but suggests the same conclusion. *Cf.* Kamen, 1985, p. 146.
44. These conclusions coincide with those of Blázquez, p. 355.
45. AHN Inq leg. 1592[1] no. 5.
46. AHN Inq lib. 742 f. 38. The rector of St Quintí was Jeroni Ferrer.
47. AHN Inq lib. 733 f. 426.
48. Details of familiars from AHN Inq leg. 2155[2]. The careers of the families Carmona and Salmell may be followed in the parish records.

49. 'Deliberació que és feu en lo Consell de Cent acerca de no fundar en la Ciutat convents nous ni ampliar los antichs', MSS. BUB MS. 1010 f. 113.

50. MSS. 'Monumentos', BUB MS. 992, chapter minutes of the late seventeenth century.

51. ADB: V vol. 74 ff. 335, 344, 347.

52. ADB: V vol. 82 ff. 120, 236, 322.

53. Braudel, 1973, vol. II, p. 835.

54. What remained of the parish records of Mediona were smuggled out and later deposited in the diocesan archive of Barcelona. The fabric of the church was restored after the civil war.

Sources

I Select Bibliography

M. Aguiló i Fuster, *Catálogo de obras en lengua catalana impresas desde 1474 hasta 1860* (reprint Barcelona, 1977).

Anselm Albareda, *Historia de Montserrat* (Montserrat, 1977).

F. Aleixandre Tena, 'Libro, imprenta y censores en Valencia bajo Carlos II', *Homenatge al doctor Sebastià Garcia Martínez*, 3 vols, Valencia 1988, II, 157–75.

Violet Alford, *Pyrenean Festivals* (London, 1937).

De l'Alphabétisation aux Circuits du Livre en Espagne, XVI–XIXᵉ siècles (Paris, 1987).

Joan Amades, *El Carnestoltes a Barcelona fins el segle XVIII* (Barcelona, 1934).

Ibid., Bruixes i bruixots (Barcelona, 1934).

Ibid., Balls populars (Tárrega, 1936).

Ibid., Costums i tradicions d'hostals i tavernes (Barcelona, 1936).

Ibid., Costumari català, El curs de l'any, 5 vols (Barcelona, 1950–6).

Ibid., 'El "ball de Diables"', *Boletín de la Biblioteca-Museo Balaguer*, II, 1954, 37–50.

Ibid., Guia de Festes Tradicionals de Catalunya (Barcelona, 1958).

Ibid., El pessebre (Barcelona, 1959).

Ibid., Folklore de Catalunya, 3 vols (Barcelona, 1980, 1982).

Joan Amades and Josep Colomines, *Els Goigs*, 2 vols (Barcelona, 1948).

Rafael d'Amat, *Costums i tradicions religiosos de Barcelona* (Barcelona, 1987).

Ibid., Calaix de Sastre, ed. Ramon Boixareu, 2 vols (Barcelona, 1987).

James Amelang, *Honored Citizens of Barcelona* (Princeton, 1986).

M. Anderson, 'The Relevance of Family History', in C. Harris (ed.), *The Sociology of the Family: New Directions for Britain* (Keele, 1979).

Ricardo del Arco y Garay, *La erudición española en el siglo XVII y el cronista de Aragón Uztarroz*, 2 vols (Madrid, 1950).

Ricardo Arias, *The Spanish Sacramental Plays* (Boston, 1980).

Philippe Ariès, *The Hour of Our Death* (London, 1981).

Philippe Ariès and André Béjin, *Western Sexuality* (Oxford, 1985).

Josep Armengou i Feliu, *La Patum de Berga* (Berga, 1968).

Othón Arróniz, *La influencia italiana en el nacimiento de la comedia española* (Madrid, 1969).

Eugenio Asensio, 'El Erasmismo y las corrientes espirituales afines', *Revista de Filología Española*, xxxvi (1952).

Antonio Astraín, *Historia de la Compañía de Jesús en la Asistencia de España*, 7 vols (Madrid, 1925).

Tarsicio de Azcona, 'Reforma de religiosas benedictinas y cistercienses de Cataluña en tiempo de los Reyes Católicos', *Studia Monastica*, 9, 1967, 75–165.

Barbara A. Babcock, ed., *The Reversible World, Symbolic Inversion in Art and Society* (Ithaca, 1978).

E. Louis Backman, *Religious Dances in the Christian Church and in Popular Medicine* (London, 1952).

Joan Bada, *Situació religiosa de Barcelona en el segle XVI* (Barcelona, 1970).

Ibid., 'Origen dels bisbes de les seus catalanes', *Questions de Vida Cristiana* (Montserrat), 113 (1982).

Ibid., 'L'origen dels clergues barcelonins en el segle XVII (1635–1717). Aproximació estadística', in *Homenatge al doctor Sebastià Garcia Martínez*, 3 vols (Valencia, 1988), II, 201–13.

Eric Baratay, 'Les animaux du Christ: le boeuf et l'âne dans la nativité du XVIIe siècle à nos jours', *Cahiers d'Histoire*, xxxiv (1989), no. 2.

Maximiliano Barrio, 'La economía de las mitras catalanas en la segunda mitad del siglo XVI', in *Jornades d'Història: Antoni Agustín i el seu temps*, vol. 2 (Tarragona, 1990), 57–72.

Marcel Bataillon, *Erasmo y España* (Mexico, 1966).

Joan B. Batlle, *Los Goigs a Catalunya* (Barcelona, 1924).

L. Batlle Prats, 'Ignaciana', *Analecta Sacra Tarraconensia* 25 (Jan–Jun, 1952).

Miquel Batllori SJ, *Vuit segles de cultura catalana a Europa* (Barcelona, 1983).

Ibid., *Humanismo y Renacimiento* (Barcelona, 1987).

Ibid., 'Temes i problemes de la història religiosa de Catalunya', in *I Congrés d'Història Moderna de Catalunya*, II, 371–9.

Josep Baucells, 'El Cant de la Sibil·la a Barcelona', *Revista Catalana de Teologia* 6 (1981).

Theodore S. Beardsley Jr, 'Spanish Printers and the Classics: 1482–1599', *Hispanic Review*, 47 (1979), 25–35.

Gabriel Beltrán *et al.*, *El Carmelo Teresiano en Cataluña 1586–1986* (Burgos, 1986).

Y-M. Bercé, *Fête et Révolte. Des mentalités populaires du XVIe au XVIIIe s* (Paris, 1976).

Philippe Berger, *Libro y lectura en la Valencia del Renacimiento*, 2 vols (Valencia, 1987).

Bibliotheca Catholica Neerlandica Impresa 1500–1727 (Hague, 1954).

Christopher Black, 'Perugia and Post-Tridentine Church Reform', *Journal of Ecclesiastical History*, 35, no. 3, July 1984, 429–51.

Juan Blázquez Miguel, *La Inquisición de Cataluña. El tribunal del Santo Oficio de Barcelona (1487–1820)* (Madrid, 1990).

José Bono, *Historia del derecho notarial español*, 2 vols (Madrid, 1979).

Antoni Borràs i Feliu SJ, 'Fundació del col·legi de Sant Andreu de la Companyia de Jesús a la Seu d'Urgell (1598–1600)', *Urgellia*, II, 1979.

Ibid., 'Els llocs de Bera, de Roda de Bera i Creixell de Mar, i el col·legi de Betlem de la Companyia de Jesús de Barcelona', XX!X Assemblea Intercomarcal d'Estudiosos (Sitges, 1985).

Fernand Braudel, The Mediterranean and the Mediterranean World in the Age of Philip II, 2 vols (London, 1973).

Ibid., The Identity of France (London, 1988).

Peter Brown, The Cult of the Saints. Its Rise and Function in Latin Christianity (Chicago, 1981).

Ibid., The Body and Society. Men, Women and Sexual Renunciation in Early Christianity (London, 1989).

Jean-Auguste Brutails, Etude sur la condition des populations rurales du Roussillon au Moyen Age (Paris, 1891) (Geneva, 1975, reprint).

J.M. de Bujanda, Index de l'Inquisition espagnole, 1551, 1554, 1559 (Geneva, 1984).

André Burguière, 'The charivari and religious repression in France during the Ancien Régime', in R. Wheaton and T. Hareven, Family and Sexuality in French History (Philadelphia, 1980).

Peter Burke, Popular Culture in Early Modern Europe (London, 1978).

Bob Bushaway, By Rite. Custom, Ceremony and Community in England 1700–1880 (London, 1982).

Andreu Caimari, 'L'antiga pietat popular entorn de Nadal', Analecta Sacra Tarraconensia, 28 (1955).

Cristina Cañedo-Argüelles, Arte y Teoria: la Contrarreforma y España (Oviedo, 1982).

Aureli Capmany, La dansa a Catalunya, 2 vols (Barcelona, 1930).

Ibid., Calendari de llegendes, costums i festes tradicionals catalanes (Barcelona, 1951).

J. Caro Baroja, 'Le charivari en Espagne', in J. Le Goff and J.C. Schmitt, Le Charivari (Paris, 1981).

Francesc Carreras i Candi and Siegfried Bosch, Desafiaments a Catalunya en el segle XVI. Extret del Butlletí de l'Acadèmia de Bones Lletres de Barcelona (Barcelona, 1936).

Venancio Carro OP, El maestro Fr Pedro de Soto OP y las Controversias político-teológicas en el siglo XVI, 2 vols (Salamanca, 1931, 1950).

Enrique Casas Gaspar, Ritos agrarios. Folklore campesino (Madrid, 1950).

James Casey, The History of the Family (Oxford, 1989).

Yves Castan, Honnêteté et relations sociales en Languedoc (1715–80) (Paris, 1974).

Narcis Castells, 'La familia a la Gerona dels segles XVI–XVII', Avenç, 66, Dec. 1983.

Henry Cavaillès, 'Une fédération pyrénéenne sous l'Ancien Régime. Les traités de lies et de passeries', in Lies et Passeries dans les Pyrénées (Tarbes, 1986).

Horace Chauvet, Traditions populaires du Roussillon (Perpignan, 1947).

Julian de Chia, La festividad del Corpus en Girona (Gerona, 1895).

William A. Christian Jr, Local Religion in Sixteenth-Century Spain (Princeton, 1981).

Ibid., Apparitions in Late Medieval and Renaissance Spain (Princeton, 1981).

Maur Cocheril, L'Abbé de Poblet Dom Père Caixal et la 'Peregrination Hispanica' de Frére Claude de Bronseval (Santes Creus, 1961).

J.M. Coll, 'Apóstoles de la devoción rosariana antes de Lepanto', Analecta Sacra Tarraconensis 28 (1955).

Conflent, Vallespir et montagnes catalanes. Actes du LIe Congrès de la Fédération historique du Languedoc méditerranéen et du Roussillon (Montpellier, 1980).

I Congrés d'Història Moderna de Catalunya, 2 vols (Barcelona, 1984).

E. Corredera, 'Una visita pastoral en el monasterio premonstratense de Santa Maria de Bellpuig de las Avellanas en 1690', *Analecta Sacra Tarraconensia* 53–4 (1980–81).

(Viaje de) Cosme de Médicis por España y Portugal (1668–1669) (Madrid, 1933).

J. Domingo Costa y Borrás, *Concilios Tarraconenses*, 2 vols (Barcelona, 1866–7).

Emilio Cotarelo y Mori, *Bibliografía de las Controversias sobre la licitud del teatro en España* (Madrid, 1904).

Dominique de Courcelles, *Les Histoires des Saints, la prière et la mort en Catalogne* (Paris, 1990).

D.W. Cruikshank, '"Literature" and the Book Trade in Golden Age Spain', *Modern Language Review*, 73 (1978).

Natalie Z. Davis, 'The Sacred and the Body Social in Sixteenth-Century Lyon', *Past and Present*, 90, Feb. 1981.

Jean-Pierre Dedieu, '"Christianisation" en Nouvelle Castille. Catéchisme, communion, messe et confirmation dans l'archevêché de Tolède, 1540–1650', *Mélanges de la Casa de Velázquez*, xv (1979).

Ibid., L'Administration de la Foi. L'Inquisition de Tolède (XVIe–XVIIIe siècle) (Madrid, 1989).

Jean Delumeau, *Rassurer et protéger. Le sentiment de sécurité dans l'Occident d'autrefois* (Paris, 1989).

M.E. Desplanque, ed., *Ville de Thuir. Inventaire sommaire des Archives Communales antérieures à 1790* (Perpignan, 1896).

Thomas Deutscher, 'Seminaries and the Education of Novarese Parish Priests, 1593–1627', *Journal of Ecclesiastical History*, 32, no. 3, July 1981, 303–19.

J.P. Devos, ed., *Description de l'Espagne par Jehan Lhermite et Henri Cock* (Paris, 1969).

Dietari de l'Antich Consell Barceloni, vols IV–VIII (Barcelona, 1892–192).

Barbara Diefendorf, *Paris City Councillors in the Sixteenth Century. The Politics of Patrimony* (Princeton, 1983).

Richard B. Donovan, *The Liturgical Drama in Medieval Spain* (Toronto, 1958).

Mary Douglas, *Natural Symbols* (London, 1970).

Manuel Durán y Bas, *Memoria acerca de las instituciones del derecho civil de Cataluña* (Barcelona, 1883).

Agustí Durán i Sanpere, *Els Cavallers de Sant Jordi* (Barcelona, 1964).

Ibid., Barcelona i la seva història, 3 vols (Barcelona, 1972).

Agustí Durán i Sanpere & Eulàlia Durán, *La Passió de Cervera. Misteri del segle XVI* (Barcelona, 1984).

Agustí Durán i Sanpere & Josep Sanabre, *Llibre de les Solemnitats de Barcelona*, 2 vols (Barcelona, 1930).

Marcel Durliat, *Art catalan* (Paris, 1963).

H.O. Evennett, *The Spirit of the Counter Reformation* (Cambridge, 1968).

Angel Fàbrega Grau, 'El P. Pedro Gil SI y sus Vidas de Santos', *Analecta Sacra Tarraconensia* 31 (1958).

Xavier Fàbregas, *Tradicions, mites i creences dels Catalans* (Barcelona, 1979).

(La) Familia en la España mediterránea (siglos XV–XIX) (Barcelona, 1987).

Arturo Farinelli, *Die Beziehungen zwischen Spanien und Deutschland in der Litteratur* (Berlin, 1892).

Jacqueline Ferreras, *Les dialogues espagnols du XVIe siècle*, 2 vols (Paris, 1985).

J.B. Ferreres SJ, *Historia del Misal Romano* (Barcelona, 1929).

Victor Ferro, *El Dret Públic Català. Les Institucions a Catalunya fins al Decret de Nova Planta* (Vic 1987).

Jeanne Ferté, *La vie religieuse dans les campagnes parisiennes (1622–95)* (Paris, 1962).

Jean-Louis Flandrin, *Families in Former Times* (Cambridge, 1979).

Ibid., Le Sexe et l'Occident (Paris, 1981).

J.L. Flecniakoska, 'Spectacles religieux dans les pueblos a travers les dossiers de l'Inquisition de Cuenca (1526–1588)', *Bulletin Hispanique*, lxxvii, July–Dec 1975, nos 3–4.

Maureen Flynn, *Sacred Charity. Confraternities and Social Welfare in Spain, 1400–1700* (London, 1989).

Eufemià Fort i Cogul, *La comunitat de pobles del Camp de Tarragona* (Barcelona, 1975).

George M. Foster, *Culture and Conquest. America's Spanish Heritage* (Chicago, 1960).

Mariano Fraile Hijosa, 'Reflexiones en torno a la publicidad del matrimonio en los primeros sinodos palentinos despues de Trento', *Publicaciones de la Institución Tello Téllez de Meneses* (Palencia, 1979), no. 42.

Margit Frenk, ' "Lectores y oidores". La difusión oral de la literatura en el Siglo de Oro', in *Actas del Septimo Congreso de la Asociación Internacional de Hispanistas*, 2 vols (Rome, 1982), I, 101–23.

J.A. Fuentes Caballero, *Concilios y sinodos en la diocesis de Palencia. . . . año 1582* (Palencia, 1980).

Francesc Vicenç Garcia, *Sonets*. A cura de G. Grilli (Barcelona, 1979).

Antonio García y García, ed., *Synodicon Hispanum* (Madrid, 1981–92).

Juan García González, 'La censura de libros en Valencia durante los siglos XVI y XVII', *Actas III Congreso de Historia de la Medicina* (Valencia, 1969), vol.II, 141–51).

Domingo Garcia Peres, *Catálogo razonado de los autores portugueses que escribieron en castellano* (Madrid, 1890).

R. García-Villoslada, ed., *Historia de la Iglesia en España*, 5 vols (Madrid, 1980).

Joaquim Garriga, *L'Epoca del Renaixement, segle XVI*. vol. IV of *Història de l'Art Català* (Barcelona, 1986).

V.A.C. Gatrell, B. Lenman and G. Parker, *Crime and the Law. The Social History of Crime in Western Europe Since 1500* (London, 1980).

Jean Gaudemet, *Le mariage en Occident* (Paris, 1987).

Josep M. Gavín, *Inventari d'esglésies* (Barcelona, 1981), vol. 10: *Alt Penedès-Baix Penedès-Garraf.*

Rafael Gay de Montellà, *Llibre del Rosselló* (Barcelona, 1959).

Clifford Geertz, 'Religion as a Cultural System', in M. Banton, ed., *Anthropological Approaches to the Study of Religion* (London, 1966).

J.E. Gelabert González, 'Lectura y Escritura en una ciudad provinciana del siglo XVI: Santiago de Compostela', *Bulletin Hispanique*, 84, 1982, nos 3–4.

Antonio Gil Ambrona, 'La mujer vista a través de la Iglesia en la sociedad catalana de los siglos XVI y XVII', *Manuscrits* (Barcelona), I, 1985, 79–94.

Carlos Gilly, *Spanien und der Basler Buchdruck bis 1600* (Basel, 1985).

J. Givanel Mas, *Una mascarada Quixotesca celebrada a Barcelona l'any 1633* (Barcelona, 1915).

Edward Glaser, *Estudios Hispano-Portugueses. Relaciones literarias del Siglo de Oro* (Madrid, 1957).

J. Goñi Gaztambide, 'La adopción de la liturgia tridentina y los libros de coro en la Diócesis de Pamplona', *Príncipe de Viana*, no. xxiv.

Ibid., *Los Navarros en el Concilio de Trento y la Reforma Tridentina en la diócesis de Pamplona* (Pamplona, 1947).

Ibid., 'La reforma de los Premonstratenses españoles del siglo XVI', *Hispania Sacra*, 13 (1960).

Myrtille Gonzalbo, 'Les pestes roussillonaises des XVIe et XVIIe siècles', mémoire de maîtrise (Université de Toulouse-Le-Mirail, 1976).

J.L. González Novalín, 'La vida religiosa en Asturias durante la edad moderna', in *Historia de Asturias, Edad Moderna I*, vol. 6 of the Historia (Oviedo, 1977).

M. González y Sugrañes, *Mendicidad y Beneficiencia en Barcelona* (Barcelona, 1903).

Jack Goody, *The Development of the Family and Marriage in Europe* (Cambridge, 1983).

Jack Goody, Joan Thirsk, E. P. Thompson, eds, *Family and Inheritance. Rural Society in Western Europe 1200–1800* (Cambridge, 1976).

Beatrice Gottlieb, 'The Meaning of Clandestine Marriage', in R. Wheaton and T. Hareven, *Family and Sexuality in French History* (Philadelphia, 1980).

Paul F. Grendler, *The Roman Inquisition and the Venetian Press, 1540–1605* (Princeton, 1977).

Kaspar von Greyerz, *Religion and Society in Early Modern Europe 1500–1800* (London, 1984).

A. Griera, *Liturgia Popular* (San Cugat, 1967).

Clive Griffin, *The Crombergers of Seville* (Oxford, 1988).

Pierre Groult, *Les mystiques des Pays-Bas et la littérature espagnole du seizième siècle* (Louvain, 1927).

J. Gudiol, 'Peregrinatges religiosos catalans', *Analecta Sacra Tarraconensia*, 3 (1927).

Asensio Gutierrez, *La France et les français dans la littérature espagnole. Un aspect de la xénophobie en Espagne (1598–1665)* (St Etienne, 1977).

C. Gutiérrez SJ, *Españoles en Trento* (Valladolid, 1951).

J.P. Gutton, *La sociabilité villageoise dans l'ancienne France* (Paris, 1979).

Ibid., 'Confraternities, curés and communities in rural areas of the diocese of Lyons under the Ancien Régime', in Greyerz, *Religion and Society* (1984).

T. Hampe Martínez, 'La difusión de libros e ideas en el Perú colonial. Análisis de bibliotecas particulares (siglo XVI)', *Bulletin Hispanique*, 89, Jan–Dec 1987, 1–4.

Christian Hermann, *L'Eglise d'Espagne sous le patronage royal (1476–1834)* (Madrid, 1988).

P. Herrera Puga, 'La mala vida en tiempo de los Austrias', *Anuario de Historia Moderna y Contemporánea* I (1974).

Ibid., *Sociedad y delincuencia en el siglo de oro* (Madrid, 1974).

Philip T. Hoffman, *Church and Community in the Diocese of Lyon, 1500–1789* (Yale University Press, 1984).

Gerhart Hoffmeister, *España y Alemania. Historia y Documentación de sus relaciones literarias* (Madrid, 1980).

R.A. Houston, *Literacy in Early Modern Europe. Culture and Education 1500–1800* (London, 1988).

Luis de Hoyos Sainz & Nieves de Hoyos, *Manual de Folklore* (Madrid, 1947).

A. Huerga, 'Sobre la catequesis en España durante los siglos XV–XVI', *Analecta Sacra Tarraconensia*, 41 (1968).

M. Hunter, 'The Problem of "Atheism" in Early Modern England', *Transactions of the Royal Historical Society*, 35, 1985.

Josep Iglésies, *Pere Gil S.I. (1551–1622) i la seva Geografia de Catalunya* (Barcelona, 1949).

Ibid., ed., *El Fogatge de 1553.* 2 vols (Barcelona, 1979).

Martin Ingram, 'Ridings, Rough Music and the "Reform of Popular Culture" in Early Modern England', *Past and Present*, 105, Nov. 1984.

Ibid., 'Religion, Communities and Moral Discipline in Late Sixteenth- and Early Seventeenth-Century England', in Greyerz, *Religion and Society* (1984).

Ibid., *Church Courts, Sex and Marriage in England, 1570–1640* (Cambridge, 1987).

Richard L. Kagan, *Students and Society in Early Modern Spain* (Baltimore, 1974).

Henry Kamen, *La España de Carlos II* (Barcelona, 1981).

Ibid., 'Clerical Violence in a Catholic Society: the Hispanic World 1450–1720', in W.J. Shiels, ed., *Studies in Church History, vol. 20. The Church and War* (Oxford, 1983).

Ibid., 'La Contrarreforma en Cataluña', *Historia 16*, year IX, no. 98 (June 1984).

Ibid., *Inquisition and Society in Spain* (London, 1985).

Ibid., *Spain 1469–1714: A Society of Conflict.* 2nd edn (London, 1991).

Ibid., in R. Scribner *et al.*, eds, *The Reformation in National Context* (Cambridge, 1993).

Robert Kingdon, 'The Plantin Breviaries', *Bibliothèque d'Humanisme et Renaissance*, 22 (1960).

Christiane Klapisch-Zuber, *Women, Family and Ritual in Renaissance Italy* (Chicago, 1985).

George Kubler, *Building the Escorial* (Princeton, 1982).

Jesús Lalinde Abadía, 'Los pactos matrimoniales catalanes', *Anuario de Historia del Derecho Español*, vol. 33 (1963).

Henry Charles Lea, *History of the Inquisition of Spain.* 4 vols (New York, 1906–8).

Gabriel Le Bras, 'La doctrine du mariage depuis l'an Mille', in *Dictionnaire de Théologie Catholique*, vol. 9, 2123–2317 (Paris, 1926).

Ibid., *L'Eglise et le Village* (Paris, 1976).

Jacques Le Goff, *Time, Work and Culture in the Middle Ages* (Chicago, 1980).

Ibid., *The Birth of Purgatory* (London, 1984).

Emmanuel Le Roy Ladurie, *Carnival. A People's Uprising at Romans 1579–1580* (New York, 1979).

Pedro de León SJ, *Grandeza y Miseria en Andalucía (1578–1616)* (Granada, 1981).

Livre et Lecture en Espagne et en France sous l'Ancien Régime (Paris, 1981).

Josep Lladonosa i Pujol, *Historia de Lleida.* 3 vols (Tárrega, 1974).

G. Llompart, 'La piedad medieval en la isla de Mallorca a través de nuevos documentos', *Analecta Sacra Tarraconensia* 51–52 (1978–79).

Ibid. 'Escarceos sobre la piedad popular postridentina', *Analecta Sacra Tarraconensia*, 40 (1967).

Ibid. 'La fiesta del Corpus en Barcelona y Mallorca (siglos XIV–XVIII)', *Analecta Sacra Tarraconensia*, 39 (1966).

Ibid. 'Penitencias y penitentes en la pintura y en la piedad catalanas bajomedievales', *Revista de Dialectología y Tradiciones Populares*, xxviii (1972), 29–49.

Ibid., 'Las danzas procesionales de Mallorca: su pasado y su presente (siglos XIV al XX)', *Actas II Congreso Nacional de Artes y Costumbres Populares*

(Saragossa, 1974), 423–38.

B. Llorca, 'Aceptación en España de los decretos del concilio de Trento', *Estudios Eclesiásticos* 39 (1964).

Antoni Llorens i Solé, *Solsona i el Solsonès en la història de Catalunya* (Lérida, 1986).

D.M. Loades, 'The Theory and Practice of Censorship in Sixteenth-Century England', *Transactions of the Royal Historical Society*, 24 (1974).

Isabel Lobato, 'Religió i Societat: processons i rogatives públiques a Barcelona, 1550–1620', *I Congrés d'Història Moderna de Catalunya*, vol.II.

Pasquale Lopez, *Inquisizione, Stampa e Censura nel Regno di Napoli tra '500 e '600* (Naples, 1974).

Juan López Martín, *Don Pedro Guerrero: Epistolario y Documentación* (Rome, 1974).

Alain Lottin, ed., *La désunion du couple sous l'Ancien Régime. L'exemple du Nord* (Paris, 1975).

Ibid., Lille, citadelle de la Contre-Réforme? (1598–1668) (Dunkirk, 1984).

J.M. Madurell i Marimón, 'Concilios Tarraconenses (1455–69)', *Analecta Sacra Tarraconensia*, 26 (1953).

Ibid., 'Diego Pérez de Valdivia en Barcelona', *Analecta Sacra Tarraconensis*, 30 (1957).

Ibid., 'Licencias reales para la impresión y venta de libros (1519–1705)', *Revista de Archivos, Bibliotecas y Museos*, 72, (1964–5).

Ibid., 'Regesta documental de Biblias manuscritas e impresas (1336–1600)', *Analecta Sacra Tarraconensis* 47 (1974) 27–63.

J.M. Madurell & Jorge Rubió y Balaguer, *Documentos para la Historia de la Imprenta y Librería en Barcelona (1474–1553)* (Barcelona, 1955).

Antonio Marín Ocete, *El arzobispo Don Pedro Guerrero y la politica conciliar española en el siglo XVI.* 2 vols (Madrid, 1970).

Antonio Martí, *La preceptiva retórica española en el siglo de oro* (Madrid, 1972).

J.M. Martí Bonet, ed., *Catàleg monumental de l'arquebisbat de Barcelona.* vols I, VI (Barcelona, 1981, 1987).

Carlos Martí Vila, *Una fiesta popular en el siglo XVII* (Barcelona, 1951).

Francisco Martín Hernández, *La formación clerical en los colegios universitarios españoles (1371–1563)* (Vitoria, 1961).

Ibid., Los Seminarios españoles (1563–1700) (Salamanca, 1964).

Linda Martz, *Poverty and Welfare in Habsburg Spain* (Cambridge, 1983).

Francisco Maspons y Anglasell, *Nostre Dret Familiar segons els autors classichs* (Barcelona, 1907).

J. Mateu Ibars, 'Catálogo de la colección bibliográfica de la Imitació Christi de la Biblioteca Central de Cataluña', *Analecta Sacra Tarraconensia*, 40 (1967).

Melveena McKendrick, *Woman and Society in the Spanish Drama of the Golden Age* (Cambridge, 1974).

Franco Meregalli, *Presenza della letteratura spagnola in Italia* (Florence, 1974).

Enrique Moliné Coll, 'La organizacion parroquial de la diócesis de Urgel, 1566–1576' (*tesina* of University of Barcelona, 1975).

Ibid., 'Les relacions de les visites "ad limina apostolorum" dels bisbes d'Urgell, 1597–1821', *Urgellia*, III, 1980.

Ibid., 'Organitzacions eclesiàstiques autónomes al Pirineu durant l'Antic Règim: les Valls d'Aneu, de Boí i d'Arán', *Urgellia*, V, 1982 & VI, 1983).

Ibid., 'Els sacerdots francesos al bisbat d'Urgell (segles XIV–XVII)', *Urgellia*, IX, 1988–9.

Jaime Moll, 'Problemas bibliográficos del libro del Siglo de Oro', *Boletín de la Real*

Academia Española, 59 (1979), 49–107.

Ibid., 'Valoración de la industria editorial española del siglo XVI', in *Livre et Lecture en Espagne et en France sous l'Ancien Régime* (Paris, 1981).

William Monter, *Frontiers of Heresy. The Spanish Inquisition from the Basque Lands to Sicily* (Cambridge, 1990).

Monumenta Historica Societatis Jesu (MHSI), S. Franciscus Borgia, 5 vols (Madrid, 1896–1908).

Robert Muchembled, *Culture populaire et culture des élites dans la France moderne (XV–XVIIIs)* (Paris, 1978).

J. Nadal and E. Giralt, *La population catalane de 1553 à 1717* (Paris, 1960).

Sara Nalle, 'Comisarios and the Spanish Inquisition', *Sixteenth-Century Journal*, XVIII, 4, (1987).

Ibid., 'Literacy and Culture in Early Modern Castile', *Past and Present*, 125, Nov 1989).

René Nelli, *Le Languedoc et le Comté de Foix. Le Roussillon* (Paris, 1958).

F.J. Norton, *Printing in Spain 1501–1520* (Cambridge, 1966).

J. Obelkevich, ed., *Religion and the People, 800–1700* (Chapel Hill, 1979).

Teodoro Olarte, *Alfonso de Castro (1495–1558). Su vida, su tiempo* (San José, 1946).

Alexandre Olivar, 'Panorama actual de la investigació historica de la liturgia a Catalunya', *Analecta Sacra Tarraconensia*, 41 (1968).

P. Andrés de Palma de Mallorca, *Mediona. Apuntes para una historia* (Barcelona, 1946).

Ibid., 'Los Capuchinos de Cataluña y el fomento de algunas devociones populares', *Analecta Sacra Tarraconensia*, 28 (1955).

Ludwig Pastor, *The History of the Popes* (London, 1929), vols XVII–XIX.

Jean Peeters-Fontainas, *Bibliographie des impressions espagnoles des Pays-Bas méridionaux*. 2 vols (Nieuwkoop, 1965).

Christian Péligry, 'El monasterio de San Lorenzo de el Escorial y la difusión de los libros litúrgicos en España (1573–1615)', *Primeras Jornadas de Bibliografía* (Madrid, 1977).

Ibid., 'Les éditeurs lyonnais et le marché espagnol aux XVIe et XVIIe siècles', in *Livre et Lecture en Espagne* (1981).

Lorenzo Pérez Martínez, 'Diego de Arnedo, reformador tridentino', *Anthologica Annua*, 6 (1958).

Ibid., *Las visitas pastorales de don Diego de Arnedo a la diócesis de Mallorca (1562–1572)*. 2 vols (Palma, 1963).

M & J.L. Peset Reig, 'El aislamiento científico español a través de los índices del inquisidor Gaspar de Quiroga', *Anthologica Annua*, 16 (1968).

C. Phythian-Adams, 'Ceremony and the Citizen: the Communal Year at Coventry 1450–1550', in P. Clark and P. Slack, eds, *Crisis and Order in English Towns 1500–1700* (London, 1972).

Jose Piñol Agulló, *Del esplendor a la decadencia de los contratos matrimoniales en Cataluña* (Barcelona, 1956).

A. Pladevall and J.M. Pons Guri, 'Particularismes catalans en els costumaris dels segles XIII–XVIII', *II Congrés Litúrgic de Montserrat, vol.III*.

A. Pladevall & A. Simón, *Guerra i vida a la Catalunya del segle XVII, segons el 'Diari' de Joan Guàrdia, pagès de l'Esquirol* (Barcelona, 1986).

(La) Pobreza y la Asistencia a los Pobres en la Cataluña medieval. 2 vols (Barcelona, 1980–2).

Guillermo Pons, 'La reforma eclesiástica en Mallorca durante el pontificado de D. Juan Vich y Manrique de Lara (1573–1604)', *Anthologica Annua*, 16 (1968).

J.S. Pons, *La littérature catalane en Roussillon au XVIIe et au XVIIIe siècle* (Toulouse, 1929).

Ibid., *La littérature catalane en Roussillon (1600–1800). Bibliographie* (Toulouse, 1929).

J.M. Puigvert i Solà, 'Parròquia, rector i comunitat pagesa', *L'Avenç* (May, 1988).

Ibid., 'El calendari festiu d'una comunitat pagesa d'antic règim mitjançant les processons', in *I Congrés d'Història Moderna de Catalunya, 1984, II*, 417–27.

Dietari de Jeroni Pujades, ed. J.M. Casas Homs. 4 vols (Barcelona, 1975–6).

B. Pullan, 'Catholics and the Poor in Early Modern Europe', *Transactions of the Royal Historical Society*, 26, 1976.

Alejandro Ramírez, *Epistolario de Justo Lipsio (1577–1606).* 2nd edn (St Louis & Madrid, 1967).

Dale B. J. Randall, *The Golden Tapestry. A Critical Survey of Non-Chivalric Spanish Fiction in English (1543–1657)* (Durham N.C, 1963).

Nolasc Rebull, *Als orígens de la sardaña* (Barcelona, 1976).

Augustin Redondo ed., *Amours légitimes, amours illégitimes en Espagne (XVIe–XVIIe siècles)* (Paris, 1985).

Ibid., ed., *Le Discours des groupes dominés* (Paris, 1986).

Ibid., 'La religion populaire espagnole au XVIe siècle: un terrain d'affrontement?', in *Culturas populares: diferencias, divergencias, conflictes* (Madrid, 1986).

Ibid., ed., *Autour des Parentés en Espagne aux XVIe et XVIIe siècles* (Paris, 1987).

Ibid., ed., *Les Parentés fictives en Espagne (XVIe–XVIIe siècles)* (Paris, 1988).

Ibid., ed., *Le Corps dans la société espagnole des XVIe et XVIIe siècles* (Paris, 1990).

Joan Reglà, *Felip II i Catalunya* (Barcelona, 1956).

Ibid., *Els Virreis de Catalunya* (Barcelona, 1980).

Robert Ricard, 'La dualité de la civilisation hispanique et l'histoire religieuse du Portugal', *Revue Hispanique* 216 (1956), 1–17.

Ibid., *The Spiritual Conquest of Mexico* (University of California, 1966).

Martí de Riquer, *Història de la Literatura Catalana*, vol.IV (Barcelona, 1985 edn).

Thomas Robisheaux, *Rural Society and the Search for Order in Early Modern Germany* (Cambridge, 1989).

Marie-Christine Rodríguez and Bartolomé Bennassar, 'Signatures et niveau culturel de témoins et accusés dans les procès d'Inquisition', *Caravelle*, 31 (1978), 17–46.

Josep Romeu, *Les Nadales tradicionals* (Barcelona, 1952).

Ibid., *La nit de Sant Joan* (Barcelona, 1953).

Lyndal Roper, *The Holy Household* (Oxford, 1989).

Basili de Rubi, *Un segle de vida caputxina a Catalunya 1564–1664* (Barcelona, 1977).

Jordi Rubió i Balaguer, *La cultura catalana del Renaixement a la Decadència* (Barcelona, 1964).

D.W. Sabean, *Power in the Blood. Popular Culture and Village Discourse in Early Modern Germany* (Cambridge, 1984).

Thomas M. Safley, 'Marital litigation in the Diocese of Constance, 1551–1620', *Sixteenth Century Journal*, XII, 2, 1981.

Ibid., *Let No Man Put Asunder: the Control of Marriage in the German Southwest: A Comparative Study 1550–1600* (Kirksville, Mo. 1984).

Núria Sales, 'Església, masia i poble (segles XVI, XVII i XVIII)', *Revista de Catalunya*, no. 16, Feb. 1988.

Juan Salvat y Bové, *Los gigantes y enanos de Tarragona*. 2nd ed (Tarragona, 1971).

Josep Sanabre, *Los sínodos diocesanos en Barcelona* (Barcelona, 1930).

Ibid., *La acción de Francia en Cataluña en la pugna por la hegemonía de Europa (1640–1659)* (Barcelona, 1956).

Pedro Sanahuja OFM, *Historia de la Seráfica Provincia de Cataluña* (Barcelona, 1959).

Miguel Sánchez, 'La familia rural al Vallès (s. XVII–XVIII)', *L'Avenç*, 66, Dec. 1983.

Juan Manuel Sánchez Gómez, 'Un discípulo del P. Mto Avila en la Inquisición de Córdoba. El Dr Diego Pérez de Valdivia', *Hispania*, 9 (1949), no. 34, 104–134.

J.L. Santos Diez, 'Política conciliar postridentina en España. El Concilio provincial de Toledo de 1565', *Anthologica Annua*, vol. 15, 1967, 309–461.

J. Sarrète, *Le Pardon de Marcevol* (Perpignan, 1902).

Ibid., *La Confrérie du Rosaire en Cerdagne* (Perpignan, 1920).

Robert Sauzet, *Contre-Réforme et Réforme Catholique en Bas-Languedoc. Le diocèse de Nimes au XVIIe siècle* (Brussels, 1979).

Adam Schneider, *Die spanischen Vorlagen der deutschen theologischen Litteratur des 17. Jahrhunderts* (Strasbourg, 1897).

R.W. Scribner, 'Ritual and Popular Religion in Catholic Germany at the Time of the Reformation', *Journal of Ecclesiastical History* 35, no. 1, Jan 1984, 47–77.

Martine Segalen, *Love and Power in the Peasant Family. Rural France in the Nineteenth Century* (Blackwell, Oxford, 1983).

Juan Sempere y Guarinos, *Historia del luxo y de las leyes suntuarias de España*. 2 vols (Madrid, 1788).

Eva Serra, *Pagesos i senyors a la Catalunya del segle XVII. Baronia de Sentmenat 1590–1729* (Barcelona, 1988).

Valeri Serra i Boldú, *Llibre d'or del Rosari a Catalunya* (Barcelona, 1925).

Ibid., *Calendari folklòric d'Urgell* (Montserrat, 1981) (orig. 1914).

Rosendo Serra y Pagès, 'La festa del Bisbetó a Montserrat', *Butlletí del Centre Excursionista*, XX (1910).

Luciano Serrano, *Correspondencia diplomática entre España y la Santa Sede*. 4 vols (Madrid, 1914).

Edward Shorter, *The Making of the Modern Family* (London, 1976).

H. D. Smith, *Preaching in the Spanish Golden Age. A Study of Some Preachers of the Reign of Philip III* (Oxford, 1978).

Tomás Sobrino Chomon, *Episcopado abulense, siglos XVI–XVIII* (Avila, 1983).

Alfred Soman, 'Press, Pulpit and Censorship in France Before Richelieu', *Proceedings of the American Philosophical Society*, 120 (1976), 439–63.

J.-F. Soulet, *Traditions et Réformes religieuses dans les Pyrénées Centrales au XVIIe siècle (Le diocèse de Tarbes de 1602 à 1716)* (Pau, 1974).

Margaret Spufford, *Contrasting Communities. English Villagers in the Sixteenth and Seventeenth Centuries* (Cambridge, 1974).

Lawrence Stone, *The Family, Sex and Marriage in England 1500–1800* (Harmondsworth, 1979).

Gerald Strauss, *Luther's House of Learning* (Baltimore, 1978).

François Taillefer, *Les Pyrénées* (Toulouse, 1974).

Victor-L. Tapié, *The Age of Grandeur. Baroque and Classicism in Europe* (London, 1957).

Juan Tejada y Ramiro, *Colección de canones y de todos los concilios*. 6 vols (Madrid, 1859).

J.I. Tellechea Idigoras, 'Biblias publicadas fuera de España secuestradas por la Inquisición de Sevilla en 1552', *Bulletin Hispanique*, 64 (1962).

Ibid., *La reforma Tridentina en San Sebastián* (San Sebastian, 1970).

Thomas N. Tentler, *Sin and Confession on the Eve of the Reformation* (Princeton, 1977).

I. Terradas, *El món històric de les masies* (Barcelona, 1984).

Keith Thomas, *Religion and the Decline of Magic* (Harmondsworth, 1973).

E. Toda y Güell, *Bibliografia Espanyola d'Italia dels origens de la impremta fins a l'any 1900*. 5 vols (Escornalbou, 1927).

A. Tomás Avila, *El culto y la liturgia en la catedral de Tarragona (1300–1700)* (Tarragona, 1963).

P. Torreilles, 'Un prêtre ermite au XVIIe siècle (moeurs religieuses de village)', *Société Agricole scientifique et littéraire des Pyrénées-Orientales*, 39 (1898).

Ibid., 'La translation du siège et du chapitre d'Elne à Perpignan', *Revue d'Histoire et d'Archéologie du Roussillon*, VI, 1905.

P. Torreilles and E. Desplanque, *L'Enseignement élémentaire en Roussillon* (Perpignan, 1895).

Jean Tosti, *L'Art et la dévotion populaire* (Ille-sur-Tet, 1989).

J. Toussaert, *Le sentiment religieux en Flandre à la fin du Moyen Age* (Paris, 1963).

Richard Trexler, 'Christianization by Children in 16th-Century New Spain', *Church and Community 1200–1600* (Rome, 1987).

Joan-Ramón Triadó, *L'Època del Barroc*. Vol. V of *Història de l'Art Català* (Barcelona, 1984).

Ibid., 'La Cultura'. Vol. V, *El Siglo de Oro*, of *Historia de España Planeta* (Madrid, 1988).

Georges Tricou, *Bibliographie Lyonnaise, par le Président Baudrier* (Geneva, 1950).

Marie-Jeanne Trogno, 'Les confréries en Roussillon aux XVIe, XVIIe et XVIIIe siècles', mémoire de maîtrise, Faculté de Paris, XII, (1975).

Victor and Edith Turner, *Image and Pilgrimage in Christian Culture* (New York, 1978).

Hugues Vanay, 'Bibliographie hispanique extra-peninsulaire', *Revue Hispanique*, XLII, 1918, 1–304.

Arnold Van Gennep, *The Rites of Passage* (Chicago, 1960).

Adriaan Van Oss, *Catholic Colonialism. A Parish History of Guatemala 1524–1821* (Cambridge, 1986).

Honorio M. Velasco, ed., *Tiempo de Fiesta* (Madrid, 1982).

Francis G. Very, *The Spanish Corpus Christi Procession* (Valencia, 1962).

Mariló Vigil, *La vida de las mujeres en los siglos XVI y XVII* (Madrid, 1986).

Pep Vila, *Festes públiques i teatre a Girona, segles XIV–XVIII* (Gerona, 1983).

Joan Vilà Valentí, *El món rural a Catalunya* (Barcelona, 1973).

Pierre Vilar, *Catalunya dins l'Espanya moderna*, 3 vols (Barcelona, 1964).

Jaime Villanueva, *Viage literario a las iglesias de España*. 22 vols (Madrid 1803–52).

Ramón Violant y Simorra, *El Pirineo español* (Madrid, 1949).
Simon Vosters, *Los paises bajos en la literatura española. Parte I: La Edad Media* (Valencia, 1978).
Ibid., 'Mas fuerte que la guerra. Intercambio cultural entre Páises Bajos y España en la Edad de Oro', *Historia 16*, 51, 1980, 39–54.
H. de Vries de Heekelingen, *Correspondance de Bonaventura Vulcanius pendant son séjour à Cologne, Genève et Bâle (1573–1577)* (La Haye, 1923).

Bruce Wardropper, *Introducción al teatro religioso del siglo de oro (La evolución del auto sacramental: 1500–1648)* (Madrid, 1953).
Donald Weinstein and Rudolph M. Bell, *Saints and Society* (Chicago, 1982).
Enid Welsford, *The Fool. His Social and Literary History* (London, 1935).
R. Wheaton & T. Hareven, *Family and Sexuality in French History* (Philadelphia, 1980).
R. Wittkower and I. Jaffe, eds, *Baroque Art: the Jesuit Contribution* (New York, 1972).

Arthur Young, *Travels During the Years 1787, 1788 and 1789*. 2nd edn. 2 vols (London, 1794).

Ernesto Zaragoza Pascual, 'Actas de Visita del Monasterio de Montserrat (1697–1817)', *Studia Monastica*, 16, 1974, 325–449.
Ibid., 'Reforma de las Benedictinas de Cataluña en el s. XVI (1589–1603)', *ibid.* 49–50, 1976–7.
Ibid., 'Documentos inéditos referentes a la reforma monástica en Cataluña durante la segunda mitad del siglo XVI (1555–1600)', *Studia Monastica*, 19, 1977, 93–203.
Ibid., 'Reforma de las Benedictinas de Cataluña en el siglo XVII (1601–1616)', *Analecta Sacra Tarraconensia* 51–2 (1978–9), 171–90.
Ibid., 'Reforma de los benedictinos y de los canónigos regulares en Cataluña. Documentos inéditos (1588–1616)', *Studia Monastica*, 23, 1981, 71–148.
Charles Zika, 'Hosts, Processions and Pilgrimages: Controlling the Sacred in Fifteenth-Century Germany', *Past and Present*, 118, Feb. 1988, 25–64.

II   Early Printed Books

These items were consulted in five libraries: the Department of Rare Books, Memorial Library, Madison; the British Library, London; the Biblioteca Nacional, Madrid; and the Biblioteca Central de Catalunya and Institut Municipal de Història, Barcelona. Dates are of the edition consulted and not necessarily of the first edition.

Christoval Acosta Affricano, *Tratado en loor de las mugeres* (Venice, 1592).
Diego Agreda y Vargas, *Novelas morales* (Barcelona, 1620).
Miquel Agustí, *Llibre dels secrets de la Agricultura* (Barcelona, 1617).
Juan de Alcocer, *Ceremonial de la Missa* (Barcelona, 1623).
Antonio Alvarez OFM, *Primera parte de la Sylva Spiritual. Segunda parte de la Sylva* (Saragossa, 1590).
Antonio Alvarez de Benavente, *Adiciones a la sylva espiritual y su tercera parte* (Barcelona, 1595).
Alfonso Alvarez Guerrero, *Tractado de la forma q se ha de tener en la celebracion del General Concilio* (Valencia, 1536).

Alexandre Amargos, *Relacio de la solemne professo ques feu en Barcelona* (Barcelona, 1601).

Alonso de Andrade, *Itinerario historical que deve guardar el hombre para caminar al cielo* (Barcelona, 1684).

Nicolás Antonio, *Biblioteca Hispana*, 2 vols (Rome, 1672).

Gregorio de Argaíz, *La Perla de Cataluña. Historia de Nuestra Señora de Monserrate* (Madrid, 1677).

Francisco Arias SJ, *Aprovechamiento espiritual* (Madrid, 1603).

Gaspar Astete SJ, *Del govierno de la familia y estado del matrimonio* (Valladolid, 1598).

Martín de Azpilcueta Navarro, *Manual de Confessores* (Barcelona, 1567).

Ibid., Tractado de alabança y murmuracion (Valladolid, 1572).

Antonio de Balbas Barona, *Restauracion de las Españas* (Madrid, 1636).

Juan Baptista, *Doctrina de sacerdotes* (Seville, 1535).

Fructuoso Bisbe y Vidal, *Tratado de las Comedias* (Barcelona, 1618).

Bisbetó, Sermó del (Barcelona, 1910).

Andreu Bosch, *Summari, Index o Epitome dels admirables y nobilissims Titols de Honor de Cathalunya, Rossello y Cerdanya* (Perpignan, 1628 [reprod. 1974 Barcelona]).

Baltasar Calderón, *Alabanças de la insigne ciudad de Barcelona* (Barcelona, 1604).

Pere Caldes, *Instructio y Doctrina que ensenye lo que deu considerar* (Barcelona, 1588).

Juan Christóbal Calvete de Estrella, *El Felicissimo Viaje del Muy Alto y Muy Poderoso Principe Don Phelippe* (Antwerp, 1552).

Marco Antonio de Camos, *Microcosmia y Govierno Universal del Hombre Christiano* (Barcelona, 1592).

Ibid., La fuente deseada (Barcelona, 1598).

Narciso Camos OP, *Jardin de Maria, plantado en Cataluña* (Barcelona, 1657).

Juan del Campo Moya, *Doctrina Christiana sobre el cathecismo* (Alcalá, 1676).

Hieronymo Campos, *Manual de oraciones de muchos padres* (Louvain, 1579).

Ibid., Sylva de varias questiones naturales y morales (Valencia, 1587).

Andreu Capella, *Sermons dels diumenges y festes principals pera utilitat dels Rectors* (Sanahuja, 1593).

Gaspar Cardillo de Villalpando, *Commentarius praecipuarum rerum Conciliis Toletanis* (Alcala, 1570).

Carnestolendas, *see* Relacion, under **Archival Sources**, Bodleian Library.

Martin Carrillo (abad de Montearagon), *Annales y memoriales cronologicas* (Madrid, 1620).

Ibid., Elogios de Mugeres insignes del viejo testamento (Huesca, 1627).

Jayme Cassador, *Advertencies y Manaments* (Barcelona, 1593).

Martín de Castañega, *Tratado de las supersticiones* (Logroño, 1529 [Madrid 1946 edn]).

Alfonso de Castro, *De iuxta haereticorum punitione* (Venice, 1549).

Tomás de Castro y Aguila, *Antidoto y Remedio Unico de Daños Publicos. Conservacion y restauracion de monarchias* (Antequera, 1649).

Thomás Cerdán de Tallada, *Visita de la carcel y de los presos* (Valencia, 1574).

Hernando Chirino de Salazar, *Practica de la frecuencia de la sagrada comunion* (Madrid, 1622).

Pedro Ciruelo, *Tratado en el qual repruevan todas las supersticiones* (Barcelona, 1628).

Miguel Ciurana, *Relacion verdadera de las solemnes fiestas en Barcelona... del Corpus* (Barcelona, 1608).

Cobles novament fetes sobre la mort de Moreu Palau (Barcelona, 1573).

Henrique Cock, *Relación del viaje hecho por Felipe II en 1585*, ed. A. Morel-Fatio (Madrid, 1876).

Pere Màrtir Coma, *Directorium Curatorum* (Barcelona, 1566).

Ibid., *Doctrina Christiana utilissima a tots los Christians* (Tarragona, 1569).

Constitutiones Sacrorum Consiliorum Tarraconensium (Barcelona, 1557).

Constitutiones Synodales Solsona (Barcelona, 1671).

Constitutiones Synodales Dioces. Barcinonen (Barcelona, 1673).

Constitutiones Synodales Vicenses (Barcelona, 1628).

Esteban de Corbera, *Cataluña Ilustrada* (Naples, 1678).

Antonio de Córdoba OFM, *Tratado de casos de consciencia* (Toledo, 1573).

Fray Martín de Córdoba, *Jardín de Nobles Donzellas*, ed. Harriet Goldberg (Chapel Hill, 1974).

Juan Cortes, *Discurso apologetico y excelencias de la medicina...este noble exercicio* (Madrid, 1638).

Juan de la Cruz OP, *Dialogo sobre la necessidad y obligacion de la oracion* (Salamanca, 1555).

Cristofor Despuig, *Los col.loquis de Tortosa. 1557* (Barcelona, 1981 edn).

Francisco Diago, *Historia de la provincia de la Orden de Predicadores de Aragon* (Barcelona, 1599).

Juan Bernal Díaz de Luco, *Aviso de Curas* (Alcalá, 1543).

Joan Dimas Loris, *Memorial de Manaments y Advertencias* (Barcelona, 1598).

Antonio Vicente Domenec, *Historia General de los Santos de Cataluña* (Gerona, 1630).

Juan de Dueñas, *Quarta, quinta y Sexta parte del Espejo de Consolacion de Tristes* (Toledo, 1591).

Joseph Dulac, *Marial de España* (Barcelona, 1680).

Enterrogatori o Confessional (Barcelona, 1535).

Desiderius Erasmus, *Colloquia et alia quaedam opuscula* (Barcelona, 1568).

Juan de Espinosa, *Dialogo en laude de las mugeres* (Milan, 1580).

Pablo de Espinosa, *Teatro de la Santa Iglesia metropolitana de Sevilla* (Seville, 1635).

Josep Elias Estrugos, *Fénix català* (Perpinyà, 1644).

Narcis Feliu de la Penya, *Anales de Cataluña*, 3 vols (Barcelona, 1709).

Alonso Fernández OP, *Historia Eclesiastica de nuestros tiempos* (Toledo, 1611).

Francisco Farfán, *Tres libros Contra el Pecado de la Simple Fornicación* (Salamanca, 1585).

Ibid., *Regimiento de Castos y remedio de Torpes* (Salamanca, 1592).

Pere Font, *Exercici Espiritual* (Barcelona, 1608).

Ibid., *Rosari de la Mare de Deu* (Barcelona, 1611).

Thomas Gage, *A New Survey of the West Indies* (London, 1655).

Francisco Garau, *El sabio instruido* (Barcelona, 1675).

Joseph Garces, *Ave Maria, La Luz mas clara* (Jaén, 1678).

Diego Garcia de Trasmiera, *De polygamia et polyviria* (Palermo, 1638).

Miguel and Joan Gassol de Conques, *Relacion fidelissima y verdadera de las fiestas y procesion con sus altares* (Barcelona, 1626).

Joseph Gavarri, *Instrucciones Predicables* (Seville, 1673).

Francisco de Gilabert, *Discursos sobre la calidad de Cataluña* (Lerida, 1616).

Juan Francisco de Gracia, *Ordinaciones del Valle de Arán* (Barcelona, 1752).

Pablo de Granada, *Causa y Origen de las felicidades de España* (Madrid, 1652).

Geronymo Gudiel, *Compendio de algunas historias de España (los Girones)* (Alcalá, 1577).

Gaspar Gutiérrez de los Rios, *Noticia General para la estimacion de las artes*

(Madrid, 1600).

Pedro de Guzmán, *Bienes de honesto trabajo* (Madrid, 1614).

Gaspar Lucas Hidalgo, *Dialogos de apacible entretenimiento* (Brussels, 1610).

Juan de Horozco y Covarruvias, *Tratado de la verdadera y falsa prophecia* (Segovia, 1588).

Ibid., *Emblemas morales* (Segovia, 1591).

Juan Huarte de San Juan, *Examen de Ingenios* (Barcelona, 1607).

Dionisio Hieronymo de Iorba, *Descripcion de las excellencias de Barcelona* (Barcelona, 1589).

Pedro de Ledesma OP, *Summa en la qual se cifra y summa todo lo que toca a los sacramentos*, 2 vols (Lisbon, 1617).

Hieronymo de Lemos, *La Torre de David moralizada* (Medina del Campo, 1583).

Antonio de León Pinelo, *Velos antiguos i modernos en los rostros de las mugeres* (Madrid, 1641).

Pedro de Luján, *Coloquios Matrimoniales* (Seville, 1550).

López Madera, *Excelencias de España* (Madrid, 1625).

Alonso Maldonado, *Preguntas y respuestas de la Doctrina Christiana* (Madrid, 1615).

Manuel Marcillo, *Crisi de Cataluña* (Barcelona, 1685).

Joseph Massot, *Compendio Historial de los Hermitaños de San Agustin del Principado de Cataluña* (Barcelona, 1699).

Pedro de Medina, *Libro de la verdad* (Alcalá, 1570).

Francisco Manuel de Mello, *Carta de Guia de casados* (Lisbon, 1651).

Felipe de Meneses, *Luz del alma cristiana*, 1554. [Madrid, 1978 edn by I. Velo Pensado].

Luis de Mercado, *De mulierum affetionibus* (Venice, 1587).

Pedro Mexía, *Dialogos eruditos* (Seville, 1570).

Vicente Mexía OP, *Saludable instrucion del estado del matrimonio* (Córdoba, 1566).

Antonio de Molina, *Instruccion de sacerdotes* (Barcelona, 1610).

Christoval Moreno, *Claridad de Simples* (Barcelona, 1586).

Gaspar Navarro, *Tribunal de la Supersticion Ladina* (Huesca, 1631).

Juan Eusebio Nieremberg, *Curiosa y oculta filosofia*, 3rd ed. (Madrid, 1643).

Nou Testament y Ultima Voluntat del Honorable Senyor Carnestoltes (Barcelona, 1625).

Benito Remigio Noydens, *Promptuario moral de questiones practicas y casos de la teologia moral, para examen de curas* (Barcelona, 1671).

Ibid., *Practica de Exorcistas* (Barcelona, 1675).

Ibid., *Practica de Curas y Confesores* (Barcelona, 1681).

Florián de Ocampo, *Los 4 libros primeros de la Crónica General de España* (Zamora, 1543).

Alonso de Orozco, *Recopilacion de todas las obras que ha escripto* (Valladolid, 1554).

Ibid., *Libro de la suavidad de Dios* (Salamanca, 1576).

Francisco Ortiz Lucio OFM, *Jardin de Amores sanctos* (Alcalá, 1589).

Ibid., *Compendio de todas las summas y recopilacion de todos los casos de conciencia* (Barcelona, 1598).

Francisco Ortiz de Salzedo, *Curia Eclesiastica, para secretarios* (Madrid, 1615).

Juan de Ovando, *Tratado Pastoral* (Salamanca, 1601).

Luis Pacheco de Narváez, *Ejemplar de las dos constantes mujeres españolas* (Madrid, 1635).

Juan Lorenzo Palmireno, *Vocabulario del humanista* (Barcelona, 1575).

Ibid., *Camino de la iglesia que el Christiano* (Barcelona, 1591).
Raphael Pastor, *A la Humildad que tuvo san Raymundo de Peñafort* (Barcelona, 1601).
Ibid., *Cobles ara novament fetes del humano al divino, al to de la serdana* (Barcelona, 1602).
Juan de Pedraza, *Summa de Casos de Conciencia* (Barcelona, 1566).
Benito de Peñalosa, *Libro de las cinco excelencias* (Pamplona, 1629).
Juan Pérez de Moya, *Comparaciones o similes para los vicios* (Alcalá, 1584).
Diego Pérez de Valdivia, *Tratado de la Alabança de la Castidad* (Barcelona, 1587).
Ibid., *Documentos saludables* (Barcelona, 1588).
Ibid., *Aviso de Gente Recogida* (Madrid, 1977 edn).
Ibid., *Platica o Lecion de las mascaras* (Barcelona, 1618).
Juan de Pineda, *Agricultura Christiana*. BAE edn (Madrid, 1963–4).
Hector Pinto, *Imagen de la vida christiana* (Saragossa, 1571).
Jayme Prades, *Historia de la adoracion y uso de las santas imagenes* (Valencia, 1597).
Pronostico y Calendario de todas las fiestas del año que se quardan en el presente Principado de Cataluña para el año de 1684 (Barcelona, 1684).
Luis de la Puente SJ, *De la perfeccion del Christiano*, 3 vols in 1 (Valladolid, 1612).
Juan Agustín Ramírez, *Norte de Pureza* (Barcelona, 1687).
Ibid., *Practica de Curas y Missioneros* (Barcelona, 1688).
Tomás Ramón OP, *Conceptos Extravagantes y peregrinos* (Barcelona, 1619).
Ibid., *Nueva Prematica de Reformacion, contra los abusos de los afeytes, calçado, trajes, y tabaco* (Saragossa, 1635).
Pedro de Ribadeneyra SJ, *Tratado de la religion y virtudes que deve tener el Principe* (Antwerp, 1597).
Miquel Ribes, *Relació breu, verdadera y molt gustosa de les famoses festes . . . en la noble ciutat de Barcelona en lo temps de Carnestoltes* (Barcelona, 1616).
Martí Rich, *Advertencias profitosas pera parrocos y curas* (Barcelona, 1657).
Alonso Rodríguez, *Exercicio de perfeccion y virtudes* (Barcelona, 1613).
Manuel Rodríguez OFM, *Summa de casos de Conciencia* (Salamanca, 1600).
Juan Gaspar Roig y Ialpi, *Grandezas y Antiguedades de Gerona* (Barcelona, 1678).
Pedro Ruiz Alcoholado, *Tractado muy util y curioso para saber bien rezar el Officio Romano* (Toledo, 1584).
Ibid., *Ceremonial Romano para misas cantadas y rezadas* (Alcalá, 1589).
Gaspar Salas, *Govern Politich de la Ciutat de Barcelona pera sustentar los pobres y evitar los vagamundos* (Barcelona, 1636).
Ambrosio Salazar, *Curieuses recherches d'Espagne* (Paris, 1612).
Juan de Salazar, *Arte de Ayudar a bien morir* (Rome, 1608).
Ibid., *Politica española* (Logroño, 1619).
Diego Sánchez Maldonado, *Agricultura alegorica o espiritual* (Burgos, 1603).
Dimas Serpi, *Tratado de Purgatorio* (Barcelona, 1604).
Juan Bautista Sicardo, *Juizio theologico moral que haze de las galas, escotados y afeites de las mugeres* (Madrid, 1677).
Ibid., *General Ruina que padece el mundo por el vicio de la Murmuracion* (Alcalá, 1675).
Ibid., *Carta Apologetica* (Alcalá n.d.).
Juan Bautista de Sossa, *Sossia perseguida* (Madrid, 1621).
Spanish and Catalan Chap-books, 2 vols (British Library).
Juan de Spinosa, *Dialogo en laude de las mugeres* (Milan, 1580).
Synodi Barcinonensis Dioecesanae (Barcelona, 1600).

Synodus Dertosana (Valencia, 1575).
Geroni Taix, *Llibre dels Miracles de Nostra Senyora del Roser* (Barcelona, 1677).
Joseph de Tamayo, *El Mostrador de la Vida humana* (Madrid, 1679).
Francisco de Toledo, *De instructione sacerdotum* (Lyon, 1613), (1st edn, 1599).
Gabriel de Toro, *Thesoro de misericordia divina y humana* (Salamanca, 1548).
Antonio de Torres SJ, *Manual del Christiano* (Saragossa, 1598).
Thomas de Truxillo OP, *Miserias del Hombre* (Barcelona, 1597).
Joan Valls, *Directori de la vida christiana* (Barcelona, 1685).
Domingo de Valtanás, *Doctrina Christiana* (Seville, 1555).
Martín de la Vera, *Instruccion de Eclesiasticos* (Madrid, 1630).
Verdadera Relació de las Festas del Corpus en Vilafranca de Panades (Barcelona, 1609).
Blas Verdu, *Engaños y desengaños del tiempo* (Barcelona, 1612).
Antonio Vilaplana, *Proposiciones christianas y juridicos* (Barcelona, 1679).
Enrique de Villalobos, *Manual de confesores* (Madrid, 1667).
Esteban Manuel de Villegas, *Las eroticas o amatorias* (Nájera, 1617–18).
Juan de Zabaleta, *El dia de Fiesta por la mañana y por la tarde*. Madrid, 1654 [1983 edn.].
Juan Zapata, *Tratado de nuestra fe christiana* (Lérida, 1576).
Francisco de Zepeda, *Resumpta Historial de España desde el diluvio hasta el año de, 1642* (Madrid, 1643).

III Archival Sources

ACA = Arxiu de la Corona d'Aragó, Barcelona
Monacales, Hacienda, vols 2079, 2568 (see MSS), 4125, 4151
Monacales, Universidad vols 9, 168, 169
ACA:CA Consejo de Aragón, Secretaría de Cataluña, legs 78, 218, 221, 234, 235, 261, 262, 264, 265, 266, 269, 342, 343, 344, 345, 346, 349, 356, 358, 367, 368, 372, 477, 547, 552
ACA:RC Real Cancillería, registros 4300, 4301, 4351, 4352, 4353, 4725, 4727, 4736, 4737, 4757, 5516, 5518.
ACL = Archivo Capitular, Lérida
Actas Capitulares, libro 32 (1569–72)
Libros de Visitas, 1 (1588–)
Constituciones sinodales, caja 5.
ACU = Arxiu Capitular d'Urgell, Seu d'Urgell
Sinodos 1610–35
Sinodos 1585–1700
ADB = Arxiu Diocesà, Barcelona
Acta Synodalia, vols 1, 2
Inquisición, legs 1623–9
Limpieza, vol 'Limpieza de religiosos d'Hebron'
Registra Ordinatorum, vol. 24
ADB:C = Comunium vols 63–81
ADB:P = Procesos, years 1596 (4 boxes), 1597 (6 boxes), 1599 (3 boxes), 1600 (6 boxes), 1601 (3 boxes), 1621, 1622 (4 boxes), 1625 (2 boxes), 1626 (5 boxes), 1660 (3 boxes), 1670 (4 boxes).
ADB:V = Visitas Pastorales, vols 34, 35, 40, 44–5, 58, 66, 71, 74, 76, 82, 84, 86
ADB:AP = Arxius parroquials

Ametlla del Vallès: vol. 53, Cofradía del Roser 1579–1667
St Pere de Vilamajor: vol. 41, Roser, seventeenth century
The parish archives of Mediona are referred to either by the name of the parish
   or, if parish manuals are cited, as follows:
   ADB:AP MP/SM = Manual parroquial, Santa Maria
   ADB:AP MP/SQ = Manual parroquial, St Quintí
      The following Mediona records were consulted (references are given as in
         the archival guide, with the modification noted):
      St Quintí:
         legs 44–5, censals.
         legs 47–9, manuals notarials.
         vol. 67, parroquial, cementiri.
      Santa Maria
         vols 1–2, baptismes.
         vol. 9, matrimonis.
         vol. 19, comunions.
         vol. 22, defuncions.
         vols 11–27: manuals parroquials (vols 12–13, 15–16 and 21–22 are in
            fact manuals of SQ, and I cite them as such)
   caixa 59, testaments.
         vols 72–4, història.
ADPO = Archives Départementales Pyrénées Orientales, Perpignan
   Série G (Archives ecclésiastiques, séculiers) registres 50, 54, 160, 164, 514, 720,
      769, 938
   Série AC (Archives communales) registres Egat no.1, 2; Escaro no. 1, 3; Nyer
      no.10.
   Série H (Archives ecclésiastiques, réguliers) registre 155 (St Martí de Canigó)
   Série BB (Llibre de Totis) registres 32, 34
ADU = Arxiu Diocesà d'Urgell, Seu d'Urgell
   Registro de Curia, vols 29, 30, 42
   Informaciones de consanguinidad, capsa 1 (1602–63)
   Libro de Visita, vol.32, 1575–6
   Procesos de Visita, 1611, 1662–99
AEV = Arxiu Episcopal, Vic
   Concilis provincials i sinodes, vol.1055 (1600–99)
   Llibres de visites, vols 1205–7
   Arxius parroquials: Orís, vol.E-H 1 (1599–1634)
   Manlleu, vol.H1 (1599–1653)
AGS = Archivo General de Simancas, Simancas
   Estado, legs 146, 148.
   Patronato Real, leg. 22.
AHAT = Arxiu Històric Arxidiocesà de Tarragona, Tarragona
   Concilio Provincial 1564–66; 1684–5
AHN = Archivo Histórico Nacional, Madrid
   Consejos Suprimidos lib. 7294
   Clero, vol. 6374.
AHN Inq = Inquisición
   Cartas al Consejo legs. 2155[1], 2155[2], 2156[1], 2157[1]
      libros 736–9, 741–5, 747–9
   Causas de fe, libros 730–3
   Visitas, legs. 1592[1], 1592[2]
AHPB = Arxiu Històric de Protocols, Barcelona
   Galcerà Francesch Devesa, leg.4, protocolos 7, año 1595

Ibid., leg.13, Pliego de Inventarios 1591–8
Miguel Cellers (menor), leg.15, Inventario de Damià Bages 1590
  Ibid., leg.17, Inventario del Dr Onofre Ferrá
Joan Terès, leg.16, Pliego de Inventarios 1593–1605
  Ibid., leg.16, Pliego de Inventarios 1594–1606
Pau Mallol, leg.18, Pliego de Inventarios 1555–86
Francesc Pedralbes, leg.36, Pliego de Inventarios (1), sin años.
Lluis Rufet, leg.26, Inventarios sueltos, 1553–80 (1)
  Ibid., leg.26, Inventarios sueltos, 1553–80 (2)
Francisco Aquiles (menor), leg.23, Pliego de Inventarios, 1612–44
Varia, Pliego de Libreros, leg.4, no.21, ss.XV–XVI
Jaume Corbera, leg.7, Inventariorum Liber, 1647–86
Pedro Saragossa, leg.16. pliego de escrituras sueltas 1521–4
Joan-Llorens Calça, leg.2, pliego de inventarios sueltos, varios años
Jeroni Llop, pliego de escrituras, varios años
Miquel-Federic Codina, leg.6, pliego de inventarios, años 1589–90
Pau Calopa, leg.13, proceso criminal por robo
Pedro Pellicer, Manual, 24 Mayo 1420–20 Mayo 1422
APP = Arxiu Parroquial, Santa Maria del Pi, Barcelona
  Llibre de la Rectoria, 1606–7
  Visites Pastorals, 1402–1918
  Comunidad: Determinacions, lletra C (1575–1606)
ARSI = Archivum Romanum Societatis Iesu, Rome
ARSI Epist Hisp = Epistola Hispaniae vols 1, 95–8, 101–3, 112–13, 133, 138, 143
ASV = Archivio Segreto del Vaticano, Vatican City
  Visita ad limina vols 111A, 212, 363A, 399A, 614, 785A, 840, 869A
BCC = Biblioteca Central de Catalunya, Barcelona
  Manuscripts from this library are listed in the section 'Contemporary manuscripts'. A couple of documents consulted from the collection Fullets Bonsoms are listed by author in the section 'Early Printed Books'; the exception is Fullet Bonsom no. 5505.
BL = British Library, London
  The item 'Spanish and Catalan Chap-books', is listed in 'Early Printed Books' but its BL reference is given in the relevant footnote to facilitate consultation.
Bodleian Library, Oxford
  'Relacion verdadera de las fiestas', Arch. Seld. A.I.14 (5).
  'Relacion ... de Carnestolendas de Barcelona, 1653', Arch. Seld. A.I.14 (5).
BUB = Biblioteca de la Universitat de Barcelona, Barcelona
  MSS vols 115, 397, 525, 629 (see MSS), 632 (see MSS), 637 (see MSS), 736, 961, 967 (see MSS), 991 (see MSS), 992 (see MSS), 1005–6 (see MSS), 1008–9–10 (see MSS), 1017, 1032, 1084–5, 1724, 1765
IMH = Institut Municipal d'Història, Barcelona
  MSS Consellers, C. XVIII, vols 2, 4, 6–8

IV   Contemporary Manuscripts

The following list includes some manuscript documents which are difficult to group since they come mainly from libraries rather than manuscript collections or archives:

MSS of the Company of Jesus in Arxiu Històric S.I., Catalonia, St Cugat:
'Cronica del Colegio de Nuestra Señora de Belén de la Compañía de Jesús', vol.I, 1545–1700. A nineteenth-century copy.
Gabriel Alvarez, 'Historia de la Provincia de Aragón de la Compañía de Jesús', 2 vols. Copy of the original in ARSI, Rome.

MSS of the Arxiu de la Corona d'Aragó (ACA):
Section Monacales, Hacienda: 'De los bienes raices del Colegio de Belén de Barcelona'. An enormous seventeenth-century volume with unique detail on the economy of the Barcelona Jesuits.

MSS of the Institut Municipal d'Història, Barcelona:
Mossèn Josep Mas, 'Notes Històriques del Bisbat de Barcelona', vols XXIII–XXIV.

MSS of Biblioteca Central de Catalunya (BCC):
'Descripcio y compte de tots los llochs tan reals com de Barons de tota la provincia de Cathaluña', BCC MS 313.
'Copiador de Cartas ... por el obispo de Urgel', 1664–74, MS 90.
Perot de Vilanova, 'Memòries pera sempre', BCC MS 501 ff.162–78. A short private memoir by a leading public person, covering the years 1560–73.
'Discurso General hecho por el Mre de campo D. Ambrosio Borsano, en que describe toda la carta topografica del Principado de Cataluña', BCC MS 2371.

MSS (microfilm) of Bibliothèque Municipale de Perpignan (BMP):
'Llibre de memories ... de la venerable comunitat de Sant Jaume', MS 84. This begins effectively in 1373 and ends in 1624. It has been published (in the original Catalan) as *Mémoires de l'Eglise Saint-Jacques de Perpignan*, Perpignan 1911.

MSS of Biblioteca de la Universitat de Barcelona (BUB):
MS 629: The first of eight volumes of sermons of Guasch, covering *c*. 1570–84. Later volumes, which I have not consulted, cover the years 1611–13.
MS 632: 'Itinerarium spirituale' of fray Pere Joan Guasch OP.
MS 967: 'Inquisición. Es de la libreria del Convento de Sta Catharina', 1720.
MS 991: 'Annales de los Carmelitas Descalços de Cathaluña', by fray Juan de San José, written in the years 1707–9.
MS 992: 'Monumentos de los Carmelitas Descalzos de Cataluña', by fray Sigismundo del Espíritu Santo. 1689.
MS 1005: 'Anals del convent de Santa Catarina', by fray Francesc Camprubi (1603–34). A valuable and lively account. Less interesting is the continuation volume, MS 1006, by other hands.
MS 1008–10: 'Miscelánea política-eclesiàstica', collected mainly by fray Gaspar Vicens OP, prior of Santa Catarina to 1635. A valuable seventeenth-century manuscript copy of contemporary documents, which includes for example Pere Gil's paper on witchcraft; and the Adrin-Cisteller controversy of 1637 on the use of Catalan.

Index

No index entries are given for commonly used terms such as Aragon, Castile, Counter Reformation, Spain. The form Sant is listed as St, and Santa as Sta.